ACCA

STUDY TEXT

Paper 3.6

Advanced Corporate Reporting

IN THIS JULY 2004 EDITION

- Targeted to the syllabus and study guide
- Quizzes and questions to check your understanding
- Clear layout and style designed to save you time
- Plenty of exam-style questions with detailed guidance from BPP
- Chapter roundups and summaries to help revision
- FRS 20 *Share based payment*, FRS 21 *Events after the balance sheet date* and FRED 32 *Disposal of non-current assets and presentation of discontinued operalions*
- Consultation Papers on convergence, the FRSSE and mineral resources
- Other convergence issues
- Amendment to FRS 5
- New rules on Operating and Financial Review

FOR EXAMS IN DECEMBER 2004 AND JUNE 2005

BPP Professional Education
July 2004

First edition 2001
Fourth edition July 2004

ISBN 07517 1672 3 (previous ISBN 07517 1204 3)

British Library Cataloguing-in-Publication Data
A catalogue record for this book is available from the British Library

Published by

BPP Professional Education
Aldine House, Aldine Place
London W12 8AW

www.bpp.com

Printed in Great Britain by Ashford Colour Press

We are grateful to the Association of Chartered Certified Accountants for permission to reproduce past examination questions and questions from the pilot paper. The answers have been prepared by BPP Professional Education.

	Page

INTRODUCTION

PART A: REGULATORY FRAMEWORK

PART B: GROUP ACOUNTS

PART C: PREPARATION OF REPORTS

PART D: INTERNATIONAL, ENVIRONMENTAL AND CURRENT ISSUES

PART E: ACCOUNTING STANDARDS

THE BPP STUDY TEXT

Aims of this Study Text

To provide you with the knowledge and understanding, skills and application techniques that you need if you are to be successful in your exams

This Study Text has been written around the **Advanced Corporate Reporting** syllabus.

- It is **comprehensive**. It covers the syllabus content. No more, no less.
- It is written at the **right level**. Each chapter is written with the ACCA's **study guide** in mind.
- It is targeted to the **exam**. We have taken account of the **pilot paper and all sittings so far**, questions put to the examiners at ACCA conferences and the assessment methodology.

To allow you to study in the way that best suits your learning style and the time you have available, by following your personal Study Plan (see page (x))

You may be studying at home on your own until the date of the exam, or you may be attending a full-time course. You may like to (and have time to) read every word, or you may prefer to (or only have time to) skim-read and devote the remainder of your time to question practice. Wherever you fall in the spectrum, you will find the BPP Study Text meets your needs in designing and following your personal Study Plan.

To tie in with the other components of the BPP Effective Study Package to ensure you have the best possible chance of passing the exam (see page (vi))

THE BPP EFFECTIVE STUDY PACKAGE

Recommended period of use	Elements of the BPP Effective Study Package
From the outset and throughout	**Learning to Learn Accountancy** Read this invaluable book as you begin your studies and refer to it as you work through the various elements of the BPP Effective Study Package. It will help you to acquire knowledge, practise and revise, efficiently and effectively.
Three to twelve months before the exam	**Study Text and i-Learn** Use the Study Text to acquire knowledge, understanding, skills and the ability to apply techniques. Use BPP's **i-Learn** product to reinforce your learning.
Throughout	**Big Picture Posters** Display these where you're studying and give yourself a feel for the overall shape of the paper and the connections between syllabus areas. Examiners have stressed that you will need to be able to link up different areas when you take the exam. The visual stimulation the posters provide will help you remember the key areas of the syllabus.
Throughout	**Virtual Campus** Study, practise, revise and take advantage of other useful resources with BPP's fully interactive e-learning site with comprehensive tutor support.
Throughout	**i-Pass** **i-Pass**, our computer-based testing package, provides objective test questions in a variety of formats and is ideal for self-assessment.
One to six months before the exam	**Practice & Revision Kit** Try the numerous examination-format questions, for which there are realistic suggested solutions prepared by BPP's own authors. Then attempt the two mock exams.
From three months before the exam until the last minute	**Passcards** Work through these short, memorable notes which are focused on what is most likely to come up in the exam you will be sitting.
One to six months before the exam	**Success Tapes and CDs** The tapes and CDs cover the vital elements of your syllabus in less than 90 minutes per subject. They also contains exam hints to help you fine tune your strategy.

HELP YOURSELF STUDY FOR YOUR ACCA EXAMS

Exams for professional bodies such as ACCA are very different from those you have taken at college or university. You will be under **greater time pressure before** the exam, as you may be combining your study with work. There are many different ways of learning and so the BPP Study Text offers you a number of different tools to help you through. Here are some hints and tips: they are not plucked out of the air, but **based on research and experience**. (You don't need to know that long-term memory is in the same part of the brain as emotions and feelings – but it's a fact anyway.)

The right approach

1 **The right attitude**

Believe in yourself	Yes, there is a lot to learn. Yes, it is a challenge. But thousands have succeeded before and you can too.
Remember why you're doing it	Studying might seem a grind at times, but you are doing it for a reason: to advance your career.

2 **The right focus**

Read through the Syllabus and Study guide	These tell you what you are expected to know and are supplemented by exam focus points in the text.
Study the Exam Paper section	Past exam papers are likely to be a reasonable guide of what you should expect in the exam.

3 **The right method**

The big picture	You need to grasp the detail – but keeping in mind how everything fits into the big picture will help you understand better. • The **Introduction** of each chapter puts the material in context. • The **Syllabus content**, **Study guide** and **Exam focus points** show you what you need to **grasp.**
In your own words	To absorb the information (and to practise your written communication skills), it helps **put it into your own words.** • **Take notes.** • Answer the **questions** in each chapter. You will practise your written communication skills, which become increasingly important as you progress through your ACCA exams. • Draw **mind maps**. We have an example for the whole syllabus. • Try 'teaching' to a colleague or friend.

Give yourself cues to jog your memory	The BPP Study Text uses **bold text** to **highlight key points** and **icons** to identify key features, such as **Exam focus points** and **Key terms.** • Try **colour coding** with a highlighter pen. • Write **key points** on cards.

4 **The right review**

Review, review, review	It is a **fact** that regularly reviewing a topic in summary form can **fix it in your memory**. Because **review** is so important, the BPP Study Text helps you to do so in many ways. • **Chapter roundups** summarise the key points in each chapter. Use them to recap each study session. • The **Quick quiz** is another review tool to ensure that you have grasped the essentials. • Go through the **Examples** in each chapter a second or third time.

Developing your personal Study Plan

The BPP Learning to Learn Accountancy book emphasises is the need to prepare (and use) a study plan. Planning and sticking to the plan are key elements of learning success.

There are four steps you should work through.

Step 1. How do you learn?

First you need to be aware of your style of learning. The BPP Learning to Learn Accountancy book commits a chapter to this **self-discovery**. What types of intelligence do you display when learning? You might be advised to brush up on certain study skills before launching into this Study Text.

> BPP's **Learning to Learn Accountancy** book helps you to identify what intelligences you show more strongly and then details how you can tailor your study process to your preferences. It also includes handy hints on how to develop intelligences you exhibit less strongly, but which might be needed as you study accountancy.

Are you a **theorist** or are you more **practical**? If you would rather get to grips with a theory before trying to apply it in practice, you should follow the study sequence on page (x). If the reverse is true (you need to know why you are learning theory before you do so), you might be advised to flick through Study Text chapters and look at questions, case studies and examples (Steps 7, 8 and 9 in the **suggested study sequence**) before reading through the detailed theory.

Step 2. How much time do you have?

Work out the time you have available per week, given the following.

- The standard you have set yourself
- The time you need to set aside later for work on the Practice & Revision Kit and Passcards
- The other exam(s) you are sitting
- Very importantly, practical matters such as work, travel, exercise, sleep and social life

		Hours
Note your time available in box A.	A	

Step 3. Allocate your time

• Take the time you have available per week for this Study Text shown in box A, multiply it by the number of weeks available and insert the result in box B.	B	
• Divide the figure in Box B by the number of chapters in this text and insert the result in box C.	C	

Remember that this is only a rough guide. Some of the chapters in this book are longer and more complicated than others, and you will find some subjects easier to understand than others.

Step 4. Implement

Set about studying each chapter in the time shown in box C, following the key study steps in the order suggested by your particular learning style.

This is your personal **Study Plan**. You should try and combine it with the study sequence outlined below. You may want to modify the sequence a little (as has been suggested above) to adapt it to your **personal style**.

BPP's *Learning to Learn Accountancy* gives further guidance on developing a study plan, and deciding when and where to study.

Suggested study sequence

Tackle the chapters in the order you find them in the Study Text. Taking into account your individual learning style, you could follow this sequence.

Key study steps	Activity
Step 1 **Topic list**	Each numbered topic is a numbered section in the chapter.
Step 2 **Introduction**	This gives you the **big picture** in terms of the **context** of the chapter. The content is referenced to the **Study Guide**, and **Exam Guidance** shows how the topic is likely to be examined. In other words, it sets your **objectives for study.**
Step 3 **Knowledge brought forward boxes**	In these we highlight information and techniques that it is assumed you have 'brought forward' with you from your earlier studies. If there are topics which have changed recently due to legislation for example, these topics are explained in more detail.
Step 4 **Explanations**	Proceed methodically through the chapter, reading each section thoroughly and making sure you understand.
Step 5 **Key terms and Exam focus points**	• **Key terms** can often earn you *easy marks* if you state them clearly and correctly in an appropriate exam answer (and they are indexed at the back of the text). • **Exam focus points** give you a good idea of what has come up in the exam and how we think the examiner intends to examine certain topics.
Step 6 **Note taking**	Take brief notes if you wish, avoiding the temptation to copy out too much.
Step 7 **Examples**	Follow each through to its solution very carefully.
Step 8 **Case examples**	Study each one, and try to add flesh to them from your own experience – they are designed to show how the topics you are studying come alive (and often come unstuck) in the real world.
Step 9 **Questions**	Make a very good attempt at each one.
Step 10 **Answers**	Check yours against ours, and make sure you understand any discrepancies.
Step 11 **Chapter roundup**	Work through it very carefully, to make sure you have grasped the major points it is highlighting.
Step 12 **Quick quiz**	When you are happy that you have covered the chapter, use the **Quick quiz** to check how much you have remembered of the topics covered.
Step 13 **Question(s) in the Question bank**	Either at this point, or later when you are thinking about revising, make a full attempt at the **Question(s)** suggested at the very end of the chapter. You can find these at the end of the Study Text, along with the **Answers** so you can see how you did. We highlight those that are introductory, and those which are of the standard you would expect to find in an exam.

Short of time: *Skim study technique*?

You may find you simply do not have the time available to follow all the key study steps for each chapter, however you adapt them for your particular learning style. If this is the case, follow the **skim study** technique below (the icons in the Study Text will help you to do this).

- Study the chapters in the order you find them in the Study Text.
- For each chapter:
  - Follow the key study steps 1-3, and then skim-read through step 4. Jump to step 11, and then go back to step 5.
  - Follow through steps 7 and 8, and prepare outline answers to questions (steps 9/10).
  - Try the Quick Quiz (step 12), following up any items you can't answer, then do a plan for the Question (step 13), comparing it against our answers.
  - You should probably still follow step 6 (note-taking), although you may decide simply to rely on the BPP Passcards for this.

Moving on...

However you study, when you are ready to embark on the practice and revision phase of the BPP Effective Study Package, you should still refer back to this Study Text, both as a source of **reference** (you should find the list of key terms and the index particularly helpful for this) and as a **refresher** (the Chapter Roundups and Quick Quizzes help you here).

And remember to keep careful hold of this Study Text – you will find it invaluable in your work.

More advice on Study Skills can be found in the BPP **Learning to Learn Accountancy** book

SYLLABUS

Aim

To ensure that candidates can exercise judgement and technique in corporate reporting matters encountered by accountants and can react to current developments or new practice.

Objectives

On completion of this paper candidates should be able to:

- Explain and evaluate the implications of an accounting standard or proposed accounting standard for the content of published financial information
- Explain and evaluate the impact on the financial statements of business decisions
- Explain the legitimacy and acceptability of an accounting practice proposed by a company
- Prepare financial statements for complex business situations
- Analyse financial statements and prepare a report suitable for presentation to a variety of users
- Evaluate current practice in the context needs of users and the objectives of financial reporting
- Evaluate current developments in corporate reporting in the context of their practical application, implications for corporate reporting and the underlying conceptual issues

  and

- Demonstrate the skills expected in Part 3

Position of the paper in the overall syllabus

This paper is the final assessment of the candidates' skills in the area of corporate reporting. The paper builds on the technical skills studied in Paper 1.1 *Preparing Financial Statements* and Paper 2.5 *Financial Reporting* by requiring candidates to demonstrate the high level technical and evaluatory skills expected of an accountant.

The paper compliments the skills acquired in studying the other core papers in Part 3 of the ACCA examination structure.

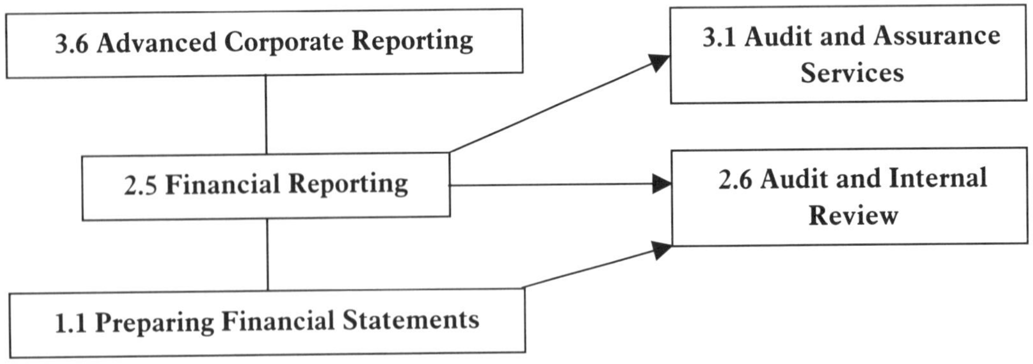

SYLLABUS

1 The UK regulatory framework

(a) Financial Reporting Standards, Financial Reporting Exposure Drafts, Discussion Papers, Urgent Issues Tasks Force Pronouncements including accounting for equity and liabilities, assets, provisions and contingencies, segments, related parties, financial instruments, taxes, leases, retirement benefits.

(b) The content of the UK regulatory framework in a given range of practical situations.

(c) The problems with the current and proposed changes to the UK regulatory framework including measurement and recognition issues.

(d) The impact of current and proposed regulations on the financial statements of the entity.

(e) The effect of business decisions and proposed changes in accounting practice by the entity on the financial statements.

(f) The legitimacy of current accounting practice and its relevance to users of corporate financial statements.

2 Preparation of the financial statements of complex business entities

(a) The financial statements of complex groups including vertical and mixed groups.

(b) Group cash flow statements.

(c) Accounting for group reorganisations and restructuring, including demergers, takeovers and group schemes.

(d) Accounting for foreign currency transactions and entities.

3 Preparation of reports for external and internal users

(a) Appraisal of financial and related information and the purchase of a business entity, the valuation of shares and the reorganisation of an entity.

(b) Appraisal of the impact of changes in accounting policies and the regulatory framework on shareholder value.

(c) Appraisal of the business performance of the entity including quantitative and qualitative measures of performance and the potential for corporate failure.

(d) The assessment of the impact of price level changes and available methods of valuation on business decisions and performance.

(e) The effectiveness of corporate governance within an entity.

4 Current issues and developments

(a) The accounting impact of environmental, cultural and social factors on the entity.

(b) The impact of the content of financial statements on users including changes in design and content of interim and year-end financial statements and alternate ways of communicating results to users.

(c) Proposed changes in the structure of national and international regulation and the impact on global harmonisation and standardisation.

(d) The applicability of the regulatory framework to small and medium sized entities.

(e) Current developments in corporate reporting.

5 Ethical considerations

(a) Ethics and business conduct.

Excluded topics

The syllabus content outlines the areas for assessment. No areas of knowledge are specifically excluded from the syllabus.

Key areas of the syllabus

Key topic areas are as follows.

- Group accounting, group cash flow statements and foreign currency translation
- Discussion papers, financial reporting exposure drafts and recent financial reporting standards
- Problems with current accounting standards and the impact of changes therein on the entity
- Preparation of reports in an advisory capacity including share valuation and purchase of a business
- Changes in organisational structure, reconstructions, demergers, etc
- The potential for business failure and problems with the business including financial analysis, corporate failure prediction and measurement of corporate performance
- Environmental and social accounting and the impact of culture
- Corporate governance and the dissemination of information to users
- Current issues

The main thrust of the syllabus will be the preparation of a set of group financial statements, advising clients on current standards and changes therein, reporting business performance including environmental and social reporting and corporate governance, and appraising current issues. It is important to realise that other areas of the syllabus will be also examined but they are not considered as important.

GROUP ACCOUNTS ARE DEALT WITH FIRST IN THIS TEXT AS THEY ARE A KEY TOPIC.

STUDY GUIDE

Paper 3.6

Advanced Corporate Reporting (GBR)

AIM

To ensure that candidates can exercise judgement and technique in corporate reporting matters encountered by accountants and can react to current developments or new practice.

OBJECTIVES

On completion of this paper candidates should be able to:

- explain and evaluate the implications of an accounting standard or proposed accounting standard for the content of published financial information
- explain and evaluate the impact on the financial statements of business decisions
- explain the legitimacy and acceptability of an accounting practice proposed by a company
- prepare financial statements for complex business situations
- analyse financial statements and prepare a report suitable for presentation to a variety of users
- evaluate current practice in the context of the needs of users and the objectives of financial reporting
- evaluate current developments in corporate reporting in the context of their practical application, implications for corporate reporting, and the underlying conceptual issues and
- demonstrate the skills expected in Part 3.

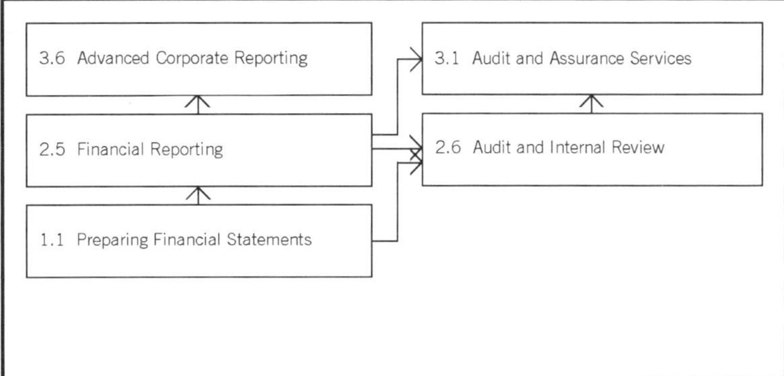

POSITION OF THE PAPER IN THE OVERALL SYLLABUS

This paper is the final assessment of the candidates' skills in the area of corporate reporting. The paper builds on the technical skills studied in Paper 1.1 Preparing Financial Statements and Paper 2.5 Financial Reporting by requiring candidates to demonstrate the high level technical and evaluatory skills expected of an accountant.

The paper complements the skills acquired in studying the other core papers in Part 3 of the ACCA examination structure.

SYLLABUS CONTENT

1 **The UK regulatory framework**

(a) Financial Reporting Standards, Financial Reporting Exposure Drafts, Discussion Papers, Urgent Issues Task Force pronouncements including accounting for equity and liabilities, assets, provisions and contingencies, segments, related parties, financial instruments, taxes, leases, retirement benefits.

(b) The content of the UK regulatory framework in a given range of practical situations.

(c) The problems with the current and proposed changes to the UK regulatory framework including measurement and recognition issues.

(d) The impact of current and proposed regulations on the financial statements of the entity.

(e) The effect of business decisions and proposed changes in accounting practice by the entity on the financial statements.

(f) The legitimacy of current accounting practice and its relevance to users of corporate financial statements.

Advanced Corporate Reporting (GBR) (Continued)

2 Preparation of the financial statements of complex business entities

(a) The financial statements of complex groups including vertical and mixed groups.

(b) Group cash flow statements.

(c) Accounting for group reorganisations and restructuring including demergers, take-overs and group schemes.

(d) Accounting for foreign currency transactions and entities.

3 Preparation of reports for external and internal users

(a) Appraisal of financial and related information, the purchase of a business entity, the valuation of shares and the reorganisation of an entity.

(b) Appraisal of the impact of changes in accounting policies and the regulatory framework on shareholder value.

(c) Appraisal of the business performance of the entity including quantitative and qualitative measures of performance and the potential for corporate failure.

(d) The assessment of the impact of price level changes and available methods of valuation on business decisions and performance.

(e) The effectiveness of corporate governance within an entity.

4 Current issues and developments

(a) The accounting impact of environmental, cultural and social factors on the entity.

(b) The impact of the content of financial statements on users including changes in design and content of interim and year-end financial statements and alternate ways of communicating results to users.

(c) Proposed changes in the structure of national and international regulation and the impact on global harmonisation and standardisation.

(d) The applicability of the regulatory framework to small and medium sized entities.

(e) Current developments in corporate reporting.

5 Ethical considerations

(a) Ethics and business conduct.

EXCLUDED TOPICS

The syllabus content outlines the areas for assessment. No areas of knowledge are specifically excluded from the syllabus.

KEY AREAS OF THE SYLLABUS

Key topic areas are as follows:

- group accounting, group cash flow statements and foreign currency translation
- discussion papers, financial reporting exposure drafts and recent financial reporting standards
- problems with current accounting standards and the impact of changes therein on the entity
- preparation of reports in an advisory capacity including share valuation, and purchase of a business
- changes in organisational structure, reconstructions, demergers, etc
- the potential for business failure and problems with the business including financial analysis, corporate failure prediction and measurement of corporate performance
- environmental and social accounting and the impact of culture
- corporate governance and the dissemination of information to users
- the move to the use of International Accounting Standards
- current issues.

The main thrust of the syllabus will be the preparation of a set of group financial statements, advising clients on current standards and changes therein, reporting business performance including environmental and social reporting and corporate governance, and appraising current issues. It is important to realise that other areas of the syllabus will be also examined.

APPROACH TO EXAMINING THE SYLLABUS

The examination is a three hour paper divided into two sections.

Section A will normally comprise one compulsory question on group financial statements including group cash flows and

Advanced Corporate Reporting (GBR) (Continued)

foreign currency translation. This question will be technically demanding and could have a discursive element in it.

Section B will comprise four questions out of which candidates should select three questions. These questions will involve advising, discussing and reporting on issues and topics in corporate financial reporting. The questions will view the subject matter from the perspective of the preparer of financial statements and from the perspective of the accountant as an advisor. Invariably a technical understanding of the subject matter will be required and candidates will have to apply their knowledge to given cases and scenarios.

Advice as to current and future reporting requirements and their impact on reported corporate performance will be an important element of these questions. Additionally current issues and developments in financial reporting will be examined on a discursive basis.

	Number of marks
Section A: One compulsory question	25
Section B: Choice of 3 from 4 questions (25 marks each)	75
	100

ADDITIONAL INFORMATION

Candidates need to be aware that questions involving knowledge of new examinable regulations will not be set until at least six months after the last day of the month in which the regulation was issued.

The Study Guide provides more detailed guidance on the syllabus. Examinable documents are listed in the 'Exam Notes' section of *student accountant*.

STUDY SESSIONS

1 Overview of UK GAAP

(a) Discuss the nature of UK GAAP

(b) Describe the applicability of UK GAAP for small companies

(c) Outline the Financial Reporting Standard for Smaller Entities (FRSSE)

(d) Discuss the solutions to differential financial reporting

(e) Discuss the implications of the first time application of International Financial Reporting Standards to financial statements drawn up under UK GAAP

2 Corporate governance

(a) Discuss the role and need for the reform of corporate governance

(b) Describe the nature of reporting under the combined code

(c) Discuss the need for corporate governance in small companies

(d) Describe the nature and content of the Operating and Financial Review (OFR)

Advanced Corporate Reporting (GBR) (Continued)

3 Group financial statements I

(a) Review the basic principles of acquisition accounting

(b) Explain and illustrate the principles of measurement relating to the fair value of the consideration and the net assets acquired

(c) Discuss the nature of step by step acquisitions

(d) Prepare consolidated financial statements where control is established by a step by step acquisition

(e) Account for complex group structures

4 Group financial statements II

(a) Explain and illustrate the basic principles relating to the disposal of group companies

(b) Discuss and illustrate the treatment of goodwill on disposal

(c) Apply the principles of accounting for partial and deemed disposals

5 Mergers

(a) Explain the basic principles and philosophy of merger accounting

(b) Account for equity eliminations, expenses and dividends of the subsidiary

(c) Prepare consolidated financial statements utilising merger accounting techniques

(d) Determine whether merger accounting could be used in specific circumstances and the relative merits of different methods of accounting for business combinations

6 Group re-organisations and restructuring

(a) Discuss of the creation of a new holding company

(b) Explain changes in the ownership of companies within a group

(c) Discuss the nature of demergers and divisionalisation

(d) Prepare group financial statements after re-organisation and reconstruction

(e) Appraise the benefits of the re-organisation and restructuring

7 Associates, joint ventures and joint arrangements that are not entities (JANE)

(a) Account for associates, joint ventures and jane's

(b) Apply the equity and gross equity methods of accounting

(c) Prepare group financial statements including accounting for associates, joint ventures and jane's

8 Foreign Currency

(a) Discuss the recording of transactions and retranslation of monetary/non-monetary items at the balance sheet date for individual entities

(b) Account for the treatment of exchange differences re the above

(c) Discuss the nature of the closing rate/net investment method and the temporal method

(d) Account for foreign equity investments financed by borrowings

(e) Prepare group financial statements incorporating a foreign subsidiary/associate

(f) Discuss problem areas in foreign currency transactions for individual and group companies

9 Group cash flow statements

(a) Discuss the usefulness of cash flow information

(b) Prepare group cash flow statements classifying cash flows by standard headings and including acquisition and disposal of subsidiaries

(c) Deal with associates, joint ventures, joint arrangements and foreign currencies

10 Fixed assets I

(a) Discuss the nature of impairment and the impairment review

(b) Apply the impairment review and deal with losses on assets

(c) Account for the amortisation of goodwill and intangible assets including impairment

11 Fixed assets II

(a) Account for revaluation gains and losses and the depreciation of revalued assets

Advanced Corporate Reporting (GBR) (Continued)

(b) Account for the disposal of revalued assets

(c) Discuss the effect of revaluations on distributable profits

(d) Discuss the problem areas in accounting for fixed assets

12 Capital instruments

(a) Account for debt instruments, share capital and the allocation of finance costs

(b) Account for fixed interest rate and convertible bonds

(c) Discuss the measurement issues relating to complex instruments – for example split accounting and the link with accounting for financial instruments

13 Financial instruments

(a) Discuss the definition and classification of a financial instrument

(b) Explain the current measurement proposals for financial instruments including the use of current values, hedging and the treatment of gains and losses

(c) Describe the nature of the disclosure requirements relating to financial instruments

(d) Discuss the key areas where consensus is required on the accounting treatment of financial instruments

14 'Off balance sheet' transactions

(a) Explain the nature of the 'off balance sheet' problem and the principle of substance over form

(b) Discuss common forms of 'off balance sheet' finance and current regulatory requirements

(c) Discuss the perceived problems of current regulatory requirements including measurement and recognition issues

15 Leases

(a) Discuss problem areas in lease accounting including classification, termination, tax variation clauses

(b) Account for sale and leaseback transactions and recognition of income by lessors

(c) Discuss and account for proposed changes in lease accounting and its impact on corporate financial statements

16 Segmental reporting

(a) Discuss the problem areas in segmental reporting including definition of segments, common costs, inter segment sales etc

(b) Discussion the different approaches used to disclose segmental information

(c) Discuss the importance of segmental information to users of financial statements

17 Accounting for Retirement Benefits

(a) Describe the nature of defined contribution, multi-employers and defined benefits schemes

(b) Explain the recognition of defined benefit schemes under current proposals

(c) Discuss the measurement of defined benefit schemes under current proposals

(d) Account for defined benefit schemes including the amounts shown in the balance sheet, statement of total recognised gains and losses, profit and loss account and notes to the account

(e) Discuss perceived problems with current proposals on accounting for retirement benefits

18 Taxation

(a) Discuss the different approaches to accounting for deferred taxation

(b) Discuss the recognition of deferred taxation in the balance sheet and performance statements under current proposals including revaluations, unremitted earnings of group companies and deferred tax assets

(c) Explain the nature of the measurement of deferred taxation under current proposals including tax rates and discounting

(d) Calculate deferred tax amounts in financial statements under current proposals

Advanced Corporate Reporting (GBR) (Continued)

19 Reporting financial performance and earnings per share

(a) Discuss proposed changes to reporting financial performance

(b) Explain the rationale behind the proposed changes in reporting financial performance

(c) Calculate diluted earnings per share by reference to dilutive potential ordinary shares, loss per share and particular types of dilutive instruments including partly paid shares, employee incentive schemes and contingently issuable shares

20 Post balance sheet events, provisions and contingencies

(a) Discuss the problems of accounting for post balance sheet events including reclassification, window dressing etc

(b) Discuss the issues relating to recognition and measurement of provisions including "best estimates", discounting, future events

(c) Explain the use of restructuring provisions and other practical uses of provisioning

(d) Discuss the problems with current standards on provisions and contingencies including definitional and discounting problems

21 Related parties and share based payment

(a) Discuss the related party issue

(b) Identify related parties (including deemed and presumed) and the disclosure of related party transactions

(c) Discuss the effectiveness of current regulations on disclosure of related party transactions

(d) Describe the current proposals for the recognition and measurement of share-based payment

(e) Show the impact of the proposals on the performance statements of the entity

22 Preparation of reports I

(a) Calculate and appraise a range of acceptable values for shares in an unquoted company

(b) Advise a client on the purchase of a business entity

(c) Analyse the impact of accounting policy changes on the value and performance on an entity

23 Preparation of reports II

(a) Discuss the financial and non-financial measures of performance

(b) Describe the procedures in designing an accounting based performance measurement system

(c) Appraise the different performance measures including return on investment, residual income and economic value added

(d) Compare target levels of performance with actual performance

24 Preparation of reports III

(a) Discuss alternative definitions of capital employed and measurement bases for assets

(b) Discuss the impact of price level changes on business performance

(c) Appraise the alternative methods of accounting for price level changes

(d) Evaluate of the potential for corporate failure

25 The impact of environmental, social and cultural factors on corporate reporting

(a) Appraise the impact of environmental, social and ethical factors on performance measurement

(b) Describe current reporting requirements and guidelines for environmental reporting

(c) Prepare an environmental report in accordance with current practice

(d) Discuss of the effect of culture on accounting and the cultural relativity of accounting

(e) Discuss of why entities might include socially orientated disclosures in performance statements

(f) Discuss the concept of a social contract and organisational legitimacy

Advanced Corporate Reporting (GBR) (Continued)

(g) Evaluate ethical conduct in the context of corporate reporting

26 International issues

(a) Evaluate the developments and the impact on companies of moves towards global and regional harmonisation and standardisation

(b) Assess proposed changes to national and international regulation

(c) Identify the reasons for major differences in accounting practices

(d) Restate overseas financial statements in line with UK accounting policies

(e) Evaluate the effect on corporate reporting of a move to International Financial Reporting Standards

(f) Understand the key differences between UK GAAP and International Financial Reporting Standards

(g) Identify the key problems for companies of a move to reporting under International Financial Reporting Standards

27 Current issues and developments

(a) Identify ways of improving communication of corporate performance, current proposals relating to year end financial reports and business reporting on the internet

(b) Identify problem areas in interim reporting

(c) Discuss current issues in corporate reporting including disclosure of accounting policies and discounting.

28 Revision

THE EXAM PAPER

The examination is a **three hour paper** divided into **two sections.**

Section A will normally comprise one compulsory question on group financial statements including group cash flows and foreign currency translation. This question will be technically demanding and could have a discursive element in it.

Section B will comprise four questions out of which candidates should select three questions. These questions will involve advising, discussing and reporting on issues and topics in corporate financial reporting. The questions will view the subject matter from the perspective of the preparer of financial statements and from the perspective of the accountant as an advisor. Invariably a technical understanding of the subject matter will be required and candidates will have to apply their knowledge to given cases and scenarios.

Advice as to current and future reporting requirements and their impact on reported corporate performance will be an important element of these questions. Additionally current issues and developments in financial reporting will be examined on a discursive basis.

		Number of Marks
Section A:	One compulsory question	25
Section B:	Choice of 3 from 4 questions (25 marks each)	75
		100

Additional information

Candidates need to be aware that questions involving knowledge of new examinable regulations will not be set until at least six months after the last day of the month in which the regulation was issued.

The Study Guide provides more detailed guidance on the syllabus. Examinable documents are listed in the 'Exam Notes' section of *Student Accountant*.

Analysis of past papers

The analysis below shows the topics which were examined in all sittings of the current syllabus so far and in the Pilot Paper.

June 2004

Section A

1 Consolidated financial statements with foreign currency

Section B

2 Segmental reporting; related parties; pensions; impairment
3 Statement of Principles; provisions; deferred tax
4 Current UK GAAP vs FRED 32
5 Social and environmental issues; human capital management

December 2003

Section A

1 Consolidation with a 'D' shaped group

Section B

2 Convergence with IAS
3 Company restructuring
4 Start up costs, hedging, foreign currency
5 Further convergence issues

June 2003

Section A

1 Consolidated profit and loss account with deemed disposal

Section B

2 Share valuation including deferred tax calculation
3 FRS 18; revenue recognition and FRS 12
4 Special purpose vehicles; reporting financial performance
5 Corporate governance: accountability, audit and effectiveness of safeguards

December 2002

Section A

1 Consolidated balance sheet with a 'D' shaped group and defined benefit pension scheme

Section B

2 International Accounting Standards; problems with GAAP reconciliations
3 Group reconstruction; effect of re-structuring plan on creditors
4 Accounting treatment of intangible assets, property and revenue
5 Problems with published financial statements: earnings figure and fair values

June 2002

Section A

1 Group cash flow statement

Section B

2 FRED 22: discussion and preparation of performance statement
3 FRS 10: impact on financial statements
4 Impact of accounting policies; EBITDA
5 Environmental reporting; convergence

December 2001

Section A

1 Consolidated financial statements and foreign currency

Section B

2 Effect of accounting treatments on EPS calculation
3 Closure of subsidiary; FRS 3, FRS 11, FRS 12, FRS 13
4 IAS requirement; share based payment; impairment
5 Reporting business performance; payment; impairment; corporate citizenship

OXFORD BROOKES BSc (Hons) IN APPLIED ACCOUNTING

The standard required of candidates completing Part 2 is that required in the final year of a UK degree. Students completing Parts 1 and 2 will have satisfied the examination requirement for an honours degree in Applied Accounting, awarded by Oxford Brookes University.

To achieve the degree, you must also submit two pieces of work based on a **Research and Analysis Project.**

- A 5,000 word **Report** on your chosen topic, which demonstrates that you have acquired the necessary research, analytical and IT skills.
- A 1,500 word **Key Skills Statement**, indicating how you have developed your interpersonal and communication skills.

BPP was selected by the ACCA and Oxford Brookes University to produce the official text *Success in your Research and Analysis Project* to support students in this task. The book pays particular attention to key skills not covered in the professional examinations.

BPP also offers courses and mentoring services.

OXFORD INSTITUTE OF INTERNATIONAL FINANCE MBA

The Oxford Institute of International Finance (OXIIF), a joint venture between the ACCA and Oxford Brookes University, offers an MBA for finance professionals.

For this MBA, credits are awarded for your ACCA studies, and entry to the MBA course is available to those who have completed their ACCA professional stage studies. The MBA was launched in 2002 and has attracted participants from all over the world.

The qualification features an introductory module (*Foundations of Management*). Other modules include *Global Business Strategy, Managing Self Development,* and *Organisational Change & Transformation.*

Research Methods are also taught, as they underpin the **research dissertation**.

The MBA programme is delivered through the use of targeted paper study materials, developed by BPP, and taught over the Internet by OXIIF personnel using BPP's virtual campus software.

For further information, please see the Oxford Institute's website: www.oxfordinstitute.org.

CONTINUING PROFESSIONAL DEVELOPMENT

ACCA is introducing a new continuing professional development requirement for members from 1 January 2005. Members will be required to complete and record 40 units of CPD annually, of which 21 units must be verifiable learning or training activity.

BPP has an established professional development department which offers a range of relevant, professional courses to reflect the needs of professionals working in both industry and practice. To find out more, visit the website: www.bpp.com/pd or call the client care team on 0845 226 2422.

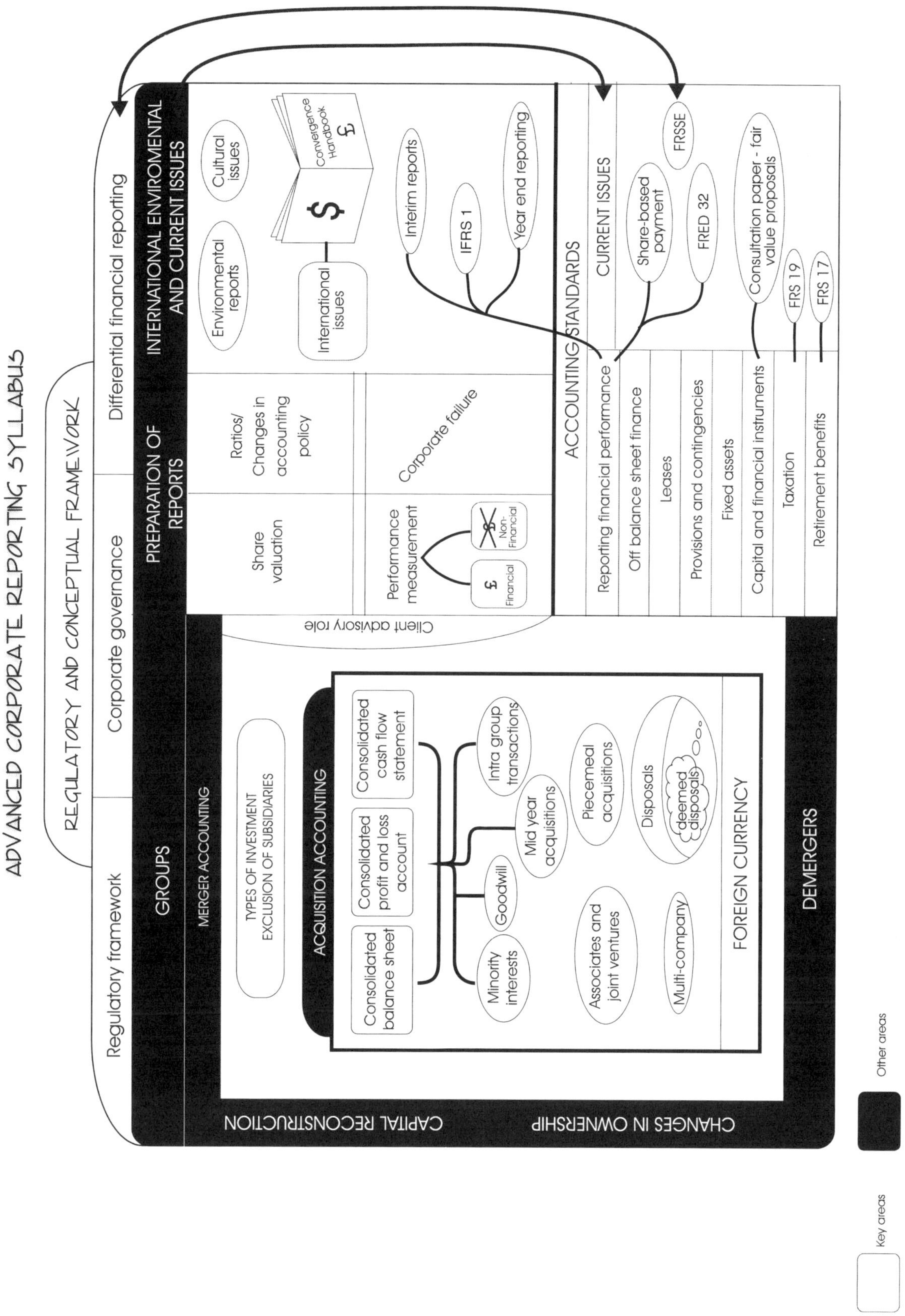

ADVANCED CORPORATE REPORTING SYLLABUS

REGULATORY AND CONCEPTUAL FRAMEWORK

Regulatory framework

Corporate governance

Differential financial reporting

GROUPS

MERGER ACCOUNTING

TYPES OF INVESTMENT
EXCLUSION OF SUBSIDIARIES

ACQUISITION ACCOUNTING

Consolidated balance sheet

Consolidated profit and loss account

Consolidated cash flow statement

Minority interests

Goodwill

Mid year acquisitions

Intra group transactions

Associates and joint ventures

Piecemeal acquisitions

Multi-company

Disposals

deemed disposals

FOREIGN CURRENCY

CAPITAL RECONSTRUCTION

CHANGES IN OWNERSHIP

DEMERGERS

Client advisory role

PREPARATION OF REPORTS

Share valuation

Ratios/ Changes in accounting policy

Performance measurement

£ Financial

Non-Financial

Corporate failure

INTERNATIONAL ENVIROMENTAL AND CURRENT ISSUES

Environmental reports

Cultural issues

International issues

$

Convergence Handbook £

Interim reports

IFRS 1

Year end reporting

ACCOUNTING STANDARDS

Reporting financial performance

Off balance sheet finance

Leases

Provisions and contingencies

Fixed assets

Capital and financial instruments

Taxation

Retirement benefits

CURRENT ISSUES

Share-based payment

FRSSE

FRED 32

Consultation paper - fair value proposals

FRS 19

FRS 17

Key areas

Other areas

Part A

Regulatory Framework

Chapter 1

OVERVIEW OF UK GAAP

Topic list		Syllabus reference
1	Regulatory framework	1(a), (b)
2	FRS for Smaller Entities	1(a), (b), 4 (d)
3	GAAP and conceptual framework	1(a), (b)
4	Corporate governance	3(e)
5	Operating and financial review	1(a), (b)

Introduction

Welcome to the Advanced Corporate Reporting paper. We must emphasise from the start that this paper is about thinking rather than rote learning. You will have met most of the accounting standards and topics covered in your earlier studies, but at Part 3 you will be required to think critically about them and show an understanding of topical issues. Put yourself in the position of an accountant giving advice to management in the light of what you know.

Study guide

Section 1 – Overview of UK GAAP

- Discussion of the nature of UK GAAP
- Describing the applicability of UK GAAP for small companies
- Outlining the FRSSE
- Discussion of the solutions to differential financial reporting

Section 2 – Corporate governance

- Discussion of the role and need for reform of corporate governance
- Describing the nature of reporting under the combined code
- Discussion of the need for corporate governance in small companies
- Describing the nature and content of the OFR

1 REGULATORY FRAMEWORK

1.1 We have covered this in your earlier studies, so only a summary is given here. However, if you have any problems or if the material is unfamiliar, look back to your earlier study material.

Knowledge brought forward from earlier studies

Regulatory framework

- The reporting environment changes constantly, through new regulations, standards etc
- International influences on UK reporting are increasing, via IASC and multinational businesses

Company law

Consolidated by the Companies Act 1985, updated by the Companies Act 1989. The Acts lay out the formats, contents and rules for the preparation of financial statements.

European Union law

The UK is obliged to comply with legal directives issued by the EU.

Stock Exchange rules

The Stock Exchange listing requirements (Yellow Book) must be complied with by companies on the market. The Alternative Investment Market (AIM) has less stringent requirements.

UK accounting standards

The standard-setting structure is as follows.

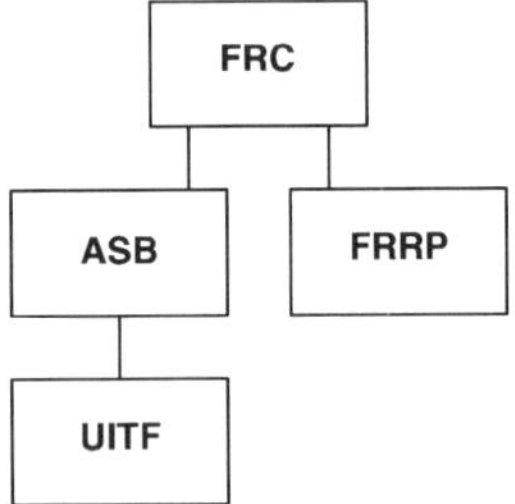

- *FRC (Financial Reporting Council)*: umbrella organisation for the standard-setting regime, responsible for financing, enforcement, appointments
- *FRRP (Financial Reporting Review Panel)*: reviews company accounts for non-compliance with accounting standards, truth and fairness, sufficient disclosure etc
- *ASB (Accounting Standards Board)*: produces FRSs from FREDs and DDs (see below)
- *UITF (Urgent Issues Task Force)*: produces 'abstracts' to tackle problem areas quickly (within one month); may be incorporated into subsequent standards

ASB and FRSs

Statement of Aims:

- *Aims*: 'to establish and improve standards of financial accounting and reporting, for the benefit of users, preparers and auditors of financial information.'
- *Achieving the aims*
  - Developing principles to provide a framework
  - Issuing new standards or amending existing ones
  - Addressing urgent issues promptly
- *Fundamental guidelines*
  1. Objectivity; represent commercial activity
  2. Clear expression; supported by analysis
  3. Inclusion of only properly researched material
  4. Due regard paid to international developments
  5. Consistency between standards and law
  6. Benefits of standards must exceed costs

Current accounting standards

1.2 The following standards are extant at the date of writing (July 2003). The SSAPs which were in force at the date the ASB was formed have been adopted by the Board. They are gradually being superseded by the new FRSs.

Accounting standards

No	*Title*	*Issue date*
	Foreword to accounting standards	Jun 93
FRS 1	Cash flow statements (revised) (see below)	Oct 96
FRS 2	Accounting for subsidiary undertakings	Jul 92
	Amendment	May 02
FRS 3	Reporting financial performance	Oct 92
FRS 4	Capital instruments	Dec 93
FRS 5	Reporting the substance of transactions	Apr 94
	Amendment to FRS 5: Revenue recognition	Nov 03
FRS 6	Acquisitions and mergers	Sep 94
FRS 7	Fair values in acquisition accounting	Sep 94
FRS 8	Related party disclosures	Oct 95
FRS 9	Associates and joint ventures	Nov 97
	Financial Reporting Standard for Smaller Entities	Dec 99
FRS 10	Goodwill and intangible assets	Dec 97
FRS 11	Impairment of fixed assets and goodwill	Jul 98
FRS 12	Provisions, contingent liabilities and contingent assets	Sep 98
FRS 13	Derivatives and other financial instruments: disclosure	Sep 98
FRS 14	Earnings per share	Oct 98
FRS 15	Tangible fixed assets	Feb 99
FRS 16	Current tax	Dec 99
FRS 17	Retirement benefits	Nov 00
FRS 18	Accounting policies	Dec 00
FRS 19	Deferred tax	Dec 00
FRS 20	Share-based payment	Apr 04
FRS 21	Events after the balance sheet date	May 04
SSAP 4	Accounting for government grants	Jul 90
SSAP 5	Accounting for value added tax	Apr 74
SSAP 9	Stocks and long-term contracts	Sep 88
SSAP 13	Accounting for research and development	Jan 89
SSAP 19	Accounting for investment properties (amended)	Nov 81
SSAP 20	Foreign currency translation	Apr 83
SSAP 21	Accounting for leases and hire purchase contracts	Aug 84
SSAP 25	Segmental reporting	Jun 90
Financial reporting exposure drafts		
FRED 23	Financial instruments: hedge accounting	May 02
FRED 24	The effects of changes in foreign exchange rates; Financial reporting in hyperinflationary economies	May 02
FRED 25	Related party disclosures	May 02
FRED 26	Earnings per share	May 02
FRED 28	Inventories; Construction contracts	May 02
FRED 29	Property, plant and equipment; Borrowing costs	May 02
FRED 30	Financial instruments: disclosure and presentation and recognition and measurement	Jun 02
FRED 30	Supplement: Fair value hedge accounting for a portfolio hedge of interest rate risk	Aug 03
FRED 30	Second supplement: Extension of scope	Jul 03
FRED 32	Disposal of non-current assets and presentation of discontinued operations	May 04

Other documents

Accounting for the effects of changing prices: a handbook - ASC (Summary and Overview)

The Cadbury Report (1992), *The Combined Code* (1998), *The Hampel Report* (Jan 1998)

Operating and Financial Review - ASB (January 1993)

Statement of Principles for Financial Reporting – ASB (Dec 99)

Consultation Paper: IASB proposals to amend certain International Accounting Standards (May 02)

Consultation Paper: IASB proposals on first-time application of International Financial Reporting Standards (July 02)

Consultation Paper: IASB proposals on business combinations, impairment and intangible assets (Dec 02)

ASB Drafts for Discussion (DDs)

Title	*Issue date*
Segmental reporting	May 96
Discounting (working paper)	Apr 97
Derivatives and other financial instruments (discussion paper)	Jul 96
Business combinations (discussion paper)	Dec 98
Leases: implementation of a new approach	Dec 99
Year end financial reports: improving communication	Feb 00
Financial instruments and similar items	Dec 00
The Convergence Handbook	Dec 00
Review of the FRSSE	Feb 01
Revenue recognition	Jul 01
Statement of Principles: Proposed interpretation for public benefit entities	May 03
IAS 13 Proposals on exploration for and evaluation of mineral resources	Jan 04
A 'one-stop shop' FRSSE	Mar 04
UK Accounting Standards: A Strategy for Convergence with IFRS	Mar 04

Statements of Recommended Practice (SORPs)

1.3 When the ASB took over from the old ASC, it adopted all the existing accounting standards. It did not, however, adopt the ASC's SORPs 1 and 2. As far as your syllabus is concerned, you need only be aware of the relevance of SORPs to financial reporting and the principal requirements of SORPs 1 and 2. SORPs are developed as an **aid to reporting** in specific industries or for specific bodies, eg pensions (SORP 1) and charities (SORP 2).

2 FRS FOR SMALLER ENTITIES

Big GAAP/little GAAP

2.1 This is a current debate in the financial accounting world. Most UK companies are **small companies**, generally owned and managed by one person or a family. The owners have invested their own money in the business and there are no outside shareholders to protect. Large companies, by contrast, particularly plcs, may have shareholders who have invested their money, possibly through a pension fund, with no knowledge whatever of the company. These shareholders need protection and the regulations for such companies need to be more stringent.

2.2 It could therefore be argued that company accounts should be of **two types**: 'simple' ones for small companies with fewer regulations and disclosure requirements and 'complicated' ones for larger companies with extensive and detailed requirements. This is the 'big GAAP/little GAAP' divide.

FRS for Smaller Entities

2.3 In November 1997 the ASB published the *Financial Reporting Standard for Smaller Entities*. This has been revised several times to take account of new FRSs. The latest revision was November 2002. It brings together in one brief document all the **accounting guidance** which UK small businesses will require to draw up their financial statements.

2.4 The FRSSE is applicable to all companies that satisfy the definition of a small company in companies legislation and is available to other entities that would meet that definition if they were companies. A company that chooses to comply with the FRSSE is exempt from all other accounting standards and UITF Abstracts.

2.5 The FRSSE contains in a simplified form the requirements from existing accounting standards that are relevant to the majority of smaller entities.

2.6 In order to keep the FRSSE as user-friendly as possible some of the requirements in accounting standards relating to more complex transactions, eg the treatment of convertible debt in FRS 4 *Capital instruments*, have not been included in the FRSSE, as they do not affect most smaller entities. Where guidance is needed on a matter not contained in the FRSSE, regard should be paid to existing practice as set out in the relevant accounting standards.

Measurement

2.7 The measurement bases in the FRSSE are the same as, or a simplification of, those in existing accounting standards. For example, under the FRSSE a lessee that is a small company could account for the finance charges on a finance lease on a straight-line basis over the life of the lease, rather than, as in SSAP 21, using a constant periodic rate of return.

Disclosure requirements

2.8 One of the many ways in which the FRSSE should reduce the burden for preparers of smaller entities' financial statements is likely to be its *reduced* disclosure requirements. For example, the FRSSE does not require an analysis of turnover and profits into continuing operations, acquisitions and discontinued operations, nor a reconciliation of movements in shareholders' funds.

Related parties

2.9 The disclosure requirements for related party transactions in the FRSSE represent a useful dispensation for smaller entities compared with those in FRS 8 *Related party disclosures*. Under FRS 8, related party transactions that are material to the related party, where that related party is an individual, are required to be disclosed in the accounts of the reporting entity even if the transaction is not material to the entity. This is not so for smaller entities adopting the FRSSE, as they need disclose only those related party transactions that are material in relation to the reporting entity.

Cash flow statement

2.10 Since small entities are already exempt from the requirements of FRS 1 *Cash flow statements* the FRSSE does not include a requirement for a cash flow statement. The ASB nevertheless believes that a cash flow statement is an important aid to the understanding of an entity's financial position and performance and the FRSSE therefore includes a 'voluntary disclosures' section, recommending that smaller entities present a simplified cash flow statement using the indirect method (ie starting with operating profit and reconciling it to the total cash generated (or utilised) in the period).

Small groups

2.11 Small groups are not required by law to prepare consolidated accounts, and therefore in practice not many do so, at least on a statutory basis. The Working Party and the Board, however, agreed with respondents that it would be unfair to those small groups that voluntarily prepare group accounts, if they were not able to take advantage of the provisions in the FRSSE. To import all the necessary requirements from accounting standards and UITF Abstracts into the FRSSE to deal with consolidated accounts would have added substantially to its length and complexity, even though it would have been of interest to only a small percentage of entities. Accordingly, the Working Party and the Board preferred to extend the FRSSE in certain areas and then require small groups adopting the FRSSE to follow those accounting standards and UITF Abstracts that deal with consolidated financial statements. This approach was supported by the majority of respondents to the Exposure Draft commenting on the matter.

Criticisms of the FRSSE

2.12 **Criticisms** of the FRSSE have been as follows.

(a) The FRSSE is unlikely to make it **easier or cheaper** to prepare financial statements.

(b) The case in favour of relaxing **measurement** GAAP for smaller companies has not yet been made convincingly. If it is ultimately decided that the only exemptions are to be from disclosure, rather than from measurement, this could be achieved more easily by simply stating in the individual FRSs and SSAPs what disclosure requirements apply to all companies and what applies only to large ones.

(c) There is concern that the FRSSE could allow smaller companies to use **different accounting measurements**, eg the straight line method rather than the current actuarial method for finance charges.

(d) It is questionable whether accounts prepared under the FRSSE would give a **true and fair view** under company law. The true and fair view requirement applies to all companies, whatever their size.

(e) The present document is not a **'stand-alone' document**. Users would still need to refer to 'mainstream' standards if they are to prepare financial statements which show a true and fair view.

2.13 However, some commentators back the concept of a financial reporting standard for smaller entities; they feel that the FRSSE provides a satisfactory and workable solution to the problems of smaller entities caused by the **increasing complexity** of accounting standards.

Future developments

2.14 With the assistance of its advisory committee, the Committee on Accounting for Smaller Entities, the ASB will update and revise the FRSSE periodically to reflect future developments in financial reporting. Any changes to the FRSSE, for example as a result of new accounting standards and UITF Abstracts, will be the subject of public consultation. Most of the December 2001 revised FRSSE is identical to its predecessor but it incorporates some changes to reflect the requirements (simplified as appropriate) introduced by FRS 16 *Current tax*, FRS 17 *Retirement benefits*, FRS 18 *Accounting polices* and FRS 19 *Deferred tax* as well as certain UITF abstracts

2.15 The FRSSE attempts to balance the conflicting views of those who commented on the proposals, ranging from those who believe small companies should be exempt from all accounting standards to those who favour retaining virtually the status quo. Given this divergence of views, the ASB believes that it is particularly important that, going forward, the FRSSE is carefully monitored. It is therefore proposed to review how the FRSSE, as a whole, is working in practice after two full years of effective operation and propose amendments as necessary, in addition to the routine periodic revisions of the FRSSE resulting from new accounting standards and UITF Abstracts.

Exam focus point

As with all topical issues, you should aim to read around the subject. Not all comments on the FRSSE have been favourable.

Discussion Paper: Review of the Financial Reporting Standard for Smaller Entities

2.16 In February 2001 the ASB issued a Discussion Paper *Review of the Financial Reporting Standard for Smaller Entities (FRSSE)*. The Discussion Paper seeks views on whether in its present form, the FRSSE best meets users' needs and whether any fundamental changes should be considered to the way in which it is prepared and presented.

2.17 The Discussion Paper asks respondents to comment on a number of issues, including the extent to which the FRSSE should be consistent with the accounting standards and UITF Abstracts on which it is based, in terms both of requirements and of drafting. The issues centre on six main questions.

(a) **Should there continue to be a FRSSE?** Is a separate reporting regime for smaller entities appropriate? If so, should the existing qualification criteria be retained or might other criteria be introduced?

(b) **Can a single FRSSE cater for the range of smaller entities?** There are different classes of smaller entity, so should there be different reporting regimes for each class?

(c) **How and when should the FRSSE be updated?** At the moment the FRSSE is a separate document, but an alternative approach might be to have a 'FRSSE section' in each new FRS. How often should the FRSSE be updated? Does the timing of changes need to correspond to changes in 'Big GAAP'?

(d) **Which aspects of smaller entities' reporting should the FRSSE cover?** For example, should it deal with the directors' report, or the Operating and Financial Review?

(e) **How should the requirements of the FRSSE be determined?** Should its requirements mirror those of Big GAAP (a 'top down' approach) or should a 'bottom up' or 'think small first' approach be taken?

(f) **How should the FRSSE be drafted and presented?** Where FRSSE requirements are derived from those of Big GAAP, should the FRSSE seek to use the same words where possible? Alternatively, should requirements be redrafted to make them as accessible as possible to preparers and users of smaller entities' financial statements?

2.18 The Discussion Paper acknowledges that these questions are interdependent. For example, whether a separate reporting regime for smaller entities is justified will depend on how different Little GAAP is from Big GAAP

Changes to small company limits

2.19 In January 2004, the thresholds for small companies, ie those eligible to use the FRSSE increased to:

(a) Turnover not more than £5.6m
(b) Balance sheet total not more than £2.8m
(c) Number of employees unchanged from the limit of 50

Discussion Paper: A 'one-stop shop' FRSSE

2.20 Companies electing to adopt the FRSSE must comply with the requirements of **companies legislation, as well as with the requirements of the FRSSE**. Entities adopting the FRSSE that are not companies should have regard to the accounting principles, presentation and disclosure requirements in companies legislation (or other equivalent legislation) that, taking into account the FRSSE, are necessary to present a true and fair view.

2.21 One of the questions arising in the 2001 review of the FRSSE was how the FRSSE might be made more accessible. The ASB received strong support for its suggestion that the FRSSE could be made more of a '**one-stop shop**' for preparers of financial statements **by including the requirements of the Companies Act 1985**.

2.22 The advantage of this approach is that it would ease the burden on the preparers of small company accounts. They would only need to refer to a single source of accounting and reporting requirements rather than having to refer to both legislation and accounting standards. The purpose of the Discussion Paper is to set out how such a 'one-stop shop' FRSSE might look and to seek views.

2.23 The consultation is limited in scope, as the ASB is aware of **related developments** which may have consequences for the FRSSE. These are as follows.

(a) The impact of the **convergence** between UK and Irish Accounting Standards and IFRSs, on which the Board will be consulting separately

(b) The **IASB's SME Project** (see Paragraph 2.24)

(c) Developments in **Company Law**, for example the changes to the limits (see Paragraph 2.19 above).

International developments

2.24 In June 2004, the **IASB** published a Discussion Paper *Preliminary Views on Accounting Standards for Small and Medium-sized Entities (SMEs)*. The purpose of the Discussion Paper is to invite comments on the IASB's preliminary views on its basic **approach to the project on accounting standards for SMEs.**

2.25 In the IASB's view, the set of accounting standards for SMEs should be a **modified version of full IFRS**, published in a separate printed volume and following the numbering system of International Financial Reporting Standards. It proposes a **rebuttable presumption that no modifications would be made to the recognition and measurement principles in IFRS**.

2.26 The IASB's proposals, if implemented, would result in standards for SMEs which differ from the FRSSE in a number of ways.

(a) The IASB project focuses on **non-public accountability** as the key test for determining who might be eligible to use the standards for SMEs. The focus, unlike that of the FRSSE, is **not on smaller entities**. If smaller entities are to enjoy a substantially reduced burden, this could imply the need for a 'three tier' system of accounting standards.

(b) **Each IFRS** and interpretation would have its **SME equivalent**. Companies would therefore be using a series of separate standards rather than the one special standard for smaller entities. Furthermore, those **SME standards would change in line with IFRS** rather than be changed at most only once a year.

(c) The IASB proposes **mandatory fallback to IFRS** for any particular accounting or measurement issue that is not addressed in the SME standards. The FRSSE, in contrast, encourages such reference only as a possible means of establishing generally accepted practice; and

(d) The IASB proposes a **'pick and mix'** approach from IFRS and IFRS for SMEs. Eligible entities could choose to follow IFRS in some areas and IFRS for SMEs in others. The FRSSE is not mandatory but once an entity has chosen to follow the FRSSE it must consider all its requirements.

3 GAAP AND CONCEPTUAL FRAMEWORK 6/04

3.1 It has been said that in the past the standard setting body took a 'fire fighting' approach to developing accounting standards. The **old SSAPs** were not based on a consistent philosophy and this led to the need for a conceptual framework of accounting.

KEY TERM

A **conceptual framework** is a constitution, a coherent system of interrelated objectives and fundamentals that can lead to consistent standards and that prescribes the nature, function and limits of financial accounting and financial statements.

Financial Accounting Standards Board (FASB)

3.2 The basic idea is to avoid the 'fire fighting' approach which characterised the development of SSAPs under the old ASC, and instead to develop an **underlying philosophy** as a basis for consistent accounting principles so that the rationale of each standard is structured into the whole framework. The process towards a conceptual framework is described briefly here.

ASC/FASB

3.3 The ASC stated in a consultative document *Setting Accounting Standards* that, whilst an agreed framework of accounting would provide a good basis on which to build accounting standards, it believed that no such framework was currently available and that conclusive results would probably not be rapidly achieved. FASB, however, began a large-scale project in 1973 to develop such a framework, with immense resources committed to the research and large volumes of material produced.

Macve Report

3.4 In the UK, a similar search for a conceptual framework was under way; a report was commissioned by the ASC from Professor Richard Macve. His report was published in 1981 and he wrote:

> 'the value of the current attempts to explore the conceptual framework lies, in my opinion, mainly in the discipline the process imposes of identifying the important areas where judgement is needed on questions of accounting policy, and of stimulating enquiry, with regard to users' needs and how to satisfy them.'

IASB's Framework

3.5 The IASB *Framework for the Preparation and Presentation of Financial Statements* is non-mandatory and it deals with:

(a) The objective of financial statements

(b) The qualitative characteristics that determine the usefulness of information in financial statements

(c) The definition, recognition and measurement of the elements from which financial statements are constructed

(d) Concepts of capital and capital maintenance

3.6 The IASB believes that further international harmonisation of accounting methods can best be promoted by focusing on these four topics since they will then lead to published financial statements that meet the common needs of most users.

Solomons Report

3.7 The Solomons Report, published in 1989 and entitled *Guidelines for Financial Reporting Standards*, proceeds in a similar way. Chapters deal with:

- The purpose of financial reporting
- Financial statements and their elements
- The qualitative characteristics of accounting information
- Recognition and measurement
- The choice of a general purpose accounting model

Advantages of a conceptual framework

3.8 The advantages arising from using a conceptual framework may be summarised by looking at some of the **problems** the old ASC had when developing SSAPs.

(a) SSAPs were developed on a **patchwork quilt** basis where a particular accounting problem was recognised by the ASC as having emerged, and resources were then channelled into standardising accounting practice in that area, without regard to whether that particular issue was necessarily the most important issue remaining at that time without standardisation.

(b) The development of certain SSAPs (eg SSAP 13) were subject to considerable **political interference** from interested parties. Where there is a conflict of interest between user groups on which policies to choose, policies deriving from a conceptual framework will be less open to criticism that the standard setters buckled under external pressure.

(c) Some SSAPs **concentrate** on the income statement (P&L account), some on the valuation of net assets (balance sheet).

(i) FRS 15 ensures that depreciation is charged on a systematic basis through the P&L account to comply with the accruals concept, but the net book value figure in the balance sheet has little meaning.

(ii) Conversely, SSAP 15 required the balance sheet provision for deferred tax to be the liability currently envisaged, but the P&L charge or credit for deferred tax has no meaning other than representing the balancing figure between a provision brought forward and carried forward in the balance sheet.

An unambiguous definition of **income** and **value** would ensure all financial statements have equal usefulness to each user group.

3.9 **Disadvantages of a conceptual framework**

(a) Financial statements are intended for a **variety of users**, and it is not certain that a single conceptual framework can be devised which will suit all users.

(b) Given the diversity of user requirements, there may be a need for a variety of accounting standards, each produced for a **different purpose** (and with different concepts as a basis).

(c) It is not clear that a conceptual framework will make the task of **preparing** and then **implementing** standards any easier than it is now.

3.10 The ASB has now focused its attention on developing a conceptual framework, based on both the IASB *Framework* and on the recommendations of the Solomons Report. The ASB conceptual framework is encompassed in a *Statement of Principles*, a summary of which is given below.

Generally Accepted Accounting Practice (GAAP)

3.11 This term has sprung up in recent years.

KEY TERM

GAAP signifies all the rules, from whatever source, which govern accounting. In the UK this is seen primarily as a combination of:

- Company law (mainly CA 1985)
- Accounting standards
- Stock exchange requirements

3.12 Although those sources are the basis for UK GAAP, the concept also includes the effects of **non-mandatory sources** such as:

- International accounting standards
- Statutory requirements in other countries, particularly the US

3.13 In other words, GAAP encompasses these regulatory influences discussed in Section 1 above. In the UK, GAAP has **no statutory or regulatory authority** or definition (unlike other countries, such as the US). The term is mentioned rarely in legislation, and only then in fairly limited terms.

3.14 GAAP is in fact a **dynamic concept**: it changes constantly as circumstances alter through new legislation, standards *and* practice. This idea that GAAP is constantly changing is recognised by the ASB in its *Statement of Aims* where it states that it expects to issue new standards and amend old ones in response to:

> 'evolving business practices, new economic developments and deficiencies identified in current practice.'

The emphasis has shifted from 'principles' to 'practice' in UK GAAP.

3.15 The problem of what is **generally accepted** is not easy to settle, because new practices will obviously not be generally adopted yet. The criteria for a practice being 'generally accepted' will depend on factors such as whether the practice is addressed by UK accounting standards or legislation, their international equivalents, and whether other companies have adopted the practice. Most importantly, perhaps: is the practice consistent with the needs of users and the objectives of financial reporting and is it is consistent with the 'true and fair' concept?

ASB Statement of Principles

3.16 You have covered this in your earlier studies, so a summary is given here.

Knowledge brought forward from earlier studies

ASB Statement of Principles

Conceptual framework

- *Definition*: a statement of generally accepted theoretical principles which form the frame of reference for financial reporting
- The previous approach was just to tackle problems as they arose; this caused overlaps, contradictions, loopholes etc
- The IASC's *Framework* document and the *Solomons Report* have been used as a basis for the ASB's *Statement of Principles*

Statement of Principles

- Will provide the conceptual basis for UK standards
- All 8 chapters now produced together in one Statement (issued December 1999)

Chapter 1 Objective of financial statements

- To provide information about *financial position*, *performance* and *financial adaptability*, useful to assess management stewardship and to make economic decisions
- Wide range of users, with some common needs, primarily meet needs of providers of risk capital
- *Users*
    - Investors
    - Employees
    - Lenders
    - Suppliers and other creditors
    - Customers

Knowledge brought forward from earlier studies (cont'd)

  - Government and their agencies
  - The public

- Investors are the defining choice of user. They require information on
  - Financial performance
  - Financial position
  - Generation and use of cash
  - Financial adaptability

Chapter 2 The reporting entity

It is important that entities that should prepare financial statements in fact do so.

The entity must be a cohesive economic unit with a determinable boundary and it is held to account for all the things it can *control.*

Control means

- Ability to deploy the economic resources
- Ability to benefit (suffer) from their deployment

Chapter 3 Qualitative characteristics of financial information

- Qualitative characteristics that relate to content are relevance and reliability
- Qualitative characteristics that relate to presentation are comparability and understandability

Chapter 4 Elements of financial statements

- *Elements*
  - Assets
  - Liabilities
  - Ownership interest
  - Gains
  - Losses
  - Contributions from owners
  - Distributions to owners
- Any item not falling under the definition of one of these should not be included in financial statements

Chapter 5 Recognition in financial statements

There are 3 stages in the recognition of assets and liabilities.

- Initial recognition
- Subsequent remeasurement
- Derecognition

Uncertainty sometimes makes it necessary to delay the recognition process.

- Element uncertainty - does the item exist and meet the definition of elements?
- Measurement uncertainty - at what monetary amount should it be recognised?

Matching is still important, but does not *drive* the recognition process.

Chapter 6 Measurement in financial statements

- *Initially*: record asset/liability at transaction cost = historical cost = current replacement cost
- *Remeasure:* in historical cost system
  - Write down *asset* to recoverable amount
  - Amend *liability* to monetary amount to be paid
- *Current value system* recommended
  - *Asset* current value = value to the business
  - *Liability* current value = market value = value to business

Knowledge brought forward from earlier studies (cont'd)

Chapter 7 Presentation of financial information

- *Components* of financial statements
  - Profit and loss account
  - Statement of total recognised gains and losses
  - Balance sheet
  - Cash flow statement

The first two are 'statements of financial performance'.

Chapter 8 Accounting for interests in other entities

This chapter deals with principles underlying consolidation, equity accounting and proportional consolidation. It focuses on the circumstances in which one business interest controls another and how to account for influence that is less than control but still significant.

Questions and answers

3.17 The original November 1995 exposure draft of the *Statement of Principles* attracted a great deal of criticism, not least from the firm Ernst & Young. In an attempt to address the criticisms raised, the ASB produced a booklet to go with the revised March 1998 exposure draft, called '*Some questions answered*'. Although these have not been incorporated into the December 1999 version, they are still valid arguments and should be used if you have to comment critically on the *Statement.* Below is an outline of the topics covered.

Status and purpose

3.18 The points made here are as follows.

(a) The *Statement* is a description of the fundamental approach that should underpin the financial statements. It is intended to be:

- Comprehensive
- Internally consistent
- Consistent with international approaches

(b) The final version is **not** an accounting standard.

(c) Its main influence on accounting practice will be through its influence on the standard-setting process. It is only one of the factors that will be taken into account.

Approach

3.19 The approach encompasses the following.

(a) There are similarities to existing practice and differences.

(b) The *Statement* is based on the International Accounting Standard Committee's framework statement and is largely consistent with the framework statements issued in Australia, Canada, New Zealand, the USA and elsewhere. This reflects the view that it will be easier to achieve harmonisation of accounting practice if standard-setters work with a common set of principles.

(c) The 'true and fair' requirement and the old SSAP 2's fundamental accounting concepts play a central role in the revised draft. The emphasis is different, however, and is reflected in FRS 18 *Accounting policies*.

(d) The *Statement's* development has not been constrained by the requirements of companies legislation because:

- It does not just apply to companies
- Legal frameworks change in response to developments in accounting thought

The use of current costs and values and current cost accounting

3.20 These points are made.

(a) The previous version of the *Statement* was criticised as heralding a move towards **current cost accounting**. However, the revised draft makes it clear that this is **not on the ASB's agenda**.

(b) The *Statement* explains that historical cost and current value are **alternative measures**. It also explains that it is envisaged that the approach now adopted by the majority of the larger UK listed companies will continue to be used. This approach involves carrying some categories of balance sheet items at historical cost and others at current value. The *Statement* then goes on to describe a framework that would guide the choice of an appropriate measurement basis for each balance sheet category.

The focus on assets and liabilities and the role of transactions

3.21 These points are made.

(a) The previous version placed great emphasis on assets and liabilities and even defined the items that are to be included in the profit and loss account in terms of assets and liabilities. This approach has been retained.

(b) The approach does not mean that the P&L is unimportant. The primary source of information provided in financial statements is the transactions undertaken by the reporting entity. The primary focus of the accounting process is to allocate these transactions to accounting periods.

(c) The *Statement* regards the profit or loss for the period as the difference between the opening and closing balance sheets adjusted for capital constructions and distributions.

Accounting standards based on the Statement

3.22 The question was raised as to whether accounting standards published in the future and therefore based on the *Statement of Principles* will be very different from past accounting standards. The ASB's view is that they won't. Some of the principles have already played very significant roles in accounting standards and have found general acceptance. The standards include:

- FRS 2 *Accounting for subsidiary undertakings*, which uses the reporting entity concept described in Chapter 2 of the draft Statement.
- FRS 4 *Capital instruments* and FRS 5 *Reporting the substance of transactions*, which use the definitions of assets and liabilities set out in Chapter 4.
- FRS 11 *Impairment of fixed assets and goodwill*, which uses the recoverable amount notion described in Chapter 6.

The way forward

3.23 At the time of writing (July 2002) the revised *Statement of Principles* has not yet had to face the barrage of criticism heaped upon the 1995 exposure draft. Watch this space!

Question: Statement of Principles

What is the purpose of the ASB's *Statement of Principles?*

Answer

The following are the main reasons why the ASB developed the *Statement of Principles.*

(a) To assist the ASB by providing a basis for reducing the number of alternative accounting treatments permitted by accounting standards and company law

(b) To provide a framework for the future development of accounting standards

(c) To assist auditors in forming an opinion as to whether financial statements conform with accounting standards

(d) To assist users of accounts in interpreting the information contained in them

(e) To provide guidance in applying accounting standards

(f) To give guidance on areas which are not yet covered by accounting standards

(g) To inform interested parties of the approach taken by the ASB in formulating accounting standards

The role of the *Statement* can thus be summed up as being to provide consistency, clarity and information.

4 CORPORATE GOVERNANCE 6/03

4.1 Your syllabus requires you to have some knowledge of topical issues relating to corporate governance. By far the most important development in this area is the report of the Cadbury Committee.

KEY TERM

Corporate governance is the system by which companies are directed and controlled.

4.2 Financial aspects of corporate governance in the UK have been addressed in the report of the Cadbury Committee, which was formed in 1991. The terms of reference of the committee were to consider, along with any other relevant matters, the following issues.

(a) The responsibilities of executive and non-executive directors for reviewing and reporting on performance to shareholders and other financially interested parties, and the frequency, clarity and form in which information should be provided

(b) The case for audit committees of the board, including their composition and role.

(c) The principal responsibilities of auditors and the extent and value of the audit

(d) The links between shareholders, boards, and auditors

4.3 The committee aimed to set out the responsibilities of each group involved in the reporting process and to make recommendations on good practice.

4.4 The **Code of Best Practice** included in the Cadbury Report is aimed at the directors of all UK public companies, but the directors of all companies are encouraged to use the Code for guidance.

4.5 Directors should state in the annual report and accounts whether they comply with the Code and give reasons for any non-compliance. **This statement of compliance should only be published after a review by the auditors.**

Provisions of the Cadbury code	
The board of directors	The **board of directors** must meet on a regular basis, retain full control over the company and monitor the executive management. A **clearly accepted division of responsibilities is necessary** at the head of the company, so no one person has complete power, answerable to no-one. The report encourages **the separation of the posts of Chairman and Chief Executive**. Where they are not separate, a strong independent group should be present on the board, with their own leader. There should be a **formal schedule of matters which must be referred to the board** stating which decisions require a single director's signature and which require several signatures. **Procedures** should be in place to make sure the schedule is followed. The schedule should include **acquisitions and disposals of assets of the company**/subsidiaries that are material to the company and **investments, capital projects, bank borrowing** facilities, **loans** and their repayment, foreign currency transactions, all above a predetermined size.
Non-executive directors	The following points are made about **non-executive directors**, who are those directors not running the day to day operations of the company. They should bring **independent judgement** to bear on important issues, including key appointments and standards of conduct. There should be **no business, financial or other connection between the non-executive directors and the company**, apart from fees and shareholdings. **Fees should reflect the time they spend on the business** of the company, so extra duties could earn extra pay. They should **not take part in share option schemes** and their service should not be pensionable, to maintain their independent status. **Appointments should be for a specified term and reappointment should not be automatic**. The board as a whole should decide on their nomination and selection. **Procedures** should exist **whereby non-executive directors may take independent advice**, at the company's expense if necessary.
Executive directors	In relation to the **executive directors,** who run companies on a day to day basis, the main points in the Code relate to service contracts (contracts of employment) and pay. The length of such contracts should be three years at most, unless the shareholders approve a longer contract. Directors' emoluments and those of the highest paid directors should be fully disclosed and analysed between salary and performance-related pay. The basis of measuring performance should also be shown. A remuneration committee of non-executive directors should decide on the level of executive pay.

Provisions of the Cadbury code	
Audit	The code states that audit is a **cornerstone of corporate governance**. It is an **objective and external check** on the **stewardship** of management. There are design problems in the framework of auditing however, including: • Choices in accounting treatments • Poor links between shareholders and auditors • Price competition associated with auditing Another problem associated with the audit is the 'expectations gap' between what an audit actually achieves and what people think it achieves, This is discussed further in Chapter 19. Some of these matters are being addressed by the APB. The threat to objectivity of auditors offered other services to audit clients should be safeguarded against by **disclosing fees for audit** in the financial statements. The code also **recommends** that the auditing profession draw **up formal guidelines concerning audit rotation**. The advantages and disadvantages of audit rotation were discussed in Chapter 2. It recommends the accountancy profession being involved in setting criteria for evaluation of **internal control** (this is discussed more in Section 4.) It recommended that auditors report on **going concern**. This has now been reflected in auditing standards and is common practice. It also recommended that auditors have guidelines about how to act in the event of suspicion of **fraud**. This is dealt with in SAS 110.

Smaller companies

4.6 Many **smaller companies** have complained that the Cadbury Code is too burdensome for them, raising fears that if its requirements are not diluted then many smaller companies will simply fail to comply with them.

4.7 In response to this, a special version of the code aimed at listed companies with market capitalisation below £250 million was published in 1994 by the City Group for Smaller Companies ('Cisco'), with the endorsement of the Cadbury Committee.

4.8 Differences between the Cisco code and the Cadbury code include reduction of the number of non-executives on a company board from three to two and not requiring smaller companies to split the roles of Chief Executive and Chairman.

The Combined Code

4.9 The Cadbury report was issued in 1992, and the comments in the table above show that some of the points have been addressed subsequently by the APB, particularly those in relation to fraud and going concern.

4.10 Since the Cadbury report, there have been several other committees, which all produced recommendations about various issues such as directors' remuneration. In 1998, the key guidance from all the reports was re-issued in the form of the combined code.

4.11 The Combined Code is issued as part of the Stock Exchange guidance and so generally relates to listed companies. However, this does not mean that following the guidance is not good practice for other companies also.

Provisions of the Combined Code	
Directors' responsibilities	
The Board	Should **meet regularly**, and have a **formal schedule of matters** reserved to it for its decision. There should be clear division of responsibilities between chairman and chief executive. **Non-executive directors** should comprise at least a third of the board. Directors should submit themselves for re-election every three years. Directors should submit themselves for re-election at regular intervals (at least every three years).
The AGM	Companies should propose **separate resolutions** at the AGM on each substantially different issue. The chairman should ensure that members of the audit, remuneration and nomination committees are available at the AGM to **answer questions**. Notice of AGMs should be sent out at least 20 days before the meeting.
Accountability and audit	The directors should **explain** their **responsibility for preparing accounts**. They should **report that the business is a going concern**, with supporting assumptions and qualifications as necessary.
Remuneration	There should be remuneration committees composed of non-executive directors to set directors' pay, which should provide pay which attracts, retains and motivates quality directors but avoids paying more than is necessary for the purpose. The company's annual report should contain a statement of remuneration policy and details of the remuneration of each director.
Internal control	The directors should review the **effectiveness of internal control** systems, at least annually, and also **review the need for an internal audit function**.
Audit committee	The board **should establish an audit committee**.
Auditors' responsibilities	
Statement of responsibilities	The auditors **should include** in their report a statement of their reporting responsibilities.

Corporate governance statement

4.12 The stock exchange rules require that, as part of the **annual report**, a company must **include** a narrative **statement of how it has applied the principles set out in the combined code**. This statement must include an explanation which allows the shareholders to evaluate how the company have applied the principles.

4.13 The statement must also provide explanation of whether the company has **complied** with the principles of the combined code.

4.14 They must also provide a statement showing how they have applied the principles relating to directors' remuneration (not examined in detail here).

4.15 The auditors must review the corporate governance statement before it is published. Their duty to review it only extends to the following items:

- Board having a formal schedule of matters for their attention
- Procedure for board members to seek independent, professional advice
- Non-executive directors having specific terms of office
- Directors being subject to election and re-election by the shareholders
- The directors and auditors stating their respective responsibilities
- The directors conducting a review of internal control effectiveness
- The board establishing an audit committee

Benefits of a voluntary code

4.16 The combined code is a **voluntary code**. The Stock Exchange requires that disclosures be made as to whether it has been complied with, but there are **no statutory requirements to comply** with it.

4.17 The main benefit in having a voluntary code is that the code can be **applied flexibly**, where management believe that it is relevant. The **disclosure** requirements ensure that **shareholders** are **aware** of the position and they can make any points they want to about compliance with the code at the AGM.

4.18 It has been argued that making such a code obligatory would have **punitive effects** on some companies, due to their size or investor make up and that legislation would create a **burden of requirement** which **could be excessive in many cases**.

4.19 Critics of the view would argue:

(a) Disclosure of non-compliance is insufficient as the AGM is still not sufficient protection for shareholders.

(b) Having a voluntary code allows some companies not to comply freely, to the detriment of their shareholders.

(c) The requirement to disclose is only a Stock Exchange requirement, and there are many unlisted companies who should be encouraged to apply the codes.

4.20 The government has shown concern for this area in the past and it is believed that it **might take action in the future to regulate this area** more heavily.

4.21 However, at the moment, having a **voluntary code is a compromise** based on the points made above.

Audit committees

4.22 A major recommendation in the Cadbury Code is that **all listed companies must establish effective audit committees** if they have not already done so.

4.23 The Code takes its example from countries such as Canada where audit committees for listed companies are compulsory.

4.24 The audit committees should have formal terms of reference dealing with their membership, authority and duties. They should meet at least three times every year and membership of the committee, which should be comprised of **non-executive directors**, should be shown in the annual report.

- The committee must have the authority, resources and means of access to investigate anything within its terms of reference.
- Review of the external auditors' management letter and the company's statement on the internal control system.

4.25 The key advantage to an auditor of having an audit committee is that a committee of independent non-executive directors provides the auditor with an independent point of reference other than the executive directors of the company, in the event of disagreement arising.

4.26 Other **advantages** that are claimed to arise from the existence of an audit committee include:

(a) It will lead to **increased confidence** in the credibility and objectivity of financial reports.

(b) By specialising in the problems of financial reporting and thus, to some extent, fulfilling the directors' responsibility in this area, it will allow the **executive** directors to **devote their attention to management.**

(c) In cases where the interests of the company, the executive directors and the employees conflict, the audit committee might provide an **impartial body** for the auditors to consult.

(d) The internal auditors will be able to report to the audit committee.

4.27 Opponents of audit committees argue that:

(a) There may be **difficulty selecting** sufficient non-executive directors with the necessary competence in auditing matters for the committee to be really effective.

(b) The establishment of such a **formalised reporting procedure** may **dissuade** the **auditors** from raising matters of judgement and limit them to reporting only on matters of fact.

(c) **Costs** may be **increased.**

4.28 In an appendix to the *Cadbury Report*, the Committee expands on the role and function of the audit committee.

> 'If they operate effectively, audit committees can bring significant benefits. In particular, they have the potential to
>
> (a) Improve the quality of financial reporting, by reviewing the financial statements on behalf of the Board
>
> (b) Create a climate of discipline and control which will reduce the opportunity for fraud
>
> (c) Enable the non-executive directors to contribute an independent judgement and play a positive role
>
> (d) Help the finance director, by providing a forum in which he can raise issues of concern, and which he can use to get things done which might otherwise be difficult
>
> (e) Strengthen the position of the external auditor, by providing a channel of communication and forum for issues of concern

(f) Provide a framework within which the external auditor can assert his independence in the event of a dispute with management

(g) Strengthen the position of the internal audit function, by providing a greater degree of independence from management

(h) Increase public confidence in the credibility and objectivity of financial statements'

4.29 In practice the main duties of the audit committee are likely to be as follows.

Review of financial statements. The committee should review both the half yearly and annual accounts. The committee should assess the **overall appearance** and **presentation** of the accounts, in particular the treatment of material changes from previous years, significant events and other exceptional items. The review should also cover.

4.30 **Liaison with external auditors**. The audit committee's tasks here will include:

(a) Being responsible for the **appointment** or **removal** of the **external auditors** as well as fixing their remuneration; the committee should also consider non-audit services provided by the external auditors, paying particular attention to whether there may be a conflict of interest

(b) Discussing the **scope** of the **external audit** prior to the start of the audit; this should include consideration of whether external audit's coverage of all areas of the business is fair, and how much external audit will rely on the work of internal audit

(c) Acting as a **forum** for **liaison** between the external auditors, the internal auditors and the finance director

(d) **Helping** the **external auditors** to **obtain** the **information** they require and in resolving any problems they may encounter

(e) Making themselves available to the external auditors for **consultation**, with or without the presence of the company's management

(f) Dealing with any **serious reservations** which the auditors may express either about the accounts, the information published with the accounts, the records, the control environment or the quality or views of the company's management

4.31 **Review of internal audit.** The review should cover the standards used, the scope of the function, the reporting arrangements and the results of internal audit work.

4.32 **Review of internal control.** The audit committee can play a significant role in reviewing internal control.

(a) Committee members can use their own experience to monitor continually the **adequacy** of **internal control systems**, focusing particularly on the control environment, management's attitude towards controls and overall management controls. The audit committee's review should cover legal compliance and ethics, for example listing rules, Financial Service Act requirements or environmental legislation.

(b) Each year the committee should be responsible for reviewing the company's statement on internal controls prior to its approval by the board.

(c) The committee should consider the recommendations of the auditors in the management letter and management's response. Because the committee's role is ongoing, it can also ensure that recommendations are publicised and see that actions are taken as appropriate.

4.33 **Investigations.** The committee will also be involved in implementing and reviewing the results of one-off investigations

Question: voluntary codes

What are the benefits of corporate governance codes being voluntary?

Answer

- Code can be applied flexibly, as is best for the company.
- Burden of statutory requirement is not created

Question: audit committees

Since 1978 all public companies in the United States of America have been required to have an audit committee as a condition of listing on the New York Stock Exchange.

(a) Explain what you understand by the term audit committee.
(b) List and briefly describe the duties and responsibilities of audit committees.
(c) Discuss their advantages and disadvantages.

Answer

(a) An **audit committee** reviews financial information and liases between the auditors and the company. It normally consists of the non-executive directors of the company, though there is no reason why other senior personnel should not also be involved.

(b) Although no specific responsibilities and duties are laid down, they would be likely to include the following.

(i) Being responsible for **recommending the appointment or removal of the external auditor** as well as for fixing their remuneration;

(ii) Helping to **ensure good relations** between the external auditors and the management as well as with the internal auditors;

(iii) **Helping the external auditors to obtain the information** they require and in resolving problems they encounter;

(iv) Making themselves **available to the external auditors** for consultation, with or without the presence of the company's management;

(v) **Dealing with any serious reservations** which the auditor may express either about the accounts, the records or the quality of management.

In addition to these responsibilities, any responsible audit committee is likely to want:

(i) To **ensure that the review procedures** for interim statements, rights documents and similar information are **adequate;**

(ii) To **review both the management accounts** used internally and the **statutory accounts** issued to shareholders for reasonableness;

(iii) To make **appropriate recommendations for improvements in management control.**

(c) There are a number of advantages and disadvantages.

Disadvantages

(i) Since the finding of audit committees are rarely made public, it is **not** always **clear what they do** or how effective they have been in doing it.

(ii) It is possible that the audit committee's **approach** may prove somewhat **pedestrian,** resolving little of consequence but acting as a drag on the drive and entrepreneurial flair of the company's senior executives.

(iii) Unless the requirement for such a body were made compulsory, as in the US, it is likely that those **firms most in need** of an audit committee would nevertheless **choose not to have**

one. (Note that the Cadbury report now requires listed companies to have an audit committee.)

Advantages

(i) By its very existence, the audit committee should make the **executive directors more aware of their duties and responsibilities.**

(ii) It could act as a **deterrent to the commission of illegal acts** by the executive directors and may discourage them from behaving in ways which could be prejudicial to the interests of the shareholders

(iii) Where **illegal or prejudicial acts** have been carried out by the executive directors, the **audit committee** provides an **independent body** to which the auditor can turn. In this way, the problem may be resolved without the auditor having to reveal the matter to the shareholders, either in his report or at the AGM.

Exam focus point

You should read the financial press to keep up to date with developments in this area.

5 OPERATING AND FINANCIAL REVIEW

5.1 The ASB's statement on the *Operating and Financial Review*, first published in 1993, also contains some useful material which demonstrates some of the problems associated with the interpretation of accounting standards. A revised version was published in January 2003.

5.2 The statement is **voluntary rather than mandatory** and it applies mainly to listed companies, but also those large corporations where there is a legitimate public interest. Such companies would be called on to produce an Operating and Financial Review (OFR) in their financial statements.

5.3 The Operating and Financial Review is intended as a **broad framework rather than a set of rules** or requirements. The directors will then apply the framework to the particular circumstances of their business. The statement says:

> 'The Operating and Financial Review (OFR) should set out the directors' analysis of the business, in order to provide to investors a historical and prospective analysis of the reporting entity "through the eyes of management". It should include discussion and interpretation of the performance of the business and the structure of its financing, in the context of known or reasonably expected changes in the environment in which it operates.'

5.4 The OFR should not duplicate information contained elsewhere in the annual report. However, it should complement the format of the annual report as a whole.

Principles

5.5 The statement contains a number of principles which need to be applied when preparing the OFR. These are as follows.

(a) **Purpose.** The OFR should set out the directors' analysis of the business to enable the user to assess future performance. There should be a discussion of:

(i) The **nature of the business**, its objectives and the strategies adopted to achieve those objectives

(ii) The **performance of the business** in the period and the main influences on performance, including the expected effect of known trends and the potential effect of risks facing the business

(iii) The **financial position**, including capital structure and treasury policy, and the factors affecting, and likely to affect, that position

(b) **Audience.** The focus will be on matters that are relevant to **investors.** The OFR must be clearly written and not assume a detailed prior knowledge of the business.

(c) **Time frame.** The OFR, in its discussion of the period's performance will identify factors relevant to future performance and long-term trends. There should be a discussion of significant post balance sheet events and of previous predictions not borne out by events.

(d) **Reliability.** Information and analysis contained in the OFR should be neutral, free from bias and complete, dealing even-handedly with both good and bad aspects.

(e) **Comparability.** The user should be able to compare the information presented with similar information about the entity for previous periods and with information about other entities in the same industry or sector.

(f) **Measures.** To enhance comparability, generally accepted measures should be used. These should be properly explained and disclosed.

Guidance

5.6 The statement goes on to give guidance as to how these principles are to be **applied**. Key features of this guidance are as follows.

The business, its objectives and strategy

5.7 This general description provides a **context** for the directors' discussion and analysis of performance and financial position. For example, it might include the business structure, the major markets and the main products and services, together with key relationships with stakeholders.

5.8 This description should identify **key financial measures** (eg turnover) and **non-financial measures** (eg customer satisfaction) which enable management to assess the achievement of its objectives.

Operating review

5.9 This should identify the main factors that underlie the business, concentrating on those that have either **varied in the past or are expected to change in the future**.

(a) **Performance in the period.** This should focus on key business segments and be discussed in the context of the long-term business objectives. It should discuss changes in the business environment, for example:

(i) Changes in market conditions
(ii) Introduction of new products and services
(iii) Changes in exchange rates and inflation rates
(iv) New activities, discontinued activities and other acquisitions and disposals

This section should also cover any special factors affecting performance and exceptional items reported in the financial statements.

(b) **Returns to shareholders.** This section will include distributions and share repurchases, and a comparison of profit and dividends. Alternative measures for earnings per share should be discussed, along with basic and diluted EPS.

(c) **Dynamics of the business.** This section considers matters which, even if they were not significant in the period under review, may affect the business in the future. There should be a discussion of the principal risks facing the business, the nature of the impact of those risks and the directors' approach to managing them. Examples of matters that could be relevant are:

(i) Scarcity of raw materials

(ii) Skill shortages and expertise of uncertain supply

(iii) Technological change

(iv) Dependence on major suppliers or customers

(v) Risks related to environmental issues

(vi) Access to markets

(vii) Product liability

(viii) Regulatory issues

(ix) Changes in demographic, political or macro-economic conditions (exchange rate fluctuations, for example)

(x) Other reputational risks

There should also be a commentary on the **strengths and resources** of the business that enable it to pursue its objectives. These might include:

(i) Corporate reputation and brand equity
(ii) Intellectual capital
(iii) Licences, patents, copyright and trademarks
(iv) Research and development
(v) Customer/ supplier relationships
(vi) Proprietary business processes
(vii) Websites and databases
(vii) Market position/dominance

(d) **Investment for the future**

The OFR should discuss how directors have sought to **maintain and improve future performance**. Examples include:

(i) Human capital policies and practices, including employee training

(ii) Pure and applied research leading to potential new products, services or processes

(iii) Development of new products and services

(iv) Investment in brand equity, through advertising and other marketing activities

(v) Technical support to customers

(vi) Refurbishment and maintenance programmes.

Information should be given about capital expenditure and the future benefits expected from this and other expenditure.

Financial Review

5.10 The principal aim of the financial review is to explain to the user of the annual report the **capital structure of the business**, its **treasury policy** and the **dynamics of its financial position** - its **sources of liquidity** and **their application**, including the implications of the financing requirements arising from its investment plans.

5.11 The main contents should be as follows.

(a) **Capital structure and treasury policy,** including maturity profile of debt, type of capital instruments used, currency, and interest rate structure. This should include comments on relevant ratios such as interest cover and debt/equity ratios, as well as short and longer-term funding plans. The OFR should discuss capital funding and treasury policies.

(b) **Cash flows.** Cash inflows and outflows during the period under review should be discussed. The principal sources of cash inflows should be identified, highlighting the relative contribution from customers and other sources. Similarly, the principal destinations of cash outflows in the period should be identified. The OFR should comment on any special factors that have influenced cash flows in the current period and those that may have a significant effect on future cash flows. Where segmental cash flows are significantly out of line with segmental profits, this should be indicated and explained.

(c) **Current liquidity** at the end of the period including comments on the current level of borrowing.

(d) **Going concern.** The going concern report required by the Combined Code may be included here.

Statement of compliance

5.12 A statement of compliance with the OFR *Statement* is **not required**, although it might be helpful to the users of the accounts.

5.13 You can see that the OFR should be of **great benefit to less sophisticated users of accounts** as it should carry out the analysis of a company's performance on the user's behalf. It should thus highlight the important items in the current year annual report, as well as drawing out those aspects of the year under review that are relevant to an assessment of future prospects.

DTI Consultative Document

5.14 In May 2004, the Government published a Consultative Document *Draft Regulations on the Operating and Financial Review and Directors' Report,* which includes a proposal that quoted companies should have to prepare a **statutory OFR** for the first time for financial years beginning on or after 1 January 2005. The Government intends to specify the ASB in legislation as the body to make the standards for a mandatory OFR.

5.15 The key aspects of the Government's proposals on the OFR require the directors of quoted companies to give a **balanced and comprehensive analysis** of their business as part of their annual reports. This will include a company's objectives, strategies and key drivers of the business, focusing more on qualitative and forward-looking information than has traditionally been included. Required information could cover **employees, environmental matters and community and social issues.**

5.16 The document **does not describe what should be in an OFR** – that is a matter for the Directors. However, the document offers suggestions on the **principles and the process** that the Directors should consider in making those decisions. Specifically, the process should:

(a) Be planned and transparent
(b) Involve stakeholders
(c) Consider all existing information
(d) Be comprehensive
(e) Maintain consistency from year to year
(f) Be subject to review.

5.17 The ASB hopes to issue an **exposure draft** of the first OFR standard in the second half of 2004, to be finalised in 2005. All companies are likely to have to produce an OFR for financial years starting in 2005. Companies that already produce one will be at an advantage. Ideally, it should help directors run a company more efficiently and reduce other requests for information. However, it is likely to increase the amount of audit work.

5.18 This new development has generally been welcomed, but some commentators have seen it as a **politically driven requirement**, which adds to the burdens businesses already have to carry.

Chapter roundup

- This is a very long but also a very important chapter. You must understand all aspects of the **regulatory environment** and the arguments behind current thinking. We have put a lot in here and you may wish to refer back to this chapter as you go through the text.
- You should be familiar using the **role and impact** of the following bodies.
  - Accounting Standards Board
  - Financial Reporting Council
  - Review Panel
  - Urgent Issues Task Force
  - European Union/European Commission
  - Company Law
  - International Accounting Standards Committee
- The ***FRS for Smaller Entities*** aims to close the big GAAP/little GAAP debate by giving small entities basic accounting and disclosure rules to follow.
- **GAAP** standards for 'Generally Accepted Accounting Practice'. It signifies all rules from whatever source, which govern accounting.
- You should be familiar with the ASB's approach to **standard setting**.
- There are some important debates raging in the financial reporting world at the moment on the *Statement of Principles* and on **corporate governance**.
- The impact of the **Cadbury Report** and the **Combined Code** is still being felt as some companies struggle to meet its requirements.
- The **Operating and Financial Review** should be of considerable benefit to less sophisticated users.

Quick quiz

1 What is the latest accounting standard?

2 What is the latest FRS?

3 The FRSSE is about to be abandoned

True ☐

False ☐

4 What is meant by GAAP?

5 Which of the following are chapters of the *Statement of Principles?* Circle all that apply.

(a) The reporting entity
(b) The quantitative characteristics of financial information
(c) Presentation of interests in other entitles
(d) Measurement in financial statements

6 The *Statement of Principles* is now a full accounting standard. True or false?

7 How does the *Statement* define assets?

8 Which accounting standard uses the 'recoverable amount' idea described in the *Statement of Principles.*

9 Name the reports that deal with corporate governance.

....

....

....

10 The Operating and Financial Review is compulsory/voluntary?

Answers to quick quiz

1 FRS 19 *Deferred tax*

2 FRS 21 *Events after the balance sheet date.*

3 False. The function and purpose of the FRSSE is under review.

4 The rules governing accounting, principally:

- Company law
- Accounting standards
- Stock exchange requirements

5 (a) and (d)

6 False. However, it will influence the standard-setting process.

7 Rights or other access to future economic benefits controlled by an entity as a result of past transactions or events.

8 FRS 11 *Impairment of fixed assets and goodwill.*

9 Cadbury
Combined Code

10 Voluntary, applying mainly to listed companies. However, it will shortly become compulsory.

Now try the questions below from the Exam Question Bank

Number	Level	Marks	Time
Q1	Introductory	n/a	n/a
Q2	Introductory	n/a	n/a

Part B

Group accounts

Chapter 2

CONSOLIDATED ACCOUNTS: SIMPLE GROUPS

Chapter topic list		Syllabus reference
1	Revision: definition of a subsidiary	2(a)
2	Revision: exclusion/exemption	2(a)
3	Revision: other provisions of FRS 2	2(a)
4	Revision: summary of techniques	

Introduction

You will have covered basic groups in your earlier studies, including the important **legislation**, **definitions** and **standards**. This is the first of six chapters on consolidation.

In Paper 3.6 the emphasis is on the more **complex aspects** of consolidation compared to the simple consolidation in your earlier studies. In this chapter, you can revise briefly the main provisions of FRS 2 *Accounting for subsidiary undertakings* and the CA 1985 provisions relating to group accounts. You can also revise some of the basic principles of consolidation by carrying out an exercise. If you have problems with this exercise, then you should go back and **revise** from your earlier study material.

Note. In all the chapters on consolidation, all undertakings are **incorporated** (ie limited companies) unless stated otherwise.

Study guide

Section 3 – Group financial statements 1

- Review the basic principles of acquisition accounting

Exam guide

While it is unlikely that you will be tested on the basic principles, you will gain marks for knowing the basics as well as the more complicated aspects.

1 REVISION: DEFINITION OF A SUBSIDIARY

1.1 From your earlier studies, as well as being able to prepare a simple group balance sheet and P&L account, you should also know:

(a) The requirements of the CA 1985 and FRS 2 *Accounting for subsidiary undertakings* regarding groups of companies

(b) The different methods which could be used to prepare group accounts

(c) The basic meaning and function of acquisition, equity and merger accounting

(d) The methods of dealing with intra-group profits

1.2 If a company has a subsidiary at its year end, it must prepare group accounts which must be in the form of **consolidated accounts.**

Knowledge brought forward from earlier studies

Definition of a subsidiary

CA 1985 defines a subsidiary undertaking as one in which the parent:

- has a majority of the **voting rights**;
- is a **member** and can appoint/remove a **majority of the board of directors** (entitled to the majority of voting rights);
- is a member and controls alone a majority of the voting rights **by agreement** with other members;
- has the right to exercise a **dominant influence** through the Memorandum and Articles or a control contract:
- has a **participating interest** and either:
    - actually exercises a dominant influence over it; or
    - manages both on a **unified basis**.

Further definition was required to stop the increasing practice of the use of the non-consolidated (quasi) subsidiary. The following extra definitions were added by FRS 2.

- **Control**: the ability of an undertaking to direct the financial and operating policies of another undertaking with a view to gaining economic benefits from its activities.
- **Dominant influence**: the ability to direct the financial and operating policies of another undertaking with a view to gaining benefits from its activities.
- **Participating interest**: an interest in shares held for the long-term for the purpose of securing a contribution to its activities by the exercise of control or influence arising from that interest.
- **On a unified basis**: two or more undertakings are managed on a unified basis if the whole of the operations of the undertakings are integrated and managed as a single unit.
- **Held on a long-term basis**: any interest held other than exclusively with a view to subsequent resale.

2 REVISION: EXCLUSION/EXEMPTION

2.1 FRS 2 and CA 1985 have **different rules** on the exclusion of subsidiaries from consolidated accounts. The rules on exemptions are much more uncontroversial and straightforward.

Knowledge brought forward from earlier studies

Exclusion/exemption

Exclusion of a subsidiary

There may be situations where consolidation would not give a true and fair view of the group's affairs: this would be exceptional.

Knowledge brought forward from earlier studies (cont'd)

- FRS 2 **requires** exclusion from consolidation under the following circumstances.

Reason	**Accounting treatment**
Severe long-term restrictions	Balance sheet: equity method up to date of severe restrictions subject to any write-down for impairment P&L a/c: dividends received only
Held exclusively for subsequent resale; never been consolidated	Current asset at the lower of cost and has net realisable value
Dissimilar activities	Equity method (see Chapter 3)

- CA 1985 **permits** exclusion from consolidation in all of the circumstances cited above, except for dissimilar activities where exclusion is **required**. CA 1985 permits exclusion for additional reasons, dismissed as invalid by the ASB.
  - The subsidiary's inclusion is not material.
  - Information cannot be obtained without disproportionate expense or undue delay.

Exemptions

- Where a company has a subsidiary but is itself at least **50% owned** by another company established in an **EU member** state, it is exempt from preparing group accounts if the intermediate holding company:
  - Does not have shares or debentures listed on a recognised SE in a member state, or
  - Is included in the audited consolidated financial statements of an EU parent
- **Minority shareholders** can request consolidation if they hold over 50% of the remaining shares in the company or 5% of the total shares.
- **Small and medium-sized groups** are not required to produce group accounts (unless they are plcs, banks etc) and cannot be required to do so by the minority shareholders.

3 REVISION: OTHER PROVISIONS OF FRS 2

3.1 The following revises some of the other important points in FRS 2 which you ought to remember.

Knowledge brought forward from earlier studies

Other provisions of FRS 2

- **Uniform accounting policies** should be used throughout the group.
  - Subsidiaries should be adjusted on consolidation
  - If this is not possible, make full disclosure of the different policies and their effects
- **Accounting period and dates**: the financial statements of all group companies should be prepared to the same accounting date and for the same accounting period; subsidiaries can prepare three months before if necessary and with appropriate adjustments and disclosure.
- **Material purchase of a subsidiary**: disclose sufficient information about the results of the subsidiary acquired to enable shareholders to appreciate its effect.
- **Effective date for acquisitions and disposals** of a subsidiary should be the date on which control passes.

> **Knowledge brought forward from earlier studies (cont'd)**
>
> - **Intra group transactions**
>   - Profits/losses on any intra group transactions should be eliminated in full
>   - Elimination of the profit/loss should be set against the interests held by the group and MI in respective proportion to their holdings in the relevant undertaking

Exposure Draft: Amendment to FRS 2 – legal changes

3.2 In March 2004, the DTI issued a Consultation Document, *Modernisation of Accounting Directives/IAS Infrastructure.* This requires EU member states to put in place **changes in the law relating to group financial reporting.**

3.3 In May 2004, the ASB published an Exposure Draft *Amendment to FRS 2 Accounting for subsidiary undertakings: legal changes.* The proposed changes are as follows.

(a) **Delete references to 'participating interest'** in the definition of a subsidiary.

(b) Reflect the proposed **exemption** from the preparation of consolidated accounts **for intermediate parent undertakings whose immediate parents are not governed by the law of a European Economic Area state**.

(c) **Remove the requirement for exclusion** from consolidation of subsidiaries with **dissimilar operations** to the parent undertaking.

4 REVISION: SUMMARY OF TECHNIQUES

4.1 The summary given below is very brief but it encompasses all the major, but basic, rules of consolidation for, firstly, the consolidated balance sheet.

> **Knowledge brought forward from earlier studies**
>
> ***Summary of technique: consolidated balance sheet***
>
> - **Net assets**: 100% H plus 100% S.
> - **Share capital**: H only.
> - **Reserves**: 100% H plus group share of post-acquisition retained reserves of S less consolidation adjustments.
> - **Minority interest**: MI share of S's consolidated assets.
>
> The method of consolidation is as follows.
>
> - Determine the **group structure**.
> - Consider **adjustments** for:
>   - Dividends
>   - Provisions for unrealised profits
>   - Revaluation to fair value
>   - Inter-company stock and cash in transit
> - Combine **net assets**, cancelling any **intra-group balances**.
>   - Current accounts
>   - Proposed dividends of subsidiary
>   - Debentures

Knowledge brought forward from earlier studies (cont'd)

- **Share capital** of H only
- Calculate the **minority interest** in net assets

MI % of share capital		X
MI % of reserves		X
MI % of revaluations to fair value		X
MI % of unrealised profit		(X)
		X

- Calculate the **goodwill**

Cost of investment		X
Pre-acquisition dividend		(X)
Assets acquired		
Share capital	X	
Pre-acquisition reserves	X	
Revaluation to fair value	X	
Group share	X%	(X)
Goodwill		X

If cost is **greater than** the share of net assets acquired then the difference is **positive** goodwill, which should be:

- Capitalised and amortised over its estimated useful life through the P&L account or
- Capitalised and retained in the balance sheet without amortising in those rare cases where its useful economic life is deemed indefinite (subject to annual impairment review).

If cost is **less than** the share of net assets acquired then the difference is **negative** goodwill.

- This should be
  - Disclosed in the intangible fixed assets category directly under positive goodwill
  - Recognised in the P&L account in the periods where **non-monetary assets** are depreciated or sold
- **Calculate reserves**

H per question		X
Post-acquisition dividends not yet accounted for		X
Proposed dividends not yet accounted for		(X)
PUP for sales made by H		(X)
		X
S per question	X	
Dividends to be proposed	(X)	
PUP for sales made by S	(X)	
Additional depreciation: transfer of fixed assets	(X)	
Less reserves at acquisition	(X)	
Group share	X%	X
Goodwill amortisation		(X)
		X

4.2 The technique for the preparation of a **consolidated P&L account** is given below, with two additional (and very important) points.

Knowledge brought forward from earlier studies

Summary of technique: consolidated P&L account

Adjustments required for consolidation of a subsidiary are as follows.

- Eliminate **intra-group sales and purchases**.

Knowledge brought forward from earlier studies (cont'd)

- Eliminate any **unrealised profits** on intra-group purchases still in stock at the year end.
- Eliminate any **intra-group dividends** received and paid, ie show only H's dividends.
- Show the **MI** as a separate line after profit after tax.
- Include the group share of any **extraordinary items** (very rare) in the subsidiary's accounts where material in a group context.

For the inclusion of a subsidiary carry out the following.

- **Combine all H and S results** from turnover to profit after tax (where the acquisition is mid-year, use a time apportioned basis).
- Exclude any **investment income** that is intra-group.
- **Calculate MI**:
  - Where there are no preference shares: MI = % × profit after tax
  - Where there are preference shares an additional working is required

Pre-acquisition dividends

There are two ways to calculate the pre-acquisition element of a dividend.

- To the extent that post-acquisition profits are **insufficient** to cover the dividend, the distribution must be out of pre-acquisition profits; this method is more commonly used in practice.
- **Apportion** the dividend on a time basis between the pre- and post-acquisition periods, so that only post-acquisition dividends are taken to H's reserves; this method is recommended in ACCA exams.
  - For **pre-acquisition dividends**: *Debit* Dividend receivable/cash, *Credit* Cost of investment.
  - For **post-acquisition dividends**: *Debit* Dividend receivable/cash, *Credit* P&L a/c.

Unrealised profits/losses

Only where **S sells to H**, allocate the unrealised profit between MI and H: *Debit* Group reserves, *Debit* Minority interest, *Credit* Stock.

4.3 After you have tried the following question and refreshed your memory on the topics listed above, we will move on to consider the usefulness and adequacy of current definitions, international definitions and the audit implications of consolidation and group accounts.

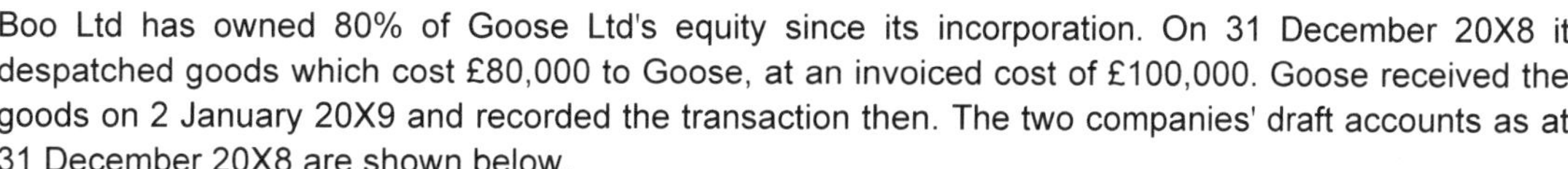

Question: simple groups

Boo Ltd has owned 80% of Goose Ltd's equity since its incorporation. On 31 December 20X8 it despatched goods which cost £80,000 to Goose, at an invoiced cost of £100,000. Goose received the goods on 2 January 20X9 and recorded the transaction then. The two companies' draft accounts as at 31 December 20X8 are shown below.

PROFIT AND LOSS ACCOUNTS

	Boo	*Goose*
	£'000	£'000
Sales	5,000	1,000
Cost of sales	2,900	600
Gross profit	2,100	400
Other expenses	1,700	320
Net profit	400	80
Tax	130	25
Profit after tax	270	55
Dividends proposed	130	40
Retained profit for the year	140	15
Retained profit brought forward	260	185
Retained profit carried forward	400	200

BALANCE SHEETS

	Boo	*Goose*
	£'000	£'000
Fixed assets		
Tangible assets	1,920	200
Investment in Goose	80	-
	2,000	200
Current assets		
Stock	500	120
Trade debtors	650	40
Bank and cash	390	35
	1,540	195
Current liabilities		
Trade creditors	910	30
Dividend payable	100	40
Tax	130	25
	1,140	95
Net current assets	400	100
	2,400	300
Capital and reserves		
Share capital	2,000	100
P&L account	400	200
	2,400	300

Required

Prepare draft consolidated financial statements.

(Assume all dividends were proposed before the year end.)

Answer

BOO GROUP
CONSOLIDATED PROFIT AND LOSS ACCOUNT
FOR THE YEAR ENDED 31 DECEMBER 20X8

	£'000
Sales (5,000 + 1,000 – 100)	5,900
Cost of sales (2,900 + 600 – 80)	3,420
Gross profit	2,480
Other expenses (1,700 + 320)	2,020
Net profit	460
Tax (130 + 25)	155
Profit after tax	305
Minority interest (20% × £55,000)	11
Group profit for the year	294
Dividend proposed (Boo only)	130
Retained profit for the year	164
Retained profit brought forward	408
Retained profit carried forward	572

CONSOLIDATED BALANCE SHEET AS AT 31 DECEMBER 20X8

		£'000	£'000
Fixed assets (1,920 + 200)			2,120
Current assets			
Stock (500 + 120 + 80)		700	
Trade debtors (650 – 100 + 40)		590	
Bank and cash (390 + 35)		425	
		1,715	
Current liabilities			
Trade creditors (910 + 30)		940	
Dividend payable:	Boo Ltd	100	
	to minority in Goose Ltd	8	
Tax (130 + 25)		155	
		1,203	
Net current assets			512
			2,632
Capital and reserves			
Share capital (Boo only)			2,000
P&L account (W)			572
Shareholders' funds			2,572
Minority interest (20% × 300)			60
			2,632

Working: group reserves

	Boo £'000	*Goose* £'000
Per question	400	200
Closing stock in transit (at cost)	80	
Inter company sale	(100)	
Dividend receivable: 80% × 40	32	
Share of Goose: 80% × 200	160	
	572	

This working is, of course, only necessary when you are not required to prepare the consolidated P & L account. Here, it serves as a proof of the consolidated P & L account as well as of the reserves figure in the balance sheet.

Exam focus point

The consolidation questions in the Paper 3.6 exam are likely to be much more difficult than those in Paper 2.5. The examiner will not bother to test basic consolidation techniques directly, although they may come up in a question: rather he will ask about one of the more complex areas which we will look at in the next few chapters.

Chapter roundup

- You should go back to your earlier study material (if necessary) and make sure you know:
  - the CA 1985 and FRS 2 **definitions** of parent and subsidiary undertakings;
  - CA 1985 requirements for **exemption** from consolidation and **exclusion** of subsidiaries;
  - the accounting requirements for **non-consolidated** subsidiaries;
  - FRS 2's regulations for **acquisition accounting**;
  - the treatment of **intra-group profits** and the situations where it arises; and
  - how to prepare **simple consolidated accounts**, including the basic treatment of goodwill and minority interests.
- Consider the nature of the **current definitions and accounting requirements**. You should be able to discuss why they are so complex and detailed.

Quick quiz

1 **Fill in the blanks** in the statements below, using the words in the box.

Per FRS 2, A is a parent of B if:

(a) A holds (1) .... in B

(b) A can appoint or remove (2) ....

(c) A has the right to exercise (3) .... over B

(d) B is a (4) .... of A

• Sub-subsidiary	• Dominant influence
• Directors holding a majority of the voting rights	• A majority of the voting rights

2 If a company holds 20% or more of the shares of another company, it has a participating interest. True or false?

3 What is dominant influence?

4 Sometimes an undertaking **may** be excluded from consolidation. Sometimes it **must** be excluded. Write 'may' or 'must' against the appropriation circumstance.

(a) Inclusion is not material.

(b) The subsidiary is held exclusively for resale and has not been consolidated previously.

(c) The subsidiary's activities are so different from those of other undertakings to be consolidated that its inclusion would be incompatible with the requirement to give a true and fair view.

5 How should a subsidiary excluded on the grounds of temporary control be accounted for in the consolidated balance sheet?

6 What are the components making up the figure of minority interest in a consolidated balance sheet?

7 Fill in the blanks to show the adjustment required before consolidation in cases where a holding company has not accounted for dividends receivable from a subsidiary.

DEBIT
CREDIT
With

8 The following diagram shows the structure of the Alpha group.

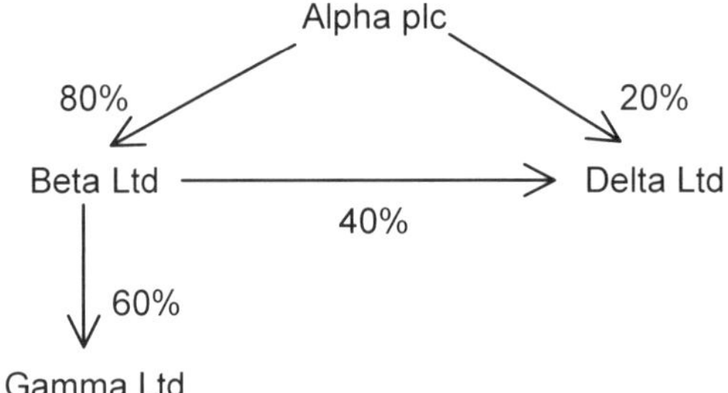

Which are the subsidiaries of Alpha plc?

A Beta Ltd
B Beta Ltd and Gamma Ltd
C Beta Ltd and Delta Ltd
D Beta Ltd, Gamma Ltd and Delta Ltd

9 Goodwill is always positive. True or false?

10 The following figures relate to Sanderstead plc and its subsidiary Croydon Ltd for the year ended 31 December 20X9.

	Sanderstead plc	*Croydon Ltd*
	£	£
Turnover	600,000	300,000
Cost of sales	(400,000)	(200,000)
Gross profit	200,000	100,000

During the year, Sanderstead plc sold goods to Croydon Ltd for £20,000 making a profit of £5,000. These goods were all sold by Croydon Ltd before the year end.

What are the amounts for turnover and gross profit in the consolidated profit and loss accounts of Sanderstead plc for the year ended 31 December 20X9?

Answers to quick quiz

1 (a) A majority of the voting rights
(b) Directors holding a majority of the voting rights
(c) Dominant influence
(d) Sub-subsidiary

2 False. Significant influence is presumed but the presumption may be rebutted.

3 Influence that can be exercised to achieve the operating and financial policies desired by the holder of the influence, notwithstanding the rights or influence of any other party.

4 (a) May
(b) Must
(c) Must

5 It should be included under current assets at the lower of cost and NRV.

6 The minority's share of ordinary shares, preference shares and reserves.

7 DEBIT Debtors (dividend receivable)
CREDIT Revenue reserves

With the parent company's share of the dividend receivable in the parent's books.

8 D Alpha has control over Beta's 40% holding in Delta and has a 20% direct holding. Thus Delta is a subsidiary.

9 False. Goodwill can be negative if the purchaser has 'got a bargain'.

10

	£
Turnover (1,600 + 300 – 20)	880
Cost of sales (400 +200 – 20)	580
Gross profit	300

Now try the question below from the Exam Question Bank

Number	Level	Marks	Time
Q3	Introductory	n/a	n/a

Chapter 3

ASSOCIATES AND JOINT VENTURES

Topic list		Syllabus reference
1	FRS 9 *Associates and joint ventures:* summary	2(a)
2	Examples	2(a)
3	Questions	2(a)

Introduction

Some investments are not subsidiaries but they may be much more than trade investments. The most important of these are associates and joint ventures, which are the subject of this chapter and of one of the ASB's recent standards FRS 9 *Associates and joint ventures.*

Study guide

Section 7 – Associates, joint ventures and JANEs

- Accounting for associates, joint ventures and JANEs
- Applying the equity and gross equity methods of accounting
- Preparation of group financial statements including accounting for associates, joint ventures and JANEs

Exam guide

Associates and joint ventures are likely to be tested as part of the compulsory group accounts in Section A. Typically you may be asked to account for a change in status from associate to subsidiary in a piecemeal acquisition, or subsidiary to associate in a disposal.

1 FRS 9 ASSOCIATES AND JOINT VENTURES: SUMMARY

1.1 You have covered FRS 9 in your earlier studies. Here we remind you of its requirements and give you some questions to practise. You must look back to your earlier studies if you are unsure.

Knowledge brought forward from earlier studies

Definition of associate

- **Associates**. FRS 9: an associate exists where:
  - Investor holds a participating interest
  - Investor exercises significant influence

  Participating interest. An interest held in the shares of another entity on a long-term basis for the purpose of securing a contribution to the investor's activities by the exercise of control or influence arising from or related to that interest.

Knowledge brought forward from earlier studies (cont'd)

Significant influence. This essentially involves participation in the financial and operating policy decisions (including dividend policy). Representation on the board is indicative but not conclusive.

- **Presumptions**
  - If ≥ 20% of equity voting rights, presumption of significant influence unless clearly demonstrated otherwise
  - If < 20% of equity voting rights, presumption of no significant influence unless clearly demonstrated otherwise

  In applying the above test, holdings of the parent company and subsidiaries should be aggregated but holdings via another associated company should be excluded.

Accounting treatment

- **Consolidated balance sheet.** Associated undertakings should be accounted for under the equity method of accounting

  Interest in associated

Investing group's share of net assets other than goodwill of the associate (after attributing FVs to net assets at time of acquisition)	X
Investing group's share of any goodwill in the associate financial statements	X
Premium paid (or discount) on the acquisition insofar as it has not already been written off or amortised	X/(X)
Investment in associate	X

- **Additional disclosures** are required where the investor's share exceeds 15% of the gross assets, liabilities or operating result of the investing group
  - Turnover
  - Fixed assets
  - Current assets
  - Current liabilities (< 1 year and > 1 year)

  If the investor's share exceeds 25% of gross assets etc, the investor's share of the following must be shown
  - Turnover
  - Profit before tax
  - Tax
  - Profit after tax
  - Fixed assets
  - Current assets
  - Liabilities < 1 year
  - Liabilities > 1 year

- **Consolidated P&L**
  - Group share of associate's operating results immediately after group operating profit
  - Amortisation of goodwill (if any)
  - Group share of associate's profit before tax included within the amounts for the group
  - Group share of tax charge of associate disclosed separately within the group tax charge

Joint ventures

- A joint venture is an entity in which the reporting entity holds an **interest on a long-term basis** and is **jointly controlled** by the **reporting entity and one or more** other venturers under a contractual arrangement.
- **Joint control**. A reporting entity jointly controls a venture with one or more other entities if none of the entities alone can control that entity but all together can do so and decisions on financial and operating policy essential to the activities, economic performance and financial position of that venture require each venturer's consent.
- Joint ventures are included in consolidated financial statements using the **gross equity method**, ie like associates but:

Knowledge brought forward from earlier studies (cont'd)

- In consolidated P&L joint venture's turnover should not be shown as part of the group turnover
- In consolidated B/S group share of gross assets and liabilities underlying the net equity amount should be shown as amplification of the net amount
- Except for profit before tax in the P&L, any supplementary information given for joint ventures, either in the P&L or B/S must be shown clearly separate from accounts for the group and must not be included in group total

- **Joint arrangements**. Participants in a joint arrangement that is not an entity (ie not a subsidiary, joint venture or associate) should account for their own assets, liabilities and cash flows measured according to the terms of the agreement governing the arrangement.

Summary

1.2 The table below, taken from the FRS, describes the **different sorts of interest that a reporting entity may have in other entities or arrangements**. The sections marked with an asterisk (*) are covered by the FRS. The defining relationships described in the table form the basis for the definitions used in the FRS.

Entity/ arrangement	*Nature of relationship*	*Description of the defining relationship - the full definitions are given in the FRS*
Subsidiary	Investor controls its investee	Control is the ability of an entity to direct the operating and financial policies of another entity with a view to gaining economic benefits from its activities. To have control an entity must have both: (a) the ability to deploy the economic resources of the investee or to direct it; and (b) the ability to ensure that any resulting benefits accrue to itself (with corresponding exposure to losses) and to restrict the access of others to those benefits.
* Joint arrangement that is not an entity	Entities participate in an arrangement to carry on part of their own trades or businesses	A joint arrangement, whether or not subject to joint control, does not constitute an entity unless it carries on a trade or business of its own.
* Joint venture	Investor holds a long-term interest and shares control under a contractual arrangement	The joint venture agreement can override the rights normally conferred by ownership interests with the effect that: • acting together, the venturers can control the venture and there are procedures for such joint action • each venturer has (implicitly or explicitly) a veto over strategic policy decisions. There is usually a procedure for settling disputes between venturers and, possibly, for terminating the joint venture.

Entity/ arrangement	*Nature of relationship*	*Description of the defining relationship - the full definitions are given in the FRS*
* Associate	Investor holds a participating interest and exercises significant influence	The investor has a long-term interest and is actively involved, and influential, in the direction of its investee through its participation in policy decisions covering the aspects of policy relevant to the investor, including decisions on strategic issues such as: (i) the expansion or contraction of the business, participation in other entities or changes in products, markets and activities of its investee; and (ii) determining the balance between dividend and reinvestment.
Simple investment		The investor's interest does not quality the investee as an associate, a joint venture or a subsidiary because the investor has limited influence or its interest is not long-term.

1.3 The table below, also taken from the FRS, sets out the **treatments in consolidated financial statements** for the different interests that a reporting entity may have in other entities and for joint arrangements that are not entities - the sections marked with an asterisk (*) are covered by the FRS.

Type of investment	*Treatment in consolidated financial statements*
Subsidiaries	The investor should consolidate the assets, liabilities, results and cash flows of its subsidiaries.
* Joint arrangements that are not entities	Each party should account for its own share of the assets, liabilities and cash flows in the joint arrangement, measured according to the terms of that arrangement, for example pro rata to their respective interests.
Joint ventures	The venturer should use the gross equity method showing in addition to the amounts included under the equity method, on the face on the balance sheet, the venturer's share of the gross assets and liabilities of its joint ventures, and, in the profit and loss account, the venturer's share of their turnover distinguished from that of the group. Where the venturer conducts a major part of its business through joint ventures, it may show fuller information provided all amounts are distinguished from those of the group.
Associates	The investor should include its associates in its consolidated financial statements using the equity method. In the investor's consolidated profit and loss account the investor's share of its associates' operating results should be included immediately after group operating results. From the level of profit before tax, the investor's share of the relevant amounts for associates should be included within the amounts for the group. In the consolidated statement of total recognised gains and losses the investor's share of the total recognised gains and losses of its associates should be included, shown separately under each heading, if material. In the balance sheet the investor's share of the net assets of its associates should be included and separately disclosed. The cash flow statement should include the cash flows between the investor and its associates. Goodwill arising on the investor's acquisition of its associates, less any amortisation or write-down, should be included in the carrying amount for the associates but should be disclosed separately. In the profit and loss account the amortisation or write-down of such goodwill should be separately disclosed as part of the investor's share of its associates' results.

Type of investment	*Treatment in consolidated financial statements*
Simple investments	The investor includes its interests as investments at either cost or valuation.

2 EXAMPLES

2.1 The following example of consolidated financial statements is taken from Appendix IV of FRS 9.

2.2 The format is illustrative only. The amounts shown for 'Associates' and 'joint ventures' are subdivisions of the item for which the statutory prescribed heading is 'Income from interests in associated undertakings'. The subdivisions may be shown in a note rather than on the face of the profit and loss account.

CONSOLIDATED PROFIT AND LOSS ACCOUNT

	£m	£m
Turnover: group and share of joint ventures	320	
Less: share of joint ventures' turnover	(120)	
Group turnover		200
Cost of sales		(120)
Gross profit		80
Administrative expenses		(40)
Group operating profit		40
Share of operating profit in		
Joint ventures	30	
Associates	24	
		54
		94
Interest receivable (group)		6
Interest payable		
Group	(26)	
Joint ventures	(10)	
Associates	(12)	
		(48)
Profit on ordinary activities before tax		52
*Tax on profit on ordinary activities**		(12)
Profit on ordinary activities after tax		40
Minority interests		(6)
Profit on ordinary activities after taxation and minority interest		34
Equity dividends		(10)
Retained profit for group and its share of associates and joint ventures		24

*Tax relates to the following:	Parent and subsidiaries	(5)
	Joint ventures	(5)
	Associates	(2)

CONSOLIDATED BALANCE SHEET

	£m	£m	£m
Fixed assets			
Tangible assets		480	
Investments			
Investments in joint ventures:			
Share of gross assets	130		
Share of gross liabilities	(80)		
		50	
Investments in associates		20	
			550
Current assets			
Stock		15	
Debtors		75	
Cash at bank and in hand		10	
		100	
Creditors (due within one year)		(50)	
Net current assets			50
Total assets less current liabilities			600
Creditors (due after more than one year)			(250)
Provisions for liabilities and charges			(10)
Equity minority interest			(40)
			300
Capital and reserves			
Called up share capital			50
Share premium account			150
Profit and loss account			100
Shareholders' funds (all equity)			300

Notes

In the example, there is no individual associate or joint venture that accounts for more than 25 per cent of any of the following for the investor group (excluding any amount for associates and joint ventures).

- Gross assets
- Gross liabilities
- Turnover
- Operating results (on a three-year average)

Additional disclosures for joint ventures (which in aggregate exceed the 15 per cent threshold)

	£m	£m
Share of assets		
Share of fixed assets	100	
Share of current assets	30	
		130
Share of liabilities		
Liabilities due within one year or less	(10)	
Liabilities due after more than one year	(70)	
		(80)
Share of net assets		50

Additional disclosures for associates (which in aggregate exceed the 15 per cent threshold)

	£m	£m
Share of turnover of associates		90
Share of assets		
Share of fixed assets	4	
Share of current assets	28	
		32
Share of liabilities		
Liabilities due within one year or less	(3)	
Liabilities due after more than one year	(9)	
		(12)
Share of net assets		20

Further aspects of FRS 9 applying to both joint ventures and associates

Principles of consolidation

2.3 As has been mentioned, when calculating the amounts to be included in the investor's consolidated financial statements, whether using the equity method for associates or the gross equity method for joint ventures, the **same principles should be applied as are applied in the consolidation of subsidiaries**. This has the following implications.

(a) **Fair values** are to be attributed to assets and liabilities on acquisition. Goodwill should be treated as per FRS 10.

(b) In arriving at the amounts to be included by the equity method, the same **accounting policies** as those of the investor should be applied.

(c) The financial statements of the investor and the associate or joint venture should be prepared to the **same accounting date** and for the **same accounting period**; associates/joint ventures can prepare three months before if necessary with appropriate adjustments and disclosure.

(d) Profits or losses resulting from **transactions between the investor and its associate/joint venture** may be included in the carrying amount of assets in either party. Where this is the case, the part relating to the **investor's share should be eliminated**. Any impairment of those or similar assets must be taken into account if evidence of it is given by the transactions in question.

Investor is a group

2.4 Where the investor is a group, it share of its associate or joint venture is the aggregate of the holdings of the parent and its subsidiaries in that entity. The holdings of any of the group's other associates or joint ventures should be ignored for this purpose. Where an associate or joint venture itself has subsidiaries, associates or joint ventures, the results and net assets to be taken into account by the equity method are those reported in that investee's consolidated financial statements (including the investee's share of the results and net assets of its associates and joint ventures), after any adjustment necessary to give effect to the investor's accounting policies.

Options, convertibles and non-equity shares

2.5 The investor may hold options, convertibles or non-equity shares in its associate or joint venture. In certain circumstances, the conditions attaching to such holdings are such that the investor should take them into account in reflecting its interest in its investee under the equity or gross equity method. In such cases, the costs of exercising the options or converting the convertibles, or future payments in relation to the non-equity shares, should also be taken into account.

Impairment

2.6 In cases where there is impairment in any goodwill attributable to an associate or joint venture the **goodwill should be written down** and the amount written off in the accounting period separately disclosed.

Commencement and cessation of relationship

2.7 The following points apply with regard to commencement or cessation of an associate or joint venture relationship.

(a) An investment **becomes an associate** on the date on which the investor begins:

(i) To hold a **participating interest**
(ii) To exercise **significant influence**

(b) An investment **ceases to be an associate** on the date when it **ceases to fulfil** either of the above.

(c) An investment **becomes a joint venture** on the date on which the investor begins to **control it jointly** with other investors, provided it has a long-term interest.

(d) On the date when an investor **ceases to have joint control**, the investment **ceases to be a joint venture.**

(e) The **carrying amount** (percentage of investment retained) should be reviewed and, if necessary, written down to the **recoverable amount**.

Joint arrangements that are not entities

2.8 A reporting entity may operate through a structure that has the appearance of a joint venture but not the reality. It may thus be a separate entity in which the participants hold a long-term interest and exercise joint management, but there may be no common interest because each venturer operates independently of the other venturers within that structure. The framework entity acts merely as an agent for the ventures with each venturer able to identify and control its share of the assets, liabilities and cash flows arising within the entity. **Such arrangements have the form but not the substance of a joint venture**.

The accounting treatment for such joint arrangements required by FRS 9 is that **each venturer should account directly for its share of the assets, liabilities and cash flows held within that structure.** This treatment reflects the substance rather than the form of the arrangement.

Investors that do not prepare consolidated accounts

2.9 A reporting entity may have an associate or joint venture, but no subsidiaries. It will thus not prepare group accounts. In such cases it should present the relevant amounts for associates and joint ventures, as appropriate, by preparing a **separate set of financial statements** or by showing the relevant amounts, together with the effects of including them, as additional information to its own financial statements. Investing entities that are exempt from preparing consolidated financial statements, or would be exempt if they had subsidiaries, are exempt from this requirement.

3 QUESTIONS

3.1 You should be familiar enough with FRS 9 to get the following questions right. If not, look back to your earlier study material.

Question: treatment of items

How should a holding company treat the following items in the financial statements for an associated company, when preparing group accounts?

(a) Turnover
(b) Inter-company profits
(c) Goodwill

Answer

(a) The holding company should not aggregate the turnover of an associated company with its own turnover.

(b) Wherever the effect is material, adjustments similar to those adopted for the purpose of presenting consolidated financial statements should be made to exclude from the investing group's consolidated financial statements such items as unrealised profits on stocks transferred to or from associated companies.

(c) The investing group's balance sheet should disclose 'interest in associated companies'. The amount disclosed under this heading should include both the investing group's share of any goodwill in the associated companies' own financial statements and any premium paid on acquisition of the interests in the associated companies in so far as it has not already been written off or amortised.

Question: associates and joint ventures (1)

Ross plc is a long established business in office supplies. The nature of its business has expanded and diversified to take account of technological changes which have taken place in recent years. Now in addition to stationery and office furniture, it also supplies photocopiers, fax machines and more recently new computer based technologies. The expansion has occurred organically but also through acquisition of existing companies and joint ventures. Ross plc's investments are as follows.

(a) *Joey Ltd.* Ross has a 40% interest in the issued share capital of Joey Ltd and representation on the board. Joey Ltd manufactures office furniture and a large proportion of what it produces is sold to Ross. Ross is therefore actively involved in decisions regarding product ranges, designs and pricing to ensure they get the products they want.

(b) *Rachel NRG.* Rachel NRG is a joint venture company which commenced operations on 1 June 20X7. The joint venturers in Rachel are Ross plc and Monica Inc, a company also in office automation, specialising in computer products. The purpose of the joint venture was to distribute their products to Asia Pacific where the demand for office automation is growing rapidly. Ross and Monica have an equal interest in Rachel.

(c) *Phoebe Ltd.* Phoebe Ltd's principal activities is the supply and fitting of bathroom suites. Its managing director is Mrs Janice Chandler, wife of Mr Paul Chandler, a director of Ross plc. Ross plc has a 25% interest in the share capital of Phoebe and the remaining shares are held by various members of the Chandler family. Mr Chandler is on the board of Phoebe as a non-executive director and this was approved at the last AGM by all the voting members of the Chandler family. The activities of Phoebe and Ross are in totally different markets, the share interest is there for historic reasons and Ross has not exercised its voting rights for several years. During the year Ross plc sold one of the company's executive cars to Phoebe Ltd for an agreed open market value of £30,000.

The following are extracts from the financial statements of Joey, Rachel and Phoebe for the year ended 31 March 20X8.

	Joey	*Rachel*	*Phoebe*
	£'000	£'000	£'000
Turnover	4,068	17,720	7,640
Operating costs	3,872	16,834	6,980
Operating profit	196	886	660
Interest payable	-	280	30
Profit before tax	196	606	630
Tax	40	152	200
Profit after tax	156	454	430
Fixed assets	360	1,720	260
Current assets	2,940	2,130	834
Creditors falling due within one year	(2,214)	(710)	(252)
Creditors falling due after one year	(26)	(1,810)	(400)
	1,060	1,330	442
Cost of investment	600	500	400

Sales of office furniture from Joey to Ross amounted to £160,000 during the year. 10% of the goods remain in the closing stock of Ross. These goods had been sold at a mark up of 25% on cost.

Required

Produce extracts from the consolidated profit and loss account and balance sheet of Ross for the year ended 31 March 20X8 indicating clearly the treatments for Joey, Rachel and Phoebe and where each item would appear.

Answer

EXTRACTS FROM THE CONSOLIDATED PROFIT AND LOSS ACCOUNT
FOR THE YEAR ENDED 31 MARCH 20X8

	£'000	£'000
Turnover	X	
Less share of joint ventures' turnover	(8,860)	
Group turnover		X
Group operating profit		X
Share of operating profit in		
Joint ventures	443	
Associates (W1)	77.2	
Interest payable		
Group	X	
Joint ventures	(140)	
Profit before tax		X
Tax (see below)		X
Profit after tax		X
Tax relates to		
Parent and subsidiary		X
Joint ventures		76
Associates		16

EXTRACTS FROM THE CONSOLIDATED BALANCE SHEET AS AT 31 MARCH 20X8

	£'000	£'000
Fixed assets		
Investments		
Investments in joint ventures		
Share of gross assets	1,925	
Share of gross liabilities	1,260	
		665.0
Investments in associates (W2)		422.8
Other investments		400.0

Workings

1 *Share of associate company profit*

	£'000
Profit of Joey per question	196.0
Less PUP (160,000 × 10% × $^{25}/_{125}$)	3.2
	192.8
Group share (40%) (rounded)	77.2

2 *Investment in associates*

	£'000
Net assets per question	1,060.0
Less PUP (W1)	(3.2)
	1,056.8
Group share (40%) (rounded)	422.8

Question: associates and joint ventures (3)

Comic plc, the holding company of the Comic Group, acquired 25% of the ordinary shares of Strip plc on 1 September 20X0 for £54 million. Strip plc carried on business as a property investment company. The draft accounts as at 31 August 20X1 are as follows.

PROFIT AND LOSS ACCOUNTS FOR THE YEAR ENDED 31 AUGUST 20X1

	Comic Group	*Strip plc*
	£m	£m
Sales	175.0	200
Profit before interest and tax	90.0	80
Exceptional profit on sale of property	20.0	-
Interest	(2.0)	(20)
	108.0	60
Taxation	(23.2)	(20)
	84.8	40
Proposed dividends	(61.0)	-
	23.8	40

BALANCE SHEETS AS AT 31 AUGUST 20X1

	Comic Group	*Strip plc*
Fixed assets	£m	£m
Tangible fixed assets	135	200
Investment in Strip plc	54	-
Current assets		
Stock	72	210
Debtors	105	50
Current liabilities		
Creditors	(95)	(20)
Overdraft	(14)	(100)
Net current assets	68	140
	257	340
Capital and reserves		
Ordinary shares of £1 each	135	50
Reserves	122	90
10% loan	-	200
	257	340

On 1 September 20X0 Comic plc sold a property with a book value of £40 million to Strip plc at its market value of £60 million. The tax suffered on this gain was £7 million. Strip plc obtained the funds to

pay the £60 million by raising a loan which is included in the 10% loan that appears in its balance sheet at 31 August 20X1.

Premiums on acquisition are amortised over 5 years. The dividends were proposed before the year end.

Required

Prepare:

(a) The consolidated profit and loss account of the Comic Group for the year ended 31 August 20X1 and a consolidated balance sheet as at that date

(b) Relevant notes to comply with the requirements of FRS 9 *Associates and joint ventures*

Answer

(a) COMIC GROUP
CONSOLIDATED PROFIT AND LOSS ACCOUNT
FOR THE YEAR ENDED 31 AUGUST 20X1

	£m	£m
Group turnover		175.00
Group operating profit		90.00
Share of operating profit in associate 20 – 5.8		14.20
		104.20
Profit on sales of property		15.00
Interest payable		
Group	2	
Associate	5	
		(7.00)
		112.20
Taxation		
Group	21.45	
Associate	5.00	
		(26.45)
		85.75
Dividends		(61.00)
Retained profit for the year		24.75

COMIC GROUP
CONSOLIDATED BALANCE SHEET
AS AT 31 AUGUST 20X1

	Notes	£m	£m
Fixed assets			
Tangible assets			135.00
Interest in associated company	2, 5		54.95
			189.95
Current assets			
Stock		72	
Debtors		105	
		177	
Current liabilities			
Creditors		95	
Bank overdraft		14	
		109	
Net current assets			68.00
			257.95
Capital and reserves			
Ordinary shares £1 each			135.00
Reserves	4		122.95
			257.95

(b) NOTES TO THE ACCOUNTS

1 *Retained profit*

	£m
Retained by Comic and its subsidiaries	14.75
Retained by Strip plc	10.00
	24.75

2 *Interest in associate*

	£m
Group's share of net assets (25% × (340 – 200))	35.00
Less unrealised profit (25% × 13)	(3.25)
Unamortised goodwill (29 – 5.8)	23.20
	54.95

Additional disclosures for associates

The group has one associate, Strip plc, in which the group's share exceeds 25 per cent with respect to the group.

	£m	£m
Share of turnover of associate		50
Share of assets		
Share of fixed assets (W5)		45
Share of current assets		65
		110
Share of liabilities		
Liabilities due within one year or less (W6)	(28.25)	
Liabilities due after more than one year	(50.00)	
		(78.25)
		31.75

Workings

1 *Premium on acquisition*

	£m
Share capital	50
Reserves at date of acquisition (90 – 40)	50
	100
Group share (25%)	25
Cost	54
Premium on acquisition	29
Amortisation (29,000 ÷ 5)	5.8

2 *Reserves*

	Comic £m	*Strip* £m
Per question	122.00	
Post acquisition (per P&L)		40
Unrealised profit	(3.25)	
Share of Strip: 40 × 25%	10.00	
Less amortisation of goodwill	(5.80)	
	122.95	

3 *Working: exceptional profit*

	£m
Profit per Comic's profit and loss account	20
Less unrealised profit (25% × 20)	(5)
	15

4 *Group tax charge*

		£m
Comic per question		23.20
Less tax on unrealised element of exceptional profit (7 × 25%)		(1.75)
		21.45

5 *Share of Strip's fixed assets*

		£m
Strip fixed assets per question		200
Unrealised profit		(20)
		180
	× 25%	45

6 *Share of Strip's liabilities within one year*

		£m
Strip liabilities per question		120
Tax element of unrealised profit		(7)
		113
	× 25%	28.25

UITF Abstract 31 Exchanges of businesses or other non-monetary assets for an interest in a subsidiary, joint venture or associate

3.2 This UITF abstract was published in October 2001. It deals with increasingly common transactions where an entity exchanges a business (or other non-monetary assets) for equity in a subsidiary, joint venture or associate. An example is where an entity forms a joint venture combining one of its businesses with that of another entity. An important issue is whether such transactions should be reported at **fair values or book values**; this affects the amounts of profits or losses and goodwill that are recognised in relation to the exchange.

3.3 The Abstract requires such transactions to be analysed in terms of **net changes in ownership interests**. The part of the business exchanged that **the entity still owns** indirectly through its new shareholding should remain at **book value**. In contrast, the entity's share of **net assets** acquired through its **new shareholding** should be accounted for at **fair value**. Goodwill is recognised in respect of the entity's newly acquired interest; a gain or loss is recognised in respect of the part of the business exchanged that the entity no longer directly or indirectly owns.

3.4 The Abstract is effective for transactions first accounted for in accounting periods commencing on or after 23 December 2001.

Chapter roundup

- **Associates** and **joint ventures** are entities in which an investor holds a **substantial but not controlling interest**.
- They are the subject of an accounting standard: **FRS 9 *Associates and joint ventures.***
- **Associates** are to be included in the investor's consolidated financial statements using the **equity method**.
    - The investor's share of its associates' results should be included immediately after group operating profit.
    - The investor's share of its associates' turnover may be shown as a memorandum item.
- **Joint ventures** are to be included in the venturer's consolidated financial statements by the **gross equity method**.
- This requires, in addition to the amounts included under the equity method, disclosure of the venturer's share of its joint ventures' turnover, gross assets and gross liabilities.
- Other **joint arrangements**, such as cost-sharing arrangements and one-off construction projects, are to be included in their participants' individual and consolidated financial statements by **each participant including directly** its share of the assets, liabilities and cash flows arising from the arrangements.

Quick quiz

1 What types of interest does FRS 9 identify?

2 A group of companies has the following shareholdings.

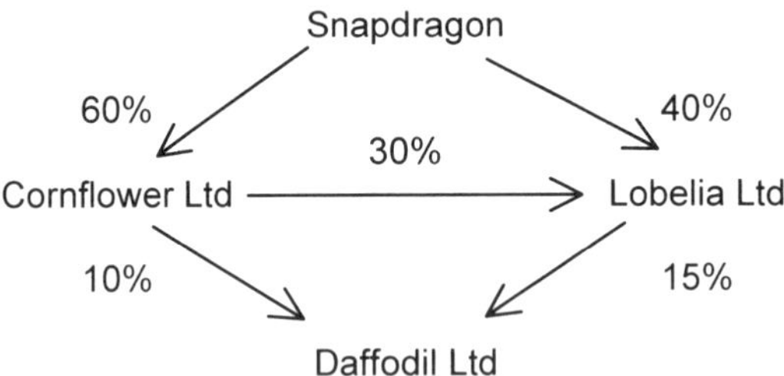

For consolidation purposes what, prima facie, is the relationship of Lobelia Ltd and Daffodil Ltd to Snapdragon plc?

3 What **additional** disclosures are required by FRS 9 when the '25% threshold' is reached (ie not also required when the '15% threshold' is reached). Circle any that apply.

(a) Fixed assets
(b) Liabilities due within one year
(c) Profit before tax
(d) Turnover
(e) Profit after tax

4 Constable plc owns 40% of Turner plc which it treats as an associated company in accordance with FRS 9. Constable plc also owns 60% of Whistler Ltd. Constable has held both of these shareholdings for more than one year. Turnover of each company for the year ended 30 June 20X0 was as follows.

	£m
Constable	400
Turner	200
Whistler	100

What figure should be shown as turnover in the consolidated profit and loss account of Constable plc?

5 Under the equity method of accounting, the balance sheet of an investing group will disclose, in respect of its associate:

A Dividends receivable but not share of net assets of the associate

B Share of net assets of the associate but not dividends receivable

C Share of net assets of the associate and dividends receivable

D Cost of investment plus goodwill on acquisition less amounts written off but not dividends receivable

Answers to quick quiz

1 Associates
Joint ventures
Joint arrangements that are not entities

2 Lobelia Ltd subsidiary; Daffodil Ltd associate

Shares held by subsidiary companies count in full. Snapdragon has control of Cornflower's 30% holding in Lobelia. It owns 40% itself, 40 + 30 gives control. Snapdragon therefore controls Lobelia's 15% in Daffodil and Cornflower's 10% in Daffodil (10 + 15 = 25 = associate).

3 (c) and (e)

4 Turnover will be 100% H + 100% S only. Associates are introduced in to the consolidated profit and loss account as a share of their operating profits in the first instance.

	£m
Constable	400
Whistler (subsidiary)	100
	500

5 C Dividends receivable from associates will be included within 'amounts owed by associated companies' and not necessarily disclosed separately. In simple terms, dividends from associates do not 'cancel out' like those from subsidiaries.

Now try the question below from the Exam Question Bank

Number	Level	Marks	Time
Q4	Exam	25	45 mins

Chapter 4

MULTI-COMPANY STRUCTURES

Introduction

This chapter introduces the first of several more complicated consolidation topics. The best way to tackle these questions is to be logical and to carry out the consolidation on a **step by step** basis.

In questions of this nature, it is very helpful to sketch a **diagram of the group structure**, as we have done. This clarifies the situation and it should point you in the right direction: always sketch the group structure as your first working and double check it against the information in the question.

Study guide

Section 3 – Group financial statements 1

- Accounting for complex group structures

1 MULTI-COMPANY STRUCTURES 12/02

1.1 In this section we shall consider how the principles of balance sheet consolidation may be applied to more complex structures of companies within a group.

(a) **Several subsidiary companies**

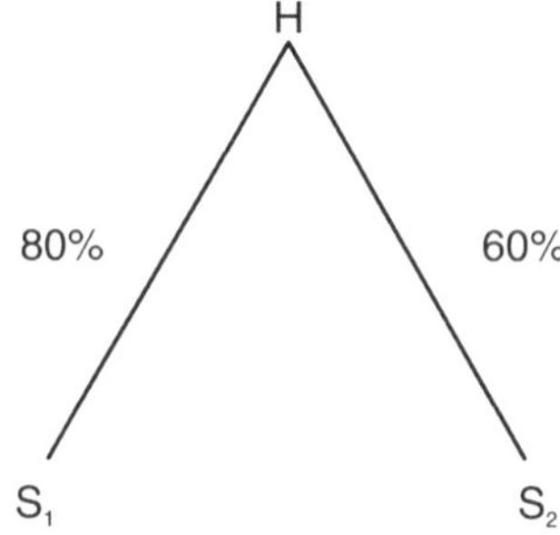

You have already seen this type of structure in your previous studies.

(b) **Sub-subsidiaries**

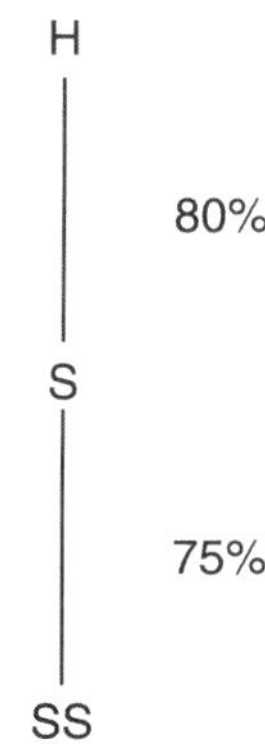

H holds a controlling interest in S which in turn holds a controlling interest in SS. SS is therefore a subsidiary of a subsidiary of H; in other words, a *sub-subsidiary* of H.

(c) **Direct holdings in sub-subsidiaries: 'D' shaped groups**

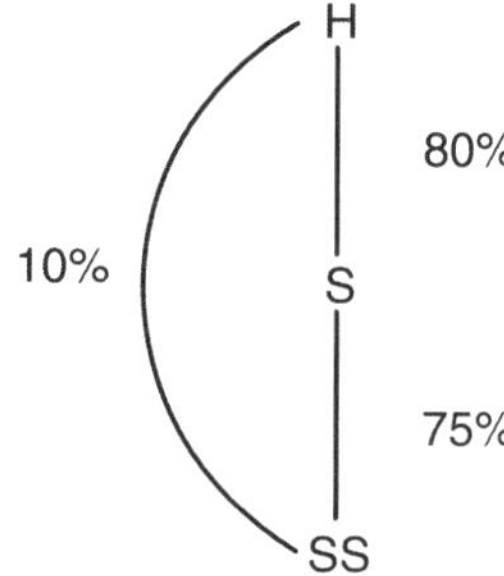

In this example, SS is a sub-subsidiary of H with additional shares held directly by H.

In practice, groups are usually larger, and therefore more complex, but the procedures for consolidation of large groups will not differ from those we shall now describe for smaller ones.

A holding company which has several subsidiaries

1.2 Where a company H has several subsidiaries S_1, S_2, S_3 and so on, the technique for consolidation is exactly as described already. **Cancellation** is from the holding company, which has assets of investments in subsidiaries S_1, S_2, S_3, to each of the several subsidiaries.

1.3 The consolidated balance sheet will show:

(a) A single figure for **minority interest**
(b) Separate totals for **goodwill** arising

A single working should be used for each of the constituents of the consolidated balance sheet: one working for goodwill, one for minority interest, one for revenue reserves, and so on, but on the consolidated balance sheet itself the separate portions of goodwill arising must each be accounted for in compliance with FRS 10.

Sub-subsidiaries

1.4 A slightly different problem arises when there are sub-subsidiaries in the group, which is how should we **identify the minority interest** in the reserves of the group? Suppose H owns 80% of the equity of S, and that S in turn owns 60% of the equity of SS.

1.5 It would appear that in this situation:

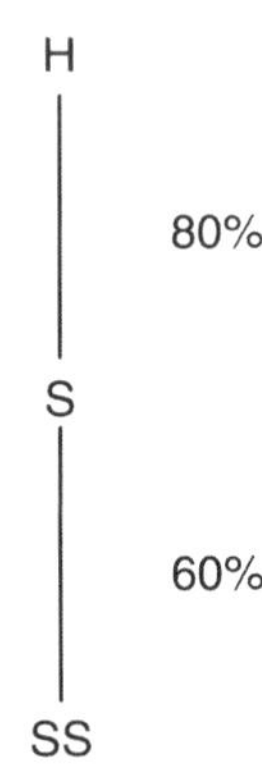

(a) H owns 80% of 60% = 48% of SS.
(b) The minority interest in S owns 20% of 60% = 12% of SS.
(c) The minority interest in SS itself owns the remaining 40% of the SS equity.

SS is nevertheless a **sub-subsidiary** of H, because it is a subsidiary of S which in turn is a subsidiary of H. The chain of control thus makes SS a sub-subsidiary of H which owns only 48% of its equity.

1.6 The total minority in SS may be checked by considering a **dividend** of £100 paid by SS where S then distributes its share of this dividend in full to its own shareholders.

		£
S will receive	£60	
H will receive	80% × £60 =	48
Leaving for the total minority in SS		52
		100

Date of effective control

1.7 The date the sub-subsidiary comes under the **control of the holding company** is one of the following.

(a) The date H acquired S if S already holds shares in SS
(b) If S acquires shares in SS later, then that later date

2 CONSOLIDATING SUB-SUBSIDIARIES

2.1 The basic consolidation method is as follows.

(a) **Net assets**: show what the group controls.

(b) **Capital and reserves**: show who owns the net assets included in the top half of the balance sheet. Reserves, therefore, are based on **effective holdings**.

2.2 As indicated earlier, the major problem on consolidation is to identify the minority interest share of the reserves of S and (especially) SS. There are **two techniques**.

(a) The two-stage (or indirect) method
(b) The single-stage (or direct) method

2.3 The two stage method is used **in practice** (where there are sub-sub-subsidiary companies it would be a three-stage method). The single-stage method is useful **in examinations,** because it is quicker and acceptable to examiners.

2.4 EXAMPLE: CONSOLIDATING SUB-SUBSIDIARIES

The draft balance sheets of H Ltd, S Ltd and SS Ltd on 30 June 20X7 were as follows.

	H Ltd		*S Ltd*		*SS Ltd*	
	£	£	£	£	£	£
Fixed assets						
Tangible assets		105,000		125,000		180,000
Investments, at cost						
80,000 shares in S Ltd		120,000		-		-
60,000 shares in SS Ltd		-		110,000		-
Current assets	80,000		70,000		60,000	
Creditors	30,000		35,000		25,000	
		50,000		35,000		35,000
		275,000		270,000		215,000
Capital and reserves						
Ordinary shares of £1 each		80,000		100,000		100,000
Reserves		195,000		170,000		115,000
		275,000		270,000		215,000

H Ltd acquired its shares in S Ltd when the reserves of S Ltd stood at £40,000; and S Ltd acquired its shares in SS Ltd when the reserves of SS Ltd stood at £50,000.

For the moment, we will assume that both acquisitions occurred on the same date.

Required

Prepare the draft consolidated balance sheet of H Group, using:

(a) The single stage method
(b) The two-stage method

Note. Goodwill should be capitalised, but amortisation can be ignored.

2.5 SOLUTION: SINGLE STAGE METHOD

Having calculated the minority interest and the H group interest (see Paragraph 1.5 above), the workings can be constructed. You should, however, note the following.

(a) **Minority interest working**: bring in the total minority interests in S Ltd's share capital and reserves (20%), and the total minority interests in SS Ltd's share capital and reserves (52%). Bring in the goodwill arising on S Ltd's acquisition of SS Ltd.

(b) **Goodwill working**: compare the costs of investments with the effective group interests acquired (80% of S Ltd and 60% of SS Ltd).

(c) **Reserves working**: bring in the share of S Ltd's and SS Ltd's post-acquisition reserves in the normal way.

1 *Minority interests*

	£	£
S Ltd		
Share capital (20% × £100,000)		20,000
Reserves (20% × £170,000)		34,000
Goodwill on acquisition of SS Ltd (20% × 20,000)		4,000
Investment in SS Ltd (20% × £110,000)		(22,000)
		36,000
SS Ltd		
Share capital (52% × £100,000)	52,000	
Reserves (52% × £115,000)	59,800	
		111,800
		147,800

Note. The rationale behind the treatment of goodwill is that on consolidation all assets are consolidated gross and minority interests shown separately. Goodwill is just another asset and should be treated in the same way.

2 *Goodwill*

	£	£	£
S Ltd			
Cost of investment			120,000
Share of net assets acquired			
as represented by			
Ordinary share capital		100,000	
Reserves		40,000	
		140,000	
Group share (80%)			112,000
Goodwill			8,000
SS Ltd			
Cost of investment		110,000	
Share of net assets acquired			
Ordinary share capital	100,000		
Reserves	50,000		
	150,000		
SS share (60%)		90,000	
Goodwill			20,000
Net goodwill			28,000

3 *Reserves*

	£
H Ltd	195,000
Share of S Ltd's post acquisition retained reserves £(170,000 – 40,000) × 80%	104,000
Share of SS Ltd's post acquisition retained reserves £(115,000 – 50,000) × 48%	31,200
	330,200

Note. This working could be presented as in earlier chapters.

H LIMITED
CONSOLIDATED BALANCE SHEET AT 30 JUNE 20X7

	£	£
Fixed assets		
Goodwill		28,000
Tangible assets		410,000
Current assets	210,000	
Creditors	90,000	
		120,000
		558,000
Capital and reserves		
Ordinary shares of £1 each fully paid		80,000
Reserves		330,200
		410,200
Minority interest		147,800
		558,000

Date of acquisition

2.6 Care must be taken when consolidating sub-subsidiaries, because (usually) either:

(a) The holding company acquired the subsidiary **before** the subsidiary bought the sub-subsidiary

(b) The holding company acquired the subsidiary **after** the subsidiary bought the sub-subsidiary

2.7 The rule to remember here, when considering pre- and post-acquisition profits, is that we are only interested in the consolidated results of the **holding company**. We will use the example above (using the single-stage method of consolidation) to demonstrate the required approach.

2.8 EXAMPLE: SUBSIDIARY ACQUIRED FIRST

Using the figures in Paragraph 2.4, assume that:

(a) H Ltd purchased its holding in S Ltd on 1 July 20X4
(b) S Ltd purchased its holding in SS Ltd on 1 July 20X5

The same reserve figures applied on the date of acquisition.

2.9 SOLUTION

The solution would be the same as that given in Paragraph 2.5. Contrast this with the situation in the next example.

2.10 EXAMPLE: SUB-SUBSIDIARY ACQUIRED FIRST

Again using the figures in Paragraph 2.4, assume that:

(a) S Ltd purchased its holding in SS Ltd on 1 July 20X4
(b) H Ltd purchased its holding in S Ltd on 1 July 20X5

The reserve figures on the respective dates of acquisition are the same, but on the date H Ltd purchased its holding in S Ltd, the reserves of *SS Ltd* were £60,000.

2.11 SOLUTION

The point here is that SS Ltd only became part of the H group on 1 July 20X5, *not* on 1 July 20X4. This means that only the reserves of SS Ltd arising *after* 1 July 20X5 can be included in the post-acquisition reserves of H Ltd group. Goodwill arising on the acquisition will be calculated by comparing the cost of the investment to the consolidated separable net assets of S (as represented by share capital and consolidated reserves, net of all goodwill).

H LIMITED
CONSOLIDATED BALANCE SHEET AS AT 30 JUNE 20X7

	£	£
Fixed assets		
Goodwill (W1)		19,200
Tangible		410,000
Current assets	210,000	
Creditors	90,000	
		120,000
		549,200

	£	£
Capital and reserves		
Ordinary shares £1 each		80,000
Reserves (W3)		325,400
Shareholders' funds		405,400
Minority interest (W2)		143,800
		549,200

Workings

1 *Goodwill*

	£	£
S Ltd		
Cost of investment		120,000
Share of net assets acquired		
Ordinary share capital	100,000	
Consolidated reserves:		
S	40,000	
SS (60 – 50) × 60%	6,000	
Goodwill (see para 2.6)	(20,000)	
	126,000	
80%		(100,800)
Goodwill		19,200

Alternative working:

	£	£	£
S Ltd (as in Paragraph 2.5)			8,000
SS Ltd			
Cost of investment (80% × 110)		88,000	
Share of net assets acquired			
Ordinary share capital	100,000		
Reserves	60,000		
	160,000		
Group share (48%)		76,800	
			11,200
Goodwill			19,200

2 *Minority interests*

	£
As para 2.5	147,800
Deduct 20% of goodwill on acquisition of SS	4,000
	143,800

3 *Reserves*

	£
H Ltd (as above)	195,000
S Ltd (as above)	104,000
SS Ltd (115 – 60) × 48%	26,400
	325,400

Question: sub-subsidiary

The balance sheets of Antelope Ltd, Yak Ltd and Zebra Ltd at 31 March 20X4 are summarised as follows.

	Antelope Ltd		*Yak Ltd*		*Zebra Ltd*	
Fixed assets	£	£	£	£	£	£
Freehold property		100,000		100,000		-
Plant and machinery		210,000		80,000		3,000
		310,000		180,000		3,000
Investments in subsidiaries						
Shares, at cost	80,000		2,200			-
Loan account	-		3,800			-
Current accounts	10,000		12,200			-
		90,000		18,200		3,000
Current assets						
Stocks	200,000		24,500		15,000	
Debtors	140,000		50,000		1,000	
Cash at bank	60,000		16,500		4,000	
	400,000		91,000		20,000	
Creditors						
Trade creditors	130,000		40,200		800	
Due to Antelope Ltd	-		12,800		600	
Due to Yak Ltd	-		-		12,600	
Taxation	40,000		7,000		-	
Unclaimed dividends	400		-		-	
Proposed dividends	50,000		-		-	
	220,400		60,000		14,000	
Net current assets		179,600		31,000		6,000
		579,600		229,200		9,000
Capital and reserves						
Ordinary share capital		200,000		100,000		10,000
Reserves		379,600		129,200		(1,000)
		579,600		229,200		9,000

Antelope Ltd acquired 75% of the shares of Yak Ltd in 20X1 when the credit balance on the reserves of that company was £40,000. No dividends have been paid since that date. Yak Ltd acquired 80% of the shares in Zebra Ltd in 20X3 when there was a debit balance on the reserves of that company of £3,000. Subsequently £500 was received by Zebra Ltd and credited to its reserves, representing the recovery of a bad debt written off before the acquisition of Zebra's shares by Yak Ltd. During the year to 31 March 20X4 Yak Ltd purchased stock from Antelope Ltd for £20,000 which included a profit mark-up of £4,000 for Antelope Ltd. At 31 March 20X4 one half of this amount was still held in the stocks of Yak Ltd. Group accounting policies are to make a full provision for unrealised inter-company profits, and to treat goodwill in accordance with FRS 10. Any dividends were proposed before the year end.

Prepare the draft consolidated balance sheet of Antelope Ltd at 31 March 20X4.

Answer

The loan account and current accounts of the three companies are self-cancelling assets and liabilities. The minority interests are as follows.

Direct minority interest in Yak Ltd		25%
Direct minority interest in Zebra Ltd	20%	
Indirect minority interest in Zebra Ltd (25% of 80%)	20%	
Total minority interest in Zebra Ltd		40%

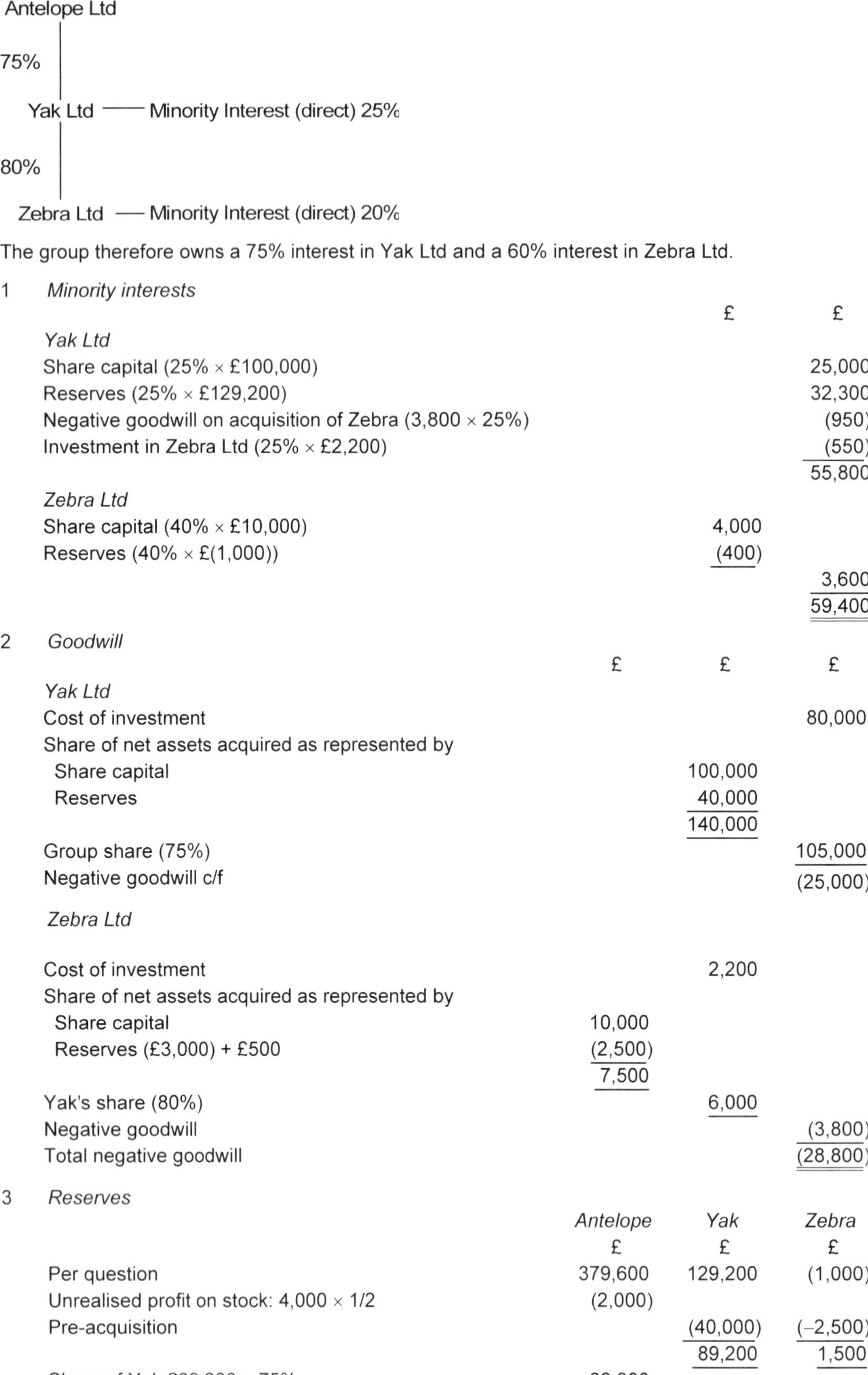

Antelope Ltd

75%

Yak Ltd — Minority Interest (direct) 25%

80%

Zebra Ltd — Minority Interest (direct) 20%

The group therefore owns a 75% interest in Yak Ltd and a 60% interest in Zebra Ltd.

1 *Minority interests*

	£	£
Yak Ltd		
Share capital (25% × £100,000)		25,000
Reserves (25% × £129,200)		32,300
Negative goodwill on acquisition of Zebra (3,800 × 25%)		(950)
Investment in Zebra Ltd (25% × £2,200)		(550)
		55,800
Zebra Ltd		
Share capital (40% × £10,000)	4,000	
Reserves (40% × £(1,000))	(400)	
		3,600
		59,400

2 *Goodwill*

	£	£	£
Yak Ltd			
Cost of investment			80,000
Share of net assets acquired as represented by			
Share capital		100,000	
Reserves		40,000	
		140,000	
Group share (75%)			105,000
Negative goodwill c/f			(25,000)
Zebra Ltd			
Cost of investment		2,200	
Share of net assets acquired as represented by			
Share capital	10,000		
Reserves (£3,000) + £500	(2,500)		
	7,500		
Yak's share (80%)		6,000	
Negative goodwill			(3,800)
Total negative goodwill			(28,800)

3 *Reserves*

	Antelope	*Yak*	*Zebra*
	£	£	£
Per question	379,600	129,200	(1,000)
Unrealised profit on stock: 4,000 × 1/2	(2,000)		
Pre-acquisition		(40,000)	(–2,500)
		89,200	1,500
Share of Yak £89,200 × 75%	66,900		
Share of Zebra £1,500 × 60%	900		
	445,400		

ANTELOPE LIMITED
CONSOLIDATED BALANCE SHEET AS AT 31 MARCH 20X4

	£	£
Fixed assets		
Negative goodwill		(28,800)
Freehold property		200,000
Plant and machinery		293,000
		464,200
Current assets		
Stocks £(239,500 – 2,000)	237,500	
Debtors	191,000	
Cash and bank	80,500	
	509,000	
Creditors: amounts falling due within one year		
Trade creditors	171,000	
Taxation	47,000	
Unclaimed dividends	400	
Proposed dividends	50,000	
	268,400	
Net current assets		240,600
		704,800
Capital and reserves		
Ordinary share capital		200,000
Reserves		445,400
Shareholders' funds		645,400
Minority interests		59,400
		704,800

IMPORTANT!

For further practice on dealing with goodwill in subsidiaries, try Question 35 Big, Small and Tiny in the Exam Question Bank.

2.12 Section summary

You should follow this **step-by-step approach** in all questions using the single-stage method. This applies to Section 3 below as well.

Step 1. Sketch the **group structure** and check it to the question

Step 2. **Add details** to the sketch of dates of acquisition, holdings acquired (percentage and nominal values) and cost

Step 3. **Minority interest working**: total MI in subsidiary plus total MI in sub-subsidiary

Step 4. **Goodwill working**: compare costs of investment with the **effective** group interests acquired. Check the question: how is goodwill to be treated? If the sub-subsidiary has already been acquired by the subsidiary, goodwill should be calculated by comparing the cost of the investments to the consolidated separable net assets of the subsidiary (net of all goodwill). If the sub-subsidiary is acquired post acquisition, include goodwill arising in the consolidated balance sheet.

Step 5. **Reserves working**: group share of subsidiary and sub-subsidiary post-acquisition reserves (effective holdings again)

Step 6. Prepare the **consolidated balance sheet** (and P&L account if required).

3 DIRECT HOLDINGS IN SUB-SUBSIDIARIES 12/03

3.1 Consider the following structure, sometimes called a '**D-shaped**' **group**.

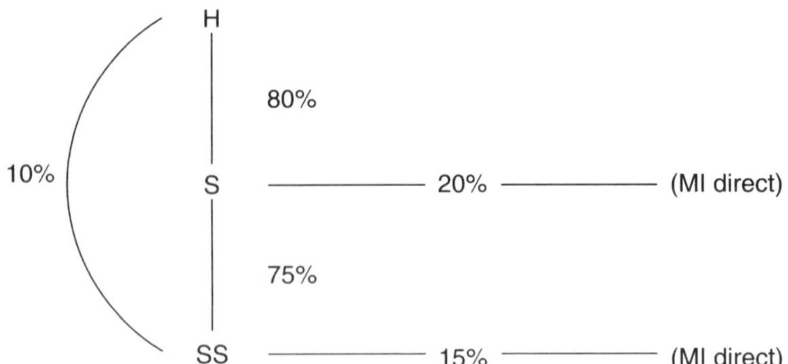

3.2 In practice several consolidations might be carried out, using procedures which are the same as in the '**two-stage**' **method** of consolidation for sub-subsidiaries:

(a) S with SS
(b) H with the S group
(c) H with SS (for the direct holding of 10%)

3.3 In an examination however, the **single-stage method** is recommended as it will save you valuable time. In the structure above, there is:

(a) A **direct** minority in S of		20%
(b) A **direct** minority in SS of	15%	
(c) An **indirect** minority in SS of 20% × 75% =	15%	
		30%

3.4 Once again, you could check a **dividend distribution** of £100 from SS.

	£
S will receive £75	
H will receive 80% of £75 =	60
H will receive 10% of £100 =	10
	70
Leaving for the total minority in SS	30

3.5 Having ascertained the structure and minority interests, proceed as for a typical sub-subsidiary situation by the single-stage method.

Question: 'D'-shaped group

The draft balance sheets of Hulk Ltd, Molehill Ltd and Pimple Ltd as at 31 May 20X5 are as follows.

	Hulk Ltd		*Molehill Ltd*		*Pimple Ltd*	
	£	£	£	£	£	£
Fixed assets						
Tangible assets		90,000		60,000		60,000
Investments in subsidiaries at cost						
Shares in Molehill Ltd	90,000		-		-	
Shares in Pimple Ltd	25,000		42,000		-	
		115,000		42,000		-
		205,000		102,000		60,000
Current assets	40,000		50,000		40,000	
Creditors due within one year						
Proposed dividends	30,000		20,000		10,000	
Other creditors	20,000		20,000		15,000	
	50,000		40,000		25,000	
Net current assets (liabilities)		(10,000)		10,000		15,000
		195,000		112,000		75,000
Creditors (falling due after one year)						
12% loan stock		-		10,000		-
		195,000		102,000		75,000

	Hulk Ltd	*Molehill Ltd*	*Pimple Ltd*
	£	£	£
Capital and reserves			
Ordinary shares of £1, allotted and fully paid	100,000	50,000	50,000
Share premium account	50,000	20,000	-
Profit and loss reserves	45,000	32,000	25,000
	195,000	102,000	75,000

(a) Hulk Ltd acquired 60% of the shares in Molehill on 1 January 20X3 when the balance on that company's profit and loss reserves was £8,000 (credit) and there was no share premium account.

(b) Hulk acquired 20% of the shares of Pimple Ltd and Molehill acquired 60% of the shares of Pimple Ltd on 1 January 20X4 when that company's profit and loss reserves stood at £15,000.

(c) There has been no payment of dividends by either Molehill or Pimple since they became subsidiaries.

(d) The proposed dividends have not yet been recorded in the books of the shareholding companies as dividends receivable.

(e) Goodwill arising on consolidation is assumed to have an indefinite life and is therefore capitalised in the balance sheet.

Required

Prepare the consolidated balance sheet of Hulk Ltd as at 31 May 20X5 using the single-stage method.

Answer

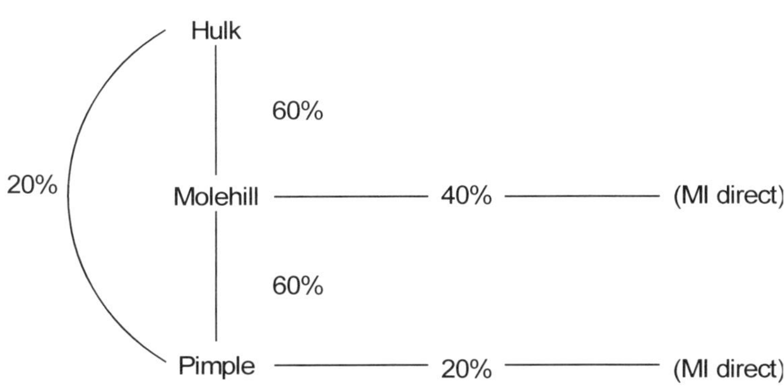

The direct minority interest in Molehill Ltd is		40%
The direct minority interest in Pimple Ltd is	20%	
The indirect minority interest in Pimple Ltd is (40% of 60%)	24%	
The total minority interest in Pimple Ltd is		44%

The group share of Molehill Ltd is 60% and of Pimple Ltd is (100 – 44)% = 56%

Dividends receivable

In Molehill Ltd's books:

DEBIT Dividends receivable	£6,000	
CREDIT Profit and loss reserves		£6,000

Being 60% of Pimple Ltd's proposed dividend

In Hulk Ltd's books:

DEBIT Dividends receivable	£14,000	
CREDIT Profit and loss reserves		£14,000

Being 20% of Pimple Ltd's proposed dividend plus 60% of Molehill Ltd's proposed dividend

1 *Minority interests*

	£	£
Molehill Ltd		
Share capital (40% × £50,000)		20,000
Share premium (40% × £20,000)		8,000
Reserves (40% × £(32,000 + 6,000))		15,200
Goodwill on acquisition of Pimple (40% × 3,000)		1,200
Investment in Pimple (40% × £42,000)		(16,800)
		27,600
Pimple Ltd		
Share capital (44% × £50,000)	22,000	
Reserves (44% × £25,000)	11,000	
		33,000
		60,600

2 *Goodwill*

	£	£	£
Molehill Ltd			
Cost of investment			90,000
Share of net assets acquired represented by			
Share capital		50,000	
Reserves		8,000	
		58,000	
Group share (60%)			34,800
Goodwill			55,200
Pimple Ltd			
Cost of direct holding		25,000	
Share of net assets acquired represented by			
Share capital	50,000		
Reserves	15,000		
	65,000		
Group share (direct interest - 20%)		13,000	
Goodwill			12,000
Cost of indirect holding		42,000	
Share of net assets acquired (60% × 65,000)		39,000	
			3,000
Total goodwill			70,200

3 *Reserves*

	Hulk	*Molehill*	*Pimple*
	£	£	£
Per question	45,000	32,000	25,000
Dividends receivable	14,000	6,000	-
Pre-acquisition		(8,000)	(15,000)
		30,000	10,000
Share of Molehill: £30,000 × 60%	18,000		
Share of Pimple: £10,000 × 56%	5,600		
	82,600		

4 *Share premium account*

	£
Hulk Ltd	50,000
Molehill Ltd: all post-acquisition (£20,000 × 60%)	12,000
	62,000

HULK LIMITED
CONSOLIDATED BALANCE SHEET AT 31 MAY 20X5

	£	£
Fixed assets		
Intangible asset: goodwill		70,200
Tangible assets		210,000
Current assets	130,000	
Creditors: amounts falling due within one year		
Minority proposed dividend	10,000	
Proposed dividend	30,000	
Other creditors	55,000	
	95,000	
Net current assets		35,000
Creditors: amounts falling due after more than one year		
12% loan stock		10,000
		305,200
Capital and reserves		
Ordinary shares of £1 allotted and fully paid		100,000
Share premium		62,000
Profit and loss reserves		82,600
Shareholders' funds		244,600
Minority interests		60,600
		305,200

Chapter roundup

- When a holding company has **several subsidiaries**, the consolidated balance sheet shows a single figure for minority interests and for goodwill arising on consolidation.
- There may also be a figure for 'capital reserve arising on consolidation'. In cases where there are several subsidiary companies the technique is to open up a **single minority interest working and a single goodwill working.**
- When dealing with **sub-subsidiaries**, there are two possible consolidation techniques. For examination purposes, the greater simplicity of the single-stage method makes it preferable to the two-stage method. However, you should understand the differences that may arise between the two methods.
- The **date of acquisition** is important when dealing with sub-subsidiaries. Remember that it is the post-acquisition reserves from a **group perspective** which are important.

Quick quiz

1 Anna plc owns 80% of Bella Ltd and 15% of Emma Ltd. Bella Ltd owns 80 % of Camilla Ltd and 40% of Emma Ltd. Camilla Ltd owns 60% of Dora Ltd. Which are the subsidiaries of Anna plc? Circle any that apply.

A Bella Ltd
B Camilla Ltd
C Dora Ltd
D Emma Ltd

2 The following diagram shows the structure of the Quince Group.

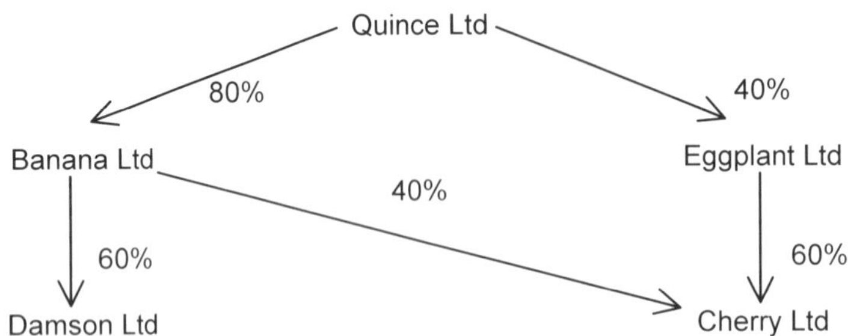

Which of these are the subsidiaries of Quince Ltd? Circle any that apply.

A Banana Ltd
B Cherry Ltd
C Damson Ltd
D Eggplant Ltd

3 What is the basic consolidation method for sub-subsidiaries?

Answers to quick quiz

1 All of them. Simply consider which company controls another.

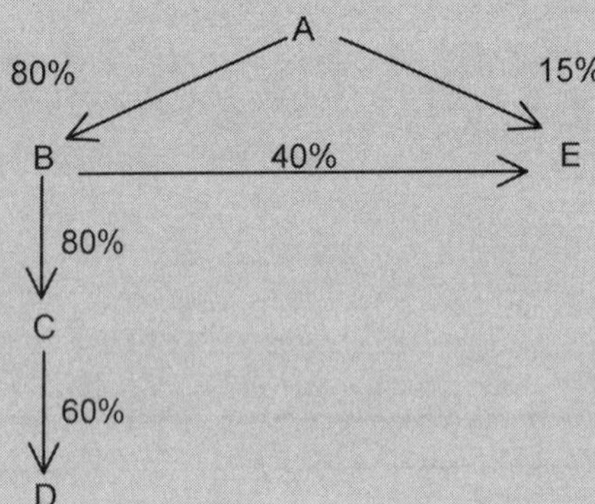

Anna controls Bella, it controls its 40% shareholdings in Emma, and 40 + 15% give control.

2 A and C. For the purposes of determining subsidiary status, shareholdings held by subsidiaries count in full, but shares held by associates do not count at all. Simply consider which company controls another. As Banana controls Damson, and as Quince controls Banana, it must control Damson. Quince does not control Eggplant.

3 (a) Net assets: show what the group controls.

(b) Capital and reserves: show who owns the net assets included in the top half of the balance sheet. Reserves, therefore, are based on effective holdings.

Now try the questions below from the Exam Question Bank

Number	Level	Marks	Time
Q5	Exam	25	45 mins
Q35	Exam	25	45 mins

Chapter 5

CHANGES IN GROUP COMPOSITION

Topic list		Syllabus reference
1	Piecemeal acquisitions	2(c)
2	Bonus issues and capital reductions	2(c)
3	Disposals	2(c)
4	Changes in direct ownership	2(c)
5	Demergers	2(c)

Introduction

Complex consolidation issues are very likely to come up in this, the final stage of your studies on financial accounting. Your approach should be the same as for more simple consolidation questions: **methodical and logical**. If you understand the basic principles of consolidation, you should be able to tackle these complicated questions.

Study guide

Section 3 – Group financial statements 1

- Discussion of the nature of step-by-step acquisitions
- Preparation of consolidated financial statements where control is established by a step-by-step acquisition

Section 4 – Group financial statements 2

- Explaining the basic principles relating to the disposal of group companies
- Discussion of the treatment of goodwill on disposal
- Applying the principles of accounting for partial and deemed disposals

Section 6 – Group reorganisations and restructuring

- Discussion of the creation of a new holding company
- Explaining changes in the ownership of companies within a group
- Discussion of the nature of demergers and divisionalisation
- Preparation of group financial statements after reorganisation and reconstruction
- Appraising the benefits of the reorganisation and restructuring

1 PIECEMEAL ACQUISITIONS

1.1 A holding company may acquire a controlling interest in the shares of a subsidiary as a result of **several successive share purchases**, rather than by purchasing the shares all on the same day. For the purpose of consolidation, it is necessary to decide which reserves of

the subsidiary are pre-acquisition profits; but since the acquisition has occurred in several stages, it is not immediately clear how to decide what they are.

1.2 If a controlling interest is achieved by means of a build-up of share acquisitions over a period of time, the present reserves may include elements which are **pre-acquisition** as regards some blocks of shares held, but **post-acquisition** as regards other blocks of shares.

1.3 There are two possible ways of dealing with the subsidiary in the accounts.

(a) Only take account of the subsidiary when **control** is achieved, in accordance with FRS 2.

(b) If the company has **already been equity accounted** for when it was an associate, then account for the **additional interest separately**.

1.4 Remember, whether the company is accounted for as an associate (equity accounted) does not depend just on the percentage of shares acquired but on whether the investor **actually exercises significant influence.** The significance of the approach taken lies in the different procedures adopted for consolidation when the partly-bought company eventually **becomes a subsidiary**. The exercise involves looking back at previous share purchases to decide on how to consolidate now that a subsidiary status (controlling interest) has been achieved.

1.5 EXAMPLE: PIECEMEAL ACQUISITION

Suppose that X Ltd bought 20,000 ordinary £1 shares in Y Ltd in 20X1 when the reserves of Y Ltd stood at £27,000 and a further 20,000 shares in 20X2 when the reserves of Y Ltd were £42,000. Finally, a purchase of 30,000 shares in 20X3 when the reserves of Y Ltd were £60,000 gave X Ltd a controlling interest over the 100,000 shares of Y Ltd. The cost of the shares purchased was £30,000 in 20X1, £34,000 in 20X2 and £56,000 for the final 30,000 shares in 20X3.

What are the pre-acquisition and post-acquisition profits of the group in Y Ltd, and what is the goodwill arising on consolidation at the date of the final acquisition in 20X3? Assume that no dividends were paid in these three years.

1.6 SOLUTION: Y LTD ACCOUNTED FOR AS AN ASSOCIATE

Purchase	*% of shares in Y Ltd bought*	*% of shares in Y Ltd now held*
20X1	20%	20%
20X2	20%	40%
20X3	30%	70% (controlling interest)

X Ltd exercises significant influence over the financial and operating policies of Y Ltd.

If X Ltd accounted for Y Ltd as an associate, we would use the **step-by-step method**. This method calculates pre-acquisition profits by computing the proportion of reserves attaching to the shares at the time of **each individual purchase**.

		£
20X1	Pre-acquisition profits of 20,000 shares (20% of £27,000)	5,400
20X2	Pre-acquisition profits of next 20,000 shares (20% of £42,000)	8,400
20X3	Pre-acquisition profits of final 30,000 shares (30% of £60,000)	18,000
	Total pre-acquisition profits	31,800

Note that post-acquisition profits would be:

		£
(a)	on shares bought in 20X1: 20% of profits since 20X1 = 20% of £(60,000 – 27,000) =	6,600
(b)	on shares bought in 20X2: 20% of profits since 20X2 = 20% of £(60,000 – 42,000) = (since no dividends were paid out on profits in this time)	3,600 10,200

Reserve working: share of Y Ltd's post acquisition retained reserves = (£60,000 × 70%) – £31,800 = £10,200.

This step-by-step calculation is only required when the company (Y Ltd) becomes a subsidiary in 20X3 and subsequent years.

Goodwill arising on consolidation would be the excess of the cost of the shares bought over their called-up value, less pre-acquisition profits: £(120,000 – 70,000 – 31,800) = £18,200.

1.7 SOLUTION: Y LTD NOT ACCOUNTED FOR AS AN ASSOCIATE

If X Ltd did not exercise a significant influence when it bought the shares of Y Ltd in 20X1 and 20X2, but only gained control when it made its final purchase in 20X3, the pre-acquisition profits would be calculated on the basis of reserves at the date of acquisition of control, ie in our example on the basis of reserves of £60,000 at the date of acquisition in 20X3.

Reserve working: share of Y Ltd's pre-acquisition retained reserves = £60,000 × 70% = £42,000.

Goodwill on consolidation would be the excess of the cost of shares over their called-up value, less pre-acquisition profits = £(120,000 – 70,000 – 42,000) = £8,000.

Suggested method

1.8 The decisive factor is whether or not the company has been equity accounted for when it was an associate. A rule-of-thumb approach to piecemeal acquisitions might be suggested as follows.

(a) Ignore share purchases which keep the buying company's share of equity **below 20%**: make no step-by-step method calculations before the bought company becomes an associated company. This is an rough and ready assumption that significant influence is not exercised on holdings of less than 20%.

(b) When the purchase of shares first takes a company's **holding above 20% (and up to 50%)**, treat all the shares purchased up to this date as a single block of purchases for the purpose of calculating pre-acquisition profits.

(c) For **future (significant) purchases** up to the time when control is eventually acquired, the step-by-step method should be applied.

Exam focus point

This question may not arise: control may be achieved after the first purchase, with a further purchase afterwards.

Question: piecemeal acquisition

A Ltd acquired shares in Z Ltd, which has issued and fully paid share capital of 100,000 £1 ordinary shares, on three separate dates.

Date	*Number of shares bought in the purchase*	*Cost*	*Reserves of Z Ltd at date of purchase*
		£	£
1 February 20X0	10,000	16,000	40,000
1 November 20X0	25,000	42,000	60,000
1 April 20X1	20,000	40,000	80,000

Required

Calculate the pre-acquisition profits of the A group in Z Ltd when Z Ltd eventually became a subsidiary on 1 April 20X1.

Answer

Step	*Date*	*% of shares bought*	*% of total holding*	
1	1 February 20X0	10%	10%	Ignore
2	1 November 20X0	25%	35%	Z Ltd achieves associated company status
3	1 April 20X1	20%	55%	Z Ltd becomes a subsidiary

A step-by-step calculation of pre-acquisition profits, assuming significant influence is exercised, would regard the first step as the purchase of shares which made Z Ltd an associated company: step 2.

	£
Pre-acquisition profits	
35% of reserves at 1 November 20X0 (35% of £60,000)	21,000
Plus 20% of reserves at 1 April 20X1 (20% of £80,000)	16,000
Total pre-acquisition profits	37,000

The minority interest at 1 April 20X1 is 45% of £80,000 =	£36,000
Post-acquisition profits are therefore £(80,000 – 37,000 – 36,000) =	£7,000

Piecemeal acquisition of a sub-subsidiary

1.9 Care may be needed in deciding the group's share of **pre-acquisition profits** when shares in a sub-subsidiary are acquired on several dates.

1.10 EXAMPLE 1: PIECEMEAL ACQUISITION OF A SUB-SUBSIDIARY

Suppose H Ltd buys 60% of the shares of S Ltd on 1 April 20X3 and 20% of the shares of SS Ltd on 1 October 20X3. S Ltd bought 70% of the shares of SS Ltd on 1 January 20X3.

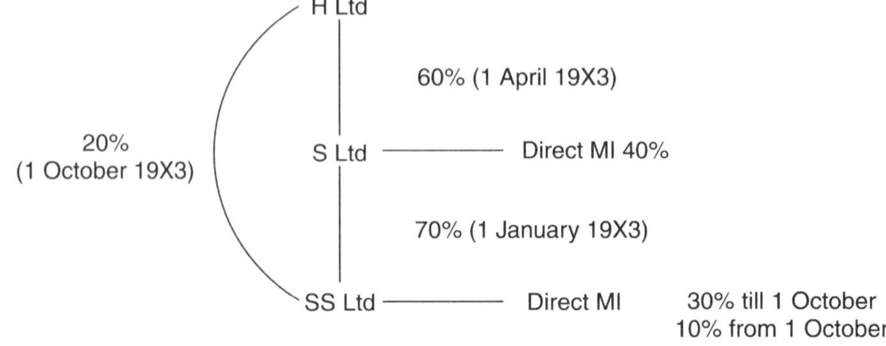

1.11 SOLUTION

Pre-acquisition profits of H Ltd in SS Ltd would be calculated as follows, by the single-stage method of consolidation:

(a) 60% × 70% = 42% of the reserves of SS Ltd at 1 April 20X3 (when the indirect minority is 40% × 70% = 28% and the total minority interest is 58%); *plus*

(b) 20% of the reserves of SS Ltd at 1 October 20X3 when the additional shares are bought.

1.12 EXAMPLE 2: PIECEMEAL ACQUISITION OF A SUB-SUBSIDIARY

Suppose instead that H Ltd buys 80% of the shares of S Ltd on 1 April 20X4 and 30% of the shares of SS Ltd on 1 November 20X4. S Ltd bought 40% of the shares of SS Ltd on 1 January 20X4.

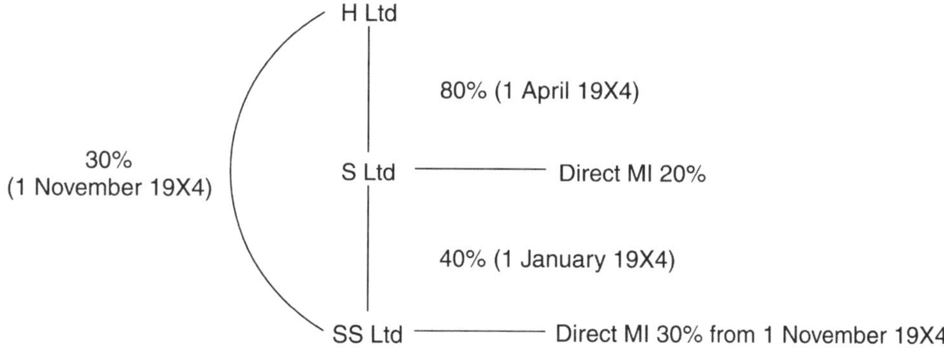

1.13 SOLUTION

In this example, SS Ltd does not come under the control of the group until 1 November 20X4 and SS Ltd is unlikely to have been equity accounted (since the original shares were bought by S Ltd before it became a subsidiary of H Ltd). The most appropriate assumption would be to calculate the pre-acquisition reserves in SS Ltd on the basis of reserves at the date of acquiring control, 1 November 20X4, so that the pre-acquisition profits in SS Ltd would be 62% of the reserves at that date.

(The indirect minority interest in SS Ltd is 20% of 40% = 8%. Therefore, the total minority interest is 38% and the group interest is 62%.)

Question: piecemeal acquisition of a sub-subsidiary

Juniper plc made the following share purchases in gaining control of Berry plc.

Date	*Voting rights and shares acquired*
1.4.X2	20%
1.4.X3	25%
1.4.X4	10%

The reserves of Berry plc were as follows.

Date	*Reserves plc*
	£'000
31.3.X2	300
31.3.X3	1,200
31.3.X4	1,500
31.3.X5	1,800

Berry plc has paid no dividends since 20X2.

Required

(a) Calculate the post-acquisition reserves for the consolidated accounts as at 31 March 20X5.
(b) Calculate the pre-acquisition reserves.
(c) Calculate the minority interest.

Answer

Year ended	*% of shares held*	*Year-end reserves*	*Post-acquisition*	
		£'000	£'000	
31.3.X2	-	300	-	
31.3.X3	20%	1,200	180	(20% × 900)
31.3.X3	45%	1,500	135	(45% × 300)
31.3.X5	55%	1,800	165	(55% × 300)
			480	

	£'000
Minority interest 45% × 1,800	810
Post-acquisition reserves, as above	480
Remainder, being pre-acquisition reserves	510
	1,800

Check

Year ended	*Year-end reserves*	*Increase in reserves*	*Pre-acquisition*	*Pre-acquisition reserves*
	£'000	£'000		£'000
31.3.X2	300		55%	165
31.3.X3	1,200	900	35% (55% – 20%)	315
31.3.X4	1,500	300	10% (55% – 45%)	30
Pre-acquisition reserves, as above				510

Note. This 'piecemeal acquisition' method is suitable only where the subsidiary has previously been equity accounted for as an associate.

1.14 Section summary

Where there is a build up of share acquisitions over time:

- What are the **pre-acquisition** profits?
- If the company has been equity accounted for when it was an associate use the **step-by-step method**.
- If it is not, use reserves at the **date control is achieved.**
- Use the same principles for piecemeal acquisitions of **sub-subsidiaries**.

2 BONUS ISSUES AND CAPITAL REDUCTIONS

Bonus issues

2.1 A bonus issue is simply a **capitalisation of reserves** and therefore there is no alteration in the percentage holding of any party. When calculating goodwill, it is easiest to ignore the effect of the bonus issue and simply use the reserves and share capital as at acquisition.

Capital reductions

2.2 A capital reduction will involve a **reduction in the nominal value of shares in issue**. In acquisition accounting, we are using calculations which show the net assets acquired (as

represented by pre-acquisition reserves and share capital), so any change in the nominal value of the shares at a later date is irrelevant and should be ignored.

3 DISPOSALS 6/03

3.1 A holding company may dispose of a subsidiary in total, or reduce the holding to the level of an associate or an investment.

Effective date of disposal

3.2 FRS 2 defines the effective date of disposal in terms of **when control passes**: 'the date for accounting for an undertaking ceasing to be a subsidiary undertaking is the date on which its former parent undertaking relinquishes its control over that undertaking'. **FRS 3** requires that the results of discontinued operations should be shown separately in the P&L account in the year of disposal (see Chapter 10). **FRS 2** states that the consolidated P&L account should include the results of a subsidiary undertaking up to the date of its disposal. We are not concerned with FRS 3 disclosure in this section, only the FRS 2 calculations.

Goodwill

3.3 When a subsidiary is disposed of, the group needs to deal with any goodwill (positive or negative) which arose when the subsidiary was purchased. If the goodwill was **written off to reserves**, it could by-pass the P&L account, thus causing a misstatement of the profit or loss on disposal.

UITF Abstract 3 *Treatment of goodwill on disposal of a business*

3.4 Consider the following situation. Cod plc purchased Chips plc on 1 January 20X4 for £15m and sold the company for £24m on 1 January 20X7. In between, the Chips plc had earned £6m profit. On acquisition the fair value of its net assets was £10.5m. The goodwill of £4.5m had been written off to reserves. The calculation of the **profit of loss on disposal** can be made in two ways.

	Option A		*Option B*	
	£m	£m	£m	£m
Sales proceeds		24.0		24.0
Carrying value				
Fair value of assets	10.5		10.5	
Retained profits	6.0		6.0	
		16.5		16.5
		7.5		7.5
Less goodwill previously written off to reserves		-		4.5
Gain on sale reported		7.5		3.0

3.5 It is clear that option B gives the **true picture** of the gain made by the company. UITF Abstract 3 outlawed the practice in option A and this was incorporated into FRS 2. Note that comparative figures should be restated where possible.

3.6 The treatment in option B may not be easy if the subsidiary has been absorbed into the group or restructured. In such cases the goodwill which was acquired is not necessarily being sold as the company is in a different form. However, CA 1985 and SSAP 22 require **records to be kept** on goodwill on acquisition, and so some sort of apportionment should be possible. Where it is not, full disclosure should be made and the reasons given. Note that

the gross goodwill figure should be used: there should be no adjustment for notional amortisation.

Exam focus point

For sometime, FRS 10 has outlawed immediate write off of goodwill to reserves, so this situation is not common in practice. However, the FRS says that goodwill previously eliminated against reserves may remain thus eliminated until the business is disposed of, so the treatment explained here is still valid.

Disposals and partial disposals

3.7 When only part of an investment is sold, but an **associate or subsidiary status** is retained, then it is necessary to decide how to account for the disposal.

Disposal: subsidiary, status retained

3.8 If the holding is still a subsidiary then it must still be **consolidated line by line**. The consolidated accounts are only adjusted in reserves and in the minority interest. A comparison of the sale proceeds and the consolidated net asset value attributable to the shares sold at the date of disposal will give the profit or loss on disposal.

3.9 EXAMPLE: PARTIAL DISPOSALS

Chalk plc bought 100% of the voting share capital of Cheese plc on 1 January 20X2 for £160,000. Cheese plc earned and retained £240,000 from that date until 31 December 20X7. At that date the balance sheets of the company and the group were as follows.

	Chalk plc	*Cheese plc*	*Consolidated*
	£'000	£'000	£'000
Investment in Cheese	160	-	-
Other net assets	800	400	1,200
	960	400	1,200
Share capital	400	160	400
Reserves	560	240	800
	960	400	1,200

On 1 January 20X8 Chalk plc sold 40% of its shareholding in Cheese plc for £280,000. The profit on disposal (ignoring tax) is calculated as follows.

	Holding company	*Group*
	£'000	£'000
Sale proceeds	280	280
40% of investment/net assets	64	160
Gain on sale	216	120

3.10 SOLUTION: SUBSIDIARY STATUS

The balance sheets immediately after the sale will appear as follows.

	Chalk plc	*Cheese plc*	*Consolidated*
	£'000	£'000	£'000
Investment in Cheese	96	-	-
Other net assets	1,080	400	1,480
	1,176	400	1,480
Minority interest			(160)
			1,320
Share capital	400	160	400
Reserves	776	240	920
	1,176	400	1,320

Disposal: subsidiary to associate status

3.11 The only difference when a subsidiary becomes an associate is that the balance sheet only carries the underlying asset on **one line**. Otherwise, the same principles apply.

3.12 SOLUTION: ASSOCIATE STATUS

Using the above example, assume that Chalk plc sold 60% of its holding in Cheese plc for £440,000. The gain or loss on disposal would be calculated as follows.

	Holding company	*Group*
	£'000	£'000
Sale proceeds	440	440
60% of investment/net assets	96	240
Profit on sale	344	200

The balance sheets would now appear as follows.

	Chalk plc	*Cheese plc*	*Consolidated*
	£'000	£'000	£'000
Investment in Cheese	64	-	160
Other net assets	1,240	400	1,240
	1,304	400	1,400
Share capital	400	160	400
Reserves	904	240	1,000
	1,304	400	1,400

Disposal: subsidiary to investment status

3.13 In these circumstances dividend income only is shown in the P&L account after the date of disposal. The investment should be left in the balance sheet at the **equity valuation at the date of disposal**. Consider whether any write down is required.

Summary of accounting treatment

3.14 Calculate the gain or loss on disposal.

(a) **In holding company**

	£
Sale proceeds	X
Less cost of investment	X
Profit/(loss): (taxable)	X/(X)

(b) **In group accounts**

(i) *Either*:

	£	£
Sale proceeds		X
Less: net assets now disposed of	X	
goodwill not yet w/off through P & L a/c	X	
		X
Profit/(loss)		X/(X)

(ii) *Or*:

	£
Profit/(loss) per holding company	X
Less post-acquisition retained reserves now disposed of	(X)
	X
Add goodwill previously written off through P & L a/c	X
	X

3.15 For a **full disposal**, apply the following treatment.

(a) **P&L account**

(i) Consolidate results to the date of disposal.

(ii) Show the group gain or loss as an exceptional item after operating profit and before interest.

(b) **Balance sheet**

There will be no minority interest and no consolidation as there is no subsidiary at the date the balance sheet is being prepared.

3.16 For **partial disposals**, use the following treatments.

(a) **Subsidiary to subsidiary**

(i) The **minority interest in the P&L account** will be based on percentage before and after disposal, ie time apportion.

(ii) The **minority interest in the balance sheet** is based on the year end percentage.

(b) **Subsidiary to associate**

(i) **P&L account**

(1) Treat the undertaking as a subsidiary up to the date of disposal, ie consolidate for the correct number of months and show the minority interest in that amount.

(2) Treat as an associate thereafter.

(ii) **Balance sheet**: use an equity valuation based on the year end holding.

(c) **Subsidiary to trade investment**

(i) **P&L account**

(1) Treat the undertaking as a subsidiary up to the date of disposal.
(2) Show dividend income only thereafter.

(ii) **Balance sheet**: leave the investment valued at its equity valuation at the date of disposal but consider whether any write-down is required.

3.17 The following comprehensive exercise should help you get to grips with disposal problems. Try to complete the whole exercise without looking at the solution, and then check your answer very carefully. Give yourself at least an hour.

Exam focus point

Questions are likely to involve part-disposals leaving investments with both subsidiary and associate status.

Question: disposal

Smith Ltd bought 80% of the share capital of Jones Ltd for £324,000 a number of years ago. At that date Jones Ltd's P&L account balance stood at £180,000. The balance sheets at 30 September 20X8 and the summarised P&L accounts to that date are given below.

	Smith Ltd	*Jones Ltd*
	£'000	£'000
Fixed assets	360	270
Investment in Jones Ltd	324	-
Net current assets	270	270
	954	540
Share capital and reserves		
£1 ordinary shares	540	180
Profit and loss account	414	360
	954	540

	£'000	£'000
Profit before tax	153	126
Tax	45	36
Retained profit	108	90
Retained profit b/f	306	270
Retained profit c/f	414	360

No entries have been made in the accounts for any of the following transactions.

Assume that profits accrue evenly throughout the year and that any goodwill has been amortised through the profit and loss account.

Ignore taxation.

Required

Prepare the consolidated balance sheet and P&L account at 30 September 20X8 in each of the following circumstances.

(a) Smith Ltd sells its entire holding in Jones Ltd for £650,000 on 30 September 20X8.

(b) Smith Ltd sells its entire holding in Jones Ltd for £650,000 on 30 June 20X8.

(c) Smith Ltd sells one quarter of its holding in Jones Ltd for £160,000 on 30 June 20X8.

(d) Smith Ltd sells one half of its holding in Jones Ltd for £340,000 on 30 June 20X8, and the remaining holding is to be dealt with:

(i) As an associate
(ii) As a trade investment

Answer

(a) *Complete disposal at year end*

CONSOLIDATED BALANCE SHEET
AS AT 30 SEPTEMBER 20X8

	£'000
Fixed assets	360
Net current assets (270 + 650)	920
	1,280
Share capital and reserves	
£1 ordinary shares	540
Profit and loss account (W3)	740
	1,280

CONSOLIDATED PROFIT AND LOSS ACCOUNT
FOR THE YEAR ENDED 30 SEPTEMBER 20X8

	£'000	£'000
Profit before tax (153 + 126)		279
Exceptional item (W1)		218
Tax (45 + 36)		81
		416
Minority interest (20% × 90)		18
Profit attributable to members of Smith Ltd		398
Retained profit brought forward		342
Retained profit carried forward (W3)		740

Workings

1 *Profit on disposal in Jones Ltd*

	£'000
Sales proceeds	650
Cost	324
Profit in Smith Ltd	326
Profit on consolidation	
Per above working	326
Less post-acquisition profits now sold	
(360 – 180) × 80%	(144)
Add goodwill fully amortised (note)	36
	218

Alternative calculation of group profit on disposal

	£'000	£'000
Sales proceeds		650
Less: net assets of Jones now sold (540 × 80%)		432
		218

Note: goodwill	£'000
Cost	324
Acquired 80% × (180 + 180)	288
	36

2 *Retained profit brought forward*

	£'000
Smith	306
Jones: 80% × (270 – 180)	72
Goodwill fully amortised (W1)	(36)
	342

3 *Retained profit carried forward*

	£'000
Smith	414
Profit on disposal (W1)	326
	740

(b) *Complete disposal mid-year*

CONSOLIDATED BALANCE SHEET
AS AT 30 SEPTEMBER 20X8

	£'000
Fixed assets	360
Net current assets (270 + 650)	920
	1,280
Share capital and reserves	
£1 ordinary shares	540
Profit and loss account (W3)	740
	1,280

CONSOLIDATED PROFIT AND LOSS ACCOUNT
FOR THE YEAR ENDED 31 SEPTEMBER 20X8

	£'000
Profit before tax (153 + ($^9/_{12} \times$ 126))	247.5
Exceptional item (W1)	236.0
Tax (45 + (36 $\times$ $^9/_{12}$))	72.0
Profit after tax	411.5
Minority interest	
(20% $\times$ 90 $\times$ $^9/_{12}$)	13.5
Profit attributable to members of Smith Ltd	398.0
Retained profit brought forward (W2)	342.0
Retained profit carried forward (W3)	740.0

Workings

1 *Profit on disposal in Smith Ltd*

	£'000
Sale proceeds	650
Cost	324
Profit in Smith Ltd	326
Profit on consolidation	
Per above working	326
Less post-acquisition profits now sold	
80% $\times$ (270 + (90 $\times$ $^9/_{12}$) – 180)	126
Add: goodwill fully amortised (note)	36
	236

Alternative calculation of group profit on disposal

	£'000
Sale proceeds	650
Less: net assets of Jones now sold	
((540 – 90) + ($^9/_{12}$ $\times$ 90)) $\times$ 80%	414
	236

2 *Retained profit brought forward*

	£'000
Smith	306
Jones: 80% $\times$ (270 – 180)	72
Goodwill fully amortised	(36)
	342

3 *Retained profit carried forward*

	£'000
Smith	414
Profit on disposal (W1)	326
	740

(c) *Partial disposal: subsidiary to subsidiary*

CONSOLIDATED BALANCE SHEET AS AT 30 SEPTEMBER 20X8

	£'000
Fixed assets (360 + 270)	630
Net current assets (270 + 160 + 270)	700
	1,330
Share capital and reserves	
£1 ordinary shares	540
Profit and loss account (W3)	574
	1,114
Minority interest (40% × 540)	216
	1,330

CONSOLIDATED PROFIT AND LOSS ACCOUNT
FOR THE YEAR ENDED 30 SEPTEMBER 20X8

	£'000	£'000
Profit before tax (153 +126)		279.0
Exceptional item (W1)		56.5
Tax (45 + 36)		81.0
Profit after tax		254.5
Minority interest		
20% × 90 × 9/12	13.5	
40% × 90 × 3/12	9.0	
		22.5
Profit attributable to members of Smith Ltd		232.0
Retained profit brought forward (W2)		342.0
Retained profit carried forward (W3)		574.0

Workings

1 *Profit on disposal in Smith Ltd*

	£'000
Sale proceeds	160
Cost (324 × 25%)	81
Profit in Smith Ltd	79
Profit on consolidation	
Per above working	79.0
Less post-acquisition profits now sold	
(270 + (90 × 9/12) – 180) × 20%	31.5
Add goodwill fully amortised (36 × 25%)	9.0
	56.5

Alternative calculation of group profit on disposal

	£'000
Sale proceeds	160.0
Less: net assets of Jones now sold	
20% × ((540 – 90) + (9/12 × 90))	103.5
	56.5

2 *Retained profit brought forward*

	£'000
Smith	306
Jones: 80% × (270 – 180)	72
Goodwill fully amortised	(36)
	342

3 *Retained profit carried forward*

	£'000
Smith	414
Profit on disposal (W1)	79
Jones 60% × (360 – 180)	108
Goodwill fully amortised	(27)
	574

(d) (i) *Partial disposal: subsidiary to associate*

CONSOLIDATED BALANCE SHEET AS AT 30 SEPTEMBER 20X8

	£'000
Fixed assets	360
Investment in associated undertaking (40% × 540)	216
Net current assets (270 + 340)	610
	1,186
Share capital and reserves	
£1 ordinary shares	540
Profit and loss account (W3)	646
	1,186

CONSOLIDATED PROFIT AND LOSS ACCOUNT
FOR THE YEAR ENDED 30 SEPTEMBER 20X8

	£'000	£'000
Profit before tax*		
(153 + (9/12 × 126)) + (3/12 × 126 × 40%)		260.1
Exceptional item (W1)		133.0
Tax (45+ (9/12 × 36)) + (3/12 × 36 × 40%)		75.6
Profit after tax		317.5
Minority interest (20% × 90 × 9/12)		13.5
Profit attributable to members of Smith Ltd		304.0
Retained profit brought forward (W2)		342.0
Retained profit carried forward (W3)		646.0

**Note.* Per FRS 9 *Associates and joint ventures* disclosure should be made of group's share of associate's operating profit. However, PBT is used here for the sake of simplicity.

Workings

1 *Profit on disposal in Smith Ltd*

	£'000
Sales proceeds	340
Cost (50% × 324,000)	162
Profit in Smith Ltd	178
Profit on consolidation	
Per above working	178
Less post-acquisition profits now sold	
40% × (270 + (90 × 9/12) – 180)	63
Add goodwill fully amortised (36 × 50%)	18
	133

Alternative calculation of group profit on disposal

	£'000	£'000
Sale proceeds		340
Less: net assets of Jones now sold		
40% × ((540 – 90) + (9/12 × 90))		207
		133

2 *Retained profit brought forward*

	£'000
Smith	306
Jones 80% × (270 – 180)	72
Goodwill fully amortised	(36)
	342

3 *Retained profit carried forward*

	£'000
Smith	414
Profit on disposal (W1)	178
Jones 40% × (360 – 180)	72
Goodwill fully amortised	(18)
	646

(ii) Partial disposal: subsidiary to trade investment

CONSOLIDATED BALANCE SHEET
AS AT 30 SEPTEMBER 20X8

	£'000
Fixed assets	360
Investment (40% × (180 + 270 + (9/12 × 90)))	207
Net current assets	610
	1,177
Share capital and reserves	
£1 ordinary shares	540
Profit and loss account	637
	1,177

CONSOLIDATED PROFIT AND LOSS ACCOUNT
FOR THE YEAR ENDED 30 SEPTEMBER 20X8

	£'000	£'000
Profit before tax (153 + (9/12 × 126))		247.5
Exceptional item (See (d)(i) above)		133.0
Tax (45 + (9/12 × 36))		72.0
Profit after tax		308.5
Minority interest		13.5
Profit attributable to members of Smith Ltd		295.0
Retained profit brought forward		342.0
Retained profit carried forward (W)		637.0

Working

Retained profit carried forward

	£'000
Smith	414
Profit on disposal	178
Jones 40% × (270 + (9/12 × 90) – 180)	63
Goodwill fully amortised	(18)
	637

Dividends

3.18 The retained reserves/net assets at the date of disposal of the subsidiary should be calculated deducting only those dividends to which the **holding company is entitled**, in other words dividends paid up to the date of disposal and dividends proposed if the shares are sold *ex-dividend*.

3.19 At the date of disposal this would be as follows.

	£
Retained profits brought forward	X
Profits after tax and extraordinary items to date of disposal	X
Dividends paid/proposed at date of disposal	(X)
	X

Disclosure requirements

3.20 The following disclosure requirements should be made when a disposal has taken place.

(a) **Results for the year**: for any material disposals the consolidated financial statements should contain significant information to enable the shareholders to appreciate the effect on the consolidated results.

(b) FRS 3 *Reporting financial performance* requires the results of **discontinued operations** to be analysed separately.

(c) The following should be disclosed in respect of each material disposal of a previously acquired business or business segment.

   (i) The **profit or loss** on the disposal

   (ii) The amount of purchased **goodwill attributable** to a disposal and how it has been treated in determining the profit or loss on disposal

   (iii) The accounting treatment adopted and the amount of the proceeds in situations where no profit or loss is recorded on a disposal because the proceeds have been accounted for as a **reduction in the cost** of the acquisition

Deemed disposals

3.21 A group does not have to dispose of shares in a subsidiary for its holding to be reduced or eliminated. An undertaking may cease to be a subsidiary undertaking, or the group may reduce its proportional interest in that undertaking, other than by actual disposal These deemed disposals may arise for a number of reasons.

(a) The subsidiary undertaking issues shares to third parties.

(b) The group does not take up its full allocation in a rights issues.

(c) The subsidiary undertaking declares special scrip dividends which are not taken up by the parent so that its proportional interest is diminished.

(d) Another party exercises it options or warrants.

3.22 FRS 2 says that the accounting for deemed disposals and direct disposals should be the same.

3.23 EXAMPLE: DILUTION IN THE HOLDING OF AN INVESTMENT IN A SUBSIDIARY UNDERTAKING

Woodward owns 1,600,000 £1 shares in Sleeman which has a share capital of £2,000,000 and net assets of £5,000,000, the balance of £3,000,000 being retained profits. Woodward owned its investment since the formation of Sleeman, and therefore has consolidated 80% of its profits (£2,400,000). Its share of Sleeman's net assets is therefore £4,000,000.

Sleeman issues 2,000,000 share to third parties for cash of £6,000,000, thereby increasing its net assets to £11,000,000. The share capital and reserves of Sleeman and the amounts attributable to Woodward (40%) are now as follows.

	Sleeman	*Attributable to Woodward*
	£	£
Share capital	4,000,000	1,600,000
Share premium account	4,000,000	1,600,000
Profit and loss account	3,000,000	1,200,000
Total	11,000,000	4,400,000

3.24 Woodward has increased its share of net assets from £4,000,000 to £4,400,000. On the face of it, FRS 2 would seem to require this gain of £400,000 to be included in Woodward's consolidated profit and loss account. However, it could be argued that this does not represent a realised profit and therefore under the Companies Act it should be included not in the profit and loss account, but in the statement of total recognised gains and losses. Also, Woodward's share of Sleeman's distributable reserves has actually declined from £2,400,000 to £1,200,000. It could also be argued that Woodward should reclassify its group reserves by making a transfer of £1,600,000 from retained profits to some other reserve,

reflecting the fact that at these profits have been replaced by a share of Sleeman's share premium account, which is not distributable. This may be the preferable route particularly if Sleeman is now to be treated as an associate of Woodward. However, FRS 2 does not give any guidance on this issue.

3.25 An example of a company recognising a profit through the profit and account in respect of a deemed disposal is shown in the following extract from the 1995 accounts of Courts.

5 Exceptional credit

	1995	*1994*
	£,000	£,000
Profit arising on deemed disposal of interest in Courts (Mauritius) Ltd)	550	-
Profit arising on sale of shares in Courts (Singapore) Ltd	-	9,428
	550	9,428

(Source: UK GAAP)

3.26 On the other hand, South African Breweries has reflected the gain through its statement of total recognised gains and losses, as illustrated below.

29 Acquisitions (extract)

The Suncrush business was purchased through the Group's subsidiary undertaking, ABI, which issued shares to Suncrush Ltd as part of the purchase consideration. The immediate effect of this was to dilute the Group's holding in ABI from 68 per cent to 53 per cent. At the same time, the Group repurchased from Suncrush Ltd a portion of the shares issued by ABI issuing shares of SAB Ltd as consideration. This resulted in the Group's holding in ABI being increased to 65 per cent. On consolidation, the reduction in the Group's holding in ABI from 68 per cent to 65 per cent has resulted in a deemed disposal of 4 per cent of ABI. The profit of US $52 million (R290 million) arising on this deemed disposal has not been realised and has been accounted for as a movement through the consolidated statement of total recognised gains and losses.

(Source: UK GAAP)

Exam focus point

If you get a deemed disposal, it is most likely to arise because a subsidiary issues shares to third parties.

3.27 Section summary

Disposals are likely to occur frequently in Paper 3.6 consolidation questions.

- The effective date of disposal is when **control passes.**
- Treatment of **goodwill** is according to UITF 3 (and FRS 2).
- Disposals may be **full** or **partial,** to subsidiary, associate or investment status.
- **Gain or loss** on disposal is calculated for the holding company and the group.
- **FRS 3** disclosure requirements are important.
- **Deemed disposals** arise when a group reduces or eliminates its holding in a subsidiary other than by actual disposal.

4 CHANGES IN DIRECT OWNERSHIP PILOT PAPER, 12/02, 12/03

4.1 Groups will reorganise on occasions for a variety of reasons.

(a) A group may want to float a business to **reduce the gearing** of the group. The holding company will initially transfer the business into a separate company.

(b) Companies may be transferred to another business during a **divisionalisation** process.

(c) The group may 'reverse' into another company to obtain a **stock exchange quotation**.

(d) Internal reorganisations may create efficiencies of group structure for **tax purposes.**

4.2 Such reorganisations involve a restructuring of the relationships within a group. Companies may be transferred to another business during a divisionalisation process. There is generally no effect on the consolidated financial statements, *provided that* no minority interests are affected, because such reorganisations are only internal. The impact on the individual companies within the group, however, can be substantial. A variety of different transactions are described here, **only involving 100% subsidiaries**.

New top holding company

4.3 A new top holding company might be needed as a vehicle for flotation or to improve the co-ordination of a diverse business. The new company, H, will issue its own shares to the holdings of the shares in S. This type of transaction will qualify as a **merger** under FRS 6 (see Chapter 6).

Subsidiary moved up

4.4 This transaction is shown in the diagram below. It might be carried out to allow S_1 to be **sold** while S_2 is retained, or to **split diverse businesses**.

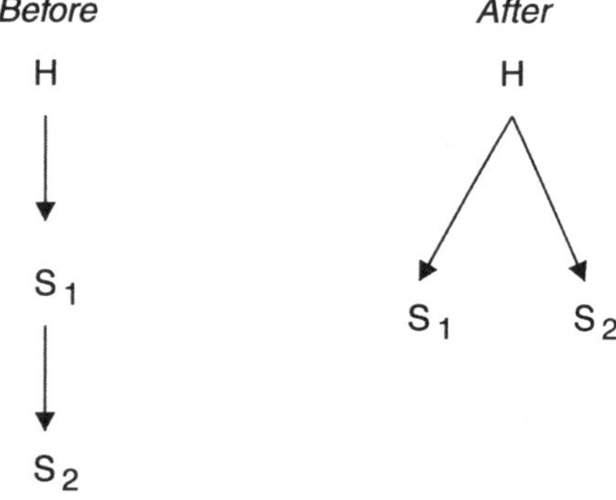

4.5 S_1 could transfer its investment in S_2 to H as a dividend *in specie* or by H paying cash. A share for share exchange is not possible because an allotment by H to S_1 is void. A **dividend in specie** is simply a dividend paid other than in cash.

4.6 S_1 must have sufficient **distributable profits** for a dividend *in specie*. If the investment in S_2 has been revalued then that can be treated as a realised profit for the purposes of determining the legality of the distribution. For example, suppose the balance sheet of S_1 is as follows.

	£m
Investment in S_2 (cost £100m)	900
Other net assets	100
	1,000
Share capital	100
Revaluation reserve	800
Profit and loss account	100
	1,000

4.7 It appears that S_1 cannot make a distribution of more than £100m; if, however, S_1 makes a distribution in kind of its investment in S_2, then the **revaluation reserve** can be treated as realised.

4.8 It is not clear how H should account for the transaction. The carrying value to S_2 might be used, but there is **no legal rule**. H will need to write down its investment in S_1 at the same time. A transfer for cash is probably easiest, but there are still legal pitfalls as to what is distributable, depending on how the transfer is recorded.

4.9 There will be **no effect** on the group financial statements as the group has stayed the same: it has made no acquisitions or disposals.

Subsidiary moved along

4.10 This is a transaction which is treated in a very similar manner to that described above.

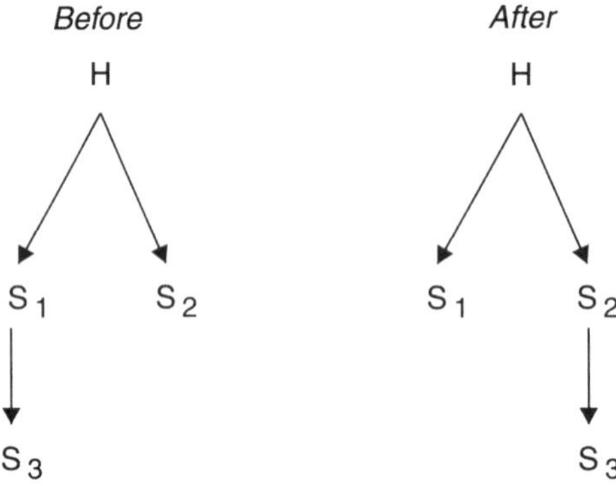

4.11 The problem of an effective distribution does not arise here because the holding company did not buy the subsidiary. There may be problems with **financial assistance** if S_2 pays less than the fair value to purchase S_3 as a prelude to S_1 leaving the group.

Subsidiary moved down

4.12 This situation could arise if H is foreign and S_1 and S_2 are UK companies. A **UK tax group** can be formed out of such a restructuring.

Before *After*

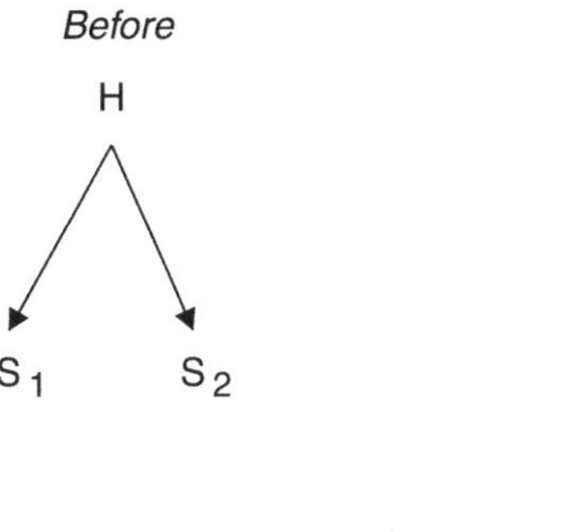

4.13 If S_1 paid cash for S_2, the transaction would be straightforward (as described above). The law is again unclear on the issue of whether H should recognise a gain or loss on the sale if S_2 is sold for more or less than carrying value. S_1 would only be deemed to have made a distribution only if the **price was excessive**.

4.14 A share for share exchange would be affected by s 132 CA 1985 which gives partial relief against the need to create a **share premium account**. A share premium account must be set up with a 'minimum premium value'. This is the amount by which the book value of the shares (or lower cost) exceeds the nominal value of the shares issued. This preserves the book value of the investment.

4.15 EXAMPLE: MINIMUM PREMIUM VALUE

Hop plc has two 100% subsidiaries, Skip and Jump. The balance sheets at 31 December 20X5 are as follows.

	Hop plc	*Skip Ltd*	*Jump Ltd*	*Group*
	£'000	£'000	£'000	£'000
Investment in Skip	1,000	-	-	-
Investment in Jump	500	-	-	-
Net assets	1,500	1,375	1,500	4,375
	3,000	1,375	1,500	4,375

	Hop plc	*Skip Ltd*	*Jump Ltd*	*Group*
	£'000	£'000	£'000	£'000
Share capital	2,500	1,000	500	2,500
P & L account	500	375	1,000	1,875
	3,000	1,375	1,500	4,375

4.16 SOLUTION

Skip Ltd issues 250,000 £1 shares in exchange for Hop plc's investment in Jump Ltd. The minimum premium value is £500,000 (carrying value) – £250,000 = £250,000. The balance sheets are now as follows.

	Hop plc	*Skip Ltd*	*Jump Ltd*	*Group*
	£'000	£'000	£'000	£'000
Investment in Skip	1,500	-	-	-
Investment in Jump	-	500	-	-
Net assets	1,500	1,375	1,500	4,375
	3,000	1,875	1,500	4,375
Share capital	2,500	1,250	500	2,500
Share premium	-	250	-	-
P & L account	500	375	1,000	1,875
	3,000	1,875	1,500	4,375

Divisionalisation

4.17 This type of transaction involves the **transfer of businesses** from subsidiaries into just one company. The businesses will all be similar and this is a means of rationalising and streamlining. The savings in administration costs can be quite substantial. The remaining shell company will leave the cash it was paid on an inter-company balance as it is no longer trading. The accounting treatment is generally straightforward.

5 DEMERGERS

5.1 A demerger will usually involve **splitting up an existing group** into two or more separate groups. This is usually done to separate different types of trade, particularly when it is intended to sell one of the resulting parts.

5.2 There are a number of ways to carry out such a transaction.

(a) H transfers shares in S_1 to its **shareholders** as a dividend *in specie*.

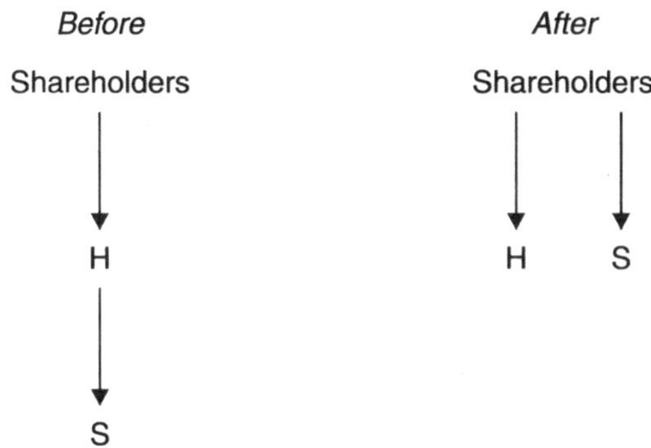

(b) H transfers a trade to **another company** S, often formed for the purpose, and in exchange S issues shares to its shareholders.

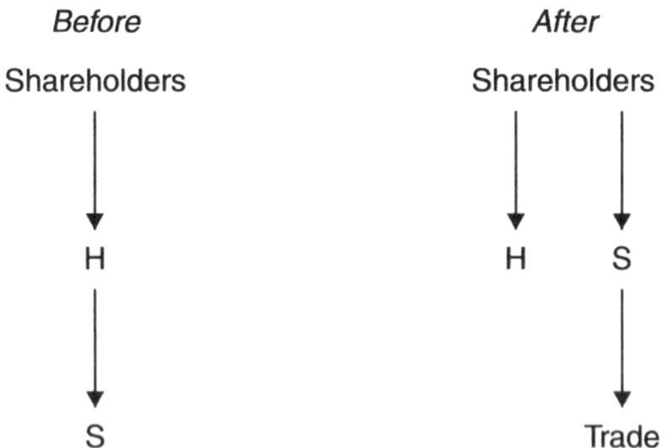

(c) H transfers shares in S_1 to **another company** S_2, who in return issues shares to the shareholders in H.

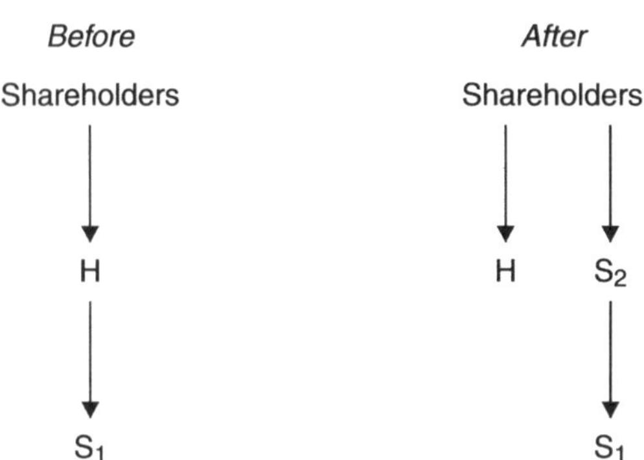

5.3 Most importantly, you should note that the transaction will *always* involve a **distribution by H to its shareholders**, even though this point may seem obscure at times.

5.4 EXAMPLE: DEMERGER

Guinevere Ltd, a subsidiary of Arthur plc, is to be demerged from the group. A new company, Lancelot Ltd, is to be created and it will issue its shares to the shareholders of Arthur in return for the investment in Guinevere. The balance sheets on the day before the demerger were as follows.

	Arthur plc	*Guinevere Ltd*	*Arthur Group*
	£'000	£'000	£'000
Investment in Guinevere	3,000	-	-
Other net assets	7,200	4,800	12,000
	10,200	4,800	12,000
Share capital	6,000	3,000	6,000
P & L account	4,200	1,800	6,000
	10,200	4,800	12,000

In exchange for Arthur's holding in Guinevere, Lancelot plc issues 3 million £1 shares to Arthur plc's shareholders.

5.5 SOLUTION

In effect this is a distribution by Arthur to its shareholders. The net assets of the company are reduced by £3m and the net assets of the group are reduced by £4.8m, the value of Guinevere. It is usual to show such treatment as movements on retained earnings.

	Company	*Group*
	£'000	£'000
Profit and loss account		
Balance at 1.1.20X5	4,200	6,000
Demerger of Guinevere	(3,000)	(4,800)
Profit for the year	2,100	2,100
Balance at 31.12.20X5	3,300	3,300

Lancelot's shares have been issued at a premium and so share premium relief ought to be taken because the transaction is in effect a merger between Guinevere and Lancelot.

5.6 Make sure you try Questions 8 and 9 in the Exam Question Bank towards the end of this text as they are comprehensive questions.

Exam focus point

The topics covered in Section 4 and 5, changes in direct ownership and demergers were the subject of a question on the Pilot Paper for 3.6.

Question: do some homework!

In between now and your examination, look for any demergers discussed in the financial press and consider the accounting implications.

Chapter roundup

- Transactions of the type described in this chapter can be very complicated and certainly look rather daunting. Remember and apply the **basic techniques** and you should find such questions easier than you expected.
- **Piecemeal acquisitions** can lead to a company becoming a fixed asset investment, an associate and then a subsidiary over time. Make sure you can deal with each of these situations.
- In piecemeal acquisitions, use the **rule-of-thumb** in Paragraph 1.8 to decide whether the step-by-step method or the one-computation-at-the-date-of-control method is more appropriate.
- **Disposals** can drop a subsidiary holding to associate status, fixed asset investment status and to zero, or a the parent might still retain a subsidiary undertaking with a reduced holding. Once again, you should be able to deal with all these situations. Remember particularly how to deal with **goodwill**.
- **Changes in direct ownership** (ie internal group reorganisations) can take many forms. Apart from divisionalisation, all other internal reorganisations will not affect the consolidated financial statements, but they will affect the accounts of individual companies within the group.
- **Demergers** are not unusual in practice and are not difficult to account for. Concentrate on the substance of the transactions undertaken.

Quick quiz

1 What is the general rule in determining pre- and post-acquisition reserves in a piecemeal acquisition?

2 When a subsidiary is disposed of, what is the required treatment of any goodwill which arose when the subsidiary was purchased?

3 Corrie Ltd acquired 70% of the 100,000 £1 ordinary shares of Brookie Ltd on 1 January 20X7 for £115,000. It sold its entire holding on 30 June 20X9 for £150,000. At acquisition Brookie Ltd had reserves of £44,000. By 1 January 20X9 the reserves had mounted to £72,000. Profit for the year ended 31 December 20X9 was £20,000, after paying a final dividend in November 20X9 of £5,000.

What is the reported exceptional item in the individual company profit and loss account?

4 Muggins Ltd had a 40% stake in Gumm Ltd which it has acquired 2 years ago for £108,000. Goodwill on acquisition was to be capitalised and amortised over five years.

The whole shareholding was sold on 31 December 20X9 for £150,000. Balance sheets were as follows

	31.12.20X7	*31.12.20X9*
	£'000	£'000
£1 ordinary shares	100	100
Share premium account	10	10
Revaluation reserve	60	90
Profit and loss account	50	120
	220	320

What is the reported consolidated profit on disposal?

5 Complete the 'after' diagrams in the following cases

New top holding company

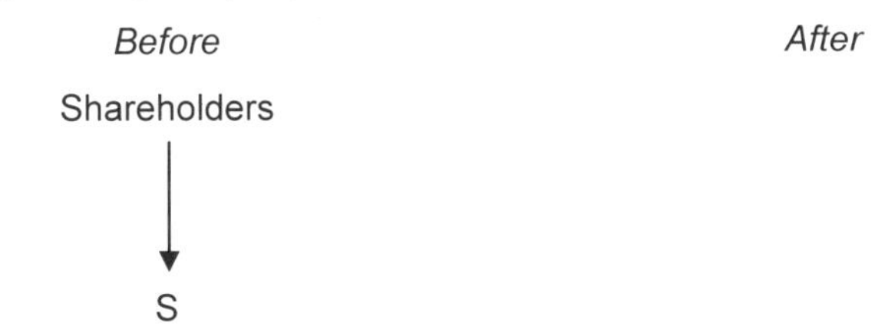

Subsidiary moved up

6 Why would a subsidiary be moved up?

7 Why would a subsidiary be moved down?

8 A demerger will always involve ....

Answers to quick quiz

1 See para 1.8

2 Any goodwill not yet written off to the profit and loss account must be deducted from the gain on disposal in the group accounts.

3 The individual company gain is simply the proceeds less the cost.

This gain will be subject to tax at the prevailing CT rate, but the tax charge is added to 'Taxation' in the profit and loss account and does not affect the reported exceptional item.

No details of goodwill policy are given. If you assume goodwill is capitalised and not amortised, the group gain would be £6,650.

		£
ie	Proceeds	150,000
	Less NA disposed 70% $[100 + 72 + \frac{6}{12} \times (25)]$	(129,150)
	Less goodwill [115 – 70% (100 + 44)]	(14,200)
		6,650

4

	£'000
Proceeds	150
Less NA sold 40% (320)	(128)
Less unamortised goodwill 3/5 (108 – 40% (220)]	(12)
	10

Alternative calculation:

	£'000
Proceeds	150
Less cost	(108)
	42
Less increase in net assets 40% (320 – 220)	(40)
Plus amortised goodwill 2/5 [108 – 40% (220)]	8
	10

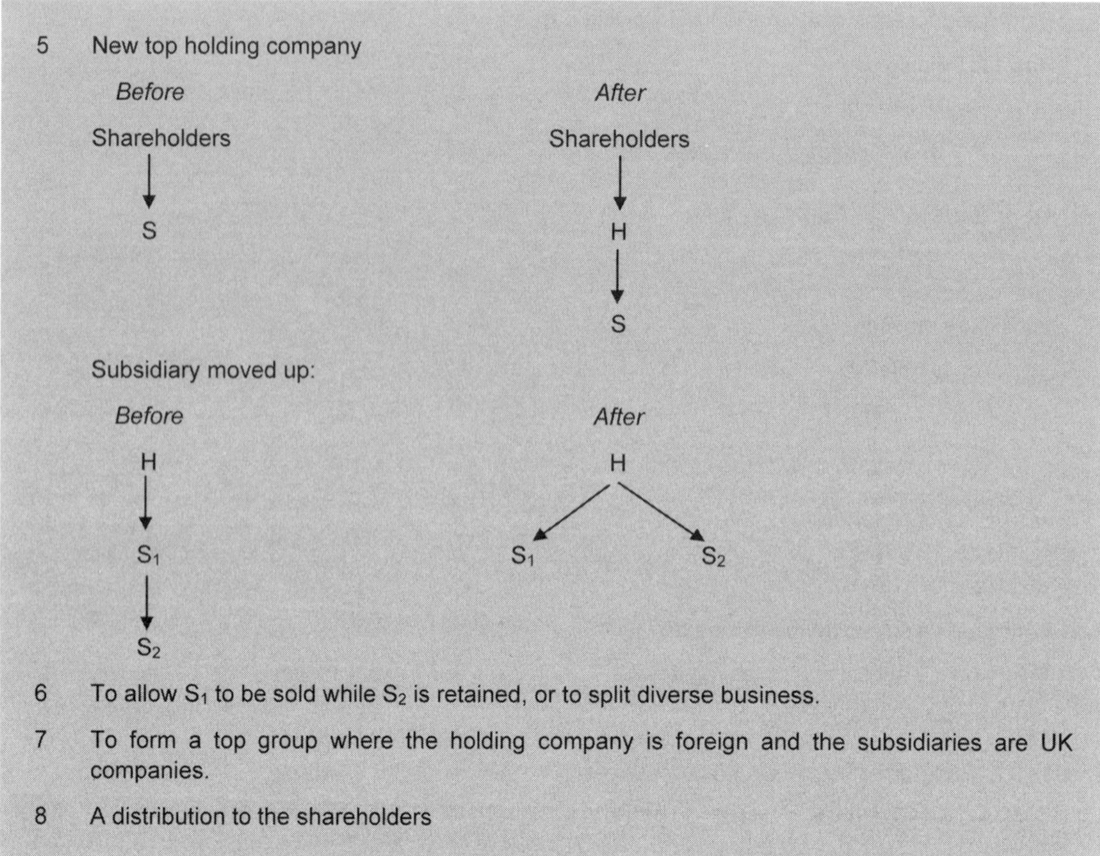

5 New top holding company

Before

Shareholders → S

After

Shareholders → H → S

Subsidiary moved up:

Before

H → S_1 → S_2

After

H → S_1, H → S_2

6 To allow S_1 to be sold while S_2 is retained, or to split diverse business.

7 To form a top group where the holding company is foreign and the subsidiaries are UK companies.

8 A distribution to the shareholders

Now try the questions below from the Exam Question Bank

Number	Level	Marks	Time
Q6	Exam	25	45 mins
Q7	Exam	25	45 mins
Q8	Exam	25	45 mins

Chapter 6

ACQUISITIONS AND MERGERS

	Topic list	Syllabus reference
1	FRS 7 *Fair values in acquisition accounting*	2(a)
2	FRS 6 *Acquisitions and mergers*	2(a)
3	Further practical issues and merger relief	2(a)

Introduction

There are **two methods** of accounting for the combination of businesses.

(a) Acquisition accounting
(b) Merger accounting

Until now in this text we have covered **acquisition accounting**, where there is in effect a 'takeover' of one entity by another. We will look at some of the problems which arise in acquisition accounting here: acquisitions during an accounting period, dividends and pre-acquisition profits, and fair values (FRS 7).

Merger accounting, where the two entities combine so that there is no takeover of one by the other, is much rarer now due to the restrictive provisions of FRS 6.

Study guide

Section 3 – Group financial statements 1

- Explaining the principles of measurement relating to the fair value of the consideration and the net assets acquired

Section 5 – Mergers

- Explaining the basic principles and philosophy of merger accounting
- Accounting for equity eliminations, expenses and dividends of the subsidiary
- Preparation of consolidated financial statements utilising merger accounting techniques
- Determining whether merger accounting could be used in specific circumstances and the relative merits of different methods of accounting for business combinations

1 FRS 7 FAIR VALUES IN ACQUISITION ACCOUNTING

1.1 FRS 10 *Goodwill and intangible assets* defines **goodwill** as the difference between the purchase consideration paid by the acquiring company and the aggregate of the 'fair values' of the identifiable assets and liabilities acquired. The balance sheet of a subsidiary company at the date it is acquired may not be a guide to the fair value of its net assets. For example, the market value of a freehold building may have risen greatly since it was acquired, but it may appear in the balance sheet at historical cost less accumulated depreciation.

Fair value calculations

1.2 Until now we have calculated goodwill as the difference between the cost of the investment and the **book value** of net assets acquired by the group. If this calculation is to comply with the definition in FRS 10 we must ensure that the book value of the subsidiary's net assets is the same as their **fair value**.

1.3 There are two possible ways of achieving this.

(a) The subsidiary company might **incorporate any necessary revaluations** in its own books of account. In this case, we can proceed directly to the consolidation, taking asset values and reserves figures straight from the subsidiary company's balance sheet.

(b) The revaluations may be made as a **consolidation adjustment** without being incorporated in the subsidiary company's books. In this case, we must make the necessary adjustments to the subsidiary's balance sheet as a working. Only then can we proceed to the consolidation.

Note. Remember that when depreciating assets are revalued there may be a corresponding alteration in the amount of depreciation charged and accumulated.

1.4 EXAMPLE: FAIR VALUE ADJUSTMENTS

H Ltd acquired 75% of the ordinary shares of S Ltd on 1 September 20X5. At that date the fair value of S Ltd's fixed assets was £23,000 greater than their net book value, and the balance of retained profits was £21,000. The balance sheets of both companies at 31 August 20X6 are given below. S Ltd has not incorporated any revaluation in its books of account.

H LIMITED
BALANCE SHEET AS AT 31 AUGUST 20X6

	£
Fixed assets	
Tangible assets	63,000
Investment in S Ltd at cost	51,000
	114,000
Net current assets	62,000
	176,000
Capital and reserves	
Ordinary shares of £1 each	80,000
Retained profits	96,000
	176,000

S LIMITED
BALANCE SHEET AS AT 31 AUGUST 20X6

	£
Tangible fixed assets	28,000
Net current assets	33,000
	61,000
Capital and reserves	
Ordinary shares of £1 each	20,000
Retained profits	41,000
	61,000

If S Ltd had revalued its fixed assets at 1 September 20X5, an addition of £3,000 would have been made to the depreciation charged in the P&L account for 20X5/X6.

Required

Prepare H Ltd's consolidated balance sheet as at 31 August 20X6.

Note. Goodwill is deemed to have an indefinite useful life and is therefore to remain in the balance sheet.

1.5 SOLUTION

S Ltd has not incorporated the revaluation in its draft balance sheet. Before beginning the consolidation workings we must therefore adjust the company's balance of profits at the date of acquisition and at the balance sheet date.

S Ltd adjusted balance of retained profits

	£	£
Balance per accounts at 1 September 20X5		21,000
Consolidation adjustment: revaluation surplus		23,000
∴ Pre-acquisition profits for consolidation purposes		44,000
Profit for year ended 31 August 20X6		
Per draft accounts £(41,000 – 21,000)	20,000	
Consolidation adjustment: increase in depreciation charge	(3,000)	
		17,000
Adjusted balance of retained profits at 31 August 20X6		61,000

In the consolidated balance sheet, S Ltd's fixed assets will appear at their revalued amount: £(28,000 + 23,000 – 3,000) = £48,000. The consolidation workings can now be drawn up.

1 *Minority interest*

	£
Share capital (25% × £20,000)	5,000
Revenue reserves (25% × £61,000)	15,250
	20,250

2 *Goodwill*

	£	£
Cost of investment		51,000
Share of net assets acquired as represented by		
Ordinary share capital	20,000	
Revenue reserves £(21,000 + 23,000)	44,000	
	64,000	
Group share (75%)		48,000
Goodwill		3,000

3 *Revenue reserves*

	H Ltd	*S Ltd*
	£	£
Per question	96,000	41,000
Depreciation increase		(3,000)
Pre-acquisition		(21,000)
		17,000
Share of S Ltd 75% × 17,000	12,750	
	108,750	

H LIMITED CONSOLIDATED BALANCE SHEET AS AT 31 AUGUST 20X6

	£
Intangible fixed asset: goodwill	3,000
Tangible fixed assets £(63,000 + 48,000)	111,000
Net current assets	95,000
	209,000
Capital and reserves	
Ordinary shares of £1 each	80,000
Retained profits	108,750
Shareholders' funds	188,750
Minority interest	20,250
	209,000

FRS 7 *Fair values in acquisition accounting*

1.6 FRS 7 and FRS 6 *Acquisitions and mergers* were published together in September 1994 in order to reform both acquisition and merger accounting practices.

1.7 As far as **acquisition accounting** is concerned, the main problem is the practice of attributing the **lowest values possible** to the net assets acquired so that the goodwill figure is correspondingly increased. Goodwill is generally deducted direct from reserves, the P&L account is by-passed, and profits are enhanced when the low asset values are subsequently charged against them in depreciation.

1.8 The commonest method of reducing the net assets acquired has been by establishing **provisions for reorganisation and restructuring costs**, reflecting the changes the acquirer intends to make to the business it has acquired. Since such provisions allow the subsequent expenditure to by-pass the P&L account, the costs disappear into a 'black hole' as far as reported profits are concerned; and the profits of the acquirer benefit from the increased earnings resulting from the reorganisation, without bearing the costs involved.

1.9 In attributing fair values to assets and liabilities acquired, FRS 7 states that the basic principle is that fair values should reflect the **circumstances at the time of the acquisition**, and should not reflect either the acquirer's intentions or events subsequent to the acquisition. Thus, the assets and liabilities recognised are restricted to those of the acquired entity that existed at the date of acquisition, and **exclude** both provisions for reorganisation costs to be carried out by the acquirer and provisions for future losses. Such items are to be treated as part of the post-acquisition results of the enlarged group.

1.10 FRS 7 also sets out specific rules on how fair values should be determined for the main categories of asset and liability. The underlying principle remains that fair values should reflect the price at which an asset or liability could be **exchanged in an arm's length transaction**. For long-term monetary assets and liabilities, fair values may be derived by **discounting**.

1.11 The standard also describes how the value attributed to the **consideration** given for the acquisition should be determined, and the acquisition expenses that may be included as part of the cost.

Objective

1.12 The objective of FRS 7 is to ensure that when a business entity is acquired by another, all the assets and liabilities that existed in the acquired entity at the date of acquisition are recorded at fair values reflecting their **condition at that date**. Any changes to the acquired

assets and liabilities, and the resulting gains and losses, that arise after control of the acquired entity has passed to the acquirer should be reported as part of the post-acquisition profits of the group.

Definitions

1.13 The following definitions are given by FRS 7; particularly note the definition of fair value.

KEY TERMS

- **Acquisition:** a business combination that is accounted for by using the acquisition method of accounting.
- **Business combination**: the bringing together of separate entities into one economic entity as a result of one entity uniting with, or obtaining control over the net assets and operations of, another.
- **Date of acquisition**: the date on which control of the acquired entity passes to the acquirer. This is the date from which the acquired entity is accounted for by the acquirer as a subsidiary undertaking under FRS 2.
- **Fair value**: the amount at which an asset or liability could be exchanged in an arm's length transaction between informed and willing parties, other than in a forced or liquidation sale.
- **Identifiable assets and liabilities**: the assets and liabilities of the acquired entity that are capable of being disposed of or settled separately, without disposing of a business of the entity.
- **Recoverable amount**: the greater of the net realisable value of an asset and, where appropriate, the value in use.
- **Value in use**: the present value of the future cash flows obtainable as a result of an asset's continued use, including those resulting from the ultimate disposal of the asset. *(FRS 7)*

Scope

1.14 FRS 7 applies to all financial statements that are intended to give a true and fair view. Although the FRS is framed in terms of the acquisition of a subsidiary undertaking by a parent company that prepares consolidated financial statements, it also applies where an **individual company** entity acquires a business other than a subsidiary undertaking. This last point means that companies cannot avoid the provisions of FRS 7 when taking over an unincorporated entity or joint venture vehicle.

Determining the fair values of identifiable assets and liabilities acquired

1.15 The basic principles stated by FRS 7 are that:

(a) All identifiable assets and liabilities should be **recognised** which are in existence at the date of acquisition

(b) Such recognised assets and liabilities should be **measured at fair values** which reflect the conditions existing at the date of acquisition

1.16 Most importantly, the FRS lists those items which do *not* affect fair values at the date of acquisition, and which are therefore to be treated as **post-acquisition items.**

(a) Changes resulting from the acquirer's **intentions or future actions**

(b) Impairments or other changes, resulting from **events subsequent to the acquisition**

(c) Provisions or accruals for **future operating losses** or for **reorganisation and integration costs** expected to be incurred as a result of the acquisition, whether they relate to the acquired entity or to the acquirer

1.17 In general terms, fair values should be determined in accordance with the acquirer's **accounting policies** for similar assets and liabilities. The standard does, however, go on to describe how the major categories of assets and liabilities should be assessed for fair values.

(a) **Tangible assets**: fair value based on:

(i) Market value, if similar assets are sold on the open market, or
(ii) Depreciated replacement cost, reflecting normal business practice.

However, fair value ≤ replacement cost.

(b) **Intangible assets**, where recognised: fair value should be based on replacement costs, which will normally be estimated market value.

(c) **Stocks and work in progress**

(i) For stocks which are replaced by purchasing in a ready market (commodities, dealing stock etc), the fair value is market value.

(ii) For other stocks, with no ready market (most manufacturing stocks), fair value is represented by the current cost to the acquired company of reproducing the stocks.

(d) **Quoted investments**: value at market price, adjusted where necessary for unusual price fluctuations or the size of the holding.

(e) **Monetary assets and liabilities**: fair values should take into account the amounts expected to be received or paid and their timing. Reference should be made to market prices (where available) or to the current price if acquiring similar assets or entering into similar obligations, or to the discounted present value.

(f) **Contingencies**: reasonable estimates of the expected outcome may be used.

(g) **Pensions and other post-retirement benefits**: the fair value of a deficiency, a surplus (to the extent it is expected to be realised) or accrued obligation should be recognised as an asset/liability of the acquiring group. Any changes on acquisition should be treated as post-acquisition items.

(h) **Deferred tax** recognised in a fair value exercise should be measured in accordance with the requirements of FRS 19 (see Chapter 22). Thus deferred tax would not be recognised on an adjustment to recognise a non-monetary asset acquired with the business at its fair value on acquisition.

Business sold or held with a view to subsequent resale

1.18 The fair value exercise for such an entity, 'sold as a single unit, within approximately one year of acquisition', should be carried out on the basis of a **single asset investment**.

'Its fair value should be based on the net proceeds of the sale, adjusted for the fair value of any assets or liabilities transferred into or out of the business, unless such adjusted net proceeds are demonstrably different from the fair value at the date of acquisition as a result of a post-acquisition event.'

Any relevant part of the business can be treated in this way if it is separately identifiable, ie it does not have to be a separate subsidiary undertaking.

1.19 Where the **first financial statements** after the date of acquisition come for approval, but the business has not been sold, the above treatment can still be applied if:

(a) A purchaser has been identified or is being sought
(b) The disposal is expected to occur within one year of the date of acquisition

1.20 The interest (or its assets) should be shown in current assets. On determination of the sales price, the original estimate of fair value should be **adjusted** to reflect the actual sales proceeds.

Investigation period and goodwill adjustments

1.21 FRS 7 states that:

> 'The recognition and measurement of assets and liabilities acquired should be completed, if possible, by the date on which the first post-acquisition financial statements of the acquirer are approved by the directors.'

Where this has not been possible, **provisional valuations** should be made, amended if necessary in the next financial statements with a corresponding adjustment to goodwill. Such adjustments should be incorporated into the financial statements in the **full year following acquisition**. After that, any adjustments (except for the correction of fundamental errors by prior year adjustment) should be recognised as profits or losses as they are identified.

Determining the fair value of purchase consideration

1.22 The cost of acquisition is the amount of **cash paid and the fair value of other purchase consideration** given by the acquirer, together with the expenses of the acquisition. Where a subsidiary undertaking is acquired in stages, the cost of acquisition is the total of the costs of the interests acquired, determined as at the date of each transaction.

1.23 The main likely components of purchase consideration are as follows.

(a) **Ordinary shares**

(i) Quoted shares should be valued at market price on the date of acquisition.

(ii) Where there is no suitable market, estimate the value using:

- the value of similar quoted securities; *or*
- the present value of the future cash flows of the instrument used; *or*
- any cash alternative which was offered.

(b) **Other securities***:* the value should be based on similar principles to those given in (a).

(c) **Cash or monetary amounts***:* value at the amount paid or payable.

(d) **Non-monetary assets***:* value at market price, estimated realisable value, independent valuation or based on other available evidence.

(e) **Deferred consideration***:* discount the amounts calculated on the above principles (in (a) to (d)). An appropriate discount rate is that which the acquirer could obtain for a similar borrowing.

(f) **Contingent consideration**: use the probable amount. When the actual amount is known, it should be recorded in the financial statements and goodwill adjusted accordingly.

1.24 **Acquisition costs** (the fees and expenses mentioned above) should be included in the cost of the investment. Internal costs and the costs of issuing capital instruments should *not* be capitalised, according to the provisions of FRS 4, ie they must be written off to the P&L account.

Summary and assessment

1.25 The most important effect of FRS 7 is the ban it imposes on making provisions for **future trading losses** of acquired companies and the costs of any related **rationalisation or reorganisation**, unless outgoing management had already incurred those liabilities. This is a controversial area, demonstrated by the dissenting view of one member of the ASB. However, this approach has been followed in FRS 12 *Provisions, contingent liabilities and contingent assets*.

1.26 Some argue that the ASB's approach **ignores the commercial reality** of the transaction by treating as an expense the costs of reorganisation that the acquirer regards as part of the capital cost of the acquisition; and that within defined limits a provision for planned post-acquisition expenditure should be permitted to be included in the net assets acquired.

1.27 The Hundred Group of finance directors gave an example. If you buy a house for, say £100,000 that you know needs £50,000 spent on it to bring it into good condition and make it equivalent to a property that sells for £150,000, then you would treat the £50,000 renovation expense as part of the cost of the house and not as part of ordinary outgoings. The group states that FRS 7 goes beyond standards set in other countries, including the US. It also recommends that abuses in this area should be dealt with by tightening existing accounting standards and through 'proper policing' by external auditors (the standard is seen to undermine the professional judgement of the auditor) and 'not by distorting accounting concepts'.

1.28 The ASB rejected this view, saying that an intention to incur revenue expenditure subsequent to the acquisition could not properly be regarded as a liability of the acquired business at the date of acquisition.

> 'Acquisition accounting should reflect the business that is acquired as it stands at the date of acquisition and ought not to take account of the changes that an acquirer might intend to make subsequently. Nor could the ASB accept the proposition that some of the inadequacies of the present system could be met by better disclosure. In the ASB's view deficient accounting cannot be put right by disclosure alone.'

Exam focus point

Questions on FRS 7 will probably involve fair values of deferred and contingent consideration and discussions on the use of provisions. You are likely to be asked about the more contentious items in Paper 3.6.

1.29 Section summary

Factors to consider when arriving at a fair value are as follows.

- **Deferred consideration**: time value of money
- **Contingent consideration**: expected amount payable/receivable
- Use of **hindsight**
- **Pension surpluses/deficiencies** unrecorded by subsidiary
- Net assets acquired should be identified and recognised using the **acquirer's accounting policies**
- No adjustments should be made for the **acquirer's future intentions**
- **Deferred tax implications** should be considered

Question: FRS 7 (1)

H Ltd acquired 100% of S Ltd for £1,000,000. At the date of acquisition S Ltd had net assets of £500,000. However, H Ltd would need to spend £200,000 on reorganising S Ltd to successfully incorporate the company into the group. The group's policy is to amortise goodwill over 5 years with a full year's amortisation in the year of acquisition.

The P&L account of H Ltd in the first year following the acquisition are as follows.

	H Ltd	*S Ltd*
	£'000	£'000
Operating profit	700	400
Reorganisation costs	-	200
Profit before tax	700	200
Tax	200	70
Profit after tax	500	130

Requirement

Calculate the goodwill and prepare the consolidated P&L account:

(a) Assuming the acquisition took place pre-FRS 7
(b) In accordance with FRS 7

Answer

Goodwill	*(a)*	*(b)*
	Pre-FRS 7	*Post-FRS 7*
	£'000	£'000
Cost of investment	1,000	1,000
Net assets acquired	(500)	500
Provision for reorganisation	200	-
Goodwill	700	500

Profit and loss account	*(a)*	*(b)*
	Pre-FRS 7	*Post-FRS 7*
	£'000	£'000
Operating profit	1,100	1,100
Goodwill amortisation (700/5 / 500/5)	(140)	(100)
Reorganisation	(200)	200
Release provision	200	
Profit before tax	960	800
Tax	270	270
Profit after tax	690	530
Profit b/fwd	-	-
Retained profit reserves c/f	690	530

Question: FRS 7 (2)

Tyzo plc prepares accounts to 31 December. On 1 September 20X7 Tyzo plc acquired 6 million £1 shares in Kono plc at £2.00 per share. The purchase was financed by an additional issue of loan stock at an interest rate of 10%. At that date Kono plc produced the following interim financial statements.

	£m		£m
Tangible fixed assets (note 1)	16.0	Trade creditors	3.2
Stocks (note 2)	4.0	Taxation	0.6
Debtors	2.9	Bank overdraft	3.9
Cash in hand	1.2	Long-term loans (note 3)	4.0
		Share capital (£1 shares)	8.0
		Profit and loss account	4.4
	24.1		24.1

Notes

1 The following information relates to the tangible fixed assets of Kono plc at 1 September 20X7.

	£m
Gross replacement cost	28.4
Net replacement cost	16.6
Economic value	18.0
Net realisable value	8.0

The fixed assets of Kono plc at 1 September 20X7 had a total purchase cost to Kono plc of £27.0 million. They were all being depreciated at 25% per annum pro rata on that cost. This policy is also appropriate for the consolidated financial statements of Tyzo plc. No fixed assets of Kono plc which were included in the interim financial statements drawn up as at 1 September 20X7 were disposed of by Kono plc prior to 31 December 20X7. No fixed asset was fully depreciated by 31 December 20X7.

2 The stocks of Kono plc which were shown in the interim financial statements at cost to Kono plc of £4 million would have cost £4.2 million to replace at 1 September 20X7 and had an estimated net realisable value at that date of £4.8 million. Of the stock of Kono plc in hand at 1 September 20X7, goods costing Kono plc £3.0 million were sold for £3.6 million between 1 September 20X7 and 31 December 20X7.

3 The long-term loan of Kono plc carries a rate of interest of 10% per annum, payable on 31 August annually in arrears. The loan is redeemable at par on 31 August 20Y1. The interest cost is representative of current market rates. The accrued interest payable by Kono plc at 31 December 20X7 is included in the trade creditors of Kono plc at that date.

4 On 1 September 20X7 Tyzo plc took a decision to rationalise the group so as to integrate Kono plc. The costs of the rationalisation (which were to be borne by Tyzo plc) were estimated to total £3.0 million and the process was due to start on 1 March 20X8. No provision for these costs has been made in any of the financial statements given above.

Required

Compute the goodwill on consolidation of Kono plc that will be included in the consolidated financial statements of the Tyzo plc group for the year ended 31 December 20X7, explaining your treatment of the items mentioned above. You should refer to the provisions of relevant accounting standards.

Answer

Goodwill on consolidation of Kono Ltd

	£m	£m
Consideration (£2.00 × 6m)		12.0
Group share of fair value of net assets acquired		
Share capital	8.0	
Pre-acquisition reserves	4.4	
Fair value adjustments		
Tangible fixed assets (16.6 – 16.0)	0.6	
Stocks (4.2 – 4.0)	0.2	
	13.2	
Group share	75%	9.9
Goodwill		2.1

Notes on treatment

(a) It is assumed that the market value (ie fair value) of the loan stock issued to fund the purchase of the shares in Kono plc is equal to the price of £12.0m. FRS 2 requires goodwill to be calculated by comparing the fair value of the consideration given with the fair value of the separable net assets of the acquired business or company.

(b) Share capital and pre-acquisition profits represent the book value of the net assets of Kono plc at the date of acquisition. Adjustments are then required to this book value in order to give the fair value of the net assets at the date of acquisition. For short-term monetary items, fair value is their carrying value on acquisition.

(c) FRS 7 states that the fair value of tangible fixed assets should be determined by market value or, if information on a market price is not available (as is the case here), then by reference to depreciated replacement cost, reflecting normal business practice. The net replacement cost (ie £16.6m) represents the gross replacement cost less depreciation based on that amount, and so further adjustment for extra depreciation is unnecessary.

(d) FRS 7 also states that stocks which cannot be replaced by purchasing in a ready market (eg commodities) should be valued at current cost to the acquired company of reproducing the stocks. In this case that amount is £4.2m.

(e) The fair value of the loan is the present value of the total amount payable, ie on maturity and in interest. If the quoted interest rate was used as a discount factor, this would give the current par value.

(f) The rationalisation costs must be reported in post-acquisition results under FRS 7, so no adjustment is required in the goodwill calculation.

---

2 FRS 6 ACQUISITIONS AND MERGERS

2.1 There are two types of business combination.

- One company takes over the business of another company for its own benefit by buying out the previous shareholders
- Two companies combine their resources for mutual benefit. There is continuity of ownership via a share for share exchange

Acquisition accounting is not appropriate in the second situation.

2.2 You have covered merger accounting in your earlier studies. Below we give a summary.

Knowledge brought forward from earlier studies

FRS 6 Acquisitions and mergers

- *Problems and abuses*
  - Two methods leads to lack of comparability
  - True mergers are difficult to define
  - Acquisition accounting can account for all combinations
  - The merger method is not used much in practice
  - There is little overseas support

FRS 6 was introduced to restrict merger accounting to **genuine mergers**.

- *Definition of a merger*

  A merger is a business combination resulting in:

  - A new reporting entity
  - Shareholders of the entities form a fairly equal partnership
  - Mutual sharing of risks and benefits
  - No dominant party for whatever reason

Knowledge brought forward from earlier studies (cont)

- *Criteria for a merger*

  FRS 6 sets out the following criteria.

  - No party to the combination is portrayed as either acquirer or acquired
  - All parties to the combination participate in establishing the management structure of the combined entity (not necessarily equal management participation)
  - The relative size of the combining entities is not so disparate that one party dominates the combined entity by virtue of its size
  - No more than an immaterial proportion of the FV of consideration received is non-equity consideration
  - No equity shareholders of any of the combining entities retains any material interest in the future performance of only part of the combined entity

- In addition, CA 1985 criteria must be met (referred to in FRS 6).

  - $\geq$ 90% of the NV of the relevant shares in the undertaking acquired must be held by the group
  - Must be achieved as a result of an arrangement providing for the issue of **equity shares** by the parent company
  - The FV of any consideration other than equity shares $\leq$ 10% NV of the equity shares issued

- *Disclosure etc*

  The disclosure requirements under FRS 6 are both comprehensive and detailed - assume everything should be disclosed.

Exam focus point

Merger accounting has now been abolished under International Financial Reporting Standards. Eventually, this will happen in the UK. It is therefore unlikely to form a major part of an exam question.

UITF Abstract 15 *Disclosure of substantial acquisitions*

2.3 In August 1995 the Stock Exchange revised its Listing Rules and they no longer refer to Class 1 transactions.

2.4 The Stock Exchange Listing Rules classify transactions by **assessing their size** relative to that of the company proposing to make the transaction. It does this by ascertaining whether any of a number of ratios (eg the net assets of the target to the net assets of the offeror) exceeds a given percentage. Class 1 transactions used to be those where the percentage exceeded 15%. Super Class 1 are those where the percentage exceeds 25%. FRS 6 uses the 15% criterion for non-listed entities.

2.5 The UITF reached a consensus that, in order to retain the ASB's original intentions for FRS 6, the reference to Class 1 transactions should be interpreted as meaning those transactions in which any of the ratios set out in the London Stock Exchange Listing Rules defining Super Class 1 transactions **exceeds 15%.**

Question: FRS 6 criteria

List the criteria for merger accounting given by FRS 6.

Answer

See KBF box.

Discussion Paper - Business Combinations

2.6 In December 1998, the ASB published a Discussion Paper *Business Combinations*, which reprinted the text of a position paper prepared for the G4+1.

2.7 If the proposals in the paper were to be implemented, all business combinations would be accounted for using acquisition accounting.

2.8 The impetus for banning merger accounting was the diversity of international practice. In the USA, in particular, although merger accounting is applied only where specific conditions are met, in practice the method is often used for large business combinations, many of which would not qualify as mergers under the criteria in FRS 6.

2.9 Generally most people who responded to the Discussion Paper were against banning merger accounting. There was widespread support instead for maintaining the approach of FRS 6, perhaps with some tightening-up of the criteria identifying mergers. The general view was that there are two different kinds of business combination - acquisitions and, more rarely, mergers of equals - and to reflect them fairly, two different methods of accounting are necessary.

2.10 The ASB shares the concerns of the G4+1 about the application of merger accounting in cases where it is not appropriate. In the light of IFRS 3 *Business combinations* it now seems very likely that it will be abolished.

3 FURTHER PRACTICAL ISSUES AND MERGER RELIEF

Merger: NV shares ≠ NV shares acquired

3.1 Where the nominal value of the shares issued is not equal to that of the shares acquired, or where there is additional consideration in some form other than equity shares, the basic method needs some modification.

Question: merger (1)

America plc has decided to combine with Europe plc and has made a successful one for one offer to the ordinary shareholders of Europe plc. Ordinary shares in America plc are quoted on the Stock Exchange at £2.20. The balance sheets of the two companies are set out below.

	America plc	*Europe plc*
	£	£
Fixed assets	2,800	2,400
Net current assets	1,400	800
	4,200	3,200
Ordinary shares of £1 each	3,000	2,000
Reserves (realised)	1,200	1,200
	4,200	3,200

Required

Prepare a consolidated balance sheet on a merger basis for America plc:

(a) Using the information given above

(b) Assuming the offer had been 3 shares in America plc for every 2 shares in Europe plc

(c) Assuming the offer had been 1 share in America plc for every 2 shares in Europe plc

(d) Assuming that America plc had paid 25p per share for Europe plc as well as giving a one for one share exchange

Answer

The investment in Europe plc shown in the accounts of America plc will be as follows.

Under (a)	£2,000
Under (b)	£3,000
Under (c)	£1,000
Under (d) (£2,000 + £500)	£2,500

CONSOLIDATED BALANCE SHEETS

	(a)	*(b)*	*(c)*	*(d)*
	£	£	£	£
Fixed assets	5,200	5,200	5,200	5,200
Net current assets	2,200	2,200	2,200	1,700
	7,400	7,400	7,400	6,900
Ordinary shares of £1 each	5,000	6,000	4,000	5,000
Unrealised reserve	-	-	1,000	-
Realised reserves	2,400	1,400	2,400	1,900
	7,400	7,400	7,400	6,900

The balance sheet in (a) shows no change in the total realised reserves. This is because the nominal value of the shares acquired exactly matches the nominal value of the shares issued.

The balance sheet in (b) reflects the fact that America plc has issued 3,000 shares, whose nominal value is £1,000 more than the nominal value of the shares taken over. The difference is deducted from realised reserves, since the group has no unrealised reserves.

The balance sheet in (c) includes an unrealised reserve, created because the nominal value of the shares issued is £1,000 less than the nominal value of the shares acquired.

The (d) balance sheet shows net current assets reduced by £500, the amount of cash paid. The difference between America's investment in subsidiary (£2,500) and the nominal value of the shares acquired (£2,000) is again deducted from realised reserves on consolidation.

3.2 It should be obvious from the above that the total net assets figure never changes (unless part of the consideration is cash). Under merger accounting consolidated reserves become in effect a **balancing figure**.

Profit and loss account

3.3 Interest in merger accounting generally focuses on the balance sheet. The P&L account aspect is really extremely simple: it involves aggregation of the individual company's figures, with normal consolidation adjustments but no attempt to distinguish between pre- and post-merger profits in the year of merger. All **comparatives are restated** as though the companies had always been merged. Note the effects of FRS 3.

Minority interest

3.4 Any minority interest (which **will never exceed 10%** under CA 1985, and under FRS 6 will be *very* rare) is accounted for in the usual way, namely:

(a) The minority interest in the subsidiary's shareholders' funds is a deferred liability

(b) Their share of any proposed dividend is a current liability

(c) Their share of the subsidiary's profits after tax is deducted in the consolidated P&L account

Merger relief

3.5 Although this section of the text is concerned with group accounts it is worthwhile to consider here the way in which a holding company records a share acquisition in its **own individual accounts**. We are mainly concerned with s 131 CA 1985.

3.6 S 131 CA 1985 provides that **no share premium account** need be created on an issue of shares provided that:

(a) the shares are issued as part of an arrangement to **acquire shares** in another company; and

(b) the investing company, after the issue, has managed to secure **at least 90%** of the equity shares in the other company. Any shares held by the investing company prior to the new issue may be counted towards the 90% but the relief under s 131 will *only* apply to the shares issued as part of the arrangement.

3.7 The exemption granted by s 131 is often referred to as **merger relief**. This has often led to confusion between two quite different things. You should be clear in your mind that the statutory provisions relate to the recording of a share issue in the **individual accounts of an investing company**; whereas merger accounting is concerned only with methods of preparing consolidated accounts.

3.8 A company taking advantage of merger relief has a **choice of accounting methods** when recording the share issue for purposes of its own (not its consolidated) accounts. Assuming an issue of shares with a nominal value of £50,000 and a market value of £220,000, the choices are as follows.

(a)

DEBIT	Investment in subsidiary	£50,000	
CREDIT	Ordinary share capital		£50,000

This method has the disadvantage that it disguises the true value of the investment acquired. The individual balance sheet will be misleading.

(b)

DEBIT	Investment in subsidiary	£220,000	
CREDIT	Ordinary share capital		£50,000
	Share premium account		£170,000

This is a most unlikely option in practice. To show a more realistic balance sheet, the company forgoes the relief available under s 131 and creates an unwelcome share premium account.

(c)

DEBIT	Investment in subsidiary	£220,000	
CREDIT	Ordinary share capital		£50,000
	Merger reserve		£170,000

This is perhaps the most likely choice. To record the investment at its 'true' cost, the company shows the share issue at its market value by setting up a reserve account; but the restrictions attaching to a share premium account are avoided by labelling the reserve a 'merger reserve'.

3.9 The method chosen from these three options will not affect the decision on the **method of consolidation** to be adopted. That decision must be taken in the light of the CA 1985 and FRS 6 criteria.

3.10 EXAMPLE: MERGER RELIEF

Comic plc acquired a 95% holding in Strip plc on 1 January 20X7 for £1,000,000 satisfied through the issue of 400,000 £1 ordinary shares in Comic plc. On 1 January 20X7 the balance sheets of the two companies were as follows (the acquisition has not yet been accounted for).

	Comic plc	*Strip plc*
	£'000	£'000
Net assets	3,000	800
Share capital	2,000	500
Profit and loss account	1,000	300
	3,000	800

Prepare the consolidated balance sheet as at 1 January 20X8 under the acquisition method, assuming merger relief is available. Goodwill is written off to reserves and the carrying value of the net assets of Strip plc approximate to their fair value.

3.11 SOLUTION

CONSOLIDATED BALANCE SHEET
AS AT 1 JANUARY 20X7

	£'000
Net assets	3,800
Share capital (2,000 + 400)	2,400
Merger reserve (1,000 – 400)	600
Profit and loss account (W2)	760
Shareholders' funds	3,760
Minority interest (W3)	40
	3,800

Workings

1 *Goodwill*

	£'000
Fair value of consideration	1,000
Net assets acquired (95% × 800)	760
Goodwill	240

2 *Profit and loss account*

	£'000
Comic plc	1,000
Strip plc: no post-acquisition retained reserves	-
Goodwill written off	(240)
	760

3 *Minority interests*

	£'000
Share of net assets (5% × 800)	40

Question: merger (2)

You are given the following information.

(a) On 30 June 20X7 Stepney plc obtained acceptance by 100% of the ordinary shareholders of Brennan plc of its offer of one new ordinary share in Stepney plc for every one ordinary share in Brennan plc. The offer was also declared unconditional on 30 June 20X7 and arrangements were made for the share exchange to take place within the next few days. On 30 June 20X7 the ordinary shares of Stepney plc had a market value of £8.50 each. The newly-formed group became known as the Stepney Group plc.

(b) It may be assumed that profits before extraordinary items of both companies accrue evenly over the year. The extraordinary charge in the accounts of Stepney plc relates to an event occurring in March 20X7.

(c) Stepney plc uses the average cost method of stock valuation while Brennan plc has used the FIFO method in preparing its 20X7 financial statements. The directors of the new group have agreed to standardise accounting practice by using average cost throughout the group. This change would have affected Brennan plc's stock values as shown below.

Stock values (Brennan plc)	*FIFO basis*	*Average cost basis*
	£'000	£'000
Stock (31 December 20X6)	2,748	2,528
Stock (31 December 20X7)	3,826	3,014

(d) SUMMARISED BALANCE SHEETS AT 31 DECEMBER 20X7

	Stepney plc	*Brennan plc*
	£'000	£'000
Fixed assets	61,376	24,299
Investment in Brennan plc	2,000	-
Current assets	22,685	8,623
	86,061	32,922
Current liabilities	12,472	5,461
Ordinary share capital	15,000 *	1,000 **
Retained profits	58,589	26,461
	86,061	32,922

* called-up share capital in ordinary shares of £1.00 each
** called-up share capital in ordinary shares of £0.50 each.

(e) SUMMARISED PROFIT AND LOSS ACCOUNTS FOR THE YEAR ENDED 31 DECEMBER 20X7

	Stepney plc	*Brennan plc*
	£'000	£'000
Turnover	41,456	15,396
Cost of sales	18,221	5,492
Gross profit	23,235	9,904
Administration expenses	2,694	1,063
Selling and distribution costs	4,143	1,824
Exceptional loss	3,904	-
Profit on ordinary activities before taxation	12,494	7,017
Taxation	3,952	2,076
Profit on ordinary activities after taxation	8,542	4,941
Dividend	2,000	-
Retained profit for year	6,542	4,941
Retained profits at 1 January 20X7	52,047	21,520
Retained profits at 31 December 20X7	58,589	26,461

You are required to prepare, on a merger accounting basis, the consolidated balance sheet at 31 December 20X7 and the consolidated P&L account for the year ended 31 December 20X7 of the Stepney Group plc. Assume that the merger requirements of FRS 6 have been met.

Answer

STEPNEY PLC
CONSOLIDATED BALANCE SHEET AS AT 31 DECEMBER 20X7

	£'000	£'000
Fixed assets		85,675
Current assets (W1)	30,496	
Current liabilities	17,933	
Net current assets		12,563
Total assets less current liabilities		98,238
Capital and reserves		
Share capital		15,000
Profit and loss account		83,238
		98,238

CONSOLIDATED PROFIT AND LOSS ACCOUNT
FOR THE YEAR ENDED 31 DECEMBER 20X7

	£'000	£'000
Turnover		56,852
Cost of sales (W3)		24,305
Gross profit		32,547
Distribution costs		5,967
Administrative expenses		3,757
Exceptional loss		3,904
Profit on ordinary activities before taxation		18,919
Tax on profit on ordinary activities		6,028
Profit on ordinary activities after taxation		12,891
Dividend		2,000
		10,891
Merger adjustment (W2)		(1,000)
Retained profit for the financial year		9,891
Retained profits brought forward		
As previously reported (52,047 + 21,520)	73,567	
Prior year adjustment (2,748 – 2,528)	(220)	
As restated		73,347
Retained profits carried forward		83,238

Workings

1 *Current assets*

	£'000	£'000
Stepney		22,685
Brennan		8,623
		31,308
Adjustment in respect of Brennan's closing stock		
FIFO cost	3,826	
Average cost	3,014	
		(812)
		30,496

2 *Merger adjustment*

	£'000
Nominal value of shares issued by Stepney	2,000
Nominal value of shares acquired by Stepney	1,000
Difference to be deducted from group reserves	1,000

3 *Cost of sales*

	£'000	£'000
Stepney		18,221
Brennan		
Unadjusted	5,492	
Adjustment in respect of stock valuation		
(3,826 – 3,014) – (2,748 – 2,528)	592	
		6,084
		24,305

Chapter roundup

- The accounting requirements and disclosures of the fair value exercise are covered by **FRS 7,** which outlaws the use of provisions for future losses and for reorganisation costs on acquisition of a subsidiary.
- **Merger accounting** is a topical issue. Make sure you know the **criteria** for merger accounting under FRS 6 and CA 1985. You should be able to discuss the **criticisms** of merger accounting. Make sure also that you can clearly differentiate acquisitions from mergers and that you can prepare accounts using both acquisition and merger accounting.
- You should also be able to explain s 131 CA 1985 **merger relief** and distinguish it clearly from merger accounting.
- **FRS 6** represents a major step in restricting the practice of businesses who use merger accounting in non-merger situations and therefore distort the true picture of their affairs.

Quick quiz

1 How is 'fair value' defined by FRS 7?

2 Which items does FRS 7 state *must* be treated as post-acquisition?

3 How is the cost of an acquisition made up?

4 On 31 March, Vellow Ltd purchased 1,800,000 of the 2,000,000 ordinary shares of £1 each in Yapton Ltd paying £1.20 per share.

At that date the values of the separable net assets of Yapton Ltd were:

Aggregate book value	£1,800,000
Aggregate fair value	£1,700,000

What is the values of the goodwill on consolidation as at 31 March?

5 On 31 March, Vellow Ltd purchased 1,800,000 of the 2,000,000 ordinary shares of £1 each in Yapton Ltd paying £1.20 per share.

At that date the value of the separable net assets of Yapton Ltd were:

Aggregate book value	£1,800,000
Aggregate fair value	£1,700,000

What is the value of the minority interest as at 31 March?

6 Fill in the blank: In merger accounting the investment in the subsidiaries is recorded as the ....

7 Goodwill never arises with merger accounting. True or false?

8 List the five FRS 6 criteria for mergers.

9 Distinguish merger accounting and merger relief.

Answers to quick quiz

1 The amount at which an asset or liability could be exchanged in an arm's length transaction between informed and willing parties other than in forced liquidation sale.

2 See Para 1.16

3 The amount of cash paid
The fair value of other purchase consideration given by the acquirer
The expenses of the acquisition

4

	£'000
Cost	2,160
Fair value of separable net assets acquired	
90% × 1,700,000	1,530
	630

5 10% × £1,700,000 = £170,000.

6 The nominal value of the consideration given

7 True

8 See Knowledge Brought Forward box

9 Merger accounting is concerned only with methods of preparing consolidated accounts. Merger relief relates to the recording of a share issue in the individual accounts of an investing company.

Now try the questions below from the Exam Question Bank

Number	Level	Marks	Time
Q9	Introductory	n/a	n/a
Q16	Introductory	n/a	n/a

Chapter 7

FOREIGN CURRENCY TRANSLATION

Introduction

Many of the largest companies in the UK, while based here, have subsidiaries and other interests all over the world: they are truly **global companies** and so foreign currency consolidations take place frequently in practice.

Study guide

Section 8 – Foreign currency 1

- Discussion of the recording of transactions and retranslation of monetary/non-monetary items at the balance sheet date for individual entities.
- Accounting for the treatment of exchange differences re the above
- Discussion of the nature of the closing rate/net investment method and the temporal method
- Accounting for foreign equity investments financed by borrowings

Section 9 – Foreign currency 2

- Preparation of group financial statements incorporating a foreign subsidiary/associate
- Discussion of problem areas in foreign currency translations for individual and group companies

Exam guide

Foreign currency consolidation questions are likely to appear frequently in Paper 3.6. Students have always found such questions difficult but, as with most financial accounting topics, you only need to adopt a **logical approach** and to **practise plenty of questions**.

1 FOREIGN CURRENCY TRANSLATION

1.1 SSAP 20 *Foreign currency translation* standardises the accounting treatment of foreign currency transactions. It explains the background and the objectives of translation.

(a) Translation should produce results which are **compatible with** the **effect of rate changes** on a company's **cash flow** and its **equity**.

(b) It should ensure that the financial statements produce a **true and fair view** of the results of management actions.

(c) **Consolidated statements** should **reflect** the financial **results** and relationships as measured in the foreign currency financial statements **before translation**.

1.2 We can distinguish between two terms here to avoid confusion.

- **Conversion** is the physical exchange of currencies.
- **Translation** is the expression of one currency in the value of another.

1.3 SSAP 20 considers the procedures which should be adopted when accounting for foreign operations in **two stages**, namely:

Stage 1. The preparation of the financial statements of an individual company; and
Stage 2. The preparation of consolidated financial statements.

2 THE INDIVIDUAL COMPANY STAGE

Monetary and non-monetary items

2.1 First of all, it is worth highlighting the difference between **monetary** and **non-monetary items** as defined by SSAP 20. This is necessary because the accounting treatments for each is different.

KEY TERMS

- **Monetary items**: are money held and amounts to be received or paid in money and should be categorised as either short-term or long-term. Short-term monetary items are those which fall due within one year of the balance sheet date. Examples include debtors, creditors, loans and bank balances.
- **Non-monetary items:** are the reverse: items which are *not* money held or amounts to be received or paid in money, eg fixed assets, investments and stock. *(SSAP 20)*

2.2 **During the period**

Step 1. Translate each transaction at the exchange rate ruling on the date the transaction occurred, ie at the **historical rate**.

Step 2. Where exchange rates do not fluctuate significantly, the **average rate** for the period may be used as an approximation.

Step 3. Where the transaction is to be settled at a **contracted rate**, that rate should be used.

Step 4. Where a trading transaction is covered by a related or matching **forward contract** the forward rate *may* by used.

Step 5. Where the transaction is settled during the period, the exchange difference is a **realised gain or loss** and is reported in the P&L account for the year.

KEY TERM

- A **forward contract** is an agreement to exchange different currencies at a specified future date and at a specified rate. The difference between the specified rate and the spot rate ruling on the date the contract was entered into is the discount or premium on the forward contract. *(SSAP 20)*

2.3 **At the balance sheet date**

Step 1. **Non-monetary assets** should not be restated, but should remain at historical rate.

Step 2. **Monetary assets and liabilities** (including long-term items) should be restated at the closing rate (or contract/forward rate as above).

Treatment of exchange differences

2.4 Exchange differences are part of the profit or loss on ordinary activities for the year. Include exchange gains or losses in one of two places.

(a) Under 'other operating income or charges' for **trading transactions**

(b) Under 'other interest receivable/payable and similar income/charges' for **financing transactions**

POINTS TO NOTE

(a) Exchange differences are **recorded separately** rather than being used to adjust the purchases figure because they result from an event (a rate change) that is separate from the original purchase or sale transaction.

(b) The exchange difference can be attributed to the delay in payment and **could have been minimised or avoided,** for example by denominating the purchase in sterling or by negotiating a forward exchange contract.

(c) The treatment of exchange differences under SSAP 20 is **comparable** to the universal treatment of **bad debts or settlement discounts,** in that they are dealt with separately rather than netted against sales or purchases.

Treatment of short-term monetary items

2.5 Exchange profits on unsettled short-term monetary items should be **included in profit,** although not realised in cash form. The justification for including such 'unrealised' gains in profit is twofold.

(a) The items involved are **short term and will be realised soon** after the year end.
(b) It provides **symmetry of treatment** with unrealised short-term losses.

Treatment of long-term monetary items

2.6 SSAP 20 takes the view that exchange gains and losses on long-term monetary items should also be **recognised in the P&L account** for the sake of symmetry. This is despite the prudence difficulties of recognising unrealised gains. The convertibility and marketability of the currency should be taken into account.

2.7 Where **unrealised gains on unsettled long-term monetary items** are taken to the P&L account this may constitute a **departure from the CA 1985** requirement that only **realised profits** should be included in the P&L account. SSAP 20 makes it clear that such a departure would be **justified by the need to give a true and fair view**. This being the case, particulars of the departure, the reasons for it and its effect should be given in a note.

Question: individual company stage

White Cliffs Ltd, whose year end is 31 December, buys some goods from Mid West Inc of the USA on 30 September. The invoice value is $40,000 and is due for settlement in equal instalments on 30 November and 31 January. The exchange rate moved as follows.

	$ = £1
30 September	1.60
30 November	1.80
31 December	1.90
31 January	1.85

Required

State the accounting entries in the books of White Cliffs Ltd.

Answer

The purchase will be recorded in the books of White Cliffs Ltd using the rate of exchange ruling on 30 September.

		£	£
DEBIT	Purchases	25,000	
CREDIT	Trade creditors		25,000

Being the sterling cost of goods purchased for $40,000 ($40,000 ÷ $1.60/£1)

On 30 November, White Cliffs must pay $20,000. This will cost $20,000 ÷ $1.80/£1 = £11,111 and the company has therefore made an exchange gain of £12,500 - £11,111 = £1,389.

		£	£
DEBIT	Trade creditors	12,500	
CREDIT	Exchange gains: P & L account		1,389
	Cash		11,111

On 31 December, the balance sheet date, the outstanding liability will be recalculated using the rate applicable to that date: $20,000 ÷ $1.90/£1 = £10,526. A further exchange gain of £1,974 has been made and will be recorded as follows.

		£	£
DEBIT	Trade creditors	1,974	
CREDIT	Exchange gains: P & L account		1,974

The total exchange gain of £3,363 will be included in the operating profit for the year ending 31 December.

On 31 January, White Cliffs must pay the second instalment of $20,000. This will cost them £10,811 ($20,000 ÷ $1.85/£1).

		£	£
DEBIT	Trade creditors	10,526	
	Exchange losses: P & L account	285	
CREDIT	Cash		10,811

3 THE CONSOLIDATED FINANCIAL STATEMENTS STAGE 12/01, 12/03, 6/04

3.1 Consider two important SSAP 20 definitions.

KEY TERMS

- A **foreign enterprise** is a subsidiary, associated company or branch whose operations are based in a country other than that of the investing company or whose assets and liabilities are denominated mainly in a foreign currency.
- A **foreign branch** is either a legally constituted enterprise located overseas or a group of assets and liabilities which are accounted for in foreign currencies. *(SSAP 20)*

3.2 In order for a UK holding company or company with a foreign branch to prepare its group accounts or final accounts for the year, the financial statements of its foreign enterprises must first be **translated into sterling**. Two main methods have been evolved, all of them involving one or both of the following types of exchange rate:

KEY TERMS

- The **closing rate** is the rate for spot transactions ruling at the balance sheet date and is the mean of the buying and selling rates at the close of business on the day for which the rate is to be ascertained.
- An **historical rate** is the rate of exchange ruling at the time a relevant transaction (or possibly revaluation) was effected. *(SSAP 20)*

3.3 The two different methods are the temporal method and the closing rate method.

Temporal method	Closing rate method
Non-monetary items that are recorded in the foreign currency financial statements on a historical cost basis are translated at the historical rates ruling when the relevant transactions occurred.	All assets and liabilities are translated at the closing rate.
Non-monetary items that have been revalued in the foreign currency financial statements are translated at the rates that existed on the dates of their revaluations.	
Monetary items are translated at the closing rate.	
Reserves is calculated as a balancing figure.	

3.4 The **temporal** and the **closing rate methods** have been the most widely used in the UK and the US and feature in SSAP 20. A brief illustration may be helpful at this stage.

3.5 EXAMPLE: TEMPORAL METHOD AND CLOSING RATE METHOD

A UK company, Stone Ltd, set up a US subsidiary on 30 June 20X1. Stone subscribed $24,000 for share capital when the exchange rate was $2 = £1. The subsidiary, Brick Inc, borrowed $72,000 in the US and bought a non-monetary asset for $96,000. Stone Ltd prepared its accounts on 31 December 20X1 and by that time the exchange rate had moved to $3 = £1. As a result of highly unusual circumstances, Brick Inc sold its asset early in

20X2 for $96,000. It repaid its loan and was liquidated. Stone's capital of $24,000 was repaid in February 20X2 when the exchange rate was $3 = £1.

Required

Account for the above transactions using both the closing rate and temporal methods.

3.6 SOLUTION

From the above it can be seen that Stone Ltd will record its initial investment at £12,000 which is the starting cost of its shares. The balance sheet of Brick Inc at 31 December 20X1 is summarised below.

	$'000
Non-monetary asset	96
Share capital	24
Loan	72
	96

This may be translated using the temporal and closing rate methods as follows.

	Temporal method	*Closing rate method*
	£'000	£'000
Non-monetary asset		
($2 = £1)	48	
($3 = £1)		32
Share capital and reserves (balancing figure)	24	8
Loan ($3 = £1)	24	24
	48	32
Exchange gain/(loss) for 20X1	12	(4)

The exchange gain and loss are the differences between the value of the original investment (£12,000) and the total of share capital and reserves as disclosed by the above balance sheets.

On liquidation, Stone Ltd will receive £8,000 ($24,000 converted at $3 = £1). The accounts of Stone Ltd will therefore need to show a loss of £16,000 (£24,000 – £8,000) in 20X2 if the temporal method is being used. No gain or loss will arise in 20X2 if the closing rate method is being used.

3.7 **What is revealed by the figures in the above example?**

(a) The exchange rate movement was such as to cause a loss to a UK company investing in the US. (If Stone Ltd had held $24,000 in cash throughout the period it would have lost £4,000.) The temporal method, however, shows an exchange gain in the accounts to 31 December 20X1. This gain is solely attributable to the loan.

	£'000
Loan translated at $2 = £1	36
Loan translated at $3 = £1	24
Exchange gain (reduction in liability)	12

The closing rate method also recognises a loss on holding the non-monetary asset.

	£'000
Asset translated at $2 = £1	48
Asset translated at $3 = £1	32
Exchange loss (fall in value of asset)	(16)
Exchange gain on loan as before	12
Net exchange loss	(4)

After taking into account the loss of £16,000 arising in 20X2 under the temporal method, the net position under the two methods will be the same. It may be argued that the closing rate method is more in line with the economic reality as it recognises the loss of £4,000 in 20X1 which is the year in which the rate change occurred. It can be seen that the closing rate method, in effect, accrues the loss caused by the exchange rate change. Whilst this may be considered acceptable and even desirable on the basis of prudence, a strict application of historical cost accounting would not allow the accrual of the unrealised gain that would have resulted had the exchange rate movement been in the opposite direction.

(b) Despite the comments made in (a) above, it is worth pointing out that the temporal method achieves its aim of representing the transactions as if they had been undertaken by the parent. The position would then have been:

	£'000
20X1 Exchange gain on loan	12
20X2 Loss on sale of asset	(16)
Net loss	(4)

(c) Under the closing rate method, the gearing ratio in the sterling accounts at 31 December 20X1 will be the same as that in the dollar accounts. This is not true for the accounts prepared under the temporal method.

The SSAP 20 approach: net investment (closing rate) vs temporal

3.8 Except in certain specified circumstances, SSAP 20 requires that the **closing rate method** of translation should be used.

(a) Exchange differences arising from the retranslation of the opening net investment in a foreign enterprise at the closing rate should be recorded as a **movement on reserves**.

(b) The P&L account of a foreign enterprise accounted for under the closing rate/net investment method should be translated at the **closing rate** *or* at an **average rate** for the period.

3.9 SSAP 20 takes the view that in most circumstances the foreign enterprise should be seen as a **single** entity operating semi-independently and as a **single business unit**. The interest of the UK company should be regarded as a '**net investment**' rather than as an investment in its many separate individual assets, liabilities and transactions. In other words, since the **foreign enterprise is a single unit**, its P&L account and balance sheet should each be translated at a **single rate**. This support for the net investment concept explains the preference given to the **closing rate method** over the temporal method by SSAP 20.

KEY TERM

The **net investment** which a company has in a foreign enterprise is its effective equity stake and comprises its proportion of such foreign enterprise's net assets; in appropriate circumstances, intra-group loans and other deferred balances may be regarded as part of the effective equity stake. *(SSAP 20)*

3.10 The vast majority of foreign enterprises are thought to fall into the category of 'net investments' and thus to necessitate use of the closing rate method. The temporal method may only be used where the enterprise trades as a **direct extension** of the investing company, rather than as a separate entity. Amongst the factors to be taken into account will be:

(a) The extent to which the **cash flows** of the enterprise have a direct impact upon those of the investing company

(b) The extent to which the **functioning** of the enterprise is dependent directly upon the investing company

(c) The **currency** in which the majority of the trading transactions are denominated

(d) The **major currency** to which the operation is exposed in its financing structure

3.11 Examples of situations where the **temporal method** may be appropriate are where the foreign enterprise:

(a) Acts as a **selling agency** receiving stocks of goods from the investing company and remitting the proceeds back to the company

(b) Produces a raw material or manufactures parts or sub-assemblies which are then shipped to the investing company for **inclusion in its own products**

(c) Is located overseas for tax, exchange control or similar reasons to act as a **means of raising finance** for other companies in the group

In other words, use the temporal method in those circumstances where the trade of the foreign enterprise is more dependent on the economic environment of the investing company's currency than that of its own reporting currency.

The closing rate method in more detail

3.12 Under the closing rate method the following treatments are used.

(a) The **assets and liabilities** shown in the foreign enterprise's balance sheet are translated at the rate of exchange ruling at the (closing) balance sheet date, regardless of the date on which those items originated. The balancing figure on the translated balance sheet represents the head office net investment in the enterprise.

(b) Amounts in the **P&L account** should be translated at either:

(i) The closing rate; OR
(ii) An average rate for the accounting period (calculated in an appropriate manner).

The method chosen should be applied **consistently** from one year to the next. Where the average rate is used and this differs from the closing rate, there will be an exchange difference (gain or loss) which should be dealt with in **reserves** and not in the P&L account for the year.

(c) Exchange differences arising from the re-translation at the end of each year of the holding company's net investment should be reported through **reserves**, not through the P&L account for the year.

The temporal method in more detail

3.13 The mechanics of this method are identical with those used in preparing the accounts of an individual company.

(a) The **P&L account** is translated using actual rates where known (an average for the period tends to be used in practice) and historical rates for non-monetary items such as opening and closing stock and depreciation.

(b) Any exchange differences are reported as **part of profit** for the year.

3.14 **Practical points for both methods**

(a) For consolidation purposes calculations are simpler if a subsidiary's share capital is translated at the **historical rate** (the rate when the investing company acquired its interest) and reserves are found as a balancing figure.

(b) **Dividends proposed** by a subsidiary should always be translated at the **closing rate** in the P&L account and at the actual rate on the date of payment. This is because the investing company will record the items at these rates in its own books.

These are both points of detail, not mentioned in SSAP 20.

Methods compared

3.15 A summary of the translation methods is given below, which shows the main steps to follow in the consolidation process.

	Closing rate method	Temporal method
Step 1. Translate the **closing balance sheet** (net assets/shareholders' funds) and use this for preparing the consolidated balance sheet in the normal way.	Under **closing rate** at the year end for all items (see note).	Use the **closing rate** at the year end for monetary items and the appropriate **historical rates** for non-monetary items. Shareholders' funds should be treated as the balancing figure (see note).
Step 2. Translate the **P&L account.** (In all cases, dividends should be translated at the rate ruling when the dividend was paid or, in the case of proposed dividends, the closing rate at the year end.)	Use the **average rate** or the **closing rate** for the year for all items (but see comment on dividends). The figures obtained can then be used in preparing the consolidated P&L a/c.	In most examination questions, translate all items apart from depreciation at the **average rate** for the year and translate depreciation at the rates ruling when the relevant fixed assets were **acquired** (or **revalued**). If however, the information is available, use the temporal rates specific to opening and closing stocks. At this stage it is not possible to prepare the consolidated P&L a/c. It may be necessary to break down costs of sales to get the translation of opening/closing sales.

	Closing rate method	**Temporal method**
Step 3. Translate the **shareholders' funds** (net assets) at the beginning of the year.	Use the **closing rate** at the beginning of the year (the opening rate for the current year).	Use the **closing rate** at the beginning of the year for monetary items and the appropriate **historical rates** for non-monetary items. In many questions it is necessary to reconstruct the **opening balance sheet.**
Step 4. Calculate the **total exchange difference** for the year as follows. £ Closing net assets at closing rate (Step 1) X Less opening net assets at opening rate (Step 3) X X Less retained profit per translated P&L a/c (Step 2) X Exchange differences X Group share (%) X It may be necessary to adjust for any profits or losses taken direct to reserves during the year.	This stage will be **unnecessary** unless you are asked to state the total exchange differences or are asked to prepare a statement of the movement on reserves, where the exchange difference will be shown. For **exam purposes** you can translate the closing shareholders' funds as follows. (a) Share capital + pre-acquisition reserves at historical rate. (b) Post-acquisition reserves as a balancing figure.	After finding the exchange differences it will be possible to prepare the **consolidated P&L a/c**. The exchange differences should be included before tax.

As mentioned above, the share capital may be translated at the historical rate (under both methods). The reserves will then be the balancing figure. The advantage of this method is that it simplifies the 'cancellation' of the share capital on consolidation.

Question: consolidated financial statements and foreign currency

The abridged balance sheets and P&L account of Darius Ltd and its foreign subsidiary, Xerxes Inc, appear below.

DRAFT BALANCE SHEET AS AT 31 DECEMBER 20X1

	Darius Ltd		Xerxes Inc	
Fixed assets	£	£	$	$
Plant at cost	600		500	
Less depreciation	(250)		(200)	
		350		300
100 $1 shares in Xerxes		25		-
		375		300
Current assets				
Stocks	225		200	
Debtors	150		100	
	375		300	
Current liabilities	100		110	
Net current assets		275		190
		650		490
Loans		50		110
		600		380
Capital and reserves				
Ordinary capital £1/$1 shares		300		100
Retained profit		300		280
		600		380

PROFIT AND LOSS ACCOUNTS
FOR THE YEAR ENDED 31 DECEMBER 20X1

	Darius Ltd	Xerxes Inc
	£	$
Profit before tax	200	160
Tax	100	80
Profit after tax, retained	100	80

The following further information is given.

(a) Darius Ltd has had its interest in Xerxes Inc since the incorporation of the company.

(b) Depreciation is 8% per annum on cost.

(c) There have been no loan repayments or movements in fixed assets during the year. The opening stock of Xerxes Inc was $120. Assume that stock turnover times are very short.

(d) Exchange rates: $4 to £1 when Xerxes Inc was incorporated
$2.5 to £1 when Xerxes Inc acquired its fixed assets
$2 to £1 on 31 December 20X0
$1.6 to £1 average rate of exchange year ending 31 December 20X1
$1 to £1 on 31 December 20X1.

Required

Prepare the summarised consolidated financial statements of Darius Ltd using:

(a) The closing rate/net investment method
(b) The temporal method

Answer: closing rate/net investment method

Step 1. The balance sheet of Xerxes Inc at 31 December 20X1 should be translated at $1 = £1.

SUMMARISED BALANCE SHEET AT 31 DECEMBER 20X1

	£	£
Fixed assets (net book value)		300
Current assets		
Stock	200	
Debtors	100	
	300	
Current liabilities	110	
Net current assets		190
		490
Loan		110
Net assets (= shareholders' funds)		380

Since Darius Ltd acquired the whole of the issued share capital on incorporation, the post-acquisition reserves including exchange differences will be the value of shareholders' funds arrived at above, less the original cost to Darius Ltd of £25. Post-acquisition reserves = £380 – £25 = £355.

SUMMARISED CONSOLIDATED BALANCE SHEET AS AT 31 DECEMBER 20X1

		£	£
Fixed assets (net book value)	£(350 + 300)		650
Current assets			
Stock	£(225 + 200)	425	
Debtors	£(150 + 100)	250	
		675	
Current liabilities	£(100 + 110)	210	
Net current assets			465
			1,115
Loans	£(50 + 110)		160
			955
Capital and reserves			
Ordinary £1 shares (Darius Ltd only)			300
Reserves	£(300 + 355)		655
			955

Note. It is quite unnecessary to know the amount of the exchange differences when preparing the consolidated balance sheet.

Step 2. The P&L account should be translated at average rate ($1.6 = £1).

SUMMARISED PROFIT AND LOSS ACCOUNT
FOR THE YEAR ENDED 31 DECEMBER 20X1

	£
Profit before tax	100
Tax	50
Profit after tax, retained	50

SUMMARISED CONSOLIDATED PROFIT AND LOSS ACCOUNT
FOR THE YEAR ENDED 31 DECEMBER 20X1

		£
Profit before tax	£(200 + 100)	300
Tax	£(100 + 50)	150
Profit after tax, retained	£(100 + 50)	150

Step 3. The equity interest at the beginning of the year can be found as follows.

	$
Equity value at 31 December 20X1	380
Retained profit for year	80
Equity value at 31 December 20X0	300
Translated at $2 = £1, this gives	£150

Step 4. The exchange difference can now be calculated.

	£
Equity interest at 31 December 20X1 (step 1)	380
Equity interest at 1 January 20X1 (step 3)	150
	230
Less retained profit (step 2)	50
Exchange gain	180

CONSOLIDATED STATEMENT OF MOVEMENTS ON RESERVES
FOR THE YEAR ENDED 31 DECEMBER 20X1

	£
Consolidated reserves at 31 December 20X0	325
Exchange gains arising on consolidation	180
Retained profit for the year	150
Consolidated reserves at 31 December 20X1	655

(*Note*. The post-acquisition reserves of Xerxes Inc at the beginning of the year must have been £150 – £25 = £125 and the reserves of Darius Ltd must have been £300 – £100 = £200. The consolidated reserves must therefore have been £325.)

Answer: temporal method

Step 1.

SUMMARISED BALANCE SHEET AS AT 31 DECEMBER 20X1

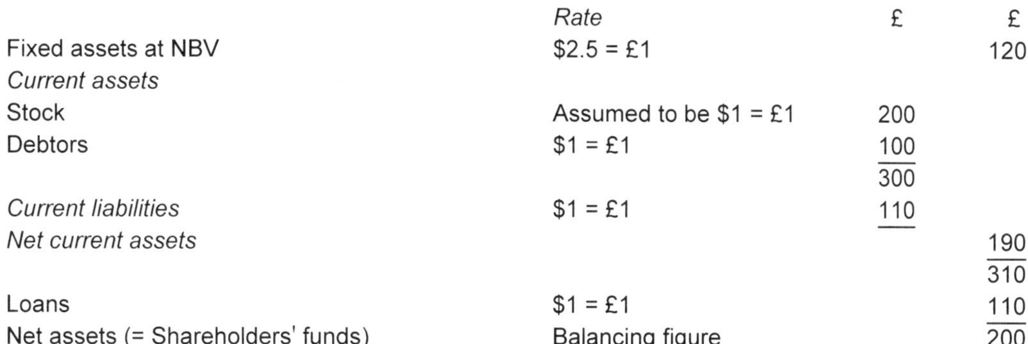

	Rate	£	£
Fixed assets at NBV	$2.5 = £1		120
Current assets			
Stock	Assumed to be $1 = £1	200	
Debtors	$1 = £1	100	
		300	
Current liabilities	$1 = £1	110	
Net current assets			190
			310
Loans	$1 = £1		110
Net assets (= Shareholders' funds)	Balancing figure		200

In arriving at the consolidated balance sheet the same comments apply as in stage 1 for the closing rate method. The post-acquisition reserves of Xerxes Inc will be £200 – £25 = £175.

SUMMARISED CONSOLIDATED BALANCE SHEET AS AT 31 DECEMBER 20X1

		£	£
Fixed assets at NBV	£(350 + 120)		470
Current assets			
Stocks	£(225 + 200)	425	
Debtors	£(150 + 100)	250	
		675	
Current liabilities	£(100 + 110)	210	
			465
			935
Loans	£(50 + 110)		160
			775
Capital and reserves			
Ordinary £1 shares			300
Reserves	£(300 + 175)		475
			775

Note. As with the closing rate method, it has been quite unnecessary to know the amount of the exchange differences when preparing the consolidated balance sheet.

Step 2. The following rates should be used for the P&L account.

	Rate
Depreciation	$2.5 = £1
Opening stock	$2.0 = £1
Closing stock	$1.0 = £1
All other items	$1.6 = £1

SUMMARISED PROFIT AND LOSS ACCOUNT FOR THE YEAR ENDED 31 DECEMBER 20X1

	$	$	*Rate*	£	£
Profit before tax, depreciation and increase in stock value		120	$1.6 = £1		75
Opening stock	120		$2.0 = £1	60	
Closing stock	200		$1.0 = £1	200	
Increase in stock value		80			140
		200			215
Depreciation (8% × $500)		40	$2.5 = £1		16
Profit before tax		160			199
Tax		80	$1.6 = £1		50
Profit after tax, retained		80			149

Step 3.

Since there were no movements in fixed assets or loan repayments, the opening balance sheet in dollars can be summarised as shown below. This has been translated at $2.5 = £1 for fixed assets and at $2.0 = £1 for monetary items and stocks.

SUMMARISED BALANCE SHEET AS AT 31 DECEMBER 20X0

	$	*Rate*	£
Fixed assets NBV $(300 + 40)	340	$2.5 = £1	136
Stocks	120	$2.0 = £1	60
Net current monetary liabilities (balancing figure)	50	$2.0 = £1	25
	410		171
Loans	110	$2.0 = £1	55
	300		116
Shareholders' funds $(380 – 80)	300	Balancing figure	116

Step 4. The exchange difference can be calculated.

	£
Shareholders' funds at 31 December 20X1	200
Less shareholders' funds at 31 December 20X0	116
	84
Less retained profit before exchange differences	149
Exchange loss	(65)

SUMMARISED CONSOLIDATED PROFIT AND LOSS ACCOUNT
FOR THE YEAR ENDED 31 DECEMBER 20X1

	£
Profit before tax £(200 + 199 – 65)	334
Tax £(100 + 50)	150
Profit after tax, retained	184
Shareholders' funds at 31 December 20X0	116
Less cost of shares	25
Post-acquisition reserves in Xerxes Inc at 31 December 20X0	91
Reserves of Darius Ltd at 31 December 20X0	200
Consolidated reserves at 31 December 20X0	291

CONSOLIDATED STATEMENT OF MOVEMENTS ON RESERVES
FOR THE YEAR ENDED 31 DECEMBER 20X1

	£
Consolidated reserves at 31 December 20X0	291
Retained profit for the year	184
Consolidated reserves at 31 December 20X1	475

Exam focus point

You could get either method in the exam, possibly with an explanation of when you would use which method.

Analysis of exchange differences

3.16 Under both the closing rate and the temporal methods, the exchange differences in the above exercise could be reconciled by splitting them into their component parts. (Such a split is not required by SSAP 20, nor is it required in your exam, but it may help your understanding of the subject.

(a) **Closing rate method**

Using the opening balance sheet reconstructed for the temporal method and translating at \$2 = £1 and \$1 = £1 gives the following.

	\$2 = £1	*\$1 = £1*	*Difference*
	£	£	£
Fixed assets at NBV	170	340	170
Stocks	60	120	60
Net current monetary liabilities	(25)	(50)	(25)
	205	410	205
Shareholders' funds	150	300	150
Loans	55	110	55
	205	410	205

Translating the P&L account arrived at for the temporal method using \$1.60 = £1 and \$1 = £1 gives the following results.

	\$1.60 = £1	*\$1 = £1*	*Difference*
	£	£	£
Profit before tax, depreciation and increase in stock values	75	120	45
Increase in stock values	50	80	30
	125	200	75
Depreciation	(25)	(40)	(15)
	100	160	60
Tax	(50)	(80)	(30)
Profit after tax, retained	50	80	30

The overall position is then:

	£	£
Gain on fixed assets (£170 – £15)		155
Loss on loan		(55)
Gain on stocks (£60 + £30)	90	
Loss on net monetary current assets/ liabilities (all other differences) (£45 – £30 – £25)	(10)	
		80
Net exchange gain: as above		180

(b) **Temporal method**

Under the temporal method there will be no gains on fixed assets or stocks so the overall position will be:

	£
Loss on net current monetary items	10
Loss on loan	55
Net exchange loss (as above)	65

3.17 Problems involving minority interests

(a) The figure for **minority interests in the balance sheet** will be the appropriate proportion of the translated share capital and reserves of the subsidiary. In addition, it may be necessary to show the proposed dividend payable to the minorities as a liability. The proposed dividend should be translated at the closing rate for this purpose.

(b) The **minority interest in the P&L account** will be the appropriate proportion of sterling profits available for distribution. In the case of the temporal method, this profit will be arrived at *after* charging or crediting the exchange differences.

3.18 EXAMPLE: MINORITY INTERESTS

The summarised accounts of Camrumite Inc are shown below.

BALANCE SHEET AS AT 31 DECEMBER 20X3

	Fr
Fixed assets	10,000
Net monetary assets	5,000
	15,000
Ordinary share capital and reserves	15,000

PROFIT AND LOSS ACCOUNT FOR THE YEAR ENDED 31 DECEMBER 20X3

	Fr
Profit after tax	3,080
Proposed final dividend	1,680
Retained profit	1,400

60% of the issued capital of Camrumite Inc is owned by Bates Ltd, a UK company.

There have been no movements in fixed assets during the year. The depreciation charge for the year was 560 Fr.

The exchange rate has moved as follows.

Date on which fixed assets were acquired	8 Fr = £1
1 January 20X3	5 Fr = £1
Average for the year ended 31.12.X3	7 Fr = £1
31 December 20X3	8 Fr = £1

You are required to calculate the figures for minority interests to be included in the consolidated accounts of Bates Ltd using:

(a) The closing rate/net investment method
(b) The temporal method

Show the movements on the minority interest accounts during the year.

3.19 SOLUTION: CLOSING RATE METHOD

Translating the shareholders' funds using the closing rate as at 31 December 20X3 gives 15,000 Fr ÷ 8 = £1,875. The minority interest in the balance sheet will be 40% × £1,875 = £750.

The proposed dividend translated at the closing rate is 1,680 Fr ÷ 8 = £210. The amount payable to the minority shareholders is 40% × £210 = £84.

The profit after tax translated at the average rate is 3,080 Fr ÷ 7 = £440. The minority interest in the P&L account is therefore 40% × £440 = £176.

At the beginning of the year the share capital and reserves must have been 15,000 Fr – 1,400 Fr = 13,600 Fr. Translating this at the rate ruling on 1 January 20X3 gives 13,600 Fr ÷ 5 = £2,720. The minority interest at 1 January 20X3 was 40% × £2,720 = £1,088.

	£	£
Shareholders' funds as at 1 January 20X3		2,720
Add: profit for year	440	
less dividends	210	
		230
		2,950
Less shareholders' funds at 31 December 20X3		1,875
Exchange loss		1,075
Minority interest therein £1,075 × 40%		430

The minority interest can be summarised as follows.

	£
Balance at 1 January 20X3	1,088
Minority interest in profit for the year	176
Minority interest in exchange losses	(430)
	834
Balance at 31 December 20X3	750
Dividend payable to minority	84
	834

3.20 SOLUTION: TEMPORAL METHOD

Shareholders' funds at 31 December 20X3

		£
Fixed assets	10,000 Fr ÷ 8	1,250
Net monetary assets	5,000 Fr ÷ 8	625
		1,875
Minority interest therein £1,875 × 40%		750

The profit after tax but before depreciation and exchange differences is 3,640 Fr. The translated P&L account before dividends will be as follows.

		£
Profit after tax but before depreciation	3,640 Fr ÷ 7	520
Depreciation	560 Fr ÷ 8	70
		450
Minority interest therein £450 × 40%		180

Shareholders' funds at 1 January 20X3

		£
Fixed assets	10,560 Fr ÷ 8	1,320
Net monetary assets (balancing figure)	3,040 Fr ÷ 5	608
Shareholders' funds	13,600 Fr	1,928
Minority interest therein £1,928 × 40%		771

	£	£
Shareholders' funds at 1 January 20X3		1,928
Add: profit for year before exchange differences	450	
less dividend	210	
		240
		2,168
Less shareholders' funds at 31 December 20X3		1,875
Exchange loss		293
Minority interest therein £293 × 40%		117

The minority interest account can be summarised as follows.

	£
Balance at 1 January 20X3	771
Minority interest in profit for the year £(180 – 117)	63
	834
Balance at 31 December 20X3	750
Dividend payable to minority	84
	834

Goodwill arising on consolidation

3.21 The calculation of goodwill should be based on the exchange rates ruling at the **date of acquisition**. It will not be altered by subsequent exchange rate changes. In other words, exchange rate differences occurring after acquisition are adjusted through post-acquisition reserves and do not affect the translation of pre-acquisition reserves. Similarly, **pre-acquisition exchange differences** are dealt with through pre-acquisition reserves.

3.22 This means that, when using the **temporal method** for translating the results of a subsidiary company acquired as a going concern, the temporal rates for non-monetary assets owned by the subsidiary at the date of acquisition will be the rate ruling on that date rather than rates ruling when the assets were originally acquired by the subsidiary and that goodwill will be the same whether the closing rate method or the temporal method is used subsequent to acquisition.

Deferred tax

3.23 Obviously, before preparing consolidated accounts it will be necessary to ensure that the accounts of foreign subsidiaries are prepared (or adjusted) in accordance with **FRS 19**.

When the accounts of foreign subsidiaries are translated using the closing rate method, the closing rate will be used for deferred tax balances. When the temporal method is used for deferred tax balances the position is not so clear cut. If the deferred tax balance is viewed as a liability, then it would seem appropriate to use the closing rate.

Foreign associated undertakings

3.24 Foreign associates will be companies with substantial autonomy from the group and so the **closing rate/net investment method** will be used when translating net assets into sterling.

3.25 Section summary

The main points to remember in this section relate to when and how to use the closing rate/net investment method or the temporal method.

- **Closing rate/net investment**
  - Use for independent subsidiary
  - Translate assets and liabilities at closing rate
  - Translate P&L account at average/closing rate
  - Exchange differences through reserves
- **Temporal**
  - Use for direct extensions of the investing company
  - Translate assets and liabilities at closing rate (monetary items) and historical rate (non-monetary)
  - Translate P&L account at actual (average) rate and historical rate (non-monetary items)
  - Exchange differences are part of profit

4 FOREIGN BORROWINGS

4.1 A special case exists where foreign equity investments are financed by foreign borrowings.

Individual company accounts

4.2 The normal treatment for exchange differences on foreign currency borrowings would be to include them in the P&L account for the year. Equally, foreign equity investments (whether in subsidiaries or not) are regarded as **non-monetary items**, which are not normally retranslated at the year end and which therefore do not give rise to any exchange differences.

4.3 There is an argument, however, that where a foreign equity investment is financed by a foreign currency loan, so that the company is **hedging the exchange risk**, gains or losses on the loan should be **offset** against losses or gains on the investment, the latter being retranslated at the closing rate.

4.4 This argument is particularly strong where the loan and the investment are in the **same foreign** currency. A loss on the loan will automatically be accompanied by a gain on the investment, and *vice versa*, and the company's exposure to exchange risks may be much reduced.

4.5 Where such hedging takes place SSAP 20 allows the equity investments to be translated at the **closing rate** and the exchange differences taken to **reserves**. The exchange gains or losses on the foreign currency borrowings should then offset these exchange differences as a reserve movement.

4.6 **Conditions**

(a) In any accounting period, exchange gains or losses arising on the borrowings may be offset **only to the extent** of exchange differences arising on the equity investments.

(b) The foreign currency borrowings, whose exchange gains or losses are used in the offset process, should not exceed, in the aggregate, the **total amount of cash** that the investments are expected to be able to generate, whether from profits or otherwise.

(c) The accounting treatment adopted should be **applied consistently** from period to period.

(d) The borrowing and the investment need *not* be denominated in the **same foreign currency**.

Consolidated accounts

4.7 Companies are permitted to offset exchange differences on foreign currency loans and foreign equity investments in the consolidated accounts, just as they can be offset in the individual company accounts. The additional requirement that the **closing rate method must be used** is logical since under the temporal method differences go through the P&L account in *all* circumstances.

> Where foreign currency **borrowings** have been used to finance, or to provide a **hedge** against, **group equity investments** in foreign enterprises, **exchange gains or losses** on the borrowings, which would otherwise have been taken to the P&L account, **may** be **offset as reserve movements against exchange differences arising on the retranslation of the net investments provided the conditions are met.**

4.8 **Conditions**

(a) The relationship between the investing company and the foreign enterprises concerned **justify the use** of the closing rate method for consolidation purposes.

(b) In any accounting period, the exchange gains and losses arising on foreign currency borrowings are offset **only to the extent** of the exchange differences arising on the net investments in foreign enterprises.

(c) The foreign currency borrowings, whose exchange gains or losses are used in the offset process, should not exceed, in the aggregate, the **total amount of cash** that the net investments are expected to be able to generate, whether from profits or otherwise.

(d) The accounting treatment is **applied consistently** from period to period.

5 DISCLOSURE AND OTHER MATTERS

5.1 **Disclosure requirements of SSAP 20**

(a) The **methods used** in the translation of the financial statements of foreign enterprises and the treatment accorded to exchange differences should be disclosed in the financial statements (as an accounting policy note).

(b) The following information should also be disclosed in the financial statements:

(i) For all companies or groups of companies, the net amount **of exchange gains and losses** on foreign currency borrowings less deposits, identifying separately:

(1) The amount offset in reserves
(2) The net amount charged/credited to the P&L account

(ii) For all companies or groups of companies, the net **movement on reserves** arising from exchange differences

5.2 Disclosure of the **basis** on which foreign currencies have been translated into sterling is also a requirement of CA 1985.

5.3 Under SSAP 20, exchange gains arising on **long-term monetary items** (ie falling due after more than one year) are deemed to be 'unrealised', and therefore the following treatment and disclosure is appropriate.

(a) Where there are doubts as to the **convertibility** of a currency, consider on the grounds of prudence whether to restrict the amount of the gain to be recognised in the P&L account.

(b) Where gains on long-term monetary items are included in the P&L account, this represents a departure from CA 1985. Here is a **specimen note** to comply with CA 1985.

> 'The P&L account includes £X of exchange gains on long-term monetary items which represents a departure from the accounting principle in the Companies Act 1985 that only realised profits should be recognised. This departure has been made in accordance with SSAP 20 in order to show a true and fair view of the results of the business.'

This covers particulars, reasons and the effect of the departure.

Criticisms of SSAP 20

5.4 Although SSAP 20 is an improvement over the previous situation, it is still criticised.

Translation of the P&L account: closing rate vs average rate

5.5 Under the closing rate method either the closing rate or the average rate may be used to translate the P&L account. This is a weakness of SSAP 20 and the problem of a **lack of comparability** between companies is exacerbated.

Advantages of closing rate	Advantages of average rate
The use of the closing rate is simpler as it avoids the need to find an average rate weighted by the volume of transactions. The use of the closing rate will preserve the relationships in the foreign currency financial statements between P&L account items and balance sheet items. (This is stated as one of the reasons for choosing the closing rate method at all.) Many UK companies prefer the closing rate, have used it for some years and would object to a change.	Profits accrue over a whole period, so the average rate will reflect the true events. There is no need to restate interim results. It is less volatile than the closing rate method. It gives greater comparability between companies with overlapping accounting periods.

Forward contracts

5.6 Two criticisms are made in relation to forward contracts and similar vehicles (currently swaps, options).

(a) There is **insufficient guidance** in the standard on accounting for such contracts, particularly the discount or premium.

(b) The use of forward rates is **optional** and so companies can ignore a related forward contract if they wish and this leads to inconsistency.

Cover method

5.7 The cover method describes where there is an **offset** of exchange differences on foreign currency loans and foreign equity investments. Again, there are several criticisms in this area.

(a) The use of the cover method is **optional**, so companies can choose not to use the cover method provisions. Again, this leads to a lack of comparability. The same applies to exchange differences in consolidated financial statements, which *may* be offset as reserve movements.

(b) Since there is no requirement that borrowings should be in the same currency as the investment, cover may not exist, in other words exchange risk is **not being hedged** unless loan *and* investment are in the same currency.

(c) Allowing borrowings to be in different currencies from the investments means that exchange differences on the borrowings will not necessarily be treated the same **each year** (some years taken to reserves, some to the P&L account).

Reserve accounting

5.8 The criticism here is that exchange differences on net investments and borrowings which are a hedge never pass through the P&L account. However, exchange differences will ultimately be reflected in **cash flows** when dividends are received from the investments or

when the investments are ultimately sold. No provisions are contained in SSAP 20 as to what should happen to the cumulative exchange differences which have arisen on the investments when the investments are sold or dividends are received. As a result, the exchange differences are usually not reflected in the P&L account at any time, even when the investment is sold.

5.9 Similarly, exchange differences on borrowings which have financed or provided a hedge against equity investments are normally taken to reserves even although they will have an impact on the **cash flows** of the company. It is therefore possible for the borrowings to have been completely repaid and none of the exchange differences thereon taken through the P&L account.

5.10 The problems associated with reserve accounting have been partly overcome by the greater prominence given to reserve movements by the **STRGL.**

Realised profits in individual companies: exchange losses

5.11 Where exchange losses have arisen, it would seem that s 275 CA 1985 is applicable. This requires that provisions should be treated as **realised losses** for the purposes of determining distributable profits. Realised losses will include those on:

- Settled transactions
- Unsettled short-term monetary items
- Long-term monetary items (to be prudent)

5.12 However, a problem exists in the case of losses on **long-term overseas borrowings** taken directly to the reserves of an individual company which uses the offset procedure in its own accounts. The question arises as to whether such losses should be treated as realised.

5.13 The cash flows can be considered where the loan **has been repaid**; in other words, where the exchange losses taken for offset to reserves relate to borrowings which have been repaid then they are **realised**. The cash flow situation where borrowings have not been repaid will be affected by the level of **dividends received** from the foreign investment before the borrowings are due to be repaid.

(a) If dividends received are sufficient, then a hedge exists and the loss on the borrowings can be treated as unrealised.

(b) If insufficient dividends are received before the borrowings are repaid, there is no hedge and the losses should be treated as realised.

5.14 This last criticism is perhaps the most serious, although the first four are bad enough as they allow a great deal of manipulation. The solution would to be an amendment to SSAP 20, taking account of the above criticisms. However, foreign currency transactions are not very high on the ASB's agenda and so revision is probably some way off.

UITF Abstract 19 *Tax on gains and losses on foreign currency borrowing that hedge an investment in a foreign enterprise*

5.15 This abstract formalises the view expressed two years ago, following changes to the tax treatment of certain exchange differences, that where exchange differences are reported in the statement of total recognised gains and losses, the related tax should also be reported in that statement.

5.16 The abstract also specifies how tax should be taken into account in applying the restrictions contained in SSAP 20 *Foreign currency translation* on the treatment of gains and losses on borrowings that finance or hedge a foreign net investment and clarifies the necessary disclosures.

5.17 Section summary

- **Disclosure**: remember the true and fair departure note for gains on long-term monetary items
- **Criticisms**: the main ones are:
  - Closing rate vs average rate arguments
  - Forward contracts: optional and insufficient guidance
  - Cover method: optional and no real hedge
  - Reserve accounting: hides results (but STRGL)
  - Realised profits/losses on long-term overseas borrowings

Question: hedging

A company operates an airline engaged in the UK charter trade. It has a number of aircraft that have been financed by US dollar loans. The aircraft earn income in sterling. At the year end there are exchange losses on the loans which are material. The company proposes to defer the exchange losses and amortise them over the life of the loans. Is the proposed treatment acceptable?

Answer

Under SSAP 20 *Foreign currency translation*, the aircraft would be translated from US dollars to sterling at the rate of exchange at the date of transaction (ie at the date(s) of purchase, not at the date(s) of payment) and this carrying value is not retranslated for subsequent changes in the rate of exchange. Exchange gains and losses on the borrowing would be taken to the P&L account each year, but no corresponding gain or loss on the 'value' of the asset will be recognised.

One exception to the above rule is where a company has used foreign currency borrowing to finance or provide a hedge against its foreign currency investment. SSAP 20 recognises that in such situations a company may be covered in economic terms against any movements in exchange rates, and states that it would be inappropriate in such cases to record an accounting profit or loss when exchange rates change.

Accordingly, where certain conditions are satisfied, the equity investment may be denominated in the appropriate foreign currency and retranslated at each year end at closing rates. Where this is done, the resulting exchange differences may be taken to reserves and the exchange gains or losses on the foreign currency borrowing should then be offset, as a reserve movement, against these exchange differences.

It should be noted that the offset treatment is also applicable to foreign branches. The standard's definition of a foreign branch includes a group of asset and liabilities that are accounted for in foreign currencies. This was further elaborated in the statement by the Accounting Standards Committee on the publication of SSAP 20 (TR 504). TR 504 includes an example of a branch comprising a ship or aircraft purchased in US dollars with a US dollar loan and which earns revenue and incurs expenses in US dollars to be accounted for under the closing rate/net investment method.

Therefore, it would be acceptable treat the aircraft as a foreign branch if they are purchased in foreign currencies and earn income in that currency.

This is not the case here, however, as the aircraft, although purchased in US dollars, do not earn income in dollars. As the aircraft fail to qualify as a foreign branch and the offset option is not open, the exchange loss should be taken to the P&L account as it arises. The company's proposed treatment is therefore not acceptable.

6 FRED 24

6.1 As part of its programme of convergence (see Chapter 13) of FRSs and International Financial Reporting Standards, in May 2002 the ASB published FRED 24 *The effects of changes in foreign exchange rates; Financial reporting in hyperinflationary economies.*

6.2 FRED 24 proposes two new standards, based on a revised IAS 21 *The effects of changes in foreign exchange rates*, and IAS 29 *Financial reporting in hyper-inflationary economies*. They would replace SSAP 20 *Foreign currency translation* and the related UITF Abstract 9.

Main points

6.3 The **main changes** from current UK GAAP are as follows.

(a) There is **no longer an option to measure the profit and loss account at closing rate**; actual (average) exchange rates should be used.

(b) **Goodwill** should be translated at the **closing rate**.

(c) Entities operating in **hyperinflationary currencies** should **restate** their financial statements using **appropriate indices**, and **not use a hard currency as the functional currency.**

6.4 The FRED is not very different from the revised IAS. However, the ASB proposes **not to introduce** in the UK the '**recycling**' from the statement of total recognised gains and losses to the profit and loss account of translation differences arising from consolidating foreign entities. As made clear in FRED 22, the ASB does not regard recycling as best practice. The IASB has, elsewhere in its work, indicated some dissatisfaction with recycling but has retained the concept in its proposed revised IAS 21.

6.5 FRED 24 introduces the terms '**functional' and 'presentation' currencies**. An entity measures items using the functional currency (that of its primary economic environment) but presents financial statements in any currency.

More detail

6.6 As FRED 24 brings in material from an IAS, there are differences of terminology and wording from SSAP 20. For example, IAS 21 and hence the FRED talk about 'integral foreign operations' rather than the 'temporal method'. There are also differences of emphasis. However, because SSAP 20 and IAS 21 were developed together as part of an international convergence project, their **requirements are similar.** This means that FRED 24 and SSAP 20 are similar.

6.7 In this section we will focus on the **changes from existing UK requirements** rather than going over the common ground.

Choice of presentation currency

6.8 SSAP 20 and FRED 24 differ in the degree of freedom permitted to entities over the choice of the currency in which they present their financial statements.

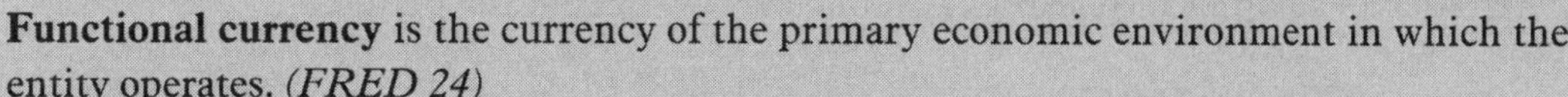

KEY TERMS

Functional currency is the currency of the primary economic environment in which the entity operates. *(FRED 24)*

Foreign currency is a currency other than the functional currency of the entity. *(FRED 24)*

Presentation currency is the currency in which the financial statements are presented. *(FRED 24)*

6.9 SSAP 20 defines a company's local currency as 'the currency of the primary economic environment in which it operates and generates net cash flows'. The SSAP does not specifically address the question of the currency in which financial statements are presented, although it implies that it will be the company's local currency (or, in the case of consolidated financial statements, the parent's local currency).

6.10 FRED 24 introduces the concepts of **functional currency** and **presentation currency**, as defined above. Functional currency is a similar concept to SSAP 20's local currency. Both SSAP 20 and FRED 24 require each entity to determine its functional currency and measure its results in that currency. However, **FRED 24** then **permits the entity to report those results in any currency (the presentation currency) it chooses.**

Preparation of consolidated financial statements

6.11 As discussed in Section 3, **SSAP 20 requires the use of different methods** for preparing consolidated financial statements - the closing rate/net investment method or the temporal method – depending on the relationship between the investing company and the foreign entity.

(a) The **closing rate/net investment method** is used where the investment of a company is in the **net worth of its foreign entity,** rather than a direct investment in the individual assets and liabilities of that entity. This method involves the translation of balance sheet amounts using the rate of exchange at the balance sheet date and the translation of profit and loss items either at the closing rate or using an average rate for the period.

(b) The **temporal method** is used where the affairs of a foreign entity are so closely **interlinked with those of the investing company** that its results are regarded as being more dependent on the economic environment of the investing company's currency than on that of its own currency. The financial statements of such a foreign entity are included in the consolidated statements as if all the entity's transactions had been entered into by the investing company itself in its own currency.

6.12 **FRED 24** proposes that there should **no longer be a different accounting treatment for integral foreign operations** (where the temporal method is used under SSAP 20).

6.13 If the affairs of a foreign entity are such that its results are 'more dependent on the economic environment of the investing company's currency than on that of its own currency', the **functional currency of the foreign entity should be the same as that of the investing company**. Therefore, although FRED 24 does not explicitly require the temporal method to be used to account for such entities, **the effect should be the same.**

6.14 For foreign entities like those in Paragraph 6.11(a), which have a different functional currency to the investing company, SSAP 20 allows the profit and loss account to be translated at either the closing rate or an average rate for the period.

6.15 However, **FRED 24 does not permit use of the closing rate to translate profit and loss account items.** Instead, the **rate of exchange at the date of the transaction** must be used, although an **average rate** for a period may often provide a **good approximation** of that rate.

Further differences

6.16 Some more differences are shown in the table below. They relate to:

- Monetary items forming part of a net investment in a foreign operation
- Translation at the contracted rate
- Deferral of foreign exchange gains
- Translation of goodwill and fair value adjustments
- Hedge accounting

SSAP 20	FRED 24
Exchange differences on a monetary item that is part of a reporting entity's **net investment** in a foreign operation must always be taken to the STRGL.	These exchange differences are recognised in the **profit and loss account** in the **separate financial statements** of the reporting entity. In the **consolidated financial statements** they are recognised in the **STRGL.**
Foreign currency transactions which are **settled at a contracted rate are recorded at the contract rate** as is any resulting asset or liability.	The transaction must be measured **initially at the spot rate** on the date of the transaction. However, a different rate may be used if hedge accounting techniques are used and FRED 23 (see later) is applied.
Exchange gains and losses on monetary items must generally be recognised in the profit and loss account. However, for long-term monetary items some or all of such **gains** (but not losses) may be **deferred.** This is **on grounds of prudence,** when there are doubts about the convertibility or marketability of the foreign currency.	**No deferral is possible** – all such items must be recognised in the profit and loss account.
SSAP 20 **does not** specifically **address** the treatment of **goodwill** and **fair value adjustments** to the carrying amounts of assets and liabilities on the acquisition of a foreign operation.	FRED 24 requires **goodwill** and **fair value adjustments** to be treated as **assets** and liabilities of the foreign operation and **translated at a closing rate**.
SSAP 20 contains certain requirements on the treatment of **hedges** of net investments in foreign operations.	FRED 24 contains **no equivalent requirements** because these will be dealt with in FRED 23 (see later).

Disclosure requirements

6.17 SSAP 20 requires disclosure of only those exchange differences included in the profit and loss account that have arisen on foreign currency borrowings less deposits. **FRED 24** goes further and requires disclosure of the **amount of exchange differences included in net profit or loss for the period.**

6.18 If the **presentation currency differs from the functional currency**, that fact, and the reason for using a different presentation currency, should be disclosed.

6.19 Any **changes in the functional currency** should be disclosed.

Financial reporting in hyperinflationary economies

6.20 UITF Abstract 9 and FRED 24 deal with accounting for operations in hyperinflationary economies when preparing consolidated financial statements. However, the scope of the proposed standard in **FRED 24 is wider than UITF Abstract 9** in that it **also deals with the accounting to be adopted in individual financial statements** when the entity has a functional currency that is the currency of a hyperinflationary economy.

6.21 **UITF Abstract 9** allows the distortions that arise in hyperinflationary economies to be eliminated in **one of two ways**.

(a) The financial statements should be **restated** to reflect the impact of price changes.
(b) The entity should **adopt a stable currency** as its functional currency.

Other approaches may be adopted if neither of these is considered appropriate.

6.22 Under **FRED 24, only alternative (a),** the **restatement** of financial statements, would be **allowed.**

Chapter roundup

- Questions on foreign currency translation have always been popular with examiners. In general you are required to prepare **consolidated accounts** for a group which includes a foreign subsidiary.
- You may have to make the decision yourself as to which method of currency translation to use, **temporal** or **closing rate**, and on whether to translate the P&L account at **average or closing rate**.
- You must be able to calculate **exchange differences** etc and also to explain the differences between the methods. You should be able to discuss the treatment of **foreign currency borrowings** to finance overseas investment.
- **Practising** examination questions is the best way of learning this topic.
- **SSAP 20** is criticised for a variety of reasons.
- **FRED 24** proposes two new standards that would **replace SSAP 20 and UITF 9**.

Quick quiz

1 Define 'monetary' and 'non-monetary' items.

2 Does SSAP 20 require that the closing rate method or the temporal method should normally be used to consolidate foreign enterprises?

3 When would the *other* method be appropriate?

4 State the three conditions which must hold before the hedging provisions of SSAP 20 can be invoked in an individual company's accounts, so that an equity investment can be retranslated at a balance sheet rate.

5 How are shareholders' funds translated using the temporal method?

6 Under FRED 24, how must the P&L be measured?

Answers to quick quiz

1 See Para 2.1

2 Yes, except is certain special circumstances.

3 (a) When the foreign enterprise acts as a selling agent.

(b) It produces raw materials or parts which are shipped to the investing company for inclusion in its own products.

(c) It acts as a means of raising finance for the companies in the group.

4 See Para 4.6.

5 Using the closing rate at the beginning of the year for monetary items and the appropriate historical rates for non-monetary items.

6 At actual or average rate. Closing rate may no longer be used.

Now try the question below from the Exam Question Bank

Number	Level	Marks	Time
Q11	Exam	25	45 mins

Chapter 8

GROUP CASH FLOW STATEMENTS

	Topic list	Syllabus reference
1	**FRS 1 (Revised) *Cash flow statements:* single company**	**1(a), (b)**
2	**Consolidated cash flow statements**	**1(a), (b)**
3	**Foreign exchange and cash flow statements**	**1(a), (b)**

Introduction

A cash flow statement is an additional primary statement of **great value** to users of financial statements for the extra information it provides.

You should be familiar with the basic principles, techniques and definitions relating to cash flow statements from your earlier studies. This chapter develops the principles and preparation techniques to include **consolidated statements** and **foreign currency problems**.

Study guide

Section 10 – Group cash flow statements

- The usefulness of cash flow information
- Preparation of group cash flow statements classifying cash flows by standard headings and including acquisition and disposal of subsidiaries
- Dealing with associates, joint ventures, joint arrangements and foreign currencies

Exam guide

A group cash flow statement is likely to appear as a compulsory 25 mark question.

1 FRS 1 (REVISED) CASH FLOW STATEMENTS: SINGLE COMPANY

1.1 We have covered this in your earlier studies, so only a summary is given here. However, if you have any problems with the question at the end of this section, look back to your earlier study material.

Knowledge brought forward from earlier studies

FRS 1 (Revised) Cash flow statements

- Information on cash flows assists the user in assessing company's viability.
    - Shows enterprise's cash generation ability
    - Shows enterprise's cash utilisation needs

Knowledge brought forward from earlier studies (cont'd)

- *Format of statement*

  Inflows and outflows of cash of an enterprise are classified between the major economic activities.

  - Operating activities
  - Dividends from associates and joint ventures
  - Returns on investments and servicing of finance
  - Taxation
  - Capital expenditure and financial investment
  - Acquisitions and disposals
  - Equity dividends paid
  - Management of liquid resources
  - Financing

  The last two headings can be shown in a single section provided a subtotal is given for each heading.

- *Notes*

  FRS 1 requires two reconciliations.

  - Operating profit to net cash flow from operating activities
  - Movement in cash in the period to movement in net debt

  Give either adjoining the statement or in a separate note.

- *Definitions*

  - Cash: cash in hand and deposits repayable on demand ... less overdrafts ... repayable on demand. Deposits are repayable on demand if they can be withdrawn at any time without notice and without penalty or if a maturity/period of notice of $\leq$ 24 hours or one working day has been agreed. Includes cash in hand and deposits in foreign currencies.

  - Liquid resources: current asset investments held as readily disposable stores of value. A readily disposable investment is one that:

    - Is disposable by the reporting entity without curtailing or disrupting its business, and is either:
    - Readily convertible into known amounts of cash at or close to its carrying amount, or
    - Traded in an active market

  - Net debt: the borrowings of the reporting entity less cash and liquid resources; may be 'net funds' rather than 'net debt'.

- *Direct and indirect methods*

  The cash flow statement may be presented using either the direct or indirect method.

  - Direct method: the components of operating cash flows (cash from customers, payments to suppliers, other cash payments) are reported under this method; encouraged because of the value of the extra information given but not required because of the recognised extra costs involved in extracting the operating cash flows

  - Indirect method: the net cash flow from operating activities is arrived at by starting with the operating profit and adjusting it for non-cash charges and credits

1.2 Summary of techniques

Remember the steps involved in preparation of a cash flow statement.

Step 1. Set out the proforma leaving plenty of space.

Step 2. Complete the reconciliation of operating profit to net cash inflow, as far as possible.

Step 3. Calculate the following where appropriate.

- Tax paid
- Dividends paid
- Purchase and sale of fixed assets
- Issues of shares
- Repayment of loans

Step 4. Work out the profit if not already given using: opening and closing balances, tax charge and dividends.

Step 5. Complete the note of gross cash flows. Alternatively the information may go straight into the statement.

Step 6. Slot the figures into the statement.

Step 7. Complete the note of the analysis of changes in net debt.

Step 8. Complete the reconciliation of net cash flow to movement in net debt.

Question: single company cash flow statement

The summarised accounts of Ashley plc for the year ended 31 December 20X8 are as follows.

ASHLEY PLC
BALANCE SHEET AS AT 31 DECEMBER 20X8

	20X8		*20X7*	
	£'000	£'000	£'000	£'000
Fixed assets				
Tangible assets		628		514
Current assets				
Stocks	214		210	
Debtors	168		147	
Cash	7		-	
	389		357	
Creditors: amounts falling due within one year				
Trade creditors	136		121	
Tax payable	39		28	
Dividends payable	18		16	
Overdraft	-		14	
	193		179	
Net current assets		196		178
Total assets less current liabilities		824		692
Creditors: amounts falling due after more than one year				
10% debentures		(80)		(50)
		744		642
Capital and reserves				
Share capital (£1 ords)		250		200
Share premium account		70		60
Revaluation reserve		110		100
Profit and loss account		314		282
		744		642

ASHLEY PLC
PROFIT AND LOSS ACCOUNT
FOR THE YEAR ENDED 31 DECEMBER 20X8

	£'000
Sales	600
Cost of sales	(319)
Gross profit	281
Other expenses (including depreciation of £42,000)	(194)
Profit before tax	87
Tax	(31)
Profit after tax	56
Dividends	(24)
Retained profit for the year	32

You are additionally informed that there have been no disposals of fixed assets during the year. New debentures were issued on 1 January 20X8. Wages for the year amounted to £86,000.

Required

Produce a cash flow statement using the direct method suitable for inclusion in the financial statements, as per FRS 1 (revised 1996).

Answer

ASHLEY PLC
CASH FLOW STATEMENT FOR THE YEAR ENDED 31 DECEMBER 20X8

	£'000	£'000
Operating activities		
Cash received from customers (147 + 600 – 168)	579	
Cash payments to suppliers (121 + 381 (W1) – 136)	(366)	
Cash payments to and on behalf of employees	(86)	
		127
Returns on investments and servicing of finance		
Interest paid		(8)
Taxation		
UK corporation tax paid (W2)		(20)
Capital expenditure		
Purchase of tangible fixed assets (W3)		(146)
		(47)
Equity dividends paid (16 + 24 – 18)		(22)
Financing		
Issue of share capital	60	
Issue of debentures	30	
Net cash inflow from financing		90
Increase in cash		21

NOTES TO THE CASH FLOW STATEMENT

1 *Reconciliation of operating profit to net cash inflow from operating activities*

	£'000
Operating profit (87 + 8)	95
Depreciation	42
Increase in stock	(4)
Increase in debtors	(21)
Increase in creditors	15
	127

2 *Reconciliation of net cash flow to movement in net debt*

	£'000
Net cash inflow for the period	21
Cash received from debenture issue	(30)
Change in net debt	(9)
Net debt at 1 January 20X8	(64)
Net debt at 31 December 20X8	(73)

3 *Analysis of changes in net debt*

	At 1 January 20X8 £'000	Cash flows £'000	At 31 December 20X8 £'000
Cash at bank	-	7	7
Overdrafts	(14)	14	-
		21	
Debt due after 1 year	(50)	(30)	(80)
Total	(64)	(9)	(73)

Workings

1 *Purchases*

	£'000
Cost of sales	319
Opening stock	(210)
Closing stock	214
Expenses (194 – 42 – 86 – 8 debenture interest)	58
	381

2 *Taxation*

TAXATION

	£'000		£'000
∴ Tax paid	20	Balance b/f	28
Balance c/f	39	Charge for year	31
	59		59

3 *Purchase of fixed assets*

	£'000
Opening fixed assets	514
Less depreciation	(42)
Add revaluation (110 – 100)	10
	482
Closing fixed assets	628
Difference = additions	146

2 CONSOLIDATED CASH FLOW STATEMENTS — Pilot Paper, 6/02

2.1 The following format is given in the standard for a group cash flow statement.

XYZ GROUP PLC
CASH FLOW STATEMENT FOR THE YEAR ENDED 31 DECEMBER 20X6

		£'000	£'000
Cash flow from operating activities (note 1)			15,672
Dividends received from associates			350
Returns on investments and servicing of finance* (note 2)			(2,239)
Taxation			(2,887)
Capital expenditure and financial investment (note 2)			(865)
Acquisitions and disposals (note 2)			(17,824)
Equity dividends paid			(2,606)
Cash outflow before use of liquid resources and financing			(10,399)
Management of liquid resources (note 2)			700
Financing (note 2)	Issue of shares	600	
	Increase in debt	2,347	
			2,947
Decrease in cash in the period			(6,752)

Reconciliation of net cash flow to movement in net debt (note 3)

Decrease in cash in the period	(6,752)	
Cash inflow from increase in debt and lease financing	(2,347)	
Cash inflow from decrease in liquid resources	(700)	
Change in net debt resulting from cash flows		(9,799)
Loans and finance leases acquired with subsidiary		(3,817)
New finance leases		(2,845)
Translation difference		643
Movement in net debt in the period		(15,818)
Net debt at 1.1.X6		(15,215)
Net debt at 31.12.X6		(31,033)

* This heading would include any dividends received *other than* those from equity accounted entities included in operating activities.

NOTES TO THE CASH FLOW STATEMENT

1 *Reconciliation of operating profit to operating cash flows*

	Continuing		*Dis-continued*	*Total*
	£'000	£'000	£'000	£'000
Operating profit		18,829	(1,616)	17,213
Depreciation charges		3,108	380	3,488
Cash flow relating to previous year restructuring provision (note 4)			(560)	(560)
Increase in stocks		(11,193)	(87)	(11,280)
Increase in debtors		(3,754)	(20)	(3,774)
Increase in creditors		9,672	913	10,585
Net cash inflow from continuing operating activities		16,662		
Net cash outflow in respect of discontinued activities			(990)	
Net cash inflow from operating activities				15,672

2 *Analysis of cash flows for headings netted in the cash flow statement*

	£'000	£'000
Returns on investments and servicing of finance		
Interest received	508	
Interest paid	(1,939)	
Preference dividend paid	(450)	
Interest element of finance lease rental payments	(358)	
Net cash outflow for returns on investments and servicing of finance		(2,239)
Capital expenditure and financial investment		
Purchase of tangible fixed assets	(3,512)	
Sale of trade investment	1,595	
Sale of plant and machinery	1,052	
Net cash outflow for capital expenditure and financial investment		(865)
Acquisitions and disposals		
Purchase of subsidiary undertaking	(12,705)	
Net overdrafts acquired with subsidiary	(5,516)	
Sale of business	4,208	
Purchase of interest in a joint venture	(3,811)	
Net cash outflow for acquisitions and disposals		(17,824)
*Management of liquid resources**		
Cash withdrawn from 7 day deposit	200	
Purchase of government securities	(5,000)	
Sale of government securities	4,300	
Sale of corporate bonds	1,200	
Net cash inflow from management of liquid resources		700

	£'000	£'000
Financing		
Issue of ordinary share capital		600
Debt due within a year		
Increase in short-term borrowings	2,006	
Repayment of secured loan	(850)	
Debt due beyond a year		
New secured loan repayable in 20Y0	1,091	
New unsecured loan repayable in 20X8	1,442	
Capital element of finance lease rental payments	(1,342)	
		2,347
Net cash inflow from financing		2,947

* XYZ Group plc includes as liquid resources term deposits of less than a year, government securities and AA rated corporate bonds.

3 *Analysis of net debt*

	At 1 Jan 20X6 £'000	*Cash flow* £'000	*Acquisition* (excl. cash and overdrafts)* £'000	*Other non-cash changes* £'000	*Exchange movement* £'000	*At 31 Dec 20X6* £'000
Cash in hand, at bank	235	(1,250)			1,392	377
Overdrafts	(2,528)	(5,502)			(1,422)	(9,452)
		(6,752)				
Debt due after 1 year	(9,640)	(2,533)	(1,749)	2,560	(792)	(12,154)
Debt due within 1 year	(352)	(1,156)	(837)	(2,560)	1,465	(3,440)
Finance leases	(4,170)	1,342	(1,231)	(2,845)		(6,904)
		(2,347)				
Current asset investments	1,240	(700)				540
Total	(15,215)	(9,799)	(3,817)	(2,845)	643	(31,033)

4 *Cash flows relating to exceptional items*

The operating cash outflows include under discontinued activities an outflow of £560,000, which relates to the £1,600,000 exceptional provision for a fundamental restructuring made in the 20X5 accounts.

5 *Major non-cash transactions*

(a) During the year the group entered into finance lease arrangements in respect of assets with a total capital value at the inception of the leases of £2,845,000.

(b) Part of the consideration for the purchases of subsidiary undertakings and the sale of a business that occurred during the year comprised shares and loan notes respectively. Further details of the acquisitions and the disposal are set out below.

6 *Purchase of subsidiary undertakings*

	£'000
Net assets acquired	
Tangible fixed assets	12,194
Investments	1
Stocks	9,384
Debtors	13,856
Taxation recoverable	1,309
Cash at bank and in hand	1,439
Creditors	(21,715)
Bank overdrafts	(6,955)
Loans and finance leases	(3,817)
Deferred taxation	(165)
Minority shareholders' interests	(9)
	5,522
Goodwill	16,702
	22,224
Satisfied by	
Shares allotted	9,519
Cash	12,705
	22,224

The subsidiary undertakings acquired during the year contributed £1,502,000 to the group's net operating cash flows, paid £1,308,000 in respect of net returns on investments and servicing of finance, paid £522,000 in respect of taxation and utilised £2,208,000 for capital expenditure.

7 *Sale of business*

	£'000
Net assets disposed of	
Fixed assets	775
Stocks	5,386
Debtors	474
	6,635
Loss on disposal	(1,227)
	5,408
Satisfied by	
Loan notes	1,200
Cash	4,208
	5,408

The business sold during the year contributed £200,000 to the group's net operating cash flows, paid £252,000 in respect of net returns on investments and servicing of finance, paid £145,000 in respect of taxation and utilised £209,000 for capital expenditure.

2.2 Cash flows that are **internal to the group** should be eliminated in the preparation of a consolidated cash flow statement. Where a subsidiary undertaking **joins or leaves** a group during a financial year the cash flows of the group should include the cash flows of the subsidiary undertaking concerned for the same period as that for which the group's P&L account includes the results of the subsidiary undertaking.

Acquisitions and disposals of subsidiary undertakings

2.3 A note to the cash flow statement should show a summary of the effects of acquisitions and disposals of subsidiary undertakings indicating how much of the **consideration comprised cash**. Material effects on amounts reported under each of the standard headings reflecting the cash flows of a subsidiary undertaking acquired or disposed of in the period should be

disclosed, as far as practicable. This information could be given by dividing cash flows between continuing and discontinued operations and acquisitions.

Consolidation adjustments and minority interests

2.4 The group cash flow statement should only deal with flows of cash and cash equivalents external to the group, so all intra-group cash flows should be eliminated. **Dividends paid to minority interests** should be included under the heading 'returns on investments and servicing of finance' and disclosed separately.

2.5 EXAMPLE: MINORITY INTERESTS

The following are extracts of the consolidated results for Jarvis plc for the year ended 31 December 20X2.

CONSOLIDATED PROFIT AND LOSS ACCOUNT (EXTRACT)

	£'000
Group profit before tax	90
Taxation	(30)
Profit after tax	60
Minority interest	(15)
Retained profit	45

CONSOLIDATED BALANCE SHEET (EXTRACT)

	20X1	*20X2*
	£'000	£'000
Minority interest	300	306

Calculate the dividends paid to the minority interest during the year.

2.6 SOLUTION

The minority interest share of profit after tax represents retained profit plus dividends paid.

	£'000
Minority interest brought forward	300
Minority interest carried forward	306
	(6)
Profit and loss account	15
Dividend paid	9

Associated undertakings

2.7 Only the actual cash flows from sales or purchases between the group and the associate, and investments in and dividends from the entity should be included. Dividends should be included as a separate item between operating activities and **returns on investments and servicing of finance**. Any other cash flows between the investment its associates should be included under the appropriate cash flow heading for the activity giving rise to the cash flow. (Note that this is the treatment prescribed by FRS 9 *Associates and joint ventures*, covered in Chapter 14.)

2.8 EXAMPLE: ASSOCIATED COMPANY

The following are extracts of the consolidated results of Pripon plc for the year ended 31 December 20X2.

CONSOLIDATED PROFIT AND LOSS ACCOUNT (EXTRACT)

	£'000	£'000
Operating profit of group		150
Share of associated undertaking profit		60
		210
Tax: group	75	
share of associate	30	
		105
Profit after tax		105

CONSOLIDATED BALANCE SHEET (EXTRACTS)

	20X1	*20X2*
	£'000	£'000
Investment in associated undertaking	264	276

Calculate the dividend received from the associated company.

2.9 SOLUTION

The associated undertaking profit before tax represents retained profit plus dividend plus tax.

	£'000	£'000
Investment brought forward		264
Investment carried forward		276
		(12)
Profit before tax	60	
Tax	(30)	
		30
Dividend from associate		18

Finance lease transactions

2.10 When rentals under a finance lease are paid the **capital and interest elements are split out** and included under the 'financing' and 'servicing of finance' headings respectively.

Exam focus point

Various complications may arise in a consolidated cash flow statement in the exam, the most important of which are covered above. The compulsory question on the Pilot paper required you to produce a revised cash flow statement, an incorrect one having been prepared by the accountant in the question. Question 2, given below, is comprehensive.

2.11 Section summary

The preparation of consolidated cash flow statements will, in many respects, be the same as those for single companies, with the following **additional complications.**

- Acquisitions and disposals of subsidiary undertaking
- Cancellation of intra-group transactions
- Minority interests
- Associated undertakings
- Finance leases
- Foreign currency (see Section 4)

Question: consolidated cash flow statement

Topiary plc is a 40 year old company producing garden statues carved from marble. In 20V9 it acquired a 100% interest in a marble importing company, Hardstuff Ltd; in 20W9 it acquired a 40% interest in a competitor, Landscapes Ltd; and on 1 January 20X7 it acquired a 75% interest in Garden Furniture Designs. The draft consolidated accounts for the Topiary Group are as follows.

DRAFT CONSOLIDATED PROFIT AND LOSS ACCOUNT
FOR THE YEAR ENDED 31 DECEMBER 20X7

	£'000	£'000
Group operating profit		4,455
Share of operating profit in associates		1,485
Income from fixed asset investment		465
Interest payable (group)		(450)
Profit on ordinary activities before taxation		5,955
Tax on profit on ordinary activities		
Corporation tax	1,308	
Deferred taxation	312	
Tax attributable to income of associated undertakings	435	
		(2,055)
Profit on ordinary activities after taxation		3,900
Minority interests		(300)
Profit for the financial year		3,600
Dividends paid and proposed		(1,200)
Retained profit for the year		2,400

DRAFT CONSOLIDATED BALANCE SHEET
AS AT 31 DECEMBER

	20X6		*20X7*	
	£'000	£'000	£'000	£'000
Fixed assets				
Tangible assets				
Buildings at net book value		6,600		6,225
Machinery: cost	4,200		9,000	
aggregate depreciation	(3,300)		(3,600)	
net book value		900		5,400
		7,500		11,625
Investments in associated undertaking		3,000		3,300
Fixed asset investments		1,230		1,230
		11,730		16,155
Current assets				
Stocks		3,000		5,925
Trade debtors		3,825		5,550
Cash		5,460		13,410
		12,285		24,885

	20X6	20X7
	£'000	£'000
Creditors: amounts falling due within one year		
Trade creditors	840	1,500
Obligations under finance leases	600	720
Corporation tax	651	1,386
Dividends	600	900
Accrued interest and finance charges	90	120
	2,781	4,626
Net current assets		
Total assets less current liabilities	9,504	20,259
Creditors: amounts falling due after more than one year	21,234	36,414
Obligations under finance leases	510	2,130
Loans	1,500	4,380
Provisions for liabilities		
Deferred taxation	39	90
Net assets	19,185	29,814
Capital and reserves		
Called up share capital in 25p shares	6,000	11,820
Share premium account	6,285	8,649
Profit and loss account	6,900	9,000
Total shareholders' equity	19,185	29,469
Minority interest	-	345
	19,185	29,814

Notes

1 There had been no acquisitions or disposals of buildings during the year.

Machinery costing £1.5m was sold for £1.5m resulting in a profit of £300,000. New machinery was acquired in 20X7 including additions of £2.55m acquired under finance leases.

2 *Information relating to the acquisition of Garden Furniture Designs*

	£'000
Machinery	495
Stocks	96
Trade debtors	84
Cash	336
Trade creditors	(204)
Corporation tax	(51)
	756
Minority interest	(189)
	567
Goodwill	300
	867
2,640,000 shares issued as part consideration	825
Balance of consideration paid in cash	42
	867

It is group policy to write off goodwill to reserves.

3 Loans were issued at a discount in 20X7 and the carrying amount of the loans at 31 December 20X7 included £120,000 representing the finance cost attributable to the discount and allocated in respect of the current reporting period.

Required

Prepare a consolidated cash flow statement for the Topiary Group for the year ended 31 December 20X7 as required by FRS 1 (revised) with supporting notes for the following.

(a) Reconciliation of operating profit to net cash flow from operating activities

(b) Analysis of cash flows netted in the cash flow statement
(c) Analysis of changes in net debt

Answer

(a) TOPIARY PLC
CONSOLIDATED CASH FLOW STATEMENT
FOR THE YEAR ENDED 31 DECEMBER 20X7

	Note	£'000	£'000
Cash flows from operating activities	1		1,116
Dividend received from associate (W2)	1		750
Returns on investments and servicing of finance	2		21
Taxation (W9)			(885)
Capital expenditure and financial investment	2		(1,755)
Acquisitions and disposals	2		294
Equity dividends paid (600 + 1,200 – 900)			(900)
Cash outflow before financing			(1,359)
Financing	2		
Issue of shares		7,359	
Increase in debt		1,950	
			9,309
Increase in cash in the period			7,950
Reconciliation of net cash flow to movement in net funds	3		
Increase in cash in the period			7,950
Cash inflow from loan issue			(2,760)
Capital element of finance lease instalments			810
Movement resulting from cash flows			6,000
Non-cash movements			
Accretion of finance costs			(120)
Additions to fixed assets under finance leases			(2,550)
Movement in net funds in period			3,330
Net funds at 1.1.X7			2,850
Net funds at 31.12.X7			6,180

NOTES TO THE CASH FLOW STATEMENT

1 *Reconciliation of operating profit to operating cash flows*

	£'000	£'000
Operating profit		4,455
Depreciation charges (W1)		975
Profit on sale of machinery		(300)
Increase in stocks (5,925 – 3,000 – 96)		(2,829)
Increase in debtors (5,500 – 3,825 – 84)		(1,641)
Increase in creditors (1,500 – 840 – 204)		456
Net cash inflow from operating activities		1,116

2 *Analysis of cash flows for headings netted in the cash flow statement*

	£'000	£'000
Returns on investments and servicing of finance		
Interest paid (W3)*	(300)	
Dividends from fixed asset investment	465	
Dividends paid to minority interest (W4)	(144)	
		21
Capital expenditure and financial investment		
Purchase of tangible fixed assets (W5)	(3,255)	
Sale of tangible fixed assets	1,500	
		(1,755)
Acquisitions and disposals		
Purchase of subsidiary undertaking		
Cash received on acquisition		336
Less cash consideration		(42)
Cash inflow		(294)

	£'000	£'000
Financing		
Issue of ordinary share capital (W6)		7,359
Debt due beyond a year (W7)	2,760	
Capital element of finance lease rental payments (W8)	(810)	
		1,950
		9,309

* There is not sufficient information in the question to identify separately interest on finance leases.

3 *Analysis of changes in net funds*

	At 1 Jan 20X7	*Cash flow*	*Other changes*	*At 31 Dec 20X7*
	£'000	£'000	£'000	£'000
Cash at bank	5,460	7,950	-	13,410
Debt due > 1yr	(1,500)	(2,760)	(120)	(4,380)
Finance leases	(1,110)	810	(2,550)	(2,850)
	-	(1,950)		-
	2,850	6,000	(2,670)	6,810

Workings

1 *Depreciation charges*

	£'000	£'000
Freehold buildings (6,600 – 6,225)		375
Plant		
Closing balance	3,600	
Opening balance	3,300	
	300	
Depreciation on disposal	300	
		600
		975

2 *Dividends from associates*

	£'000	£'000
Opening balance		3,000
Share of profit	1,485	
Taxation	(435)	
		1,050
		4,050
Closing balance		3,300
		750

3 *Interest*

	£'000
Accrued interest b/f	90
P & L account	450
Discount	(120)
Less accrued interest c/f	(120)
	300

4 *Minority interests*

	£'000
Opening balance	-
Profit for year	300
On acquisition	189
	489
Closing balance	(345)
Cash outflow	144

5 *Purchase of tangible fixed assets: machinery*

	£'000	£'000
Cost at 31 December 20X7		9,000
Cost at 1 January 20X7		4,200
		4,800
Disposal		1,500
		6,300
On acquisition	495	
Leased	2,550	
		(3,045)
Cash outflow		3,255

6 *Issue of ordinary share capital*

	£'000	£'000
Closing balance		
Shares	11,820	
Premium	8,649	
		20,469
Non-cash consideration		
Shares	660	
Premium	165	
		(825)
Opening balance		
Shares	6,000	
Premium	6,285	
		(12,285)
Cash inflow		7,359

7 *Issue of loan stock*

	£'000
Closing balance	4,380
Opening balance	1,500
	2,880
Finance cost	120
Cash inflow	2,760

8 *Capital payments under leases*

	£'000	£'000
Opening balances		
Current		600
Long-term		510
		1,110
New lease commitment		2,550
Closing balances		
Current	720	
Long-term	2,130	
		(2,850)
Cash outflow		810

9 *Taxation*

	£'000	£'000
Opening balance		
Corporation tax	651	
Deferred tax	39	
		690
Profit and loss account transfer (1,308 + 312)		1,620
Closing balances		
Corporation tax	1,386	
Deferred tax	90	
		(1,476)
		834
On acquisition		51
Cash outflow		885

3 FOREIGN EXCHANGE AND CASH FLOW STATEMENTS

Individual companies

3.1 Receipts and payments should be translated into the reporting currency at the **rate ruling** at the date on which the receipt or payment is made.

Exchange differences **do not give rise to cash flows** and therefore they would not be reflected in the cash flow statement.

Group companies

3.2 The main problems relating to foreign exchange differences are when dealing with the cash flows of an overseas subsidiary. FRS 1 requires that all cash flows relating to an overseas subsidiary be translated into sterling using the **same exchange rate** as is used for the translation of the subsidiary's P&L account. Where the net investment method has been used to consolidate the subsidiary's results (as will be the case most of the time) then the subsidiary's cash flows will be translated using either the average or the closing rate.

3.3 If the **closing rate** is used, then the group cash flow statement can be prepared by using only the opening and closing group balance sheets. If the **average rate** is used, then merely using the balance sheets would not be appropriate as the resulting cash flow statement would not comply with FRS 1, some items being translated at the closing rate. The practical answer to this problem is to use the following method (which would be time consuming in practice).

Step 1. Produce a cash flow statement for each subsidiary.

Step 2. Translate each into sterling using the average rate.

Step 3. Consolidate them into the group cash flow statement (after eliminating inter-company items).

3.4 The other main point to note is that the exchange differences on translation must be **analysed into their constituent parts**, namely fixed assets, debtors, cash, creditors and minority interests and so forth. You may be asked to perform this exercise in the examination although, in the example shown below, the split is given.

Hedging transactions

3.5 Cash flows that result from a transaction undertaken to hedge another should be reported under the **same standard heading** as the transaction which is the subject of that hedge. This does *not* apply to hedging investments in foreign subsidiaries.

3.6 EXAMPLE: FOREIGN CURRENCY TRANSLATION

The draft balance sheets and P&L account of Guinevere plc are as follows.

CONSOLIDATED BALANCE SHEETS
AS AT 31 DECEMBER

	20X2	20X1
	£'000	£'000
Fixed assets		
Tangible assets	32,907	22,926
Investments	6,300	6,300
	39,207	29,226
Current assets		
Stock	21,735	18,300
Debtors	19,230	21,633
Cash in bank and in hand	2,859	495
	43,824	40,428
Creditors: amounts falling due within one year		
Trade creditors	5,760	5,070
Dividend payable by Guinevere plc	801	720
Dividend payable to minority	225	180
Corporation tax	8,232	8,454
	15,018	14,424
Net current assets	28,806	26,004
Creditors: amounts falling due after more than one year		
Loans	3,006	4,230
Minority interest	7,557	5,991
	57,450	45,009

	20X2	20X1
	£'000	£'000
Capital and reserves		
Called up share capital	15,000	15,000
Share premium	9,000	9,000
Profit and loss account	33,450	21,009
	57,450	45,009

There were no fixed asset disposals during the year. The depreciation charge for the year was £5,931,000. There were no fixed asset creditors at either year end.

Debtors as at 31 December 20X2 include called up share capital not paid of £3,705,000 (20X1: £8,238,000).

DRAFT CONSOLIDATED PROFIT AND LOSS ACCOUNT
FOR THE YEAR ENDED 31 DECEMBER 20X2

	£'000
Group operating profit	20,865
Income from fixed asset investments	192
Interest payable	522
Group profit before tax	20,535
Tax: corporation tax	8,490
tax credits on dividends	48
Group profit after tax	11,997
Minority interest	678
Profit attributable to members of Guinevere plc	11,319
Dividends	1,800
Retained profit	9,519
Reserves as at 1 January 20X1	21,009
Exchange gain on translation (note 1)	4,068
Exchange loss on loan	(1,146)
Reserves as at 31 December 20X2	33,450

Note: exchange gain

The exchange gain on translation is made up as follows.

	£'000
Fixed assets	3,684
Stocks	1,179
Debtors	633
Cash	117
Creditors	(189)
Minority interest	(1,356)
	4,068

Required

Prepare the group cash flow statement for Guinevere plc for the year ended 31 December 20X2, in accordance with FRS 1 (revised).

3.7 SOLUTION

CASH FLOW STATEMENT FOR THE YEAR ENDED 31 DECEMBER 20X2

	Note	£'000	£'000
Operating activities	1		23,544
Returns on investments and servicing of finance			
Interest paid		(522)	
Dividends received		144	
Dividends paid to minority interest			
(5,991 + 180 + 678 + 1,356 – 7,557 – 225)		(423)	
Taxation			
Corporation tax paid (8,454 + 8,490 – 8,232)			(8,712)
Capital expenditure			
Payments to acquire tangible fixed assets			
(5,931 + 32,907 – 22,926 – 3,684)			(12,228)
Equity dividends paid (720 + 1,800 – 801)			(1,719)
Financing			
Proceeds of share issue		4,533	
Repayment of loans		(2,370)	
			2,163
Increase in cash			2,247

Reconciliation of net cash flows to movements in net debt (note 2)

	£'000
Increase in cash in the period	2,247
Cash outflow from decrease in debt	78
Change in net debt resulting from cash flows	2,325
Translation difference	1,263
Movement in net debt in period	3,568
Net debt at 1.1.X2	(3,735)
Net debt at 31.12.X2	(147)

NOTES TO THE CASH FLOW STATEMENT

1 *Reconciliation of operating profit to net cash inflow from operating activities*

	£'000
Operating profit	20,865
Depreciation	5,931
Increase in stocks (21,735 – 18,300 – 1,179)	(2,256)
Increase in debtors (19,230 – 3,705 – 21,633 + 8,238 – 633)	(1,497)
Increase in creditors (5,760 – 5,070 – 189)	501
	23,544

2 *Analysis of net debt*

	At 1.1.X2	*Cash flows*	*Exchange movement*	*At 31.12.X2*
	£'000	£'000	£'000	£'000
Cash in hand	495	2,247	117	2,859
Debt due > 1 year	(4,230)	78	1,146	(3,006)
Net debt	(3,735)	2,325	1,263	(147)

An analysis of the cash flow statement above shows that a major inflow of cash relates to the proceeds of a share issue even though the called up share capital has not altered, because it was called up but not paid at the beginning of the year and therefore included in debtors.

Chapter roundup

- You must be able to produce a **single company cash flow statement**. You should also know the scope, formats and definitions given in FRS 1 (revised).
- **Consolidated cash flows** should not present a great problem if you understand how to deal with acquisitions and disposals of subsidiaries, minority interests and dividends.
- A **foreign exchange difference** in a group cash flow statement must be analysed into its constituent parts.

Quick quiz

1 List the standard headings of a cash flow statement under the revised FRS 1.

2 How should an acquisition or disposal of a subsidiary be shown in the cash flow statement?

3 How should an associate be reported in the cash flow statement?

4 What is the net cash inflow from financing giving the following?

Receipts	£	*Payments*	£
Share issue	5,000	Loan repayments	2,200
Loan	9,000	Expense of share issue	500

Included in loan repayments are £300 interest.

5 Extracts from Net Ltd accounts are given below.

	20X9	*20X8*
	£'000	£'000
Current assets		
Treasury bills	140	120
Cash	40	30
Creditors after one year:		
Debenture loans	200	500
Ordinary share capital	200	100
Share premium account	120	20

What amount will be shown as the change in net debt for the year from 20X8 to 20X9?

Answers to quick quiz

1 See Knowledge Brought Forward box.

2 A note to the cash flow statement should show a summary of the effects of acquisitions and disposals of subsidiary undertakings indicating how much of the consideration comprised cash.

3 Only the actual cash flows from sales or purchases between the group and the associate, and investment in and dividends from the entity should be included.

4

		£'000
Inflows:	Issue	5,000
	Loan	9,000
		14,000
Outflows:	Shares expenses	(500)
	Loan repayments (net of interest)	(1,900)
		11,600

5

	£'000
Cash inflow	10
Cash used to acquire liquid resources	20
Cash used to repurchase debentures	300
	330

Now try the questions below from the Exam Question Bank

Number	Level	Marks	Time
Q12	Exam	25	45 mins
Q13	Introductory	n/a	n/a
Q14	Exam	25	45 mins

Part C

Preparation of reports

Chapter 9

SHARE VALUATION

Topic list		Syllabus reference
1	Reasons for share valuations	3(a)
2	Methods of valuing shares	3(a)

Introduction

This chapter calls on knowledge and techniques from **financial management**. Most of the methods available for calculating share valuations use the earnings basis and the asset value basis. However, some of the different methods mentioned here may be appropriate for given situations. Refer to your financial management study material for further guidance.

Study guide

Section 23 – Preparation of reports 1

- Calculating and appraising a range of acceptable values for shares in an unquoted company
- Advising a client on the purchase of a business entity

Exam guide

This topic is relevant to the client advisory role that the examiner for this paper sets great store by. For example, when advising a client on whether to accept a takeover bid, the accountant must be able to produce a relevant share calculation.

1 REASONS FOR SHARE VALUATIONS

1.1 It may be wondered why, given quoted share prices on the Stock Exchange, there is any need to devise techniques for estimating the value of a share. A share valuation will be necessary in various cases.

(a) **For quoted companies,** when there is a takeover bid and the offer price is an estimated 'fair value' in excess of the current market price of the shares

(b) **For unquoted companies,** when:

  (i) The company wishes to 'go public' and must fix an issue price for its shares
  (ii) There is a scheme of merger, and each company's shares must be assessed
  (iii) Shares are sold
  (iv) Shares need to be valued for the purposes of taxation
  (v) Shares are pledged as collateral for a loan

(c) **For subsidiary companies,** when the group's holding company is negotiating the sale of the subsidiary to a management buyout team or to an external buyer

1.2 Valuing **unquoted companies** presents some special considerations.

(a) It may not be sensible to use P/E ratios of a quoted company for comparative purposes because the market value of a quoted company is likely to include a premium to reflect the marketability of its shares.

(b) A small unquoted company may be highly sensitive to the loss of key employees which may follow a merger or buyout. An arrangement of tie key employees in to the enterprise could be very costly.

1.3 Our main interest is with methods of valuing the **entire equity** in a company, perhaps for the purpose of making a takeover bid, rather than with the value of small blocks of shares which an investor might choose to buy or sell on the stock market or, in the case of unquoted companies, privately.

2 METHODS OF VALUING SHARES 6/03

2.1 The most common methods of valuing shares are as follows.

(a) Earnings (P/E ratio)
(b) Accounting rate of return
(c) Net assets
(d) Dividend yield
(e) Use of the CAPM
(f) Super-profits
(g) DCF-based valuations

Each method will give a different share valuation.

2.2 It is unlikely that one method would be used in isolation. **Several valuations** are made using different techniques or assumptions. The valuations can then be compared, and a final price reached as a compromise between the different values.

Issues in share valuation

2.3 The method(s) of valuation chosen will depend on a variety of issues.

(a) Is the company a **going-concern**? If not, only a break-up valuation is required, future earnings are irrelevant; the value of net assets is important.

(b) From which **perspective** are you viewing the valuation (buyer's or seller's)? If it is the buyer the lowest possible value should be used as a starting point, if the seller then **vice versa**.

(c) What **percentage of share capital** is to be bought or sold? A premium will usually be required for a participating interest (>20%) and a greater premium for a controlling interest (>50%). For a controlling interest the ability to sell the assets of the company means both net assets and earnings will be of great interest. But bear in mind that a small holding can be key when its sale could give another shareholder control or more power.

(d) Is the company **quoted**? A private company will usually be valued at a discount against a similar quoted company due to the lack of marketability of its shares.

(e) How **marketable** is the share? This can have an impact on the method applied and the solution.

The P/E ratio (earnings) method of valuation

2.4 This is a common method of **valuing a controlling interest** in a company, where the owner can decide on dividend and retentions policy. The P/E ratio relates earnings per share to a share's value.

$$\text{Since P/E ratio} = \frac{\text{Market value}}{\text{EPS}}$$

$$\text{Market value} = \text{EPS} \times \text{P/E ratio}$$

2.5 The concept of the P/E ratio can be used to make an earnings-based valuation of shares. This is done by deciding a **suitable P/E ratio** and multiplying this by the EPS for the shares which are being valued. The EPS could be historical or prospective.

2.6 For a given EPS figure, a higher P/E ratio will result in a higher price. A **high P/E ratio** may indicate various factors.

(a) **Expectations** that the EPS will grow rapidly in the years to come, so that a high price is being paid for future profit prospects. Many small, but successful and fast-growing companies are valued on the stock market on a high P/E ratio.

(b) **Security of earnings**: a well-established low-risk company would be valued on a higher P/E ratio than a similar company whose earnings are subject to greater uncertainty.

(c) **Status**: if a quoted company made a share-for-share takeover bid for an unquoted company, it would normally expect its own shares to be valued on a higher P/E ratio than the target company's shares. This is because a quoted company ought to be a lower-risk company; but in addition, there is a clear advantage in having shares which are quoted on a stock market: the shares can be readily sold. As a general guideline, the P/E ratio of an unquoted company's shares might be around 50% to 60% of the P/E ratio of a similar public company with a full Stock Exchange listing (and perhaps 70% of that of a company whose shares are traded on the AIM).

2.7 EXAMPLE: P/E RATIO OF VALUATION

Spider plc is considering the takeover of an unquoted company, Fly Ltd. Spider's shares are quoted on the Stock Exchange at a price of £3.20 and since the most recent published EPS of the company is 20p, the company's P/E ratio is 16. Fly Ltd is a company with 100,000 shares and current earnings of £50,000, 50p per share. How might Spider plc decide on an offer price?

2.8 SOLUTION

The decision about the offer price is likely to be based on deciding first of all what a reasonable P/E ratio would be.

(a) If Fly Ltd is in the same industry as Spider plc, its P/E ratio ought to be lower, because of its lower status as an unquoted company.

(b) If Fly Ltd is in a different industry, a suitable P/E ratio might be based on the P/E ratio that is typical for quoted companies in that industry.

(c) If Fly Ltd is thought to be growing fast, so that its EPS will rise rapidly in the years to come, the P/E ratio that should be used for the share valuation will be higher than if only small EPS growth is expected.

(d) If the acquisition of Fly Ltd would contribute substantially to Spider's own profitability and growth, or to any other strategic objective that Spider has, then Spider should be willing to offer a higher P/E ratio valuation, in order to secure acceptance of the offer by Fly's shareholders.

Of course, the P/E ratio on which Spider bases its offer will probably be lower than the P/E ratio that Fly's shareholders think their shares ought to be valued on. Some haggling over the price might be necessary.

(a) Spider might decide that Fly's shares ought to be valued on a P/E ratio of 60% × 16 = 9.6, that is, at 9.6 × 50p = £4.80 each.

(b) Fly's shareholders might reject this offer, and suggest a valuation based on a P/E ratio of, say, 12.5, that is, 12.5 × 50p = £6.25.

(c) Spider's management might then come back with a revised offer, say valuation on a P/E ratio of 10.5, that is, 10.5 × 50p = £5.25.

The haggling will go on until the negotiations either break down, or succeed in arriving at an agreed price.

2.9 When a company is thinking of acquiring an **unquoted company** in a takeover, the final offer price will be agreed by negotiation, but a list of some of the factors affecting the valuer's choice of P/E ratio is given below.

(a) General economic and financial **conditions**.

(b) The type of **industry** and the prospects of that industry.

(c) The **size** of the undertaking and its status within its industry. If an unquoted company's earnings are growing annually and are currently around £300,000 or so, then it could probably get a quote in its own right on the AIM and a higher P/E ratio should therefore be used when valuing its shares.

(d) **Marketability**: the market in shares which do not have a Stock Exchange quotation is always a restricted one and a higher yield is therefore required. As noted above, for examination purposes you should normally take a figure around one half to two thirds of the industry average when valuing an unquoted company.

(e) The **diversity of shareholdings** and the financial status of any principal shareholders.

(f) The **reliability** of profit estimates and the past profit record.

(g) **Asset backing** and liquidity.

(h) The **nature of the assets**, eg whether some of the fixed assets are of a highly specialised nature, and so have only a small break-up value.

(i) **Gearing**: a relatively high gearing ratio will generally mean greater financial risk for ordinary shareholders and call for a higher rate of return on equity.

(j) The extent to which the business is dependent on the technical skills of one or more **individuals**.

Exam focus point

In an exam question you might be asked to adjust earnings to reflect expected results post-acquisition and then apply a P/E ratio.

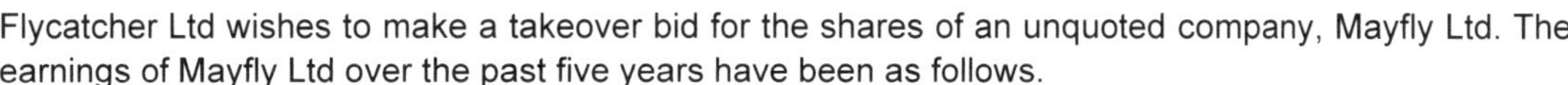

Question: share valuations

Flycatcher Ltd wishes to make a takeover bid for the shares of an unquoted company, Mayfly Ltd. The earnings of Mayfly Ltd over the past five years have been as follows.

20X0	£50,000	20X3	£71,000
20X1	£72,000	20X4	£75,000
20X2	£68,000		

The average P/E ratio of quoted companies in the industry in which Mayfly Ltd operates is 10. Quoted companies which are similar in many respects to Mayfly Ltd are:

(a) Bumblebee plc, which has a P/E ratio of 15, but is a company with very good growth prospects;

(b) Wasp plc, which has had a poor profit record for several years, and has a P/E ratio of 7.

What would be a suitable range of valuations for the shares of Mayfly Ltd?

Answer

(a) *Earnings.* Average earnings over the last five years have been £67,200, and over the last four years £71,500. There might appear to be some growth prospects, but estimates of future earnings are uncertain.

A low estimate of earnings in 20X5 would be, perhaps, £71,500.

A high estimate of earnings might be £75,000 or more. This solution will use the most recent earnings figure of £75,000 as the high estimate.

(b) *P/E ratio.* A P/E ratio of 15 (Bumblebee's) would be much too high for Mayfly Ltd, because the growth of Mayfly Ltd earnings is not as certain, and Mayfly Ltd is an unquoted company.

On the other hand, Mayfly Ltd's expectations of earnings are probably better than those of Wasp plc. A suitable P/E ratio might be based on the industry's average, 10; but since Mayfly is an unquoted company and therefore more risky, a lower P/E ratio might be more appropriate: perhaps 60% to 70% of 10 = 6 or 7, or conceivably even as low as 50% of 10 = 5.

The valuation of Mayfly Ltd's shares might therefore range between:

(i) high P/E ratio and high earnings: 7 × £75,000 = £525,000; and
(ii) low P/E ratio and low earnings: 5 × £71,500 = £357,500.

2.10 When one company is thinking about taking over another, it should look at the target company's **forecast earnings**, not just its historical results. Forecasts of the future earnings of a target company might be attempted by managers in the company which is planning to make the takeover bid. Quite commonly, however, the management of the predator company will make an initial approach to the board of directors of the target company, to sound them out about a possible takeover bid. If the target company's directors are amenable to a bid, they might agree to produce forecasts of their company's future earnings and growth. These forecasts (for the next year and possibly even further ahead) might then be used by the predator company in choosing an offer price.

2.11 Forecasts of earnings growth should **only be used** if:

(a) There are good reasons to believe that earnings growth will be achieved
(b) A reasonable estimate of growth can be made
(c) Any forecasts supplied by the target company's board of directors are made in good faith

2.12 There are **problems** with using price earnings multiples.

(a) The calculation of the earnings figure is arbitrary.
(b) Selecting a suitable P/E ratio is difficult.
(c) Any discounting of the selected P/E ratio of a quoted company is to an extent arbitrary.

The accounting rate of return (ARR) method of share valuation

2.13 This method considers the accounting rate of return which will be **required from the company** whose shares are to be valued. It is therefore distinct from the P/E ratio method, which is concerned with the market rate of return required. The following formula should be used.

$$\text{Value} = \frac{\text{Estimated future profits}}{\text{Required return on capital employed}}$$

2.14 For a takeover bid valuation, it will often be necessary to **adjust the profits figure** to allow for expected changes after the takeover. Those arising in an examination question might include:

(a) New levels of **directors' remuneration**

(b) New levels of **interest charges** (perhaps because the predator company will be able to replace existing loans with new loans at a lower rate of interest, or because the previous owners had lent the company money at non-commercial rates)

(c) A charge for **notional rent** where it is intended to sell existing properties or where the rate of return used is based on the results of similar companies that do not own their own properties

(d) The effects of **product rationalisation** and **improved management**

2.15 EXAMPLE: ARR METHOD OF SHARE VALUATION

Chambers Ltd is considering acquiring Hall Ltd. At present Hall Ltd is earning, on average, £480,000 after tax. The directors of Chambers Ltd feel that after reorganisation, this figure could be increased to £600,000. All the companies in the Chambers group are expected to yield a post-tax accounting return of 15% on capital employed. What should Hall Ltd be valued at?

2.16 SOLUTION

$$\text{Valuation} = \frac{£600{,}000}{15\%} = £4{,}000{,}000$$

This figure is the maximum that Chambers should be prepared to pay. The first offer would probably be much lower.

2.17 An ARR valuation might be used in a takeover when the acquiring company is trying to assess the **maximum amount** it can afford to pay. This is because it is a measure of management efficiency and the rate used can be selected to reflect (among other things) the return which the acquiring company thinks should be obtainable after any post-acquisition reorganisation has been completed. A valuation on this basis should then be compared with the stock market price (for quoted companies) or a price arrived at using the P/E ratio of similar quoted companies.

2.18 There are **problems** associated with this method of valuation.

(a) It is difficult to calculate an accurate figure for post-acquisition profits, having taken into account the changing cost profile following the takeover.

(b) The method does not take account of future growth in profits.

The net assets method of share valuation

2.19 Using this method of valuation, the value of a share in a particular class is equal to the **net tangible assets** attributable to that class, divided by the number of shares in the class. Intangible assets (including goodwill) should be excluded, unless they have a market value (for example patents and copyrights, which could be sold).

(a) Goodwill, if shown in the accounts, is unlikely to be shown at a true figure for purposes of valuation, and the value of goodwill should be reflected in another method of valuation (for example the earnings basis, the dividend yield basis or the super-profits method).

(b) Development expenditure, if shown in the accounts, would also have a value which is related to future profits rather than to the worth of the company's physical assets.

2.20 EXAMPLE: NET ASSETS METHOD OF SHARE VALUATION

The balance sheet of Cactus Ltd is as follows.

	£	£
Fixed assets		
Land and buildings		160,000
Plant and machinery		80,000
Motor vehicles		20,000
		260,000
Goodwill		20,000
		280,000
Current assets		
Stocks	80,000	
Debtors	60,000	
Short-term investments	15,000	
Cash	5,000	
	160,000	
Current liabilities		
Creditors	60,000	
Taxation	20,000	
Proposed ordinary dividend	20,000	
	100,000	
Net current assets		60,000
		340,000
12% debentures		60,000
Deferred taxation		10,000
		270,000
Capital and reserves		
Ordinary shares of £1		80,000
Reserves		140,000
		220,000
4.9% preference shares of £1		50,000
		270,000

What is the value of an ordinary share using the net assets basis of valuation?

2.21 SOLUTION

If the figures given for asset values are not questioned, the valuation would be as follows.

	£	£
Total value of net assets		340,000
Less intangible asset (goodwill)		20,000
Total value of tangible assets (net)		320,000
Less: preference shares	50,000	
debentures	60,000	
deferred taxation	10,000	
		120,000
Net asset value of equity		200,000
Number of ordinary shares		80,000
Value per share		£2.50

2.22 The difficulty in an asset valuation method is establishing the **asset values to use**. Values ought to be realistic. The figure attached to an individual asset may vary considerably depending on whether it is valued on a going concern or a break-up basis.

2.23 The following list should give you some idea of the **factors** that must be considered.

(a) Do the assets need **professional valuation**? If so, how much will this cost?

(b) Have the **liabilities** been accurately quantified, eg deferred taxation? Are there any contingent liabilities? Will any balancing tax charges arise on disposal?

(c) How have the **current assets** been valued? Are all debtors collectable? Is all stock realisable? Can all the assets be physically located and brought into a saleable condition? This may be difficult in certain circumstances where the assets are situated abroad.

(d) Can any **hidden liabilities** be accurately assessed? Would there be redundancy payments and closure costs?

(e) Is there an **available market** in which the assets can be realised (on a break-up basis)? If so, do the balance sheet values truly reflect these break-up values?

(f) Are there any **prior charges** on the assets?

2.24 The net assets basis of valuation should be used in the following circumstances.

(a) **As a measure of the 'security' in a share value**. A share might be valued using the earnings basis, and this valuation might be:

   (i) Higher than the net asset value per share. If the company went into liquidation, the investor could not expect to receive the full value of his shares when the underlying assets were realised

   (ii) Lower than the net asset value per share. If the company went into liquidation, the investor might expect to receive the full value of his shares (perhaps much more) when the underlying assets were realised

   The asset backing for shares thus provides a measure of the possible loss if the company fails to make the expected earnings or dividend payments. It is often thought to be a good thing to acquire a company with valuable tangible assets, especially freehold property which might be expected to increase in value over time.

(b) **As a measure of comparison in a scheme of merger**. For example, if company A, which has a low asset backing, is planning a merger with company B, which has a high asset backing, the shareholders of B might consider that their shares' value ought to reflect this. It might therefore be agreed that something should be added to the value of the company B shares to allow for this difference in asset backing.

For these reasons, it is always advisable to calculate the net assets per share.

The dividend yield method of share valuation

2.25 The dividend yield method of share valuation is suitable for the valuation of **small shareholdings in unquoted companies.** It is based on the principle that small shareholders are mainly interested in dividends, since they cannot control decisions affecting the company's profits and earnings. A suitable offer price would therefore be one which compensates them for the future dividends they will be giving up if they sell their shares. You might be expected to value shares using gross dividend yield rather than net dividend yield. Read any examination question carefully.

2.26 The simplest dividend capitalisation technique is based on the assumption that the level of dividends in the future will be **constant**. A dividend yield valuation would be:

$$\text{Value} = \frac{\text{Dividend in pence}}{\text{Expected dividend yield\%}}$$

2.27 It may be possible to use expected future dividends for a share valuation and to predict **dividend growth**. For this purpose, it is first necessary to predict future earnings and then to decide how changes in earnings will be reflected in the company's dividend policy.

2.28 The **dividend growth model** for share valuation, you may recall from your other studies, is as follows.

$$MV = \frac{d_0(1+g)}{(r-g)}$$

where	MV	is the current market value ex-dividend
	d_0	is the current dividend
	g	is the expected annual growth in dividend, so
	$d_0(1 + g)$	is the expected dividend next year
	r	is the return required

2.29 There are **problems** with these methods of share valuation.

(a) Predicting future earnings and hence dividends.

(b) Calculating an appropriate discount rate. An investor may be prepared to accept a lower rate of return where he achieves significant influence (>20%), or where he can block the company on special resolutions (>25%).

The CAPM and share price valuations

2.30 The CAPM might be used to value shares, particularly when pricing shares for a **stock market listing**. The CAPM would be used to establish a required equity yield.

2.31 EXAMPLE: CAPM AND SHARE PRICE VALUATIONS

Suppose that Mackerel plc is planning to obtain a Stock Exchange listing by offering 40% of its existing shares to the public. No new shares will be issued. Its most recent summarised results are as follows.

	£
Turnover	120,000,000
Earnings	1,500,000
Number of shares = 3,000,000	

The company has low gearing. It regularly pays 50% of earnings as dividends, and with reinvested earnings is expected to achieve 5% dividend growth each year.

Summarised details of two listed companies in the same industry as Mackerel plc are as follows.

	Salmon plc	*Trout plc*
Gearing (total debt/total equity)	45%	10%
Equity beta	1.50	1.05

The current Treasury bill yield is 7% a year. The average market return is estimated to be 12%. The new shares will be issued at a discount of 15% to the estimated post-issue market price, in order to increase the prospects of success for the share issue.

What will the issue price be?

2.32 SOLUTION

Using the CAPM, we begin by deciding on a suitable β value for Mackerel's equity. We shall assume that since Mackerel's gearing is close to Trout's, a β of 1.05 is appropriate.

The cost of Mackerel equity is 7% + 1.05 (12 – 7)% = 12.25%

This can now be used in the dividend growth model. The dividend this year is 50% of £1,500,000 = £750,000.

The total value of Mackerel's equity is $\dfrac{£750{,}000(1.05)}{(0.1225-0.05)}$ = £10,862,068

There are 3,000,000 shares, giving a market value per share of £3.62.

Since the shares that are offered to the public will be offered at a discount of about 15% to this value, the share price for the market launch should be about 85% of £3.62 = £3.08.

The super-profits method of share valuation

2.33 This method starts by applying a 'fair return' to the net tangible assets and comparing the result with the expected profits. Any **excess of profits** (the super-profits) is used to calculate goodwill.

The goodwill is normally taken as a fixed number of years super-profits. The goodwill is then added to the value of the target company's tangible assets to arrive at a value for the business. Profits should be adjusted for any directors' rewards beyond their value to the business.

2.34 EXAMPLE: SUPER-PROFITS METHOD OF SHARE VALUATION

Light Ltd has net tangible assets of £120,000 and present earnings of £20,000. Doppler Ltd wants to take over Light Ltd and considers that a fair return for this type of industry is 12%, and decides to value Light Ltd taking goodwill at three years super-profits.

2.35 SOLUTION

	£
Actual profits	20,000
Less fair return on net tangible assets: 12% × £120,000	14,400
Super-profits	5,600
Goodwill: 3 × £5,600	£16,800
Value of Light Ltd: £120,000 + £16,800	£136,800

2.36 The principal **drawbacks** to this valuation method are as follows.

(a) The rate of return required is chosen subjectively.

(b) The number of years purchase of super-profits is arbitrary. In the example above, goodwill was valued at three years of super-profits, but it could have been, for example, two years or four years of super-profits.

While this method is unscientific, it is widely used, particularly in the sale of smaller businesses for which there are very often yardsticks set within in a trade.

The discounted future profits method of share valuation

2.37 This method of share valuation may be appropriate when one company intends to **buy the assets** of another company and to make further investments in order to improve profits in the future.

2.38 EXAMPLE: DISCOUNTED FUTURE PROFITS METHOD OF SHARE VALUATION

Diversification Ltd wishes to make a bid for Tadpole Ltd. Tadpole Ltd makes after-tax profits of £40,000 a year. Diversification Ltd believes that if further money is spent on additional investments, the after-tax cash flows (ignoring the purchase consideration) could be as follows.

Year	*Cash flow (net of tax)*
	£
0	(100,000)
1	(80,000)
2	60,000
3	100,000
4	150,000
5	150,000

The after-tax cost of capital of Diversification Ltd is 15% and the company expects all its investments to pay back, in discounted terms, within five years.

What is the maximum price that the company should be willing to pay for the shares of Tadpole Ltd?

2.39 SOLUTION

The maximum price is one which would make the return from the total investment exactly 15% over five years, so that the NPV at 15% would be 0.

Year	*Cash flows ignoring purchase consideration*	*Discount factor*	*Present value*
	£	@ 15%	£
0	(100,000)	1.000	(100,000)
1	(80,000)	0.870	(69,600)
2	60,000	0.756	45,360
3	100,000	0.658	65,800
4	150,000	0.572	85,800
5	150,000	0.497	74,550
Maximum purchase price			101,910

2.40 This method is unusually **unworkable in practice** because of:

(a) the difficulty of predicting future cash flows; and

(b) the problem of choosing an appropriate discount rate.

2.41 Section summary

Which of the above methods you use in an exam depends on the **requirements of the question** and the **circumstances given**. Remember the following points.

- Adjustments to earnings for post-acquisition changes
- Quoted vs unquoted companies
- Availability of information
- Size of shareholding to be acquired (<20%, 20-50%, 50%+)

Question: seven valuations

Black Raven Ltd is a prosperous private company, whose owners are also the directors. The directors have decided to sell their business, and have begun a search for organisations interested in its purchase. They have asked for your assessment of the price per ordinary share a purchaser might be expected to offer.

Relevant information is as follows.

BALANCE SHEET (MOST RELEVANT)

	£'000	£'000
Fixed assets (net book value)		
Land and buildings		800
Plant and equipment		450
Motor vehicles		55
Patents		2
		1,307
Current assets		
Stock	250	
Debtors	125	
Cash	8	
	383	
Current liabilities		
Creditors	180	
Taxation	50	
	230	
Net current assets		153
		1,460
Long-term liability		
Loan secured on property		400
		1,060
Capital and reserves		
Share capital (300,000 ordinary shares of £1)		300
Reserves		760
		1,060

The profits after tax and interest but before dividends over the last five years have been as follows.

		£
Year	1	90,000
	2	80,000
	3	105,000
	4	90,000
	5 (most recent)	100,000

The annual dividend has been £45,000 (gross) for the last six years.

The company's five year plan forecasts an after-tax profit of £100,000 for the next 12 months, with an increase of 4% a year over each of the next four years.

As part of their preparations to sell the company, the directors of Black Raven Ltd have had the fixed assets revalued by an independent expert, with the following results.

	£
Land and buildings	1,075,000
Plant and equipment	480,000
Motor vehicles	45,000

The dividend yields and P/E ratios of three quoted companies in the same industry as Black Raven Ltd over the last three years have been as follows.

	Aardvark plc		*Bullfinch plc*		*Crow plc*	
	Div. yield	*P/E ratio*	*Div. yield*	*P/E ratio*	*Div. yield*	*P/E ratio*
	%		%		%	
Recent year	12	8.50	11.0	9.0	13.0	10.0
Previous year	12	8.00	10.6	8.5	12.6	9.5
Three years ago	12	8.50	9.3	8.0	12.4	9.0
Average	12	8.33	10.3	8.5	12.7	9.5

Large companies in the industry apply an after-tax cost of capital of about 18% to acquisition proposals when the investment is not backed by tangible assets, as opposed to a rate of only 14% on the net tangible assets.

Your assessment of the net cash flows which would accrue to a purchasing company, allowing for taxation and the capital expenditure required after the acquisition to achieve the company's target five year plan, is as follows.

	£
Year 1	120,000
Year 2	120,000
Year 3	140,000
Year 4	70,000
Year 5	120,000

Required

Use the information provided to suggest seven valuations which prospective purchasers might make.

Answer

(a) *An assets basis valuation*

If we assume that a purchaser would accept the revaluation of assets by the independent valuer, an assets valuation of equity would be as follows.

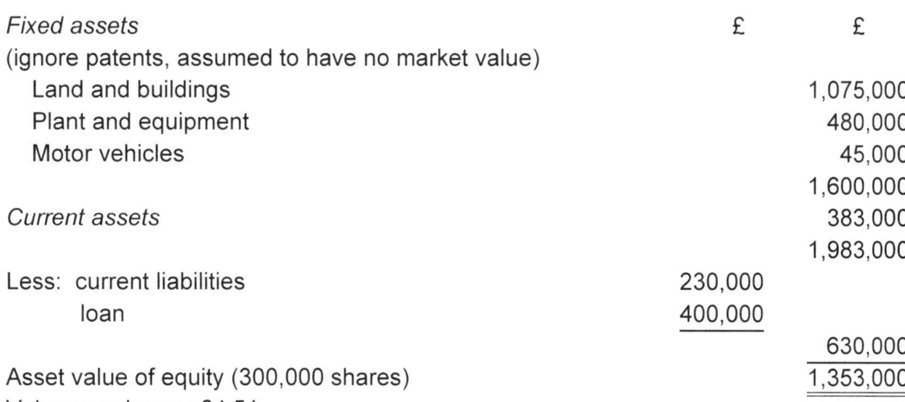

	£	£
Fixed assets		
(ignore patents, assumed to have no market value)		
Land and buildings		1,075,000
Plant and equipment		480,000
Motor vehicles		45,000
		1,600,000
Current assets		383,000
		1,983,000
Less: current liabilities	230,000	
loan	400,000	
		630,000
Asset value of equity (300,000 shares)		1,353,000
Value per share = £4.51		

Unless the purchasing company intends to sell the assets acquired, it is more likely that a valuation would be based on earnings.

(b) *Earnings basis valuations*

If the purchaser believes that earnings over the last five years are an appropriate measure for valuation, we could take average earnings in these years, which were

$$\frac{£465,000}{5} = £93,000$$

An appropriate P/E ratio for an earnings basis valuation might be the average of the three publicly quoted companies for the recent year. (A trend towards an increase in the P/E ratio over three years is assumed, and even though average earnings have been taken, the most recent year's P/E ratios are considered to be the only figures which are appropriate.)

	P/E ratio	
Aardvark plc	8.5	
Bullfinch plc	9.0	
Crow plc	10.0	
Average	9.167	(i)
Reduce by about 40% to allow for unquoted status	5.5	(ii)

Share valuations on a past earnings basis are as follows.

	P/E ratio	*Earnings*	*Valuation*	*Number of shares*	*Value per share*
		£'000	£'000		
(i)	9.167	93	852.5	300,000	£2.84
(ii)	5.5	93	511.5	300,000	£1.71

Because of the unquoted status of Black Raven Ltd, purchasers would probably apply a lower P/E ratio, and an offer of about £1.71 per share would be more likely than one of £2.84.

Future earnings might be used. Forecast earnings based on the company's five year plan will be used.

		£	
Expected earnings:	Year 1	100,000	
	Year 2	104,000	
	Year 3	108,160	
	Year 4	112,486	
	Year 5	116,986	
	Average	108,326.4	(say £108,000)

A share valuations on an expected earnings basis would be as follows.

P/E ratio	*Average future earnings*	*Valuation*	*Value per share*
5.5	£108,000	£594,000	£1.98

It is not clear whether the purchasing company would accept Black Raven's own estimates of earnings.

(c) *A dividend yield basis of valuation with no growth*

There seems to have been a general pattern of increase in dividend yields to shareholders in quoted companies, and it is reasonable to suppose that investors in Black Raven would require at least the same yield.

An average yield for the recent year for the three quoted companies will be used. This is 12%. The only reliable dividend figure for Black Raven Ltd is £45,000 a year gross, in spite of the expected increase in future earnings. A yield basis valuation would therefore be:

$$\frac{£45,000}{12\%} = £375,000 \text{ or } £1.25 \text{ per share.}$$

A purchasing company would, however, be more concerned with earnings than with dividends if it intended to buy the entire company, and an offer price of £1.25 should be considered too low. On the other hand, since Black Raven Ltd is an unquoted company, a higher yield than 12% might be expected.

(d) *A dividend yield basis of valuation, with growth*

Since earnings are expected to increase by 4% a year, it could be argued that a similar growth rate in dividends would be expected. We shall assume that the required yield is 17%, rather more than the 12% for quoted companies because Black Raven Ltd is unquoted. However, in the absence of information about the expected growth of dividends in the quoted companies, the choice of 12%, 17% or whatever, is not much better than a guess.

$$MV = \frac{d_0\,(1+g)}{(r-g)} = \frac{45,000(1.04)}{(0.17-0.04)} = £360,000 \text{ or } £1.20 \text{ per share}$$

(e) *The discounted value of future cash flows*

The present value of cash inflows from an investment by a purchaser of Black Raven Ltd's shares would be discounted at either 18% or 14%, depending on the view taken of Black Raven Ltd's assets. Although the loan of £400,000 is secured on some of the company's property, there are enough assets against which there is no charge to assume that a purchaser would consider the investment to be backed by tangible assets.

The present value of the benefits from the investment would be as follows.

Year	*Cash flow*	*Discount factor*	*PV of cash flow*
	£'000	14%*	£'000
1	120	0.877	105.24
2	120	0.769	92.28
3	140	0.675	94.50
4	70	0.592	41.44
5	120	0.519	62.28
			395.74

* $\frac{1}{1.14}, \frac{1}{(1.14)^2}$ etc

A valuation per share of £1.32 might therefore be made. This basis of valuation is one which a purchasing company ought to consider. It might be argued that cash flows beyond year 5 should be considered and a higher valuation could be appropriate, but a figure of less than £2 per share would be offered on a DCF valuation basis.

(f) *The accounting rate of return method*

If a company wishing to take over Black Raven Ltd expects to make an accounting rate of return of, say, 20%, and assuming that a return of £100,000 is assumed for this purpose the valuation of Black Raven Ltd might be

$\frac{£100,000}{20\%}$ = £500,000, or £1.67 per share.

(g) *The super-profits method*

If we assume that the normal rate of profit is 5% on net assets, the normal profits might be as follows (although 'net assets' could be defined in other ways).

	£
Asset value of equity (see (a))	1,353,000
Add asset value of loan stock	400,000
Net assets	1,753,000
Actual (current) profit	100,000
Less normal profit after taxation (5%)	87,650
Super-profits	12,350
Goodwill (say two years purchase of super-profits)	£24,700

The total purchase consideration for equity would be £1,353,000 + £24,700 = £1,377,700 or £4.59 per share.

(h) *Summary*

Any of the preceding valuations might be made, but since share valuation is largely a subjective matter, many other prices might be offered. In view of the high asset values of the company an asset stripping purchaser might come forward.

Chapter roundup

- There are a number of different ways of putting a value on a business, or on shares in an unquoted company. It makes sense to use **several methods of valuation**, and to compare the values they produce.
- At the end of the day, however, what really matters is the final price that the **buyer and the seller agree.** The purchase price for a company will usually be discussed mainly in terms of:
  - P/E ratios, when a large block of shares, or a whole business is being valued;
  - alternatively, a DCF valuation;
  - to a lesser extent, the net assets per share.
- When advising on the price of a block of shares you must always take into account the **size of the holding** under consideration ie is it 5-10%? >20% or >50%?
- The dividend yield method is more relevant to **small shareholdings**.

Quick quiz

1 Give four circumstances in which the shares of an unquoted company might need to be valued.

2 How is the P/E ratio related to EPS?

3 What is meant by 'multiples' in the context of share valuation?

4 Value = Estimated future profits/Required return on capital employed. What is the name of this valuation model?

Answers to quick quiz

1
- Setting an issue price if the company is floating its shares
- When shares are sold
- For tax purposes
- When shares are pledged as collateral for a loan

2 P/E ratio = Share price/EPS.

3 The P/E ratio: the multiple of earnings at which a company's shares are traded.

4 Accounting rate of return method.

Now try the question below from the Exam Question Bank

Number	Level	Marks	Time
Q15	Exam	25	45 mins

Solution

4 $\frac{7.8p}{(1.12)^4} + \frac{7.8p}{(1.12)^5} + ... = \frac{7.8p}{0.12} \times \frac{1}{(1.12)^3} = \frac{65p}{(1.12)^3}$ = 46.26p, say 46p

Chapter 10

RATIO ANALYSIS

Topic list		Syllabus reference
1	Sources of information and the role of regulation	3(b)
2	The broad categories of ratios	3(b)
3	Profitability and return on capital	3(b)
4	Liquidity and working capital	3(b)
5	Long-term solvency: debt and gearing	3(b)
6	Shareholders' investment ratios	3(b)

Introduction

You should be very familiar with many of the **ratios** discussed in this chapter from your earlier studies. They are covered in full again here, because it is very unusual for a Paper 3.6 exam not to have some financial analysis in it somewhere. Such questions will often draw in more complex matters, which we will look at in the next few chapters.

You must be able to **explain the results** of your analysis in the Paper 3.6 exam: numbers alone are never enough.

Study guide

Section 23 – Preparation of reports 1

- Analysing the impact of accounting policy changes on the value and performance of an entity

1 SOURCES OF INFORMATION AND THE ROLE OF REGULATION

1.1 The accounts of a business are designed to provide users with information about its performance and financial position. The bare figures, however, are not particularly useful and it is only through **comparisons** (usually of ratios) that their significance can be established. Comparisons may be made with previous financial periods, with other similar businesses or with averages for the particular industry. The choice will depend on the purpose for which the comparison is being made and the information that is available.

1.2 Various groups are interested in the performance and financial position of a company.

(a) **Management** will use comparisons to ensure that the business is performing efficiently and according to plan

(b) **Employees,** trade unions and so on

(c) **Government**

(d) Present and potential **investors** assess the company to judge if it is a good investment

(e) **Lenders** and **suppliers** will want to judge its creditworthiness

1.3 This text is concerned with financial rather than management accounting and the ratios discussed here are therefore likely to be calculated by external users. The main sources of information available to external users are:

(a) Published accounts and interim statements
(b) Documents filed at Companies House
(c) Statistics published by the government
(d) Other published sources eg *Investors Chronicle*, *The Economist*, Extel

Financial analysis

1.4 The **lack of detailed information** available to the outsider is a considerable disadvantage in undertaking ratio analysis. The first difficulty is that there may simply be insufficient data to calculate all of the required ratios. A second concerns the availability of a suitable 'yardstick' with which the calculated ratios may be compared.

Inter-temporal analysis

1.5 Looking first at inter-temporal or trend analysis (comparisons for the same business over time), some of the **problems** include:

(a) Changes in the nature of the business
(b) Unrealistic depreciation rates under historical cost accounting
(c) The changing value of the pound
(d) Changes in accounting policies

1.6 Other factors will include changes in government incentive packages, changes from purchasing equipment to leasing and so on.

Cross-sectional analysis

1.7 When undertaking 'cross-sectional' analysis (making comparisons with other companies) the position is even more difficult because of the problem of identifying companies that are comparable. **Comparability** between companies may be impaired because of:

(a) Different degrees of diversification

(b) Different production and purchasing policies (if an investor was analysing the smaller car manufacturers, he would find that some of them buy in engines from one of the 'majors' whilst others develop and manufacture their own)

(c) Different financing policies (eg leasing as opposed to buying)

(d) Different accounting policies (one of the most serious problems particularly in relation to fixed assets and stock valuation)

(e) Different effects of government incentives

1.8 The major **inter-company comparison organisations** (whose results are intended for the use of participating companies and are not generally available) go to considerable length to adjust accounts to comparable bases. The external user will rarely be in a position to make such adjustments. Although the position is now improved by increases in disclosure requirements (especially the more detailed P&L accounts required by CA 1985 and FRS 3), direct comparisons between companies will inevitably, on occasion, continue to give rise to misleading results.

Social and political considerations

1.9 Social considerations tend to be **shortlived** or 'fashionable' and therefore each set of statements can be affected by a different movement or fad. In recent years, the social aspect much in evidence has been that of environmental issues. Companies have gone for a 'green' image, although this has been more in evidence in glossy pictures than in the accounts themselves.

1.10 **Political considerations** have been more far reaching. The new regulatory regime was set up by statute (CA 1989), which was a direct result of UK membership of the EU, and politicians have kept the pressure up after disasters like Polly Peck and BCCI. In general, however, self-regulation is encouraged in the UK through bodies such as the Competition Commission, Stock Exchange and Takeover Panel.

Multinational companies

1.11 Multinational companies have great difficulties sometimes because of the need to comply with **legislation** in a large number of countries. As well as different reporting requirements, different rules of incorporation exist, as well as different directors' rules, tax legislation and so on. Sometimes the local rules can be so harsh that companies will avoid them altogether. In California, for example, multinational companies with operations there are taxed on their *world wide* profits, not just their US profits. Local tax regimes may also require information about the group as a whole because of the impact of internal transfer pricing on tax.

1.12 Different local reporting requirements will also make **consolidation** more difficult. The results of subsidiaries must be translated, not only to the company's base currency, but also using the accounting rules used by head office. This is a requirement in the UK in company law as 'uniform accounting policies' are called for.

The efficient market hypothesis and the Stock Exchange

1.13 It has been argued that the UK and US stock markets are **efficient capital markets**, that is, markets in which:

(a) The prices of securities bought and sold reflect all the relevant information which is available to the buyers and sellers. In other words, share prices change quickly to reflect all new information about future prospects

(b) No individual dominates the market

(c) Transaction costs of buying and selling are not so high as to discourage trading significantly

1.14 If the stock market is efficient, share prices should vary in a **rational way**, ie reflecting the known profits or losses of a company and the state of return required based on interest states.

1.15 Research in both Britain and the USA has suggested that market prices anticipate mergers several months before they are formally announced, and the conclusion drawn is that the stock market in these countries *do* exhibit **semi-strong efficiency**. It has also been argued that the market displays sufficient efficiency for investors to see through 'window dressing' of accounts by companies which use accounting conventions to overstate profits (ie creative accounting).

1.16 Evidence suggests that stock markets show efficiency that is **at least weak form**, but tending more towards a semi-strong form. In other words, current share prices reflect all or most publicly available information about companies and their securities. However, it is very difficult to assess the market's efficiency in relation to shares which are not usually actively traded.

1.17 **Fundamental analysis** and **technical analysis** carried out by analysts and investment managers play an important role in creating an efficient stock market. This is because an efficient market depends on the widespread availability of cheap information about companies, their shares and market conditions, and this is what the firms of market makers and other financial institutions *do* provide for their clients and for the general investing public. In a market which demonstrates strong-form efficiency, such analysis would not identify profitable opportunities, ie where shares are undervalued, because such information would already be known and reflected in the share price.

1.18 On the other hand, the crash of October 1987, in which share prices fell suddenly by 20% to 40% on the world's stock markets, raised serious questions about the validity of the **fundamental theory of share values** and the efficient market hypothesis. If these theories are correct, how can shares that were valued at one level on one day suddenly be worth 40% less the next day, without any change in expectations of corporate profits and dividends? On the other hand, a widely feared crash late in 1989 failed to happen, suggesting that stock markets may not be altogether out of touch with the underlying values of companies.

2 THE BROAD CATEGORIES OF RATIOS

2.1 Ratio analysis involves comparing **one figure against another** to produce a ratio, and assessing whether the ratio indicates a weakness or strength in the company's affairs.

Exam focus point

You are unlikely to be asked to calculate many ratios in the Paper 3.6 exam, or directly at any rate. If, say, you were asked to comment on a company's past or potential future performance, you would be expected to select your own ratios in order to do so. The skill here is picking the key ratios in the context of the question and not calculating a lot of useless ratios.

The broad categories of ratios

2.2 Broadly speaking, basic ratios can be grouped into five categories.

- Profitability and return
- Short-term solvency and liquidity
- Long-term solvency and stability
- Efficiency (turnover ratios)
- Shareholders' investment ratios

2.3 Ratio analysis on its own is **not sufficient** for interpreting company accounts, and that there are other items of information which should be looked at, for example:

(a) **Comments** in the chairman's report, the directors' report and the operating and financial review (see Chapter 1)

(b) The age and nature of the **company's assets**

(c) Current and future **developments** in the company's markets, at home and overseas, recent acquisitions or disposals of a subsidiary by the company

(d) Any other **noticeable features** of the report and accounts, such as post balance sheet events, contingent liabilities, a qualified auditors' report, the company's taxation position, and so on

2.4 The following sections summarise what you already know about ratio analysis from your earlier studies. You should then perform the comprehensive questions given in this chapter. The following three chapters look at more complex areas of analysis and interpretation, which build on the knowledge in this chapter.

Exam focus point

It cannot be emphasised enough that a deeper level of analysis is required for Paper 3.6. You **must** answer the question from the viewpoint of the person needing the ratios - banker, prospective investor/predator.

3 PROFITABILITY AND RETURN ON CAPITAL

3.1 One profit figure that should be calculated and compared over time is **PBIT, profit before interest and tax**, the amount of profit which the company earned before having to pay interest to the providers of loan capital. By providers of loan capital, we usually mean longer-term loan capital, such as debentures and medium-term bank loans, which will be shown in the balance sheet as 'creditors: amounts falling due after more than one year'. Also, tax is affected by unusual variations which have a distorting effect.

3.2 Profit before interest and tax is therefore:

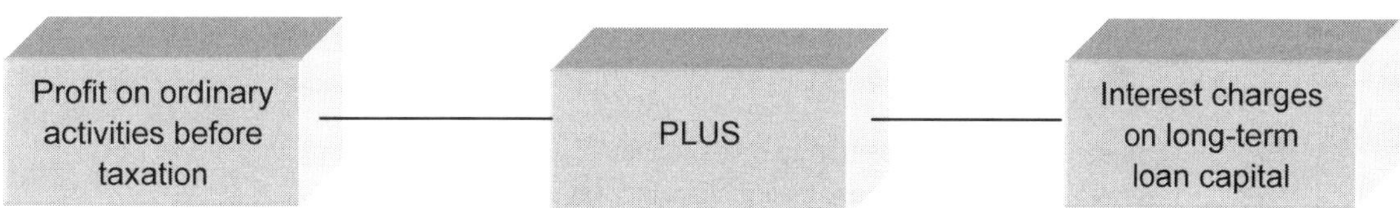

Published accounts do not always give sufficient detail on interest payable to determine how much is interest on long-term finance.

Knowledge brought forward from earlier studies

Profitability

Return on capital employed

$$\text{ROCE} = \frac{\text{PBIT}}{\text{Capital employed}} = \frac{\text{PBIT}}{\text{Total assets less current liabilities}}$$

When **interpreting** ROCE look for the following.

- How risky is the business?
- How capital intensive is it?
- What ROCE do similar businesses have?

Knowledge brought forward from earlier studies (cont'd)

Problems: which items to consider to achieve comparability:

- Revaluation reserves
- Policies, eg goodwill, R & D
- Bank overdraft: short/long-term liability
- Investments and related income: exclude

The following **considerations** are important.

- Change year to year
- Comparison to similar companies
- Comparison with current market borrowing rates

Return on equity

$$\text{ROE} = \frac{\text{Profit after tax and pref div}}{\text{Ordinary share capital + reserves}}\%$$

This gives a more **restricted view** of capital than ROCE, but the same principles apply.

Secondary ratios

Profit margin × Asset turnover = ROCE

Profit margin

$$\text{Profit margin} = \frac{\text{PBIT}}{\text{Turnover}}\% \quad \text{Gross profit margin} = \frac{\text{Gross profit}}{\text{Turnover}}\%$$

It is useful to compare profit margin to gross profit % to investigate movements which do not match. Take into account:

- **Gross profit margin**
  - Sales prices, sales volume and sales mix
  - Purchase prices and related costs (discount, carriage etc)
  - Production costs, both direct (materials, labour) and indirect (overheads both fixed and variable)
  - Stock levels and stock valuation, including errors, cut-off and stock-out costs
- **Net profit margin**
  - Sales expenses in relation to sales levels
  - Administrative expenses, including salary levels
  - Distribution expenses in relation to sales levels

  Depreciation should be considered as a separate item for each expense category.

Asset turnover

$$\text{Asset turnover} = \frac{\text{Turnover}}{\text{Total assets less current liabilities}}$$

This measures the **efficiency** of the use of assets. Amend to just fixed assets for capital intensive businesses.

A warning about comments on profit margin and asset turnover

3.3 It might be tempting to think that a high profit margin is good, and a low asset turnover means sluggish trading. In broad terms, this is so. But there is **a trade-off** between profit margin and asset turnover, and you cannot look at one without allowing for the other.

(a) A high profit margin means a high profit per £1 of sales, but if this also means that sales prices are high, there is a strong possibility that sales turnover will be depressed, and so asset turnover lower.

(b) A high asset turnover means that the company is generating a lot of sales, but to do this it might have to keep its prices down and so accept a low profit margin per £1 of sales.

4 LIQUIDITY AND WORKING CAPITAL

4.1 Profitability is of course an important aspect of a company's performance and debt or gearing is another. Neither, however, addresses directly the key issue of liquidity in the **short term**.

4.2 **Liquidity** is the amount of cash a company can put its hands on quickly to settle its debts (and possibly to meet other unforeseen demands for cash payments too). Liquid funds consist of:

(a) Cash

(b) Short-term investments for which there is a ready market (short-term investments are distinct from investments in shares in subsidiaries or associated companies)

(c) Fixed-term deposits with a bank or building society, for example, a six month high-interest deposit with a bank

(d) Trade debtors (because they will pay what they owe within a reasonably short period of time)

(e) Bills of exchange receivable (because like ordinary trade debtors, these represent amounts of cash due to be received within a relatively short period of time)

4.3 A company can obtain liquid assets from sources other than sales, such as the issue of shares for cash, a new loan or the sale of fixed assets. But a company cannot rely on these at all times, and in general obtaining liquid funds depends on making sales and profits. Even so, **profits do not always lead to increases in liquidity**. This is mainly because funds generated from trading may be immediately invested in fixed assets or paid out as dividends.

4.4 **Efficiency ratios** indicate how well a business is controlling aspects of its working capital.

Knowledge brought forward from earlier studies

Liquidity and working capital

This was very topical in the late 1980s as interest rates were high, and there was a recession Can a company meet its short-term debts.

Current ratio

$$\text{Current ratio} = \frac{\text{Current assets}}{\text{Current liabilities}}$$

Assume assets realised at book level ∴ theoretical. 2:1 acceptable? 1.5:1? It depends on the industry.

Quick ratio

$$\text{Quick ratio (acid test)} = \frac{\text{Current assets - Stock}}{\text{Current liabilities}}$$

Eliminates illiquid and subjectively valued stock. Care is needed: it could be high if **overtrading** with debtors, but no cash. Is 1:1 OK? Many supermarkets operate on 0.3.

Knowledge brought forward from earlier studies (cont'd)

Collection period

$$\text{Average collection period} = \frac{\text{Trade debtors}}{\text{Credit turnover}} \times 365$$

Is it **consistent** with quick/current ratio? If not, investigate.

Stock turnover

$$\text{Stock turnover} = \frac{\text{Cost of sales}}{\text{Stock}} \quad \text{Stock days} = \frac{\text{Stock}}{\text{Cost of sales}} \times 365$$

Higher the better? But remember:

- Lead times
- Seasonal fluctuations in orders
- Alternative uses of warehouse space
- Bulk buying discounts
- Likelihood of stock perishing or becoming obsolete

Creditors' payment period

$$\text{Creditors' payment period} = \frac{\text{Trade creditors}}{\text{Purchases}} \times 365$$

Use **cost of sales** if purchases are not disclosed.

Cash cycle

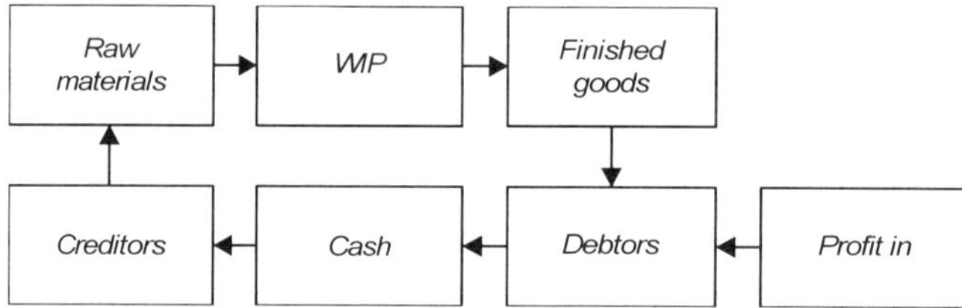

- Cash flow timing does not match sales/cost of sales timing as credit is taken
- Holding stock delays the time between payments for goods and sales receipts

Reasons for changes in liquidity

- **Credit control** efficiency altered
- Altering **payment period** of creditors as a source of funding
- Reduce **stock holdings** to maintain liquidity

5 LONG TERM SOLVENCY: DEBT AND GEARING

5.1 Debt and gearing ratios are concerned with a company's **long-term stability**: how much the company owes in relation to its size, whether it is getting into heavier debt or improving its situation, and whether its debt burden seems heavy or light.

(a) When a company is heavily in debt, banks and other potential lenders may be unwilling to advance further funds.

(b) When a company is earning only a modest profit before interest and tax, and has a heavy debt burden, there will be very little profit left (if any) over for shareholders after the interest charges have been paid. And so if interest rates were to go up (on bank overdrafts and so on) or the company were to borrow even more, it might soon be incurring interest charges in excess of PBIT. This might eventually lead to the liquidation of the company.

Knowledge brought forward from earlier studies

Debt and gearing

Debt/equity

$$\text{Debt/equity ratio} = \frac{\text{Interest bearing net debts}}{\text{Shareholders' funds}} \% \quad (> 100\% = \text{high})$$

There is **no definitive answer**; elements included are subjective. The following could have an impact.

- Convertible loan stock
- Preference shares
- Deferred tax
- Goodwill and development expenditure capitalisation
- Revaluation reserve

Gearing ratio

$$\text{Gearing ratio} = \frac{\text{Prior charge capital}}{\text{Total capital}}$$

Interest cover

$$\text{Interest cover} = \frac{\text{PBIT(incl int receivable)}}{\text{Interest payable}}$$

Is this a better way to **measure gearing**? Company must generate enough profit to cover interest. Is a figure of 3+ safe?

The implications of high or low gearing

5.2 Gearing is, amongst other things, an attempt to quantify the **degree of risk** involved in holding equity shares in a company, both in terms of the company's ability to remain in business and in terms of expected ordinary dividends from the company. The problem with a highly geared company is that, by definition, there is a lot of debt. Debt generally carries a fixed rate of interest (or fixed rate of dividend if in the form of preference shares), hence there is a given (and large) amount to be paid out from profits to holders of debt before arriving at a residue available for distribution to the holders of equity.

5.3 The more highly geared the company, the greater the risk that little (if anything) will be available to distribute by way of dividend to the ordinary shareholders. The more highly geared the company, the greater the percentage change in profit available for ordinary shareholders for any given percentage change in profit before interest and tax. The relationship similarly holds when profits increase. This means that there will be greater **volatility** of amounts available for ordinary shareholders, and presumably therefore greater volatility in dividends paid to those shareholders, where a company is highly geared. That is the risk. You may do extremely well or extremely badly without a particularly large movement in the PBIT of the company.

5.4 The risk of a company's ability to remain in business was referred to earlier. Gearing is relevant to this. A highly geared company has a large amount of interest to pay annually. If those borrowings are 'secured' in any way (and debentures in particular are secured), then the holders of the debt are perfectly entitled to force the company to realise assets to pay their interest if funds are not available from other sources. Clearly, the more highly geared a company, the more likely this is to occur when and if profits fall. Note that problems related

to **off balance sheet finance** hiding the level of gearing have gradually become rarer, due to standards such as FRS 2 and SSAP 21.

5.5 Companies will only be able to increase their gearing if they have **suitable assets** to offer for security. Companies with assets which are depreciated rapidly or which are at high risk of obsolescence will be unable to offer sufficient security, eg computer software companies. On the other hand, a property company will have plenty of assets to offer as security whose value is fairly stable (but note the effect of a property slump as in the late 1980s).

5.6 Ideally, the following **gearing profiles** would apply, so that only certain types of company could have higher gearing.

Type of company	Assets	Profits
Highly geared companies	Holding value, long-term	Stable, steady trends
Low geared companies	Rapid depreciation/change	Erratic, volatile

The effect of GAAP on gearing

5.7 **Variations in accounting policy** can have a significant impact on gearing and it will be necessary to consider the individual policies of companies. The main areas which are likely to require consideration area as follows.

(a) FRS 4 *Capital instruments* has halted the practice of classifying an instrument as equity when the true nature is that of debt and also of accounting for debt at an amount lower than its repayable amount (see Chapter 18).

(b) Revaluation of fixed assets will have an impact on equity and it will be necessary to consider the frequency of such revaluations (see Chapter 16).

(c) Assets held under leases may be excluded from a company's balance sheet if the leases are classified as operating leases (see Chapter 20).

(d) The treatment of deferred development expenditure will have an impact on gearing, ie capitalise or write off (see Chapter 17 on SSAP 13).

(e) The structure of group accounts and methods of consolidation will also have a substantial impact on gearing (use of acquisition/merger/equity accounting; exclusion of subsidiaries; FRSs 2 and 6 in Chapters 2 and 6).

6 SHAREHOLDERS' INVESTMENT RATIOS

6.1 These are the ratios which help equity shareholders and other investors to assess the value and quality of an investment in the **ordinary shares** of a company.

6.2 The value of an investment in ordinary shares in a **listed company** is its market value, and so investment ratios must have regard not only to information in the company's published accounts, but also to the current price.

6.3 Earnings per share is a valuable indicator of an ordinary share's performance and you should refer to Chapter 23 to study its calculation. We have also looked at some of the other ratios in the context of share valuation in Chapter 9.

Knowledge brought forward from earlier studies

Investors' ratios

Dividend yield

$$\text{Dividend yield} = \frac{\text{Div per share}}{\text{Mid-market price}}\%$$

- **Low yield**: the company retains a large proportion of profits to reinvest
- **High yield**: this is a risky company or slow-growing

Dividend cover

$$\text{Dividend cover} = \frac{\text{EPS}}{\text{Net div per share}}$$

$$\text{Or} \quad \frac{\text{Profit after tax and pref div}}{\text{Div on ordinary shares}}$$

This shows **how safe the dividend is**, or the extent of profit retention. Variations are due to maintaining dividend when profits are declining.

P/E ratio

$$\text{P/E ratio} = \frac{\text{Mid - market price}}{\text{EPS}}$$

The **higher the better** here: it reflects the confidence of the market. A rise in EPS will cause an increase in P/E ratio, but maybe not to same extent: Look at the context of the market and industry norms.

Earnings yield

$$\text{Earnings yield} = \frac{\text{EPS}}{\text{Mid - market price}}$$

This shows the dividend yield if there is no retention of profit. It allows you to compare companies with **different dividend policies**, showing growth rather than earnings.

Net assets per share

$$\text{Net assets per share} = \frac{\text{Net assets}}{\text{No of shares}}$$

This is a **crude measure** of value of a company, liable to distortion.

See also **EPS** and **dividend per share**

Exam focus point

It cannot be overemphasised that question practice is *vital* in this area. By answering as many questions as possible you will become more and more adept at spotting the major issues in these types of question - which means you will gain most of the marks!

Question: ratio analysis (1)

RST plc is considering purchasing an interest in its competitor XYZ Ltd. The managing director of RST plc has obtained the three most recent P&L accounts and balance sheets of XYZ Ltd as shown below.

XYZ LIMITED
PROFIT AND LOSS ACCOUNTS FOR YEARS ENDED 31 DECEMBER

	20X0	*20X1*	*20X2*
	£'000	£'000	£'000
Turnover	18,000	18,900	19,845
Cost of sales	10,440	10,340	11,890
Gross profit	7,560	8,560	7,955
Distribution costs	1,565	1,670	1,405
Administrative expenses	1,409	1,503	1,591
Operating profit	4,586	5,387	4,959
Interest payable on bank overdraft	104	215	450
Interest payable on 12% debentures	600	600	600
Profit on ordinary activities before taxation	3,882	4,572	3,909
Taxation on ordinary activities	1,380	2,000	1,838
Profit on ordinary activities after taxation	2,502	2,572	2,071
Proposed dividend	1,600	1,693	1,800
Retained profit	902	879	271

XYZ LIMITED
BALANCE SHEETS AS AT 31 DECEMBER

	20X0		*20X1*		*20X2*	
	£'000	£'000	£'000	£'000	£'000	£'000
Fixed assets						
Land and buildings	11,460		12,121		11,081	
Plant and machinery	8,896		9,020		9,130	
		20,356		21,141		20,211
Current assets						
Stock	1,775		2,663		3,995	
Trade debtors	1,440		2,260		3,164	
Cash	50		53		55	
	3,265		4,976		7,214	
Current liabilities						
Trade creditors	390		388		446	
Bank	1,300		2,300		3,400	
Taxation	897		1,420		1,195	
Proposed dividend	1,600		1,696		1,800	
	4,187		5,804		6,841	
Net current assets/(liabilities)		(922)		(828)		373
12% debentures 20X5 - 20X8		(5,000)		(5,000)		(5,000)
		14,434		15,313		15,584
Share capital		8,000		8,000		8,000
Profit and loss account		6,434		7,313		7,584
		14,434		15,313		15,584

Required

Prepare a report for the managing director of RST plc commenting on the financial position of XYZ Ltd and highlighting any areas that require further investigation.

(Marks will be awarded for ratios and other financial statistics where appropriate.)

Answer

To: MD of RST plc
From: An Accountant
Date: XX.XX.XX
Subject: *The financial position of XYZ* Ltd

Introduction

This report has been prepared on the basis of the three most recent P&L accounts and balance sheets of XYZ Ltd covering the years 20X0 to 20X2 inclusive. Ratio analysis used in this report is based on the calculations shown in the appendix attached.

Performance

Sales have increased at a steady 5% per annum over the three year period.

In contrast, the gross profit percentage has increased from 42% in 20X0 to 45% in 20X1 before dropping back to 40% in 20X2. Similarly, operating profit as a percentage of sales was 26% in 20X0, 28.5% in 20X1 and 25% in 20X2. This may indicate some misallocation of costs between 20X1 and 20X2 and should be investigated or it may be indicative of a longer downward trend in profitability.

Return on capital employed, as one would expect, has shown a similar pattern with an increase in 20X1 with a subsequent fall in 20X2 to a level below that of 20X0.

Debt and liquidity

The debt ratio measures the ratio of a company's total debt to its total assets. Although we have no information as to the norm for the industry as a whole, the debt ratios appear reasonable. However, it should be noted that it has risen steadily over the three year period.

When reviewing XYZ Ltd's liquidity the situation has improved over the period. The current ratio measures a company's ability to meet its current liabilities out of current assets. A ratio of at least 1 should therefore be expected. XYZ Ltd did not meet this expectation in 20X0 and 20X1.

This ratio can be misleading as stock is included in current assets. Because stock can take some time to convert into liquid assets a second ratio, the quick ratio, is calculated which excludes stock. As can be seen, the quick ratio, although improving, is low and this shows that current liabilities cannot be met from current assets if stock is excluded. As a major part of current liabilities is the bank overdraft, the company is obviously relying on the bank's continuing support with short-term funding. It would be useful to find out the terms of the bank funding and the projected cash flow requirements for future funding.

Efficiency ratios

The efficiency ratios, debtors ratio and stock turnover, give a useful indication of how the company is managing its current assets.

As can be seen from the appendix the debtors collection period has increased over the three years from 29 days to 58 days. This may indicate that the company is failing to follow up its debts efficiently or that it has given increased credit terms to some or all of its customers.

Looking at stock turnover, this has also risen from 62 days to 122 days. This may be an indication of over-stocking, stocking up on the expectation of a substantial sales increase or the holding of obsolete or slow-moving stock items which should be written down. More investigation needs to be done on both debtors and stock.

The financing of additional debtors and stock has been achieved in the main through the bank overdraft as the trade creditors figure has not increased significantly.

Conclusion

The review of the three year financial statements for XYZ Ltd has given rise to a number of queries which need to be resolved before a useful conclusion can be reached on the financial position of XYZ Ltd. It may also be useful to compare XYZ Ltd's ratios to those of other companies in the same industry in order to obtain some idea of the industry norms.

APPENDIX TO MEMORANDUM

	20X0	*20X1*	*20X2*
% sales increase		5%	5%
Gross profit %	42%	45%	40%
Operating profit %	25.5%	28.5%	25%

Return on capital employed

= $\frac{\text{Profit before interest and tax}}{\text{Capital employed}}$	$\frac{4,586-104}{14,434+5,000}$	$\frac{5,387-215}{15,313+5,000}$	$\frac{4,959-450}{15,584+5,000}$
× 100%	= 23%	= 25.5%	= 21.9%

	20X0	20X1	20X2
Debt ratio			
= Total debt / Total assets × 100%	$\frac{4,187 + 5,000}{20,356 + 3,265}$ = 38.9%	$\frac{5,804 + 5,000}{21,114 + 4,976}$ = 41.4%	$\frac{6,841 + 5,000}{20,211 + 7,214}$ = 43.2%
Current ratio			
= Current assets / Current liabilities	$\frac{3,265}{4,187}$ = 0.78	$\frac{4,976}{5,804}$ = 0.86	$\frac{7,214}{6,814}$ = 1.06
Quick ratio			
= (Current assets – stock) / Current liabilities	$\frac{3,265 - 1,775}{4,187}$ = 0.36	$\frac{4,976 - 2,663}{5,804}$ = 0.40	$\frac{7,214 - 3,995}{6,814}$ = 0.47
Debtors ratio			
= Trade debtors / Sales × 365 days	$\frac{1,440}{18,000}$ = 29.2 days	$\frac{2,260}{18,900}$ = 43.6 days	$\frac{3,164}{19,845}$ = 58.2 days

	20X0	20X1	20X2
Stock turnover			
= Stock / Cost of sales × 365 days	$\frac{1,775}{10,440}$ = 62 days	$\frac{2,663}{10,340}$ = 94 days	$\frac{3,995}{11,890}$ = 122.6 days

Question: ratio analysis (2)

You are the management accountant of Fry plc. Laurie plc is a competitor in the same industry and it has been operating for 20 years. Summaries of Laurie plc's P&L accounts and balance sheets for the previous three years are given below.

SUMMARISED PROFIT AND LOSS ACCOUNTS
FOR THE YEAR ENDED 31 DECEMBER

	20X0	20X1	20X2
	£m	£m	£m
Turnover	840	981	913
Cost of sales	554	645	590
Gross profit	286	336	323
Selling, distribution and administration expenses	186	214	219
Profit before interest	100	122	104
Interest	6	15	19
Profit on ordinary activities before taxation	94	107	85
Taxation	45	52	45
Profit on ordinary activities after taxation	49	55	40
Dividends	24	24	24
Retained profit for year	25	31	16

SUMMARISED BALANCE SHEETS AS AT 31 DECEMBER

	20X0	20X1	20X2
	£m	£m	£m
Fixed assets			
Intangible assets	36	40	48
Tangible assets at net book value	176	206	216
	212	246	264
Current assets			
Stocks	237	303	294
Debtors	105	141	160
Bank	52	58	52
	606	748	770
Creditors: amounts falling due within one year			
Trade creditors	53	75	75
Other creditors	80	105	111
	133	180	186
Creditors: amounts falling due after more than one year			
Long-term loans	74	138	138
	207	318	324
Shareholders' interest			
Ordinary share capital	100	100	100
Retained profits	299	330	346
	606	748	770

You may assume that the index of retail prices has remained constant between 20X0 and 20X2.

Required

Write a report to the finance director of Fry plc:

(a) Analysing the performance of Laurie plc and showing any calculations in an appendix to this report

(b) Summarising five areas which require further investigation, including reference to other pieces of information which would complement your analysis of the performance of Laurie plc

Answer

(a) To: Finance Director
From: Management accountant
Subject: *Performance of Laurie plc 20X0 to 20X2*

An appendix is attached to this report which shows the ratios calculated as part of the performance review.

Profitability

The gross profit margin has remained relatively static over the three year period, although it has risen by approximately 1% in 20X2. ROCE, while improving very slightly in 20X1 to 21.5% has dropped dramatically in 20X2 to 17.8%. The net profit margin has also fallen in 20X2, in spite of the improvement in the gross profit margin. This marks a rise in expenses which suggests that they are not being well controlled. The utilisation of assets compared to the turnover generated has also declined reflecting the drop in trading activity between 20X1 and 20X2.

Trading levels

It is apparent that there was a dramatic increase in trading activity between 20X0 and 20X1, but then a significant fall in 20X2. Turnover rose by 17% in 20X1 but fell by 7% in 20X2. The reasons for this fluctuation are unclear. It may be the effect of some kind of one-off event, or it may be the effect of a change in product mix. Whatever the reason, it appears that improved credit terms granted to customers (debtors payment period up from 46 to 64 days) has not stopped the drop in sales.

Working capital

Both the current ratio and quick ratio demonstrate an adequate working capital situation, although the quick ratio has shown a slight decline. There has been an increased investment over the period in stocks and debtors which has been only partly financed by longer payment periods to trade creditors and a rise in other creditors (mainly between 20X0 and 20X1).

Capital structure

The level of gearing of the company increased when a further £64m was raised in long term loans in 20X1 to add to the £74m already in the balance sheet. Although this does not seem to be a particularly high level of gearing, the debt/equity ratio did rise from 18.5% to 32.0% in 20X1. The interest charge has risen to £19m from £6m in 20X0. The 20X1 charge was £15m, suggesting that either the interest rate on the loan is flexible, or that the full interest charge was not incurred in 20X1. The new long-term loan appears to have funded the expansion in both fixed and current assets in 20X1.

APPENDIX

Ratio	*Working*	*20X0*	*20X1*	*20X2*
Gross profit margin	(1)	34.0%	34.3%	35.4%
ROCE	(2)	21.1%	21.5%	17.8%
Profit margin	(3)	11.9%	12.4%	11.4%
Assets turnover	(4)	1.78	1.73	1.56
Gearing ratio	(5)	15.6%	24.3%	23.6%
Debt/equity ratio	(6)	18.5%	32.0%	30.9%
Interest cover	(7)	16.7	8.1	5.5
Current ratio	(8)	3.0	2.8	2.7
Quick ratio	(9)	1.2	1.1	1.1
Debtor's payment period (days)	(10)	46	52	64
Stock turnover period (days)	(11)	156	171	182
Creditor's turnover period	(12)	35	42	46

Workings (all in £m)

		20X0	*20X1*	*20X2*
1	Gross profit margin	$\frac{286}{840}$	$\frac{336}{981}$	$\frac{323}{913}$
2	ROCE *	$\frac{100}{473}$	$\frac{122}{568}$	$\frac{104}{584}$
3	Profit margin	$\frac{100}{840}$	$\frac{122}{981}$	$\frac{104}{913}$
4	Assets turnover	$\frac{840}{473}$	$\frac{981}{568}$	$\frac{913}{584}$
5	Gearing ratio	$\frac{74}{74+399}$	$\frac{138}{138+430}$	$\frac{138}{138+446}$
6	Debt/equity ratio	$\frac{74}{399}$	$\frac{138}{430}$	$\frac{138}{446}$
7	Interest cover	$\frac{100}{6}$	$\frac{122}{15}$	$\frac{104}{19}$
8	Current ratio	$\frac{394}{133}$	$\frac{502}{180}$	$\frac{506}{186}$
9	Quick ratio	$\frac{157}{133}$	$\frac{199}{180}$	$\frac{212}{186}$
10	Debtors' payment period	$\frac{105}{840} \times 365$	$\frac{141}{981} \times 365$	$\frac{160}{913} \times 365$
11	Stock turnover period	$\frac{237}{554} \times 365$	$\frac{303}{645} \times 365$	$\frac{294}{590} \times 365$
12	Creditors' payment period	$\frac{53}{554} \times 365$	$\frac{75}{645} \times 365$	$\frac{75}{590} \times 365$

* ROCE has been calculated here as:

$$\frac{\text{Profit on ordinary activities before interest and taxation (PBIT)}}{\text{Capital employed}}$$

where capital employed = shareholders' funds plus creditors falling due after one year and any long-term provision for liabilities and charges. It is possible to calculate ROCE using net profit after taxation and interest, but this admits variations and distortions into the ratio which are not affected by *trading* activity.

(b) Areas for further investigation include the following.

(i) *Long-term loan*

There is no indication as to why this loan was raised and how it was used to finance the business. Further details are needed of interest rate(s), security given and repayment dates.

(ii) *Trading activity*

The level of sales has fluctuated in quite a strange way and this requires further investigation and explanation. Factors to consider would include pricing policies, product mix, market share and any unique occurrence which would affect sales.

(iii) *Further breakdown*

It would be useful to break down some of the information in the financial statements, perhaps into a management accounting format. Examples would be:

(1) sales by segment, market or geographical area;
(2) cost of sales split, into raw materials, labour and overheads;
(3) stocks broken down into raw materials, work in progress and finished goods;
(4) expenses analysed between administrative expenses, sales and distribution costs.

(iv) *Accounting policies*

Accounting policies may have a significant effect on certain items. In particular, it would be useful to know what the accounting policies are in relation to intangible assets (and what these assets consist of), and whether there has been any change in accounting policies.

(v) *Dividend policy*

The company has maintained the level of dividend paid to shareholders (although it has not been raised during the three year period). Presumably the company would have been able to reduce the amount of long-term debt taken on if it had retained part or all of the dividend during this period. It would be interesting to examine the share price movement during the period and calculate the dividend cover.

Tutorial note. Other matters raised could have included:

(1) working capital problems, particularly stock turnover and control over debtors; and

(2) EPS (which cannot be calculated here as the number of shares is not given) and other related investor statistics, such as the P/E ratio.

Chapter roundup

- Keep the various **sources of financial information** in mind and the effects of insider dealing, the efficient market hypothesis and Stock Exchange regulations.
- Much of the material here on **basic ratios** should have been revision for you. The next few chapters will cover much more complicated aspects of financial analysis.
- Make sure that you can **define** all the ratios. Look out for variations in definitions of ratios which might appear in questions.
- Always remember that 'profit' and 'net assets' are fairly **arbitrary figures**, affected by different accounting policies and manipulation.

Quick quiz

1 Apart from ratio analysis, what other information might be helpful in interpreting a company's accounts?

2 In a period when profits are fluctuating, what effect does a company's level of gearing have on the profits available for ordinary shareholders?

3 Name three areas where variations in accounting policy can have a significant impact on gearing.

4 The acid test or quick ratio should include:

A Stocks of finished goods
B Raw materials and consumables
C Long-tem loans
D Trade debtors

5 The asset turnover of Taplow Ltd is 110% that of Stoke Ltd.

The return on capital of Taplow Ltd is 80% of that of Stoke Ltd.

Calculate Taplow Ltd's profit margin expressed as a percentage of Stoke Ltd's.

6 Deal Ltd has the following capital structure:

	£'000
£1 ordinary shares	55,000
6% £1 Preference shares	15,000
Reserves	12,000
	82,000
8% debentures	30,000
	112,000

What is the most appropriate measure of the debt/equity ratio for a potential equity investor?

7 Below is an extract of the profit and loss account of Public plc.

		£	£
Operating profit			1,260,000
Interest payable on loan stock			60,000
Profit before tax			1,200,000
Taxation at 30%			360,000
Profit after taxation			840,000
Dividends:	preference	65,000	
	ordinary	100,000	
			(165,000)
			675,000

Treating the preference shares as part of the borrowing of the company, what is the interest cover?

Answers to quick quiz

1 See Para 1.2.

2 There is more risk that there will be little to distribute by way of a dividend as the percentage change in profit available for shareholders fluctuates more.

3 (a) Classification of debt and equity instruments
(b) Revaluation of fixed assets
(c) Classification of leases
(d) Treatment of deferred development expenditure
(e) Structure of group accounts

4 D Acid test ratio = $\frac{\text{CA - stock}}{\text{CL}}$

5 $\frac{80}{110} = 73\%$

6 Debt = 30 + 15 = 45
Equity = 55 + 12 = 67
$\therefore$ 45/67 × 100 = 67.2%

7 Interest cover = $\frac{\text{PBIT}}{\text{Interest} + \text{Pref dividend} \times 100/70}$

$= \frac{1{,}200 + 60}{60 + (65 \times 100/70)}$

The preference dividend is paid from post tax profits and therefore needs grossing up by the tax rate.

Now try the question below from the Exam Question Bank

Number	Level	Marks	Time
Q16	Exam	25	45 mins

Chapter 11

MEASUREMENT OF PERFORMANCE

Introduction

This chapter looks at a wide variety of issues connected with performance measurement, ranging from the general aspects of a business that need to be measured to specific techniques specified in your Study Guide for Paper 3.6.

Study guide

Section 24 – Preparation of reports 2

- Discussion of the financial and non-financial measures of performance
- Describing the procedures in designing an accounting based performance measurement system
- Appraising the different performance measures, including return on investment, residual income and economic value added
- Comparing target levels of performance with actual performance

Exam guide

Since these are financial management topics and new to this syllabus, it is not clear how they will be examined.

1 PERFORMANCE MEASUREMENT

1.1 Performance measurement aims to establish **how well** something or somebody is doing in relation to the **planned activity** and **desired results**. The 'thing' may be a machine, a factory, a subsidiary company or an organisation as a whole. The 'body' may be an individual employee, a manager, or a group of people.

1.2 A typical business requires performance measurement in the following areas.

(a) In relation to **external parties** (customers, market, suppliers, competitors)
(b) **Across the organisation** as a whole (divisional performance measurement)
(c) **Within** each of the main sub-divisions of the business
(d) At the level of **individual activities**

1.3 Measurement can be in terms of **profitability**, **activity** and **productivity**.

Point of reference	Comment
Profitability	Profit has two components: cost and income. All parts of an organisation and all activities within it incur costs, and so their success needs to be judged in relation to cost. Only some parts of an organisation receive income, and their success should be judged in terms of both cost and income.
Activity	All parts of an organisation are also engaged in activities (activities cause costs). Activity measures could include the following. • Number of orders received from customers, a measure of the effectiveness of marketing • Number of deliveries made, a measure of the effectiveness of distribution • Number of production runs achieved by a particular factory Each of these items could be measured in terms of physical numbers, monetary value, or time spent.
Productivity	This is the quantity of the product or service produced in relation to the resources put in, for example so many units produced per hour, or per employee, or per tonne of material. It defines how *efficiently* resources are being used.

Question: performance measurement

An invoicing assistant works in a department with three colleagues. She is paid £8,000 per annum. The department typically handles 10,000 invoices per week. One morning she spends half an hour on the phone to her grandfather, who lives in Australia, at the company's expense. The cost of the call proves to be £32.

Required

From this scenario identify as many different performance measures as possible, explaining what each is intended to measure. Make any further assumptions you wish.

Answer

Invoices per employee per week: 2,500 (activity)
Staff cost per invoice: £0.06 (cost/profitability)
Invoices per hour: 2,500/(7 × 5) = 71.4 (productivity)
Cost of idle time: £32 + £2.14 = £34.14 (cost/profitability)

You may have thought of other measures and probably have slight rounding differences.

Profit and other objectives

1.4 A traditional view has been that a desire to achieve greater profitability often entails a **sacrifice** in some other aspect of performance. One obvious example is quality: if cheaper materials are used to make a product or less highly trained workers deliver a service, money will be saved (increasing profits), but quality will fall.

1.5 In other cases there may not be a clear link between an objective and the profitability objective. A company may aim to improve **working conditions** for its staff, and measure its success in terms of the cost of improved facilities, falls in staff turnover, or absenteeism and

so on. Some of the successes are directly contrary to profitability, while others can only with difficulty be linked to extra productivity.

1.6 A third example is where a company aims to fulfil its **social and moral responsibilities**, for example by incurring costs to make a manufacturing process more environmentally friendly.

Control and performance measurement

1.7 Performance measurement is a vital part of **control**: it is the part of the control process where **feedback** is compared with the plan, and it is also a means of **feedforward control** in the sense that it sets targets to be aimed at in the future.

Exam focus point

An exam question might refer to the need to exercise control over the process of performance measurement and ask how measurement itself acted as a control mechanism.

Measuring productivity

1.8 Earlier we identified **productivity** as a key area for measurement of a business, so let us see how that might be 'controlled', in other words how we can make sure that the 'right' productivity gets measured.

KEY TERM

Productivity expresses a relationship between outputs from a system and the inputs which go into their creation, as output ÷ input.

1.9 The lower the input and the higher the output, the higher will be the resulting productivity. However it needs to be understood by those measuring and those being measured that **high productivity is not a virtue** in itself. It might be possible to produce a larger number of items by spreading the inputs available more thinly, but **if the final output does not then serve its intended purpose** high productivity is worthless.

1.10 **Inputs** should be measured accurately and fairly.

(a) In some cases it is very **easy** to measure inputs: the material inputs for a mass-produced product can be **weighed** or **counted** and a standard established. The more finished items that can be got out of standard inputs the more productive the process is.

(b) Sometimes it can be more **difficult**, however, perhaps because **people** do not keep accurate records of the time they put into a task (or falsify records), or because satisfactory outputs depend upon **quality** of input rather than quantity.

(c) Arguably, a fair measure should be **neutral**, that is, not manipulated by the measurer to encourage certain behaviour. An example might be the exclusion from time measurements of an arbitrary allowance for time that management considers to be 'wasted' chatting to colleagues.

1.11 **Outputs** must also be measured fairly and accurately.

(a) In a manufacturing context outputs are likely to consist of finished products, but a fair measurement should also take account of goods subsequently **returned** for repair or replacement.

(b) In a service context (for example, the delivery of products or after-sales care), outputs can be difficult to define: ***how* satisfied** is a satisfied customer, for example?

1.12 The measure needs to exhibit all the qualities of **good information**. For example it needs to be understood by those using it to make decisions, it needs to be available to them on time so that they can act if necessary, it should not cost more to obtain and calculate the measurement than the benefit derived from it, and so on.

1.13 The measurement should be **interpreted in context**. Low productivity in a particular month may be an isolated occurrence or part of a worsening trend. High productivity in one part of the factory may be overburdening workers in the next part of the process, causing them to cut corners and produce less satisfactory finished output.

1.14 As a **means of control**, productivity measures can be used in the following ways.

(a) They can be linked to, and so help to achieve, the organisation's overall **strategy** and **objectives**. (A certain level of productivity may, in fact, be an objective itself.)

(b) Once established they can be used to **predict** future performance.

(c) They can indicate when and **where action is needed** to correct a process that is out of control.

(d) They can be used as a **motivation** device if appropriate incentives are offered for achieving productivity targets (or disincentives for failing to achieve them).

Critical success factors

1.15 The use of critical success factors (CSFs) can help to determine the information requirements of senior management.

KEY TERM

Critical success factors are the few key areas of the job where things must go right for the organisation to flourish. They are all critical to the furtherance of the organisation's aims and the organisation cannot afford to fall behind in any of these areas.

1.16 There are usually **fewer than ten** of these factors that any one executive should monitor. They are very **time dependent**, so they should be **re-examined** as often as necessary to keep abreast of the current business climate.

1.17 Critical success factors are derived from the concerns of senior management and cover such areas as industry trends, market positioning and the wider business environment. Here are four sources of CSFs.

(a) The **industry** that the business is in

(b) The **company** itself and its situation within the industry

(c) The **environment**, for example consumer trends and the economy

(d) **Temporal organisational factors** (areas of corporate activity which are currently **unacceptable** and represent a cause of concern, such as high stock levels)

Case example

A famous study of GEC examined a management reporting system that produced reports on the following factors.

(a) Profitability
(b) Market share
(c) Productivity
(d) Product leadership
(e) Personnel development
(f) Employee attitudes
(g) Public responsibility
(h) Balance between short-range and long-range goals

1.18 One approach to asking users to define the factors which are critical to success in performing their functions or making decisions is as follows.

Step 1. List the organisation's corporate objectives and goals.

Step 2. Determine which factors are critical for accomplishing the objectives.

Step 3. Determine a small number of prime measures for each factor.

1.19 Two separate types of critical success factor can be identified. A **monitoring** CSF is used to keep abreast of existing activities and operations. A **building** CSF helps to measure the progress of new initiatives and is more likely to be relevant at senior executive level.

Behavioural implications of performance measurement

1.20 If people **know** that their performance is being measured then this will affect the standard of their performance, particularly if they know that they will be **rewarded** for achieving a certain level of performance.

1.21 Ideally, performance measures will be devised that reward behaviour that maximises the **corporate good**. In practice, however, it is not quite so simple.

(a) There is a danger that managers and staff will concentrate **only** upon what they know is being measured. This is not a problem if every important issue has a measure attached to it, but such a system is difficult to devise and implement.

(b) Individuals have their own **personal goals**, but performance that satisfies their own sense of what is important will not necessarily work towards the corporate good.

1.22 Point (b) is the problem of **goal congruence**.

Attitudes

1.23 There are a number of factors which may affect the **attitude** of staff to their work.

(a) The feeling of **belonging** to a group with similar aims can be a great motivating force.

(b) The feeling of having **fulfilled one's personal potential** by introducing a new method or receiving praise from a customer can motivate staff.

(c) The amount of **resources** available will affect how staff work. If resources provided are inadequate they will feel as if their task is almost impossible.

(d) **Pay, promotion** prospects and bonuses will also be influencing factors.

1.24 Staff attitude can be measured in a number of ways.

(a) By the level of **quality** of their work and their **productivity** relative to other staff.
(b) By responses to **customer questionnaires** about the attitude of staff.
(c) By reviews written by **colleagues** and **bosses**.

2 FINANCIAL PERFORMANCE MEASURES

2.1 Financial measures (or *monetary* measures) are very familiar to you. Here are some examples, accompanied by comments from a single page of the *Financial Times*.

Measure	Example
Profit	*Profit* is the commonest measure of all. Profit maximisation is usually cited as the main objective of most business organisations: 'ICI increased pre-tax profits to £233m'; 'General Motors... yesterday reported better-than-expected first-quarter net income of $513 (£333m).
Revenue	'the US businesses contributed £113.9m of total group turnover of £409m'.
Costs	'Sterling's fall benefited pre-tax profits by about £50m while savings from the cost-cutting programme instituted in 1991 were running at around £100m a quarter'; 'The group interest charge rose from £48m to £61m'.
Share price	'The group's shares rose 31p to 1,278p despite the market's fall'.
Cash flow	'Cash flow was also continuing to improve, with cash and marketable securities totalling $8.4bn on March 31, up from $8bn at December 31'.

2.2 Note here that monetary amounts stated are only given meaning in **relation to something else**. Here is a list of yard-sticks against which financial results are usually placed so as to become measures, perhaps in the form of **variances.**

- Budgeted **sales, costs** and **profits**
- **Standards** in a standard costing system
- The **trend** over time (last year/this year, say)
- The results of **other parts** of the business
- The results of **other businesses**
- The **economy** in general
- **Future potential**

Modern trends: customer profitability analysis

2.3 In certain circumstances a useful approach to performance evaluation may be the analysis of **profitability by customer** or customer group. Profitability can vary widely between different customers because various overhead costs are, to some extent, variable and '**customer-driven**'. These overheads include things like discounts and distribution costs.

2.4 Customer profitability analysis relates these variabilities in cost to individual customers or customer groups. Managers can use this information to check whether or not individual customers are actually profitable to sell to, and to assess whether profitability can be improved for any customer by switching effort from one type of overhead activity to another, or by reducing spending on some overhead activities.

Modern trends: activity based costing

2.5 The implications of ABC for performance measurement are highly significant. For example if a large part of production overheads used to be known as 'warehousing', but are now recognised as 'materials handling costs' that are incurred in relation to the number of production runs, then a materials handling rate per production run can be established. Many such insights will become possible using ABC and they are useful not only for costing products, but also as a **measurement** that will help in the **management** of costs.

Modern trends: benchmarking

2.6 **Benchmarking** has been described as 'the formalisation of the basic notion of comparing practices. It is a **systematic analysis of one's own performance against that of another organisation** ... the overall objective of benchmarking is to improve performance by learning from the experience of others' (Smith). Benchmarking, which is becoming increasingly popular, therefore aims to **achieve competitive advantage** by **learning from others' experiences and mistakes**, finding **best practice** and translating this best practice into **use in the organisation**.

Types of benchmarking

2.7 **External benchmarking** involves comparing the performance of an organisation with that of a **direct competitor** - ideally one that is acknowledged to be the 'best in class' (**competitive benchmarking**) or comparing the performance of an internal function with those of the best **external practitioners of those functions**, regardless of the industry within which they operate (**functional benchmarking**). Given that the benchmark is the 'best' in a particular field, it provides a meaningful target towards which the organisation should aim.

Internal benchmarking, on the other hand, involves comparing the performance of **one part of a business with that of a different part of the same business** with the aim of establishing best practice throughout an organisation. Some external benchmarking is still required, however, in order to establish best practice.

2.8 A 1994 survey of the *The Times* Top 1000 companies (half of which were in manufacturing) revealed that the business functions most subjected to benchmarking in the companies using the technique were **customer services, manufacturing, human resources** and **information services.**

Why benchmark?

2.9 'Perhaps performance measures, when done correctly, help everyone in the company focus on the right things in the right place at the right time. However ... there are many stories of dysfunctional behaviour - the telephone company which pledged to have at least 90% of payphones working, then achieving this figure by simply removing all public payphones from those areas most often vandalised. Or the bus operator which, plagued by delays, decided to pay bonuses to drivers who arrived at the terminus on time. As a result, most buses arrived at the terminus on time - however, drivers no longer tended to stop for passengers along the way!

Measuring performance by itself has no meaning. Meaning can only be achieved through comparison, either against poor performance, which usually provides no true indication of future or competitive position, or through benchmarking.' (*Management Accounting,* November 1996)

Limitations

2.10 Both approaches to benchmarking suffer from a number of **limitations**.

(a) **Limitations of external benchmarking**

- Deciding which activities to benchmark
- Identifying which organisation is the 'best in class' at an activity
- **Persuading that organisation to share information**
- Successful practices in one organisation may not transfer successfully to another

(b) The principal limitation of **internal benchmarking** centres on the **relevance of the other part of the business.**

- The amount of resources devoted to the units may differ.
- There may be local differences (use of different computer hardware).
- Inputs and outputs may be difficult to define.

2.11 Benchmarking **works,** it is claimed, **for the following reasons.**

(a) The comparisons are carried out by the **managers who have to live with any changes implemented** as a result of the exercise.

(b) Benchmarking focuses on improvement in key areas and sets **targets** which are **challenging but 'achievable'**. What is *really* achievable can be discovered by examining what others have achieved: managers are thus able to accept that they are not being asked to perform miracles.

2.12 Benchmarking can also provide **early warning of competitive disadvantage** and should lead to a greater incidence of **teamworking** and **cross-functional learning.**

3 NON-FINANCIAL PERFORMANCE MEASURES

Quantitative and qualitative performance measures

3.1 As you know it is possible to distinguish between **quantitative** information, which is capable of being expressed in numbers, and **qualitative** information, which can only be expressed in numerical terms with difficulty.

3.2 An example of a **quantitative** performance measure is 'You have been late for work *twice* this week and it's only Tuesday!'. An example of a **qualitative** performance measure is 'My bed is *very* comfortable'.

3.3 The first measure is likely to find its way into a staff appraisal report. The second would feature in a bed manufacturer's customer satisfaction survey. Both are indicators of whether their subjects are doing as good a job as they are required to do.

3.4 Qualitative measures are by nature **subjective** and **judgmental** but this does not mean that they are not valuable. They are especially valuable when they are derived from several different sources because then they can be expressed in a mixture of quantitative and qualitative terms which is more meaningful overall.

3.5 Consider the following statement.

'Seven out of ten customers think our beds are very comfortable.'

This is a **quantitative** measure of customer satisfaction as well as a **qualitative** measure of the perceived performance of the beds. (But it does not mean that only 70% of the total beds produced are comfortable, nor that each bed is 70% comfortable and 30% uncomfortable: 'very' is the measure of comfort.)

Non-financial indicators (NFIs)

3.6 Financial measures do not convey the full picture of a company's performance, especially in a **modern business environment**.

> 'In today's worldwide competitive environment companies are competing in terms of product quality, delivery, reliability, after-sales service and customer satisfaction. None of these variables is directly measured by the traditional responsibility accounting system, despite the fact that they represent the major goals of world-class manufacturing companies.'

3.7 Many companies are discovering the usefulness of quantitative and qualitative **non-financial indicators (NFIs)** such as the following.

- Quality
- Lead times
- Rework
- Delivery to time
- Non-productive hours
- System (machine) down time, and so on
- Number of customer complaints and warranty claims

3.8 Unlike traditional variance reports, measures such as these can be provided quickly for managers, per shift, **daily** or even **hourly** as required. They are likely to be easy to calculate, and easier for non-financial managers to understand and therefore to use effectively.

3.9 The beauty of non-financial indicators is that **anything can be compared** if it is **meaningful** to do so. The measures should be **tailored** to the circumstances so that, for example, number of coffee breaks per 20 pages of Study Text might indicate to you how hard you are studying!

3.10 Many suitable measures combine elements from the chart shown below. The chart is not intended to be prescriptive or exhaustive.

Errors/failure	Time	Quantity	People
Defects	Second	Range of products	Employees
Equipment failures	Minute	Parts/components	Employee skills
Warranty claims	Hour	Units produced	Customers
Complaints	Shift	Units sold	Competitors
Returns	Cycle	Services performed	Suppliers
Stockouts	Day	kg/litres/metres	
Lateness/waiting	Month	m^2/m^3	
Misinformation	Year	Documents	
Miscalculation		Deliveries	
Absenteeism		Enquiries	

3.11 Traditional measures derived from these lists like 'kg (of material) per unit produced' or 'units produced per hour' are fairly obvious, but what may at first seem a fairly **unlikely combination** may also be very revealing. 'Absenteeism per customer', for example, may be of no significance at all or it may reveal that a particularly difficult customer is being avoided, and hence that some action is needed.

3.12 There is clearly a need for the information provider to work more closely with the managers who will be using the information to make sure that their needs are properly understood. The measures used are likely to be **developed and refined over time**. It may be that some will serve the purpose of drawing attention to areas in need of improvement but will be of no further relevance once remedial action has been taken. A flexible, responsive approach is essential.

Question: non-financial indicators

Using the above chart make up five non-financial indicators and explain how each might be useful.

Answer

Here are five indicators, showing you how to use the chart, but there are many other possibilities.

(a) Services performed late v total services performed
(b) Total units sold v total units sold by competitors (indicating market share)
(c) Warranty claims per month
(d) Documents processed per employee
(e) Equipment failures per 1,000 units produced

Don't forget to explain how the ones that you chose might be useful.

NFIs and financial measures

3.13 Arguably, NFIs are less likely to be **manipulated** than traditional profit-related measures and they should, therefore, offer a means of counteracting short-termism, since short-term profit at any (non-monetary) expense is rarely an advisable goal. The ultimate goal of commercial organisations in the long run is likely to remain the maximisation of **profit**, however, and so the financial aspect cannot be ignored.

3.14 There is a danger that too many such measures could be reported, leading to **information overload** for managers, providing information that is not truly useful, or that sends conflicting signals. A further danger of NFIs is that they might lead managers to pursue detailed **operational goals** and become blind to the **overall strategy** in which those goals are set.

3.15 A **combination** of financial and non-financial indicators is therefore likely to be most successful.

Question: operational performance

What do the following indicate about an organisation's operational performance?

(a) Actual late deliveries as a percentage of total orders are greater than the budgeted figure.
(b) Actual process losses as a percentage of input are greater than the budgeted figure.
(c) Actual sales volumes are lower than budgeted sales volumes.

Answer

(a) This could indicate problems with either production planning or distribution.

(b) This could indicate faulty material, poor quality work or machine faults.

(c) This could indicate a fall in demand or too great a proportion of replacements or too many losses in process so that production cannot meet demand.

Ratios

3.16 **Ratios** (covered in Chapter 10) are a useful way of measuring performance for a number of reasons.

(a) It is easier to look at **changes over time** by comparing ratios in one time period with the corresponding ratios for periods in the past.

(b) Ratios are often **easier to understand than absolute measures** of physical quantities or money values. For example, it is easier to understand that 'productivity in March was 94%' than 'there was an adverse labour efficiency variance in March of £3,600'.

(c) Ratios **relate one item to another**, and so help to put performance into context. For example the profit/sales ratio sets profit in the context of how much has been earned per £1 of sales, and so shows how wide or narrow profit margins are.

(d) Ratios can be used as **targets**. In particular, targets can be set for ROI, profit/sales, asset turnover, capacity fill and productivity. Managers will then take decisions which will enable them to achieve their targets.

(e) Ratios provide a way of **summarising** an organisation's results, and **comparing** them with similar organisations. For example, the results of one investment centre/profit centre/company can be compared directly with the results of another.

Percentages

3.17 A **percentage** expresses one number as a proportion of another and gives meaning to absolute numbers. Examples are as follows.

(a) **Market share**. A company may aim to achieve a 25% share of the total market for its product, and measure both its marketing department and the quality of the product against this.

(b) **Capacity levels** are usually measured in this way. 'Factory A is working at 20% below full capacity' is an example which indicates relative inefficiency.

(c) **Wastage** is sometimes expressed in percentage terms. 'Normal loss' may be 10%, a measure of *in*efficiency.

(d) **Staff turnover** is often measured in this way. In the catering industry for example, staff turnover is typically greater than 100%, and so a hotel with a lower percentage could take this as an indicator both of the experience of its staff and of how well it is treating them.

Indices

3.18 **Indices** show how a particular variable has changed **relative to a base value**. The base value is usually the level of the variable at an earlier date. The 'variable' may be just one particular item, such as material X, or several items, such as 'raw materials' generally.

3.19 In its simplest form an index is calculated as (current value/base value) × 100. Thus if materials cost £15 per kg in 20X0 and now (20X3) cost £27 per kg, the 20X0 value would be expressed in index form as 100 (15/15 × 100) and the 20X3 value as 180 (27/15 × 100). If you find it easier to think of this as a percentage, then do so.

4 BENEFITS AND PROBLEMS OF PERFORMANCE MEASURES

4.1 George Brown's article on performance measurement ('Accountability and performance measurement' *ACCA Students' Newsletter*, August 1998) includes Berry, Broadbent and Otley's list of **benefits of performance measures**.

1 'Clarifying the objectives of the organisation
2 Developing agreed measures of activity
3 Greater understanding of the processes
4 Facilitating comparison of performance in different organisations
5 Facilitating the setting of targets for the organisation and its managers
6 Promoting accountability of the organisation to its stakeholders'

4.2 Their list of **problems of performance measures** is also included in the article.

Problem	Comment
Tunnel vision	Undue focus on performance measures to the detriment of other areas
Sub-optimisation	Focus on some objectives so that others are not achieved
Myopia	Short-sightedness leading to the neglect of longer-term objectives
Measure fixation	Measures and behaviour in order to achieve specific performance indicators which may not be effective
Misrepresentation	'Creative' reporting to suggest that a result is acceptable
Misinterpretation	Failure to recognise the complexity of the environment in which the organisation operates
Gaming	Deliberate distortion of a measure to secure some strategic advantage
Ossification	An unwillingness to change the performance measure scheme once it has been set up

4.3 The article suggests ways in which the **problems may be reduced**, and they are summarised here.

(a) **Involvement of staff** at all levels in the development and implementation of the scheme should help to reduce gaming and tunnel vision.

(b) A **flexible use** of performance measures should help to reduce measure fixation and misrepresentation.

(c) Keeping the performance measurement system under **constant review** should help to overcome the problems of ossification and gaming.

(d) Give careful consideration to the **dimensions of performance**. Quantifying all objectives should help to overcome sub-optimisation, while a focus on measuring customer satisfaction should reduce tunnel vision and sub-optimisation.

(e) Consideration should be given to the **audit of the system**. Expert interpretation of the performance measurement scheme should help to provide an idea of the incidence of the problems, while a careful audit of the data used should help to reduce the incidence and impact of measure fixation, misinterpretation and gaming.

(f) **Recognition of the key feature** necessary in any scheme (a long-term view/perspective amongst staff, a sensible number of measures, benchmarks which are independent of past activity) should help to overcome the range of problems listed above.

5 MEASURING DIVISIONAL PERFORMANCE: ROI, RI AND EVA

Meaningful comparisons

5.1 **Like should be compared with like.** When comparing the financial performance of divisions there is a great deal of scope for different treatments of certain items. Problems that may affect comparability include the following.

- How are **assets valued** (NBV, current cost, market value, etc)?
- What **charge is made**, if any, for the use of **jointly owned or centrally owned** assets?
- How are **common costs** allocated between separate units?
- Do units control their own **working capital** or is this centrally managed? Are charges made for the use of **company funds?**
- Do different units exchange goods or services. What **transfer pricing** system is used?
- **What 'profit'** is used if profit is compared (gross profit, profit before interest and tax, etc)?

Return on investment (ROI)

KEY TERM

Return on investment (ROI) shows how much profit has been made in relation to the amount of capital invested.

ROI = (profit/capital employed) × 100%

5.2 Return on investment is inevitably a **widely-used** measure of company or divisional performance.

(a) It **ties in directly with the (financial) accounting process and is identifiable from the profit and loss account and balance sheet**.

(b) If a measurement of the return on investment for a division or company as a single entire unit is wanted, ROI is the only measure of performance available that has gained acceptance.

5.3 ROI is a simple measure to compute in theory: it is the percentage given by dividing the profit made by a business by the amount of capital invested in order to make that profit. However, **both elements of the ROI fraction present problems in practice**.

Measuring investment

5.4 'Investment' is likely to comprise the fixed assets of a business plus its net current assets. For the business as a whole these figures may be easy to identify, but when judging the performance of the separate operations that make up the business it will be **hard to decide what element of assets shared by several different operations should be taken into account.** For example, debtors and creditors may be managed centrally by head office; motor vehicles used by individual shops for deliveries might be part of a pool covering several shops in a region.

5.5 Even if the assets used by separate operations can be identified there is the further **problem of ascribing a value to them.**

(a) If assets are valued at historic cost then an older asset will have a lower value than an identical one acquired more recently.

(b) If the value is restated at current cost, this may disguise the impact of the relative inefficiency of older assets compared with newer ones (for example repair costs and lack of technological improvements).

(c) If depreciation is taken into account, are all similar assets being depreciated according to the same accounting policy?

5.6 The ROI measure may, in any case, not be a reliable guide to the quality of the management of the various operations.

(a) There is a considerable difference between the return likely to be achievable by a factory on its assets compared with a shop and its, quite different, assets. **Like should be compared with like**, or allowances should be made for differences, otherwise the exercise has no validity.

(b) **If investment decisions are made centrally** it may not be fair to measure a manager's ability to earn a return on assets that he or she might not have chosen to invest in, in the first place.

(c) Managers may **manipulate short-term levels** to improve the ratio.

(d) If managers have control over the assets in use in their operation, they may be inclined to under-**invest in new assets** in order to keep the investment figure low and their ROI high. This is unlikely to be in the interests of the company as a whole. This point is developed in the following paragraphs. First try a question.

Question: short-termism

How can the short-termism associated with traditional performance measures be overcome?

Answer

Here are some suggestions.

- Measure ROI (for example) over a period of more than one year
- Use non-profit-related performance indicators
- Use the balanced scorecard approach
- Focus incentive schemes on long-term aims
- Set easily-attainable short-term targets
- Specify in management contracts that performance will be judged on achieving long-term organisation objectives
- Offer bonuses relating to increases in share price over a certain time period
- Adopt an economic value added approach (see below)

Dysfunctional decisions

5.7 It might be group policy that investments earning 12% or more should be undertaken, but if a subsidiary is currently earning a ROI of, say, 30%, its manager might want to reject a proposed project whose return would be, say, 20%, because it would reduce the centre's overall ROI to below 30%. The **investment might be desirable from the group's point of view**, but would **not be in the individual investment centre's 'best interest'** to undertake. This would be an example of **sub-optimality** and a **lack of goal congruence** in decision making.

5.8 A similar misguided decision would occur where a divisional manager is worried about the low ROI of his division, and decides to **reduce his investment by scrapping some machinery** which is not currently in use. The reduction in both depreciation charges and assets would **immediately improve the ROI**. When the machinery is eventually required the manager would then be **obliged to buy new equipment**. Such a situation may seem bizarre, but it does occur in real life.

5.9 ROI should not be used to guide management decisions but there is a difficult motivational problem. If management performance is measured in terms of ROI, any decisions which benefit the company in the **long term** but which reduce the ROI in the immediate short term would reflect badly on the manager's reported performance. In other words, **good investment decisions would make a manager's performance seem worse than if the wrong investment decision were taken instead.**

Residual income (RI)

5.10 An alternative way of measuring the performance of an investment centre, instead of using ROI, is residual income (RI).

KEY TERM

Residual income (RI) is a measure of an investment centre's profits after deducting a notional or imputed interest cost.

- The divisional profit is after deducting depreciation on capital equipment.
- The imputed cost of capital might be the organisation's cost of borrowing or its weighted average cost of capital. Alternatively, the cost of capital can be adjusted to allow for the risk characteristics of each investment centre.

Question: residual income

A division with capital employed of £7m currently earns a ROI of 16%. It can make an additional investment of £1m for a 4 year life with nil residual value. The average net profit from this investment would be £200,000 after depreciation. The division's cost of capital is 8%. Calculate the residual income before and after the investment.

Answer

	Before investment	*After investment*
	£'000	£'000
Divisional profit	1,120	1,320
Imputed interest	560	640
Residual income	560	680

Make sure you understand how these figures are calculated.

The advantages and weaknesses of RI compared with ROI

5.11 The **advantages of using RI** are as follows.

- Residual income will **increase** when **investments earning above the cost of capital are undertaken** and when **investments earning below the cost of capital are eliminated.**

In this respect, it is a better measure than ROI for reasons explained in the following paragraphs.

- Residual income is **more flexible** since a different cost of capital can be applied to investments with different risk characteristics.

5.12 The **weakness of RI** is that it **does not facilitate comparisons** between investment centres **nor does it relate the size of a centre's income to the size of the investment**. In this respect, ROI is a better measure of performance, and RI is not much used in practice.

5.13 **Residual income does not always point to correct investment decisions,** because notional interest on accounting capital employed is not the same as DCF yield on cash investment. However, residual income is **more likely than ROI to improve when managers make correct investment/divestment decisions**, and so is probably a 'safer' basis than ROI on which to measure performance.

Annuity depreciation

5.14 The use of annuity depreciation with residual income attempts to avoid the problems of straight line depreciation. **With straight line depreciation and constant profits, the residual income will increase as asset values fall**. This could lead to dysfunctional behaviour and sub-optimal decision making. **With annuity depreciation and constant profits RI will remain constant if profits are constant.**

Question: annuity depreciation

A project requires an investment of £200,000 and will last for five years. The cost of capital is 9%. Cash inflows will be £70,000 per annum. Calculate the interest charges and depreciation charges using annuity depreciation.

Answer

Annual 'repayment' = £200,000/9% annuity factor (5 years) = £200,000/3.890 = £51,414

Year	*Annual repayment*	*Interest at 9% on outstanding capital*	*Depreciation*	*Capital outstanding*
	£	£	£	£
0				200,000
1	51,414	18,000	33,414	166,586
2	51,414	14,993	36,421	130,165
3	51,414	11,715	39,699	90,466
4	51,414	8,142	43,272	47,194
5	51,414	4,220 (rounded)	47,194	-

Economic value added

KEY TERM

Economic value added (EVA) 'A measure which approximates a company's profit. Traditional financial statements are translated into EVA statements by reversing distortions in operating performance created by accounting rules and by charging operating profit for all of the capital employed. For example, written-off goodwill is capitalised, as are extraordinary losses and the present value of operating leases. Extraordinary gains reduce capital.' *(CIMA Official Terminology)*

5.15 Such an approach contrasts favourably with information based on traditional accounting concepts and conventions. The prudence concept, for example, requires revenue expenditure (such as maintenance expenditure on plant and machinery) to be written off to the profit and loss account in the accounting period in which it is incurred. This is to reflect the fact that such expenditure may have no long term benefits. It is therefore not very surprising that if management are assessed using performance measures calculated using traditional accounting policies, they are unwilling to invest in or spend money on activities which immediately reduce current year's profit.

5.16 It is claimed that EP provides the basis for a useful management performance appraisal measure because **while EP increases, so does the market value added for a company and shareholder value.**

5.17 EXAMPLE OF EVA

Recommend which plc, X or Y, to invest funds in. Justify your decision.

Profit and loss account for the previous year (£m's)

	X	*Y*
Sales	26.0	62.0
Cost of sales	18.0	47.0
Gross profit	8.0	15.0
Production overheads	1.2	2.4
Advertising	0.6	2.0
Depreciation	1.1	1.6
Training	0.1	1.8
R&D	0.6	2.0
Bad debt expense	0.2	0.3
PBIT	4.2	4.9
Investment base	26.5	40.6

5.18 SOLUTION

Traditional ROI techniques would give X plc 15.8% and Y plc 12.1%, and therefore choose X plc for investment. However, this ignores the fact that Y is more heavily involved in developing the long term future of its company by spending on training and R&D. These items, under EVA, would be added back to obtain a comparison using operational expenses.

Adjusted ROI

	X	*Y*
Original profit	4.2	4.9
Training	0.1	1.8
Advertising	0.6	2.0
R&D	0.6	2.0
New profit	5.5	10.7
New ROI	20.8%	26.4%

5.19 There is still a lack of information here to make a final decision, although the original analysis and decision to invest in X plc has been considerably refined. Business risk, market dynamics, previous year's results, competitor comparisons and investment portfolio issues will affect the analysis.

5.20 '**Economic value added** is the best indicator of business performance. When it is projected for future years and discounted to the present value, it represents the net present value of all past and future investments and cash flows. Therefore, by making increases in EP a

priority, the economic value added of a company will increase, which will, in turn, lead to increases in a company's market value (and therefore its share price)'.

(John Mayfield, 'Economic value management: the route to shareholder value', *Management Accounting*, September 1997)

Chapter roundup

- Key areas for performance measurement are **profitability, activity** and **productivity**. Profitability is often a key objective but other '**success factors**' are also critical. **Benchmarking** is increasingly common.
- Both quantitative and qualitative performance measures are equally valuable.
- Financial measures generally derive from the accounting system (or other businesses' accounting systems).
- An imaginative approach to performance measurement is becoming a necessity in the modern business environment, and many businesses now recognise the need to supplement traditional financial measures with other, **non-financial indicators.**
- Non-monetary measures also include **ratios**, **percentages** and **indices**.
- **Indices** can be used in a variety of ways in performance measurement, for example in **forecasting** and for **inter-company comparisons**.
- A recent article by the examiner considers the **benefits and problems of performance measures**.
- **Return on investment (ROI)** is a convenient measure, which ties in easily with the firm's accounts. However, there are measurement and valuation decisions which are not in the firm's best long-term interest. ROI does not easily account for risk.
- ROI is based on **organisation structure**, not business processes, and is only suitable to products at the mature phase of the life cycle.
- **Residual income** (RI) gets around some of the problems of ROI, by deducting from profit an imputed interest charge for the use of assets.
- **Economic value** management hinges on the idea of an **economic profit,** which is derived after adjusting traditional accounting profits for the write offs that are made for **value building expenditures** such as training and advertising. By adding such expenditure back to accounting profit, better comparison can be made between companies.

Quick quiz

1 What is the aim of performance management?

2 What is a critical success factor?

3 Which of the following are examples of non-financial indicators? Circle all that apply.

- Number of customer complaints
- Lead times
- Cash flow
- Delivery to time
- Revenue

4 Financial indicators are superior to non-financial indicators.

True ☐

False ☐

5 What is the main problem associated with ROI as a performance measure?

6 ROI is a form of ROCE

True ☐

False ☐

7 Residual income (RI) is a measure of the centre's profits after deducting a notional or imputed ………… cost.

8 A division with capital employed of £400,000 currently earns a ROI of 22%. It can make an additional investment of £50,000 for a 5 year life with nil residual value. The average net profit from this investment would be £12,000 after depreciation. The division's cost of capital is 14%. Calculate the residual income before and after the investment.

9 Economic value added is more sophisticated form of residual income.

True ☐

False ☐

Answers to quick quiz

1 To establish how well something or somebody is doing in relation to the planned activity and desired results.

2 An area of the job where things must go right for the organisation to flourish.

3 Number of customer complaints
Lead times
Delivery to time

4 False. A **combination** of financial and non-financial indicators is desirable.

5 It is mainly to do with the problem of accurate measurement of the value of the assets used to produce the return. For example, it is probably most common to use return on net assets. Inflation and technological change alter the cost of fixed assets, so that it becomes difficult to compare the performance of different divisions.

6 True

7 Interest

8

	Before investment	After investment
	£	£
Divisional profit	88,000	100,000
Imputed interest		
(400,000 × 0.14)	56,000	
(450,000 × 0.14)		63,000
Residual income	32,000	37,000

9 True

Now try the question below from the Exam Question Bank

Number	Level	Marks	Time
Q17	Introductory	n/a	n/a

Chapter 12

PRICE CHANGES AND CORPORATE FAILURE

Introduction

Some companies publish **current cost information** (particularly the utilities). You should be able to analyse this type of information and indicate where accounting ratios will differ compared to historical costs.

The state of the economy in recent years has emphasised the need to **monitor companies** carefully for signs of difficulty. This is important, not just for the investors or creditors of a company, but also for a company's managers. After all, they frequently have as much to lose as their shareholders!

Study guide

Section 25 – Preparation of reports 3

- Discussion of alternative definitions of capital employed and measurement bases for assets
- Discussion of the impact of price level changes on business performance
- Appraising the alternative methods of accounting for price level changes
- Evaluation of the potential for corporate failure

1 ANALYSIS OF CURRENT VALUE FINANCIAL STATEMENTS

1.1 Why might historical cost accounts analysis not be as useful as it first appears? Why would it be better to analyse current value accounts?

Numerator/denominator

1.2 The numerator and the denominator of a given ratio should be **consistent**: profit available to shareholders should be related to shareholders' capital employed; profit before interest should be related to all long-term capital employed and so on. In addition, the numerator and denominator should be expressed in measurement scales which are comparable and which thus produce a meaningful result. For example, the ratio of liquid assets (in £) to current liabilities (also in £) produces a meaningful result (the proportionate excess, or shortfall, of liquid assets over current liabilities), whereas a ratio of sales (in £) to the average age of fixed assets (in years) does not.

1.3 On the face of it, the ratios we have examined in Chapter 24 appear to produce meaningful results: the measurement scales appear to be in harmony. For each ratio both the numerator and denominator are expressed in pounds (£). But consider: what is the aim of producing any ratio? We are interpreting historical data in order to obtain **predictive information**. We are interested in the current year's amount of sales revenue generated per £1 of capital invested largely as a basis for predicting future years' sales revenues (and, eventually, cash flows). Would an extra £1 invested at the beginning of 1984 generate an additional £2 of sales revenue now? It is unlikely because the numerator and the denominator of this ratio are not in fact consistent with each other. It is not sufficient that they are both expressed in £s. The sales figure is expressed in £s reflecting current prices, but the long-term capital figure comprises amounts invested over a period of many years.

Sales/net profit

1.4 Although sales are expressed in current prices, net profit is not. Many components of net profit are expressed in current prices (sales, wages, rent, rates and so on) but **depreciation,** in particular, is based upon prices which existed at the time of purchase of the relevant assets. As we have already noted these assets may have been bought a long time ago. Similar problems can occur if older items of stock are included in cost of goods sold. Both problems can be avoided by the use of current costs in the P&L account.

Return on investment

1.5 The potential usefulness of a **return on investment figure**, both as an indicator of overall performance and as a guide to future performance, would appear to demand that the constituent elements of the P&L account and the balance sheet be expressed in comparable current prices. If some form of 'current' cost accounting is used, the return on investment ratio would provide a much better indication of management's efficiency in using resources. For example, if asset values and operating costs were based on replacement costs, the ratio would provide an indicator of management's ability to generate sufficient funds to replace assets as they are used, and hence to ensure the long-run survival of the company.

1.6 In times of rising prices we would expect historical cost returns on historical capital employed (net assets) to be **higher** than replacement cost (operating) returns on replacement cost capital employed, where capital employed is defined in terms of operating capacity (holding gains are taken into the balance sheet rather than the P&L account). However, the difference between the two returns will not be identical for each company. This is due in part to the differential effects which price changes can have on different industries as a result of differences in the nature and size of fixed assets and stocks, and because different industries traditionally have different debtor/creditor relationships.

1.7 The usefulness of **other profitability ratios** is similarly limited if costs are measured on an historical rather than a current cost basis. For example, an organisation exhibiting a satisfactory gross profit percentage (a surplus of sales revenue over the historical cost of stock used), may not be generating sufficient funds either to replace the stock at current prices or to meet its operating costs.

Return on owners' capital

1.8 Similar criticisms can be levelled at the ratio expressing the return on owners' capital employed. This is based on the historical value of capital provided, both in the form of capital paid in and in the form of retained profits (reserves). As far as shareholders are concerned, the real cost of their investment in the company (the 'opportunity cost' of their investment) is represented by the amount sacrificed by not selling their shares: the **market value** of their shares. The same is true for potential buyers of shares who have to pay the market value rather than the book value to acquire shareholdings.

1.9 This problem would still exist if the company used some form of current cost accounting, although the differences between the 'book' figures used in the ratio and the 'relevant' return and income figures described above might be smaller. The return to ordinary shareholders depends on the **dividends** they receive and expect to receive and on the **market value** of their shares. Neither of these is included in the calculation of return on owners' capital based on the company's P&L account and balance sheet, although, in practice, a quoted company's net profit (or earnings) to its price-earnings ratio is often used as an indicator of success.

1.10 In addition, **profit after interest** may have little relationship to **cash** paid to or available for the owners of the company. The owners' return depends both on the cash distributed by the business during the period and on the value of the business at the end of the period, which in turn depends on the cash expected to be distributed in future periods.

Exam focus point

The following question links this section back to your earlier studies on accounting for changing prices and should be a useful test of your understanding of this area.

Question: current value financial statements

You are a financial analyst specialising in the analysis of the profitability of organisations in the engineering sector. One such company is Darton Ltd. The directors of Darton Ltd have always been interested in the impact of price changes on the performance of their business and have adopted the practice of including current cost accounts (using the 'real terms' system) alongside the historical cost accounts in the published financial statements. Extracts from the published financial statements for the year ended 31 March 20X6 are given below.

PROFIT AND LOSS ACCOUNTS FOR THE YEAR ENDED 31 MARCH 20X6

	Historical cost	*Current cost*	
	£'000	£'000	£'000
Sales	30,000		30,000
Operating costs (note 1)	16,000		19,000
Operating profit	14,000		11,000
Interest payable	2,000		2,000
Profit before taxation	12,000		9,000
Taxation	3,500		3,500
Profit after taxation	8,500		5,500
Holding gains arising during the year	-	3,500	
Inflation adjustment to shareholders' funds	-	(2,000)	
Real gains	-		1,500
Profit for the year	8,500		7,000
Dividends	7,000		7,000
Retained profit	1,500		-

BALANCE SHEET AS AT 31 MARCH 20X6

	£'000	£'000
Tangible fixed assets	20,000	24,000
Current assets (note 2)	16,000	19,000
Current liabilities	(10,000)	(10,000)
Loans	(15,000)	(15,000)
	11,000	18,000
Shareholders' funds	11,000	18,000

Notes

	Historical cost £'000	*Current cost* £'000
1 *Operating costs*		
Cost of sales (excluding depreciation)	8,000	10,000
Depreciation	5,000	6,000
Other operating costs	3,000	3,000
	16,000	19,000

	Historical cost £'000	*Current cost* £'000
2 *Current assets*		
Stocks	6,000	9,000
Debtors	9,000	9,000
Cash	1,000	1,000
	16,000	19,000

Required

(a) Compute (under *both* conventions) three accounting ratios for Darton Ltd which differ under the two conventions.

(b) Explain, for each ratio you have computed, the reason why the current cost elements included in the ratio differ from the historical cost elements.

(c) Explain the adjustments 'holding gains arising during the year' and 'inflation adjustment to shareholders' funds'.

Answer

(a) *Three accounting ratios*

		Historical cost	*Current cost*
Return on shareholders' funds	$= \frac{\text{Profit for the year}}{\text{Shareholders' funds}}$	$\frac{8,500}{11,000} = 77\%$	$\frac{5,500}{18,000} = 31\%$
Operating profit to sales	$= \frac{\text{Operating profit}}{\text{Sales}}$	$\frac{14,000}{30,000} = 47\%$	$\frac{11,000}{30,000} = 37\%$
Payment ratio	$= \frac{\text{Dividend}}{\text{Profit for year}}$	$\frac{7,000}{8,500} = 82\%$	$\frac{7,000}{7,000} = 100\%$

(b) *Return on shareholders' funds*

There is a significant difference between the ratios calculated under historical and current cost. Part of this is due to the reduction in net profit (net profit to sales for historical and current costs are 28% and 23% respectively). This results from the higher cost of sales under current cost accounts because of the effects of inflation, ie post-inflation costs are used. In addition, depreciation is higher under current costs as it is based on the replacement cost of assets, not their historical costs. The overall effect is to match truly current sales values to the current cost of resources used, rather than historical cost.

In the denominator of the equation, the shareholders' funds under current costs represent what it would cost to replace the net assets of the business. This means that the ratio shows the return on shareholders' funds *after* sufficient funds have been retained to maintain the operating capability of the business. The ratio is a great deal higher under historical costs because low pre-inflation costs are matched against current value sales and the resulting profit figure is compared to low pre-inflation shareholders' funds.

Operating profit to sales

The company's profitability seems much worse under current cost than under historical cost. Under current cost, realised holding gains of £3m have been excluded from operating costs. Cost of sales under current cost reflects the replacement cost of the stocks used up to produce the sales, not the low pre-inflation values of the historical cost accounts. The depreciation increase reflects the portion of current cost consumed during the year (ie a proportion of the asset replacement costs). Under historical cost the depreciation set aside is based on the original cost of the asset, and is insufficient to fund its replacement.

Payment ratio

Under historical costs Dambon Ltd appears to have paid out only a proportion of the profit for the year. The current cost accounts show that, after setting aside funds to retain the operating capability of the company (ie to maintain capital employed at current prices), the whole of the profit for the year has been distributed and therefore no funds have been retained to fund growth.

(c) *Holding gains arising during the year*

If assets are held for a period during which inflation exists, then they will be worth more in money terms at the time they are used, or at the accounting date if they are still held then. This adjustment is made to reflect this increase in value, from historical to current cost of resources used (realised holding gains) or held at the period end (unrealised holding gains). If this adjustment is not made before profit calculation and asset valuation for the financial statements, then profit would be overstated and capital employed would be understated. In effect, this adjustment indicates the amount of shareholders' funds which are not available for distribution as they are necessary to maintain the business's operating capability.

Inflation adjustment to shareholders' funds

This is an adjustment based on the concept of financial capital maintenance. By applying a general price index to shareholders' funds, it shows how much is needed to maintain the purchasing power of the shareholders' investment. Any holding gains which exceed this represent a 'real' gain to the shareholder, although this is not distributable. Under the real terms system, if the adjustment is greater than holding gains calculated, the deficit must be made up by an appropriation from profit.

---

2 IMPACT OF INFLATION ON TREND ANALYSIS

2.1 If the main aim of interpretation is **comparison**, then we need to build in the effects of inflation to ensure that a year on year comparison is valid, ie we need to **analyse trends.** Although CCA takes account of specific price changes, the results are still expressed in pounds for the year in question. The old ASC recognised this problem and put forward suggestions to tackle the issue in a discussion paper, *Corresponding amounts and ten year summaries in current cost accounting.*

2.2 The paper suggested two methods of adjusting past figures.

(a) Using specific costs and indices
(b) Using a general price index

Specific costs and indices

2.3 This method is unsatisfactory from a practical and theoretical viewpoint because it involves creating a completely **new set of accounts** for past periods which would be difficult to

interpret. The residuals in such accounts, such as profits, would be subject to unpredictable fluctuations. Volume changes are highlighted using this method where sales and product mix is comparatively unchanged.

2.4 EXAMPLE: SPECIFIC COSTS AND INDICES

Dunky has the following stock figures at two consecutive year ends.

	£
At 31 December 20X1: 8,000 items at £7.00	56,000
At 31 December 20X2: 9,000 items at £8.70	78,300
Increase in historical cost figures	22,300

2.5 SOLUTION

This change represents nearly 40% of the opening stock figure. Compare this with the rise in volume (12.5%) and the rise in price (24%).

Adjusting the opening figure for price reveals the following.

	£
At 31 December 20X1: £56,000 × 8.70/7.00	69,600
At 31 December 20X2	78,300
12.5% increase in volume	8,700

2.6 This method can be useful on occasion but not as a general method of adjusting past figures.

General price index

2.7 This method measures **financial changes**. It is useful to compare it with the problem of foreign currencies: we cannot add English pounds and French francs together without changing one of them into the other. In a similar way, the figures for the current year must be restated in terms of something at a point in the past to make it more meaningful.

2.8 The ASC suggested that the **General Index of Retail Prices (RPI)** might be used as a suitable index to reflect the change in the value of money for a general adjustment of this type. It is suitable in these circumstances because:

(a) It is published monthly
(b) It is published quickly after the end of the month
(c) It is not revised subsequent to publication
(d) It demonstrates trends which are similar to more accurate methods

Exam focus point

An exam question might look at the problems of comparison of results over time *and* between different companies.

Question: trend analysis

Extracts from the recently published five year summary of Daggers plc are shown below.

Year ended 31 March	*20X2*	*20X3*	*20X4*	*20X5*	*20X6*
	£m	£m	£m	£m	£m
Turnover	236	268	335	386	429
Current cost profit before tax	11	12	14	17	33
Current cost net assets per share	315p	359p	503p	556p	630p

The retail price index over the last five years has been as follows.

	Average	Year end
20X2	160.0	165.8
20X3	173.4	179.7
20X4	196.7	210.7
20X5	232.1	242.5
20X6	259.6	271.7

Required

(a) State the alternative methods which could be used to achieve greater comparability of the figures over five years.

(b) Prepare a revised five year summary for Daggers plc. Give reasons for the adjustments you have made.

(c) Comment on any significant trends which are revealed by the revised five year summary in (b).

Answer

(a) CCA takes account of specific price changes but each year's results are expressed in the pounds of that year. Comparison is therefore not complete. This problem can be solved by calculation of 'pure ratios': numerator and denominator are both expressed in terms of pounds of the same year. The ratio can then be compared with that achieved in other years. Examples of pure ratios include:

$$\frac{\text{Current cost operating profit}}{\text{Average net operating profit}}$$

$$\frac{\text{Net borrowings}}{\text{Equity interest}}$$

where they are based on current cost accounts.

A more complete answer would be to adjust figures by use of indices.

The following decisions must then be made:

(i) Whether to deflate the figures to a base period or update past figures to current year values

(ii) Whether to use a general price or specific index

(iii) Whether the index used should be an average for the year or that governing at the balance sheet date

(b) DAGGERS PLC
FIVE YEAR SUMMARY

Year ended 31 March	*20X2*	*20X3*	*20X4*	*20X5*	*20X6*
	£m	£m	£m	£m	£m
Turnover (W1)	401	420	463	452	449
Current cost profit before tax	19	19	19	20	35
Current cost net assets					
per share (W2)	516p	543p	649p	623p	630p

Workings

1 *Turnover and current cost profit before tax*

These figures should be adjusted from average pounds for each year to the figure at 31 March 20X6.

	Turnover	*Profit*	*Update*	*Turnover*	*Profit*
	£m	£m		£m	£m
20X2	236	11	271.7 ÷ 160.0	401	19
20X3	268	12	271.7 ÷ 173.4	403	19
20X4	335	14	271.7 ÷ 196.7	463	19
20X5	386	17	271.7 ÷ 232.1	452	20
20X6	429	33	271.7 ÷ 259.6	449	35

2 *Current cost net assets per share*

These figures should be adjusted from year end pounds each year to the figure at 31 March 20X6.

	Current cost net assets per share (p)	*Update*	*Net assets per share (p)*
20X2	315	271.7 ÷ 165.8	516
20X3	359	271.7 ÷ 179.7	543
20X4	503	271.7 ÷ 210.7	649
20X5	556	271.7 ÷ 242.5	623
20X6	630	271.7 ÷ 271.7	630

(c) The figures in the five year plan in (b) are much more informative now. The growth in turnover halted in 20X4 and has declined since, although at a slowing rate. Profit, which has remained fairly constant for some years, has suddenly risen by 75% in 20X6, a dramatic increase. The net asset per share figure has improved in 20X6, presumably because of the leap in profits, halting the decline from 20X4 to 20X5. Further investigations might reveal the meaning of these figures, but the main point is that the revised five year plan is much more informative.

3 CORPORATE FAILURE PREDICTION

3.1 The often unexpected collapse of large companies during the early 1990s and more recently in 2002 has led analysts to look for ways of predicting company failure. We will look at one of the most popular methods shortly. First of all, we need to consider what leads companies into insolvency, particularly those that appear successful.

Major causes of insolvency

3.2 A company is technically insolvent when it **cannot pay its debts as they fall due**. Insolvency law prevents companies from continuing trading in such situation, mainly to prevent preferential payments to creditors. Directors who allow companies to carry on trading while insolvent become personally liable for company debts and may be prosecuted.

3.3 The obvious major cause of insolvency is **no money**! Lack of funds can occur for a variety of reasons, and we have already identified how cash can be used up rapidly in the working capital cycle. This situation can lead to insolvency, but for a healthy and growing company, lack of short-term funds can be remedied by the injection of long-term equity or loan capital. The market will be willing to invest in sound companies and thereby fund expansion.

Example of company failure: property developers

3.4 The recent recession hit **property development companies** particularly hard. These companies present a typical high risk profile: high value stocks (land and developments in progress), high gearing and reliance on economic prosperity. Once the recession and the collapse of the property market came along, such companies faced such a large drop in income that they could not service their debt and continue with existing projects.

3.5 These companies also saw their balance sheets decimated by the fall in property values. Property companies frequently **capitalised interest** in the cost of development, avoiding passing the interest through the P&L account until income was received on the project. This was justified under the accruals concept as a matching of income with expenditure. As property prices fell, this treatment could no longer be justified as the prudence concept was being breached (stocks were valued at more than their net realisable value). Such companies

therefore wrote off large interest costs, often built up over several years, without the benefit of any related income.

Interest rates

3.6 Increases in interest rates are obviously a great problem for **highly geared companies**. Companies which carry existing long-term fixed interest debt at lower interest rates are obviously at a great advantage. New debt at higher or variable rates and short-term debt will become much more expensive. The combination of higher interest costs and reduced income because of economic factors can drive a company into insolvency.

Loan covenants

3.7 Another problem can arise when assets have to be written down. Companies with high debt will often undertake covenants with their lenders. Such covenants are often based on the relationship between total debt and **balance sheet values of assets**, or perhaps balance sheet totals. The covenants may also be based on interest cover. If debt covenants are breached, then the lender can usually appoint a receiver. This is still a last resort in most situations and companies and lenders will normally renegotiate the covenants, although the company may have to compensate the lender for agreeing to take on extra risk.

Working capital problems

3.8 Working capital difficulties can arise for reasons other than overtrading. Businesses which rely on **one large customer** (or just a few) are in a very dangerous position. The loss of such a customer can have such a severe impact on cash flow that a company cannot find new customers in time to avoid disasters. Losing customers because they themselves go bankrupt is even worse: they might owe you a significant amount of money which as an unsecured creditor you would not be able to recover. Large customers can also impose trading terms which are unfavourable, but which must be accepted to avoid loss of business. For example, one of the large supermarket chains cut suppliers' prices for certain produce across the board and with no consultation. The suppliers had no choice but to 'take on their share of margin reductions'.

Exam focus point

You may find some aspects of this chapter worth mentioning if you are asked to analyse the financial statements of a company which is obviously in difficulties, particularly if you are asked to comment from a creditor's point of view.

4 MULTI-VARIATE ANALYSIS

4.1 The analysis of financial ratios is largely concerned with the **efficiency and effectiveness** of the use of resources by a company's management, and also with the **financial stability** of the company. Investors, including holding companies, will wish to know:

(a) Whether additional funds could be lent to the company with reasonable safety;
(b) Whether the company would fail without additional funds.

Z scores

4.2 **E I Altman** researched into the simultaneous analysis of several financial ratios as a combined predictor of business failure. Altman analysed 22 accounting and non-accounting variables for a selection of failed and non-failed firms in the USA, and from these five key indicators emerged. These five indicators were then used to derive a **Z score**. Firms with a Z score above a certain level would be predicted to be financially sound, and firms with a Z score below a certain level would be expected to fail. Altman also identified a range of Z scores in between the non-failure and failure categories in which eventual failure or non-failure was uncertain.

4.3 Altman's **Z score model** (derived in 1968) emerged as:

$$Z = 1.2X_1 + 1.4X_2 + 3.3X_3 + 0.6X_4 + 1.0X_5$$

Where

X_1 = working capital/total assets
X_2 = retained earnings/total assets
X_3 = earnings before interest and tax/total assets
X_4 = market value of equity/book value of total debt (a form of gearing ratio)
X_5 = sales/total assets.

4.4 In Altman's model, a Z score of 2.7 or more indicated non-failure, and a Z score of 1.8 or less indicated failure.

4.5 Altman's sample size was small, and related to US firms. Subsequent research based on the similar principle of identifying a Z score predictor of business failure has produced **different prediction models**, using a variety of financial ratios and different Z score values as predictors of failure. It could be argued, for example, that different ratios and Z score values would be appropriate for conditions in the UK.

Question: Z score

Earlier in this Study Text you were asked to obtain copies of company annual reports. Try to apply Altman's Z score model to one or more of them.

The value of Z scores

4.6 A current view of the link between financial ratios and business failure is as follows.

(a) The financial ratios of firms which fail can be seen in retrospect to have **deteriorated significantly** prior to failure, and to have been worse than the ratios of non-failed firms. In retrospect, financial ratios can be used to suggest why a firm has failed.

(b) No fully accepted model for **predicting future business failures** has yet been established, although some form of Z score analysis would appear to be the most promising avenue for progress. In the UK, several Z score-type failure prediction models exist, and are used by consultancy firms to assist clients (such as banks).

4.7 Because of the use of X_4: market value of equity/book value of debt, Z score models cannot be used for unquoted companies which lack a market value of equity. Alternative **K score models**, which are not limited in this way, have been developed.

Argenti's failure model

4.8 From historical data on a wide range of actual cases, J Argenti developed a model which is intended to predict the likelihood of company failure. The model is based on calculating

scores for a company based on (a) defects of the company; (b) management mistakes and (c) the symptoms of failure. For each of the scores (a), (b) and (c) there is a **danger mark**.

4.9 Among the most important factors in the model are the following.

(a) **Defects**

(i) Autocratic chief executive (Robert Maxwell is an example here)
(ii) Passive board
(iii) Lack of budgetary control

(b) **Mistakes**

(i) Over-trading (expanding faster than cash funding)
(ii) Gearing - high bank overdrafts/loans
(iii) Failure of large project jeopardises the company (for example Laker Airways)

(c) **Symptoms**

(i) Deteriorating ratios
(ii) Creative accounting - signs of window-dressing
(iii) Declining morale and declining quality

Other indicators of financial difficulties

4.10 You should not think that ratio analysis of published accounts and score analysis are the only ways of spotting that a company might be running into financial difficulties. There are other possible indicators too.

(a) **Other information in the published accounts**

Some information in the published accounts might not lend itself readily to ratio analysis, but can still be an indicator of financial difficulties, eg:

(i) Very large increases in intangible fixed assets

(ii) A worsening cash plus cash equivalents position shown by the cash flow statement

(iii) Very large contingent liabilities

(iv) Important post balance sheet events

(b) **Information in the chairman's report and the directors' report**

The report of the chairman or chief executive that accompanies the published accounts might be very revealing. Although this report is not audited, and will no doubt try to paint a rosy picture of the company's affairs, any difficulties the company has had and not yet overcome will probably be discussed in it. There might also be warnings of problems to come in the future.

The directors' report is usually restricted to the minimum information required by law, but it might be interesting to check whether there have been any changes in the composition of the board since last year. Have many of last year's directors gone? Are there many new directors, and if so, what are their qualifications?

(c) **Published information in the press**

Newspapers and financial journals are a source of information about companies, and the difficulties or successes they are having. There may be reports of strikes, redundancies and closures. Newspapers also report when directors of listed companies sell their shares: what does this mean?

There are often articles in newspapers which focus on particular companies. If a company is in financial difficulty, adverse comments might well appear in one of these articles.

(d) **Published information about environmental or external matters**

There will also be published information about matters that will have a direct influence on a company's future, although the connection may not be obvious. Examples of external matters that may affect a company adversely are as follows.

(i) New legislation, eg on product safety standards or pollution controls, which affect a company's main products

(ii) International events, eg political disagreements with a foreign country, leading to a restriction on trade between the countries

(iii) New and better products being launched on to the market by a competitor

(iv) A big rise in interest rates, which might seriously affect a highly-geared company

(v) A large movement in foreign exchange rates, which might affect a major importer or exporter seriously

Chapter roundup

- Ratios based on **current cost accounts** are more useful for trend analysis over time than ratios based on historical cost accounts.
- Financial analysis is not a precise science. The **nature of accounting information** means that distortions and differences will always exist between sets of accounts, not only from company to company, but also over time.
- There are various ways of taking account of **inflation** in trend analysis. Current cost accounts must be adjusted by using a deflator or an index to bring all the results to a base period or to the current results.
- **Corporate failure prediction** is extremely important, particularly in recessionary periods.
- The **major causes of insolvency** can be summarised as follows.
  - Industry in decline
  - Overtrading
  - Empire building
  - Lack of financial controls
  - General economic conditions
- **Sophisticated techniques**, such as **multi-variate analysis**, have been developed to help predict company failures. They are not accurate and it cannot be guaranteed that the prediction made will be fulfilled.

Quick quiz

1. When prices are rising, HCA returns on HCA capital employed would be higher/lower than the equivalent replacement cost ratio. (Delete as applicable)
2. Why have property companies been so badly affected by the current recession?
3. A company with one large customer is at less risk than a company with many small customers?

   True ☐

   False ☐
4. What are the major aims of multi-variate analysis?
5. Reproduce Altman's Z score model.
6. Upon what factors is Argenti's failure model based? Defects, mistakes and ....
7. Highlight some other important indicators of financial difficulties.

Answers to quick quiz

1. Higher
2. They are high risk: high value stocks, high gearing and reliance on economic prosperity.
3. False. It is more risky to have 'all your eggs in one basket'.
4. To determine whether additional funds can safely be lent to the company and whether the company would fail without additional funds
5. $Z = 1.2X_1 + 1.4X_2 + 3.3X_3 + 0.6X_4 + 1.0X_5$

   Where

   X_1 = working capital/total assets
   X_2 = retained earnings/total assets
   X_3 = earnings before interest and tax/total assets
   X_4 = market value of equity/book value of total debt (a form of gearing ratio)
   X_5 = sales/total assets.
6. Symptoms
7. See paragraph 4.10 (a)

Now try the questions below from the Exam Question Bank

Number	Level	Marks	Time
Q18	Exam	25	45 mins
Q19	Introductory	n/a	n/a

Part D

International, environmental and current issues

Chapter 13

INTERNATIONAL ISSUES

Introduction

As business expands on an **international scale** so financial reporting must be viewed as it operates on an international rather than a national level. In studying the impact of the international environment we will look at the influences on accounting in a number of countries. These influences vary from country to country and include legal, political, socio-cultural and economic conditions prevailing at any time.

Study guide

Section 27 – International issues

- Evaluating the developments in global harmonisation and standardisation
- Assessing proposed changes to national and international regulation
- Identifying the reasons for major differences in accounting practices
- Restating overseas financial statements in line with UK accounting policies

Exam guide

In view of the move towards IAS for listed companies in the EU, this is a 'hot topic', and, as such, ripe for examination

1 INTERNATIONAL HARMONISATION 12/01, 6/02, 12/02, 12/03

1.1 Before we look at any other countries in particular, we must consider what barriers there are to international harmonisation and why harmonisation is considered so desirable, before looking at comparative accounting systems.

Barriers to harmonisation

1.2 There are undoubtedly many barriers to international harmonisation: if there were not then greater progress would probably have been made by now. The main problems are as follows.

(a) **Different purposes of financial reporting**. In some countries the purpose is solely for tax assessment, while in others it is for investor decision-making.

(b) **Different legal systems**. These prevent the development of certain accounting practices and restrict the options available.

(c) **Different user groups**. Countries have different ideas about who the relevant user groups are and their respective importance. In the USA investor and creditor groups are given prominence, while in Europe employees enjoy a higher profile.

(d) **Needs of developing countries**. Developing countries are obviously behind in the standard setting process and they need to develop the basic standards and principles already in place in most developed countries.

(e) **Nationalism** is demonstrated in an unwillingness to accept another country's standard.

(f) **Cultural differences** result in objectives for accounting systems differing from country to country.

(g) **Unique circumstances**. Some countries may be experiencing unusual circumstances which affect all aspects of everyday life and impinge on the ability of companies to produce proper reports, for example hyperinflation, civil war, currency restriction and so on.

(h) **The lack of strong accountancy bodies**. Many countries do not have strong independent accountancy or business bodies which would press for better standards and greater harmonisation.

1.3 These are difficult problems to overcome, and yet attempts are being made continually to do so. We must therefore consider what the perceived advantages of harmonisation are, which justify so much effort.

Advantages of global harmonisation

1.4 The advantages of harmonisation will be based on the benefits to users and preparers of accounts, as follows.

(a) **Investors**, both individual and corporate, would like to be able to compare the financial results of different companies internationally as well as nationally in making investment decisions. Differences in accounting practice and reporting can prove to be a barrier to such cross-border analysis. There is a growing amount of investment across borders and there are few financial analysts able to follow shares in international markets. For example, it is not easy for an analyst familiar with UK accounting principles to analyse the financial statements of a Dutch or German company. Harmonisation would therefore be of benefit to such analysts.

(b) **Multinational companies** would benefit from harmonisation for many reasons including the following.

(i) Better access would be gained to foreign investor funds.

(ii) Management control would be improved, because harmonisation would aid internal communication of financial information.

(iii) Appraisal of foreign enterprises for take-overs and mergers would be more straightforward.

(iv) It would be easier to comply with the reporting requirements of overseas stock exchanges.

(v) Consolidation of foreign subsidiaries and associated companies would be easier.

(vi) A reduction in audit costs might be achieved.

(vii) Transfer of accounting staff across national borders would be easier.

(c) **Governments of developing countries** would save time and money if they could adopt international standards and, if these were used internally, governments of developing countries could attempt to control the activities of foreign multinational companies in their own country. These companies could not 'hide' behind foreign accounting practices which are difficult to understand.

(d) **Tax authorities.** It will be easier to calculate the tax liability of investors, including multinationals who receive income from overseas sources.

(e) **Regional economic groups** usually promote trade within a specific geographical region. This would be aided by common accounting practices within the region.

(f) **Large international accounting firms** would benefit as accounting and auditing would be much easier if similar accounting practices existed throughout the world.

Progress with harmonisation to date

1.5 The barriers to harmonisation may be daunting but some progress has been made. There are various bodies which are working on different aspects of harmonisation and these are discussed below. The most important of these bodies, in the light of recent developments, is the IASB.

International Accounting Standards Board (IASB)

1.6 The function and role of the IASB was covered in your earlier studies. In particular, the effect of the IASB's *Framework for the Preparation and Presentation of Financial Statements* on the UK standard setting regime has been profound.

1.7 The IASB is tackling the issue of harmonisation through a review of its International Accounting Standards (IASs). This review was embodied in a Statement of Intent *Comparability of Financial Statements,* published in mid-1990. This statement laid out proposed revisions of certain IASs and the programme of amendment should be completed soon.

1.8 The IASB has been around for 30 years. The current list of IASs is as follows.

International Accounting Standards

IAS 1 (revised)	Presentation of financial statements
IAS 2 (revised)	Inventories
IAS 7	Cash flow statements
IAS 8 (revised)	Accounting policies, changes in accounting estimates and errors
IAS 10 (revised)	Events after the balance sheet date
IAS 11	Construction contracts
IAS 12 (revised)	Income taxes
IAS 14 (revised)	Segment reporting
IAS 16 (revised)	Property, plant and equipment
IAS 17 (revised)	Leases
IAS 18	Revenue
IAS 19 (revised)	Employee benefits
IAS 20	Accounting for government grants and disclosure of government assistance
IAS 21	The effects of changes in foreign exchange rates

IAS 23	Borrowing costs
IAS 24 (revised)	Related party disclosures
IAS 26	Accounting and reporting by retirement benefit plans
IAS 27 (revised)	Consolidated and separate financial statements
IAS 28	Investments in associates
IAS 29	Financial reporting in hyperinflationary economies
IAS 30	Disclosure in the financial statements of banks and similar financial institutions
IAS 31	Interests in joint ventures
IAS 32	Financial instruments: disclosure and presentation
IAS 33	Earnings per share
IAS 34	Interim financial reporting
IAS 36 (revised)	Impairment of assets
IAS 37	Provisions, contingent liabilities and contingent assets
IAS 38 (revised)	Intangible assets
IAS 39	Financial instruments: recognition and measurement
IAS 40	Investment property
IAS 41	Agriculture
IFRS 1	First-time application of International Financial Reporting Standards
IFRS 2	Share based payment
IFRS 3	Business combinations
IFRS 4	Insurance contracts
IFRS 5	Non-current assets held for sale and discontinued operations

IASB and IOSCO

1.9 At the international level, the International Organisation of Securities Commissions (IOSCO) is looking to the IASB to provide a set of **mutually acceptable international standards of accounting** and disclosure that can be used in the financial statements of any company looking to list its securities, on any stock exchange. This effort is directed primarily at companies that are involved in **multinational securities offerings** and which have multiple listings of their securities.

1.10 The major breakthrough in the recognition of worldwide standards came in July 1995 when an agreement was made between the IASB and IOSCO (which is the international organisation representing securities market regulators). IOSCO agreed a four year timetable for the IASB to revise its '**core standards**', after which IOSCO members will be recommended to recognise these rules for cross-border capital raisings and listings.

1.11 On 17 May 2000, IOSCO gave its qualified backing to 30 International Accounting Standards. It recommended that its members allow multinationals to use them in cross-border listings. This is a significant step towards global harmonisation.

1.12 However, the endorsement was not wholehearted and IOSCO has identified 'outstanding substantive' issues that require 'supplemental treatment'.

IASB and current developments

1.13 America and Japan have been two of the developed countries which have been most reluctant to accept accounts prepared under IASs, but recent developments suggest that such financial statements may soon be acceptable on these important stock exchanges. The Japanese situation was discussed above.

1.14 In **America**, the Securities and Exchange Commission (SEC) agreed in 1993 to allow foreign issuers (of shares, etc) to follow IASB treatments on business combinations, goodwill and subsidiaries in hyper-inflationary economies, and to file cash flow statements

under IAS 7. The SEC also allowed foreign issuers to use proportional consolidations (favoured by the IASB) to report interests in joint ventures. The overall effect is that, where IASB treatments differ from US GAAP, these treatments will now be acceptable. The SEC is now supporting the IASB because it wants to attract foreign listings.

1.15 This SEC decision was supported by the findings of a report by Professor Trevor Harris of the University of Columbia on the reporting practices of several large multi-national companies. His report concludes that on both measurement issues and disclosure, the revised IASs had reduced differences between IASs and US GAAP where differences still existed. IAS treatments or disclosures were often as good as or even better than US GAAP. In addition, in early 1996, the FASB and IASB approved similar draft codes on the disclosure of EPS.

1.16 This **close conformity between IASs and US GAAP** could, however, **cause problems for the IASB**. Some countries will see these moves as an attempt to force an international version of US GAAP on the rest of the world. It is not only developing countries which have reservations; the IOSCO review of IASs highlighted a number of European and Japanese issues which are outstanding. The IASC agreement with IOSCO has added substance to the perception that the IASC attaches more importance to American issues than to those of Europe or Japan.

1.17 The IASB therefore runs a fine balancing act between various strong interests. It must maintain support from all areas in order to ensure that pronouncements are accepted worldwide and this is a difficult political talk. The main methods of achieving this will be by:

(a) Ensuring the quality of the IASB's technical work

(b) Involving national standard-setting bodies (and multi-national companies) in the IASB's work

1.18 This will also help to ensure that IASs are 'marketed' as the best approach based on accepted principles, rather than 'lowest-common denominator' standards.

ASB and international standards

1.19 The ASB considers the development of international standards of **fundamental importance**. In addition, the ASB meets on a formal, and regular basis with standard-setters around the world.

Exam focus point

FRS 20 *Share based payment* is almost identical to IFRS 2 of the same name.

The EC regulation

1.20 As we have already seen, the EC regulations form one part of a broader programme for the harmonisation of company law in member states. The commission is uniquely the only organisation to produce **international** standards of accounting practice which are legally enforceable, in the form of directives which must be included in the national legislation of member states. The directives have been criticised as they might become constraints on the application of world-wide standards and bring accounting standardisation and harmonisation into the political arena.

1.21 The EC has adopted a regulation stating that **by 2005 consolidated accounts of listed companies will be required to comply with international accounting standards.** The implications of this proposal are far reaching. A detailed comparison of international and national accounting standards has been carried out, called *The Convergence Handbook*. In conjunction with other developments, this has led to the development of a Strategy for Convergence (see Section 2).

1.22 Many commentators believe that, in the light of the above, it is only a matter of time before national standard setting bodies like the ASB are, in effect, replaced by the IASB and national standards fall into disuse. However, national standards were designed for the national environment, which includes small companies (see Chapter 2). Moreover, the IASB will need input and expertise from valued national standard setters like the ASB.

The situation today and in the future

1.23 Many organisations committed to global harmonisation have done a great deal of work towards this goal. It is the case at present, however, that fundamental disagreements exist between countries and organisations about the way forward. One of the major gulfs is between the reporting requirements in developed countries and those in non-developed countries. It will be some time before these difficulties can be overcome. The IASB is likely to be the lead body in attempting to do so, as discussed above.

2 CONVERGENCE 6/02, 12/03

2.1 As explained in Section 1, The **Convergence Handbook** is a detailed comparison between International Accounting Standards (IASs) and UK financial reporting requirements. Implementation of the Handbook's recommendations will require changes to UK accounting standards or IASs— and in many cases to both.

2.2 The ASB asked for the research to be carried out in the light of the **European Commission's** regulation that, in order to improve the harmonisation of accounting within the single market, consolidated accounts of listed companies should be required to **comply with IASs by 2005**.

2.3 The ASB's intention in asking for a comparison to be made was to reveal in detail the differences between the two sets of accounting requirements. This will enable the financial and business community in the UK and in the Republic of Ireland to examine the differences and inform the ASB whether they would wish the domestic requirements to be altered to conform with IASs. Alternatively, where the UK requirements are thought to be of a higher quality, the ASB can seek to persuade IASB to change IASs.

Recommendations for convergence

2.4 It is outside the scope of your syllabus to go into all the differences between UK GAAP and IAS. However, an outline of the Handbook's recommendations is given here.

2.5 The authors believe that there is now a **strong case for greater convergence** of UK GAAP and IAS and that any changes should happen quickly.

2.6 Complete convergence could be achieved by the ASB replacing all current accounting standards with FRSs that are identical to IAS. However, the authors do not support this approach, as some IAS are simply inferior to FRSs.

2.7 Alternatively, complete convergence could be achieved by the IASB replacing all current IAS with UK standards. Even if this approach were acceptable internationally (unlikely), the authors believe that some IAS are superior or more up to date than FRSs and are not constrained by company law. The authors believe that **convergence should be achieved by changes to both UK standards and IAS.**

2.8 The Handbook's recommended approach is twofold.

Stage 1. The **ASB** should undertake a **convergence project** to deal with **revisions to UK GAAP** (Table 1) and seek any necessary changes in company law (Table 2).

Stage 2. The **IASB** should undertake a further **improvements project** (Table 3) to deal with the **revisions to IAS**.

Exam focus point

Skim read the tables below and move to paragraph 2.9 on recent developments.

Table 1: ASB convergence project

Aim – improve existing UK GAAP by eliminating optional accounting treatments and by adopting superior IAS treatments.

SSAP 4 *Accounting for government grants*

Require disclosure of any unfulfilled conditions attached to government assistance.
Clarify treatment of subsidies relating to cost of inventories (stocks).

SSAP 9 *Stocks and work in progress*

Replace SSAP 9 with IAS 2, IAS 11 and appropriate section of IAS 18 (provided that changes are made to these three IASs in accordance with Table 3).

SSAP 13 *Accounting for research and development*

Require demonstration of future benefits as a criterion for the recognition of development costs as an asset.

SSAP17 *Accounting for post balance sheet events*

Require dividends payable to be recognised only when declared.

SSAP 19 *Accounting for investment properties*

Add guidance on the determination of fair value.
Add guidance on transfers to and from investment properties.

SSAP 20 *Foreign currency translation*

Require all exchange differences on monetary items to be included in the income statement.
Require the use of average rate for the translation of the income statement.

On a business combination:

(i) Require fair value adjustments on acquired assets and liabilities to be treated as foreign currency items

(ii) Consider whether goodwill should be treated as a foreign currency item

SSAP 21 ***Accounting for leases (pending a comprehensive review)***

Require the use of the net investment method for the recognition of finance income be lessors.

Conform the requirements on sale and leaseback transactions that result in finance leases with the requirements for sale and repurchase agreements in FRS 5.

Add guidance on the treatment of operating lease incentives by lessors.

Conform disclosures with IAS 17.

SSAP 25 ***Segmented reporting (pending a review of new standards)***

Conform disclosure requirements (but not definitions of segments etc) with IAS 14.

FRS 3 ***Reporting financial performance***

Replace existing requirements for discontinued operations with IAS 35 requirements for discontinuing operations.

FRS 4 ***Capital instruments***

Require an issuer's instruments to be classified as equity or liabilities according to their substance.

Require own shares, including those held in employee share ownership plans (EOSPs), to be deducted from shareholders' equity.

Extend disclosures of terms and conditions of capital instruments.

FRS 6 ***Acquisitions and mergers***

Require the recognition of contingent purchase consideration when it meets the definition and recognition criteria for provisions.

FRS 7 ***Fair values in acquisition accounting***

Require adjustment of goodwill on the recognition of tax assets after the one-year investigation period when such assets existed at the date of acquisition and their subsequent recognition is unavoidable.

FRS 8 ***Related party disclosures***

Require disclosure of pricing policies for all material related party transactions.

FRS 10 ***Goodwill and Intangible assets***

Disclose the location of amortisation expense in the profit and loss account.

FRS 11 ***Impairment of fixed assets and goodwill***

Remove exception in estimation of cash flows for impairment reviews for newly acquired income generating units.

Require allocation of impairment losses on an income generating unit to asset within that unit in the following order: specific impaired assets; goodwill; other asset on a pro rata basis.

Allow reversal of impairment losses on intangible assets.

Add further guidance on impairment tests on goodwill, including IAS 36's 'bottom-up' test.

Add disclosures about impairment losses for each class of assets.

FRS 15 ***Tangible fixed assets***

Require revaluation losses to be taken to the statement of total recognised gains and losses unless there is a clear consumption of benefits.

Require exchange of dissimilar assets to be measured at fair value.

FRS 17 *Retirement benefits*

Extend scope to deal with employee benefits other than retirement benefits.

Extend scope to deal with insured benefits.

Revise terminology and style to conform with IAS 19.

Define plan assets.

Require deferred tax relating to employee benefits to be included with other deferred tax rather than being deducted from retirement benefit liabilities and assets.

FRS 19 *Deferred tax*

Reconsider non-recognition of deferred tax on revaluation gains that are included in the statement of total recognised gains and losses.

Interim reports

Require that frequency of reporting should not affect annual results.
Require disclosure of diluted earnings per share.

Revenue

Adopt IAS 18 as a FRS (provided that changes are made to IAS 18 in accordance with Table 3).

Table 2: UK Company Law changes

Companies Act 1985

Modify reference to realised profits to conform with the *Statement of Principles* and the IASB's *Framework for the Preparation and Presentation of Financial Statements* (if necessary, seek modifications to the EU Fourth Directive).

Require that dividends payable should be recognised only when declared.

Table 3: IASB Improvements project

Aim – improve existing IAS by eliminating optional accounting treatments and by adopting superior UK GAAP treatments.

IAS 1 *Presentation of financial statements*

Require basic disclosures about the reporting company and its directors.

IAS 2 *Inventories*

Require that measurement methods provide the fairest practicable approximation of cost.
Prohibit use of LIFO formula.
Extend guidance on the allocation of overheads.
Require disclosure of cost of sales.

IAS 11 *Construction contracts*

Add guidance on the balance sheet presentation of construction contracts.

IAS 14 *Segment reporting*

Rewrite to remove unnecessary complexity and length.

IAS 16 *Property, plant and equipment*

Require impairment test for property, plant and equipment with long useful lives.

IAS 17 *Leases*

Reconsider the accounting for sale and leaseback transactions.

IAS 18 *Revenue*

Conform with the *Framework for the Preparation and Presentation of Financial Statements.*

Add more guidance on different types of revenue, including consignment stocks and sale and repurchase agreements

Add guidance on the balance sheet presentation of long-term contracts.

IAS 19 *Employee benefits*

Require immediate recognition of all actuarial gains and losses.

Add guidance on valuation of defined benefit plan assts and expected return on those assets.

Require disclosure of:

(i) Outstanding or prepaid contributions to a defined contribution scheme
(ii) Actuarial assumptions about inflation and pension increases
(iii) Analysis of actuarial gains and losses
(iv) Differences between expected and actual return on plan assets over five years

IAS 21 *The Effects of changes in foreign exchange rates*

Reconsider inclusion of certain foreign exchange differences in the cost of inventories and property, plant and equipment.

On a business combination:

(i) Require fair value adjustment on acquired assets and liabilities to be treated as foreign currency items

(ii) Reconsider whether goodwill should be treated as a foreign currency item

IAS 22 *Business combinations*

Require the recognition of contingent purchase consideration when it meets the definition and recognition criteria for provisions.

Require the recognition and measurement of acquired assets and liabilities at fair value.

Require that fair values should reflect conditions at the date of the acquisition.

Require impairment reviews when an acquisition gives rise to negative goodwill.

Allow indefinite useful lives for goodwill (subject to annual impairment test).

IAS 32 *Financial instruments: disclosure and presentation*

Require disclosure of sensitivity to currency movements.

IAS 33 *Earnings per share*

Add guidance on share consolidations that have the effect of a share repurchase at fair value.

Add guidance on employee share and incentive plans.

Add guidance on contingently issuable shares.

Require presentation of a line item on the face of the income statement for all per share amounts of components of net profit.

IAS 34 *Interim reporting*

Require disclosure of effects of changes in accounting policies.
Require disclosure of tax effects of exceptional items.

IAS 36 *Impairment of assets*

Require allocation of impairment losses on a cash generating unit to assets within that unit in the following order: specific impaired assets; goodwill; other assets on a pro rata basis.

Require inclusion of impairment losses in operating profit.

Require comparisons over five years of cash flow actuals with forecasts used in impairment reviews.

IAS 38 *Intangible assets*

Require an item to be separable in order to meet the definition of an intangible asset.

Require capitalisation of internally generated intangible assets when there is a readily ascertainable market value.

Allow indefinite useful lives for intangible assets (subject to annual impairment test).

IAS 39 *Financial instruments: recognition and measurement*

Deal with proceeds of issuances of equity shares and warrants.

IAS 40 *Investment property*

Prohibit cost alternative for investment property.

Allow long-leasehold properties to be classified as investment property.

Recent developments: FREDs, revised and new IAS and Discussion Paper

2.9 Rather than 'sit tight' using its own Standards until 2005, the ASB is proposed to **revise** a number of **UK Standards** to bring them into line with the (revised and improved) IAS. To this end, in May 2002 it has published for comment nine Financial Reporting Exposure Drafts. It also published three Consultation Papers, two of which describe certain changes proposed by the IASB to its standards and one of which gives guidance on first-time application. This is a record in terms of the amount of material issued in such a short time. The documents are as follows.

FRED 23 *Financial instruments: hedge accounting*

FRED 24 *The effects of changes in foreign exchange rates; Financial reporting in hyperinflationary economies*

FRED 25 *Related party disclosures*

FRED 26 *Earnings per share*

FRED 27 *Events after the balance sheet date**

FRED 28 *Inventories*

FRED 29 *Property, plant and equipment; Borrowing costs*

FRED 30 *Financial instruments: Disclosure and Presentation; recognition and measurement*

FRED 31 *Share-based payment**

Consultation Paper *IASB proposals to amend certain International Accounting Standards**

Consultation Paper *IASB proposals for first-time application of International Financial Reporting Standards**

Consultation Paper *IASB proposals on business combinations, impairment and intangible assets**

Moving on

2.10 The items marked with an asterisk (*) have been developed further, since they were first issued.

(a) FRED 27 *Events after the balance sheet date* has now become a full standard (FRS 21), covered in Chapter 25.

(b) FRED 31 *Share based payment* has now become a full standard (FRS 20) (identical to IFRS 2, covered in Chapter 24).

(b) The Consultation Paper on first-time application of IFRS is now IFRS 1 *First time adoption of International Financial Reporting Standards* and is covered in Chapter 15.

(d) The changes proposed in the other consultation papers have been effected by revising IAS 1, 2, 8, 10, 16, 17, 24, 27, 28, 33, 36, 38 and 40 and issuing IFRS 3 *Business combinations.*

Exam focus point

You will need to know these in terms of the main changes from UK practice.

Discussion Paper: UK accounting standards: a strategy for convergence with IFRS

2.11 In March 2004, the ASB issued a Discussion Paper *UK accounting standards: a strategy for convergence with IFRS.* The EU Regulation requiring the accounts of UK listed companies to comply with international standards has **significant consequences for the ASB** and for the future of **UK accounting standards**.

2.12 The objective of the Discussion Paper is to set out the ASB's views on the possible development of UK accounting standards and to consult on its plans.

2.13 The approach taken by the ASB reflects two fundamental propositions.

(a) There can be no **case for the use in the UK of two sets of wholly different accounting standards in the medium term.**

(b) should **not** seek to issue **new standards** that are **more demanding or restrictive than** International Financial Reporting Standards ('**IFRS**')

2.14 The intention of the ASB is to bring UK accounting standards into line with IFRS as quickly as possible, whilst:

(a) **Avoiding the burden of excessive changes** in any one year

(b) Minimising the cases in which an entity using UK standards may be required to make **successive changes of accounting policy** in respect of the same matter

Phased approach

2.15 Accordingly, the ASB has proposed a **phased approach** to the convergence.

Phase 1 New standards effective in 2005 and 2006 that will **enhance** existing UK financial reporting requirements and keep them in step with changes in the law.

Phase 2 A series of '**step changes**', replacing one or more existing UK accounting standards with standards **based on IFRS as prospective IASB projects are completed**.

2.16 In order to avoid two changes of accounting policy on the same issue within a short period, the Paper discusses a number of ongoing IASB projects for which the ASB recommends retaining the equivalent UK standards at present.

Phase 1: standards for 2005 to 2006

2.17 The new standards effective in 2005 and 2006 will address the following areas.

(a) **Share options.** FRS 20 *Share based payment* (see Chapter 24) is based on IFRS 2 of the same name.

(b) **Financial instruments.** Standards will be issued based on IAS 32 and much of IAS 39 from 2005. This is covered in FRED 30, second supplement (see Chapter 18).

(c) **Retirement benefits.** FRS 17 (see Chapter 21) will replace SSAP 24 in 2005 so that, consistent with IASB proposals for IAS 19 *Employee benefits*, actuarial gains and losses are fully recognised in the period in which they arise.

(d) **Events after the balance sheet date** (post balance sheet events). FRS 21 *Events after the balance sheet date* (see Chapter 25) was issued in May 2004. The standard replaces SSAP 17 from 2005 and brings UK GAAP into line with the revised IAS 10.

(e) **Earnings per share.** A UK standard (applicable to listed companies only) based on IAS 33 will replace FRS 14 from 2005. This will follow FRED 26 (see Chapter 23).

(f) **Related party disclosures.** A standard based on IAS 24 will replace FRS 8 from 2006. This will follow FRED 25 (see Chapter 24).

(g) **Subsidiary undertakings.** An exposure draft was published in May 2004 proposing a minor amendment arising from the Government's expected change to the legal definition of a subsidiary undertaking (see Chapter 2).

(h) **Agriculture and leases.** After considering responses to the discussion paper, the ASB may issue exposure drafts for a UK standard based on IAS 41 *Agriculture* and revised disclosures in respect of operating lease commitments based on those in IAS 17 *Leases.*

Phase 2: Standards to be retained

2.18 Phase 2 involves replacing one or more existing UK standards with standards based on IFRS as IASB projects are completed. The Discussion Paper mentions a number of ongoing IASB projects for which the ASB recommends retaining the equivalent UK standards at present.

(a) **FRS 5.** This plays a critical role in the context of UK financial reporting and should be retained until it becomes clear that its most important requirements, including those on revenue recognition, have adequate counterparts under IFRS.

(b) **SSAP 9 and FRS 5 Application Note G (Revenue recognition).** The ASB favours retaining these until the IASB's project on revenue recognition results in a standard. Then UK standards based on IAS 2 and IAS 11 would be introduced, as well as the new standard on revenue recognition.

(c) **Financial instruments.** The ASB does not intend to implement the sections of IAS 39 relating to recognition and derecognition at this time; it believes that the requirements of FRS 5, which cover a wider scope than the derecognition of financial assets dealt with in IAS 39, should be retained for the present. Further delays relate to fair value and hedging.

Phase 2: 'Step changes' awaiting completion of IASB projects

2.19 In most of these cases, an IASB project would affect several UK standards. Implementing the changes would therefore entail replacing several UK standards at the same time with new standards based on IFRS. Thus UK standards would converge with IFRS in a series of

significant, but discrete, steps rather than a number of piecemeal changes being introduced over a number of years.

(a) **Reporting comprehensive income.** FRS 3 was introduced to combat the focus on one measure of performance, such as EPS by requiring a STRGL as well as a profit and loss account. It also prohibits 'recycling' gains and losses, that is transferring them to the profit and loss account in a subsequent period, for example, when the gain or loss is 'realised'. UK standards are in contrast to US standards, which sometimes require it and IFRS, which sometimes allow it, eg IAS 39 and IAS 21. This issue remains unresolved. The ASB does not therefore propose IFRS based standards to replace FRS 1 *Cash flow statements*, FRS 3 *Reporting financial performance* or SSAP 25 *Segmental reporting*. It would also be necessary to retain FRS 18 *Accounting policies*, as the corresponding requirements in IFRS are contained in IAS 1 *Presentation of financial statements* and IAS 8 *Accounting policies, changes in accounting estimates and errors* which may also be revised as a result of the project on comprehensive income.

(b) **Disposal of non-current assets and presentation of discontinued operations.** IFRS 5 on this topic has been published. However, as it is part of reporting comprehensive income and would also require changes to FRS 15, the ASB is awaiting the outcome of this project and revisions to IAS 16 *Property, plant and equipment.*

(c) **Fixed assets and investment properties.** There is an international project on measurement. Until completion of this, FRS 15 and SSAP 19 are to be retained.

(d) **Business combinations, impairment and intangibles.** The first phase of the IASB project is reflected in IFRS 3 *Business combinations*. The IASB is continuing its work on accounting for business combinations and further international exposure drafts will be published. Introduction of standards based on IFRS resulting from the completed IASB project would be likely to involve replacing SSAP 13, FRS 6, FRS 7, FRS 10 and FRS 11. The ASB will await the completion of the IASB business combinations project before introducing UK standards based on IFRS.

(e) **Provisions, contingent liabilities and contingent assets.** The IASB is considering modifying IAS 37, so the ASB will await the revised IAS before revising FRS 12.

(f) **Government grants.** IAS 20 on government grants is to be withdrawn, therefore it will not be brought into the UK in its present form.

(g) **Consolidation, associates and joint ventures.** This is the subject of an IASB project, therefore FRS 2 and FRS 9 will be retained for now.

(h) **Taxation and leasing.** Replacement of or changes to FRS 16 and 19 are awaiting the completion of IASB and FASB considerations.

(i) **Insurance.** IFRS 4 on insurance has recently been published, but may be subject to further changes, and therefore its requirements will not at this stage be introduced into the UK.

(j) **Small companies.** As mentioned in Chapter 1, the IASB's consideration of smaller companies is at an early stage (discussion paper), so the FRSSE will be retained for now.

Role of the ASB

2.20 The ASB plans to continue to devote significant resources to **working with, and influencing the work of**, the IASB, the International Financial Reporting Interpretations Committee ('IFRIC') and other international bodies, including the European Financial Reporting Advisory Group ('EFRAG'). The ASB will continue to maintain its dialogue with

constituents in the UK and Republic of Ireland and encourage them to make their views known directly to such bodies.

2.21 The ASB also intends to:

(a) Address issues that arise in the context of UK standards either through UK accounting standards or through its Urgent Issues Task Force

(b) Maintain the FRSSE

(c) Oversee the development of Statements of Recommended Practice ('SORPs') where these give appropriate sectoral guidance.

Exam focus point

This information is up to date as of July 2004. It is vital that you read *Student Accountant* to keep up to date with developments in this area. It will also help you in practice to know what's coming next, in this rapidly changing financial reporting environment.

3 ACCOUNTING OVERSEAS

Europe

3.1 You would expect that countries which are members of the EU, and which are therefore bound by European Commission directives (particularly the 4th and 7th), would have very similar reporting and accounting requirements. This is not necessarily the case, however, and many influences have shaped financial reporting practices, even events as far back as the Second World War. In an effort to understand what differences exist between European countries, we will examine four areas and their impact on financial reporting:

- The legal system
- The taxation system
- The forms of organisations
- The accounting profession

We have limited the scope of our comparison to France and Germany, which will give you a good idea of the differences which can exist across Europe.

Exam focus point

The discussion that follows on the differences in these four areas is useful background reading, so that you can understand why international differences exist. Try to get an overview.

Legal system

3.2 European countries have historically had either a **common law system**, such as in the UK, or a **Roman codified system**, such as in France and Germany. These different systems have had a direct effect on the development of the variety of accounting practices found in Europe.

3.3 In **France** the Roman codified system is made up of commercial codes and related decrees and amendments. The significant influence of legislation on French financial accounting

reflects the national planning policy of the government, which requires a high level of standardised accounting practice and reporting. This process is aided by the use of a national plan. The plan has been adopted by almost all enterprises in the country, and provides:

(a) A national uniform chart of accounts
(b) Definitions and explanations of terminology
(c) Details of bookkeeping entries
(d) Principles of accounting measurement (valuation)
(e) Standard forms of financial statements
(f) Details of permitted cost accounting methods

3.4 The main principles of the French plan reflect **conservatism** and adherence to legal form rather than economic substance. This is similar to the situation in Germany, whose system influenced the French during the 1930s and 1940s.

3.5 In **Germany** the provision of detailed accounting requirements by law has a long history, during which period these **legal regulations** have remained dominant in the field of prescribing basic accounting practices. The majority of the current legislation is laid down in the Commercial Code (first established in 1897), the Corporation Act 1965 and tax laws. The Commercial Code regulates the maintenance of accounting records in accordance with 'principles of proper bookkeeping' and the preparation of periodic financial statements. The Corporation Act 1965 regulates the accounting standards and practices that should be adopted in preparing financial statements.

3.6 A feature of German financial accounting which is important is the legal and revenue reserves that are required, plus the '**secret reserves**', which exist because revaluation of appreciating assets is not allowed and depreciation in line with the tax rules is often in excess of that which is required to measure the periodic cost of depreciating assets. Such reserves have no exact UK equivalent.

Taxation system

3.7 In some European countries the tax system, in line with the legal system, has a **considerable effect** on financial accounting practices while in others, including the UK, it has only a minor indirect influence.

3.8 The **French** tax system is an imputation system and has a very strong influence on French accounting practices including the values incorporated in financial statements. **Accounting profit measurement rules are the same as those for tax profit measurement**, mainly because for an item to be allowed as a tax deduction it must be included in the financial accounts. Depreciation rules, for example, are based on tax rules and assets are only revalued in line with tax regulations. Voluntary revaluations are permitted but are unlikely to occur as income tax is payable on the unrealised profit on revaluation. A French company's tax return will therefore look like a detailed copy of the financial statements.

3.9 In **Germany** the tax system is an integral part of the legal system. For example, there is a fundamental legal principle that values of profit/assets and liabilities in financial accounts may be no higher or lower, respectively, than their counterparts allowed for tax purposes. The financial accounts should agree with the tax requirements, and so changes in accounting practice are often made in the name of changes in the accounting requirements of the tax system.

3.10 The **emphasis on compliance** with the tax rules and regulations limits the usefulness of German financial statements for decision making by readers. The reported profit and the valuations contained in the statements will reflect the most favourable tax position. This may not reflect the economic profitability and position of the company, making them too conservative for readers to (say) estimate the future net cash flows due to the company. This is obviously not the objective of German financial reporting.

Forms of organisation

3.11 The types of organisation and their ownership will also have varying effects on a nation's accounting practices. In some countries ownership is mainly in the **hands of a family** and finance is provided by the banks. Both these parties have access to internal financial information concerning the business and therefore there is little demand for the development of forms of external financial reporting.

3.12 In other countries the ownership of the business organisation is in the hands of **external widely dispersed shareholders** (as in the UK and US). Such providers of finance will probably not have direct access to internal financial information and will therefore demand some form of external reporting to provide them with the information they require to make investment decisions. The existence and importance of shareholders will determine the influence of the national stock exchange.

3.13 A wide spectrum of organisations exist in **France** including:

- Partnerships (Société en nom Collectif)
- Companies (Société Anonyme (SA) and Société à Responsibilité Limitée (SARL))
- Family holdings

The accounts produced by all these organisations are governed by the National Plan; the stock exchange (Bourse) has not had a particularly strong influence over financial reporting practices.

3.14 There are various forms of organisations in **Germany** and the distinction is important because financial reporting and disclosure requirements are dependent on the organisational form of business. Public companies consist of the following.

(a) 'Aktiengesellschaft' (AG). This is similar to a large UK public company, although the shares are usually 'bearer'. These companies have a supervisory body; 50% is appointed by shareholders and 50% by employees. This board appoints a management board and approves the annual accounts.

(b) 'Kommanditgesellschaft auf Aktien' (KGaA). This is a form of limited partnership and company combined. One shareholder is liable to the creditors in full, while the others enjoy limited liability. It is not a particularly popular form of company.

3.15 Another form of company is a 'Gesellschaft mit beschränkter Haftung' (GmbH). It is not quoted on the stock exchange and is subject to different legal reporting requirements. It is similar to, but not the same as, a UK private company. There are numerous organisations operating as partnerships or sole traders. Banks and other lenders are an important source of finance in Germany, and therefore the **German stock exchange**, while being an efficient medium for raising new finance, **does not appear to have a great influence** on financial reporting.

Accounting profession

3.16 The accounting profession in a country has **varying levels of influence** on national accounting practices. However, care must be taken in interpreting the influence of the accounting profession because in some countries an 'accountant' may not be considered to be part of the 'profession'.

3.17 In **France**, the accounting profession is split into two distinct organisations:

- **Accountants** (Ordre des Experts Comptables et des Comptables Agrées)
- **Auditors** (Compaigne Nationale des Commissaires aux Agrées)

3.18 Most members of the auditors' organisation are also members of the more important accountants' organisation. Examinations, work experience and articles are similar to those of the UK accountancy bodies, but there are only an estimated 11,000 qualified accountants in France. The profession's main influence is through the issue of non-mandatory opinions and recommendations of accounting principles relevant to the implementation of the National Plan.

3.19 The main professional body in **Germany** is the Institute of Certified Public Accountants (Institut der Wirtschafstprüfer). Members of this institute carry out all the statutory audits, and are required to have very high educational and experience qualifications. The Institute issues a form of auditing standard but this is tied very closely to legislation. As well as auditing, members are mainly involved in tax and business management, with no obvious significant role in establishing financial accounting principles and practices. There is no independent accounting standard-setting body.

Former communist and developing countries

3.20 The sophisticated regulatory frameworks discussed above, along with those in the UK and the USA, contrast sharply with the situation in former communist and developing countries. The problems in these countries are covered briefly here.

3.21 In socialist countries the economic system has usually been **resource constrained** and enterprise management operating within such an environment required quantity data on resource availability and resource utilisation. The accounting function was **passive**. Price signals were not influential and enterprises did not need to be 'profitable'. There was not the same call for accounting development and innovation that exists where accounting is **active** (as in capitalist countries).

3.22 For the country trying to recover from events such as revolution or war, such a system is appropriate but after the short-term resource problems have been solved the economy needs to develop along the lines of the demand constrained economy. Many socialist and former socialist countries are currently attempting to move to such a system which includes enterprise independence and market conditions of supply and demand. Accounting will therefore (hopefully) develop in these socialist countries into a more active information source.

3.23 Developing countries are often defined as such by using *per capita* **gross national product**, relating development to economic growth and social improvements. The general characteristics of such countries include unbalanced distribution of wealth, few exports (agricultural/mineral), basic but developing domestic industries, long-term balance of payments deficits, authoritarian political systems and inadequate education.

3.24 Both developing and former socialist countries have the same problems in relation to financial accounting and many will be overcome in the same way. In general, most of these countries are **adopting financial reporting systems** from developed countries and adjusting them to suit the individual needs of the country concerned. This is a long and slow process as such sophisticated reporting systems are rarely suitable and require a great deal of modification. The local workers do not have the requisite skills, which have to be imported from abroad. More sophisticated financial reporting may be required by multinational companies who have subsidiaries or investments in such countries.

Other countries

3.25 Of the other **main developed countries**, such as Canada, Australia and New Zealand, some have developed framework projects like the IASB and some have detailed standards, often with the force of law. The country which has had most impact on world financial reporting, however, is the USA (as we shall see in the next section).

Question: US GAAP accounts

In recent years, only two German companies, Daimler Benz and Veba, have filed accounts prepared under US GAAP, although other German companies are likely to follow suit. Why should German companies take the trouble to produce such accounts, and what do you think was the impact on reported results?

Answer

The reasons given by Veba for producing US GAAP accounts were based on the fact that, although Veba still earns 70% of its revenues within Germany, only about 44% of its equity is held in Germany, with 15% held in the US. The company saw the need to become 'more international' and US GAAP accounts would increase transparency and shareholder value. An article in the *Financial Times* on 28 March 1996 stated the following.

> 'Converting accounts to US accounting standards has been problematic for German companies, many of whom prefer the inscrutability of the German accounting system. It enables them to build up reserves which might otherwise be paid out to shareholders.
>
> Mr Kurt Lauk, Veba's finance director, said he had conducted 'difficult' negotiations with the Securities and Exchange Commission, the agency supervising the New York Stock Exchange, for two years before all differences were resolved.
>
> Mr Lauk said Veba had chosen GAAP over the rival IAS accounting standard, widely used by large European companies, because the latter did not permit a listing in New York.'

The likely effect and reported results can be difficult to judge. One might expect that German accounting rules, generally perceived as more conservative than UK/US GAAP, would produce lower profits and shareholder funds. This was the case recently when BMW reported its results, including Rover, a British subsidiary.

'BMW, the German carmaker, yesterday reported that Rover, its UK subsidiary, lost DM355m (£157m) last year, in spite of having earlier reported a 9 per cent rise in profits before interest and tax to £91m for the same period.

The discrepancy came from the 'stricter valuation criteria' applied by BMW compared with its UK subsidiary, according to the German company.' (*Financial Times,* 3 April 1996)

This is not always the case, however, as was demonstrated when Daimler Benz first produced US GAAP accounts. Analysts were shocked when a substantial loss was reported under US GAAP rather than the modest profit under German rules. (DM 949m loss vs DM 168m profit, 1991 half year results). This was partly because the company was caught during a slump, but it demonstrates how dramatic the differences can be under the different accounting regimes.

4 FINANCIAL REPORTING IN THE USA

4.1 Standard setting in the USA is characterised by a **plethora of highly detailed legislative rules**. These have largely obscured the concept of 'fair presentation', despite the development of a conceptual framework as discussed below. The Financial Accounting Standards Board (FASB) has produced well over 100 Statements of Financial Accounting Standards (SFASs).

A conceptual framework in the USA

4.2 The FASB has been developing a conceptual framework since 1973. According to the FASB, the conceptual framework was expected:

(a) To **guide the body** responsible for establishing standards

(b) To provide a **frame of reference** for resolving accounting questions in the absence of a specific promulgated standard

(c) To determine **bounds for judgement** in preparing financial statements

(d) To increase financial statement **users' understanding** of and confidence in financial statements

(e) To enhance **comparability**

Comparison with UK/IASB view

4.3 The ASB has acknowledged that, in drafting the *Statement of Principles,* it drew heavily on the **work done in previous projects** in other countries, mainly the FASB concept statements *and* the IASB *Framework.* This is particularly true of the early chapters, and indeed Chapter 1 opens with the statement that 'the objective of financial statements is to provide information ... that is useful to a wide range of users in making economic decisions', almost a repetition of the FASB wording. The ASB has, however, extended this function to include showing the results of the stewardship of management.

4.4 The IASB's *Framework* was **based very closely** on the FASB's concept statements, and it is perceived as an attempt by the IASC to justify the *status quo*; the IASB tried to make the proposed framework consistent with current external financial reporting practice. The ASB stated that it would use the IASB *Framework* as much as possible in its own work on the conceptual framework. It remains to be seen whether the flaws in both the FASB's concept statements and the IASB's *Framework* will be tackled adequately by the ASB.

5 UK GAAP VS IAS VS US GAAP

5.1 Your syllabus requires you to identify **major differences** between UK GAAP, IASs and US GAAP. An **overview** is given in the table below.

Exam focus point

A **detailed knowledge of IAS and US GAAP is not necessary.** Such questions tend to be both interesting and relatively straightforward, requiring only a general overview of IAS and US GAAP.

Subject	UK GAAP	US GAAP	IAS
Goodwill	FRS 10 requires goodwill to be amortised over its expected life. In some cases the life may be indefinite, in which case there is no amortisation. There is a rebuttable presumption that the life of goodwill will be no more than 20 years. If more than 20 years perform annual impairment reviews.	Goodwill must be capitalised and is then carried in the balance sheet, subject to annual impairment reviews.	IFRS 3 requires goodwill to be calculated and then carried in the balance sheet, subject to annual impairment reviews.
Merger accounting **Uniting of interests 'merger accounting'**	Merger accounting **must** be used if the criteria in FRS 6 are met.	All business combinations must be accounted for as acquisitions; 'pooling of interests' cannot be used.	IFRS 3 prohibits uniting of interest accounting; all combinations must be treated as acquisitions
Research and development	SSAP 13 permits but does not require capitalisation. No time period is specified.	Development expenditure must be written off to the income statement under all circumstances.	Development costs recognised as an asset should be amortised normally over a maximum of 5 years.
Capitalisation of borrowing costs	FRS 15 permits capitalisation of borrowing costs but **does not require** it. The policy as regards capitalisation must be **consistent**.	Under **US** GAAP, interest **must** be capitalised in certain circumstances.	IAS 23 states that such costs should be recognised as an expense, but allows capitalisation as an alternative.
Stock (inventory) valuation	The **LIFO** method is **not** permitted under UK GAAP, so the stock must be valued using a method such as FIFO (first in first out)	In the USA stock may be valued using the **LIFO** (last in first out) method. Under this method, assuming prices are rising, closing stock has a lower value than using FIFO	IAS 2 no longer permits LIFO as an allowed alternative; FIFO or AVCO must be used.

6 RESTATING OVERSEAS AND UK ACCOUNTS 12/02

6.1 In your examination, as well as written questions on this topic, you may be asked to reproduce a sets of overseas accounts using **UK accounting principles**. Multi-national companies already provide this type of information if they have a large number of investors in another country, say the USA. Here is an example of such a reconciliation.

UK vs US GAAP

6.2 The following is a summary of the differences between UK and US GAAP which you might expect to find in the notes to the accounts of a **multinational company**. It is not comprehensive, but gives you a good idea of the type of reconciling items you will find.

SUMMARY OF DIFFERENCES BETWEEN UK AND US GAAP

Deferred taxation

The main difference between UK and US GAAP in respect of deferred tax is that UK GAAP requires that deferred taxation is provided using the liability method whereby taxation is provided at the same rates at which timing differences are expected to reverse; under US GAAP, the deferred method is currently used whereby deferred taxation is provided at the rates applicable to the year when provision is made.

Pension costs

The methods used to determine the annual pensions costs for defined benefit schemes under both UK GAAP and US GAAP are similar in that they required pension costs to be spread over the expected service lives of employees. However, the use of different actuarial methodologies and assumptions gives rise to a difference in reported pension costs.

Ordinary dividends

Under UK GAAP, ordinary dividends proposed are provided for in the year in respect of which they are recommended by the Board of Directors for approval by the shareholders. Under US GAAP, such dividends are not provided for until declared by the Board of Directors.

The following is a summary of the estimated material adjustments to profit and ordinary shareholders' equity which would be required if US GAAP had been applied instead of UK GAAP.

PROFIT FOR THE YEAR ENDED 31 DECEMBER

	20X2	*20X1*
	£m	£m
Profit under UK GAAP	1,033	912
US GAAP adjustments		
Deferred taxation	(18)	(35)
Pension costs	(4)	-
Net income under US GAAP	1,011	877
Income per ordinary share of 25p under US GAAP	33.5p	28.0p

ORDINARY SHAREHOLDERS' EQUITY
AS AT 31 DECEMBER

	20X2	*20X1*
	£m	£m
Ordinary shareholders' equity under UK GAAP	3,572	3,208
US GAAP adjustments		
Deferred taxation	(218)	(199)
Pension costs	(1)	-
Dividend proposed	331	292
Ordinary shareholders' equity under US GAAP	3,684	3,307

Question: GAAP reconciliation (1)

The following are the main US accounting principles which differ from those generally accepted in the United Kingdom as applied by XYZ plc in its financial statements.

Revaluation of land and buildings

Periodically land and buildings are revalued on an existing use basis by professionally qualified external valuers and such assets are written up to the appraised value. Depreciation is, where applicable, calculated on these revalued amounts. When revalued properties are sold, the gain or loss on sale is calculated based on revalued carrying amounts and reflected in income and any revaluation surplus thus realised is reclassified directly to retained earnings. Under US GAAP such revaluations would not be reflected in financial statements and the gain or loss on sale would be calculated based on original cost and reflected in income. The amount of additional depreciation charged in respect of the revalued properties is not material (net effect: profit and loss account nil; balance sheet £166m).

Timberlands

Reforestation costs are charged to the profit and loss account when incurred and depletion of timberlands is only provided to the extent that the amount of timber harvested exceeds the estimated growth of standing timber. Under US GAAP depletion on a unit of production basis is charged to the profit and loss account and reforestation costs are capitalised as part of the carrying cost of timberlands (net effect: profit and loss account £36m; balance sheet £60m).

Foreign currencies

Revenues, expenses, assets and liabilities relating to overseas subsidiaries are translated at the year end rate. Under US GAAP assets and liabilities are translated as under UK GAAP; however, revenues and expenses are translated at average rates for the year (net effect: profit and loss account £11m; balance sheet nil).

Pensions

The accounting policy of the group has not been to account for exceptional past pension surpluses. Under US GAAP, such surpluses are recognised and credited over an appropriate future period (net effect: profit and loss account £52m; balance sheet £189m).

Other information

Profit available for appropriation under UK GAAP = £1,089m.

Ordinary shareholders' equity under UK GAAP = £4,224m

Required

Provide the reconciliation to US GAAP for:

(a) Profit available for appropriation
(b) Ordinary shareholders' equity

Answer

		£m
(a)	Profit available for appropriation as reported in the consolidated profit and loss account	1,089
	Estimated adjustments	
	Foreign currency translation	(11)
	Pensions	52
	Timberlands depletion and reforestation	(36)
	Estimated profit available for appropriation (net income) as adjusted to accord with US GAAP	1,094

		£m
(b)	Ordinary shareholders' equity as reported in the consolidated balance sheet	4,224
	Estimated adjustments	
	Revaluation of land and buildings	(166)
	Pensions	189
	Timberlands depletion and reforestation	(60)
	Estimated ordinary shareholders' equity as adjusted to accord with US GAAP	4,187

Question: GAAP reconciliation (2)

In the group's annual report, the following appears as a note to the group's consolidated profit and loss account.

INCOME STATEMENT RECONCILIATION
FOR THE YEAR ENDED 31 DECEMBER 20X6

	£m
UK GAAP: net profit	130
US GAAP: adjustments net of tax	
Amortisation of capitalised interest	(8)
Additional depreciation and amortisation of goodwill for acquisition accounting	(280)
Results eliminated arising pre-merger	(200)
US GAAP: estimated loss as adjusted	(358)

There is also a reconciliation between equity as reported under UK GAAP and US GAAP.

Required

(a) Explain to your managing director why it is considered that greater harmonisation of accounting policies and disclosures on an international level would be beneficial. Note the barriers which exist to such harmonisation.

(b) In relation to the above income statement reconciliation, explain why each adjustment has been made.

(c) Will equity under US GAAP be greater or less than equity reported under UK GAAP if the adjustments made in the equity reconciliation relate to those given in the income statement reconciliation? Explain your answer

(d) Supposing that a final dividend was proposed, and that under US GAAP this had to be included in the year in which the dividend is to be *paid*, state the effect on equity.

Answer

(a) The **advantages of harmonisation** will be based on the benefits to users and preparers of accounts, as follows.

Investors, both individual and corporate, would like to be able to compare the financial results of different companies internationally as well as nationally in making investment decisions. Differences in accounting practice and reporting can prove to be a barrier to such cross-border analysis. There is a growing amount of investment across borders and there are few financial analysts able to follow shares in international markets. For example, it is not easy for an analyst familiar with UK accounting principles to analyse the financial statements of a Dutch or German company. Harmonisation would therefore be of benefit to such analysts.

Multinational companies would benefit from harmonisation for many reasons including the following.

(i) Better access would be gained to foreign investor funds.

(ii) Management control would be improved, because harmonisation would aid internal communication of financial information.

(iii) Appraisal of foreign enterprises for takeovers and mergers would be more straightforward.

(iv) It would be easier to comply with the reporting requirements of overseas stock exchanges.

(v) Consolidation of foreign subsidiaries and associated companies would be easier.

(vi) A reduction in audit costs might be achieved.

(vii) Transfer of accounting staff across national borders would be easier.

Governments of developing countries would save time and money if they could adopt international standards and, if these were used internally, governments of developing countries could attempt to control the activities of foreign multinational companies in their own country. These companies cold not 'hide' behind foreign accounting practices which are difficult to understand.

For **tax authorities** it will be easier to calculate the tax liability of investors, including multinationals who receive income from overseas sources.

Regional economic groups usually promote trade with a specific geographical region. This would be aided by common accounting practices within the region.

Large international accounting firms would benefit as accounting and auditing would be much easier if similar accounting practices existed throughout the world.

The main **barriers to international harmonisation** are as follows.

(i) **Different purposes of financial reporting.** In some countries the purpose is solely for tax assessment, while in others it is for investor decision-making.

(ii) **Different legal systems.** These prevent the development of certain accounting practices and restrict the options available.

(iii) **Different user groups.** Countries have different ideas about who the relevant user groups are and their respective importance. In the USA investor and creditor groups are given prominence, while in Europe employees enjoy a higher profile.

(iv) **Needs of developing countries.** Developing countries are obviously behind in the standard setting process and they need to develop the basic standards and principles already in place in most developed countries.

(v) **Nationalism** is demonstrated in an unwillingness to accept another country's standard.

(vi) **Cultural differences** result in objectives for accounting systems differing from country to country.

(vii) **Unique circumstances.** Some countries may be experiencing unusual circumstances which affect all aspects of everyday life and impinge on the ability of companies to produce proper reports, for example hyperinflation, civil war, currency restriction and so on.

(viii) **The lack of strong accountancy bodies**. Many countries do not have strong independent accountancy or business bodies which would press for better standards and greater harmonisation.

(b) *Amortisation of interest costs*
Under UK GAAP companies have the choice of expending or capitalising interest as there is no accounting standard governing this area. Under US GAAP the group has capitalised the interest (whereas in the UK it appears to have been written off) and the amortisation charge relating to this interest is £8m.

Merger accounting adjustments
It appears that a merger has taken place during the year which satisfies UK criteria for the use of merger accounting (per FRS 6). This is not allowed under US GAAP so adjustments have been made to adopt acquisition accounting, including the removal of £200m of pre-acquisition profits and the additional depreciation and amortisation of £280m.

(c) The effect of the above items on the UK/US GAAP equity reconciliation is as follows.

Amortisation of interest costs
Any unamortised balance outstanding will increase equity under US GAAP (ie this balance will not be part of UK GAAP equity).

Merger accounting adjustment
The adjustments required to switch UK GAAP merger accounting to US GAAP acquisition accounting will probably cause an increase in equity because of the uplift to net assets given by a fair value exercise (a fall is possible, but unlikely).

(d) If such a dividend was proposed, the effect on equity would be to increase it because under UK GAAP the dividend must be accounted for in the fiscal year to which it relates. Under US GAAP the reduction in equity caused by the dividend is delayed until 20X7.

Chapter roundup

- **Harmonisation** in accounting is likely to come from international accounting standards, but not in the near future. There are enormous difficulties to overcome, both technical and political.
- You should be able to discuss the **barriers to harmonisation** and the advantages of and **progress towards harmonisation**.
- The EC has proposed that **by 2005** consolidated accounts of all listed companies should **comply with IAS.**
- This led to the publication of the **Convergence Handbook.**
- The IASB is working on an **Improvements Project** to bring IAS up to the quality of FRS.
- The **convergence project** is well underway with a number of FREDs based on IAS, new standards and revisions to IAS.
- The ASBs **Discussion Paper on Convergence** sets out the strategy. The aim is to minimise the burden of change. The strategy is twofold.
  - New standards effective in 2005/06 to enhance UK financial reporting
  - 'Step changes', replacing UK standards as and when IASB projects are completed
- We have concentrated on certain countries in our **comparison** between UK and overseas accounts, but you should be able to highlight the differences to UK accounting if you are presented with a set of accounts from any other country.
- You may be given a **set of accounts from another country**, with their accounting policies, and asked to discuss how the statements would appear **under UK accounting conventions** and disclosure rules.

Quick quiz

1. Which preparers and users of accounts can be expected to benefit from global harmonisation of accounting?
2. How many IASs are in existence at the moment?
3. What does IOSCO stand for?
4. Fill in the blanks: IAS ...... is almost identical to FRS ......
5. Why was *The Convergence Handbook* published?
6. German financial statements may be less useful than UK ones for decision-making purposes. Why?
7. Goodwill has been identified as an area where UK GAAP differs from US GAAP. In what way?
8. US GAAP permits but does not require capitalisation of development expenditure. True or false?
9. Fill in the blanks.

   The LIFO method of stock valuation is not permitted under ....

   LIFO is permitted under ....
10. What other areas of difference are there between UK GAAP, US GAAP and IAS?
11. Why were so many new FREDs published in recent years?
12. International rules on discontinued operations will be introduced in the UK in 2005.

    True ☐

    False ☐

Answers to quick quiz

1 Investors, multinational companies, governments of developing countries, the authorities (overseas income), regional economic groups, large international accounting firms.

2 41

3 International Organisation of Securities Commissions

4 IAS *37* is almost identical to FRS *12*.

5 To determine, in the light of the EC harmonisation proposal, whether domestic requirements should change to fit in with IAS or vice versa.

6 Because of the emphasis on compliance with tax rules.

7 UK GAAP allows the possibility of an indefinite useful life, while US GAAP does not.

8 False. Under US GAAP, development expenditure must be written off to the profit and loss account under all circumstances.

9 Not permitted under UK GAAP and now under IAS. Permitted under US GAAP and IASs.

10 Merger accounting, capitalisation of borrowing of costs, research and development.

11 To bring UK Standards into line with IAS in good time for the changeover to IAS in 2005.

12 False. An IAS-based standard awaits the outcome of the project on reporting comprehensive income.

Now try the question below from the Exam Question Bank

Number	Level	Marks	Time
Q20	Exam	25	45 mins

Chapter 14

ENVIRONMENTAL AND CULTURAL ISSUES

	Topic list	Syllabus reference
1	Environmental reporting	4(a)
2	Boundary management	5(a)
3	The social and ethical environment	5(a)
4	Social responsibility	5(a)
5	Ethics in organisations	5(a)

Introduction

Environmental issues are very topical. Just because these topics are discursive does not mean that you can 'waffle'. Social responsibility and ethical issues relate to many aspects of the firm: its environment, its culture and management practice. However, it is the nature of ethics to deny easy answers; furthermore, in the context of business, ethical prescriptions have to be practical to be of any use.

Study guide

Section 26 –The impact of environmental, social and cultural factors on corporate reporting

- Appraising the impact of environmental, social and ethical factors on performance measurement
- Describing current reporting requirements and guidelines for environmental reporting
- Preparing an environmental report in accordance with current practice
- Discussion of the effect of culture on accounting and the cultural relativity of accounting
- Discussion of why entities might include socially orientated disclosures in performance statements
- Discussion of the concept of a social contract and organisational legitimacy
- Evaluating ethical conduct in the context of corporate reporting

Exam guide

Environmental reporting was tested in the Pilot Paper, so the examiner clearly regards it as important.

1 ENVIRONMENTAL REPORTING — Pilot paper, 6/02, 6/04

1.1 At the end of the 1980s there were perhaps only two or three companies in the world issuing environmental reports. At the time of writing (June 2001) there are around 2,000. It is likely that by the end of 2001, almost all the UK FTSE 100 will be producing them. Worldwide there are around 20 award schemes for environmental reporting, notably the ACCA's. This section looks at environmental reporting mainly under three headings:

- The effect of environmental matters on management information and accounting
- External reporting and auditing
- Possible future developments

1.2 Let us consider the major areas of impact on (any) accountant's job caused by consideration of environmental matters.

(a) **Management accountant**

(i) Investment appraisal: evaluation of environmental costs and benefits.

(ii) Incorporating new costs, capital expenditure and so on, in to budgets and business plans.

(iii) Undertake cost/benefit analysis of any environmental improvements.

(b) **Financial accountant**

(i) The effect of revenue costs: site clean up costs, waste disposal or waste treatment costs and so on, which will affect the profit and loss account.

(ii) Gauging balance sheet impacts, particularly liabilities, contingencies, provisions *and* valuation of assets.

(iii) The effect of environmental matters, and particularly potential liabilities, on a company's relationship with bankers, insurers and major shareholders (institutional shareholders).

(iv) Environmental performance evaluation in annual reports.

(c) **Project accountant**

(i) Environmental audit of proposed takeovers, mergers and other planning matters.
(ii) Investment appraisal.

(d) **Internal auditor**: environmental audit.

(e) **Systems accountant**: effect on, and required changes to management and financial information systems.

What is environmental accounting?

1.3 The following list encompasses the major aspects of environmental accounting.

'(a) Recognising and seeking to **mitigate the negative environmental effects of conventional accounting** practice.

(b) Separately **identifying environmentally related costs and revenues** within the conventional accounting systems.

(c) Devising new forms of financial and non-financial accounting systems, information systems and control systems to **encourage more environmentally benign management decisions.**

(d) Developing new forms of **performance measurement**, reporting and appraisal for both internal and external purposes.

(e) Identifying, examining and seeking to **rectify** areas in which conventional (financial) criteria and environmental criteria are in **conflict**.

(f) Experimenting with ways in which, **sustainability** may be assessed and incorporated into organisational orthodoxy.'

Accounting for the Environment Bob Gary (with Jan Bebbington and Diane Walters)

1.4 The whole environmental agenda is **constantly changing** and businesses therefore need to monitor the situation closely. Most businesses, certainly those in the UK, have generally ignored environmental matters in the past. How long will they be able to do so?

Management information and accounting

1.5 The means of codifying a company's attitude towards the environment is often the creation of a published **environmental policy document** or charter. This may be internally generated or it may be adopted from a standard environmental charter, such as the **Valdez Principles**.

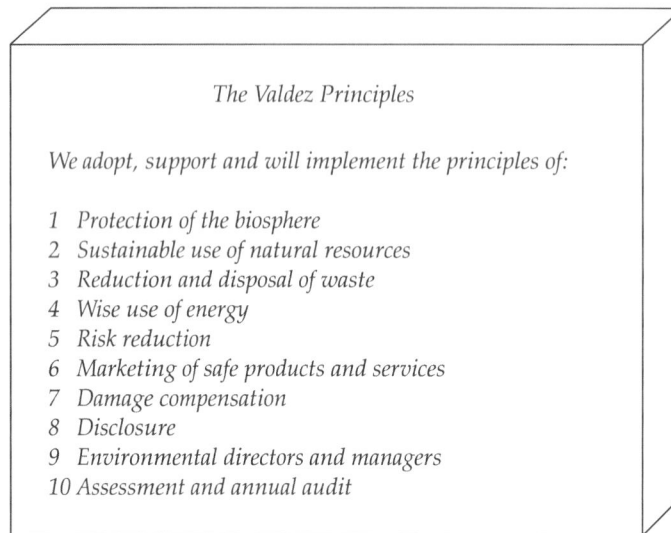

The Valdez Principles

We adopt, support and will implement the principles of:

1 Protection of the biosphere
2 Sustainable use of natural resources
3 Reduction and disposal of waste
4 Wise use of energy
5 Risk reduction
6 Marketing of safe products and services
7 Damage compensation
8 Disclosure
9 Environmental directors and managers
10 Assessment and annual audit

1.6 The problem here, as with other similar principles or charters, is that the commitment required from companies is generally too high and the fear exists that the principles may have legal status which could have a severe effect on a company's liability. Other documents available which are similar to the *Valdez Principles* are:

- The International Chamber of Commerce **Business Charter for Sustainable Developments**
- The Chemical Industries Association **Responsible Care Programme**
- The Confederation of British Industry **Agenda for Voluntary Action**
- Friends of the Earth Environmental **Charter for Local Government**

1.7 Adopting such a charter is one thing; implementing and monitoring it are more important and generally more difficult to achieve.

Environmental audit

1.8 Environmental auditing is exactly what it says: auditing a business to assess its impact on the environment, or as the CBI expressed it 'the systematic examination of the interactions between any business operation and its surroundings'.

1.9 The audit will cover a range of areas and will involve the performance of different types of testing. The scope of the audit must be determined and this will depend on each individual

organisation. There are, however, some aspects of the approach to environmental auditing which are worth mentioning.

(a) **Environmental Impact Assessments (EIAs)** are required, under EC directive, for all major projects which require planning permission and have a material effect on the environment. The EIA process can be incorporated into any environmental auditing strategy.

(b) **Environmental surveys** are a good way of starting the audit process, by looking at the organisation as a whole in environmental terms. This helps to identify areas for further development, problems, potential hazards and so forth.

(c) **Environmental SWOT analysis**. A 'strengths, weaknesses, opportunities, threats' analysis is useful as the environmental audit strategy is being developed. This can only be done later in the process, when the organisation has been examined in much more detail.

(d) **Environmental Quality Management (EQM).** This is seen as part of TQM (Total Quality Management) and it should be built in to an environmental management system. Such a strategy has been adopted by companies such as IBM, Dow Chemicals and by the Rhone-Poulenc Environmental Index which has indices for levels of water, air and other waste products.

(e) **Eco-audit**. The European Commission has adopted a proposal for a regulation for a voluntary community environmental auditing scheme, known as the eco-audit scheme. The scheme aims to promote improvements in company environmental performance and to provide the public with information about these improvements. Once registered, a company will have to comply with certain on-going obligations involving disclosure and audit.

(f) **Eco-labelling**. Developed in Germany, this voluntary scheme will indicate those EC products which meet the highest environmental standards, probably as the result of an EQM system. It is suggested that eco-audit *must* come before an eco-label can be given.

(g) **BS 7750 Environmental Management Systems**. BS 7750 also ties in with eco-audits and eco-labelling and with the quality BSI standard BS 5750. Achieving BS 7750 is likely to be a first step in the eco-audit process.

(h) **Supplier audits,** to ensure that goods and services bought in by an organisation meet the standards applied by that organisation.

Case example

In June 1999 BP Amoco commissioned KPMG to conduct an independent audit of its greenhouse gas emissions in the first ever environmental audit.

Financial reporting

1.10 There are **no disclosure requirements relating to environmental matters in the UK**, so any disclosures tend to be **voluntary** unless environmental matters happen to fall under standard accounting principles (eg recognising liabilities).

(a) In most cases disclosure is descriptive and unquantified.

(b) There is little motivation to produce environmental information and many reasons for not doing so, including secrecy.

(c) The main factor seems to be apathy on the part of businesses but more particularly on the part of shareholders and investors. The information is not demanded, so it is not provided.

1.11 Environmental matters may be reported in the accounts of companies in the following areas.

- Contingent liabilities
- Exceptional charges
- Operating and financial review comments
- Profit and capital expenditure forecasts

1.12 The voluntary approach contrasts with the position in the United States, where the SEC/FASB accounting standards are obligatory.

1.13 While nothing is compulsory, there are a number of **published guidelines** and **codes of practice**, including:

- The *Valdez Principles*
- The Confederation of British Industry's guideline *Introducing Environmental Reporting*
- The ACCA's *Guide to Environment and Energy Reporting*
- The Coalition of Environmentally Responsible Economies (CERES) formats for environmental reports
- The Friends of the Earth *Environmental Charter for Local Government*
- The Eco Management and Audit Scheme Code of Practice

1.14 EXAMPLE: ENVIRONMENTAL LIABILITIES

You have met FRS 12 *Provisions, contingent liabilities and contingent assets* in your earlier studies. FRS 12 deals with the issue of whether environmental liabilities should be provided for. The example below is taken from an article by Alan Pizzey which appeared in the February 1998 edition of *CIMA Student*. Study the example and attempt the question which follows it.

MegaBux plc is a multinational holding company. During the year a number of situations have arisen and the board is to meet soon to determine an appropriate treatment .

Site A

This site is occupied by a small refinery. The site and some adjacent land has been contaminated by chemical spillages. The cost of remedying the contamination is £20m, but under local laws there is no requirement to clean up the site.

Site B

Similar contamination has arisen but the local government, and a neighbouring land owner, require the contamination to be remedied soon. The cost of cleaning up the site is £15m, but an extra £5m could be spent to raise the standard of the operation in line with undertakings given to the local community ten years ago.

1.15 SOLUTION

Site A

The mere existence of contamination does not establish an obligation on the part of the company and without an obligation there is no need for a provision.

Site B

An obligation does exist which the local government and a neighbour can prove in court. At least £15m must be provided, but there may be a constructive obligation, wider than a legal obligation, to spend an extra £5m to raise the standard of rectification. Concern for its long term reputation may influence the company to honour its undertaking given to the local community.

Question: environmental liabilities

Site C

Considerable contamination needs to be remedied, but the managing director is arguing that no provision is required this year since the amount concerned cannot be estimated with accuracy.

Site D

Spillage of chemicals has reduced the value of the site from £25m, its book value, to £10m, its current realisable value. By spending £5m on rectification, the site value will be increased to £20m. The spillage has seeped into a local river and fines of £3m are now payable.

Answer

Site C

Whilst the exact amount of the expenditure may not be known with certainty, it should be possible to arrive at a realistic and prudent estimate. It is not acceptable to omit a liability on the grounds that its amount is not known with certainty – this would be a distortion.

Site D

The fines of £3m are a current cost to be charged to the profit and loss account. The spillage has impaired the value of the site, which must be written down to its new market value of £20m after rectification. The cost of the write-down (£5m) and the cost of the rectification (£5m) are charged to the profit and loss account. The site is now carried in the books at its recoverable amount.

The environmental report and the exam

1.16 You may be asked in the exam to prepare an environmental report. Your report should distinguish between:

(a) Transactions that affect the financial statements, for example provisions that need to be made under FRS 12

(b) Information to be disclosed elsewhere, for example in the operating and financial review, or in a separate environmental report.

Exam focus point

Have a go at the Pilot Paper question in the Exam Question Bank. This distinguishes between environmental matters that affect the financial statements and those which do not, but are nevertheless important.

1.17 EXAMPLE: ENVIRONMENTAL REPORT

A good example of an environmental report is the Boots report for 1999/2000. This was published as a separate report consisting of around 20 pages. Extracts from the report are reproduced below to give you a feel for it. Note that the report is based around 'key

performance indicators'. These are monitored against targets. We emphasise that this is not the only possible approach to environmental reporting.

'Environmental policy statement

We have a responsibility as a company to take proper care of the environment on behalf of our shareholders, customers, staff and the communities in which we operate. Caring for the environment is an essential part of the way we run our business.

We are committed to managing responsibly the way in which our activities affect the environment by:

- Optimising the use of energy
- Ensuring efficient use of materials
- Encouraging re-use and recycling
- Incorporating the principle of sustainable development.

By integrating environmental considerations into our everyday activities, the environment will be managed alongside other business considerations such as safety, quality and value.

Management

We will set objectives and targets for those activities which significantly affect the environment and we will measure our performance over time. Details of our progress will be published at least annually.

Environmental audits and inspections will be undertaken to monitor our progress against this policy.

Within the individual businesses there is a clear structure of responsibility devolved into each business via an appointed manager with overall environmental responsibility. At a corporate level, the Environmental Affairs team co-ordinates environmental issues for the company through the Environmental Working Party.

The company's significant impacts have been assessed and Key Performance Indicators (KPIs) have been selected to track performance over time. Data to monitor these is generated via environmental management systems that are incorporated into business systems and regularly audited.

Environmental management is integrated into everything we do from product development to the supply chain and staff training.

Key performance indicators 99/00

Energy

In 1999/2000 total company energy use decreased by 5.3 per cent, while energy efficiency improved by 10.2 per cent.

Over the last four years energy efficiency, as measured by kWh per £ thousand turnover, has improved by 12 per cent overall, maintaining a positive trend.

Transport

Commercial transport efficiency improved by 2 per cent.

Alongside the ongoing internal data verification programme, improvements to data management systems have resulted in additional transport data being reported for 1998/99. Transport efficiency over the last three years, as measured by litres of diesel consumed per £ million turnover, maintained a positive trend overall with a 2 per cent improvement recorded over the last year.

The efficiency of stock delivery, as measured by the volume of stock delivered per 1000 litres of fuel, reduced by 3.7 per cent at Boots The Chemists. This is due to a combination of factors, including new store openings and the closure of an old warehouse in an urban centre (see Progress against targets). The move to lower sulphur diesel for commercial fleets has also had a negative impact on fuel efficiency. Trials of alternative fuel vehicles have continued.

Carbon dioxide and global warming

In the last year, like-for-like CO2 emissions decreased by 4.4 per cent.

The main greenhouse gas associated with the company's operations is CO2 arising primarily from energy use in manufacturing and retailing, and emissions from its transport fleets. Some 84 per cent of total emissions relate to energy consumption. Similarly, around 85 per cent of transport emissions relate to commercial fleets, with around 8 per cent to company cars.

The company's modern combined heat and power (CHP) energy centre on the head office site continues to contribute to a global reduction in annual CO2 emissions of around 44,000 tonnes compared with purchasing electricity from third party suppliers. This represents a reduction in the company's total CO2 emissions of around 15 per cent each year. The saving is achieved through the re-use of waste heat from the electricity generation process to generate usable steam.

Waste

Around 26,000 tonnes of waste was recovered through recycling or incineration with heat recovery.

As the business is primarily retailing, the largest proportion of waste (91 per cent) is transit packaging and general office waste that is mainly non-hazardous. Other wastes arise from manufacturing processes, laboratories, garage and pharmacy operations.

Of the 54,000 tonnes of material identified as waste, some 26,000 tonnes (48 per cent) was recovered through recycling or incineration with heat recovery. The majority of the remaining 28,000 tonnes of waste (94 per cent) was disposed to landfill.

Quantifying the weight of non-hazardous waste is difficult due to small quantities of unweighed waste being collected from a large number of retail locations by multiple collection vehicles, and shopping centres amalgamating non-hazardous waste from a number of retailers for bulk collection. Because of this, although the company's data collection systems for waste have continued to improve, it is unlikely that year-on-year comparisons will be meaningful for some time to come.

Packaging

In the last year the company handled some 162,000 tonnes of packaging.

Minimising packaging is a complex business challenge where a number of considerations have to be balanced. These include evaluating the wide variety of roles performed by packaging (from improved keeping qualities for food and medical products to optimal shapes for efficient stacking and transportation) together with aspects such as design, quality, performance, cost and environment.

In addition, several factors mask the performance that can be directly attributed to packaging management. In particular, consumer and business demands in retailing require ongoing changes to the scale of product ranges and the general product mix within stores, which can produce conflicting trends in packaging use.

The issue will remain as a key performance indicator given its perceived environmental impact in the retail and manufacturing sectors, but it is unlikely that a valid, quantitative comparison of company performance will be developed in this area.

Water and effluent

In the last year Boots Contract Manufacturing reduced the effluent load per unit produced by more than 18 per cent.

Centralised monitoring of water consumption continued with substantial effort being put into the development of robust data management systems. This section relates mainly to Boots Contract Manufacturing, but from April 2000 the data available will include all business units and will be comparable across future years. The acquisition of historical water consumption data proved more difficult than expected, so the overall picture for the company is currently incomplete. Information has been included in the data section where meaningful.

Water conservation in Boots Contract Manufacturing, across all production areas, has again been an area of considerable focus. Improvements such as the elimination of 'once-through' water cooling systems have been implemented in key areas. Fitting improved temperature controls to a tempering belt reduced steam demand as well as saving cooling water.

Water use has been benchmarked across departments and factories to enable sharing of best practice in successful conservation strategies. A computerised data reporting system in the main factory on the Nottingham site allows water use profiles to be analysed. This has been a significant factor in bringing about change. For example, over the past four years water consumption in the factory over the Christmas shutdown period has been reduced from 60 per cent to less than 10 per cent of that on a normal working day. This experience has been shared and improved water metering is now being installed at the Airdrie factory.

In other areas external factors, such as the reduced use of preservatives in products and third party customer specifications that predefine equipment-cleaning procedures, resulted in some increased

water use. Overall, water use per unit of production was reduced by 2.6 per cent against a target of 3 per cent.

Reducing waste discharged as effluent has been targeted in several key areas. Process changes have brought about material savings at Nottingham and, at Airdrie, a new system for cleaning pipes between product batches has reduced the amount of water required for this operation by 90 per cent. Together, all these initiatives reduced the loss of material to drain by more than 18 per cent (as measured by chemical oxygen demand and solids load per unit 'produced').'

2 BOUNDARY MANAGEMENT

2.1 A business supplies goods and services to customers, and employs people; **it is an integral part of society and is subject to the pressures of that society**. Many companies share similar aspirations.

- To seek a good public image
- To protect the environment from pollution, and the waste of non-renewable resources
- To be good employers
- To provide facilities or welfare to the local community or the country as a whole (eg the sponsorship of sports, which is not always associated with a blaze of advertising and publicity, donations to charity)

2.2 There are differing views about the extent to which external pressures modify business objectives and form boundaries to the exercise of management discretion.

(a) **The stakeholder view of company objectives** is that many groups of people have a stake in what the company does. Shareholders own the business, but there are also suppliers, managers, workers and customers. A business depends on appropriate relationships with these groups, otherwise it will find it hard to function. Each of these groups has its own objectives, so that a compromise or balance is required. **Management must balance the profit objective with the pressures from the non-shareholder groups in deciding the strategic targets of the business.**

(b) **The consensus theory of company objectives** was developed by *Cyert and March*. They argued that managers run a business but do not own it and that 'organisations do not have objectives, only people have objectives'. Managers do not necessarily set objectives for the company, but rather they look for objectives which suit their own inclinations. However, objectives emerge as a consensus of the differing views of shareholders, managers, employees, suppliers, customers and society at large, but (in contrast to the stakeholder view) **they are not all selected or controlled by management**.

2.3 *Ansoff* suggested that a company has a number of **different levels of objectives**.

(a) A **primary economic objective**, aimed at optimising the efficiency and effectiveness of the firm's 'total resource-conversion process'.

(b) **Non-economic, social objectives**, which are secondary and modify management behaviour. These social objectives are the result of inter-action among the individual objectives of the differing groups of stakeholders.

(c) **Responsibilities** are obligations which a company undertakes, but which do not form a par t of its 'internal guidance or control mechanism'. Responsibilities would include charitable donations, contributions to the life of local communities.

(d) **Boundaries** are rules that restrict management's freedom of action, and include government legislation (on, for instance, pollution levels, health and safety at work, employment protection, redundancy and monopolies) and agreements with trade unions.

3 THE SOCIAL AND ETHICAL ENVIRONMENT 12/01, 6/04

KEY TERM

Ethics: a set of moral principles to guide behaviour

3.1 Whereas the political environment in which an organisation operates consists of laws, regulations and government agencies, the social environment consists of the customs, attitudes, beliefs and education of society as a whole, or of different groups in society; and the ethical environment consists of a set (or sets) of well-established rules of personal and organisational behaviour.

3.2 Social attitudes, such as a belief in the merits of education, progress through science and technology, and fair competition, are significant for the management of a business organisation. Other beliefs have either gained strength or been eroded in recent years:

(a) There is a growing belief in preserving and improving the quality of life by reducing working hours, reversing the spread of pollution, developing leisure activities and so on. Pressures on organisations to consider the environment are particularly strong because most environmental damage is irreversible and some is fatal to humans and wildlife.

(b) Many pressure groups have been organised in recent years to protect social minorities and under-privileged groups. Legislation has been passed in an attempt to prevent racial discrimination and discrimination against women and disabled people.

(c) Issues relating to the environmental consequences of corporate activities are currently debated, and respect for the environment has come to be regarded as an unquestionable good.

3.3 The ethical environment refers to justice, respect for the law and a moral code. The conduct of an organisation, its management and employees will be measured against ethical standards by the customers, suppliers and other members of the public with whom they deal.

Ethical problems facing managers

3.4 Managers have a duty (in most enterprises) to aim for profit. At the same time, modern ethical standards impose a duty to guard, preserve and enhance the value of the enterprise for the good of all touched by it, including the general public. Large organisations tend to be more often held to account over this than small ones.

3.5 In the area of **products and production**, managers have responsibility to ensure that the public and their own employees are protected from danger. Attempts to increase profitability by cutting costs may lead to dangerous working conditions or to inadequate safety standards in products. In the United States, product liability litigation is so common that this legal threat may be a more effective deterrent than general ethical standards. The

Consumer Protection Act 1987 and EU legislation generally is beginning to ensure that ethical standards are similarly enforced in the UK.

3.6 Another ethical problem concerns **payments by companies to government or municipal officials** who have power to help or hinder the payers' operations. In *The Ethics of Corporate Conduct, Clarence Walton* refers to the fine distinctions which exist in this area.

(a) **Extortion**. Foreign officials have been known to threaten companies with the complete closure of their local operations unless suitable payments are made.

(b) **Bribery**. This refers to payments for services to which a company is not legally entitled. There are some fine distinctions to be drawn; for example, some managers regard political contributions as bribery.

(c) **Grease money**. Multinational companies are sometimes unable to obtain services to which they are legally entitled because of deliberate stalling by local officials. Cash payments to the right people may then be enough to oil the machinery of bureaucracy.

(d) **Gifts**. In some cultures (such as Japan) gifts are regarded as an essential part of civilised negotiation, even in circumstances where to Western eyes they might appear ethically dubious. Managers operating in such a culture may feel at liberty to adopt the local customs.

3.7 Business ethics are also relevant to competitive behaviour. This is because a market can only be free if competition is, in some basic respects, fair. There is a distinction between competing aggressively and competing unethically. The dispute between British Airways and Virgin centred around issues of business ethics.

Examples of social and ethical objectives

3.8 Companies are not passive in the social and ethical environment. Many organisations pursue a variety of social and ethical objectives.

3.9 **Employees**

(a) A minimum wage, perhaps with adequate differentials for skilled labour

(b) Job security (over and above the protection afforded to employees by government legislation)

(c) Good conditions of work (above the legal minima)

(d) Job satisfaction

3.10 **Customers** may be regarded as entitled to receive a produce of good quality at a reasonable price.

3.11 **Suppliers** may be offered regular orders and timely payment in return for reliable delivery and good service.

3.12 **Society** as a whole

(a) Control of pollution

(b) Provision of financial assistance to charities, sports and community activities

(c) Co-operation with government authorities in identifying and preventing health hazards in the products sold

3.13 As far as it is possible, social and ethical objectives should be expressed quantitatively, so that actual results can be monitored to ensure that the targets are achieved. This is often easier said than done - more often, they are expressed in the organisation's mission statement which can rarely be reduced to a quantified amount.

3.14 Many of the above objectives are commercial ones - for example satisfying customers is necessary to stay in business. The question as to whether it is the business of businesses to be concerned about wider issues of social responsibility *at all* is discussed shortly.

4 SOCIAL RESPONSIBILITY

4.1 Not only does the environment have a significant influence on the structure and behaviour of organisations, but also organisations have some influence on their environment.

4.2 Since organisations have an effect on their environment, it is arguable that they should act in a way which shows **social awareness and responsibility**.

> 'A society, awakened and vocal with respect to the urgency of social problems, is asking the managers of all kinds of organisations, particularly those at the top, what they are doing to discharge their social responsibilities and why they are not doing more.'
>
> Koontz, O'Donnell and Weihrich

4.3 Social responsibility is expected from all types of organisation.

(a) **Local government** is expected to provide services to the local community, and to preserve or improve the character of that community, but at an acceptable cost to the ratepayers.

(b) **Businesses** are expected to provide goods and services, which reflect the needs of users and society as a whole. These needs may not be in harmony - arguably, the development of the Concorde aeroplane and supersonic passenger travel did not contribute to the public interest, and caused considerable inconvenience to residents near airports who suffer from excessive aircraft noise. A business should also be expected to anticipate the future needs of society; examples of socially useful products might be energy-saving devices and alternative sources of power.

(c) **Pollution control** is a particularly important example of social responsibility by industrial organisations, and some progress has been made in the development of commercial processes for re-cycling waste material. British Coal attempts to restore the environment by planting on old slag heaps.

(d) **Universities and schools** are expected to produce students whose abilities and qualifications will prove beneficial to society. A currently popular view of education is that greater emphasis should be placed on vocational training for students.

(e) In some cases, **legislation** may be required to enforce social need, for example to regulate the materials used to make crash helmets for motor cyclists, or to regulate safety standards in motor cars and furniture. Ideally, however, organisations should avoid the need for legislation by taking **earlier self-regulating action**.

Social responsibility and businesses

4.4 Arguably, institutions like hospitals, schools and so forth exist because health care and education are seen to be desirable social objectives by government at large, if they can be afforded.

4.5 However, where does this leave businesses? How far is it reasonable, or even appropriate, for businesses to exercise 'social responsibility' by giving to charities, voluntarily imposing strict environmental objectives on themselves and so forth?

4.6 One school of thought would argue that **the management of a business has only one social responsibility, which is to maximise wealth for its shareholders**. There are two reasons to support this argument.

(a) If the business is owned by the shareholders the assets of the company are, ultimately, the shareholders' property. Management has no moral right to dispose of business assets (like cash) on non-business objectives, as this has the effect of reducing the return available to shareholders. The shareholders might, for example, disagree with management's choice of beneficiary. Anyhow, it is for the shareholders to determine how their money should be spent.

(b) A second justification for this view is that management's job is to maximise wealth, as this is the best way that society can benefit from a business's activities.

(i) Maximising wealth has the effect of increasing the tax revenues available to the state to disburse on socially desirable objectives.

(ii) Maximising wealth for the few is sometimes held to have a 'trickle down' effect on the disadvantaged members of society.

(iii) Many company shares are owned by pension funds, whose ultimate beneficiaries may not be the wealthy anyway.

4.7 This argument rests on certain assumptions.

(a) The first assumption is, in effect, the opposite of the stakeholder view. In other words, it is held that the *rights* of legal ownership are paramount over all other *interests* in a business: while other stakeholders have an interest, they have few legal or moral rights over the wealth created.

(b) The second assumption is that a business's *only* relationship with the wider social environment is an economic one. After all, that is what businesses exist for, and any other activities are the role of the state.

(c) The defining purpose of business organisations is the maximisation of the wealth of their owners.

4.8 *Henry Mintzberg* (in *Power In and Around Organisations*) suggests that simply viewing organisations as vehicles for shareholder investment is inadequate.

(a) In practice, he says, organisations are rarely controlled effectively by shareholders. Most shareholders are passive investors.

(b) Large corporations can manipulate markets. Social responsibility, forced or voluntary, is a way of recognising this.

(c) Moreover, businesses do receive a lot of government support. The public pays for roads, infrastructure, education and health, all of which benefits businesses. Although businesses pay tax, the public ultimately pays, perhaps through higher prices.

(d) Strategic decisions by businesses always have wider social consequences. In other words, says Mintzberg, the firm produces two outputs: **goods and services** and the **social consequences of its activities** (eg pollution).

Externalities

4.9 If it is accepted that businesses do not bear the total social cost of their activities, then the exercise of social responsibility is a way of compensating for this.

4.10 An example is given by the environment. Industrial pollution is injurious to health: if someone is made ill by industrial pollution, then arguably the polluter should pay the sick person, as damages or in compensation, in the same way as if the business's builders had accidentally bulldozed somebody's house.

4.11 In practice, of course, while it is relatively easy to identify statistical relationships between pollution levels and certain illnesses, mapping out the chain of cause and effect from an individual's wheezing cough to the dust particles emitted by Factory X, as opposed to Factory Y, is quite a different matter.

4.12 Of course, it could be argued that these external costs are met out of general taxation: but this has the effect of spreading the cost amongst other individuals and businesses. Moreover, the tax revenue may be spent on curing the disease, rather than stopping it at its source. Pollution control equipment may be the fairest way of dealing with this problem. Thus advocates of social responsibility in business would argue that business's responsibilities then do not rest with paying taxes.

4.13 However, is there any justification for social responsibility outside remedying the effects of a business's direct activities. For example, should businesses give to charity or sponsor the arts? There are several reasons why they should.

(a) If the **stakeholder concept** of a business is held, then the public is a stakeholder in the business. A business only succeeds because it is part of a wider society. Giving to charity is one way of encouraging a relationship.

(b) Charitable donations and artistic sponsorship are a useful medium of **public relations** and can reflect well on the business. It can be regarded, then, as another form of promotion, which like advertising, serves to enhance consumer awareness of the business, while not encouraging the sale of a particular brand.

4.14 The arguments for and against social responsibility of business are complex ones. However, ultimately they can be traced to different assumptions about society and the relationships between the individuals and organisations within it.

Question: social responsibility

The Heritage Carpet Company is a London-based retailer which imports carpets from Turkey, Iran and India. The company was founded by two Europeans who travelled independently through these countries in the 1970s. The company is the sole customer for carpets made in a number of villages in each of the source countries. The carpets are hand woven. Indeed, they are so finely woven that the process requires that children be used to do the weaving, thanks to their small fingers. The company believes that it is preserving a 'craft', and the directors believe that this is a justifiable social objective. Recently a UK television company has reported unfavourably on child exploitation in the carpet weaving industry. There were reports of children working twelve hour shifts in poorly lit sheds and cramped conditions, with consequent deterioration in eyesight, muscular disorders and a complete absence of education. The examples cited bear no relation to the Heritage Carpet Company's suppliers although children are used in the labour force, but there has been a spate of media attention. The regions in which the Heritage Carpet Company's supplier villages are found are soon expected to enjoy rapid economic growth.

What boundary management issues are raised for the Heritage Carpet Company?

Answer

Many. This is a case partly about boundary management and partly about enlightened self-interest and business ethics. The adverse publicity, although not about the Heritage Carpet Company's own suppliers, could rebound badly. Potential customers might be put off. Economic growth in the area may also mean that parents will prefer to send their children to school. The Heritage Carpet Company as well as promoting itself as preserving a craft could reinvest some of its profits in the villages (eg by funding a school), or by enforcing limits on the hours children worked. It could also pay a decent wage. It could advertise this in a 'code of ethics' so that customers are reassured that the children are not simply being exploited. Alternatively, it could not import child-made carpets at all. (This policy, however, would be unlikely to help communities in which child labour is an economic necessity. Children already living on the margins of subsistence might end up even more exploited, in begging or prostitution.)

5 ETHICS IN ORGANISATIONS

5.1 Ethics is a code of moral principles that people follow with respect to what is right or wrong. Ethical principles are not necessarily enforced by law, although the law incorporates moral judgements (murder is wrong ethically, and is also punishable legally).

5.2 Companies have to follow legal standards, or else they will be subject to fines and their officers might face similar charges. Ethics in organisations relates to **social responsibility** and **business practice.**

5.3 People that work for organisations bring their own values into work with them. Organisations contain a variety of ethical systems.

(a) **Personal ethics** (eg deriving from a person's upbringing, religious or non-religious beliefs, political opinions, personality). People have different ethical viewpoints at different stages in their lives. Some will judge situations on 'gut feel'. Some will consciously or unconsciously adopt a general approach to ethical dilemmas, such as 'the end justifies the means'.

(b) **Professional ethics** (eg ACCA's ethical rules).

(c) **Organisation cultures** (eg 'customer first'). Culture, in denoting what is normal behaviour, also denotes what is the right behaviour in many cases.

(d) **Organisation systems**. Ethics might be contained in a formal code, reinforced by the overall statement of values. A problem might be that ethics does not always save money, and there is a real cost to ethical decisions. Besides, the organisation has different ethical duties to different stakeholders. Who sets priorities?

Case example

Organisation systems and targets do have ethical implications. The Harvard Business Review reported that the US retailer, Sears, Roebuck was deluged with complaints that customers of its car service centre were being charged for unnecessary work: apparently this was because mechanics had been given targets of the number of car spare parts they should sell.

Leadership practices and ethics

5.4 The role of culture in determining the ethical climate of an organisation can be further explored by a brief reflection on the role of leaders in setting the ethical standard. A culture is partly a collection of symbols and attitudes, embodying certain truths about the organisation. Senior managers are also symbolic managers; inevitably they decide priorities;

they set an example, whether they like it or not. Remember, too, that one of the roles of managers, according to Mintzberg is the **ceremonial one**.

5.5 **There are four types of cultural leadership in organisations**. (Note that these should *not* be confused with leadership styles.)

(a) **Creative**. The culture of an organisation often reflects its founder, and it is therefore reasonable to expect that the founding visionary should set the ethical tone. Such leaders create the ethical style.

(b) **Protective**. Such leaders sustain, or exemplify, the organisation's culture: for example a company which values customer service may have leaders who are 'heroic' in their efforts to achieve it.

(c) **Integrative**. Other leaders aim to create consensus through people, and perhaps flourish in an involvement culture. The danger is that this can turn to political manipulation; the 'consensus' created should work towards some valued cultural goal.

(d) **Adaptive**. These leaders change an existing culture or set of ethics. (When appointed to run *British Airways*, *Colin Marshall* changed the sign on his door from Chief Executive to his own name.) However, a leader has to send out the right signals, to ensure that competitive behaviour remains ethical, to avoid bad publicity if nothing else.

Two approaches to managing ethics

5.6 *Lynne Paine* (*Harvard Business Review*, March-April 1994) suggests that ethical decisions are becoming more important as penalties, in the US at least, for companies which break the law become tougher. (This might be contrasted with UK, where a fraudster whose deception ran into millions received a sentence of community service.) Paine suggests that there are two approaches to the management of ethics in organisations.

- Compliance-based
- Integrity-based

Compliance-based approach

5.7 **A compliance-based approach is primarily designed to ensure that the company acts within the letter of the law, and that violations are prevented, detected and punished**. Some organisations, faced with the legal consequences of unethical behaviour take legal precautions such as those below.

- Compliance procedures
- Audits of contracts
- Systems for employees to inform superiors about criminal misconduct without fear of retribution
- Disciplinary procedures

5.8 Corporate compliance is limited in that it refers only to the law, but legal compliance is 'not an adequate means for addressing the full range of ethical issues that arise every day'. This is especially the case in the UK, where **voluntary** codes of conduct and self-regulation are perhaps more prevalent than in the US.

5.9 An example of the difference between the **legality** and **ethicality** of a practice is the sale in some countries of defective products without appropriate warnings. 'Companies engaged in

international business often discover that conduct that infringes on recognised standards of human rights and decency is legally permissible in some jurisdictions.'

5.10 The compliance approach also overemphasises the threat of detection and punishment in order to channel appropriate behaviour. Arguably, some employers view compliance programmes as an insurance policy for senior management, who can cover the tracks of their arbitrary management practices. After all, some performance targets are impossible to achieve without cutting corners: managers can escape responsibility by blaming the employee for not following the compliance programme, when to do so would have meant a failure to reach target.

5.11 Furthermore, mere compliance with the law is no guide to **exemplary** behaviour.

Integrity-based programmes

5.12 'An integrity-based approach combines a concern for the law with an **emphasis on managerial responsibility** for ethical behaviour. Integrity strategies strive to define companies' guiding values, aspirations and patterns of thought and conduct. When integrated into the day-to-day operations of an organisation, such strategies can help prevent damaging ethical lapses, while tapping into powerful human impulses for moral thought and action.

5.13 It should be clear to you from this quotation that an integrity-based approach to ethics treats ethics as an issue of organisation culture.

5.14 Ethics management has several tasks.

- To define and give life to an organisation's defining values.
- To create an environment that supports ethically sound behaviour
- To instil a sense of shared accountability amongst employees.

5.15 The table below indicates some of the differences between the two main approaches.

	Compliance	**Integrity**
Ethos	Knuckle under to external standards	Choose ethical standards
Objective	Keep to the law	Enable legal and responsible conduct
Originators	Lawyers	Management, with lawyers, HR specialists etc
Methods (both includes education, and audits, controls, penalties)	Reduced employee discretion	Leadership, organisation systems
Behavioural assumptions	People are solitary self-interested beings	People are social beings with values
Standards	The law	Company values, aspirations (including law)
Staffing	Lawyers	Managers and lawyers
Education	The law, compliance system	Values, the law, compliance systems

	Compliance	Integrity
Activities	Develop standards, train and communicate, handle reports of misconduct, investigate, enforce, oversee compliance	Integrate values *into* company systems, provide guidance and consultation, identify and resolve problems, oversee compliance

5.16 In other words, an integrity-based approach **incorporates** ethics into corporate culture and systems.

Case example

Charles Hampden-Turner (in his book *Corporate Culture*) notes that attitudes to safety can be part of a corporate *culture*. He quotes the example of a firm called (for reasons of confidentiality) *Western Oil*.

Western Oil had a bad safety record. 'Initially, safety was totally at odds with the main cultural values of productivity (management's interests) and maintenance of a macho image (the worker's culture) ... Western Oil had a culture which put safety in conflict with other corporate values.' In particular, the problem was with its long-distance truck drivers (which in the US have a culture of solitary independence and self reliance) who drove sometimes recklessly with loads large enough to inundate a small town. The company instituted *Operation Integrity* to improve safety, in a lasting way, changing the policies and drawing on the existing features of the culture but using them in a different way.

The culture had five dilemmas.

- *Safety-first vs macho-individualism.* Truckers see themselves as 'fearless pioneers of the unconventional lifestyle ... "Be careful boys!" is hardly a plea likely to go down well with this particular group'. Instead of trying to control the drivers, the firm recommended that they become *road safety consultants* (or design consultants). Their advice was sought on improving the system. This had the advantage that 'by making drivers critics of the system their roles as outsiders were preserved and promoted'. It tried to tap their heroism as promoters of public safety.
- *Safety everywhere vs safety specialists.* Western Oil could have hired more specialist staff. However, instead, the company promoted cross functional safety teams from existing parts of the business, for example, to help in designing depots and thinking of ways to reduce hazards.
- *Safety as cost vs productivity as benefit.* 'If the drivers raced from station to station to win their bonus, accidents were bound to occur .... The safety engineers rarely spoke to the line manager in charge of the delivery schedules. The unreconciled dilemma between safety and productivity had been evaded at management level and passed down the hierarchy until drivers were subjected to two incompatible injunctions, work fast and work safely'. To deal with this problem, safety would be built into the reward system.
- *Long-term safety vs short-term steering.* The device of recording 'unsafe' acts in operations enabled them to be monitored by cross-functional teams, so that the causes of accidents could be identified and be reduced.
- *Personal responsibility vs collective protection.* It was felt that if 'safety' was seen as a form of management policing it would never be accepted. The habit of management 'blaming the victim' had to stop. Instead, if an employee reported another to the safety teams, the person who was reported would be free of *official* sanction. Peer presence was seen to be a better enforcer of safety than the management hierarchy.

5.17 It has also been suggested that the following institutions can be established.

- An **ethics committee** is a group of executives (perhaps including non-executive directors) appointed to oversee company ethics. It rules on misconduct. It may seek advice from specialists in business ethics.
- An **ethics ombudsperson** is a manager who acts as the corporate conscience.

5.18 Accountants can also appeal to their professional body for ethical guidance.

5.19 **Whistle-blowing** is the disclosure by an employee of illegal, immoral or illegitimate practices on the part of the organisation. In theory, the public ought to welcome the public trust: however, confidentiality is very important in the accountants' code of ethics. Whistle-blowing frequently involves **financial loss** for the whistleblower.

- The whistle-blower may lose his or her job.
- If the whistle-blower is a member of a professional body, he or she cannot, sadly, rely on that body to take a significant interest, or even offer a sympathetic ear. Some professional bodies have narrow interpretations of what is meant by ethical conduct. For many the duties of **commercial confidentiality** are felt to be more important.

Exam focus point

The ethics codes described above can be related to mission, culture and control strategies. A compliance-based approach suggest that bureaucratic control is necessary; an integrity based approach relies on cultural control.

Chapter roundup

- Although not compulsory, environmental reports are becoming increasingly important. You should distinguish
  - Items that affect the financial statements (eg FRS 12)
  - Items that affect the OFR or environmental report
- The stakeholder view holds that there are many groups in society with an interest in the organisation's activities. Some firms have objectives for these issues. Some argue, however, that a business's only objective should be to make money: the state, representing the public interest, can levy taxes to spend on socially desirable projects or can regulate organisational activities.
- Firms have to ensure they obey the law: but they also face ethical concerns, because their reputations depend on a good image.
- Inside the organisation, a compliance based approach highlights conformity with the law. An integrity based approach suggests a wider remit, incorporating ethics in the organisation's values and culture.
- Organisations sometimes issue codes of conduct to employees. Many employees are bound by professional codes of conduct.

Quick quiz

1 Give an example of a recent environmental audit.

2 Name four areas of company accounts where environmental matters may be reported.

3 If a site is contaminated, a provision must be made.

True ☐

False ☐

4 Distinguish between responsibilities and boundaries.

5 What ethical problems face management?

6 What objectives might a company have in relation to wider society?

7 To whom might management have responsibilities, and what are some of these responsibilities?

8 Why does Mintzberg say that the profit motive is not enough?

9 Describe two approaches to the management of ethics in an organisation.

10 What systems of ethics might you find in an organisation?

11 What is whistle blowing?

Answers to quick quiz

1 In 1999 KPMG conducted an audit of the greenhouse gas emissions of BP Amoco.

2 Contingent liabilities
Exceptional charges
Operating and financial review comments
Profit and capital expenditure forecasts

3 False. an **obligation** must be established.

4 In Ansoff's analysis, boundaries are imposed rules; they restrict management's freedom of action. Responsibilities are voluntarily undertaken obligations such as charitable donations.

5 There is a constant tension between the need to achieve current profitability, the need to safeguard the stakeholders' long term investment and the expectations of wider society.

6 Protection of the environment, support for good causes, a responsible attitude to product safety.

7 Managers of businesses are responsible to the owners for economic performance and to wider society for the externalities related to their business operations.

8 Large businesses are rarely controlled by their shareholders; they receive a lot of support from public funds; and their activities have wider consequences.

9 A compliance–based approach aims to remain within the letter of the law by establishing systems of audit and review so that transgressions may be detected and punished. An integrity-based approach tries to promote an ethical culture in which individuals will do the right thing.

10 Personal ethics, professional ethics, organisation culture, organisation systems.

11 Informing outside regulatory agencies about transgressions by one's organisation.

Now try the question below from the Exam Question Bank

Number	Level	Marks	Time
Q21	Exam	25	45 mins

Chapter 15

CURRENT ISSUES

Topic list		Syllabus reference
1	Communication of corporate performance	4(b)
2	Interim reports	4(b)
3	IFRS 1 First time adoption of International Financial Reporting Standards	4(b)
4	Current issues in corporate reporting	l(d),(f), 4(e)

Introduction

This chapter deals with a number of current issues and developments. Section 4 highlights the latest developments in FRSs, FREDs and Discussion Papers. These are dealt with within the relevant chapters of this text.

You should be familiar with the accounting standards covered in Part E. If you are in a hurry or revising, go straight to the sections highlighted in this chapter as current issues.

Study guide

Section 28 – Current issues and developments

- Identifying ways of improving communication of corporate performance, current proposals relating to year end financial reports and business reporting on the internet
- Problem areas in interim reporting
- Current issues in corporate reporting including disclosure of accounting policies and discounting

Exam guide

The examiner has explicitly stated that he intends to test current issues, and the Pilot Paper bears this out, so make sure you read this chapter carefully.

1 COMMUNICATION OF CORPORATE PERFORMANCE

Discussion paper

1.1 Companies' **financial statements**—the principal documents circulated to shareholders at present, aim to meet the information needs of institutional investors and other expert users. However, concern has been expressed that they are now **too long and complex for the average private shareholder**. As a result, the main messages that non-expert shareholders want to receive become **lost in the detail**.

1.2 In February 2000 the ASB published a discussion paper *Year-end financial reports: improving communication*. The paper examines how companies could simplify their annual financial statements to make them more accessible to private shareholders.

Summary financial statements as main statements

1.3 We have seen that the law already allows listed companies to offer their shareholders **summary financial statements** instead of the full audited financial statements. The Discussion Paper proposes that this option should be **given greater emphasis**.

(a) A **summarised version** of the full financial statements would form the **basis** of the annual report and accounts that listed companies are required to **send to their shareholders**.

(b) The content of this summarised version could be the **same as the minimum** recommended for companies' **preliminary announcements**.

(c) **Detailed financial statements** would continue to be compiled in **plain paper form** for filing purposes and for shareholders who required them.

Simple review

1.4 The Discussion Paper acknowledges that some shareholders, in particular those with very small shareholdings, might not be inclined to read even summary financial statements. Companies should be allowed to offer such shareholders an **even shorter and simpler narrative financial review** instead. Such an option might be most attractive to companies, such as the utility companies, that have **very large numbers of small private shareholders.**

1.5 The diagram below illustrates the proposed structure

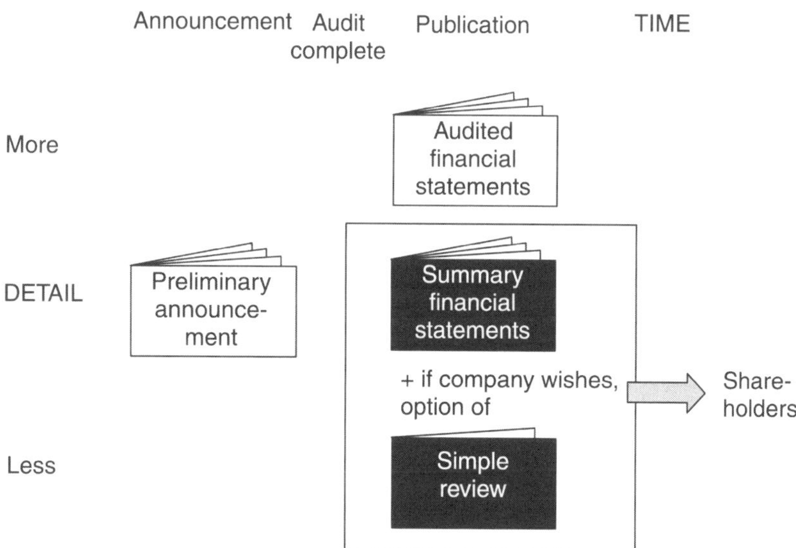

Figure 1: Proposed year-end reporting structure

1.6 The changes proposed in the Discussion Paper would require **amendments to company law**. These could be considered as part of the present Company Law Review. The ASB therefore plans to pass its suggestions and comments received on them to the Department of Trade and Industry.

1.7 Commenting on the Discussion Paper's proposals, the ASB's Chairman, Sir David Tweedie, said:

> Financial reporting is useless if it fails to communicate. As the financial world has become more complex, financial statements have had to mirror those changes through new measurement techniques and disclosures. For the expert this has led to new insights into a company's financial position and performance. For the informed layman, however, there is a danger that the central features of a company's performance and financial position may get lost in a welter of detail. This

development has left even further behind those many private shareholders for whom accounting has always been something of a mysterious black art.

The Board's proposals are intended to address these issues. In essence, the Board is proposing horses for courses and formalising what many of our best companies already do in trying to ensure that all shareholders and not simply the experts can understand what the company has (or has not) achieved in the past financial year.

Financial reporting on the internet

1.8 The Discussion Paper points towards a move away from the conventional paper-based report and accounts and expresses the ASB's belief that users of accounts will benefit from financial reporting on the internet. However, the paper also indicates that there are risks.

1.9 **Benefits**

(a) Large companies can significantly **reduce the substantial costs** of printing and posting annual reports.

(b) The information can be accessed by a **much larger audience** than conventional reports.

(c) **Websites can be kept up to date**, while paper reports have a short shelf life.

(d) **Sophisticated analytical tools** can be used to manipulate the data.

(e) '**Hyperlinks**' enable users to jump from one area of the financial statements to another where the same topic is discussed. Thus users can bypass the detailed analysis of aspects they are not interested in and go straight to the page or topic that they see as relevant.

1.10 **Risks**

(a) **Errors** may creep in when the site is updated, or the information may not be entered accurately.

(b) Information may be provided on the website that is inconsistent with the audited financial statements. Some information is audited and some is unaudited, but the **audit status of information may not be clear**.

(c) Similarly, users may not know what information is prepared in accordance with **regulations** and what is not.

1.11 A possible way round these last two problems is to **separate the information** in the annual report, which is regulated and audited, from other information on the website by making a clear visual distinction and by prompting the user when leaving the annual report section with the question, 'You are now leaving the annual report. Do you wish to continue? Y/N'

1.12 In summary, reporting on the internet is likely to become increasingly important, but there are **still problems that need resolving**, for accountants and auditors alike.

1.13 At this point it would be useful to outline two recent UITF abstracts, which relate to the internet.

UITF Abstract 26 Barter transactions for advertising

1.14 An entity such as a publisher or broadcaster may agree to provide advertising in exchange for advertising services provided by its customer, rather than for a cash consideration. For example, it has recently become common for companies that provide commercial Websites

to display advertisements in exchange for advertising of their own services on another Website. Such an exchange gives rise to the question of what amount, if any, should be included in reported turnover and expense.

1.15 The UITF consensus is that **turnover and costs in respect of barter transactions for advertising should not be recognised unless** there is persuasive **evidence of the value** at which the advertising would have been sold for cash in a similar transaction. In these circumstances that value should be included in turnover and costs. Persuasive evidence of the value of advertising exchanged will exist only where it can be demonstrated that similar advertising has been sold for cash. This will be the case only where the entity has a history of selling similar advertising for cash and where substantially all the turnover from advertising within the accounting period is represented by cash sales.

UITF Abstract 29 Website development costs

1.16 Abstract 29 clarifies the circumstances in which an entity should recognise as an asset the costs of developing a website for its own use.

1.17 The Abstract requires an entity to **capitalise and amortise costs** (other than planning costs) of developing a website **provided that certain criteria** are met. The criteria restrict in particular the circumstances in which an entity should capitalise amounts spent on creating the design, appearance and content of the website.

2 INTERIM REPORTS

2.1 In September 1997 the ASB published a 'best practice' statement on *Interim reports*. This takes forward a recommendation made by the **Cadbury Committee** (see Chapter 1). The Statement is non-mandatory but is designed to be a guide to best practice. The ASB strongly encourages listed companies to adopt the recommendations when preparing interim reports and its use is recommended by the Financial Reporting Council, the Hundred Group of Finance Directors, the London Stock Exchange and the Irish Stock Exchange.

2.2 Interim reports are produced by **large listed companies** when they release half-yearly figures to the markets. Recent surveys have disclosed that current practices in interim reporting vary and have evolved considerably from the reporting requirements of the London Stock Exchange. The Statement sets out the recommended contents and measurement basis of interim reports and is designed to improve the consistency, comparability and quality of interim reporting.

2.3 The **IASB** who also had interim reporting on its agenda issued an IAS in 1998. The IAS is on similar lines to, though more detailed than, the ASB's statement.

Basis of presentation

2.4 Interim reports should be drawn up using the same measurement and recognition bases and accounting policies as used in the preparation of annual financial statements, with the specific exception of taxation: the **'discrete' approach**. Under the discrete approach, the interim period is treated as a **distinct accounting period**, not as part of the annual reporting cycle. Therefore incomplete transactions are treated using the same accounting principles as are applied at the year-end.

2.5 The Statement does not favour the alternative '**integral' approach**, which views the interim period as part of the **larger annual reporting period**, predominantly to predict and explain the full year's financial information. Under the integral approach, revenues and expenses are therefore recognised in interim periods as a proportion of estimated annual amounts.

2.6 As taxation can be determined only at the end of the financial year the Statement requires that an interim period's tax charge should be based on an estimate of the **annual effective tax rate**, applied to the interim period's results.

Content

2.7 Interim reports should contain the following.

- Management commentary
- Summarised profit and loss account
- Statement of total recognised gains and losses, where relevant
- Summarised balance sheet
- Summarised cash flow statement

2.8 The **management commentary** should highlight and explain significant events and trends since the previous annual financial statements. Attention should be drawn to events and changes within the period that are likely to have a significant effect on the succeeding period despite having had relatively little impact in the current period. The commentary should describe and explain any seasonal activity and draw attention to a summarised balance sheet and cash flow statement.

2.9 The management commentary should also analyse turnover and profit **by segment** in a similar manner to that disclosed in the annual financial statements. In addition, discontinued operations and, where possible, acquisitions should be separately disclosed for turnover and operating profit.

2.10 Basic **earnings per share** should also be disclosed, as well as earnings per share using other bases, if they are also disclosed in the annual financial statements.

2.11 A **Statement of total recognised gains and losses** should be included to provide a link between the P&L account and the balance sheet. It is not required, however, if there are no other material gains and losses to report in the interim period, other than operating profit.

2.12 The summarised **balance sheet** should, for consistency, be based on similar classifications to those used in the annual financial statements. Current assets should be separated into their key component parts, mentioning stock, debtors and cash, to assist users' analyses.

2.13 The **cash flow statement** should be summarised using the headings required by FRS 1. Reconciliations of operating profit to operating cash flow and of cash in the period to the movement in net debt should also be disclosed.

3 IFRS 1: FIRST TIME ADOPTION OF INTERNATIONAL FINANCIAL REPORTING STANDARDS

3.1 IFRS 1 sets out the precise way in which companies should implement a **change from local accounting standards (their previous GAAP) to IASs and IFRSs**.

Exam focus point

Although this is on IFRS, it is more relevant to the UK stream, as it deals with questions of transition. Accordingly, it is examinable.

3.2 One of the main reasons for issuing a new standard is that listed companies in the EU will be required to prepare their consolidated financial statements in accordance with IFRSs from 2005 onwards. Many companies in the EU (for example, in the UK) will be making the transition to IFRS over the next few months.

3.3 The standard is intended to ensure that an entity's **first IFRS financial statements** contain **high quality information** that is transparent for users and comparable over all periods presented; provides a suitable starting point for accounting under IFRSs; and can be generated at a cost that does not exceed the benefits to users.

KEY TERMS

Date of transition to IFRSs. The beginning of the earliest period for which an entity presents full comparative information under IFRSs in its first IFRS financial statements.

Deemed cost An amount used as a surrogate for cost or depreciated cost at a given date.

Fair value The amount for which an asset could be exchanged, or a liability settled, between knowledgeable, willing parties in an arm's length transaction.

First IFRS financial statements The first annual financial statements in which an entity adopts International Financial Reporting Standards (IFRSs), by an explicit and unreserved statement of compliance with IFRSs.

Opening IFRS balance sheet An entity's balance sheet (published or unpublished) at the date of transition to IFRSs.

Previous GAAP The basis of accounting that a first time adopter used immediately before adopting IFRSs.

Reporting date The end of the latest period covered by financial statements or by an interim financial report. *(IFRS 1)*

3.4 IFRS 1 **only applies** where an entity prepares IFRS financial statements **for the first time**. Changes in accounting policies made by an entity that already applies IFRSs should be dealt with by applying either IAS 8 or specific transitional requirements in other standards.

Making the transition to IRFS

3.5 An entity should:

(a) Select accounting policies that comply with IFRSs **at the reporting date** for the entity's first IFRS financial statements.

(b) Prepare an **opening IFRS balance sheet** at the **date of transition to IFRSs.** This is the starting point for subsequent accounting under IFRSs. The date of transition to IFRSs is the beginning of the earliest comparative period presented in an entity's first IFRS financial statements.

(c) **Disclose the effect** of the change in the financial statements.

3.6 EXAMPLE: REPORTING DATE AND OPENING IFRS BALANCE SHEET

An EU listed company has a 31 December year-end and will be required to comply with IFRSs from 1 January 2005.

Required

What is the date of transition to IFRSs?

3.7 SOLUTION

The company's first IFRS financial statements will be for the **year ended 31 December 2005**.

IFRS 1 requires that at least one year's comparative figures are presented in the first IFRS financial statements. The comparative figures will be for the year ended 31 December 2004.

Therefore the date of transition to IFRSs is **1 January 2004** and the company prepares an opening IFRS balance sheet at this date.

Preparing the opening IFRS balance sheet

3.8 IFRS 1 states that in its opening IFRS balance sheet an entity must:

(a) **Recognise all assets and liabilities** whose recognition is required by IFRSs

(b) Not recognise items as assets or liabilities if IFRSs do not permit such recognition

(c) **Reclassify items** that it recognised under previous GAAP as one type of asset, liability or component of equity, but are a different type of asset liability or component of equity under IFRSs

(d) **Apply IFRS in measuring** all recognised assets and liabilities

3.9 This involves restating the balance sheet prepared at the same date under the entity's previous GAAP so that it complies with IASs and IFRSs in force **at the first reporting date**. In our example above, the company prepares its opening IFRS balance sheet at **1 January 2004**, following accounting policies that comply with IFRSs in force at **31 December 2005**.

3.10 The accounting policies that an entity uses in its opening IFRS balance sheet may differ from those it used for the same date using its previous GAAP. The resulting adjustments are recognised directly **in retained earnings** (in equity) **at the date of transition**. (This is because the adjustments arise from events and transactions before the date of transition to IFRS.)

Exemptions from other IFRSs

3.11 A business may elect to use **any or all** of a range of exemptions. These enable an entity not to apply certain requirements of specific accounting standards retrospectively in drawing up

its opening IFRS balance sheet. Their purpose is to ensure that the cost of producing IFRS financial statements does not exceed the benefits to users.

Business combinations

3.12 IFRS 3 need not be applied retrospectively to business combinations that occurred before the date of the opening IFRS balance sheet. This has the following consequences.

(a) Combinations keep the **same classification** (eg, acquisition, uniting of interests) as in the previous GAAP financial statements.

(b) **All acquired assets and liabilities are recognised** other than:

(i) Some financial assets and financial liabilities derecognised under the previous GAAP (derivatives and special purpose entities must be recognised);

(ii) Assets (including goodwill) and liabilities that were not recognised under previous GAAP and would not qualify for recognition under IFRSs.

Any resulting change is recognised by **adjusting retained earnings** (ie equity) unless the change results from the recognition of an intangible asset that was previously subsumed within goodwill.

(c) **Items which do not qualify for recognition** as an asset or liability under IFRSs must be excluded from the opening IFRS balance sheet. For example, intangible assets that do not qualify for separate recognition under IAS 38 must be reclassified as part of goodwill.

(d) The carrying amount of **goodwill** in the opening IFRS balance sheet is the same as its carrying amount **under previous GAAP**. However, goodwill must be tested for impairment at the transition date.

Property, plant and equipment

3.13 An entity may measure an item of property, plant and equipment at its **fair value at the transition** date and then use the fair value as its **deemed** cost at that date.

3.14 An entity may use a **previous GAAP revaluation,** or a valuation for the purpose of a privatisation or initial public offering, as the deemed cost at the transition date, so long as the revaluation was **broadly comparable** to fair value or depreciated replacement cost at the date of the valuation.

3.15 These exemptions are also available for:

(a) Investment properties measured under the cost model in IAS 40 *Investment property*

(b) Intangible assets that meet the recognition criteria and the criteria for revaluation in IAS 38 *Intangible assets*

Employee benefits

3.16 Under IAS 19 an entity may elect to use a 'corridor' approach that leaves some actuarial gains and losses unrecognised. A first time adopter **may elect to recognise all cumulative actuarial gains and losses** at the date of transition to IFRSs, even if it uses the corridor approach for later actuarial gains and losses. If this election is used it must apply to all plans.

Cumulative translation differences

3.17 IAS 21 requires some exchange differences is to be classified as a separate component of equity, for example, differences arising when a the financial statements of a foreign operation are translated. The cumulative translation differences must be included in the gain or loss on disposal of the foreign operation. Under the exemption, the **cumulative translation differences for all foreign operations are deemed to be zero at the transition date**. The gain or loss on a subsequent disposal of a foreign operation will exclude translation differences that arose before the transition date. Later translation differences will be included.

Compound financial instruments

3.18 IAS 32 requires compound financial instruments to be split at inception into separate liability and equity components. If the liability component is no longer outstanding at the date of the translation to IFRSs, the split is not required.

Designation of previously recognised financial instruments

3.19 When financial instruments are first recognised, they may be designated as financial assets or financial liabilities 'at fair value through profit or loss' or as 'available for sale' under IAS 39. An entity may make such a designation at the date of transition to IFRSs.

Share-based payment transactions

3.20 An entity is encouraged, but not required to apply IFRS 2 to:

(a) Equity instruments that were granted and vested before the date of transition to IFRSs or 1 January 2005 (whichever is the later)

(b) Liabilities arising from share-based payment transactions that were settled before the date of transition to IFRSs

Exceptions to retrospective application of other IFRSs

3.21 IFRS 1 prohibits retrospective application of some other aspects of IFRSs.

(a) **Derecognition of financial assets and financial liabilities:** the requirements in IAS 39 **are applied prospectively** from 1 January 2001 (the effective date of IAS 39). This means that financial assets and liabilities derecognised under previous GAAP before this date are not recognised.

(b) **Hedge accounting:** the **conditions** to qualify for hedge accounting apply **prospectively** from the date of transition to IFRSs.

(c) **Estimates:** Estimates under IFRSs at the date of transition must be **consistent** with those made **at the same date under previous GAAP**, (after adjustments to reflect any difference in accounting policies), unless there is objective evidence that those estimates were in error.

Question 4: Adoption of IFRS

Russell Co will adopt International Financial Reporting Standards (IFRSs) for the first time in its financial statements for the year ended 31 December 20X4.

In its previous financial statements for 31 December 20X2 and 20X3, which were prepared under local GAAP, the company made a number of routine accounting estimates, including accrued expenses. It

also recognised a general provision for liabilities, calculated at a fixed percentage of its retained profits for the year. This is required under its local GAAP.

Subsequently, some of the accruals were found to be overestimates and some were found to be underestimates.

Required

Discuss how the matters above should be dealt with in the IFRS financial statements of Russell Co for the year ended 31 December 20X4.

Answer

Provided that the routine accounting estimates have been made in a manner consistent with IFRSs no adjustments are made in the first IFRS financial statements. The only exception to this is if the company has subsequently discovered that these estimates were in error. Although there were some overestimates and some underestimates, this is probably not the case here.

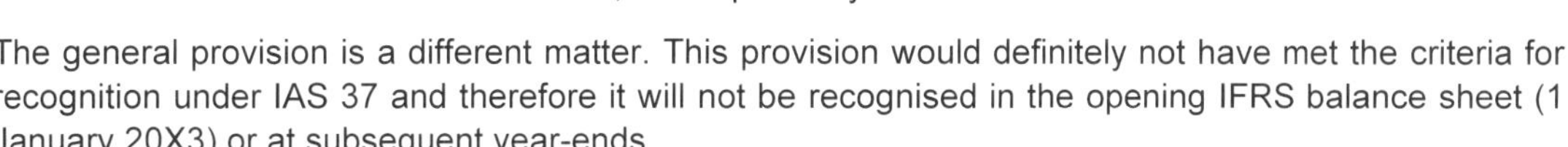

The general provision is a different matter. This provision would definitely not have met the criteria for recognition under IAS 37 and therefore it will not be recognised in the opening IFRS balance sheet (1 January 20X3) or at subsequent year-ends.

Presentation and disclosure

3.22 An entity's first IFRS financial statements must include **at least one year of comparative information.**

3.23 Comparative information need not comply with IAS 32 and IAS 39; instead the entity may apply its previous GAAP and disclose this fact together with the nature of the main adjustments that would make the information comply with IAS 32 and IAS 39.

3.24 An entity must also **explain the effect** of the transition from previous GAAP to IFRSs on its financial position, financial performance and cash flows by providing **reconciliations**:

(a) Of **equity** reported under previous GAAP to equity under IFRSs at the **date of transition and at the balance sheet date**

(b) Of the **profit or loss** reported under previous GAAP to profit or loss reported under IFRSs for the period

The reconciliations must give sufficient detail to enable users to understand the material adjustments to the balance sheet and income statement.

3.25 If an entity presented a cash flow statement under its previous GAAP, it should also explain the material **adjustments to the cash flow statement.**

3.26 If an entity recognised or reversed any **impairment losses** for the first time in preparing its opening IFRS balance sheet, it must provide the disclosures that IAS 36 *Impairment of assets* would have required if the entity had recognised those impairment losses or reversals in the period beginning with the date of transition to IFRSs.

3.27 If an entity corrects **errors made under previous GAAP**, the reconciliations must distinguish the correction of errors from changes in accounting policies.

3.28 Where **fair value has been used as deemed cost** for a non-current asset in the opening IFRS balance sheet as deemed cost for a non-current asset, the financial statements must disclose the aggregate of fair values and the aggregate adjustments to the carrying amounts reported under previous GAAP for each line in the opening IFRS balance sheet.

Interim financial reports

3.29 IFRS 1 applies to any interim financial report that an entity presents under IAS 34 *Interim financial reporting* for part of the period covered by the first IFRS financial statements.

3.30 Where interim financial reports are presented, an entity should provide the same reconciliations required for full financial statements and described in 5.24 above. Material adjustments to the cash flow statement, if any, should also be disclosed.

Managing the change to International Standards

3.31 The implementation of the above technical aspects is likely to entail careful management in most companies. Here are some of the **change management considerations** that should be addressed.

(a) **Accurate assessment of the task involved**. Underestimation or wishful thinking may hamper the effectiveness of the conversion and may ultimately prove inefficient.

(b) **Proper planning**. This should take place at the overall project level, but a **detailed** task **analysis** could be drawn up to **control work performed**.

(c) **Human resource management**. The project must be properly structured and staffed.

(d) **Training**. Where there are **skills gaps**, remedial training should be provided.

(e) **Monitoring and accountability**. A relaxed 'it will be alright on the night' attitude could spell danger. Implementation **progress** should be **monitored** and **regular meetings** set up so that participants can **personally account for what they are doing** as well as **flag up any problems** as early as possible. **Project drift should be avoided**.

(f) **Achieving milestones**. Successful completion of key steps and tasks should be appropriately acknowledged, ie what managers call 'celebrating success', so as to **sustain motivation and performance**.

(g) **Physical resourcing.** The need for IT **equipment** and **office space** should be properly assessed.

(h) **Process review**. Care should be taken not to perceive the change as a one-off quick fix. Any charge in **future systems** and processes should be assessed and properly implemented.

(i) **Follow-up procedures**. As with general good management practice, the **follow up procedures** should be planned in to **make sure that the changes stick** and that any further changes are identified and addressed.

3.32 Section summary

You need to be able to advise an entity making the change from previous GAAP to IFRSs on:

- The **general rules** (including the date of the **opening IFRS balance sheet**)
- The **exemptions** available
- How to deal with **estimates** in previous financial statements
- **Explaining the effects** of the change on the financial statements (preparing reconciliations)
- The **practical aspects** of managing the change.

4 CURRENT ISSUES IN FINANCIAL REPORTING

4.1 The examiner for Paper 3.6 is very keen indeed on current issues and has said that there will be even more emphasis than previously on these issues.

Consultation paper: IASB Proposals on exploration for and evaluation of mineral resources: main proposals

4.2 An entity may elect to **continue** to recognise and measure exploration and evaluation assets in accordance **with its existing accounting policies**, except that **certain expenditure cannot be included** in the initial measurement of exploration and evaluation assets.

(a) The development of a mineral resource once technical feasibility and commercial viability of extracting a mineral resource have been established

(b) Administration and other general overhead costs

4.3 Exploration and revaluation assets are measured in the same way as other non-current assets (initially at cost; then according to either the cost model or the revaluation model in IAS 16 and IAS 38).

4.4 If an entity elects to continue to use its previous accounting policies for exploration and evaluation assets must **only change those policies if** the change makes the financial statements **more relevant** to the decision making needs of users and **reliable**.

4.5 An entity that has recognised exploration and evaluation assets must **assess those assets for impairment annually** and recognise any resulting impairment loss in accordance with IAS 36. (However, an entity can elect to apply the impairment test at a different level from that normally required by IAS 36.)

4.6 An entity must **disclose information** that identifies and explains the amounts recognised in its financial statements that arise from the exploration for and evaluation of mineral resources.

UITF 37 Purchases and sales of own shares

4.7 The *Statement of Principles* addresses the treatment of increases or decreases in an entity's ownership interest that result from transactions with owners in their capacity as owners. Such transactions are referred to as 'contributions from owners" and 'distributions to owners'; these elements of financial statements do not give rise to gains or losses. Distributions to owners include the payment of dividends and the return of capital. The Statement gives the purchase by a company of its own shares as an example of a return of capital, which is reflected in financial statements by reducing the amount of ownership interest. Ownership interest is defined as a residual interest, ie the amount that results from deducting all of an entity's liabilities from all of its assets.

4.8 An entity's purchase of its own shares gives rise to a **reduction in the entity's ownership interest, not an asset**. Transactions in own shares do not give rise to gains or losses in the issuing entity's profit and loss account or statement of total recognised gains and losses.

4.9 This is reflected in FRS 4. Whether a transaction in own shares relates to equity or non-equity shares, there is no effect on reported profit as it is a transaction affecting only shareholders' interests. Any difference between the carrying amount of shareholders' funds attributable to non-equity shares and the consideration paid for their purchase is reported

as an appropriation of profits in the same manner as FRS 4 requires for finance costs in respect of non-equity shares.

4.10 **UITF 37** states that:

(a) **Consideration paid for an entity's own shares** should be **deducted** in arriving at **shareholders' funds**.

(b) **No gain or loss** should be recognised in the **profit and loss account** or statement of total recognised gains and losses on the purchase, sale or cancellation of an entity's own shares.

(c) **Consideration** paid or received for the purchase or sale of an entity's own shares should be shown as **separate amounts** in the reconciliation of movements in shareholders' funds.

(d) The **amounts of reductions to shareholders' funds** for an entity's own shares held, and the number of own shares held, should be **disclosed separately**.

4.11 Where shares in a holding company are purchased, held or sold by a subsidiary, the requirements apply in the holding company's consolidated financial statements.

UITF Abstract 38 *Accounting for ESOP trusts*

4.12 This Abstract supersedes UITF Abstract 13 of the same name. Abstract 13 dealt with two issues.

(a) The **nature and extent** of the sponsoring company's assets and liabilities that should be recognised under employee share ownership plans (ESOPs

(b) The **timing** of expense recognition under such arrangements

4.13 Abstract 38 addresses (a) above. The principal change from Abstract 13 concerns the treatment of an interest in an entity's own shares arising through an ESOP trust. Abstract 13 required that such shares should be recognised as assets of the sponsoring entity. This Abstract reflects the principle in UITF Abstract 37 *Purchases and sales of own shares*, which is consistent with International Financial Reporting Standards (IFRSs), that an **entity that reacquires its own equity instruments should present them as a deduction in arriving at shareholders' funds rather than as assets**. The sponsoring company of an ESOP trust should recognise the assets and liabilities of the trust in its own accounts whenever it has de facto control of those assets and liabilities:

(a) Until such time as the company's own shares held by the ESOP trust vest unconditionally in employees, the consideration paid for the shares should be deducted in arriving at shareholders' funds.

(b) Other assets and liabilities (including borrowings) of the ESOP trust should be recognised as assets and liabilities of the sponsoring company.

(c) Consideration paid or received for the purchase or sale of the company's own shares in an ESOP trust should be shown as separate amounts in the reconciliation of movements in shareholders' funds.

(d) No gain or loss should be recognised in the profit and loss account or statement of total recognised gains and losses on the purchase, sale, issue or cancellation of the company's own shares.

(e) Finance costs and any administration expenses should be charged as they accrue and not as funding payments are made to the ESOP trust.

(f) Any dividend income arising on own shares should be excluded in arriving at profit before tax and deducted from the aggregate of dividends paid and proposed. The deduction should be disclosed if material. Under FRS 14 *Earnings per share*, the shares are treated as if they were cancelled when calculating earnings per share.

4.14 Some current issues have been dealt with in this chapter, but some are more appropriately dealt with in the chapters on the individual topics. The table below is a guide to what is 'hot' and where to find it in the Study Text.

Hot topic	Where to find it
First time adoption of IFRS	Chapter 15
Discussion paper on convergence	Chapter 13
'One-stop-shop' FRSSE – Discussion Paper	Chapter 1
FRED 32 Disposal of non-current assets and presentation of discontinued operations	Chapter 23
Revenue recognition and FRS 5 amendment	Chapter 19
FRED 23	Chapter 18
FRED 24	Chapter 7
FRED 25	Chapter 24
FRED 26	Chapter 23
FRED 28	Chapter 19
FRED 29	Chapter 16
FRED 30	Chapter 18
FRS 20 Share based payment	Chapter 24
FRS 21 Events after the balance sheet date	Chapter 25

Exam focus point

Keep your eye out for articles on these topics in *Student Accountant*, a good indication that the topic will be examined.

Chapter roundup

- A new **discussion paper** proposes significant changes to year end reporting. Summary financial statements would become the norm rather than the exception.
- Increasingly companies are publishing their accounts on the **internet**. There are **benefits** to this (cheaper, wider audience, flexible data) and **risks** (errors, audit status unclear).
- You should know which are the **current issues** and concentrated your studying on these.
- IFRS 1 sets out the precise way in which an entity should implement a change from local accounting standards to IASs and IFRSs.

Quick quiz

1 What is the main proposal in the Discussion Paper on year-end reporting?

2 Why can this change not be made right now?

3 Auditors are responsible for company information that appears on the internet.

True ☐

False ☐

4 What approach is favoured in the ASB's *Statement* on Interim Reporting? Discrete/integral

5 IFRS 1 prohibits retrospective application of hedge accounting?

True ☐

False ☐

Answers to quick quiz

1 Summary financial statements are to be the norm.

2 A review of company law needs to be completed

3 False. Opinions differ on this and the matter has yet to be resolved.

4 Discrete

5 True. This is a specific exception

Now try the question below from the Exam Question Bank

Number	Level	Marks	Time
Q22	Introductory	n/a	n/a

Part E

Accounting Standards

Chapter 16

FIXED ASSETS: TANGIBLE ASSETS

	Topic list	Syllabus reference
1	**Definitions and statutory requirements**	**1(a) 1(d)**
2	**FRS 15 *Tangible fixed assets***	**1(a) 1(d)**
3	**Revaluation**	**1(a) 1(d)**
4	**SSAP 19 *Accounting for investment properties***	**1(a) 1(d)**
5	**SSAP 4 *Accounting for government grants***	**1(a) 1(d)**
6	**FRED 29**	**1(a) 1(d)**

Introduction

FRS 15 is a fairly recent standard, so it is covered in full here, although you may have met it in your earlier studies. The main purpose of the standard was to codify **best practice** on accounting for tangible fixed assets.

SSAPs 4 and 19 should be familiar to you. Try the questions and go back to your earlier studies if you have any problems.

Study guide

Section 12 – Fixed assets 2

- Accounting for revaluation gains and losses and the depreciation of revalued assets
- Accounting for the disposal of revalued assets
- Discussion of the effect of revaluations on distributable profits
- Discussion of the problem areas in accounting for fixed assets

Exam guide

This part of the Study Text deals with accounting standards, most of which you should already know about. However, the approach at Paper 3.6 is very different from that in our earlier studies – you will need to think critically and deal with controversial areas.

1 DEFINITIONS AND STATUTORY REQUIREMENTS

1.1 Assets have been defined in many different ways and for many purposes. The definition of an asset is important because it directly affects the **treatment** of such items. A good definition will prevent abuse or error in the accounting treatment: otherwise some assets might be treated as expenses, and some expenses might be treated as assets.

1.2 Let us begin with a simple definition from the CIMA *Official Terminology*.

KEY TERM

An **asset** is any tangible or intangible possession which has value.

This neat, quick definition seems to cover the main points: **ownership** and **value**. An asset is so called because it is owned by someone who values it. However, this definition leaves several questions unanswered.

- What determines ownership?
- What determines value?

Accounting Standards Board (ASB)

1.3 In the ASB's *Statement of Principles*, Chapter 4 *The Elements of Financial Statements*, currently assets are defined as follows.

KEY TERM

Assets are rights or other access to future economic benefits controlled by an entity as a result of past transactions or events. *Statement of Principles*

1.4 The *Statement* goes on to discuss various aspects of this definition, and it is broadly consistent with the **IASB's** *Framework*. The *Statement* then goes further in discussing the complimentary nature of assets and liabilities.

Financial Accounting Standards Board (FASB)

1.5 The definition given by the FASB in the USA in its *Statement of Concepts* is very similar.

KEY TERM

Assets are probable future economic benefits obtained or controlled by a particular entity as a result of past transactions or events.

'Probable' is given in its general meaning merely to reflect the fact that no future outcome can be predicted with total certainty.

Comparison of definitions

1.6 It is clear from what we have seen so far that a general consensus seems to exist in the standard setting bodies as to the definition of an asset. That definition encompasses **three important characteristics**.

(a) Future economic benefit
(b) Control (ownership)
(c) The transaction to acquire control has already taken place

Definition of a fixed asset

1.7 Fixed assets are defined by CA 1985.

KEY TERM

A **fixed asset** as one intended for use on a continuing basis in the company's activities, ie it is not intended for resale.

Statutory requirements relating to fixed assets

1.8 You have already come across these in you earlier studies, besides which FRS 15 now deals much more comprehensively with the important issues from CA 85. For completeness, a summary is given here.

Summary: statutory requirements relating to fixed assets

Initial cost

- Purchase price plus any expenses incidental to its acquisition.
- Where an asset is produced by a company for its own use, its 'production cost' must include the cost of raw materials, consumables and other attributable direct costs (such as labour). Production cost may additionally include a reasonable proportion of indirect costs, together with the interest on any capital borrowed to finance production of the asset.

Valuation: alternative accounting rules

- Historical cost is the norm, but revalued amount/current cost may be used.
- Depreciation may be provided on the basis of the new valuation.
- Where an asset is revalued, the gain or loss goes to a revaluation reserve.
- There are three alternative bases for valuation: current cost, market value and directors' valuation (for investments)

FRS 3 and revaluations

1.9 Note the effect here of FRS 3. The **statement of recognised gains and losses** (STRGL) shows the profit or loss for the period along with all other movements on reserves which reflect recognised gains and losses attributable to shareholders. It does *not* deal with the **realisation** of gains in previous periods, nor with transfers between reserves.

IMPORTANT RULE TO LEARN

The excess of the revalued amount over historical cost will *never* be recognised in the P&L account; profit or loss on disposal will be calculated as the difference between the net proceeds and the net carrying amount

1.10 This is a very important FRS 3 rule; previously, on disposal of a revalued asset, companies could transfer the surplus in the revaluation reserve which related to the asset to the P&L

account. The difference between historical cost depreciation and depreciation on a revaluation will appear in the **note of historical cost profits and losses**.

UITF Abstract 5 *Transfer from current assets to fixed assets*

1.11 This abstract requires transfers from current assets to fixed assets to be made at the **lower of cost and net realisable value**, in order to prevent the practice of transfers being made at a value higher than NRV. This practice avoided charging the P&L account with any diminution in value of what were, in effect, unsold trading assets. Once transferred to fixed assets, the CA 1985 alternative accounting rules could be used to take the debit reflecting the diminution in value to a revaluation reserve. This abstract follows the *Statement of Principles*. This was triggered by a Review Panel judgement on Trafalgar House's 1991 accounts.

2 FRS 15 TANGIBLE FIXED ASSETS

2.1 FRS 15 *Tangible fixed assets* goes into a lot more detail than the Companies Act. It replaced SSAP 12 but not SSAP 19. Investment properties are still accounted for in accordance with SSAP 19 (see Section 4).

Objective

2.2 FRS 15 deals with accounting for the initial measurement, valuation and depreciation of tangible fixed assets. It also sets out the information that should be disclosed to enable readers to understand the impact of the accounting policies adopted in relation to these issues.

Initial measurement

2.3 A tangible fixed asset should **initially be measured at cost**.

KEY TERM

Cost is purchase price and any costs directly attributable to bringing the asset into working condition for its intended use.

2.4 Examples of directly attributable costs are:

- **Acquisition costs**, eg stamp duty, import duties
- Cost of **site preparation** and clearance
- Initial **delivery and handling** costs
- **Installation** costs
- **Professional fees** eg legal fees
- The estimated cost of **dismantling and removing** the asset and restoring the site, to the extent that it is recognised as a provision under FRS 12 *Provisions, contingent liabilities and contingent assets* (discussed later).

2.5 Any abnormal costs, such as those arising from design error, industrial disputes or idle capacity are not directly attributable costs and therefore should not be capitalised as part of the cost of the asset.

Question: start-up costs

Seafood 'n' Eatitt, a trendy restaurant, opens on 1 January 20X9 with a skeleton staff. The first month is not expected to bring in many customers as it will take time to build up a reputation. Could the costs incurred in January be capitalised as start-up costs?

Answer

No. The restaurant *could* operate at normal levels immediately so the start up costs are not essential.

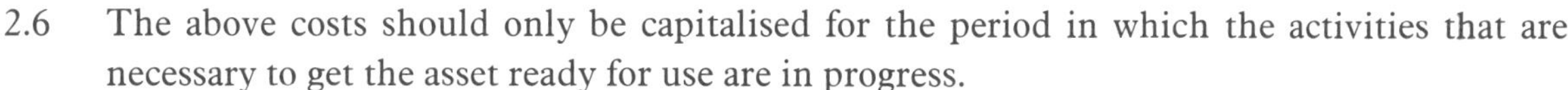

2.6 The above costs should only be capitalised for the period in which the activities that are necessary to get the asset ready for use are in progress.

Finance costs

2.7 The **capitalisation of finance costs**, including interest, is **optional**. However, if an entity does capitalise finance costs they must do so **consistently**.

2.8 All finance costs that are **directly attributable** to the construction of a tangible fixed asset should be capitalised as part of the cost of the asset.

KEY TERM

Directly attributable finance costs are those that would have been avoided if there had been no expenditure on the asset.

2.9 If finance costs are capitalised, capitalisation should start when:

- Finance costs are being incurred
- Expenditure on the asset is being incurred
- Activities necessary to get the asset ready for use are in progress

2.10 Capitalisation of finance costs should cease when the asset is ready for use.

2.11 Sometimes construction of an asset may be completed in parts and each part is capable of being used while construction continues on other parts. An example of such an asset is a business park consisting of several units. In such cases **capitalisation of borrowing costs relating to a part should cease when substantially all the activities that are necessary to get that part ready for use are completed.**

Question: capitalisation

Why would this not apply in the case of a steel mill?

Answer

A steel mill is an industrial plant involving several processes that are carried out **in sequence** at different parts of the plant within the same site.

2.12 **Disclosures in respect of capitalisation of borrowing costs**

(a) The accounting policy adopted

(b) The amount of borrowing costs capitalised during the period

(c) The amount of borrowing costs recognised in the profit and loss account during the period

(d) The capitalisation rate used to determine the amount of capitalised borrowing costs

Recoverable amount

2.13 The amount recognised when a tangible fixed asset is acquired or constructed should **not exceed its recoverable amount**.

2.14 It is not necessary to review tangible fixed assets for impairment when they are acquired or constructed. They need to be reviewed for impairment only if there is some indication that impairment has occurred. Such indications are specified in FRS 11 *Impairment of fixed assets and goodwill.*

Subsequent expenditure

2.15 **Subsequent expenditure** is repairs and maintenance expenditure which ensures that an asset maintains it originally assessed standard of performance. An example of such expenditure is the cost of servicing or overhauling plant and equipment. Without this expenditure, the depreciation expense would be increased because the useful life and perhaps the residual value of the asset would be reduced.

Rule to learn

Subsequent expenditure (repairs and maintenance expenditure) should be recognised in the profit and loss account as it is incurred.

2.16 There are three exceptions to this.

(a) It enhances the economic benefits over and above those previously estimated. An example might be modifications made to a piece of machinery that increases its capacity or useful life.

(b) A component of an asset that has been treated separately for depreciation purposes (because it has a substantially different useful economic life from the rest of the asset) has been restored or replaced.

(c) It relates to a major inspection or overhaul that restores economic benefits that have been consumed and reflected in the depreciation charge.

Question: subsequent expenditure (1)

A building is repainted. How should this expenditure be treated?

Answer

It should be written off to the profit and loss account. This expenditure is too regular an occurrence to be seen as a separate 'component'.

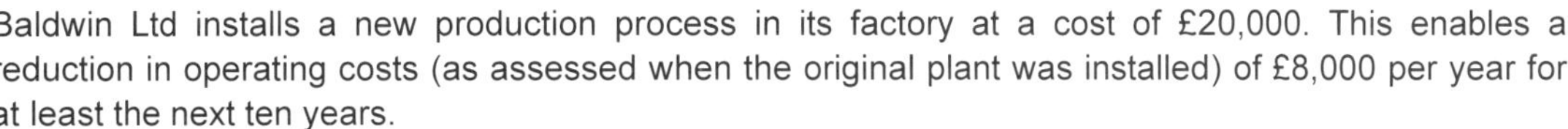
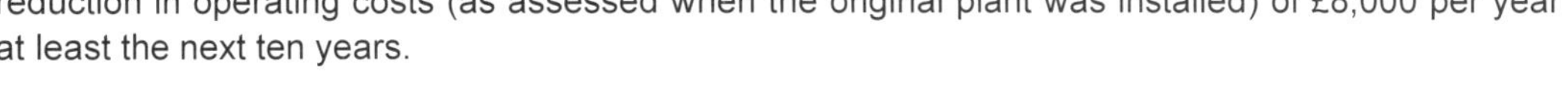

Question: subsequent expenditure (2)

Baldwin Ltd installs a new production process in its factory at a cost of £20,000. This enables a reduction in operating costs (as assessed when the original plant was installed) of £8,000 per year for at least the next ten years.

How should the expenditure be treated?

Answer

It should be capitalised and added to the original cost of the plant as it results in enhancement of economic benefits.

2.17 An entity often has to spend material amounts on a major refit or refurbishment every few years, in order to stay in business. For example, a furnace may require relining every few years.

Rule to learn

Each component is depreciated over its individual useful economic life, so that the depreciation profile over the whole asset more accurately reflects the actual consumption of the asset's economic benefits.

2.18 The same approach is applied to major inspections and overhauls of tangible fixed assets.

2.19 EXAMPLE: MAJOR OVERHAUL

An aircraft is required by law to be overhauled once every three years. Unless the overhaul is undertaken the aircraft cannot continue to be flown. The cost of the overhaul is capitalised when incurred because it restores the economic benefits of the tangible fixed asset. The carrying amount representing the cost of the benefits consumed is removed from the balance sheet.

2.20 This works in exactly the same way as when an asset is divided into separate components for depreciation. Suppose a company owns an aircraft with a useful economic life of ten years, but the aircraft needs a major overhaul every three years. The depreciation will be the estimated overhead cost written off over three years and the rest of the cost of the aircraft written off over ten years. Then in three years time, when the overhaul work is done, the cost and accumulated depreciation of the 'overhaul' portion of the asset are removed from the balance sheet and the cost of the work done is capitalised.

Valuation

2.21 FRS 15 supplements and clarifies the rules on revaluation of fixed assets which the Companies Act allows. Revaluation is discussed in the next section.

Depreciation

2.22 As noted earlier, the Companies Act 1985 requires that all fixed assets having a limited economic life should be depreciated. FRS 15 gives a useful discussion of the purpose of depreciation and supplements the statutory requirements in important ways.

KEY TERM

Depreciation is defined in FRS 15 as the measure of the cost or revalued amount of the economic benefits of the tangible fixed asset that have been consumed during the period. Consumption includes the wearing out, using up or other reduction in the useful economic life of a tangible fixed asset, whether arising from use, effluxion of time or obsolescence through either changes in technology or demand for the goods and services produced by the asset.

2.23 This definition covers the amortisation of assets with a pre-determined life, such as a leasehold, and the depletion of wasting assets such as mines.

2.24 FRS 15 contains **no detailed guidance** on the calculation of depreciation or the suitability of the various depreciation methods, merely stating the following two **general principles**.

> 'The depreciable amount of a tangible fixed asset should be allocated on a **systematic** basis over its useful economic life. The depreciation method used should reflect as fairly as possible the pattern in which the asset's economic benefits are consumed by the entity. The depreciation charge for each period should be recognised as an expense in the profit and loss account unless it is permitted to be included in the carrying amount of another asset.'
>
> 'A variety of methods can be used to allocate the depreciable amount of a tangible fixed asset on a systematic basis over its useful economic life. The method chosen should result in a **depreciation charge throughout the asset's useful** economic life and not just towards the end of its useful economic life or when the asset is falling in value.'

REMEMBER!

Systematic and throughout.

Two of the most common methods – the straight line and the reducing balance method are mentioned, the former to be used where the pattern of consumption of an asset's economic benefits is uncertain.

Factors affecting depreciation

2.25 FRS 15 states that the following factors need to be considered in determining the useful economic life, residual value and depreciation method of an asset.

(a) The **expected usage** of the asset by the entity, assessed by reference to the asset's expected capacity or physical output

(b) The **expected physical deterioration** of the asset through use or effluxion of time; this will depend upon the repair and maintenance programme of the entity both when the asset is in use and when it is idle

(c) **Economic or technological obsolescence**, for example arising from changes or improvements in production, or a change in the market demand for the product or service output of that asset

(d) **Legal or similar limits** on the use of the asset, such as the expiry dates of related leases

2.26 If it becomes clear that the **original estimate** of an asset's useful life was **incorrect**, it should be **revised**. Normally, no adjustment should be made in respect of the depreciation charged in previous years; instead the remaining net book value of the asset should be depreciated over the new estimate of its remaining useful life.

2.27 FRS 15 also states that a **change from one method** of providing depreciation **to another** is permissible only on the grounds that the new method will give a **fairer presentation** of the results and of the financial position. Such a change does **not**, however, constitute a **change of accounting policy**; the carrying amount of the tangible fixed asset is depreciated using the revised method over the remaining useful economic life, beginning in the period in which the change is made.

Two or more components of a fixed asset

2.28 A fixed asset may comprise two or more major components with substantially different useful economic lives. In such cases each component should be accounted for separately for depreciation purposes and depreciated over its individual useful economic life. Examples include:

- Land and buildings
- The structure of a building and items within the structure, such as general fittings

Question: components

What about the trading potential associated with a property valued as an operational entity, such as a hotel or pub? Should this be treated as a separate component?

Answer

No. The value and life of any trading potential is inherently inseparable from that of the property.

2.29 In calculating the useful economic life of an asset it is assumed that **subsequent expenditure** will be undertaken to **maintain the originally assessed standard** of performance of the asset (for example the cost of servicing or overhauling plant and equipment). Without such expenditure the depreciation expense would be increased because the useful life and/or residual value of the asset would be reduced. This type of expenditure is **recognised as an expense when incurred**.

2.30 **Subsequent expenditure** may be undertaken that results in a **restoration or replacement of a component** of the asset that has been depreciated or an **enhancement of economic benefits** of the asset in excess of the originally assessed standard of performance. This type of expenditure may result in an **extension of the useful economic life** of the asset.

IMPORTANT!

Subsequent expenditure does not obviate the need to charge depreciation. The subsequent expenditure is **capitalised as it is incurred and depreciated** over the asset's (or, where the expenditure relates to a component, the component's) useful economic life.

2.31 Tangible fixed assets other than non depreciable land, should be **reviewed for impairment** at the end of the reporting period where:

- No depreciation is charged on the grounds that it would be immaterial
- The estimated remaining useful economic life exceeds 50 years.

The review should be in accordance with FRS 11 *Impairment of fixed assets and goodwill*, discussed in the next chapter

2.32 Many companies carry fixed assets in their balance sheets at **revalued amounts**, particularly in the case of freehold buildings. When this is done, the **depreciation charge** should be calculated **on the basis of the revalued amount** (not the original cost), in spite of the alternative accounting rules in CA 1985.

2.33 Where the **residual value** is material, it should be **reviewed** at the end of each reporting period to take account of reasonably expected technological changes. A **change** in the estimated residual value should be **accounted for prospectively over the asset's remaining useful economic life**, except to the extent that the asset has been impaired at the balance sheet date.

Disclosure requirements of FRS 15

2.34 The following information should be disclosed separately in the financial statements for each class of tangible fixed assets.

(a) The depreciation **M**ethods used

(b) The **U**seful economic lives or the depreciation rates used

(c) **T**otal depreciation charged for the period

(d) Where material, the **F**inancial effect of a change during the period in either the estimate of useful economic lives or the estimate of residual values

(e) The **C**ost or revalued amount at the beginning of the financial period and at the balance sheet date

(f) The **C**umulative amount of provisions for depreciation or impairment at the beginning of the financial period and at the balance sheet date

(g) A **R**econciliation of the movements, separately disclosing additions, disposals, revaluations, transfers, depreciation, impairment losses, and reversals of past impairment losses written back in the financial period

(h) The **N**et carrying amount at the beginning of the financial period and at the balance sheet date

REMEMBER!

Man **U**nited **T**rials in **F**ootball **C**an **C**reate **R**aw **N**erves

Criticisms of FRS 15

2.35 FRS 15 has been largely welcomed, particularly the rules on revaluations (see below). However, some commentators have found problematic the treatment of subsequent expenditure where there is a major overhaul. The treatment has been described as 'contrived'.

UITF 24 Accounting for start up costs **12/03**

2.36 The issue is whether start-up costs that cannot be included in the cost of a fixed asset may nevertheless be carried forward, for example as a prepayment, deferred expenditure or other kind of asset. FRS 15 *Tangible fixed assets* addresses the accounting for costs associated with a start-up or commissioning period. Paragraph 14 states that such costs should be included in the cost of a tangible fixed asset only where the asset is available for use but incapable of operating at normal levels without such a start-up or commissioning period.

2.37 The consensus was that **start-up costs should be accounted for on a basis consistent with the accounting treatment of similar costs incurred as part of the entity's ongoing activities**. In cases where there are no such similar costs, start-up costs that do not meet the criteria for recognition as assets under a relevant accounting standard should be recognised as an expense when they are incurred.

2.38 If start-up costs meet the definition of exceptional items they should be disclosed in accordance with FRS 3 *Reporting financial performance*. Disclosure regarding start-up costs in the Operating and Financial Review is also encouraged.

3 REVALUATION

3.1 Before FRS 15, companies could pick and choose which of their assets they wished to revalue and when. This allowed companies to flatter their balance sheet figures through the inclusion of meaningless out of date valuations, thereby hindering comparability between companies from year to year. **FRS 15 puts a stop to this 'cherry picking'**.

3.2 An entity may adopt a policy of **revaluing tangible fixed assets**. Where this policy is adopted **it must be applied consistently** to all assets of the same class.

KEY TERM

A **class of fixed assets** is 'a category of tangible fixed assets having a similar nature, function or use in the business of an entity'. *(FRS 15)*

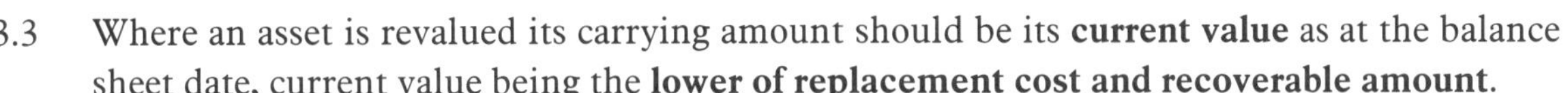

3.3 Where an asset is revalued its carrying amount should be its **current value** as at the balance sheet date, current value being the **lower of replacement cost and recoverable amount**.

3.4 To achieve the above, the standard states that a **full valuation** should be carried out **at least every five years** with an **interim valuation in year 3**. If it is likely that there has been a material change in value, interim valuations in years 1, 2 and 4 should also be carried out.

3.5 A full valuation should be conducted by either a **qualified external valuer** or a **qualified internal valuer**, provided that the valuation has been subject to review by a qualified external valuer. An interim valuation may be carried out by either an external or internal valuer.

3.6 For certain types of assets (other than properties) eg company cars, there may be an **active second hand market for the asset** or appropriate indices may exist, so that the directors can establish the asset's value with reasonable reliability and therefore avoid the need to use the services of a qualified valuer.

Basis

Property type	Valuation method
Specialised properties	Depreciated replacement cost Specialised properties are those which, due to their specialised nature, are rarely, if ever, sold on the open market for single occupation for a continuation of their existing use, except as part of a sale of the business in occupation. Eg oil refineries, chemical works, power stations, or schools, colleges and universities where there is no competing market demand from other organisations using these types of property in the locality.
Non-specialised properties	Existing use value (EUV)
Properties surplus to an entity's requirements	Open market value (OMV)

3.7 Where there is an indication of impairment, an **impairment review** should be carried out in accordance with FRS 11. The asset should be recorded at the lower of revalued amount (as above) and recoverable amount.

3.8 Tangible fixed assets other than properties should be valued using market value or, if not obtainable, depreciated replacement cost.

Reporting gains and losses on revaluation

3.9 Revaluation **gains** are recognised in the **statement of total recognised gains and losses (STRGL)** except to the extent that they reverse revaluation losses on the same assets, in which case they should be recognised in the profit and loss account.

3.10 All revaluation **losses** that are caused by a clear consumption of economic benefit (eg physical damage or a deterioration in the quality of the service provided by the asset) are recognised in the **profit and loss account**, ie the asset is clearly impaired.

3.11 **Other losses** are recognised in the **STRGL until the carrying amount reaches depreciated historical cost** and **thereafter in the profit and loss account**. However, if it can be demonstrated that the recoverable amount of the asset is more than its revalued amount, the loss will be recognised in the STRGL to the extent that the recoverable amount exceeds the revalued amount. This is because the difference between recoverable amount and revalued amount is not an impairment and should therefore be recognised in the STRGL as a valuation adjustment, rather than the profit and loss account.

3.12 EXAMPLE: ACCOUNTING FOR REVALUATION LOSSES

The following details are available in relation to a non specialised property.

Carrying value	£960,000
Depreciated historic cost	£800,000
Recoverable amount	£760,000
Existing use value	£700,000

How should the revaluation loss be treated?

3.13 SOLUTION

(a) The revaluation loss on the property is £260,000 (ie carrying value of £960,000 compared with EUV of £700,000).

(b) The fall in value from carrying value (£960,000) to depreciated historic cost (£800,000) of £160,000 is recognised in the STRGL.

(c) The fall in value from depreciated historic cost (£800,000) to recoverable amount (£760,000) of £40,000 is recognised in the profit and loss account.

(d) The difference between recoverable amount (£760,000) and EUV (£700,000) is recognised in the STRGL.

4 SSAP 19 ACCOUNTING FOR INVESTMENT PROPERTIES

4.1 A summary of the main provisions of SSAP 19 *Accounting for investment properties* is given below, and these should be familiar to you from your earlier studies.

Knowledge brought forward from earlier studies

SSAP 19 *Accounting for investment properties*

Definition

- **Investment property:** an interest in land and/or buildings in respect of which construction work and development have been completed, and which is held for its investment potential, rental income being negotiated at arm's length.
- **Exceptions**: property owned and occupied by a company for its own purposes; and property let to and occupied by another group company (in company and group accounts). An associated company is not a group company.

Accounting treatment

- Such properties are **not depreciated**, except where a leasehold has an unexpired term of less than 20 years.
- **Revalue** each year to open market value.
- The increase in value is taken to the **IRR** (Investment Revaluation Reserve).
- For **diminutions** in value the treatment varies (this required an amendment to SSAP 19).
  - If **permanent**, it is charged to the P&L a/c.
  - If **temporary**, a temporary IRR deficit is allowed.
- **Disposals**: per FRS 3,
  - Profit/loss represents the sales proceeds less the carrying amount
  - Revaluation surplus transferred to the P&L a/c (as realised profits)

Disclosures

- Investment properties and the IRR should be **displayed prominently**.
- **Disclose**:
  - the name of the valuer;
  - whether the valuer is an employee or officer of the company; and
  - the basis of valuation used.
- **Non-compliance with CA 1985** for a true and fair view should be noted as required by UITF Abstract 7 (see below).

4.2 This chart will help to determine the application of SSAP 19.

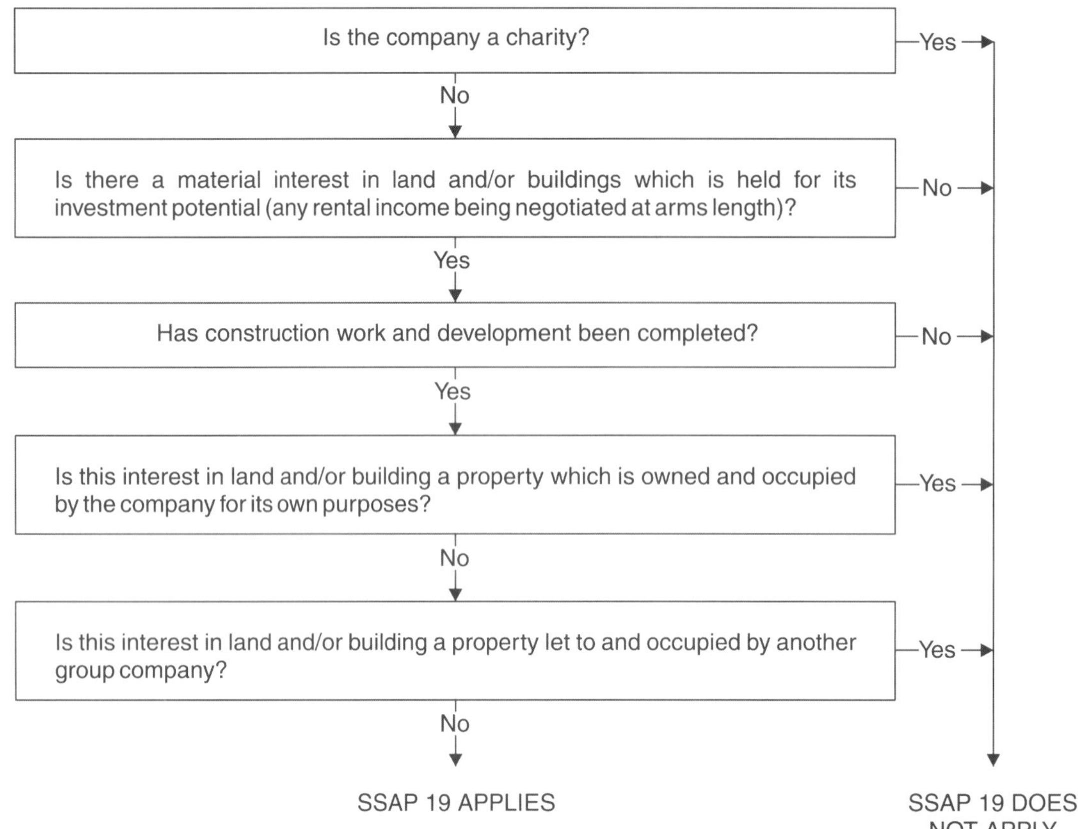

Question: investment properties

The managing director of your company has always been unhappy at depreciating the company's properties because he argues that these properties are in fact appreciating in value. Recently he heard of another company which has investment properties and does not depreciate those properties.

You are required to write a report to your managing director explaining:

(a) The consequences of not depreciating the company's existing properties
(b) The meaning of investment properties
(c) The accounting treatment of investment properties in published financial statements

Answer

REPORT

From: Finance Director
To: Managing Director — Date: 31 October 20X2
Subject: *Depreciation of property*

(a) All fixed assets that have a finite economic life should be depreciated in a systematic manner over that period. While it is recognised that, generally, freehold land has an indefinite economic life, the same is not true of buildings. Even if they are properly maintained, most industrial and commercial buildings will become economically obsolete in time, even if they remain structurally sound.

The failure to provide depreciation on industrial and commercial buildings over their period of use overstates the profits of the company and this could lead to over-distribution of profit.

(b) An investment property is defined in the relevant accounting standard (SSAP 19) as one which is held for its investment potential and for which a rental is negotiated at arms length (and where construction is complete). It cannot be one which is owned and occupied by a company or its affiliated companies for its own purposes.

This means that our properties, which are used for the purposes of the company's own manufacturing, distribution and administrative activities, do not qualify for treatment as investment properties.

It also means that they could not be made to qualify as investment properties by transferring them to another group company and renting them back.

(c) Under SSAP 19 investment properties are not depreciated but are shown in the accounts at open market value. Increases in market value are credited to an investment revaluation reserve and decreases are charged to it. The open market valuation, which is related to rentals, is likely to vary considerably over time and large charges against profits could occur during periods of weakness in the property market. This could lead to greater volatility of earnings than if the properties had been depreciated, but it reflects more accurately the realities of the property market.

Problems with SSAP 19

4.3 It is likely that SSAP 19 will be amended to fit in with the new FRS 15 from which it is excluded. There are criticisms of the standard, mainly because it does give a clear definition of 'market value'. The Royal Institution of Chartered Surveyors defines **market value** as the best price at which the sale of an interest in property might reasonably be expected to have been completed unconditionally for cash consideration on the date of valuation, assuming a 'willing seller'. There is no mention of a 'willing buyer'.

4.4 There are perceived to be various difficulties with this definition.

(a) **A market transaction** cannot take place without both a seller and a buyer.

(b) The concept of '**willing seller**' (but not a willing buyer) is largely theoretical in depressed market conditions where no willing seller really exists, only unwilling and even forced sellers.

(c) This 'willing seller' concept inevitably leads to an over-emphasis on comparable evidence, forcing the valuer to look **backwards** rather than forwards.

(d) Following on from (c), such an approach cannot cope with **specialised assets**, such as large regional shopping centres, for which no ready market exits.

4.5 The deficiencies in the current definition of open market value do not become apparent **in normal market conditions** where there is a liquid market in actively traded properties. However, at the extremes of the cycle, the current definition is quite inadequate, producing over-valuation in times of boom and under-valuation in times of slump, exacerbating market cycles in an extremely damaging way.

5 SSAP 4 ACCOUNTING FOR GOVERNMENT GRANTS

5.1 SSAP 4 is summarised here as it is very straightforward and you have already studied it, look back to your previous studies if necessary.

Knowledge brought forward from earlier studies

SSAP 4 Accounting for government grants

Problems

- There is a **conflict** of the accruals concept vs the prudence concept.
- **Matching** is difficult if the expenditure is not specified to which the grant should be applied.
- It is necessary to distinguish between **revenue** and **capital grants**.

Accounting treatment

- **Government grants** should be matched in the P&L a/c with the expenditure for which they are contributed.

> **Knowledge brought forward from earlier studies (cont'd)**
>
> - For **fixed assets**, the grant is recognised over the useful economic life of the asset.
> - The method of reducing the acquisition cost of the fixed asset by the amount of the grant and depreciating the net amount is **in conflict with CA 1985**.
> - Grants are not recognised in the P&L a/c until **conditions of receipt** are complied with.
> - If part or all recognition is **deferred**, treat this as deferred income.
> - Any **potential liabilities** to repay should be provided for to the extent that repayment is probable.
>
> *Disclosure*
>
> - **Accounting policy note**
> - Effect of **government grants** on the results for the period and/or the position at the B/S date.
> - Any **potential liability** to repay grants according to FRS 12.

6 FRED 29

6.1 As part of the ASB's programme of convergence between FRS and IFRS (see Chapter 13), in May 2002 it issued FRED 29 *Property, plant and equipment; Borrowing costs.*

Main points

6.2 FRED 29 includes the text of a revised IAS 16 *Property, plant and equipment* and IAS 23 *Borrowing costs.* Like FRS 15, IAS 23 permits a **choice** between **capitalising certain borrowing costs** and treating all such costs as an **expense**.

6.3 The **principles for initial measurement and depreciation are the same** in both IAS 16 and FRS 15 *Tangible fixed assets.* Both standards allow the option of revaluing assets or keeping them at depreciated cost. But there are some significant differences, of which the most important is in relation to revaluation. Where the **UK uses a 'value to the business' model, the international standard uses a 'fair value' model.**

Revaluation proposals

6.4 Currently proposals on the revaluation of fixed assets are being developed by the 'Revaluation Group', which includes representatives of national standard setters from countries where revaluation is permitted (Australia, New Zealand, South Africa and the UK). The group have proposed that **assets should be stated at entry value** unless disposal would be the more economically rational course of action, in which case exit value should be used. In the absence of a market for the asset, its value would be based on an assessment of cash flows or on replacement cost.

6.5 In the light of these proposals, it is possible that **IAS 16 may undergo further revision**, with regard to its revaluation rules.

ASB's approach

6.6 FRED 29 proposes that the UK should replace FRS 15 with the revised IAS 16 and IAS 23, unless there are further changes to the IAS 16 requirements on revaluation.

6.7 Other changes from existing UK requirements are:

(a) There will be **no requirement for annual impairment reviews** where **no depreciation** is **charged**.

(b) **Capitalisation of interest** would be allowed on certain **inventories**.

(c) **Renewals accounting** would **not** be **allowed**.

More detail on FRED 29

6.8 There is much overlap between FRS 15 *Tangible fixed assets* and FRED 29 *Property, plant and equipment; Borrowing costs.* They are similar in scope, and have **similar principles** for initial measurement, valuation and depreciation of tangible fixed assets. Both standards allow a choice of revaluing assets or keeping them at cost subject to depreciation.

6.9 There are **differences of terminology**, the most obvious being 'property, plant and equipment', which is the international version, in place of the UK terminology, 'tangible fixed assets', but these terms have a similar meaning. (It is worth noting that other IAS refer to 'non-current assets', where in the UK we would say 'fixed assets'.)

Exam focus point

For the purposes of your exam, there is little to be gained by going over the common ground where the differences are only in terminology or wording. You would advice to concentrate on the **proposed changes from existing UK requirements,** as you may be asked to **compare** the current and the proposed treatment. These changes are covered in the remainder of this section.

Exchanges of assets

6.10 An item of property, plant and equipment may be acquired in exchange or part exchange for another item of property, plant and equipment or another asset. FRED 29 introduces a requirement that is not found in existing UK standards. It requires that the cost of such an item must normally be measured at the **fair value of the asset given up**, adjusted by the amount of any cash or cash equivalents transferred.

6.11 The **fair value of the asset received** is used to measure its cost **if it is more clearly evident** than the fair value of the asset given up.

6.12 The only **exception** to the above requirements is where fair value **cannot be determined reliably,** for example when comparable market transactions are infrequent.

Donated assets

6.13 **FRED 29 does not address the treatment of donated assets** received by charities, presently covered in FRS 15.

Depreciation

6.14 FRED 29 generally contains the **same principles** as FRS 15 regarding **depreciation**. However, there is an **exception**, which relates to **residual values.**

6.15 **Both** FRS 15 and FRED 29 require that, where residual values are material, they should be **reviewed at each balance sheet date**. **FRED 29** states that residual value should be revised using **current prices at the date of revision.** This is a change from **FRS 15**, which generally requires prices at the **date of acquisition or latest valuation** to be used, in order to provide a consistent basis for the recalculation of depreciation.

Situations where no depreciation is charged

6.16 Both the FRS and the FRED state that subsequent expenditure on assets does not negate the need to recognise depreciation. However, unlike FRED 29, FRS 15 addresses the situation where no depreciation is charged or the depreciation period is very long, and where there is therefore a risk that the asset's recoverable amount will fall below its carrying amount.

6.17 **FRS 15 requires annual impairment reviews** to be carried out on assets where no depreciation is charged because it would be immaterial, or where the remaining useful life is greater than 50 years. It also **gives guidance** on **when** uncharged depreciation may be regarded as **immaterial**.

6.18 **FRED 29 does not include** equivalent requirements and guidance.

Renewals accounting

6.19 FRS 15 includes specific industry guidance on the use of renewals accounting as a method of estimating the depreciation to be charged on certain infrastructure assets. **The FRED does not address renewals accounting**, and therefore does not depart from the principle that the depreciation expense is determined by reference to an asset's depreciable amount. For assets carried at historical cost, this would be cost less residual value.

Revaluation of assets

6.20 FRS 15 and FRED 29 have much **in common**

(a) Both **allow the option of revaluing** property, plant and equipment.

(b) Both require that where a policy of revaluation is adopted, **all assets of the same class must be revalued.**

(c) Both require that valuations must be **kept up to date.**

6.21 However, there is an important **difference of principle**, which is that **FRED 29** requires revaluation to **fair value,** whereas **FRS 15** requires revaluation to current value defined in terms of the '**value to the business**' model.

6.22 **FRED 29** states that **fair value** of land and buildings, plant and equipment is usually its **market value.** Where there is no evidence of market value because of the asset's specialised nature, depreciated replacement cost should be used instead.

6.23 The **value to the business model used by FRS 15**, and which the ASB has generally preferred for current value, seeks to provide a value that is relevant to economic decision making. It is the loss that the entity would suffer if it were deprived of the asset. As stated earlier, it is the **lower of replacement cost and recoverable amount.**

6.24 Look back to Paragraph 3.6 to see how FRS 15 reflects this valuation. You will see that **FRS 15 differs from FRED 29 in requiring non-specialised properties to be valued at existing use value (EUV).** FRED 29 states that fair value is usually market value, which can generally be assumed to be the same as open market value (OMV).

6.25 The difference will come into play **when OMV is greater than EUV,** for example where the property can be developed for an alternative use. FRS 15 would not allow the higher value for the alternative use to be reflected in an entity's balance sheet (unless the property is surplus to its requirements). But **FRED 29** does not restrict this value to EUV, and would therefore show a **higher value** in such cases.

6.26 On the other hand, suppose **EUV is less than OMV**. This would be the case if a property has been adapted to the needs of the current occupier, and there is little prospect of finding a buyer in the market who could use those adaptations.

6.27 In such a case, **FRED 29** would require OMV to be used, which would result in a **lower value than under FRS 15.** The exception would be if it were a specialised property, in which case depreciated replacement cost would be used.

Frequency of valuations

6.28 Both FRS 15 and FRED 29 require that valuations should be kept up to date and both require the use of qualified valuers for property. However, the requirements of FRED 29 are not as detailed or specific, as shown in the following table.

FRS 15	FRED 29
Requires five-yearly valuations with interim updates.	No maximum interval specified – valuations must be undertaken as frequently as is necessary to ensure fair values do not differ materially from carrying values. However, it does indicate that 'volatile' assets may need annual revaluations where every three or five years would be sufficient for less volatile assets.
Contains detailed guidance on the process of performing full and interim valuations and on an appropriate index for use by the directors in valuing plant and machinery.	No such guidance provided.
Contains a requirement to take account of notional directly attributable acquisition or selling costs where material.	Not addressed.
Contains detailed guidance on the valuation of properties valued on a trading basis and the treatment of specialised 'adaptation works'	No such guidance provided.

Reporting revaluation gains and losses

6.29 There are differences between FRS 15 and IAS 16 *Property, plant and equipment* regarding the reporting of revaluation losses. These reflect the use in FRS 15 of the value to the business model.

6.30 As discussed in Paragraph 6.4, revaluation is the subject of a project currently being undertaken by the 'Revaluation Group', which may result in further changes to IAS 16. Meanwhile, the ASB believes that it is appropriate to argue the case for IAS 16 to be amended to incorporate principles of revaluation similar to those in FRS 15.

6.31 The upshot of this is that **FRED 29 adopts, for now, the IAS 16 model,** with the wording amended to reflect the use in the UK of the statement of total recognised gains and losses. **The position may change depending on changes to IAS 16.** The table below compares the treatment.

FRS 15	FRED 29
A revaluation loss that exceeds an existing revaluation surplus in respect of an asset should be recognised in the STRGL to the extent that the asset's recoverable amount is greater than its revalued amount (ie there is no impairment).	A revaluation loss that exceeds an existing revaluation surplus in respect of an asset should be recognised in the STRGL until the carrying amount reaches its depreciated historical cost and thereafter in the profit and loss account.
FRS 15 requires any revaluation loss that is clearly caused by the consumption of economic benefits, ie an impairment, to be charged as an expense in the profit and loss account. This is irrespective of whether there is an existing revaluation surplus in respect of the asset.	Any revaluation loss must be charged to the STRGL to the extent that there is an existing revaluation surplus in respect of the asset.

Borrowing costs

6.32 **FRED 29** also incorporates most of IAS 23 *Borrowing costs.* Like FRS 15, IAS 23 – and hence FRED 29 – **permits entities to choose** whether or not to **capitalise** borrowing costs, provided the policy is applied **consistently.**

6.33 The IASB has considered this issue as part of its Improvements Project, being inclined to eliminate the choice and require all borrowing costs to be reported as an expense as incurred. However, as this raises a number of issues, it decided not to eliminate the choice at this stage, but to consider it as part of the wider issue of measurement of an asset and initial recognition.

6.34 FRS 15's requirements regarding the capitalisation of finance costs were modelled on IAS 23, so the two standards are similar in most respects, even wording. Although the style of the IAS is to present the optional treatment as the 'benchmark treatment' and the 'allowed alternative' treatment, this does not imply that one treatment is preferred to the other.

6.35 However, one difference not adopted by the ASB is that IAS 23 allowed certain **exchange differences** to be included in borrowing costs eligible for capitalisation. **FRED 29 does not allow this.**

6.36 A difference that **FRED 29** has adopted is that as well as covering interest capitalisation on tangible fixed assets, it also applies to **certain inventories**. These are included within its definition of 'qualifying assets'.

6.37 A further change to existing UK practice concerns the type of borrowing costs eligible for capitalisation if **specific borrowings** are raised to fund a qualifying asset. **FRS 15** only permits the capitalisation of the interest arising on the amount of borrowings that has been spent on the asset to date; **interest paid and received any portion unused and reinvested is recognised in the profit and loss account. FRED 29**, which follows IAS 23, **permits capitalisation of the actual borrowing costs less any investment income received from the temporary investment of unutilised borrowings**.

6.38 Finally, FRED 29 does not require disclosure of the aggregate amount of finance costs included in the cost of tangible fixed assets and the amount recognised in the profit and loss account. Both are required by FRS 15.

6.39 Section summary

- FRED 29 proposes two new standards which would eventually replace FRS 15.
- There would be no requirement for annual impairment reviews where no depreciation is charged.
- Renewals accounting would not be allowed.
- 'Fair value' would be used for revalued assets rather than 'value to the business'
- Capitalisation of interest would be allowed on certain inventories.

Chapter roundup

- **Assets** have been defined in various ways. The most recent definition is contained in the ASB's *Statement of Principles*, Chapter 4 *Elements of financial statements*.
- CA 1985 maintains **historical cost** principles, modified by the revaluations of certain assets.
- **FRS 15** sets out **uniform principles** relating to tangible fixed assets with regard to:
  - Initial measurement
  - Valuation
  - Depreciation
- **SSAP 19** conflicts with the statutory requirement to depreciate all fixed assets with a limited economic life, by stating that investment properties need not ordinarily be depreciated. Companies taking advantage of this provision need to justify their departure from statute as being necessary to provide a true and fair view.
- **FRED 29** *Property, plant and equipment; Borrowing costs* proposes replacing FRS 15 with the revised IASs of those names.

Quick quiz

1 How does the ASB's *Statement of Principles* define an asset?

2 Can finance costs be capitalised?

3 Can subsequent expenditure on a fixed asset be capitalised?

4 Define depreciation.

5 What accounting treatment is required if the estimated useful life of a fixed asset is revised?

6 When properties are revalued, how often, per FRS 15, is a full valuation needed?

7 Specialised properties should be valued on the basis of:

A Existing value in use
B Open market value
C Depreciated replacement cost
D Net realisable value

8 Which of the following is not a directly attributable cost associated with bringing a tangible fixed asset into working condition?

A Cost of site preparation and clearance
B Installation costs
C Stamp duty
D Design errors

9 What is the main difference between FRS 15 and FRED 29?

Answers to quick quiz

1 See key term.

2 Yes. This is optional. If an entity does capitalise finance costs, they must do so consistently.

3 Yes, in three cases.

   (a) It enhances the economic benefits over and above those previously estimated.

   (b) A component treated separately for depreciation purposes has been restored or replaced

   (c) It relates to a major inspection or overhaul that restores economic benefits that have been consumed and reflected in the depreciation charge.

4 See para 2.21.

5 The net book value of the asset should be depreciated over the new estimate of its remaining useful life.

6 Every 5 years.

7 C

8 D Abnormal costs, such as those arising from design errors, industrial disposals and idle capacity, should not be capitalised as part of the cost.

9 For revaluations, FRED 29, for now, proposes fair value, whereas FRS 15 uses 'value to the business'.

Now try the question below from the Exam Question Bank

Number	Level	Marks	Time
Q23	Exam	25	45 mins

Chapter 17

FIXED ASSETS: INTANGIBLE ASSETS

	Topic list	Syllabus reference
1	FRS 10 *Goodwill and intangible assets*	1(a) – 1(d)
2	FRS 11 *Impairment of fixed assets and goodwill*	1(a) – 1(d)
3	SSAP 13 *Accounting for research and development*	1(a) – 1(d)
4	Investments	1(a) – 1(d)

Introduction

Probably the most important, and certainly the most contentious intangible fixed asset is **goodwill**. This is the subject of **FRS 10** *Goodwill and intangible assets* which was covered in your earlier studies.

The section on **SSAP 13** should be revision of a fairly straightforward topic, but you should make sure that you know SSAP 13's provisions.

FRS 11 *Impairment of fixed assets and goodwill* is a recent standard that you need to know about.

Study guide

Section 11 – Fixed assets 1

- Discussion of the nature of impairment and the impairment review
- Applying the impairment review and dealing with losses on assets
- Accounting for the amortisation of goodwill and intangible assets including impairment

1 FRS 10 GOODWILL AND INTANGIBLE ASSETS 6/02, 12/02

1.1 You should be familiar with FRS 10 *Goodwill and intangible assets* from your earlier studies. Below is a summary of the requirements, together with one or two questions. Look back to your earlier study material if you are unsure.

Knowledge brought forward from earlier studies

FRS 10 Goodwill and intangible assets

Accounting treatment

- Under FRS 10 both purchased goodwill and intangible assets should be capitalised as assets in the B/S. Thereafter treatment depends on the nature of investment.
  - There is a rebuttable presumption that the useful economic lives (UEL) of purchased goodwill and intangible assets are limited and do not exceed 20 years from acquisition.
  - The UEL may be regarded as greater than 20 years or even indefinite, but only if the goodwill is capable of continued measurement so that annual impairment reviews can be performed

Knowledge brought forward from earlier studies cont.

- **Positive purchased goodwill and intangible assets**
  - Where goodwill and intangible assets are regarded as having limited UEL they should be amortised
  - Where they are regarded as having indefinite UEL they should not be amortised
  - Where they are not amortised or are amortised over more than 20 years, impairment reviews should be performed each year under FRS 11
- **Negative goodwill**

  Negative goodwill should be recognised and separately disclosed on the face of the balance sheet immediately below the goodwill heading. It should be recognised in the profit and loss account in the periods in which the non monetary assets acquired are depreciated or sold
- **Internally generated goodwill**

  Internally generated goodwill should not be capitalised and internally developed intangible assets should be capitalised only where they have a readily ascertainable market value

Question: goodwill

The circumstances where an indefinite useful economic life longer than 20 years may be legitimately presumed are limited. What factors determine the durability of goodwill?

Answer

FRS 10 mentions the following.

(a) The nature of the business
(b) The stability of the industry in which the acquired business operates
(c) Typical lifespans of the products to which the goodwill attaches
(d) The extent to which the acquisition overcomes market entry barriers that will continue to exist
(e) The expected future impact of competition on the business

Question: negative goodwill

Brookie plc acquired its investment in Stenders Ltd in the year ended 31 December 20X8. The goodwill on acquisition was calculated as follows.

	£'000	£'000
Cost of investment		200
Fair value of net assets acquired (remaining useful life - 7 years)		
Fixed assets	350	
Stock	50	
Net monetary assets	100	
		(500)
Negative goodwill		(300)

Required

Calculate the amount relating to negative goodwill as reflected in the profit and loss account and balance sheet for the year ended 31 December 20X8.

Answer

Amortisation in the profit and loss account for 20X8

Non-monetary assets recognised through the profit and loss account for the year ended 31 December 20X8:

	£'000
Stock	50
Depreciation (£350,000 ÷ 7)	50
	100

Proportion recognised this year	¼

This means that a credit of £75,000 (£300,000 × ¼) of the negative goodwill will be charged to the profit and loss account for the year ended 31.12.X8. The remaining £225,000 will be carried in the balance sheet as a deduction from positive goodwill as part of intangible fixed assets.

Over the next six years (the remaining useful life of the non-monetary assets originally purchased), it will be released into the profit and loss account (£37,500 a year).

Criticisms of FRS 10

1.2 The new rules have meant significant changes to the accounts of many companies. Over 95% of companies in the UK adopted the 'immediate write off' treatment permitted under the old SSAP 22. Some commentators have suggested that some deals will not be done because of the new, tougher rules. This is probably an exaggeration, but it is certainly possible that FRS 10 will not be popular.

1.3 More seriously, criticisms have been made of the thinking behind the standard by the firm Ernst & Young. The main criticisms are as follows.

(a) FRS 10 **still allows a choice** of accounting treatments. Companies can follow a regime that permits the goodwill to be carried as a permanent asset. This may allow some spurious assets to remain indefinitely in the balance sheet, potentially providing fuel for criticism of the profession in the next wave of accounting scandal.

(b) The **impairment review**, based on FRS 11, applies 'labyrinthine methodologies to very soft numbers'. In other words, it is **subjective**, not least in determining how the business is to be segmented. Forecasting cashflows is also problematic.

(c) The importance of **negative goodwill** has been underestimated. It is more likely to arise now that FRS 7 bans reorganisation provisions, thus raising the value of the net assets acquired.

(d) The treatment of **negative goodwill** is 'strange'. It is a '**dangling credit**' in the balance sheet and the profit and loss account treatment simply mirrors that required for depreciation without regard to the fact that this is a **credit** to the profit and loss account.

UITF Abstract 27 Revision to estimates of the useful economic life of goodwill and intangible assets

1.4 This Abstract states that a change from non-amortisation of goodwill or intangible assets, on the grounds that the life of the asset is indefinite, to amortisation over a period of 20 years or less should not be reported as a change in accounting policy. In such a circumstance, the carrying amount of the goodwill or intangible asset should be amortised over the revised remaining useful life.

2 FRS 11 IMPAIRMENT OF FIXED ASSETS AND GOODWILL 12/01

2.1 It is accepted practice that a **fixed asset** should **not be carried in the financial statements at more than its recoverable amount**, ie the higher of the amount for which it could be sold and the amount recoverable from its future use.

FRS 11 *Impairment of fixed assets and goodwill*

2.2 While statute provides some guidance, it provides none on how the recoverable amount should be measured and when impairment losses should be recognised. As a result, practice is inconsistent and perhaps some impairments may not be recognised on a timely basis.

2.3 Under FRS 10, where goodwill and intangible assets have a useful life in excess of twenty years or one that is indefinite, the recoverable amount of the goodwill and intangible assets has to be reviewed every year.

2.4 **Objective of FRS 11**

(a) Fixed assets and goodwill are recorded in the financial statements at no more than their **recoverable amount**.

(b) Any resulting **impairment loss** is measured and recognised on a **consistent basis**.

(c) **Sufficient information** is **disclosed** in the financial statements to enable users to understand the impact of the impairment on the financial position and performance of the reporting entity.

2.5 The FRS applies to subsidiary undertakings, associates and joint ventures but excludes fixed assets governed by FRS 13 and SSAP 19.

Indications of impairment

2.6 A **review for impairment** of a fixed asset or goodwill should be carried out if events or changes in circumstances indicate that the carrying amount of the fixed asset or goodwill may not be recoverable.

KEY TERM

Impairment: a reduction in the recoverable amount of a fixed asset or goodwill below its carrying amount. *(FRS 11)*

2.7 Impairment occurs due to

- Something happening to the **fixed asset** itself
- Something occurring in the **environment** within which the asset operates.

2.8 **Indicators of impairment**

(a) There is a **current period operating loss** or **net cash outflow** from operating activities, combined with *either*:

(i) **past** operating losses or net cash outflows from operating activities; *or*

(ii) an expectation of **continuing** operating losses or net cash outflows from operating activities.

(b) A **fixed asset's market value has declined** significantly during the period.

(c) Evidence is available of **obsolescence or physical damage** to the fixed asset.

(d) There is a **significant adverse change** in any of the following.

(i) Either the **business or the market** in which the fixed asset or goodwill is involved, such as the entrance of a major competitor.

(ii) The **statutory or other regulatory environment** in which the business operates.

(iii) Any **indicator of value** (eg multiples of turnover) used to measure the fair value of a fixed asset on acquisition.

(e) A commitment by management to undertake a **significant reorganisation**.

(f) A major loss of **key employees**.

(g) **Market interest rates** or other market rates of return have increased significantly, and these increases are likely to affect materially the fixed asset's recoverable amount.

2.9 Where any of these occur, then an impairment review should be carried out. In the case of tangible fixed assets, if there is no cause to suspect any impairment, then **no impairment review** is necessary. Intangible assets and goodwill may, however, still require review.

KEY TERMS

Intangible assets: non-financial fixed assets that do not have physical substance but are identifiable and controlled by the entity through custody or legal rights.

Purchased goodwill: the difference between the cost of an acquired entity and the aggregate of the fair values of that entity's identifiable assets and liabilities.

Tangible fixed assets: assets that have physical substance and are held for use in the production or supply of goods or services, for rental to others, or for administrative purposes on a continuing basis in the reporting entity's activities.

(FRS 11)

The impairment review

2.10 The impairment review will consist of a **comparison of the carrying amount** of the fixed asset or goodwill **with its recoverable amount** (the higher of net realisable value, if known, and value in use). To the extent that the **carrying amount exceeds the recoverable amount, the fixed asset or goodwill is impaired and should be written down. The impairment loss should be recognised in the profit and loss account unless it arises on a previously revalued fixed asset.**

2.11 An impairment **loss** on a **revalued fixed asset** should be recognised in the **profit and loss account** if it is caused by a **clear consumption of economic benefits. Other impairments** of revalued fixed assets should be recognised in the **statement of total recognised gains and losses** until the carrying amount of the asset reaches its **depreciated historical cost** and **thereafter in the profit and loss account**.

KEY TERMS

- **Net realisable value**: the amount at which an asset could be disposed of, less any direct selling costs.
- **Recoverable amount**: the higher of net realisable value and value in use.
- **Value in use**: the present value of the future cash flows obtainable as a result of an asset's continued use, including those resulting from its ultimate disposal.

2.12 Note the following **rules** here.

(a) If NRV *or* value in use is higher than the carrying amount, there is no impairment.

(b) If a reliable estimate of NRV cannot be made, the recoverable amount is its value in use.

(c) If NRV is less than the carrying amount, then value in use must be found to see if it is higher still. If it is higher, recoverable amount is based on value in use, not NRV.

2.13 When an impairment loss on a fixed asset or goodwill is recognised, the **remaining useful economic life** should be reviewed and revised if necessary. The revised carrying amount should be depreciated over the revised estimate of the useful economic life.

Calculation of net realisable value

2.14 The net realisable value of an asset that is **traded on an active market** will be based on **market value**. Disposal costs should include only the essential selling costs of the fixed asset and *not* any costs of reducing or reorganising the business.

Calculation of value in use

2.15 Value in use is **not always easy** to estimate.

(a) The value in use of a fixed asset should be estimated **individually** where reasonably practicable.

(b) Where it is not reasonably practicable to identify cash flows arising from an individual fixed asset, value in use should be calculated at the level of **income-generating units**.

(c) The **carrying amount of each income-generating unit** containing the fixed asset or goodwill under review should be compared with the **higher of the value in use and the net realisable value** (if it can be measured reliably) of the unit.

KEY TERM

An **income generating unit** is defined as a group of assets, liabilities and associated goodwill that generates income that is largely independent of the reporting entity's other income streams. The assets and liabilities include those already involved in generating the income and an appropriate portion of those used to generate more than one income stream.

2.16 Because it is necessary to identify only material impairments, in some cases it may be acceptable to consider a **group of income generating units together** rather than on an individual basis.

2.17 In some cases a detailed calculation of value in use will not be necessary. A **simple estimate** may be sufficient to demonstrate that either value in use is higher than carrying value, in which case there is no impairment, or value in use is lower than net realisable value, in which case impairment is measured by reference to net realisable value.

Identification of income generating units

2.18 Income generating units should be identified by **dividing the total income of the entity into as many largely independent income streams as is reasonably practicable**. Each of the entity's identifiable assets and liabilities should be attributed to, or apportioned between, one or more income generating unit(s). However, the following are **excluded**.

- Deferred tax balances
- Interest bearing debt
- Dividends payable
- Other financing items

2.19 In general terms, the income streams identified are likely to **follow** the way in which **management** monitors and makes decisions about continuing or closing the different lines of business of the entity. **Unique intangible assets**, such as brands and mastheads, are generally seen to generate income independently of each other and are usually **monitored separately**. Hence they can often be used to identify income-generating units. **Other income streams** may be identified by **reference to major products or services.**

2.20 EXAMPLE: IDENTIFICATION OF INCOME GENERATING UNITS

A transport company runs a network comprising trunk routes fed by a number of supporting routes. Decisions about continuing or closing the supporting routes are not based on the returns generated by the routes in isolation but on the contribution made to the returns generated by the trunk routes.

2.21 SOLUTION

An income-generating unit comprises a trunk route plus the supporting routes associated with it because the cash inflows generated by the trunk routes are not independent of the supporting routes.

Question: income generating unit

Identify the income generating unit in the following cases.

(a) A manufacturer can produce a product at a number of different sites. Not all the sites are used to full capacity and the manufacturer can choose how much to make at each site. However, there is not enough surplus capacity to enable any one site to be closed. The cash inflows generated by any one site therefore depend on the allocation of production across all sites.

(b) A restaurant chain has a large number of restaurants across the country. The cash inflows of each restaurant can be individually monitored and sensible allocations of costs to each restaurant can be made.

Answer

(a) The income-generating unit comprises all the sites at which the product can be made.

(b) Each restaurant is an income-generating unit by itself. However, any impairment of individual restaurants is unlikely to be material. A material impairment is likely to occur only when a number of restaurants are affected together by the same economic factors. It may therefore be acceptable to consider groupings of restaurants affected by the same economic factors rather than each individual restaurant.

Question: impairment loss

Ashley Ltd has an income-generating unit which has a carrying value of £4,000,000 at 31 December 20X7. This carrying value comprises £1,000,000 relating to goodwill and £3,000,000 relating to net assets. The goodwill is not being amortised as its useful life is believed to be indefinite. In 20X8, changes in the regulatory framework surrounding its business mean that the income-generating unit has a value in use of £3,200,000. As a result of losses, net assets have decreased to £2,800,000 reducing the total carrying value of the unit to £3,800,000 which has thus suffered an impairment loss of £600,000. This is charged to the profit and loss account. The carrying value of goodwill is reduced to

£400,000. In 20X9 the company develops a new product with the result that the value in use of the income-generating unit is now £3,400,000. Net tangible assets have remained at £2,800,000.

Can all or any of the impairment loss be reversed?

Answer

No. Despite the value in use of the business unit now being £3,400,000 compared to its carrying value of £3,200,000, it is not possible to reverse £200,000 of the prior year's impairment loss of £600,000 since the reason for the increase in value of the business unit (the launch of the new product) is not the same as the reason for the original impairment loss (the change in the regulatory environment in which the business operates).

Central assets

2.22 Assets and liabilities that are directly involved in the production and distribution of individual products may be attributed directly to one unit. Central assets, such as group or regional head offices and working capital may have to be apportioned across the units as on a logical and systematic basis. The **sum of the carrying amounts of the units must equal the carrying amount of the net assets (excluding tax on finance) of the equity as a whole**.

2.23 It **may not be possible** to **apportion certain central assets** meaningfully **across the income generating units** to which they contribute. Such assets **may be excluded from** the **individual income generating units**.

- An additional impairment review should be performed on the excluded central assets.
- The income generating units to which the central assets contribute should be combined and their combined carrying amount (including that of the central assets) should be compared with their combined value in use.

Capitalised goodwill

2.24 This **should be attributed to income generating** units or groups of similar units.

Cash flows

2.25 The expected future cash flows of the income-generating unit, including any allocation of central overheads but excluding cash flows relating to financing and tax, should be based on **reasonable and supportable assumptions**. The cash flows should be **consistent with the most up-to-date budgets** and plans that have been formally approved by management. Cash flows for the period beyond that covered by formal budgets and plans should assume a steady or declining growth rate.

2.26 **Future cash flows** must be estimated for income generating units in their **current condition**, ie exclude:

(a) Benefits expected to arise from a **future reorganisation** for which provision has not been made

(b) **Future capital expenditure** that will improve or enhance the income generating units more than originally assessed

2.27 For the **five years** following each impairment review where the recoverable amount has been based on value in use, the **cash flows achieved should be compared with those forecast**.

(a) If the actual cash flows are so much less than those forecast that use of the actual cash flows could have required recognition of an impairment in previous periods, the original **impairment calculations should be re-performed** using the actual cash flows.

(b) Any **impairment** identified should be **recognised in the current period** unless the impairment has reversed.

Discount rate

2.28 The present value of the income-generating unit under review should be calculated by discounting the expected future cash flows of the unit.

(a) The discount rate used should be an **estimate of the rate that the market would expect** on an **equally risky investment**.

(b) It should **exclude the effects of any risk for which the cash flows have been adjusted** and should be calculated on a pre-tax basis.

Allocation of impairment loss

2.29 Allocation of any impairment loss calculated (ie where carrying amount exceeds value in use) should be allocated in stages

Step 1. To any **goodwill** in the unit

Step 2. To any **capitalised intangible asset**

Step 3. To the **tangible assets** (pro-rata or other method).

No asset with a readily ascertainable market value should be written down to below NRV.

Reversal of past impairments

2.30 Tangible fixed assets and investments are treated differently from goodwill and intangible assets.

Tangible fixed assets and investments

2.31 **If**, after an impairment loss has been recognised, the **recoverable amount** of a tangible fixed asset or investment (in subsidiaries, associates and joint ventures) **increases because of a change in economic conditions**, the resulting **reversal** of the impairment loss should be **recognised in the current period**. However, recognition is ***only* to the extent that it increases the carrying amount of the fixed asset up to the amount that it would have been had the original impairment not occurred**. The reversal of the impairment loss should be recognised in the **profit and loss account unless** it arises on a **previously revalued fixed asset** (see below).

2.32 Such events would be the reverse of those given above (Paragraph 2.8) to trigger an impairment review. Increases in value from the passage of time or through the passing of cash outflows do *not* give rise to the reversal of an impairment loss.

IMPORTANT

An increase in value above the original carrying value is a **revaluation**, and this is the case with goodwill and intangibles too.

Goodwill and intangible assets

2.33 The reversal of an impairment loss on intangible assets and goodwill should be **recognised in the current period if, and only if**:

(a) an **external event** caused the recognition of the impairment loss in previous periods, and subsequent external events clearly and demonstrably reverse the effects of that event in a way that was not foreseen in the original impairment calculations; or

(b) the impairment loss related to an intangible asset with a readily ascertainable market value and the **net realisable value based on that market value** has increased **to above the intangible asset's impaired carrying amount**.

2.34 The reversal of the impairment loss should be **recognised to the extent that it increases the carrying amount of the goodwill or intangible asset up to the amount that it would have been had the original impairment not occurred**. However, the reversal of an impairment loss recognised under (b) above should *not* be recognised **beyond the extent that it increases the carrying amount of the intangible asset to its net realisable value.**

KEY TERM

Readily ascertainable market value, in relation to an intangible asset, is the value that is established by reference to a market where:

(a) The asset belongs to a homogeneous population of assets that are equivalent in all material respects

(b) An active market, evidenced by frequent transactions, exists for that population of assets *(FRS 11)*

Question: reversal of impairment loss

An income-generating unit comprising a factory, plant and equipment etc and associated purchased goodwill becomes impaired because the product it makes is overtaken by a technologically more advanced model produced by a competitor. The recoverable amount of the income-generating unit falls to £60m, resulting in an impairment loss of £80m, allocated as follows.

	Carrying amounts before impairment	*Carrying amounts after impairment*
	£m	£m
Goodwill	40	-
Patent (with no market value)	20	-
Tangible fixed assets	80	60
Total	140	60

After three years, the entity makes a technological breakthrough of its own, and the recoverable amount of the income-generating unit increases to £90m. The carrying amount of the tangible fixed assets had the impairment not occurred would have been £70m.

Required

Calculate the reversal of the impairment loss.

Answer

The reversal of the impairment loss is recognised to the extent that it increases the carrying amount of the tangible fixed assets to what it would have been had the impairment not taken place, ie a reversal of the impairment loss of £10m is recognised and the tangible fixed assets written back to £70m. Reversal of the impairment is not recognised in relation to the goodwill and patent because the effect of the external event that caused the original impairment has not reversed - the original product is still overtaken by a more advanced model.

2.35 The **reversal of past impairment losses** is **recognised** when the **recoverable amount** of a tangible fixed asset or investment in a subsidiary, an associate or a joint venture has **increased because of a change in economic conditions or in the expected use of the asset**. Increases in the recoverable amount of goodwill and intangible assets are recognised only when:

(a) an external event caused the recognition of the impairment loss in previous periods; and

(b) subsequent external events clearly and demonstrably reverse the effects of that event in a way that was not foreseen in the original impairment calculations.

RULES TO LEARN

(a) **Impairment losses** are recognised in the **profit and loss account, unless** they arise on a **previously revalued fixed asset.**

(b) Impairment losses on **revalued fixed assets** are recognised in the **statement of total recognised gains and losses** until the carrying value of the asset falls **below depreciated historical** cost unless the impairment is clearly caused by a **consumption of economic benefits,** in which case the loss is recognised in the **profit and loss account.**

(c) Impairments **below depreciated historical** cost are recognised in the **profit and loss account.**

Presentation and disclosure

2.36 **Impairment losses recognised in the profit and loss account** should be included within **operating profit** under the **appropriate statutory heading**, and disclosed as an exceptional item if appropriate. Impairment losses recognised in the STRGL should be **disclosed separately** on the face of that statement.

2.37 In **the notes** to the financial statements in **accounting periods after the impairment**, the impairment loss should be treated as follows.

(a) For assets held on a **historical cost basis**, the impairment loss should be included **within cumulative depreciation**: the cost of the asset should not be reduced.

(b) For **revalued assets held at a market value** (eg existing use value or open market value), the impairment loss should be included **within the revalued carrying amount**.

(c) For **revalued assets held at depreciated replacement** cost, an impairment loss **charged to the profit and loss account** should be included **within cumulative depreciation**: the carrying amount of the asset should not be reduced; an **impairment loss charged to the STRGL** should be **deducted from the carrying amount** of the asset.

2.38 If the impairment loss is measured by reference to **value in use** of a fixed asset or income-generating unit, the **discount rate applied to the cash flows should be disclosed**. If a risk-free discount rate is used, some indication of the risk adjustments made to the cash flows should be given.

2.39 Where an impairment loss recognised in a previous period is **reversed** in the current period, the financial statements should **disclose the reason for the reversal**, including any changes in the assumptions upon which the calculation of recoverable amount is based.

2.40 Where an impairment loss would have been recognised in a previous period had the forecasts of future cash flows been more accurate but the impairment has reversed and the reversal of the loss is permitted to be recognised, the impairment now identified and its subsequent reversal should be disclosed.

2.41 Where, in the measurement of value in use, the period before a steady or declining long-term growth rate has been assumed extends to more than five years, the financial statements should **disclose the length of the longer period** and the circumstances justifying it.

2.42 Where, in the measurement of value in use, the long-term growth rate used has exceeded the long-term average growth rate for the country or countries in which the business operates, the financial statements should **disclose the growth rate assumed** and the circumstances justifying it.

2.43 Section summary

The main aspects of FRS 11 to remember are:

- **Indications** of impairment
- Identification of **income-generating** unit
- How an **impairment review** is carried out
- **Restoration of past losses** (tangibles vs intangibles)
- Impairment and restoration of **revalued fixed assets**

3 SSAP 13 ACCOUNTING FOR RESEARCH AND DEVELOPMENT

3.1 In many companies, especially those which produce food, or 'scientific' products such as medicines, or 'high-technology' products, the expenditure on research and development is considerable. When R & D is a large item of cost, its accounting treatment may have a significant influence on the profits of a business and its balance sheet valuation. SSAP 13 is relatively straightforward, and you have met it in your previous studies. A summary is given below, along with a revision question.

Knowledge brought forward from earlier studies

SSAP 13 Accounting research and development

Definitions

- **Pure/basic research** is experimental/theoretical work with no commercial end in view and no practical application.
- **Applied research** is original investigation directed towards a specific practical aim/objective.
- **Development** is the use of scientific/technical knowledge in order to produce new/substantially improved materials, devices, processes etc.

Accounting treatment

- **Pure and applied research** should be written off as incurred.

Knowledge brought forward from earlier studies cont.

- **Development expenditure** should be written off in year of expenditure, *except* in certain circumstances when it *may* be deferred to future periods.

  S Separately defined project
  E Expenditure separately identifiable
  C Commercially viable
  T Technically feasible
  O Overall profit expected
  R Resources exist to complete the project

- Show **deferred development costs** as an intangible asset amortised from the beginning of commercial production, systematically by reference to sales, etc.
- Deferred costs should be **reviewed annually**; where the above criteria no longer apply, write off the cost immediately.
- Development expenditure previously written off can be **reinstated** if the uncertainties which led to it being written off no longer apply.
- **R & D fixed assets** should be capitalised and written off over their estimated economic lives.
- Deferral of costs should be **applied consistently** to all projects.
- SSAP 13 **does not apply to**:
  - Fixed assets used for R&D (except amortisation)
  - The cost of locating mineral deposits in extractive industries
  - Expenditure where there is a firm contract for reimbursement

Disclosure

- R&D activities should be disclosed in the **directors' report**.
- Private companies outside groups which include a plc are **exempt** from disclosing R & D expenditures (except amortisation) if they meet the criteria for a medium-sized company × 10.
- **Disclose**:
  - Movements on deferred development expenditure
  - R&D charged to the P&L a/c analysed between current year expenditure and amortisation
  - An accounting policy note

R & D in practice

3.2 In a recent survey of company accounts, it was found that 25% did not show the amount spent on R & D, even when it had been disclosed in the chairman's report that money had been spent during the period. This contradicts SSAP 13. It is obviously misleading for companies to state that they spend money on R & D unless the amount was **material**. If it was material the amount should be disclosed.

3.3 The importance of R & D disclosure was emphasised in another survey of what users really needed in financial statements. UK institutional investors said the top requirement was **future prospects and plans** (84%). R & D is seen to form a crucial quantitative element of prospects and plans. When specifically asked about R & D, 64% of UK investors said the data was very, or extremely, important to them. Unfortunately, the top companies analysed failed dismally to provide the information required. There is a wide variety of treatment and information given on R & D and improvements are required in the reporting of R & D.

3.4 The emergence of new and quickly growing **computer software companies** has brought SSAP 13, a previously uncontroversial standard, back into the spotlight. These companies have complained about the high level of write-offs of R & D costs, which has a significant impact on profits. Such costs have to be written off because they are often incurred on

speculative software which is high risk and may never be produced commercially. It is unlikely, however, that the ASB will look at this topic in the near future.

Question: R & D

Forkbender Ltd develops and manufactures exotic cutlery and has the following projects in hand.

	Project				
	1	*2*	*3*	*4*	*5*
	£'000	£'000	£'000	£'000	£'000
Deferred development expenditure b/f 1.1.X2	280	-	450	-	-
Development expenditure incurred during the year					
Salaries, wages and so on	35	29	-	60	20
Overhead costs	2	5	-	-	3
Materials and services	3	13	-	11	4
Patents and licences	1	2	-	-	-
Market research	-	10	-	2	-

Project 1 was originally expected to be highly profitable but this is now in doubt, since the scientist in charge of the project is now behind schedule, with the result that competitors are gaining ground.

Project 2: £370,000 development expenditure on this project has been written off in previous years. Directors now believe, on the best advice, that the project will in future earn revenue considerably in excess of all development costs and they therefore wish to reinstate the expenditure of previous years.

Project 3: commercial production started during the year. Sales were 20,000 units in 20X2 and future sales are expected to be: 20X3 30,000 units; 20X4 60,000 units; 20X5 40,000 units; 20X6 30,000 units. There are no sales expected after 20X6.

Project 4: these costs relate to a new project, which meets the criteria for deferral of expenditure and which is expected to last for three years.

Project 5 is another new project, involving the development of a 'loss leader', expected to raise the level of future sales.

The company's policy is to defer development costs, where permitted by SSAP 13. Expenditure carried forward is written off evenly over the expected sales life of projects, starting in the first year of sale.

Required

Show how the above projects should be treated in the accounting statements of Forkbender Ltd for the year ended 31 December 20X2 in accordance with best accounting practice. Justify your treatment of each project.

Answer

Project 1 expenditure, including that relating to previous years, should all be written off in 20X2, as there is now considerable doubt as to the profitability of the project.

Project 2 expenditure for 20X2 can be deferred and the expenditure relating to previous years can be reinstated.

Since commercial production has started under project 3 the expenditure previously deferred should now be amortised. This will be done over the estimated life of the product, as stated in the question.

Project 4 the development costs may be deferred.

Since project 5 is not expected to be profitable its development costs should not be deferred.

BALANCE SHEET AS AT 31 DECEMBER 20X2 (extract)

	£'000
FIXED ASSETS	
Intangible assets	
Development costs (Note 2)	850

NOTES TO THE ACCOUNTS

1 *Accounting policies*

Research and development

Research and development expenditure is written off as incurred, except that development expenditure incurred on an individual project is carried forward when its future recoverability can be foreseen with reasonable assurance. Any expenditure carried forward is amortised over the period of sales from the related project.

2 *Development costs*

	£'000	£'000
Balance brought forward 1 January 20X2		730
Development expenditure reinstated		370
Development expenditure incurred during 20X2	188	
Development expenditure amortised during 20X2	438	
		(250)
Balance carried forward 31 December 20X2		850

Note. SSAP 13 does not permit the inclusion of market research in deferred development expenditure. The costs might, however, be carried forward separately under the accruals principle.

Workings

	1	*2*	*3*	*4*	*5*	*Total*
	£'000	£'000	£'000	£'000	£'000	£'000
B/F	280	-	450	-	-	730
Expenditure previously written off, reinstated	-	370	-	-	-	370
Salaries etc.	35	29	-	60	20	144
Overheads	2	5	-	-	3	10
Materials etc.	3	13	-	11	4	31
Patents etc.	1	2	-	-	-	3
C/F	-	(419)	(360)	(71)	-	(850)
Written off	321	-	90	-	27	438

* *Note.* An alternative basis for amortisation would be:

$$\frac{20}{180} \times 450 = 50$$

The above basis is more prudent, however, in this case.

4 INVESTMENTS

4.1 The last category of fixed assets we need to consider is investments. Not all investments are held by a company for the long term and it will be convenient to deal with **fixed asset investments** and **current asset investments** together. Investments intended to be retained by a company on a continuing basis (for use in the company's activities) should be treated as fixed assets, while any other investments should be taken to be current assets.

4.2 All the terms relating to investments in **group companies** were explained in Part B of this Study Text.

Fixed asset investments

4.3 The provisions relating to fixed assets in general, which were given in the previous chapter, embrace investments which are held as fixed assets. But investments will not normally have a limited economic life, so that the requirement of **systematic depreciation does not apply**.

4.4 The **alternative accounting rules** allow the following bases of valuation, other than cost, for fixed asset investments.

(a) **Market value**: if this is higher than the stock exchange value, the latter should also be disclosed

(b) **Directors' valuation**

(c) **Equity method**: this method will be explained during your studies of accounting for associated companies

4.5 As always when advantage is taken of the alternative accounting rules, **disclosure** must be made of:

- The items affected
- The basis of valuation adopted
- The comparable amounts determined according to the historical cost convention

Current asset investments

4.6 Current asset investments should be shown, in accordance with the **prudence concept**, at the lower of purchase price and net realisable value.

Listed vs unlisted

4.7 Investments, whether fixed assets or current assets, must be split between any listed investments and those which are unlisted. **Income** from listed investments need not be disclosed. Shares dealt with on the Alternative Investment Market (AIM) are not 'listed' (but they are 'quoted').

Chapter roundup

- The treatment of **goodwill and intangibles** is a controversial and complex area. You must ensure that you can discuss the current thinking on the nature of fixed assets, intangible assets and goodwill and that you can discuss all the possible treatments of positive and negative goodwill in accounts and the arguments on brand accounting. You should be familiar with, and be able to explain, the ASB's requirements as set out in FRS 10 *Goodwill and intangible assets.*
- FRS 11 *Impairment of fixed assets and goodwill* was introduced to ensure that
  - Fixed assets and goodwill are recorded at no more than their **recoverable amount**
  - Any **impairment loss** is **correctly measured**
  - **Sufficient information** is disclosed
- **SSAP 13** on the other hand is a standard which is generally accepted and well understood. You should already be very familiar with its provisions, but make sure that you learn the disclosure requirements.
- **Investments** are treated according to the percentage holding of votes and shares.

Quick quiz

1 What is the normal treatment prescribed by FRS 10 for positive purchased goodwill?

2 The useful economic life of goodwill or intangible assets is always 20 years or less. True or false?

3 Which of the following criteria need to be met in order that internally developed intangible assets can be capitalised per FRS 10 on the balance sheet? Circle any that apply.

(a) The asset is unique.
(b) The asset is a member of a group of homogeneous assets.
(c) There is an active market for that group of assets, evidenced by frequent transactions.

4 Per FRS 10, negative goodwill arising in the year on the acquisition of a subsidiary should be accounted for in the consolidated balance sheet in which of the following ways?

A Credited to the profit and loss reserve.

B Netted off against any positive goodwill arising on other acquisitions and the net balance shown on the face of the balance sheet as an intangible asset.

C Recognised on the face of the balance sheet as a negative intangible asset directly after any positive goodwill which has arisen on other acquisitions.

D Credited to a capital reserve.

5 What is the correct treatment for central assets under FRS 11?

6 A machine is presently recognised in the accounts at its historical cost NBV of £150,000. An impairment in value has been identified due to the machine becoming damaged in the year. Due to the damage the scrap value of the asset is now expected to be only £75,000 and £2,000 of selling expenses would need to be incurred. The alternative to selling the asset is to continue to use it in the business. The economic value is deemed to be £76,000 or £74,500 at present values.

At what value should the asset be recognised in the balance sheet?

7 What is the accounting treatment of a laboratory purchased for R&D activity?

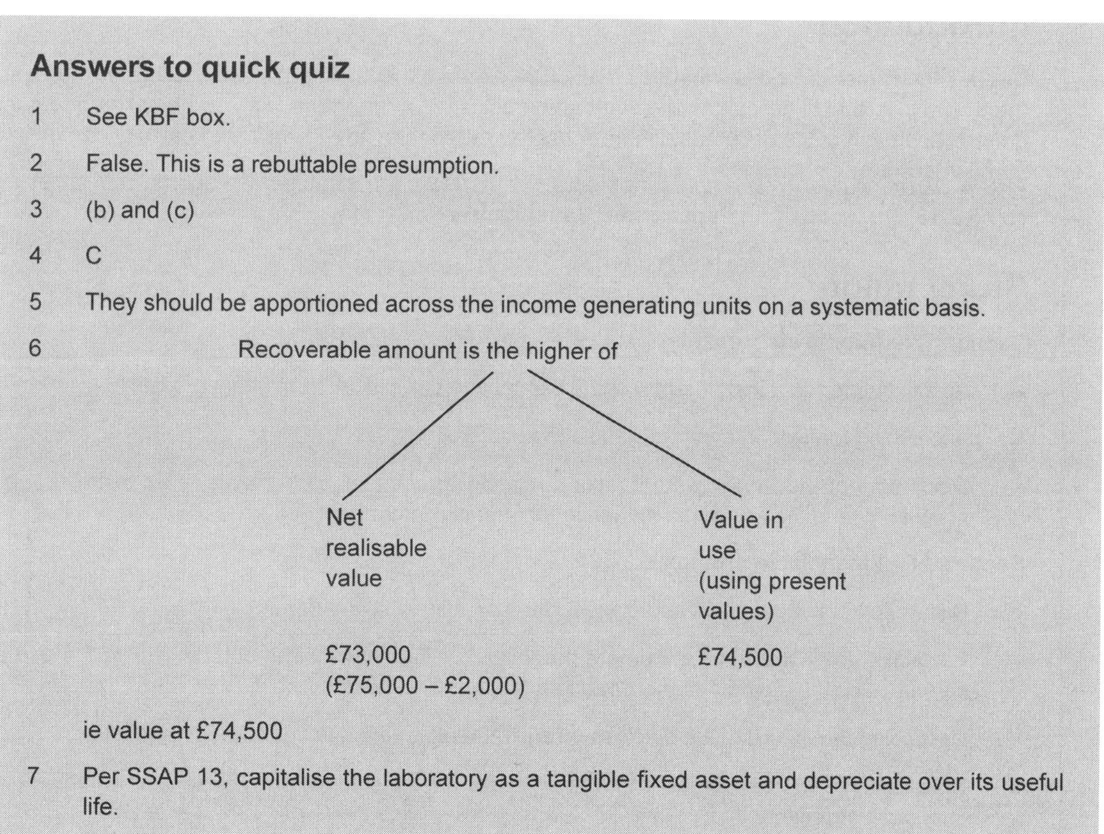

Answers to quick quiz

1 See KBF box.

2 False. This is a rebuttable presumption.

3 (b) and (c)

4 C

5 They should be apportioned across the income generating units on a systematic basis.

6 Recoverable amount is the higher of

Net realisable value	Value in use (using present values)
£73,000 (£75,000 – £2,000)	£74,500

ie value at £74,500

7 Per SSAP 13, capitalise the laboratory as a tangible fixed asset and depreciate over its useful life.

Now try the questions below from the Exam Question Bank

Number	Level	Marks	Time
Q24	Introductory	n/a	n/a
Q25	Introductory	n/a	n/a

Chapter 18

CAPITAL AND FINANCIAL INSTRUMENTS

	Chapter topic list	Syllabus reference
1	FRS 4 *Capital instruments*	1(a) – 1(f)
2	Treatment of certain capital instruments	1(a) – 1(f)
3	Derivatives: measurement and hedge issues	1(a) – 1(f)
4	FRED 23 *Financial Instruments: hedge accounting*	1(a) – 1(f)
5	FRS 13 *Derivatives and other financial instruments: disclosures*	1(a) – 1(f)
6	Current proposals: the Consultation Paper and FRED 30	1(a) – 1(f)

Introduction

Capital instruments and **derivatives** are often extremely complex in business but in the exam there is a limit to how difficult a question can be asked. You are more likely to be asked about the general approach of the documents in this chapter, rather than any complicated calculations.

FRS 4 *Capital instruments* requires most attention here but the examiner is keen on current issues so **FRS 13**, the **Discussion Paper** or the **Consultation Paper** may also come up.

Study guide

Section 13 – Capital instruments

- Accounting for debt instruments, share capital and the allocation of finance costs
- Accounting for fixed interest rate and convertible bonds
- Discussion of the measurement issues relating to complex instruments – for example, split accounting and the link with accounting for financial instruments

Section 14 – Financial instruments

- Discussion of the definition and classification of a financial instrument
- Explaining the current measurement proposals for financial instruments, including the use of current values, hedging and the treatment of gains and losses
- Describing the nature of the disclosure requirements relating to financial instruments
- Discussion of the key areas where consensus is required on the accounting treatment of financial instruments

Exam guide

The examiner said that there will be a lot of emphasis on capital and financial instruments under this syllabus.

1 FRS 4 CAPITAL INSTRUMENTS

1.1 **Capital instruments** are instruments which are issued to raise finance. There are many different types. FRS 4 addresses how issuers should account for capital instruments. The standard covers all capital instruments **except** leases, options or warrants granted under employee share schemes and equity shares issued in a business combination accounted for as a merger.

KEY TERM

- **Capital instrument**: all instruments that are issued by reporting entities as a means of raising finance, including shares, debentures, loans and debt instruments, options and warrants that give the holder the right to subscribe for or obtain capital instruments. In the case of consolidated financial statements the term includes capital instruments issued by subsidiaries except those that are held by another member of the group included in the consolidation. *(FRS 4)*

1.2 Other important **definitions** are given in FRS 4.

KEY TERMS

- **Debt:** capital instruments that are classified as liabilities.
- **Equity shares**: shares other than non-equity shares.
- **Finance costs**: the difference between the net proceeds of an instrument and the total amount of the payments (or other transfer of economic benefits) that the issuer may be required to make in respect of the instrument.
- **Issue costs**: the costs that are incurred directly in connection with the issue of a capital instrument, that is, those costs that would not have been incurred had the specific instrument in question not been issued.
- **Net proceeds**: the fair value of the consideration received on the issue of a capital instrument after deduction of issue costs.
- **Non-equity shares**: shares possessing any of the following characteristics.
  - (a) Any of the rights of the shares to receive payments (whether in respect of dividends, in respect of redemption or otherwise) are for a limited amount that is not calculated by reference to the company's assets or profits or the dividends on any class of equity share.
  - (b) Any of their rights to participate in a surplus in a winding up are limited to a specific amount that is not calculated by reference to the company's assets or profits and such limitation had a commercial effect in practice at the time the shares were issued or, if later, at the time the limitation was introduced.
  - (c) The shares are redeemable either according to their terms, or because the holder, or any party other than the issuer, can require their redemption.
- **Participating dividend**: a dividend (or part of a dividend) on a non-equity share that, in accordance with a company's memorandum and articles of association is always equivalent to a fixed multiple of the dividend payable on an equity share.

KEY TERMS (CONT'D)

- **Share**: share in the share capital of the reporting company (or, in the context of consolidated financial statements, the holding company of a group) including stock.
- **Shareholders' funds**: the aggregate of called up share capital and all reserves, excluding minority interests.
- **Term (of a capital instrument)**: the period from the date of issue of the capital instrument to the date at which it will expire, be redeemed, or be cancelled.

  If either party has the option to require the instrument to be redeemed or cancelled and, under the terms of the instrument, it is uncertain whether such an option will be exercised, the term should be taken to end on the earliest date at which the instrument would be redeemed or cancelled on exercise of such an option.

  If either party has the right to extend the period of an instrument, the term should not include the period of the extension if there is a genuine commercial possibility that the period will not be extended.
- **Warrant**: an instrument that requires the issuer to issue shares (whether contingently or not) and contains no obligations for the issuer to transfer economic benefits.

(FRS 4)

Scope

1.3 The standard applies to all financial statements intended to give a true and fair view of a reporting entity's financial position and profit or loss (or income and expenditure). **No exemptions** have been given on the grounds of size, ownership or industry. Comparative figures may require restatement where the effect on prior years is material.

Distinguishing between debt and equity

1.4 One of the key users' ratios is the **gearing ratio**, ie the measure of the proportion of debt to equity. In order for this measure to be meaningful there must be consistency in the allocation of financial instruments between these two categories. (Minority interests in consolidated financial statements represent a minor category, discussed below.)

1.5 Capital instruments should be included in one of two categories in the balance sheet: **liabilities** or **shareholders' funds**. The rules for distinguishing between debt and equity are based on the accounting model being developed in the ASB's *Statement of Principles*. They require:

(a) A company's **shares** to remain in **shareholders' funds**

(b) **Capital instruments** to be reported as **liabilities** if they contain an 'obligation to transfer economic benefits'

(c) **Capital instruments** to be reported as **shareholders' funds** if they do not contain an 'obligation to transfer economic benefits'

1.6 Some capital instruments have features of **both debt and equity**. The common example of such 'hybrid' instruments is convertible debt, which is economically equivalent to conventional debt plus a warrant to acquire shares in the future.

(a) If the individual components of such instruments are **physically separable**, the FRS requires that they should be **accounted for separately**.

(b) Where the components are **inseparable**, the instrument should be accounted for as a **single instrument**, eg a convertible bond should not be notionally 'split' into debt and an option to acquire shares.

1.7 The rule for determining whether a capital instrument is a **liability** is widely drawn. An 'obligation to transfer economic benefits' means any requirement to make cash payments (usually) or transfer other kinds of property (more rarely) even if the requirement is only contingent. Hence, convertible debt instruments are usually liabilities.

1.8 The standard says that the effect of applying these criteria is that the classification of capital instruments will be consistent with their **substance**, rather than their **legal form**. (A number of observers have said exactly the opposite.)

Disclosure: general

1.9 A fundamental part of FRS 4's approach on hybrid instruments and other less conventional forms of finance is that their issuers must make **considerable disclosures**.

1.10 In order to distinguish shares with debt characteristics from other share capital, the FRS contains a definition of **non-equity shares**. Broadly speaking, these are shares that contain preferential rights to participate in the company's profits or assets (for example preference shares) or are redeemable.

1.11 The main new disclosure requirement is the analysis of the following items in the balance sheet.

Item	Analysed between	
Shareholders' funds	Equity interests	Non-equity interests
Minority interests in subsidiaries	Equity interests in subsidiaries	Non-equity interests in subsidiaries
Liabilities	Convertible liabilities	Non-convertible liabilities

Such analysis is usually to be given on the **face of the balance sheet**. Dividends to shareholders and the minority interests' share of the results for the year should be analysed similarly in the P&L account. Considerable disclosure is also required about the rights and terms of each class of non-equity share and convertible debt.

1.12 The overall effect is to provide the users of financial statements with quite a **detailed analysis of shareholders' funds** showing the amounts pertaining to each separate class of share and a summary of the rights of the holders.

Question: classification of instrument

A company issues a convertible instrument which does not pay a coupon and is mandatorily convertible into shares of the issuer after 3 years. The holder is compensated through the conversion rights attached to the instrument. Although it is mandatorily convertible, the holders will rank as creditors in the event of insolvency of the issuer.

How should the instrument be classified?

Answer

Under FRS 4, this instrument should be classified in shareholders' funds as there is no 'obligation to transfer economic benefits'. Hence, this will be accounted for like a 'fully-paid' warrant. Its impact will be to dilute shareholders' interests in the future.

(Source: *Capital Instruments: A Guide to FRS 4*, Ernst & Young)

Accounting for debt instruments

1.13 Debt should be recorded in the balance sheet at the **fair value** of the consideration received less **costs incurred** directly in connection with the issue of the instrument. Such issue costs are narrowly defined and sometimes have to be written off immediately, but otherwise are spread over the life of the debt.

1.14 The carrying amount of debt should be **increased by the finance cost** in respect of the reporting period and **reduced by payments** made in respect of the debt in that period.

1.15 The **finance cost** of debt is the difference between the **total payments** required to be made and the **initial carrying value of the debt** (that is the interest cost or the dividends plus any premium payable on redemption or other payments). This should be charged to the profit and loss account over the term of the instrument at a **constant rate of interest** on the outstanding amount of the debt. The effective rate of interest implicit in the debt instrument will be required for that purpose.

1.16 Note that under s 130 CA 1985 **discounts** on the issue of debentures may be taken against the share premium account. This would be shown as a transfer in reserves.

Question: debt instrument

On 1 January 20X4, an entity issued a fixed rate debt instrument and received £900,000. Interest is payable annually in arrears at a rate of 5% on the stated principal amount of £1,000,000. The instrument has a 5 year term and the stated principal will be repaid at maturity. Issue costs of £50,000 were incurred.

The effective rate of interest implicit in this instrument is the discount rate which equates the present value of future cash flows to the net proceeds received. This has been calculated as 8.84%.

State the disclosure of the instrument in the profit and loss account and the balance sheet for each year of the term.

Answer

The net proceeds of this issue are £850,000. The finance cost of this instrument is £400,000, being the difference between the total future payments (ie £1,250,000, see column (a) below) and the net proceeds from the issue.

The interest charge for the year (column (b) below) is calculated by applying this rate to the carrying value of the debt in the balance sheet during the year.

	(a)	*(b)*	*(c)*
	Cash flows	*Interest charge*	*Carrying value in the balance sheet*
	£'000	£'000	£'000
At January 20X4	(850)		850.0
At 31 December 20X4	50	75.1	875.1
At 31 December 20X5	50	77.4	902.5
At 31 December 20X6	50	79.8	932.3
At 31 December 20X7	50	82.4	964.7
At 31 December 20X8	1,050	85.3	-
Total	400	400.0	

(Source: *Capital Instruments: A Guide to FRS 4, Ernst & Young*)

1.17 If debt is **repurchased** or **settled** before its maturity, any gains or losses should be recognised immediately in the P&L account.

Convertible debt

1.18 FRS 4 requires that **conversion of debt** should *not* be anticipated but rather reported in liabilities with the finance cost calculated on the assumption that the debt will *never* be converted. When the debt is converted, the amount of consideration recognised in respect of the shares should be the amount of the liability for the debt at the date of conversion.

Disclosure: debt

1.19 (a) **Maturity of debt**. The financial statements or notes should include an analysis of the maturity of debt showing amount falling due:

(i) In one year or less, or on demand
(ii) In more than one year but not more than two years
(iii) In more than two years, but not more than five years
(iv) In more than five years

The maturity of the debt should be determined by reference to the **earliest date** on which the lender can demand repayment.

(b) **Convertible debt** should be stated separately from other liabilities. The following details must be given:

(i) The date of redemption
(ii) The amount payable on redemption
(iii) The number and class of shares into which the debt may be converted
(iv) The period in which the conversion may take place
(v) Whether conversion is at the option of the issuer or holder

Repurchase of own debt

1.20 Any profits or losses arising on the repurchase of debt should be recognised in the **year of repurchase**. This applies to debt repurchased or settled early. Gains or losses should be separately disclosed in the P&L account within, or adjacent to, 'interest payable and similar charges'.

1.21 This is consistent with the treatment previously required by UITF Abstract 8 *Repurchase of own debt* (which FRS 4 replaced), although the wording in the standard makes it clear that this treatment should be applied to debt that is settled early as well as debt that is repurchased. Abstract 8 stated that there were **two circumstances** where it would not be appropriate to recognise any gain or loss on the repurchase of debt:

(a) where the transaction was **not undertaken at a fair value**, but there were other relevant terms to the total transaction (which would often imply, but not require, that the transaction had taken place with a party connected with the company in some way); and

(b) where the debt was **replaced with new debt** on virtually identical terms, except for a difference in the rate of finance cost.

1.22 The basic text of FRS 4 ignores these issues, although they are mentioned in the notes on the development of the standard. The notes mention that such situations may need to be considered in the light of FRS 5 *Reporting the substance of transactions*. Under FRS 5, the transactions would need to be treated as linked, and accounted for as a whole rather than individually. Although not quite as specific or clear as UITF Abstract 8, this is usually likely to arrive at the same result. The apparent profit or loss would need to be considered

together with all the other implications of the group of transactions, and it seems likely that this would often lead to deferral of the gain or loss.

Accounting for shares

1.23 Share issues should be recorded at the **fair value** of the consideration received less **issue costs**. Issue costs should be written off directly to reserves and should not be reported in the STRGL, ie those relating directly to the issue of the instrument should be accounted for as a reduction in the proceeds of a capital instrument.

Question: issue costs

A company issues 100 £1 ordinary shares at par. Issue costs of £2 are incurred.

State how this transaction should be recorded and disclosed.

Answer

If there is a share premium account in existence, the share issue may be recorded by increasing share capital by £100 and setting off the issue costs against share premium account. In the analysis of total shareholders' funds, the equity interests will have increased by £98.

If there is no share premium account, share capital will be increased by £100 but the issue costs would be deducted from another reserve (usually profit and loss account reserve) subject to the provisions of the company's articles. Prior to FRS 4, companies in this situation had to charge the issue costs to the P&L account. The equity interest within shareholders' funds also increases by £98 in this case.

(Source: *Capital Instruments: A Guide to FRS 4, Ernst & Young*)

1.24 As stated above, under FRS 4 the balance sheet should show the amount of **shareholders' funds attributable** to equity interests and the amount attributable to non-equity interests.

1.25 The **finance cost** of non-equity shares should be calculated on the same basis as for debt instruments. Dividends in respect of non-equity shares have to be accounted for on an accruals basis. The only exception is where there are insufficient distributable profits and the dividend rights are non-cumulative. Arrears of preference dividends must therefore be provided for rather than simply disclosed.

Warrants

1.26 Warrants should be included in shareholders' funds at the **net proceeds** of the issue. If the warrant **lapses unexercised**, the amount paid for it becomes a gain and should be taken to the STRGL. If the warrant is **exercised**, the shares issued should be recorded at the aggregate of the net proceeds received when the warrant was issued and the fair value of the consideration received on exercise less issue costs of the shares.

Scrip dividends

1.27 If **shares are issued in lieu of dividends**, the value of the shares issued, being equal to the value of the dividend payable, should be reflected in the P&L account as an appropriation of profit.

Disclosure: shares

1.28 The following disclosures should be made.

(a) **Analysis of shares** between equity and non-equity interests.

(b) The **rights of each class** of shares should be summarised detailing:

   (i) The rights to dividends

   (ii) The dates at which shares are redeemable and the amounts payable in respect of redemption

   (iii) Their priority and amounts receivable on a winding up

   (iv) Their voting rights

(c) Where **warrants or convertible debt** are in issue that may require the company to issue shares of a class not currently in issue the details in (b) above must be given.

(d) The **aggregate dividends** for each class of shares should be disclosed.

Minority interests

1.29 In consolidated financial statements, shares of subsidiary companies which are not owned by the group are accounted for as minority interests (either equity or non-equity). There is **one exception to this rule**. In some situations (for example where the parent or another group company has guaranteed their dividends or redemption), such shares become **liabilities** from the perspective of the group and therefore have to be reported as such on consolidation. For other capital instruments of a subsidiary, if the subsidiary has classified a capital instrument as debt, then the consolidated accounts will also do so.

UITF Abstract 11 *Capital instruments: issuer call options*

1.30 This abstract states that where a capital instrument includes a call option that can be exercised **only by the issuer**, the payment required on exercise of that option does not normally form part of the finance costs of the instrument in accordance with the requirement of FRS 4. Thus any gain or loss arising on repurchase or early settlement will reflect the amount payable on exercise.

Exam focus point

The examiner said that there is more emphasis on capital instruments in the new syllabus than in the old.

1.31 Section summary

FRS 4 is technically extremely complex. You should be able to discuss the main provisions of the standard.

- **Definitions**, particularly of capital instruments, debt, equity/non-equity shares and shareholders' funds
- **General disclosure**: shareholders' funds, minority interests and liabilities
- Accounting for **debt instruments**
- Accounting for **shares**
- **Minority interests**

2 TREATMENT OF CERTAIN CAPITAL INSTRUMENTS

2.1 The application notes of FRS 4 contain guidance on the treatment of **specific types** of capital instrument. The list is not exhaustive and each complex capital instrument must be assessed on its individual terms and features.

Auction Market Preferred Shares (AMPS)

2.2 AMPS are **preference shares** that are entitled to dividends determined in accordance with an auction process in which a panel of investors participates, the shares being transferred at a fixed price to the investor who will accept the lowest dividend. If the auction process fails, for example because no bids are received, the shares remain in the ownership of the former holder and the dividend is increased to a rate, known as the default rate, that is calculated in accordance with a prescribed formula.

Analysis and required accounting

2.3 As AMPS are shares, dividends cannot be paid in respect of them except out of distributable profits, nor can they be redeemed unless the redemption is financed out of distributable profits or by a fresh issue of shares. Because they are redeemable at a fixed amount and because the dividend rights are limited, AMPS constitute **non-equity shares**.

2.4 AMPS should be reported within shareholders' funds as non-equity shares and included in the amount attributable to non-equity shares. The **finance cost** for each period should be the dividend rights accruing in respect of the period.

Capital contributions

2.5 Capital contributions are sometimes made by a holding company to its wholly-owned subsidiary in order to provide the finance necessary for the subsidiary, where it is not desired that this should be by way of debt and there would be adverse consequences (for example, tax consequences) arising from a subscription for new shares. Whilst a capital contribution enhances the value of the holding company's investment in its subsidiary, there is no requirement for the subsidiary to bear any servicing cost, nor can it be required to repay the contribution.

Analysis and required accounting

2.6 From the standpoint of the subsidiary, a capital contribution does not contain an obligation to transfer economic benefits. In accordance with FRS 4 it should be reported within **shareholders' funds**. In the year in which the capital contribution is made, it should be reported in the reconciliation of movements in shareholders' funds.

Convertible capital bonds

2.7 The detailed provisions of convertible capital bonds vary but the following are typical. Convertible capital bonds are debt instruments on which interest is paid periodically, issued by a special purpose subsidiary incorporated outside the UK. Prior to maturity they my be exchanged for shares of the subsidiary which, at the option of the bondholder, are either immediately redeemed or immediately exchanged for ordinary shares of the parent. The bonds and payments in respect of the shares of the subsidiary are guaranteed by the parent. The parent has the right to issue convertible redeemable preference shares of its own in substitution for the bonds should it wish to do so.

Analysis and required accounting

2.8 From the standpoint of the **subsidiary**, convertible capital bonds are clearly debt since the obligation to pay interest is an obligation to transfer economic benefits. In addition, FRS 4

requires that conversion of debt should *not* be anticipated. In the subsidiary's financial statements the bonds should therefore be accounted for as **debt**.

2.9 From the standpoint of the **group** they are also **liabilities**. Even though the parent has the option to issue convertible preference shares in substitution for the bonds, the requirements of FRS 4 again entail that such conversion should *not* be anticipated. Whilst non-equity shares have a particular legal status that justifies their inclusion in shareholders' funds, this does not justify reporting within shareholders' funds an instrument that does not have that status and may never be converted into one that does.

2.10 Since the liabilities are convertible, the amount attributable to convertible capital bonds should be included in the amount of **convertible debt**, which should be stated separately from other liabilities.

Convertible debt with a premium put option

2.11 Convertible debt with a premium put option contains an option for the holder to demand redemption (either at the maturity of the debt or at some earlier date) for an amount that is in excess of the amount originally received for the debt. At the time the debt is issued, it is uncertain whether the debt will be converted before the redemption option my be exercised, and hence whether the premium on redemption will be paid.

Analysis and required accounting

2.12 The premium put option provides a higher guaranteed return to the holder of the debt that would be received on identical debt without such a put option. Often this higher return corresponds to that which the holder would have expected to receive on non-convertible debt. The holder's decision as to whether to exercise the option will depend on the relative values of the shares to which he would be entitled on conversion and the cash receivable, including the premium, on exercise of the option.

2.13 The term of convertible debt with a premium put option should be considered to end on the **earliest date** at which the holder has the option to require redemption. The **premium** payable on exercise of the premium put option should be included in the calculation of the finance costs for the debt.

On conversion, the proceeds of the shares issued should be deemed to be the carrying amount of the debt, including accrued premium, immediately prior to conversion.

Convertible debt with enhanced interest

2.14 As an alternative to the premium put structure discussed above, convertible debt may contain an undertaking that the interest will be increased at a date in the future. At the time the debt is issued, it is uncertain whether the debt will be converted before the enhanced interest is payable.

Analysis and required accounting

2.15 The enhanced rate of interest increases the guaranteed return to the holder. Often this higher return corresponds to that which the holder would have expected to receive on non-convertible debt. The holders' decision as to whether to convert the debt will take into account the interest forgone by such a decision.

2.16 The interest for the **full term** of the convertible debt should be taken into account in the allocation of finance costs, which should be allocated at a **constant rate**.

2.17 EXAMPLE: CONVERTIBLE DEBT WITH ENHANCED INTEREST

Convertible debt is issued on 1 January 2000 for £1,000 and is redeemable at the same amount on 31 December 2014. It carries interest of £59 a year (a nominal rate of 5.9%) for the first five years, after which the rate rises to £141 a year (a nominal rate of 14.1%).

2.18 The finance costs should be allocated to accounting periods at the rate of 10% a year. The movement on the carrying amount over the term of the debt would be as follows.

Year ending	*Balance at beginning of year*	*Finance costs for year (10%)*	*Cash paid during year*	*Balance at end of year*
	£	£	£	£
31.12.2000	1,000	100	(59)	1,041
31.12.2001	1,041	104	(59)	1,086
31.12.2002	1,086	109	(59)	1,136
31.12.2003	1,136	113	(59)	1,190
31.12.2004	1,190	119	(59)	1,250
31.12.2005	1,250	125	(141)	1,234
31.12.2006	1,234	124	(141)	1,217
31.12.2007	1,217	122	(141)	1,198
31.12.2008	1,198	120	(141)	1,177
31.12.2009	1,177	118	(141)	1,154
31.12.2010	1,154	116	(141)	1,129
31.12.2011	1,129	113	(141)	1,101
31.12.2012	1,101	110	(141)	1,070
31.12.2013	1,070	107	(141)	1,036
31.12.2014	1,036	105*	(141 + 1,000)	-

* Increased by £1 rounding difference.

Debt issued with warrants

2.19 Debt is sometimes issued with warrants. The issue is often made for the par value of the debt and the debt will be redeemed at the same amount. The warrants and the debts are capable of being transferred separately.

Analysis and required accounting

2.20 The proceeds of the issue should be allocated between the **debt** and the **warrants**. As a result, the amount of the proceeds deemed to relate to the debt will be less than par value. The discount on issue should be treated as **finance costs** and apportioned to accounting periods so that the total finance costs on the debt will have a constant relationship to the outstanding obligation.

2.21 Accounting for warrants is discussed above in Section 1.26.

2.22 EXAMPLE: DEBT ISSUED WITH WARRANTS

Debt and warrants are issued together for £1,250. The debt is redeemable at the same amount. The term of the debt is five years from 1 January 2000 and it carries interest at 4.7% (£59 a year). It is determined (for example by reference to the market values for the

debt and the warrants immediately after issue) that the fair value of the debt and the warrants are respectively £1,000 and £250.

2.23 The debt would initially be recognised at £1,000. The finance cost of the debt is the difference between the payments required by the debt which total £1,545 ((5 × £59) + £1,250) and the deemed proceeds of £1,000, that is £545. In order to allocate these costs over the term of the debt at a constant rate on the carrying amount they must be allocated at the rate of 10%. The movements on the carrying amount of the debt over its term would be as follows.

Year ending	*Balance at beginning of year*	*Finance costs for year (10%)*	*Cash paid during year*	*Balance at end of year*
	£	£	£	£
31.12.2000	1,000	100	(59)	1,041
31.12.2001	1,041	104	(59)	1,086
31.12.2002	1,086	109	(59)	1,136
31.12.2003	1,136	113	(59)	1,190
31.12.2004	1,190	119	(1,250 + 59)	-

Deep discount bonds

2.24 Deep discount bonds are bonds that carry a low nominal rate of interest and accordingly are issued at a discount to the value at which they will be redeemed. In the extreme case where no interest at all is payable they are sometimes referred to as **zero coupon bonds**.

Analysis and required accounting

2.25 The cost to the borrower of issuing a deep discount bond comprises the discount on issue as well as any interest payments. It is clear that deep discount bonds represent **liabilities** of the issuer since they contain an obligation to make cash payments. The **finance costs** will constitute the difference between the net proceeds and the total payments that the issuer may be required to make in respect of the instrument and will be allocated to periods at a constant rate on the carrying amount, with the result that the carrying amount of the bond immediately prior to redemption will equate to the amount at which it is to be redeemed. The discount should *not* be treated as an asset.

2.26 The example shown above under debt issued with warrants illustrates the accounting treatment of a deep discount bond.

Income bonds

2.27 The distinctive feature of income bonds is that interest is payable only in the event that the issuer has sufficient reported profits (after allowing for interest on other kinds of debt) to make the payment. If profits are insufficient the issuer is not in default and no additional rights accrue to the holder of the bond, although interest payments may be redeemed by the issuer at a fixed amount on a specific date.

Analysis and required accounting

2.28 The requirement to redeem the bonds is an obligation to transfer economic benefits. The bonds must therefore be accounted for as a **liability**.

Index linked loans

2.29 Sometimes loan agreements do not state a specific amount for the payments: instead they include a formula to be used for their calculation. For example, in the case of floating rate loans, the amount of periodic payments of interest will be calculated by reference to a basic rate, eg LIBOR + 2%. Another example is that of index linked loans which may be redeemable at the principal amount multiplied by an index.

Analysis and required accounting

2.30 **Finance costs** contingent on uncertain events such as changes in an index should be adjusted to reflect those events only once they have occurred. The effect is that the initial carrying amount will take no account of those events but the carrying amount at each subsequent balance sheet date will be recalculated to take account of the changes occurring in that reporting period. The resulting change in carrying amount is accounted for as an increase or decrease in finance costs for the period.

2.31 EXAMPLE: INDEX LINKED LOAN

A loan of £1,250 is issued on 1 January 2000 on which interest of 4% (£50) is paid annually and the principal amount is repayable based on an index. The balance at the end of each year is found by multiplying the original principal amount by the index at the end of the year: the change in the amount is treated as additional finance costs.

Year ending	*Balance at beginning of year*	*Finance costs for year (10%)*	*Cash paid during year*	*Balance at end of year*	*Index at end of year*
	£	£	£	£	
31.12.2000	1,250	125	(50)	1,325	106
31.12.2001	1,325	100	(50)	1,375	110
31.12.2002	1,375	75	(50)	1,400	112
31.12.2003	1,400	150	(50)	1,500	120
31.12.2004	1,500	175	(1,625 + 50)	-	130

Limited recourse debt

Features

2.32 Sometimes debt is raised on terms that the lender's recourse is limited. Although the borrower is expected to meet the obligations of the debt out of his general resources, in the event of default the lender can obtain repayment only by enforcing his rights against the particular security that is identified in the loan agreement. If the proceeds of the security are insufficient to repay the loan, the lender must bear the loss and has no further rights against the borrower.

Analysis and required accounting

2.33 Limited recourse debt constitutes an obligation on the part of the borrower to repay, and hence should be accounted for as a ***liability***. The borrower will normally have all the benefits of the security (including the right to receive the sale proceeds) and will have to meet the obligation to repay the debt in order to preserve these rights. If the security declines in value the borrower may be able to elect to hand it over to the lender and thus avoid any further liability in respect of the debt. However, such an eventuality would be unusual, and therefore should not be reflected in the accounting until the asset is transferred.

2.34 Limited recourse debt is one of the kinds of debt envisaged in FRS 4 in that its **legal nature** differs from that usually associated with debt. A brief description of its nature should be given.

Participating preference shares

2.35 Participating preference shares are similar to other familiar kinds of preference shares except that they are entitled, in addition to a fixed dividend for each accounting period, to a proportion of the dividends paid on equity shares.

Analysis and required accounting

2.36 Because participating preference shares contain an entitlement to share in profits that is of a restricted amount and has priority over the other classes of shares, they are *non*-**equity shares** and their interest in **shareholders' funds** should be presented in the balance sheet within the aggregate amount attributable to non-equity shares. The fixed and participating elements of the dividend will be disclosed separately.

Perpetual debt

2.37 Perpetual debt is debt in respect of which the issuer has neither the right nor the obligation to repay the principal amount of the debt. Usually, interest is paid at a constant rate, or at a fixed margin over a benchmark rate such as LIBOR.

Analysis and required accounting

2.38 Sometimes it is suggested that as the principal amount will never be repaid there is no need for the balance sheet to reflect a liability in respect of the debt. However, the obligation to pay interest is an obligation to transfer economic benefits and hence the instrument is a **liability**. As there are no repayments of principal the burden of this liability never diminishes.

2.39 FRS 4 is based on the principle that debt should be accounted for having regard to all the payments required by the debt, irrespective of their legal description, in the determination of the appropriate finance charge and capital repayment for each accounting period. In the case of perpetual debt where interest is paid at a constant rate, or at a fixed margin over a benchmark, the correct **finance charge** will be equal to the coupon payable for each period. Hence no part of the repayments will reduce the carrying amount of net proceeds.

Repackaged perpetual debt

2.40 Sometimes perpetual debt is issued that carries interest at a relatively high rate for a number of years ('the primary period'), and then bears no further interest, or only a nominal amount. As the debt cannot be required to be redeemed, its value after the primary period has expired is negligible and, in practice, there will usually be arrangements to transfer it to a party friendly to the issuer or to enable the issuer to elect, in effect, to redeem the debt for a token amount.

Analysis and required accounting

2.41 The substance of such an arrangement is that the debt is repaid over the primary period. The payments required by the debt should be apportioned between a finance charge for each accounting period and the effective reduction of the principal amount. It would be necessary to make full disclosure of the arrangement in the financial statements.

2.42 The **finance costs** of the debt will be the difference between the net proceeds and the payments which the issuer is required to make. This will be allocated to periods over the primary period at a constant rate on the carrying amount.

2.43 EXAMPLE: REPACKAGED PERPETUAL DEBT

On 1 January 2004 a company borrows £1,250 which is stated to be irredeemable and to carry interest of 16.275% for the first ten years after which no further payments are required. The annual payments would be £203. The substance of the arrangement is that the ten payments of £203 would repay the amount borrowed and the finance charge would be allocated using a rate of 10 per cent. The accounting would be as follows.

Year ending	*Balance at beginning of year*	*Finance costs for year (10%)*	*Cash paid during year*	*Balance at end of year*
	£	£	£	£
31.12.2004	1,250	125	(203)	1,172
31.12.2005	1,172	117	(203)	1,086
31.12.2006	1,086	108	(203)	991
31.12.2007	991	99	(203)	887
31.12.2008	887	88	(203)	772
31.12.2009	772	77	(203)	646
31.12.2010	646	64	(203)	507
31.12.2011	507	50	(203)	354
31.12.2012	354	35	(203)	186
31.12.2013	186	17*	(203)	-

* Reduced by £1 rounding difference.

Stepped interest bonds

2.44 The stated rate of interest payable in respect of stepped interest bonds increases progressively over the period of issue.

Analysis and required accounting

2.45 In the case of stepped interest bonds, the stated rate of interest for each accounting period does not reflect the true economic cost of borrowing in any period during the time the bond is outstanding, since low rates of interest in one period are compensated for by higher rates in another.

2.46 The pattern of the interest payments does not affect the **allocation of finance costs**. The payments required by the debt should be apportioned between a finance charge for each accounting period at a constant rate on the outstanding obligation and a reduction of the carrying amount. The effect of this accounting on a stepped interest bond is that the overall effective interest cost will be charged in each accounting period: an accrual will be made in addition to the cash payments in earlier periods and will reverse, partially offsetting the higher cash payments, in later periods. It would be necessary to make full disclosure of the arrangement in the financial statements.

2.47 EXAMPLE: STEPPED INTEREST BOND

A loan of £1,250 is entered into on 1 January 2004 under which interest is payable according to the following schedule.

Year ending	*Rates of interest (as a % nominal amount)*	*Interest paid*
		£
31.12.2004	6.0	75
31.12.2005	8.0	100
31.12.2006	10.0	125
31.12.2007	12.0	150
31.12.2008	16.4	205

2.48 The overall effective rate can be found to be 10%. The movement on the loan over its period in issue would be as follows.

Year ending	*Balance at beginning of year*	*Finance costs for year (10%)*	*Cash paid during year*	*Balance at end of year*
	£	£	£	£
31.12.2004	1,250	125	(75)	1,300
31.12.2005	1,300	130	(100)	1,330
31.12.2006	1,330	133	(125)	1,338
31.12.2007	1,338	134	(150)	1,322
31.12.2008	1,322	133	(1,250 + 205)	-

Subordinated debt

2.49 Subordinated debt is debt under which the rights of the lender are not as great as those of other creditors of the issuer. The methods of subordination vary widely. One method of subordination is a prohibition on repayment of the debt whilst other creditors remain unpaid.

Analysis and required accounting

2.50 Irrespective of the means of subordination that is used, the lender on subordinated terms does not forgo the right to be repaid: he simply accepts that under certain conditions repayment will be postponed. It follows that, despite the subordination, the company has an obligation to repay (that it, an obligation to transfer economic benefits) and therefore subordinated debt should be accounted for as a **liability**.

2.51 Subordinated debt is one of the kinds of debt envisaged in FRS 4 in that its **legal nature** differs from that usually associated with debt. A brief description of its nature should be given.

UITF Abstract 33 Obligations in capital instruments

2.52 The Abstract was issued in February 2002. It addresses in particular the presentation of certain complex instruments that are not shares but contain obligations that the issuer can choose to settle by paying cash or by issuing equity shares. The Abstract sets out circumstances where the substance of such instruments requires them to be treated as liabilities rather than as shareholders' funds; these include cases where the issuer may issue shares to the value of a specified amount.

2.53 Section summary

There is no need for you to learn all the descriptions and treatments given above. They are provided only as illustrations of the more common types of capital investments. You should read about each type carefully and try to understand *why* the relevant treatments are required in relation to the analysis given of FRS 4 in the previous section.

Exam focus point

Remember that, in an exam, you should judge each instrument on its individual terms.

3 DERIVATIVES: MEASUREMENT AND HEDGE ISSUES

3.1 Derivatives present problems worldwide for users and preparers of financial statements. In July 1996 the ASB produced a discussion paper on the subject: *Derivatives and other financial instruments*. The paper deals with two main groups of issues.

(a) **Measurement and hedge accounting issues:** the ASB expects it will be several years before a standard is produced.

(b) **Disclosure**: the ASB feels there is an urgent need for improvement here, and in fact FRS 13 has already been produced which supersedes this part of the paper (see Section 4).

3.2 Do not get too worried about what 'derivatives' are: as we will see in Section 4 they are simply defined as financial instruments that derive their value from the price or rate of some underlying item(s), eg the interest rate of some debt. If you read the *Financial Times* or an equivalent paper or journal regularly, you may already know about derivatives.

Reasons for the project

3.3 The ASB gives four main reasons why this project was considered necessary.

(a) The **significant growth of financial instruments** over recent years has outstripped the development of guidance for their accounting (there is no UK accounting standard which covers derivatives).

(b) The topic is of **international concern**; other national standard-setters and the IASC are involved.

(c) There have been recent **high-profile disasters** involving derivatives (eg Barings) which, while not caused by accounting failures, have raised questions about accounting and disclosure practices.

(d) **Comments received** as both FRS 4 and FRS 5 were developed showed the need for a wider project on financial instruments.

Scope of project

3.4 What are **financial instruments**? Examples are forward contracts, futures, swaps and options. The ASB will produce an all-encompassing definition of financial instruments in terms of contracts for cash flows (ie monetary assets and liabilities) and equity instruments. This general definition will thereby capture newly devised instruments, without the need for constant updating.

3.5 Certain items which meet this definition will, however, be **excluded**.

(a) Operating leases
(b) Pensions and other post-retirement benefits
(c) Shares in subsidiaries/associates
(d) Obligations to employees under employee share schemes
(e) The reporting entity's own equity shares and warrants/options on them

Measurement

3.6 At present, financial instruments are measured on a **variety of different bases**. Although historical cost is the most widely used basis, some use is made of current value. For example:

(a) instruments held for **trading purposes** are commonly measured at market value;

(b) monetary assets and liabilities denominated in a **foreign currency** are translated at the rate of exchange at the balance sheet date;

(c) **current asset investments** are valued at the lower of cost and net realisable value; and

(d) **fixed asset investments** are written down to reflect any permanent diminution in value.

This mixed measurement basis complicates the picture given by the accounts. It also gives rise to a need for hedge accounting (see below) which involves many conceptual and practical difficulties.

3.7 There is also concern that the most widely used basis, **historical cost**, is not suitable for all financial instruments. In general, with historical cost, only the initial outlay on an instrument is recorded in the accounts until such time as the instrument is realised by sale or payment of a cash flow. **Unrealised gains and losses** resulting from changes in value in the interim are ignored. In brief, this gives rise to the following difficulties.

(a) Using realisation as the trigger for reporting gains and losses means that reported profits do not reflect the **events of the year** in question. Unrealised gains and losses, which are not recognised, may be overlooked. In addition, companies can manage reported profits by 'cherry picking' which gains and losses to realise.

(b) **Active risk management** is not adequately reflected by historical cost.

(c) Derivatives whose **cost is nil** are not recorded in the balance sheet at all under a historical cost system, even though they may represent substantial assets or liabilities of the company and expose it to significant risks.

(d) Using historical costs impairs the ability of users to **compare** one company with another. Different amounts may be recorded in both the P&L account and the balance sheet for identical instruments that were acquired at different times. This is a particular problem given that the values of financial instruments can change rapidly and by large amounts.

(e) Using historical cost gives rise to a need for **hedge accounting** to correct the anomaly that results where risk on an instrument that is measured at cost is mitigated by an instrument that is measured at current value.

Rejected measurement proposals

3.8 As a result, the ASB has decided that current measurement practices are inadequate. Before we look at the recommendations on measurement, a brief mention should be given to several potential **halfway house** approaches considered by the ASB. Under these, some instruments would be measured at cost and some at current value, depending on various suggested distinctions.

(a) Distinction based on **kind of entity:** 'simple' company at cost vs 'sophisticated' company at current value

(b) Distinction based on **management intent**: to hold to maturity or to hedge at cost vs to trade at current value

(c) Distinction based on whether the instrument is a **derivative:** derivatives at current value vs non-derivatives at cost

(d) Distinction based on whether the instrument is **either a derivative** or is **hedged by a derivative:** use current value for all of these, but other instruments at cost

3.9 These approaches were all **rejected** for a variety of reasons, including lack of comparability, changes in management intention, hampering the way companies manage risk and so on.

ASB's measurement proposals

3.10 The ASB's conclusion is that none of the above approaches is viable in the long term. In the light of the recent growth of derivatives, the trend for companies to manage risk actively on a portfolio basis and the ease with which gains and losses on financial instruments can be realised, the ASB believes that all financial instruments have to be measured at **current value** with all **gains and losses recognised** as they occur.

It would be inappropriate, however, for all gains and losses to be reported in the P&L account, for two main reasons.

(a) Some gains and losses, such as those on fixed rate borrowings, are clearly of a **different nature** from the results generated by the entity's ongoing operations and it seems right that they should be reported separately.

(b) For **borrowings**, this might be thought to imply that fixed rate borrowings are 'risky' (since their value varies with interest movements) and floating rate borrowings are 'risk-free' (since their value does not vary with interest rate movements). At least for a non-financial institution, this is not always the case.

3.11 The ASB therefore (tentatively) favours an approach whereby all financial instruments are **measured at current value**, but some changes in value are reported in the P&L account and others in the statement of total recognised gains and losses (STRGL). In particular, the **STRGL** should report gains and losses, both realised and unrealised, on:

(a) fixed rate borrowings;

(b) interest rate derivatives used to manage the interest basis of borrowings; and

(c) currency borrowings and currency derivatives where these are used to manage the currency translation risk of a group's investments in overseas operations (currency gains and losses on the investments themselves and any associated borrowings are already reported in the STRGL under SSAP 20: it therefore seems right that the effects of any derivatives that mitigate these gains and losses should also be shown in the STRGL).

3.12 In addition, the P&L account should continue to report an **interest expense** calculated in accordance with FRS 4 (namely, at an effective yield to maturity calculated on a historical cost basis). This has the effect that, provided a fixed rate borrowing is held to maturity, any changes in its value arising from interest rate movements that are initially recorded in the STRGL would reverse out in later years, also in the STRGL.

3.13 These proposals would only be applied to **listed and similar public interest companies**.

Hedge accounting

3.14 Entities often acquire derivatives to mitigate or 'hedge' the risks arising from other assets and liabilities. The practice of hedge accounting has grown up whereby gains and losses on an instrument that is classed as a 'hedge' are **deferred** so that they can be included in the P&L account in the same period(s) as those on the 'hedged position'.

3.15 The **three kinds of situation** where hedge accounting is used are as follows.

(a) Measurement anomalies
(b) Recognition anomalies
(c) Uncontracted future transactions: existence differences

These matters should be familiar from your financial management studies.

3.16 The **problems** perceived with hedge accounting are as follows.

(a) As entities have become more sophisticated in their approach to risk management, hedge accounting has become more **difficult to implement**; risks are aggregated and managed on a portfolio basis, so there is no one-to-one linkage of a 'hedge' to a 'hedged position'.

(b) Given the advent of sophisticated active risk management, the **dividing line** between hedging (for which gains and losses are deferred) and trading (for which gains and losses are recognised as they occur) is increasingly difficult to draw.

(c) The accounts are **less easy to understand** if hedge accounting is used since it gives rise to debits and credits in the balance sheet that are not assets and liabilities (but losses and gains).

(d) The classification of a derivative as a hedge is based on **management intent**.

(e) Use of hedge accounting has traditionally depended on the hedge reducing risk. However **risk** is a term whose meaning is not agreed.

(i) Risk could be seen as the chance of both gain and loss or as merely the chance of loss.

(ii) Risk could be seen as exposure to changes in cash flows or as exposure to changes in market values.

(iii) Does there need to be a reduction of risk or merely a change in risk to achieve a desired risk profile that may or may not reduce risk?

ASB's proposals on hedging

3.17 If the ASB proposals on measurement of all financial instruments at current value are adopted then the need for hedge accounting would be reduced as many of the measurement anomalies would cease to exist. On the question of whether hedge accounting should be

used and, if it is, what criteria should be met for its use, the **ASB is split in three**, expressing in turn these views.

(a) **No hedge accounting** should be used (exception to the normal accounting rules is not justified).

(b) **Hedge accounting is permitted** only where it corrects measurement and recognition anomalies (ie for assets and liabilities measured at cost and for firm contracts).

(c) **Hedge accounting can be used** as in (b), but also for hedges of some uncontracted future transactions (ie uncontracted sales and purchases, but the entity must be 'commercially committed').

3.18 If some hedge accounting is allowed, there are four options given as to how it should be achieved.

(a) Leave the **hedge at cost** (present practice).

(b) Measure the hedge at **current value** in the balance sheet and take the resulting gain or loss to **equity** (against the spirit of FRS 3).

(c) Measure the hedge at **current value** in the balance sheet and record the resulting gain/loss within **liabilities/assets** respectively.

(d) Measure the hedge at current value in the balance sheet and put the resulting gain or loss to the **STRGL**. The gain or loss would then be 'recycled' (ie transferred) from the STRGL to the P&L account in a later period when the hedged transactions occurs.

In the Discussion Paper, the ASB favours (c) or (d) or a combination of the two. However, it now proposes to adopt the international rules (see Section 4 on FRED 23).

3.19 Section summary

All these matters are a long way from becoming a standard, but the issue of disclosure has gone further, resulting in FRS 13, discussed in the next section. For **measurement and hedging** issues, the following points are important.

- A standard is needed because of the huge growth in the **use and complexity** of financial instruments.
- Different **measurement bases** are currently used for different instruments/intentions.
- **Historical cost** is not always appropriate because of **unrealised gains and losses**.
- ASB measurement proposals: **current value**, with gains/losses taken to the **STRGL**.
- **Hedge accounting** creates many problems.

4 FRED 23 FINANCIAL INSTRUMENTS: HEDGE ACCOUNTING

4.1 Entities often enter into transactions to **mitigate or 'hedge' the risks** arising from assets, liabilities and other exposures that they have. To account for such transactions, the practice has grown up whereby gains and losses on the hedging instrument are deferred so that they can be included in the profit and loss account in the same period (or periods) as those on the hedged item. This practice is known as **hedge accounting**. FRED 23 *Financial instruments: hedge accounting* was published in May 2002. It sets out proposed restrictions on the use of hedge accounting. The proposal is that an accounting standard based on the FRED should come into effect for financial statements ending on or after a date in early 2003.

Main points

4.2 The FRED's proposals focus exclusively on the use of hedge accounting to account for financial instruments. Not all hedging instruments are financial instruments and not all hedged risks arise from financial instruments, so only some types of hedge accounting are covered by the FRED.

4.3 The view of the ASB on **hedge accounting** is that its use **should be restricted**. However, to date it has not issued a standard on hedge accounting because the wider project on financial instruments is still underway.

4.4 IAS 39 *Financial instruments: recognition and measurement* is an interim standard, and is undergoing revision. However, it is becoming increasingly likely that the measurement model set out in IAS 39 will be adopted. As a result, the ASB believes that it is now appropriate, in the interests of convergence, to develop a standard on hedge accounting.

4.5 The FRED allows hedge accounting only when certain **conditions** are met.

(a) The hedging relationship is **clearly defined**.
(b) The hedging relationship is **measurable**.
(c) The hedge is **effective**.

4.6 This approach accords with the approach in IAS 39, and, as far as possible, the same wording is used. However, IAS 39 contains more detailed requirements and hedge accounting techniques. The proposed UK standard contains only those requirements necessary to implement the main principles described in Paragraph 4.5.

Why do we need an accounting standard on hedge accounting for financial instruments?

4.7 The use of hedge accounting can have a significant effect on an entity's reported financial performance and financial position. However, there are **few explicit restrictions** in existing UK accounting literature on the use of hedge accounting. An FRS on hedge accounting will **fill a gap that might otherwise appear in UK accounting literature**, when SSAP 20, which contains requirements on hedges of net investments in foreign operations, is replaced by a new standard (currently FRED 24) which does not.

4.8 Another important factor is **convergence** (see Chapter 13). EU Ministers have proposed that, from 1 January 2005, all listed companies in the EU should prepare their consolidated financial statements in accordance with adopted international accounting standards. The ASB is pursuing a programme of work to align UK accounting standards with IFRSs wherever practicable. The ASB is proposing to do this in the main by means of a phased replacement of existing UK standards with new UK standards based on the equivalent IFRSs. The FRED's proposals if implemented would be part of this process because, as explained below, much of the **material** in the proposed standard is **drawn from IAS 39** *Financial instruments: recognition and measurement.*

Objective of the proposed FRS

4.9 The objective of FRED 23 is to ensure that **hedge accounting is used only when it is appropriate** to do so. In summary, it does that by specifying that:

(a) If hedge accounting is to be used, the relationship between the hedging instrument and the hedged item should have been **designated as a hedge** at the **outset**.

(b) The hedge needs to meet certain **hedge effectiveness criteria**.

KEY TERMS

Hedge: A contract (the hedging instrument) that individually, or with other contracts, has a value or cash flow that is expected, wholly or partly, to move inversely with changes in the value of or cash flows arising from another contract or other exposure (the hedged item).

Hedge accounting: An accounting treatment that alters the accounting that would otherwise apply so that gains and losses on the hedging instrument are recognised in the same performance statement (in other words, the profit and loss account or statement of total recognised gains and losses as appropriate) and in the same period(s) as offsetting gains and losses on the hedged item.

Hedge effectiveness: The degree to which offsetting changes in fair value or cash flows attributable to a hedged risk are achieved by the hedging instrument.

4.10 EXAMPLES: HEDGING RELATIONSHIP

In the following cases there is no hedging relationship. (Assume historical cost is being used.)

(a) If a derivative acquired at no cost moves into a loss position (or the market value of a financial instrument carried at cost falls below that cost), that position would be reflected immediately in the financial statements by recognising a loss in the current period's performance statement (usually the profit and loss account).

(b) If a financial instrument is sold, the gain or loss arising on the sale would be recognised immediately in the current period's performance statement (usually the profit and loss account).

(c) If a non-financial asset is being bought for an amount expressed in a currency other than the reporting entity's local or functional currency, that asset, when acquired, would be recognised initially in the entity's balance sheet at an amount that is equal to the purchase price converted at the rate of exchange on the date on which the asset was acquired (or, if a rate was specified in the purchase contract, at that contract rate).

How would the accounting change if a hedging relationship is involved?

4.11 SOLUTION

When a hedging relationship is involved, this accounting may be varied so that gains and losses on the hedging instrument are recognised in the same performance statement and in the same period(s) as offsetting gains and losses on the hedged item.

(a) If the derivative is being held as a hedging instrument the entity might defer recognition in the performance statements of the loss on the derivative until the offsetting gain on the hedged item is recognised.

(b) Assuming the derivative sold was held as a hedging instrument in an ongoing hedge, the hedge accounting technique adopted might involve deferring the recognition in the

performance statements of the realised gain or loss on the derivative until the offsetting losses and gains on the hedged item are recognised.

(c) If the entity entered into a forward foreign exchange purchase agreement to hedge the currency exposure on the asset's purchase contract, the hedge accounting technique used might involve converting the foreign currency purchase price of the asset at the exchange rate inherent in the forward foreign exchange purchase agreement.

Scope

4.12 The proposed FRS would apply to all financial statements that are intended to give a true and fair view of a reporting entity's financial position and profit or loss (or income and expenditure) for a period, except for reporting entities applying the FRSSE.

Hedge accounting criteria

4.13 A financial instrument qualifies for hedge accounting if, and only if, it is held as a hedging instrument in a hedge that meets:

(a) The **hedging relationship criteria** (including the pre-designation criterion)
(b) The **hedge effectiveness criteria**

Hedging relationship criteria

4.14 The hedging relationship criteria that must be met are as follows.

(a) At the inception of the hedge there is **formal documentation of the hedging relationship and the entity's risk management objective and strategy for undertaking the hedge**. That documentation should include **identification** of the **hedging instrument**, the related **hedged item**, the **nature of the risk** being hedged, and **how the entity will assess the hedging instrument's effectiveness** in offsetting the exposure to changes in the hedged item's fair value or cash flows that is attributable to the hedged risk.

(b) The **effectiveness** of the hedge can be **reliably measured**, that is, the fair value or cash flows of the hedged item and the fair value or cash flows of the hedging instrument can be reliably measured.

(c) If a **forecast transaction** is being hedged, it must be **highly probable** and must present an exposure to variations in cash flows that could ultimately affect reported net profit or loss.

4.15 It is not necessary for the whole of the financial instrument that is the hedging instrument to have hedging benefits; it is acceptable for just a portion of an instrument to be a hedging instrument or for the instrument to hedge just a portion of a hedged item. **Different portions of an instrument can be designated as hedges of different exposures.**

4.16 Essentially, it is not the nature of the hedging 'instrument' or hedged 'item' that is important so much as whether the pre-designation and effectiveness criteria set out in FRED 23 are met.

Hedge effectiveness criteria

4.17 The following hedge effectiveness criteria need to be met.

(a) The hedge was **expected at the outset to be highly effective** in achieving offsetting changes in fair value or cash flows attributable to the hedged item, consistent with the originally documented risk management strategy for that particular hedging relationship.

(b) The hedge has, since its commencement, been assessed on an ongoing basis and **determined actually to have been highly effective** throughout the financial reporting period.

4.18 How do we determine whether a hedge is highly effective? We apply the following test.

(a) At inception and throughout the life of the hedge, the entity can expect **changes** in the fair value or cash flows of the **hedged item** to be almost fully **offset** by the **changes** in the fair value or cash flows of the **hedging instrument**.

(b) Actual results are within a **range of 80 per cent to 125 per cent**.

4.19 EXAMPLE: HEDGE EFFECTIVENESS

The loss on a hedging instrument is 120 and the gain on the hedged instrument is 100. Offset can be measured by 120/100, which is 120 per cent, or by 100/120, which is 80 per cent. The entity will conclude that the hedge is highly effective.

4.20 An entity may adopt different methods for assessing the effectiveness of different types of hedges.

4.21 If the principal terms of the hedging instrument and of the entire hedged item are the same, the changes in fair value and cash flows attributable to the risk being hedged are offset fully, both when the hedge is entered into and thereafter until completion. For instance, an interest rate swap is likely to be an effective hedge if the notional and principal amounts, term, repricing dates, dates of interest and principal receipts and payments, and basis for measuring interest rates are the same for the hedging instrument and the hedged item.

4.22 On the other hand, sometimes the hedging instrument will offset the hedged risk only partially. For instance, a hedge would not be fully effective if the hedging instrument and hedged item are denominated in different currencies and the two do not move in tandem. Also, a hedge of interest rate risk using a derivative would not be fully effective if part of the change in the fair value of the derivative is due to the counterparty's credit risk.

4.23 It is not enough for the hedge to relate to overall entity business risk. It must relate to a specific identified and designated risk. **Ultimately it must affect the entity's net profit or loss.**

4.24 FRED 23 **does not specify a single method** for assessing the effectiveness of a hedge. An entity must document its hedging strategy and include within that documentation its procedures for assessing effectiveness. The time value of money will generally need to be considered.

Accounting for hedges

4.25 Hedge accounting can take different forms, and in general **FRED 23 does not require or prohibit the adoption of any particular form of hedge accounting**. However, the FRED

does stipulate that if a hedge accounting technique is adopted, that technique should meet the following **requirements**.

(a) For a hedge of a **net investment in a foreign operation**:

   (i) The **portion** of the gain or loss on the hedging instrument that is determined to be an **effective hedge** should be **recognised immediately in the statement of total recognised gains and losses** and should thereafter be treated in the same way as gains and losses on the hedged item.

   (ii) The **ineffective portion** should be **reported immediately in the profit and loss account.**

(b) If a hedge of something **other than a net investment in a foreign operation** is involved, any **ineffective portion** of the gain or loss on the hedging instrument that would have been recognised had hedge accounting not been adopted should be **recognised immediately in the profit and loss account**.

4.26 If, and only if, a hedge no longer meets the hedging relationship criteria and the hedge effectiveness criteria, a hedging instrument will then **cease to qualify for hedge accounting**. In such circumstances, or if the hedging instrument expires or is sold terminated or exercised, hedge accounting should be **discontinued prospectively**.

(a) If hedge accounting has been discontinued because a forecast transaction that was being hedged is no longer expected to occur, the net cumulative gain or loss on the hedging instrument that has not to date been recognised in the profit and loss account should be recognised in the profit and loss account immediately.

(b) If hedge accounting has been discontinued for a reason other than the one described in (a), the net cumulative gain or loss on the hedging instrument that has not to date been recognised in the profit and loss account (or statement of total recognised gains and losses if appropriate) should be recognised in the profit and loss account (or statement of total recognised gains and losses if appropriate) so as to offset the gains and losses arising on the hedged item.

5 FRS 13 DERIVATIVES AND OTHER FINANCIAL INSTRUMENTS: DISCLOSURES 12/01

5.1 FRS 13 appeared in September 1998. Although the measurement and hedging issues discussed above will take a long time to resolve, the disclosure of derivatives and other financial instruments is much less controversial.

Objectives

5.2 The objective of FRS 13 is to ensure that reporting entities falling within its scope provide in their financial statements disclosure necessary to enable users to assess:

(a) the **risk profile** of the entity for each of the main risks that arise in connection with financial instruments, commodity contracts with similar characteristics; and

(b) the **significance** of such instruments and contracts, regardless of whether they are on balance sheet (recognised) or off balance sheet (unrecognised), to an entity's reported financial position, performance and cash flows.

Scope

5.3 FRS 13 applies to an entity that:

(a) has any of its capital instruments **listed** or **publicly traded** on a stock exchange or market; and

(b) prepares financial statements that are intended to give a true and fair view of the entity's financial position and profit or loss (or income and expenditure) for a period.

5.4 The FRS is in three parts:

(a) **Reporting entities other than financial institutions** and financial institution groups
(b) **Banks,** banking groups and similar institutions
(c) **Other financial institutions** and financial institution groups

We will concentrate on Part (a) as this is more relevant to your syllabus.

5.5 There are various **exclusions** encompassing all interests in group companies (except where held exclusively for resale) pensions, share options, obligations under operating leases (see SSAP 21), insurance contracts, equity shares and warrants and options on equity shares issued by the entity.

Definitions

5.6 The following important definitions are given in FRS 13 (among others).

KEY TERMS

- **Borrowings**: an entity's borrowings are its debt (as defined in FRS 4) together with its obligations under finance leases (as defined in SSAP 21).
- **Capital instruments**: defined as in FRS 4.
- **Derivative financial instrument**: a financial instrument that derives its value from the price or rate of some underlying item.
- **Equity instrument:** any instrument that evidences an ownership interest in an entity, ie a residual interest in the assets of the entity after deducting all of its liabilities.
- **Fair value:** The amount at which an asset or liability could be exchanged in an arm's length transaction between informed and willing parties, other than in a forced or liquidation sale.
- **Financial asset**: any asset that is:

  (a) cash;

  (b) a contractual right to receive cash or another financial asset from another entity;

  (c) a contractual right to exchange financial instruments with another entity under conditions that are potentially favourable; or

  (d) an equity instrument of another entity.
- **Financial instrument**: a financial instrument is any contract that gives rise to both a financial asset of one entity and a financial liability or equity instrument of another entity.

KEY TERMS (CONT'D)

- **Financial liability**: any liability that is a contractual obligation:

  (a) to deliver cash or another financial asset to another entity; or

  (b) to exchange financial instruments with another entity under conditions that are potentially unfavourable.

- **Functional currency**: the currency of the primary economic environment in which an entity operates and generates net cash flows.

- **Short term debtors and creditors**: Financial assets and liabilities which meet all the following criteria.

  (a) They would be included under one of the following balance sheet headings if the entity was preparing its financial statements in accordance with Schedule 4 to the Companies Act 1985:

    (i) debtors;

    (ii) prepayments and accrued income;

    (iii) creditors: amounts falling due within one year, other than items that would be included under the 'debenture loans' and 'bank loans and overdrafts' subheadings;

    (iv) provisions for liabilities and charges; or

    (v) accruals and deferred income.

  (b) They mature or become payable within 12 months of the balance sheet date.

  (c) They are not a derivative financial instrument.

- **Trading in financial assets and financial liabilities**: Buying, selling, issuing or holding financial assets and financial liabilities in order to take advantage of short-term changes in market prices or rates or, in the case of financial institutions and financial institution groups, in order to facilitate customer transactions.

(FRS 13)

Instruments to be dealt with in the disclosures

5.7 The FRS applies to all financial assets and financial liabilities, except those mentioned in Paragraph 4.5 above. Note also:

(a) Short-term debtors and creditors - **either all** of those should be included in the disclosures **or none of these**.

(b) **All non-equity** shares should be dealt with in the disclosures in the same way as financial liabilities except they should be **disclosed separately**.

Types of risks arising from financial instruments

5.8 This FRS is all about the disclosure of risk, so the different aspects of risk are analysed in some depth.

5.9 The two most familiar risks arising from financial instruments are credit risk and liquidity risk.

> **KEY TERMS**
>
> - **Credit risk**: the possibility that a loss may occur from the failure of another party to perform according to the terms of a contract.
> - **Liquidity risk** (also referred to as funding risk): the risk that an entity will encounter difficulty in realising assets or otherwise raising funds to meet commitments associated with financial instruments. *(FRS 13)*

5.10 These are **familiar** and they tend to be the types of risk disclosed in financial statements, eg debtors' provisions indicate credit risk; borrowing conditions, current ratio and quick ratio indicate liquidity risk.

5.11 Financial instruments, however, entail two other important types of risk: **cash flow risk** and **market price risk**.

> **KEY TERMS**
>
> - **Cash flow risk**: the risk that future cash flows generated by a monetary financial instrument will fluctuate in amount.
> - **Market price risk:** the possibility that future changes in market prices may change the value, or the burden, of a financial instrument. *(FRS 13)*

5.12 The main components of **market price risk** likely to affect most entities are also defined.

> **KEY TERMS**
>
> - **Interest rate risk**: the risk that the value of a financial instrument will fluctuate because of changes in market interest rates.
> - **Currency risk**: the risk that the value of a financial instrument will fluctuate because of changes in foreign exchange rates.
> - **Other market price risk**: the risk that the value of a financial instrument will fluctuate as a result of changes in market prices caused by factors other than interest rates or currencies. This category includes risk stemming from commodity prices and share prices. *(FRS 13)*

5.13 Until now information on these types of risk has been 'scant and often lacking in focus'. The fact that market price risk and cash flow risk are **diametrically opposed** is rarely mentioned; but the relationship between them has a significant impact on the risk profile. This can be illustrated as follows.

Financial instrument	Market price risk	Cash flow risk
Fixed rate interest-earning asset	Exposure	No exposure
Floating rate interest-earning asset	No exposure	Exposure

5.14 Depending on **management's attitude** to these particular risks, transactions may be undertaken to reduce one of the risks at the expense of increasing the other. Consequently,

the choice of which risk it seeks to reduce will have an important bearing on the entity's financial position, financial results and cash flows.

Summary of requirements

5.15 FRS 13 requires entities that have any of their capital instruments listed or publicly traded on a domestic or foreign stock market, and all other banks and insurance companies, to disclose in their financial statements certain information, including information about **risk** on the derivatives and other financial instruments that they hold or have issued. This is to enable users to understand the major aspects of the risk profile that might affect the entity's performance and financial condition and how this risk profile is being managed.

5.16 The FRS requires **narrative disclosures** that put into context the entity's chosen risk profile. These narrative disclosures set the scene for, and are supplemented by, a range of **numerical disclosures** that show how the entity's objectives and policies were implemented in the period and provide supplementary quantitative information for evaluating significant or potentially significant exposures. Together, these disclosures will provide a broad overview of the financial instruments held or issued and of the risk position created by them, focusing on those risks and instruments that are of greatest significance.

5.17 The **extent** of information disclosed will vary according to the nature of an entity's activities and the relative importance and complexity of transactions involving financial instruments. The vast majority of companies are not involved in complex transactions. The FRS also encourages an appropriate degree of **aggregation** to avoid excessively detailed disclosures.

Narrative disclosures

5.18 An entity is required to provide an explanation of the role of financial instruments in **creating or changing the risks** faced by an entity during the period. This discussion should also include a description of the entity's objectives, policies and strategies for holding and issuing derivatives and other financial instruments. The disclosures may be summarised as follows.

(a) An explanation of the **objectives and policies** of holding financial instruments

(b) **Significant changes** in these objectives or policies

(c) An explanation of how the period end **numerical disclosures reflect the policies** and explanations presented

5.19 Although this disclosure is mandatory, the FRS permits the information to be given in a statement other than the financial statements, eg the **operating and financial review (OFR)**, provided that it is incorporated into the financial statements by reference.

5.20 The FRS offers the following **example** of discursive disclosure, which would probably be given in the OFR.

> 'The Group's financial instruments, other than derivatives, comprise borrowings, some cash and liquid resources, and various items, such as trade debtors, trade creditors etc, that arise directly from its operations. The main purpose of these financial instruments is to raise finance for the Group's operations.
>
> The Group also enters into derivatives transactions (principally interest rate swaps and forward foreign currency contracts). The purpose of such transactions is to manage the interest rate and currency risks arising from the Group's operations and its sources of finance.

It is, and has been throughout the period under review, the Group's policy that no trading in financial instruments shall be undertaken.

The main risks arising from the Group's financial instruments are interest rate risk, liquidity risk and foreign currency risk. The Board reviews and agrees policies for managing each of these risks and they are summarised below. These policies have remained unchanged since the beginning of 20X0.

Interest rate risk

The Group finances its operations through a mixture of retained profits and bank borrowings. The Group borrows in the desired currencies at both fixed and floating rates of interest and then uses interest rate swaps to generate the desired interest profile and to manage the Group's exposure to interest rate fluctuations. The Group's policy is to keep between 50 per cent and 65 per cent of its borrowings at fixed rates of interest. At the year-end, 62 per cent of the Group's borrowings were at fixed rates after taking account of interest rate swaps.

Liquidity risk

As regards liquidity, the Group's policy has throughout the year been that, to ensure continuity of funding, at least 50 per cent of its borrowings should mature in more than five years. At the year-end, 57 per cent of the Group's borrowings were due to mature in more than five years.

Short-term flexibility is achieved by overdraft facilities.

Foreign currency risk

The Group has one significant overseas subsidiary - Foreign - which operates in the USA and whose revenues and expenses are denominated exclusively in US dollars. In order to protect the Group's sterling balance sheet from the movements in the US dollar/sterling exchange rate, the Group finances its net investment in this subsidiary by means of US dollar borrowings.

About one-third of the sales of the Group's UK businesses are to customers in continental Europe. These sales are priced in sterling but invoiced in the currencies of the customers involves. The Group's policy is to eliminate all currency exposures on sales at the time of sale through forward currency contracts. All the other sales of the UK businesses are denominated in sterling.'

Numerical disclosures

5.21 The FRS requires specific numerical disclosures. So they do not become so detailed that their message is obscured, the FRS encourages, and in some cases requires, a high degree of aggregation. The required disclosures are as follows.

(a) **Interest rate risk.** The carrying amount of financial liabilities should be analysed to show those liabilities at fixed interest rates and those at floating rates. Under this heading, operating entities will need to provide:

(i) The weighted average interest rate for fixed debt
(ii) The weighted average period for which interest rates are fixed
(iii) A benchmark for determining floating rate interest charges (eg LIBOR)

(b) **Currency risk**. Monetary assets and liabilities should be analysed by principal currency (ignoring those assets and liabilities denominated in the entity's functional currency)

(c) **Liquidity risk**. Disclose:

(i) The maturity profile of the carrying amount of financial liabilities
(ii) The maturity profile of undrawn committed borrowing facilities

(d) **Fair values** and book values of financial assets and liabilities must be disclosed, along with an indication of how the fair value was ascertained (eg discounting cash flows, market price)

(e) **Financial instruments used for trading.** Disclose:

(i) The net gain or loss included in the P&L, analysed by type of financial instrument, business activity or risk

(ii) Their period end value, including the average fair value where this is untypical.

(f) **Financial instruments used for hedging.** Disclose:

(i) The cumulative aggregate gains and losses that are unrecognised at the balance sheet date

(ii) The cumulative aggregate gains and losses carried forwards at the balance sheet date pending their recognition in the profit and loss account

(iii) The extent to which (i) and (ii) are expected to be recognised in the profit and loss account in the next accounting period

(iv) Amounts of gains and losses included in the period's profit and loss account that arose in previous years and were unrecognised and carried forward

(g) Certain **commodity contracts**

(h) **Market price risk** (encouraged, not required)

Exam focus point

This is a long and rather dull list to learn by heart. Think carefully about **why** the disclosures are required. Remember, **it's all about risk**.

Question: disclosures

Why do you think FRS 13 requires disclosure of the following?

(a) The maturity profile of the carrying amount of financial liabilities

(b) The maturity profile of undrawn committed borrowing facilities

(c) The carrying amount of financial liabilities analysed to show those liabilities at fixed interest rates and those at floating rates

Answer

(a) This will tell us about patterns of cash flow in the foreseeable future - will we have to pay a big loan off soon; how great is our exposure to debt?

(b) An example of 'undrawn committed borrowing facilities' might be an overdraft facility whose limit is, say, three times our actual overdraft. Such a facility provides a **cushion** against other risks, and gives us flexibility, or, in the words of the *Statement of Principles* 'financial adaptability'.

(c) Again, this is about risk - a floating interest rate liability will be more risky than a fixed rate one, although this risk can go in our favour.

5.22 The FRS gives **examples** of numerical disclosures, as follows.

'*Interest rate risk profile of financial assets and financial liabilities*

Financial assets

The Group has no financial assets, other than short-term debtors and an immaterial amount of cash at bank.

Financial liabilities

After taking into account the various interest rate swaps and forward foreign currency contracts entered into by the Group, the interest rate profile of the Group's financial liabilities at 31 December 20X1 was:

Currency	*Total*	*Floating rate financial liabilities*	*Fixed rate financial liabilities*	*Financial liabilities on which no interest is paid*
	£m	£m	£m	£m
Sterling	415	150	250	15
US dollar	200	80	120	-
Total	615	230	370	15

	Fixed rate financial liabilities		*Financial liabilities on which no interest is paid*
Currency	*Weighted average interest rate*	*Weighted average period for which rate is fixed*	*Weighted average period until maturity*
	%	Years	Years
Sterling	10	5	1.4
US dollar	7	8	-
Total	-	6	1.4

The floating rate financial liabilities comprise:

- Sterling denominated bank borrowings and overdrafts that bear interest at rates based on the six-month LIBOR; and
- US dollar denominated bank borrowings that bear interest at rates based on the US Prime rate.

Currency exposures

As at 31 December 20X1, after taking into account the effects of forward foreign exchange contracts the Group had no currency exposures.

Maturity of financial liabilities

The maturity profile of the Group's financial liabilities at 31 December 20X1 was as follows.

	£m
In one year or less, or on demand	200
In more than one year but not more than two years	15
In more than two years but not more than five years	60
In more than five years	340
	615

Borrowing facilities

The Group has various undrawn committed borrowing facilities. The facilities available at 31 December 20X1 in respect of which all conditions precedent had been met were as follows.

	£m
Expiring in one year or less	40
Expiring in more than one year but not more than two years	7
Expiring in more than two years	3
	50

Fair values of financial assets and financial liabilities

Set out below is a comparison by category of book values and fair values of the Group's financial assets and liabilities as at 31 December 20X1.

	Book value £m	Fair value £m
Primary financial instruments held or issued to finance the Group's operations:		
Short-term financial liabilities and current portion of long-term borrowings	(215)	(223)
Long-term borrowings	(400)	(370)
Financial assets	7	8
Derivative financial instruments held to manage the interest rate and currency profile:		
Interest rate swaps	-	15
Forward foreign currency contracts	-	(5)

The fair values of the interest rate swaps, forward foreign currency contracts and sterling denominated long-term fixed rate debt with a carrying amount of £250 million have been determined by reference to prices available from the markets on which the instruments involved are traded. All the other fair values shown above have been calculated by discounting cash flows at prevailing interest rates.

Gains and losses

The Group enters into forward foreign currency contracts to eliminate the currency exposures that arise on sales denominated in foreign currencies immediately those sales are transacted. It also uses interest rate swaps to manage its interest rate profile. Changes in the fair value of instruments used as hedges are not recognised in the financial statements until the hedged position matures. An analysis of these unrecognised gains and losses is as follows:

	Gains £m	Losses £m	Total net gains/(losses) £m
Unrecognised gains and losses on hedges at 1.1.X1	9	12	(3)
Gains and losses arising in previous years that were recognised in 20X1	8	9	1
Gains and losses arising before 1.1.X1 that were not recognised in 20X1	1	3	(2)
Gains and losses arising in 20X1 that were not recognised in 20X1	18	6	12
Unrecognised gains and losses on hedges at 31.12.X1	19	9	10
Of which:			
Gains and losses expected to be recognised in 20X2	12	6	6
Gains and losses expected to be recognised in 20X3 or later	7	3	4

Market price risk

The Group's exposure to market price risk comprises interest rate and currency risk exposures. It monitors these exposures primarily through a process known as sensitivity analysis.

On the basis of the Group's analysis, it is estimated that a rise of one percentage point in all interest rates would have reduced 20X1 profit before tax by approximately 1.5 per cent and that a three percentage point increase would have reduced such profits by 4.2 per cent. This is well within the ranges that the Group regards as acceptable.'

Criticisms of FRS 13

5.23 As a disclosure standard applying only to quoted companies, banks and similar institutions, FRS 13 would not appear to present too many implementation problems. However, some criticisms have been voiced about the detail of the disclosures.

(a) Not all companies will have systems which enable the data on hedging to be easily collected.

(b) The requirement to fair-value financial assets and liabilities will involve extra time and costs.

(c) Not all the disclosures are particularly meaningful.

5.24 Section summary

Concentrate on getting an overall picture of the FRS 13 disclosures.

- **Definitions**: financial instruments, derivatives, financial assets/liabilities
- **Risk**: understand market price risk and cash flow risk and their relationship
- **Disclosure**: overall narrative and numerical disclosure requirements

6 CURRENT PROPOSALS: THE CONSULTATION PAPER AND FRED 30

6.1 In December 2000, the ASB issued a consultation paper *Financial Instruments and Similar Items*, which presents the text of a paper prepared by the Financial Instruments Joint Working Group of standard setters (JWG). The ASB believes that the publication of this paper represents an important step in its financial instruments project.

6.2 The paper sets out the JWG's proposals on the recognition (and derecognition), measurement, presentation and disclosure of financial instruments. It is prepared in the form of a draft accounting standard and application guidance. It also incorporates a lengthy explanation of the reasoning behind its proposals and of the reasons for rejecting alternative arguments (the 'Basis for Conclusions').

6.3 **Main proposals**

(a) Virtually all financial instruments should be measured at **fair value.**

(b) Virtually all gains and losses arising from **changes** in those fair values should be **recognised immediately in the profit and loss account**.

(c) There should be **no** special accounting (ie **hedge accounting**) for financial instruments that are hedged or are used as a hedging instrument.

(d) A **new approach** is required **to the derecognition** of financial assets and to the way in which transfers of financial assets are accounted for. This approach, if implemented in the UK, would require changes to be made to FRS 5 *Reporting the substance of transactions* and would involve fundamental changes to the accounting for most securities sale and repurchase arrangements and most stock-lending transactions.

(e) There should be **changes** to the way in which **gains and losses** on financial instruments are **presented** in the profit and loss account, and changes in the way that financial instruments are presented in the balance sheet.

(f) There should be some **refinement of the note disclosures** on financial instruments, particularly those dealing with the financial risks arising from them.

6.4 The ASB has already made it clear that it is concerned about existing accounting practice for financial instruments and that it believes that significant changes in practice are necessary. Furthermore, it regards the development of an accounting standard on financial instruments as a priority for standard-setters throughout the world.

Criticisms of the new approach

6.5 Ron Paterson (*Accountancy,* March 2001) criticises what he calls the 'snapshot valuation' approach on several grounds.

(a) All companies will be reporting instant profits on their fixed-rate borrowings whenever there is a general rise in interest rates and losses whenever there is a fall, even when the cash flows are unaffected and the gain or loss will be reversed by adjusting the interest rates.

(b) Interest expense will always be measured at current rates, regardless of what rate the borrowers have contracted to pay; the impact of the rates they have negotiated will be found only in the revaluations.

(c) The revaluation has to take account, not only of market interest rates that apply to all companies, but of the specific rates that would be offered to your company. This means that even if general interest rates remain unchanged, a company in financial difficulty will report profits on its borrowings simply because its credit rating is declining.

(d) The approach is symptomatic of a tendency in recent accounting standards to pay little regard to management intent or to what is likely to happen in the future. The directors may plan to keep the loan for its full term and regard its fluctuating value in the meantime as irrelevant. Nevertheless, changes of value are recognised as they occur.

(e) The effect of this is to portray all companies as active traders in their financial assets and liabilities whether they are or not.

FRED 30 *Financial instruments: Disclosure and presentation; Recognition and measurement*

6.6 FRED 30 presents two new UK standards, based on the IASB's June 2002 proposals for a revised IAS 32 *Financial instruments: disclosure and presentation* and a revised IAS 39 *Financial Instruments: recognition and measurement*. These standards would replace FRS 4 *Capital instruments* (and the related UITF Abstracts 11 and 33) and FRS 13 *Derivatives and other financial instruments: disclosures,* and would involve amendments to various other standards.

6.7 The FRED was issued as part of the ASB's 'convergence project'. More detail on the convergence project can be found in Chapter 13; basically the intention is to bring UK financial reporting standards into line with international standards in time for 2005, when listed companies adopt international standards.

6.8 To summarise, FRED 30 proposes that (subject to certain exceptions) in 1 January 2004 new UK **standards based on IASs 32 and 39 should come into effect**.

6.9 This proposal is based on two assumptions: that, by 2004, legislative changes will have been made to eliminate the inconsistencies that exist at the moment between IASs 32 and 39 and companies legislation; and that, by 2004, it will be clear that no further changes are to be made to either international standard before 2005.

6.10 The **main changes** to UK practice would be as follows.

Disclosure and presentation

6.11 IAS 32 sets out the criteria a company should use to decide whether its own capital instruments should be presented as liabilities or equity. If its requirements are implemented in the UK, the presentation implications would be as follows.

(a) The **categories** into which capital instruments will be classified will change from **'liabilities' and 'shareholders' funds' to 'liabilities' and 'equity'**. Instruments, including shares, will be classified in accordance with the **substance of the contractual arrangements** involved.

(b) The overall effect of this change will be to **increase liabilities** at the expense of shareholders' funds/equity, because some instruments that are currently treated as shareholders' funds will henceforth be treated as liabilities. For example, those preference shares which are in substance liabilities will be treated as liabilities under the proposals.

(c) **Only income payments on instruments classified as equity will be treated as dividends**; income payments on all other instruments (including preference shares that are in substance liabilities) will be treated as an interest expense. The overall effect of this will be to **increase the amount of interest expense** recognised in the profit and loss account. Furthermore, income payments treated as dividends will no longer be reported in the profit and loss account.

(d) FRS 4 currently requires convertible debt to be classified as a liability. The FRED proposes that instruments, such as **convertible debt**, that comprise an equity element and a liability element should be broken in two, with the equity element reported as equity and the liability element treated as a liability. This is often referred to as '**split accounting**'. The liability component is measured first and the difference between the proceeds of the bond issue and the fair value of the liability is assigned to the equity component.

(e) The FRED proposes one other change to the existing requirements on the presentation of financial instruments. FRS 5 *Reporting the substance of transactions* currently contains provisions specifying when balance sheet debits and credits should be shown together as a single asset or liability (in other words, when balance sheet items should be offset). The FRED proposes that those provisions be replaced by the offset provisions in IAS 32. The effect of this will be to allow balance sheets **debits and credits** to be **offset more often** than they are at present.

6.12 Regarding **disclosure**, FRS 13 requires UK entities to provide a range of narrative and numerical risk disclosures about their financial instruments. Those requirements are both extensive and relatively detailed. The FRED proposes that they should be replaced by a UK standard based on IAS 32 disclosure requirements. IAS 32's requirements mirror the broad thrust of the existing UK requirements (although there are a number of detailed differences) but are **less detailed**. The main effect of this change will therefore be to give entities **greater flexibility** as to the form of the disclosures they provide.

6.13 EXAMPLE: DEBT/EQUITY SPLIT

On 1 January 20X1 Russell plc issues 4,000 convertible bond. The bonds are issued at par with a nominal value of £2,000 per bond and are redeemable at par in three years' time. Interest is payable annually in arrears at an interest rate (based on nominal value) of 6%. Each bond is convertible at any time up to maturity into 500 ordinary shares.

When the bonds are issued, the prevailing market interest rate for similar debt without the conversion options is 9%.

Discount factors at 9% are:

Amount payable in 3 years' time: 0.772

Cumulative present value of amounts payable at the end of each year for 3 years: 2.531

Required

Show how the bond would be split into debt and equity.

6.14 SOLUTION

	£	£
Proceeds of bond issue: 4,000 × £2,000		8,000,000
Less liability component		
Present value of principle: £8m × 0.772	6,176,000	
Present value of interest: £8m × 6% × 2.531	1,214,880	
Total liability component		7,390,880
Equity component		609,120

Recognition and measurement

6.15 The proposed revised IAS 39 contains the following requirements.

(a) All derivatives and all financial assets and financial liabilities that are in fact (or are designated as) **held for trading** are to be measured at **fair value** with all **changes** in those fair values **recognised immediately in the profit and loss account**.

(b) **All other liabilities**, all other **loans and receivables originated by the reporting entity** and all **other financial assets** that are being **held to maturity** by the reporting entity are to be measured at **cost**.

(c) **All other financial assets** are to be measured at **fair value** with **gains and losses** recognised immediately in the **statement of total recognised gains and losses**.

Under existing UK accounting, only financial institutions tend to measure any of their financial instruments at fair value, so the implementation of the above measurement requirements will be the **first time that many entities have used fair values** in their financial statements.

6.16 IAS 39 also contains requirements setting out the criteria that need to be met if **hedge accounting** techniques are to be applied. The principle in IAS 39 is that hedge accounting should be available only if the hedging relationship has been documented at the beginning of the hedge and the hedge has since proved to date to be effective. IAS 39 also specifies the hedge accounting techniques that are permitted to be used. The effect of these provisions will be to **prohibit the use of hedge accounting** in some of the circumstances in which it is currently used.

6.17 It is expected that, from 2005, listed entities will be required to adopt IAS 39's hedge accounting requirements in their consolidated financial statements. The FRED suggests that UK standards should require IAS 39's **hedge accounting requirements** (as amended in this FRED) to be complied with by **unlisted entities** and for the individual financial statements of listed entities **only if the fair value accounting rules are adopted** in the financial statements involved.

Question: hedging

Is the FRED 30 approach to hedging the same as the FRED 23 approach?

Answer

In principle the approach is the same. Much of FRED 23's wording is in fact drawn from IAS 39. However, IAS 39 contains a number of detailed requirements that are not in FRED 23 and so it is more

restrictive. Since hedge accounting is to be less widely available under IAS 39, the accounting numbers will become more volatile.

Question: measurement

To what extent will the following companies be affected by the measurement rules proposed in FRED 30?

(a) High Street Bank plc has a balance sheet that consists almost entirely of financial instruments. It marks its trading books to market and measures its 'banking books', including customer loans and advances, on a cost basis.

(b) Bog Standard plc is financed mainly by ordinary shares but has some debt capital.

(c) Talbot Manufacturing plc is a manufacturing company with sophisticated financing and treasury function.

Answer

(a) Banks will not be required to fair value their customer loans and advances, so the FRED 30 measurement rules will not change things very much. However, the proposed standard could have a significant impact on the bank's use of hedge accounting and possibly on the hedging strategies it adopts. This is partly because the proposed standard restricts hedge accounting, but also because of the proposed use of fair value.

(b) Provided Bog Standard plc does not have activities that generate large amounts of financial instruments, it will be largely unaffected by the measurement and hedge accounting requirements of FRED 30. Regarding the debt capital, as long as it does not use derivatives and other financial instruments to manage the financial risks, it should be unaffected.

(c) The company will find itself marking to market all its derivatives and many of its other financial assets and studying the hedge accounting restrictions in detail.

Differences between FRED 30 and proposed IFRSs

6.18 Not all the provisions of IAS 39 have been taken up.

(a) **Recognition and derecognition**. The ASB wishes to retain the 'risks and rewards' approach of FRS 5. The proposed IFRS is based on the 'control of components' approach. This is based around contractual rights: derecognition of an asset occurs when the contractual rights are transferred and the company has no continuing involvement in it.

(b) **Measurement and hedge accounting.** There are two main differences.

(i) *Recycling.* IAS 39 requires certain gains and losses to be recognised initially outside the profit and loss account (ie in equity) and then, at a later date, recognised in the profit and loss account. The **ASB does not support the use of recycling** and would not allow this.

(ii) *Scope.* IAS 39's measurement and hedging requirements are mandatory for all entities. FRED 30 proposes that **only those entities choosing to adopt fair value accounting** should be required to comply with these requirements.

(iii) *Disclosure.* The IFRS requirements apply to all entities, but the UK requirements would apply **only to banks and listed entities** and not to the individual financial statements of entities that are also providing the disclosures for their group in the consolidated financial statements.

Potential problems

6.19 The **measurement and hedging requirements** are regarded as particularly **controversial**.

(a) IAS 39 is a very **long and complex** standard which is difficult and time-consuming to implement. Some believe that it is too difficult to implement consistently and is therefore flawed.

(b) Managers and accountants have traditionally been more focussed on cash flows and cash flow risk than on fair values and fair value risk. Many perhaps **do not see fair value as important** and do not see that it should determine a significant part of financial performance.

(c) Some may view the **hedging requirements** as unnecessarily **restrictive**.

FRED 30 Second Supplement: extension of scope

6.20 In April 2004, the ASB issued a second supplement to FRED 30 (the first is not examinable) entitled *Financial instruments: extension of scope.*

6.21 The original FRED 30 proposed that that its draft measurement and disclosure requirements should be mandatory for some entities only. The supplement sets out the ASB's proposals to extend the scope of those requirements so that they apply to certain entities that did not fall within the scope of the original proposals.

6.22 The ASB's proposals in FRED 23 and FRED 30 were an attempt to regulate the use of fair value measurement and hedge accounting techniques. However, it was recognised that this was only a partial solution, because fair value measures were not compulsory, and only those entities choosing to adopt fair value measures would be subject to the full hedge accounting requirements. The solution was seen as a stepping stone to more comprehensive requirements.

6.23 The problem with this 'half-way house' was that it was too complex. The ASB therefore decided to adopt a single approach for all entities that converges with IFRS and deals more comprehensively with measurement.

6.24 The ASB is therefore proposing a **phased implementation of IAS 39, commencing with those entities—listed companies—where public interest is greatest.**

Measurement and hedge accounting

6.25 FRED 30 proposed that the measurement requirements of IAS 39 should apply only to those entities adopting the fair value basis of measurement under the amendments to be made to the Companies Act 1985 as a result of the Fair Value Directive.

6.26 The ASB is now proposing to bring within the scope of those requirements **all listed entities**, other than those that either are required or choose to adopt IFRS following the IAS Regulation.

6.27 The **advantages** of this proposal are as follows

(a) It **addresses a weakness** in the existing requirements.

(b) This is an **internationally agreed solution**, bringing together UK standards for listed entities with IFRS.

(c) It ensures **comparablility**, in the important area of measurement of financial instruments between listed groups and listed entities that are not groups.

(d) For listed groups it ensures **consistency** between consolidated financial statements and the single entity financial statements of the parent.

Disclosure

6.28 **FRED 30** proposed that, although the presentation requirements of IAS 32 (primarily concerned with the equity/liability distinction) would apply to all entities, **unlisted companies other than banks would be exempted** from the disclosure requirements. This proposal reflected the exemptions in FRS 13.

6.29 In the five years since FRS 13 was issued the quality of financial instrument disclosures has improved, such that the ASB considers that it is appropriate to extend the requirements to a wider range of entities.

6.30 The **FRED 30 supplement proposes widening the scope of the disclosure requirements**, applying them to **all entities** reporting under UK standards (other than those falling within the scope of the FRSSE and those entities that are either required or choose to adopt IFRS).

Chapter roundup

- FRS 4 *Capital instruments* is a complex standard. It has been issued to halt abuses in the accounting for **debt** and **equity**.
- The important things to remember in relation to **FRS 4** are:
  - Definitions
  - Accounting treatment
  - Disclosure
- Although the **application notes** to FRS 4 examine the treatment of certain capital instruments, each one must be judged on its own terms.
- The ASB has started a project to tackle the problems with accounting for **derivatives and other financial instruments**. The main problems surround:
  - Measurement
  - Hedge accounting
  - Disclosure
- **Measurement** and **hedge accounting** are considered in a discussion paper. Hedge accounting is also the subject of **FRED 23**.
- **Disclosure matters** relating to derivatives have already been developed in **FRS 13**. You should understand the major definitions and the different types of risk.
- FRED 30 proposes bringing in the disclosure and presentation rules of IAS 32 and the recognition and measurement rules of IAS 39.

Quick quiz

1 How should debt and equity be distinguished under FRS 4?

2 How should hybrid instruments be disclosed?

3 How does FRS 4 define:

(a) Capital instruments?
(b) Shareholders' funds?

4 FRS 4 requires certain items to be analysed in the balance sheet. Without cheating, fill in the gaps in the table below.

Item	Analysed between	
Shareholders' funds		
Minority interests in subsidiaries		
Liabilities		

5 Both shares and debt should be recorded as the fair value of the consideration received less issue costs. True or false?

6 FRED 23 prohibits hedging. True or false?

7 Define derivative financial instrument.

8 A fixed rate interest-earning asset is exposed to cash flow risk. True or false?

9 FRS 13 requires narrative disclosures to be given in the financial statements. True or false?

10 Deep plc has issued a deep discount bond. Would this need to be held at fair value under FRED 30?

Answers to quick quiz

1 See Para 1.5.

2 See Para 1.6.

3 (a) 'All instruments that are issued by the reporting entity as a means of raising finance, including shares, debentures, loans and debt instruments, options and warrants that give the holder the right to subscribe for or obtain instruments.'

(b) 'The aggregate of called up share capital and all reserves, excluding minority interests.'

4

Item	Analysed between	
Shareholders' funds	Equity interests	Non-equity interests
Minority interests in subsidiaries	Equity interests in subsidiaries	Non-equity interests in subsidiaries
Liabilities	Convertible liabilities	Non-convertible liabilities

5 True

6 False. FRED 23 specifies the strict criteria under which it is allowed.

7 See key term.

8 False. It is exposed to market price risk.

9 False. They may be given elsewhere, for example in the operating and financial review.

10 Not unless it was held for trading purposes. If it is not held for trading purposes, it is correct, under FRED 30, to carry it at amortised cost.

Now try the question below from the Exam Question Bank

Number	Level	Marks	Time
Q26	Exam	25	45 mins

Chapter 19

OFF BALANCE SHEET FINANCE

	Topic list	Syllabus reference
1	Off balance sheet finance explained	1(a) – 1(f)
2	Substance over form	1(a) – 1(f)
3	FRS 5 *Reporting the substance of transactions*	1(a) – 1(f)
4	Common forms of off balance sheet finance	1(a) – 1(f)
5	Revenue recognition	1(a) – 1(f)

Introduction

FRS 5 is a very important standard. It shows the *Statement of Principles* in action. The examiner tested it fairly regularly in old syllabus papers, and, as you have the same examiner for the new syllabus, you can assume that it will come up a lot.

Study guide

Section 15 – Off balance sheet transactions

- Explain the nature of the 'off balance sheet' problem and the principle of substance over form
- Discussion of common forms of 'off balance sheet' finance and current regulatory requirements
- Discussion of the perceived problems of current regulatory requirements including measurement and recognition issues

1 OFF BALANCE SHEET FINANCE EXPLAINED

KEY TERM

Off balance sheet finance is the funding or refinancing of a company's operations in such a way that, under legal requirements and existing accounting conventions, some or all of the finance may not be shown on its balance sheet.

1.1 Off balance sheet transactions may involve the **removal of assets** from the balance sheet, as well as liabilities, and they are likely to have a significant impact on the P&L account.

1.2 **Why off balance sheet finance exists**

(a) To **keep gearing low**, probably because of the views of some analysts and brokers.

(b) A company may need to keep its gearing down in order to **stay within the terms of loan covenants** imposed by lenders.

(c) A listed company with high borrowings is often expected (by analysts and others) to declare a **rights issue** in order to reduce gearing. This has an adverse effect on a company's share price and so off balance sheet financing is used to reduce gearing *and* the expectation of a rights issue.

(d) Analysts' short term views are a problem for companies **developing assets** which are not producing income during the development stage. Such companies will match the borrowings associated with such developing assets, along with the assets themselves, off balance sheet. They are brought back on balance sheet once income is being generated by the assets. This process keeps return on capital employed higher than it would have been during the development stage.

(e) Groups of companies have **excluded subsidiaries** from consolidation in an off balance sheet transaction because they carry out completely different types of business and have different characteristics. The usual example is a leasing company (in say a retail group) which has a high level of gearing.

1.3 The overriding motivation is to **avoid misinterpretation**. The company does not trust the analysts or other users to understand the reasons for a transaction and so avoids any effect such transactions might have by taking them off balance sheet. Unfortunately, the position of the company is then **misstated** and the user of the accounts is misled.

1.4 Not all forms of 'off balance sheet finance' are undertaken for cosmetic or accounting reasons. Some transactions are carried out to **limit or isolate risk**, to reduce interest costs and so on. These transactions **are in the best interests of the company**, not merely a cosmetic repackaging of figures which would normally appear in the balance sheet. Also, not all off balance sheet financing schemes derive from an intention to mislead. There may be genuine reasons for exclusion.

The off balance sheet finance problem

1.5 The main argument used for disallowing off balance sheet finance is that the true **substance** of the transactions should be shown, not merely the **legal form**, particularly when it is exacerbated by poor disclosure.

2 SUBSTANCE OVER FORM

KEY TERM

Substance over form: transactions and other events should be accounted for and presented in accordance with their substance and financial reality and not merely with their legal form. *(IAS 1)*

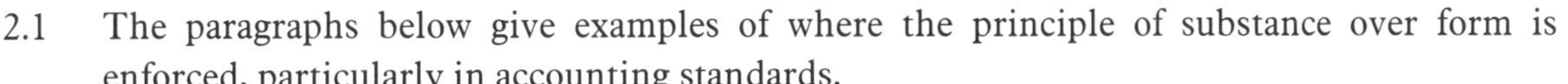

2.1 The paragraphs below give examples of where the principle of substance over form is enforced, particularly in accounting standards.

SSAP 21 *Accounting for leases and hire purchase* contracts

2.2 There is an explicit requirement that if the lessor transfers substantially all the **risks and rewards of ownership** to the lessee, even though the legal title has not passed, the item being leased should be **shown as an asset** in the balance sheet of the lessee and the amount due to the lessor should be shown as a liability.

FRS 8 *Related party disclosures*

2.3 FRS 8 requires financial statements to disclose fully material transactions undertaken with a related party by the reporting entity, **regardless of any price charged**.

SSAP 9 *Stocks and long-term contracts*

2.4 In SSAP 9 there is a requirement to account for **attributable profits** on long-term contracts under the accruals convention. However, there may be a problem with realisation, since it is arguable whether we should account for profit which, although attributable to the work done, may not have yet been invoiced to the customer. It is argued that the convention of substance over form is applied to justify ignoring the strict legal position.

FRS 2 *Accounting for subsidiary undertakings*

2.5 This is perhaps the most important area of off balance sheet finance which has been prevented by the application of the **substance over form** concept. The use of quasi-subsidiaries was very common in the 1980s.

KEY TERM

A **quasi-subsidiary** of a reporting entity is a company, trust, partnership or other vehicle that, though not fulfilling the definition of a subsidiary, is directly or indirectly controlled by the reporting entity and gives rise to benefits for that entity that are in substance no different from those that would arise were the vehicle a subsidiary. *(FRS 5)*

2.6 The main off balance sheet transactions involving quasi-subsidiaries were:

(a) **Sale of assets.** The sale of assets to a quasi-subsidiary was carried out to remove the associated borrowings from the balance sheet and so reduce gearing; or perhaps so that the company could credit a profit in such a transaction. The asset could then be rented back to the vendor company under an operating lease (no capitalisation required by the lessee).

(b) **Purchase of companies or assets**. One reason for such a purchase through a quasi-subsidiary is if the acquired entity is expected to make losses in the near future. Post-acquisition losses can be avoided by postponing the date of acquisition to the date the holding company acquires the purchase from the quasi-subsidiary.

(c) **Business activities conducted outside the group**. Such a subsidiary might have been excluded through a quasi-subsidiary or not consolidated under the 'dissimilar activities' requirement in FRS 2. Exclusion from consolidation might be undertaken because the activities are high risk and have high gearing.

2.7 CA 1989 introduced a new definition of a subsidiary based on **control** rather than just ownership rights and this definition (along with other related matters) was incorporated into FRS 2, thus substantially reducing the effectiveness of this method of off-balance sheet finance. FRS 5 defines control.

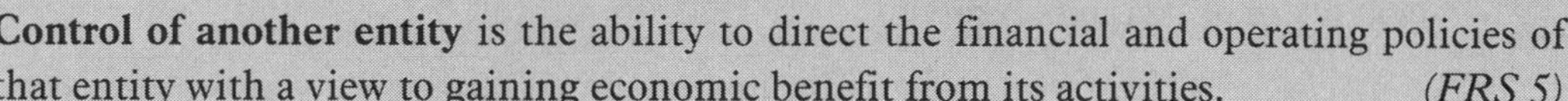

KEY TERM

Control of another entity is the ability to direct the financial and operating policies of that entity with a view to gaining economic benefit from its activities. *(FRS 5)*

FRS 9 Associates and joint ventures

2.8 FRS 9 was considered in Chapter 5. The aspect which is relevant to substance over form is the required treatment for **joint arrangements which are not** entities . The section of the standard dealing with such arrangements is headed 'a structure with the **form but not the substance of a joint venture**'. Such structures are **not** to be accounted for as joint ventures.

2.9 You may also hear the term **creative accounting** used in the context of reporting the substance of transactions. This can be defined simply as the manipulation of figures for a desired result. Remember, however, that it is very rare for a company, its directors or employees to manipulate results for the purpose of fraud. The major consideration is usually the effect the results will have on the company's share price. Some areas open to abuse (although some of these loopholes have been closed) are given below and you should by now understand how these can distort a company results.

(a) Income recognition and cut-off
(b) Use of merger accounting
(c) Manipulation of reserves
(d) Revaluations and depreciation
(e) Window dressing
(f) Changes in accounting policy

Question: creative accounting

Creative accounting, off balance sheet finance and related matters (in particular how ratio analysis can be used to discover these practices) often come up in articles in, for example, the *Financial Times* and *The Economist*. Find a library, preferably a good technical library, which can provide you with copies of back issues of such newspapers or journals and look for articles on creative accounting. Alternatively look on the Web.

3 FRS 5 REPORTING THE SUBSTANCE OF TRANSACTIONS

FRS 5 *Reporting the substance of transactions*

3.1 FRS 5 *Reporting the substance of transactions* is a daunting document, running to well over 100 pages, although the standard section itself is relatively short. The overriding principle of FRS 5 is that transactions should be accounted for according to their **substance rather than their legal form,** as we discussed above.

3.2 As stated in Chapter 3 of the *Statement of Principles,* accounting for items according to substance and economic reality and not merely legal form is a key determinant of reliable information.

(a) For the majority of transactions there is **no difference** between the two and therefore no issue.

(b) For other transactions **substance and form diverge** and the choice of treatment can give different results due to non-recognition of an asset or liability even though benefits or obligations result.

FRS 5 makes clear that full disclosure is not enough: all transactions must be **accounted for** correctly, with full disclosure of related details as necessary to give the user of accounts a full understanding of the transactions.

Relationship to other standards

3.3 The interaction of FRS 5 **with other standards and statutory requirements** is also an important issue; whichever rules are the more specific should be applied. Leasing provides a good example. **Straightforward leases** which fall squarely within the terms of **SSAP 21** should continue to be accounted for without any need to refer to FRS 5. Where their terms are **more complex**, or the lease is only one element in a larger series of transactions, then **FRS 5** comes into play.

Basic principles

3.4 As stated above, FRS 5's fundamental principle is that the substance of an entity's transactions should be reflected in its accounts. The key considerations

- Whether a transaction has given rise to new assets and liabilities
- Whether it has changed any existing assets and liabilities.

3.5 The characteristics of transactions whose substance is not readily apparent are as follows.

(a) The **legal title** to an item is separated from the ability to enjoy the principal benefits, and the exposure to the main risks associated with it.

(b) The transaction is **linked to one or more others** so that the commercial effect of the transaction cannot be understood without reference to the complete series.

(c) The transaction includes **one or more options**, under such terms that it makes it highly likely that the option(s) will be exercised.

Definitions of assets and liabilities

KEY TERMS

- **Assets** are rights or other access to future economic benefits controlled by an entity as a result of past transactions or events.
- **Liabilities** are an entity's obligations to transfer economic benefits as a result of past transactions or events. *(FRS 5)*

3.6 Identification of **who has the risks** relating to an asset will generally indicate **who has the benefits** and hence **who has the asset**. If an entity is, in certain circumstances unable to avoid an **outflow of benefits**, this will provide evidence that it has a liability.

KEY TERMS

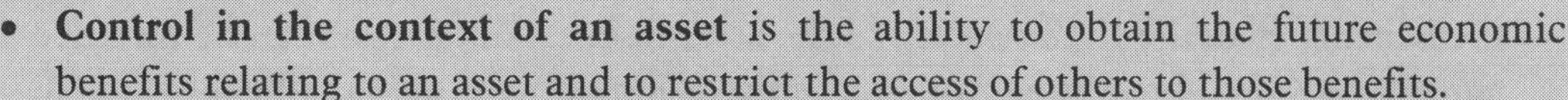

- **Control in the context of an asset** is the ability to obtain the future economic benefits relating to an asset and to restrict the access of others to those benefits.

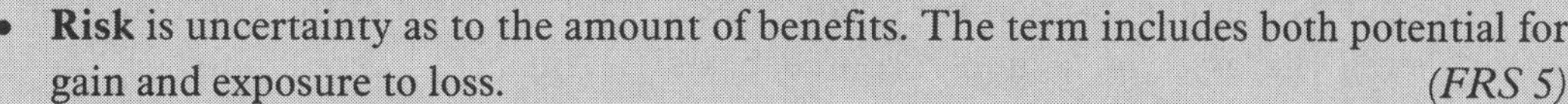

- **Risk** is uncertainty as to the amount of benefits. The term includes both potential for gain and exposure to loss. *(FRS 5)*

Recognition

KEY TERM

Recognition is the process of incorporating an item into the primary financial statements with the appropriate headings. It involves depiction of the items in words and by a monetary amount and inclusion of that amount in the statement totals. *(FRS 5)*

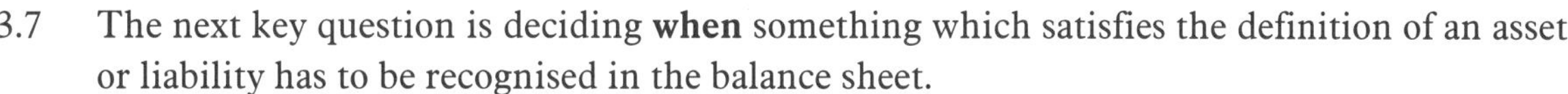

3.7 The next key question is deciding **when** something which satisfies the definition of an asset or liability has to be recognised in the balance sheet.

Criterion 1. There is sufficient evidence of the existence of the item (including, where appropriate, evidence that a future inflow or outflow of benefit will occur)

Criterion 2. The item can be measured at a monetary amount with sufficient reliability.

Derecognition

3.8 This is the question of when to **remove from the balance sheet** the assets and liabilities which have previously been recognised. FRS 5 addresses this issue only in relation to assets, not liabilities, and its rules are designed to determine one of three outcomes.

- **Complete derecognition**
- **No derecognition**
- The in-between case, **partial derecognition**

3.9 The issue of derecognition is perhaps one of the most common aspects of off balance sheet transactions: **has an asset been sold or has it been used to secure borrowings**? The concept of partial derecognition attempts to deal with the in-between situation of where sufficient benefits and risks have been transferred to warrant at least some derecognition of an asset.

Complete derecognition

3.10 In the simplest case, where a transaction results in the transfer to another party of all the **significant benefits and risks** relating to an asset, the entire asset should cease to be recognised. In this context, the word 'significant' is explained further: it should not be judged in relation to all the conceivable benefits and risks that could exist, but only in relation to those that are **likely to occur in practice**.

No derecognition

3.11 At the other end of the spectrum, where a transaction results in **no significant change** to the benefits or to the risks relating to the asset in question, no sale can be recorded and the entire asset should continue to be recognised. Retaining **either** the benefits or the risks is sufficient to keep the asset on the balance sheet. This means that the elimination of risk by financing the asset on a **non-recourse basis** (ie finance secured only on the asset in question) will not remove it from the balance sheet; it would be necessary to dispose of the upside as well in order to justify recording a sale. A further possible treatment, the special case of a '**linked presentation**', is discussed below.

3.12 The standard says that **any transaction** that is **in substance a financing** will **not qualify for derecognition**; the item will therefore stay on the balance sheet, and the finance will be introduced as a liability.

Partial derecognition

3.13 As can be seen, the above criteria are relatively restrictive. The standard therefore goes on to deal with circumstances where, although not all significant benefits and risks have been transferred, the transaction is more than a mere financing and has transferred enough of the benefits and risks to warrant at least some derecognition of the asset. It addresses three such cases.

(a) **Where an asset has been subdivided**

Where an identifiable part of an asset is separated and sold off, with the remainder being retained, the asset should be split and a partial sale recorded. Examples include the sale of a proportionate part of a loan receivable, where all future receipts are shared equally between the parties, or the stripping of interest payments from the principal of a loan instrument.

(b) **Where an item is sold for less than its full life**

The seller retains a residual value risk by offering to buy the asset back at a predetermined price at a later stage in the asset's life. Such an arrangement is sometimes offered in relation to commercial vehicles, aircraft, and so on. In such cases the original asset will have been replaced by a residual interest in the asset together with a liability for its obligation to pay the repurchase price.

(c) **Where an item is transferred for its full life but some risk or benefit is retained**

This may arise, for example, where a company gives a warranty or residual value guarantee in relation to the product being sold. This does not prevent the recording of the sale so long as the exposure under the warranty or guarantee can be assessed and provided for if necessary. Companies may also sometimes retain the possibility of an upward adjustment to the sale price of an asset based on its future performance, eg when a business is sold subject to an earn-out clause, but again this should not prevent the recognition of the sale.

3.14 In all of these cases of partial disposals, the amount of the initial profit or loss may be **uncertain**. The normal rules of prudence should be applied, but also that the uncertainty should be disclosed if it could have a material effect on the accounts.

Linked presentation

3.15 A 'linked presentation' requires **non-recourse finance** to be shown on the face of the balance sheet as a deduction from the asset to which it relates (rather than in the liabilities

section of the balance sheet), provided certain **stringent criteria** are met. This is really a question of how, rather than whether, to show the asset and liability in the balance sheet, so it is not the same as derecognition of these items, although there are some similarities in the result.

3.16 Linked presentation should be used when an asset is financed in such a way that:

(a) the finance will be repaid only from **proceeds generated by the specific item** it finances and there is no possibility whatsoever of a claim on the entity being established other than against funds generated by that item; *and*

(b) there is no provision whereby the entity may either **keep the item** on repayment of the finance or **reacquire** it at any time.

There are also several more specific conditions which elaborate on these principles.

3.17 An obvious example where linked presentation applies is when **debts are factored.** Debt factoring is discussed in more detail in the next section, but in simplified terms such a transaction would appear as follows.

Current assets	£'000
Debtors	500
Less non-returnable amounts received on sale of debtor	(425)
	75

In this case 85% of the debtor balances are received on a non-returnable basis.

Question: linked presentation

The managing director of your company has read an article about FRS 5 relating to linked presentation. The company is seeking to structure a financing of its head office in such a way that the asset and the funding could be 'linked' on the balance sheet.

As the company's finance director, draft a reply to the managing director, stating whether this treatment is possible.

Answer

The 'linked presentation' is a layout that shows the amount of borrowing or proceeds raised that has been deducted from the original asset amount, on the assets side of the balance sheet. It was developed in response to the ASB's difficulties in settling an appropriate accounting treatment for securitisations, but the criteria for its use are expressed in general terms; it is not reserved solely for securitisations.

Nevertheless, the provisions of FRS 5 relating to linked presentation are drawn extremely strictly. And even though companies should in general interpret FRS 5 in terms of its spirit and reasoning, the ASB's intention in the case of linked presentation was to limit its application by requiring the criteria to be met 'to the letter' before a linked presentation could be adopted.

It is a question of fact whether the proposed financial transaction meets the criteria in FRS 5, although, apart from some securitisations and factoring arrangements, the transactions it does apply to are likely to be very rare. The main criteria are that the finance that is shown as linked should be non-recourse, ie secured only on the asset in question, and that the company must not keep the asset when the finance is paid off, or reacquire it at any time.

In this case, the transaction is unlikely to be effective, as presumably the company will want to continue to use its head office after the finance is repaid.

Offset

3.18 FRS 5 makes it clear that assets and liabilities which qualify for recognition should be accounted for individually, rather than netted off. Offset is allowed by the standard only where the debit and credit balances are **not really separate assets and liabilities**, eg where there are amounts due to and from the same third party and there is a legal right of set-off. The key consideration is whether the entity can **enforce** a right of set-off so that there is no possibility of having to pay the creditor balance without recovering the debtor amount.

3.19 The detailed criteria which permit offset and **all of which must apply** are set out in FRS.

(a) The parties owe each other **determinable monetary amounts**, denominated either in the same currency or in different but freely convertible currencies.

(b) The reporting entity has the ability to insist on a **net settlement**, which can be enforced in all situations of default by the other party.

(c) The reporting entity's ability to insist on a net settlement is **assured beyond doubt**. This means that the debit balance must be receivable no later than the credit balance requires to be paid, otherwise the entity could be required to pay the other party and later find that it was unable to obtain payment itself. It also means that the ability to insist on a net settlement would survive the insolvency of the other party (which may require detailed examination in group situations).

Disclosure

3.20 FRS 5 has a general requirement to disclose transactions in sufficient detail to enable the reader to understand their **commercial effect**, whether or not they have given rise to the recognition of assets and liabilities. This means that where transactions or schemes give rise to assets and liabilities which are *not* recognised in the accounts, disclosure of their nature and effects still has to be considered in order to ensure that the accounts give a true and fair view.

3.21 A second general principle is that an explanation should be given where there are any assets or liabilities whose **nature is different** from that which the reader might expect of assets or liabilities appearing in the accounts under that description. There are specific disclosures in relation to the use of the linked presentation, the inclusion of quasi-subsidiaries in the accounts, and the various transactions dealt with in the application notes (see below).

Question: treatment of off balance sheet finance

Explain the accounting treatment and disclosure requirements for off balance sheet finance.

Answer

In the past neither accounting standards nor company law provided fully effective means for outlawing all off balance sheet practices either by specifying an accounting treatment or by adequate disclosure. Some may consider that the requirement for accounts to provide a true and fair view implies that disclosure is required of the existence and financial effect of, say, a controlled non-subsidiary. On the other hand, it was common practice to rely on the letter of the law to avoid this.

The ASB strengthened the principle of 'substance over form' by introducing definitions of assets and liabilities that require recognition of most forms of off balance sheet financing. FRS 5 requires recognition of the true economic and commercial effects of such transactions regardless of the form that they take.

In addition, individual laws or standards outlaw specific practices. For example, the 1989 Companies Act, which implements the EC 7th Directive on consolidated accounts, amended the Companies Act

1985 so that it now applies tests regarding control over, rather than ownership of another company to determine whether or not it should be consolidated. This deals with the above situation, where control is exercised even in the absence of majority ownership. These changes were incorporated into FRS 2 by the ASB.

These moves indicate that there is decreasing sympathy in the accounting profession and in the business community for off balance sheet financing. Thus, we can expect the auditors to take a firmer line on this topic than in the past and the investment community and the financial press pay more attention to it.

Exam focus point

Examination questions are likely to ask for calculations, accounting treatment and disclosure for a variety of transactions, including sale and leaseback transactions and debt factoring agreements. Question practice in this area is very worthwhile.

Private finance initiative

3.22 In 1999 the ASB published an *Application Note to FRS 5 Reporting the substance of transactions*.

3.23 The accounting treatment of PFI has become the subject of much debate. To fulfil a PFI contract, a private sector 'operator' typically constructs a capital asset (eg a road, bridge, hospital, prison, computer system or school) and uses that asset to provide services to a public sector 'purchaser'. The key accounting question is:

- Whether the purchaser has an asset of the property used to provide the contracted services together with a corresponding liability to pay the operator for it; or, alternatively
- Whether the operator has an asset of the property used to provide the contracted services or a financial asset being a debt due from the purchaser.

3.24 FRS 5 has a two-stage test.

Stage 1. Exclude any separable elements of the contract that relate only to services (such as cleaning, laundry, catering etc), rather than to the capital asset. Any such **service** elements are not relevant to determining which party has the **asset** and should be ignored.

Stage 2. Assess what remains to see if the leasing standard (SSAP 21) or FRS 5 should be applied.

3.25 Section summary

The diagram should help to explain a sensible approach to FRS 5 in examination questions. Important points to remember are:

- **Substance over form**
- Definitions of **assets** and **liabilities**
- Definition of **recognition**
- Different degrees of **derecognition**: complete, partial and none
- When **linked presentation** is used
- When **offset** is allowed

Accounting treatment for the recognition of assets and liabilities

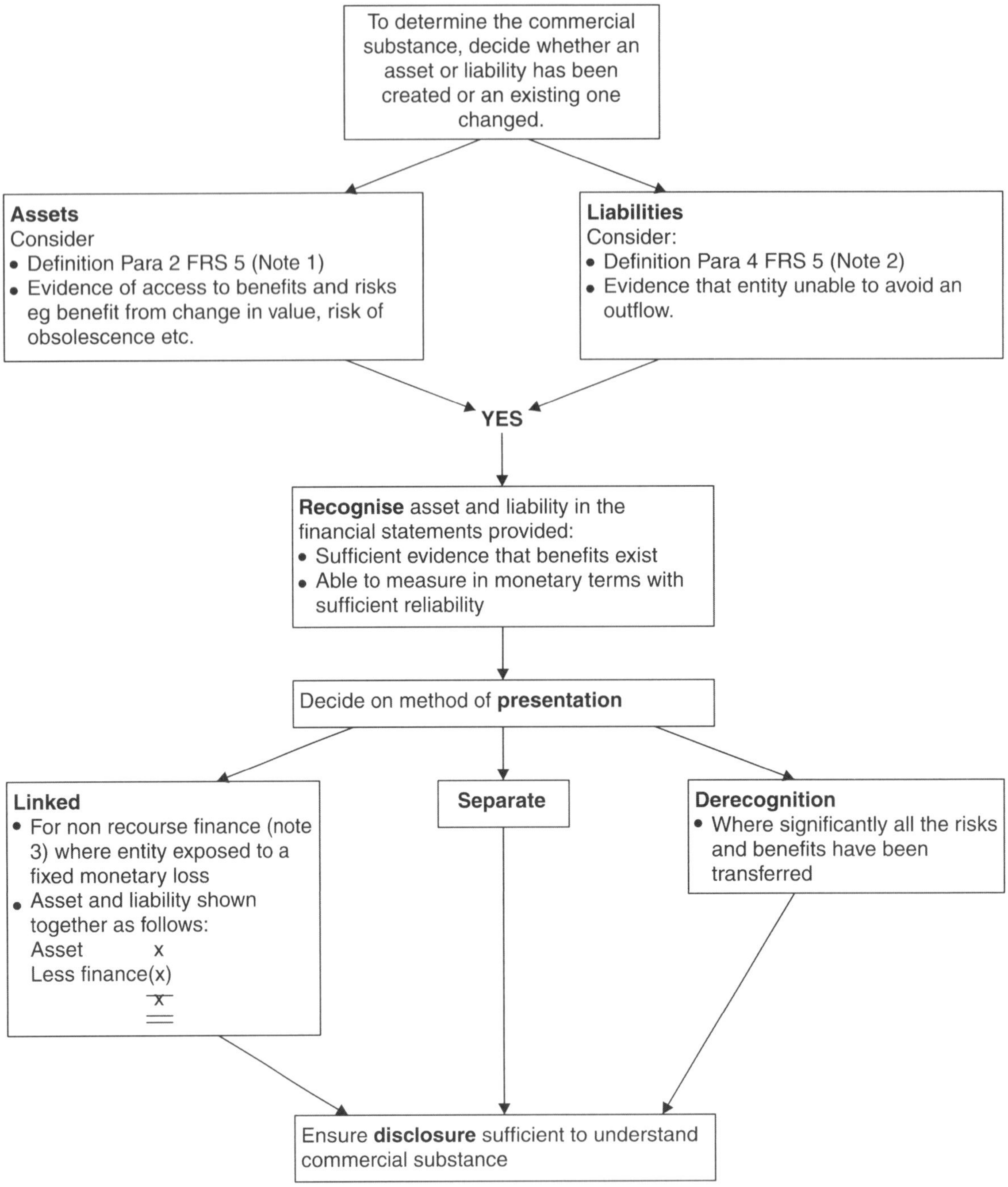

To determine the commercial substance, decide whether an asset or liability has been created or an existing one changed.

Assets
Consider
- Definition Para 2 FRS 5 (Note 1)
- Evidence of access to benefits and risks eg benefit from change in value, risk of obsolescence etc.

Liabilities
Consider:
- Definition Para 4 FRS 5 (Note 2)
- Evidence that entity unable to avoid an outflow.

YES

Recognise asset and liability in the financial statements provided:
- Sufficient evidence that benefits exist
- Able to measure in monetary terms with sufficient reliability

Decide on method of **presentation**

Linked
- For non recourse finance (note 3) where entity exposed to a fixed monetary loss
- Asset and liability shown together as follows:

Asset	x
Less finance	(x)
	x

Separate

Derecognition
- Where significantly all the risks and benefits have been transferred

Ensure **disclosure** sufficient to understand commercial substance

Notes

1 *Assets*: rights or other access to future economic benefits controlled by an entity as a result of past transactions or events.

2 *Liabilities*: an entity's obligations to transfer future economic benefits as a result of past transactions or events.

3 *Non-recourse finance*: there is no (or limited) recourse to the seller for losses.

4 COMMON FORMS OF OFF BALANCE SHEET FINANCE

4.1 FRS 5 deals with certain specific aspects of off balance sheet finance in detailed **application notes**. These cover the following topics.

- Consignment stock
- Sale and repurchase agreements
- Factoring of debts
- Securitised assets
- Loan transfers

4.2 The application notes explain how to apply the standard to the particular transactions which they describe, and also contain specific disclosure requirements in relation to those transactions. The application notes are **not exhaustive** and they do not override the general principles of the standard itself, but they are regarded as authoritative insofar as they assist in interpreting it.

4.3 Note that in *all* cases **full disclosure** of the transaction should be given, whatever its accounting treatment. This will particularly hold where a **linked presentation** is used.

Consignment stock

4.4 Consignment stock is an arrangement where stock is held by one party (say a distributor) but is owned by another party (for example a manufacturer or a finance company). Consignment stock is common in the motor trade and is similar to goods sold on a 'sale or return' basis.

4.5 To identify the correct treatment, it is necessary to identify the point at which the distributor or dealer acquired the benefits of the asset (the stock) rather than the point at which legal title was acquired.

(a) If the manufacturer has the right to require the return of the stock, and if that right is likely to be exercised, then the stock is *not* an asset of the dealer.

(b) If the dealer is rarely required to return the stock, then this part of the transaction will have little commercial effect in practice and should be ignored for accounting purposes.

(c) The potential liability would need to be disclosed in the accounts.

Summary of indications of asset status

4.6 The following analysis is given in FRS 5.

Indications that the stock is *not an asset* of the dealer at delivery	**Indications that the stock *is an asset* of the dealer at delivery**
Manufacturer can require dealer to **return stock** (or transfer stock to another dealer) without compensation; or	Manufacturer cannot require dealer to **return or transfer stock**; or
Penalty paid by the dealer to prevent returns/transfers of stock at the manufacturer's request.	**Financial incentives** given to persuade dealer to transfer stock at manufacturer's request.

Indications that the stock is *not an asset* of the dealer at delivery	Indications that the stock *is an asset* of the dealer at delivery
Dealer has unfettered **right to return stock** to the manufacturer without penalty and actually exercises the right in practice.	Dealer has **no right to return stock** or is commercially compelled not to exercise its right of return.
Manufacturer bears **obsolescence risk,** eg: (a) obsolete stock is returned to the manufacturer without penalty; or (b) financial incentives given by manufacturer to prevent stock being returned to it (eg on a model change or if it becomes obsolete).	Dealer bears **obsolescence risk**, eg: (a) penalty charged if dealer returns stock to manufacturer; or (b) obsolete stock cannot be returned to the manufacturer and no compensation is paid by manufacturer for losses due to obsolescence.
Stock **transfer price** charged by manufacturer is based on manufacturer's list price at date of transfer of legal title.	Stock **transfer price** charged by manufacturer is based on manufacturer's list price at date of delivery.
Manufacturer bears **slow movement risk,** eg: transfer price set independently of time for which dealer holds stock, and there is no deposit.	Dealer bears **slow movement risk**, eg: (a) dealer is effectively charged interest as transfer price or other payments to manufacturer vary with time for which dealer holds stock; or (b) dealer makes a substantial interest-free deposit that varies with the levels of stock held.

Required accounting

4.7 Where it is concluded that the stock **is in substance an asset** of the dealer:

(a) Recognise the stock as such on the dealer's balance sheet, together with a corresponding liability to the manufacturer.

(b) Deduct any deposit from the liability and classify the excess as a trade creditor.

(c) Give full disclosure in the notes to the financial statements.

4.8 Where it is concluded that the stock is **not in substance an asset** of the dealer:

(a) Do not include the stock on the dealer's balance sheet until the transfer of title has crystallised.

(b) Include any deposit under 'other debtors'.

(c) Give full disclosure in the notes to the financial statements.

Question: consignment stock

Daley Motors Ltd owns a number of car dealerships throughout Essex. The terms of the arrangement between the dealerships and the manufacturer are as follows.

(a) Legal title passes when the cars are either used by Daley Ltd for demonstration purposes or sold to a third party.

(b) The dealer has the right to return vehicles to the manufacturer without penalty. (Daley Ltd has rarely exercised this right in the past.)

(c) The transfer price is based on the manufacturer's list price at the date of delivery.

(d) Daley Ltd makes a substantial interest-free deposit based on the number of cars held.

Should the asset and liability be recognised at the date of delivery?

Answer

(a) Legal form is irrelevant.
(b) Yes: only because rarely exercised (otherwise 'no').
(c) Yes: per FRS 5.
(d) Yes: the dealership is effectively forgoing the interest which could be earned on the cash sum.

Sale and repurchase agreements

4.9 These are arrangements under which the company sells an asset to another person on terms that allow the company to **repurchase the asset** in certain circumstances. A common example is the sale and repurchase of maturing whisky stocks. The key question is whether the transaction is a **straightforward sale**, or whether it is, in effect, a **secured loan**. It is necessary to look at the arrangement to determine who has the rights to the economic benefits that the asset generates, and the terms on which the asset is to be repurchased.

4.10 If the seller has the right to the benefits of the **use of the asset**, and the repurchase terms are such that the **repurchase is likely** to take place, the transaction should be accounted for as a **loan**.

Summary of indications of the sale of the asset

4.11 FRS 5 gives the following summary.

Indications of *sale* of original asset to buyer (nevertheless, the seller may retain a different asset)	Indications of *no sale* of original asset to buyer (secured loan)
	Sale price does not equal market value at date of sale.
No commitment for seller to repurchase asset, eg call option where there is a real possibility the option will fail to be exercised.	Commitment for seller to repurchase asset, eg: • put and call option with the same exercise price; • either a put or a call option with no genuine commercial possibility that the option will fail to be exercised; or • seller requires asset back to use in its business, or asset is in effect the only source of seller's future sales.
Risk of **changes in asset value** borne by buyer such that buyer does not receive solely a lender's return, eg both sale and repurchase price equal market value at date of sale/repurchase	Risk of **changes in asset value** borne by seller such that buyer receives solely a lender's return, eg: • Repurchase price equals sale price plus costs plus interest

Indications of *sale* of original asset to buyer (nevertheless, the seller may retain a different asset)	Indications of *no sale* of original asset to buyer (secured loan)
	• Original purchase price adjusted retrospectively to pass variations in the value of the asset to the seller • Seller provides residual value guarantee to buyer or subordinated debt to protect buyer from falls in the value of the asset.
Nature of the asset is such that it will be used over the life of the agreement, and seller has no rights to **determine its use**. Seller has no rights to determine asset's development or future sale.	Seller retains right to **determine asset's use**, development or sale, or rights to profits therefrom.

Required accounting

4.12 Where the substance of the transaction is that of a **secured loan**:

(a) The seller should continue to recognise the original asset and record the proceeds received from the buyer as a liability

(b) Interest, however designated, should be accrued

(c) The carrying amount of the asset should be reviewed and provided against if necessary

(d) Full disclosure should be made in the notes to the financial statements

4.13 Where the transaction is a **sale and leaseback**, no profit should be recognised on entering in to the arrangement and no adjustment made to the carrying value of the asset. As stated in the guidance notes to SSAP 21, this represents the substance of the transactions, 'namely the raising of finance secured on an asset that continues to be held and that is not disposed of'.

4.14 Where the **seller has a new asset or liability** (eg merely a call option to repurchase the original asset), it should recognise or disclose that new asset or liability on a prudent basis in accordance with the provisions of FRS 12. In particular, the seller should recognise (and not merely disclose) a liability for any kind of unconditional obligation it has entered into.

Question: sale and repurchase

A construction company, Mecanto plc, agrees to sell to Hamlows Bank some of the land within its landbank. The terms of the sale are as follows.

(a) The sales price is to be at open market value.

(b) Mecanto plc has the right to develop the land on the basis that it will pay all the outgoings on the land plus an annual fee of 5% of the purchase price.

(c) Mecanto has the option to buy back the land at any time within the next five years. The repurchase price is based on:

(i) Original purchase price
(ii) Expenses relating to the purchase
(iii) An interest charge of base rate + 2%
(iv) Fewer amounts received from Mecanto by Hamlows.

(d) At the end of five years Hamlows Bank may offer the land for sale generally. Any shortfall on the proceeds relative to the agreed purchase price agreed with Mecanto has to be settled by Mecanto in cash.

Should the asset continue to be recognised and the sales proceeds treated as a loan?

Answer

(a) No: the sales price is as for an arms' length transaction.

(b) Yes: Mecanto has control over the asset.
Yes: Mecanto has to pay a fee based on cash received.

(c) Yes: interest is charged on the proceeds paid to Mecanto.
Yes: the repurchase price is based on the lender's return

(d) Yes: options ensure that Mecanto bears all the risk (both favourable and unfavourable) of changes in the market value of the land.

Factoring of debts

4.15 Where debts are factored, the original creditor **sells the debts to the factor**. The sales price may be fixed at the outset or may be adjusted later. It is also common for the factor to offer a credit facility that allows the seller to draw upon a proportion of the amounts owed.

4.16 In order to determine the correct accounting treatment it is necessary to consider whether the benefit of the debts has been passed on to the factor, or whether the factor is, in effect, providing a loan on the security of the debtors. If the seller has to **pay interest** on the difference between the amounts advanced to him and the amounts that the factor has received, and if the seller bears the **risks of non-payment** by the debtor, then the indications would be that the transaction is, in effect, a loan. Depending on the circumstances, either a linked presentation or separate presentation may be appropriate.

Summary of indications of appropriate treatment

4.17 FRS 5 gives the following summary of indicators of the appropriate treatment.

Indications that derecognition is appropriate (debts are *not an asset* of the seller)	**Indications that a *linked presentation* is appropriate**	**Indications that a separate presentation is appropriate (debts are an *asset* of the seller)**
Transfer is for a single non-returnable fixed sum.	Some non-returnable proceeds received, but seller has rights to further sums from the factor (or vice versa) whose amount depends on whether or when debtors pay.	Finance cost varies with speed of collection of debts, eg: • by adjustment to consideration for original transfer or • subsequent transfers priced to recover costs of earlier transfers.
There is **no recourse** to the seller for losses.	There is either **no recourse** for losses, or such recourse has a fixed monetary ceiling.	There is **full recourse** to the seller for losses.

Indications that derecognition is appropriate (debts are *not an asset* of the seller)	**Indications that a *linked presentation* is appropriate**	**Indications that a separate presentation is appropriate (debts are an *asset* of the seller)**
Factor is paid **all amounts** received from the factored debts (and no more). Seller has no rights to further sums from the factor.	Factor is paid only out of **amounts collected** from the factored debts, and seller has no right or obligation to repurchase debts.	Seller is required to **repay** amounts received from the factor on or before a set date, regardless of timing or amounts of collections from debtors.

Required accounting

4.18 **Derecognition**. Where the seller has retained no significant benefits and risks relating to the debts and has no obligation to repay amounts received from the factors, the debtors should be removed from its balance sheet and no liability shown in respect of the proceeds received from the factor. A profit or loss should be recognised, calculated as the difference between the carrying amount of the debts and the proceeds received.

4.19 **Linked presentation**. Where the conditions for a linked presentation are met, the proceeds received, to the extent they are non-returnable, should be shown deducted from the gross amount of the factored debts (after providing for bad debts, credit-protection charges and any accrued interest) in the face of the balance sheet. The interest element of the factor's charges should be recognised as it accrues and included in the P&L account with other interest charges.

4.20 **Separate presentation**. Where neither derecognition nor a linked presentation is appropriate, a separate presentation should be adopted: a gross asset (equivalent in amount to the gross amount of the debts) should be shown on the balance sheet of the seller within assets, and a corresponding liability in respect of the proceeds received from the factor should be shown within liabilities. The interest element of the factor's charges should be recognised as it accrues and included in the P&L account with other interest charges. Other factoring costs should be similarly accrued and included in the P&L account within the appropriate caption.

Securitised assets

4.21 Securitisation is very common in the financial services industry, and the assets that are most commonly securitised are mortgages and credit card accounts, although hire purchase loans, trade debts and even property and stocks are sometimes securitised. **Blocks of assets** are thus financed, rather than the company's general business.

4.22 The normal procedure is for the assets to be transferred by the person who held them (the originator) to a special purpose company (the issuer) in exchange for cash. The issuer will use the proceeds of an issue of debentures or loan notes to pay for the assets. The shares in the issuer are usually held by a third party so that it does not need to be consolidated. The issuer will usually have a very small share capital, and so most of the risk will be borne by the people who lent it the money through the debentures to pay for the assets. For this reason there is usually some form of insurance taken out on the assets to give some security for the lenders.

Summary of indications as to accounting treatment

4.23 FRS 5 gives the following summary of indications of the appropriate treatment.

Indications that derecognition is appropriate (securitised assets are *not an asset* of the seller)	**Indications that a *linked presentation* is appropriate**	**Indications that a separate presentation is appropriate (securitised assets are *assets* of the originator)**
	Originator's individual financial statements	
Transaction price is **arm's length price** for an outright sale.	Transaction price **is not arm's length price** for an outright sale.	Transaction price is **not arm's length price** for an outright sale.
Transfer is for a **single, non-returnable fixed sum**.	Some **non-returnable proceeds** received, but originator has rights to further sums from the issuer, the amount of which depends on the performance of the securitised assets.	Proceeds received are **returnable**, or there is a provision whereby the originator may keep the securitised assets on repayment of the loan notes or re-acquire them.
There is **no recourse** to the originator for losses.	There is either **no recourse** for losses, or such recourse has a fixed monetary ceiling.	There is or may be **full recourse** to the originator for losses, eg: • Originator's directors are unable or unwilling to state that it is not obliged to fund any losses • Noteholders have not agreed in writing that they will seek repayment only from funds generated by the securitised assets
	Originator's consolidated financial statements	
Issuer is owned by an **independent third party** that made a substantial capital investment, has control of the issuer, and has the benefits and risks of its net assets.	Issuer is a **quasi-subsidiary** of the originator, but the conditions for a linked presentation are met from the point of view of the group.	Issuer is a **subsidiary** of the originator.

Required accounting: originator's financial statements

4.24 **Derecognition**. Where the originator has retained no significant benefits and risks relating to the securitised assets and has no obligation to repay the proceeds of the note issue, the asset should be removed from its balance sheet, and no liability shown in respect of the proceeds of the note issue. A profit or loss should be recognised, calculated as the difference between the carrying amount of the assets and the proceeds received.

4.25 **Linked presentation**. Where the conditions for a linked presentation are met, the proceeds of the note issue (to the extent they are non-returnable) should be shown deducted from the securitised assets on the face of the balance sheet within a single asset caption. Profit should be recognised and presented in the manner set out in FRS 5. The disclosure requirements are extensive, including a description of the securitised assets and all relevant terms, income and expenses, claims on proceeds, etc.

4.26 **Separate presentation**. Where neither derecognition nor a linked presentation is appropriate, a separate presentation should be adopted, ie a gross asset (equal in amount to the gross amount of the securitised assets) should be shown on the balance sheet of the originator within assets, and a corresponding liability in respect of the proceeds of the note issue shown within liabilities. No gain or loss should be recognised at the time the securitisation is entered into (unless adjustment to the carrying value of the asset independent of the securitisation is required).

Required accounting: issuer's financial statements

4.27 The requirements set out in the paragraphs above for the originator's individual financial statements also apply to the issuer's financial statement. In most cases the issuer will be required to adopt a **separate presentation**, in which case the provisions of Paragraph 4.26 will apply.

Loan transfers

4.28 These are arrangements where a loan is transferred to a transferee from an original lender. This will usually be done by the **assignment of rights and obligations** by the lender, or the **creation of a new agreement** between the borrower and the transferee. The same principles apply to loan transfers as to debt factoring and securitised assets.

Summary of indications of appropriate treatment

4.29 FRS 5 gives the following summary.

Indications that *derecognition* is appropriate (off lender's balance sheet)	**Indications that a *linked presentation* is appropriate**	**Indications that a *separate presentation* is appropriate (on lender's balance sheet**
Transfer is for a single, non-returnable fixed sum.	Some non-returnable proceeds received, but lender has rights to further sums whose amount depends on whether or when the borrowers pay.	The proceeds received are returnable in the event of losses occurring on the loans.
There is no recourse to the lender for losses from any cause.	There is either no recourse for losses, or such recourse has a fixed monetary ceiling.	There is full recourse to the lender for losses.
Transferee is paid all amounts received from the loans (and no more), as and when received. Lender has no rights to further sums from the loans or the transferee.	Transferee is paid only out of amounts received from the loans, and lender has no right or obligation to repurchase them.	Lender is required to repay amounts received from the transferee on or before a set date, regardless of the timing or amount of payments by the borrowers.

Required accounting

4.30 **Derecognition**. Where the lender has retained no significant benefits and risks relating to the loans and has no obligation to repay the transferee, the loans should be removed from its balance sheet and no liability shown in respect of the amounts received from the transferee. A profit or loss may arise for the lender. Where the profit or loss is realised in cash it should be recognised, calculated as the difference between the carrying amount of the loans and the cash proceeds received. Where, however, the lender's profit or loss is not realised in cash and there are doubts as to its amount, full provision should be made for any expected loss but recognition of any gain, to the extent it is in doubt, should be deferred until cash has been received.

4.31 **Linked presentation**. Where the conditions for a linked presentation are met, the proceeds received, to the extent they are non-returnable, should be shown deducted from the gross amount of the loans on the face of the balance sheet. Profit should be recognised and presented as set out in FRS 5.

4.32 **Separate presentation**. Where neither derecognition not a linked presentation is appropriate, a separate presentation should be adopted, ie a gross asset (equivalent in amount to the gross amount of the loans) should be shown on the balance sheet of the lender within assets, and a corresponding liability in respect of the amounts received from the transferee should be shown within creditors. No gain or loss should be recognised at the time of the transfer (unless adjustment to the carrying value of the loan independent of the transfer is required).

Exam focus point

In spite of FRS 5 and its application notes, there are *still* opportunities to manipulate results.

UITF Abstract 32 Employee benefit trusts and other intermediate payment arrangements

4.33 This Abstract was published in December 2001. It applies where an entity sets up and provides funds to an employee benefit trust (or other intermediary) and the trust's accumulated assets are used to remunerate the entity's employees (or other service providers).

4.34 Abstract 32 clarifies how the principles of FRS 5 *Reporting the substance of transactions* should be applied to determine:

(a) Whether a payment to the intermediary should be charged as an expense when the payment is made

(b) If the payment is not an expense, what assets and liabilities the sponsoring entity should recognise after the payment

4.35 The Abstract requires that when an entity transfers funds to an employee benefit trust or other intermediary there should be a rebuttable presumption that the entity has exchanged one asset (usually cash) for another (such as restricted cash) and that the payment itself does not represent an immediate expense. The expense is incurred when a liability for the employee costs arises. This means that in most circumstances sponsoring entities should recognise the assets (and any liabilities) of employee benefit trusts as their own until, for example, the assets vest unconditionally in identified beneficiaries.

UITF Abstract 36 *Contracts for sale of capacity*

4.36 In some industries, entities enter into contracts that convey the right to use some or all of the capacity of a physical assets. For example, in the telecommunications and electricity industries, entities may buy and sell capacity on each others' network. Some contracts give the right to use identifiable physical assets, whilst others convey the right to use a specified amount of capacity.

4.37 This type of transaction gives rise to three questions.

(a) Should the seller **report the transaction as a sale** of an asset or should the seller **continue to recognise existing assets** in their entirety?

(b) Should gains and losses arising be **presented as operating revenues/costs**, or should they be presented as gains /losses on disposal of fixed assets?

(c) How should transactions involving **exchanges** of network capacity be accounted for?

4.38 UITF Abstract 36, which was issued in March 2003, addresses these issues. In general terms, the principles of FRS 5 are applied.

Reporting the transaction as a sale

4.39 A seller of a right to use capacity should **not** report the transaction as the **sale of an asset** or component of a larger asset unless all of the following **conditions** can be satisfied.

(a) The purchaser's right of use is **exclusive and irrevocable**.

(b) The asset component is **specific and separable**. (The buyer's exclusivity is guaranteed and the seller has no right to substitute other assets.)

(c) The term of the contract is for a **major part of the asset's useful economic life**.

(d) The attributable cost or carrying value can be **measured reliably**.

(e) **No significant risks are retained** by the seller.

Turnover or disposal of fixed asset

4.40 If a transaction is reported as the sale of an asset, the proceeds will generally be reported as a **fixed asset disposal**. Only if the assets were designated as held for resale may the proceeds be reported as turnover.

Exchanges of network capacity

4.41 An entity may sell capacity on a network in exchange for receiving capacity on another entity's network in cases where the two capacities are of similar value. These types of transactions are often referred to as **reciprocal transactions**. They fall into two categories.

(a) Contracts to provide capacity in exchange for receiving capacity (no cash involved)
(b) Transactions entered into wholly or in part for a cash consideration

4.42 The UITF states that turnover or gains in respect of reciprocal transactions should be **recognised only** if the assets or services provided or received have a **readily ascertainable market value**.

4.43 **No accounting recognition** should be given to transactions that are **artificial or lacking in substance**.

4.44 FRS 5 is counted as one of the ASB's successes. However, it is not without its critics. It is very long, dense and in places difficult to understand. Moreover, the linked presentation requirement is controversial, and some commentators think it is wrong.

5 REVENUE RECOGNITION 12/02, 6/03

The problem

5.1 The recognition and measurement of revenue are of fundamental importance to proper financial reporting. Furthermore, revenue recognition has been in the news recently. There has been much discussion about the range of different accounting policies adopted by software companies, with pressure from analysts and shareholders to achieve greater consistency of reporting in that sector. The Auditing Practices Board issued a Consultation Paper at the end of June focusing on 'aggressive earnings management', with revenue recognition being one of the concerns at the heart of that debate.

5.2 The basic problem is that, with the increasing complexity of business activities, **traditional drivers of revenue**—such as 'earning', realisation, accruals/matching and prudence—are becoming harder to apply.

5.3 Faced with difficult questions over revenue recognition, different companies are finding different answers, and **practices** are developing that are in some respects **inconsistent** from one industry to another and within a single industry. The ASB believes that this inconsistency is not merely a practical issue: it also reflects different views of what revenue should represent, and of how financial statements should portray a business's operating activities.

5.4 Nor is this a problem confined to the UK and the Republic of Ireland. Although revenue accounting standards elsewhere are based on underlying concepts, those concepts are not always explored in sufficient depth to ensure their consistent application. For example, in the USA accounting for revenue is driven by underlying concepts of revenue being both **earned** and **realised**, but considerable judgement can be required in interpreting and applying these concepts.

ASB Discussion Paper

5.5 In July 2001, the ASB published a Discussion Paper *Revenue recognition.* The Paper does not discuss revenue recognition issues arising in specific industries, such as the software industry. Rather, it **focuses on the underlying proble**m, which is that, with the increasing complexity of business activities, traditional drivers of revenue are becoming harder to apply.

5.6 The ASB aims to develop a single accounting standard that sets out general principles for revenue recognition, but in sufficient depth to avoid some of the inconsistencies that exist at present. It hopes to **establish a framework** that can be used consistently to address revenue issues arising in different contexts. It's main content is summarised below.

Chapter 1: What should revenue represent?

5.7 This chapter asks what 'revenue' - which may be referred to by various names, including sales, fees, interest, dividends and royalties - should represent in financial statements. It proposes the following definitions.

KEY TERMS

In the context of a business operating cycle, **revenue** is the class of gains, before deduction of associated costs, arising as a result of **benefit being transferred to a customer** in an **exchange transaction** (ie under a contract).

An **operating cycle** is a sequence of business activities, carried out with a view to profit, which involves the **transfer of benefit to customers in exchange for consideration** (ie payment).

Chapter 2: Revenue and contractual performance

5.8 Chapter 2 develops this definition of revenue, by exploring how benefit is transferred to customers in exchange transactions. It concludes that benefit is transferred when the seller honours the promises it has made under the contract - in other words, 'performs' its contractual obligations. In that light, the chapter builds on the definition of revenue from Chapter 1.

In the context of a business operating cycle, revenue arises as a result of benefit being transferred to a customer through the **seller's performance under a contract.**

Chapter 3: Accounting for incomplete contractual performance

5.9 Chapter 3 extends this discussion of performance to contracts where the seller's contractual performance is incomplete. It concludes that **full performance is only sometimes necessary for revenue to arise**, and suggests the following general principle for determining the extent to which revenue should be recognised on the basis of partial performance.

Where contractual performance **is incomplete**, revenue should be recognised **to the extent that the seller has performed** and that performance has resulted **in benefit accruing to the customer.**

5.10 The Chapter then considers, at a very high level, various techniques by which this general principle might be applied in practice. It acknowledges, however, that dealing with **incomplete performance is likely to be the biggest single difficulty arising in practice,** and that the application of the above proposal to specific industries will be an important part of the next stage of this project.

Chapter 4: Rights of return and post performance options

5.11 Chapter 4 considers how the approach developed above is affected by customer rights of return, which in effect give a customer the ability to unwind a contract after performance by the supplier has occurred. The chapter proposes the following two possible approaches to accounting for rights of return and asks for views on which is more appropriate.

(a) **Expected sale approach.** Where goods are transferred along with a right of return, revenue should be recognised on the transfer of benefit, with an appropriate adjustment to reflect the risk of returns.

(b) **Accounting policy approach.** Where goods are transferred along with a right of return, an entity should select and consistently apply whichever of the following accounting policies is **most appropriate** to its circumstances.

  (i) *Either* revenue should be recognised on the transfer of benefit, with an appropriate adjustment to reflect the risk of returns

  (ii) *Or* revenue should be recognised on the expiry of the right to return

5.12 The most appropriate accounting policy should be judged by reference to the objectives and constraints set out in FRS 18 *Accounting policies*, giving due weight to the objective of comparability between entities operating within the same industry.

Chapter 5: Measuring consideration

5.13 Chapter 5 discusses measurement principles as opposed to recognition principles. It makes the following proposal for measurement of revenue.

Revenue should be **measured as the change in fair value** arising from the **seller's performance** of:

(a) **Assets** representing rights or other access to consideration, and
(b) **Liabilities** in respect of consideration received in advance of performance

5.14 Because revenue is restricted to gains that arise from the seller's performance, measurement of revenue is not distorted by the timing of payment from a customer. **Changes** to the value of consideration **that do not arise from performance**, for example, the **time value of money** where a customer pays a long time in advance, **do not form part of the measurement of revenue.**

5.15 Chapter 5 also considers barter transactions and asks if these should give rise to revenue. What is important is the role that the transaction has in the entity's operating cycle.

A transaction is with a customer – and hence gives rise to revenue – if, on its completion, the entity has been rewarded for **eliminating the risks previously outstanding in the relevant operating cycle.**

Chapter 6: Other issues relating to contracts and performance

5.16 This chapter considers

- Pre-performance options
- Which activities constitute performance
- 'Two-way' trading arrangements

5.17 It asks how customer payments for options should be dealt with and puts forward the following proposals.

When a customer pays for an **option** to require future performance from a seller, that payment gives rise to a liability which should be **released as revenue only when the future performance to which it relates occurs.**

> Because the number of options that will lapse unexercised cannot be known with certainty, the relationship between proceeds and **performance should be estimated at the outset and estimates should be revised over the period of performance.**

5.18 The chapter goes on to consider which activities of a seller should be taken into account when assessing the extent to which performance has occurred. It concludes that in order to be considered as part of the performance of the contract, it must be a **necessary part of the contract.** It must be specific to the customer and it must be an activity that would not have taken place had the contract not existed.

5.19 Two contracts should be accounted for separately if they are genuinely independent of one another. However, they should be treated as one larger contract if one is conditional or dependent on the other, either legally or economically.

5.20 This kind of economic dependence may arise if, for example, contract prices are set so far from fair value that there is no realistic prospect that the second contract will not follow from the first.

Chapter 7: Agency

5.21 This chapter considers certain aspects of agency agreements. Its main proposals are as follows.

(a) When a **principal transacts with a customer through a disclosed agent**, the principal's revenue should reflect the **full consideration payable by the customer** in the transaction. The principal should treat any **commission** or other amounts payable to the agent **separately as an expense and not as a reduction of revenue.**

(b) When an **entity acts as a disclosed agent**, its revenue should reflect the amount of **commission or other income receivable** from its principal.

(c) When an entity acts as an **undisclosed agent**, it should **account for revenue in the same way as a principal.**

FRED 28 *Inventories; Construction and service contracts*

5.22 As part of the ASB's programme of convergence between FRS and IFRS (see Chapter 13), in May 2002 it issued FRED 28 *Inventories; Construction and service contracts.*

Main points

5.23 This FRED covers material from three IAS: IAS 2 *Inventories,* IAS 11 *Construction contracts* and a small amount of material from IAS 18 *Revenue.*

5.24 There are no major differences between the accounting required by the proposals in FRED 28 and the existing requirements of SSAP 9.

5.25 The topic of revenue recognition is being considered by the ASB and other standard setters, and is currently the subject of a Discussion Paper (see paragraphs 5.1-5.21). For this reason, the ASB does not currently propose that the UK should adopt the full text of IAS 18.

5.26 The main difference between SSAP 9 and FRED 28 is in the **terminology**, most obviously in the title. International accounting standards talk about 'inventory' rather than 'stocks' and 'construction and service contracts' rather than 'long-term contracts'. **Stocks and long-term contracts are not examinable at. Paper 3.6**, so we focus below on the material from IAS 18 on revenue recognition, which will be new to you.

Main changes proposed to existing UK requirements

5.27 There are **no major differences** between the accounting required in FRED 28 and the existing requirements of SSAP 9. However, SSAP 9 requires 'prudently calculated attributable profit' to be recognised in the profit and loss account when the outcome of a contract can be assessed with 'reasonable certainty'. Appendix I to the standard, contains similar references to prudence and reasonable certainty. FRED 28 requires the recognition of contract revenue and contract costs when the outcome of a contract can be **estimated reliably**. In emphasising reliability rather than prudence, the approach of the draft standard is more in keeping with the ASB's *Statement of Principles* and FRS 18 *Accounting policies*.

5.28 FRED 28 requires that **amounts received from the customer before the related work is performed** are recognised as a **separate liability** ('advances'). However, there are **no requirements relating to the further analysis** of the remaining balance sheet amount. (Paragraph 42 requires it to be presented as a single asset or liability, the 'gross amount due to/from customers for contract work'.) SSAP 9 requires the separate disclosure of 'amounts recoverable on contracts' (a debtor), 'payments on account' (a creditor), 'long-term contract balances' (stock) and foreseeable losses (a provision or creditor).

5.29 **FRED 28** allows the requirements of the standard to be applied to the **separately identifiable components of a single contract or to a group of contracts together**, if that would reflect the substance of a contract or a group of contracts. SSAP 9 itself does not include an equivalent requirement.

5.30 The appendix to SSAP 9 indicates that, in some businesses, it will be most appropriate to treat parts of a long-term contract separately, but does not mention the combination of more than one contract. A similar treatment to that of the draft standard should be achieved by applying SSAP 9 in the context of FRS 5 *Reporting the substance of transactions.*

5.31 The remainder of this section deals with the material on contracts for services from IAS 18.

Rendering of services

5.32 The rendering of services typically involves the performance by the enterprise of a contractually agreed task over an agreed period of time. The services may be rendered within a single period or over more than one period.

5.33 Some contracts for the rendering of services are directly related to construction contracts, for example those for the services of project managers and architects. These are dealt with in accordance with the requirements for construction contracts.

5.34 When the outcome of a transaction involving the rendering of services can be estimated reliably, the associated revenue should be recognised by reference to the **stage of completion of the transaction** at the balance sheet date. The outcome of a transaction can be estimated reliably when *all* these conditions are satisfied.

(a) The amount of revenue can be **measured reliably**

(b) It is probable that the **economic benefits** associated with the transaction will flow to the enterprise

(c) The **stage of completion** of the transaction at the balance sheet date can be measured reliably

(d) The **costs incurred** for the transaction and the costs to complete the transaction can be measured reliably

5.35 The parties to the transaction will normally have to agree the following before an enterprise can make reliable estimates.

(a) Each party's **enforceable rights** regarding the service to be provided and received by the parties

(b) The **consideration** to be exchanged

(c) The **manner and terms of settlement**

5.36 There are various methods of determining the stage of completion of a transaction, but for practical purposes, when services are performed by an indeterminate number of acts over a period of time, revenue should be recognised on a **straight line basis** over the period, unless there is evidence for the use of a more appropriate method. If one act is of more significance than the others, then the significant act should be carried out *before* revenue is recognised.

5.37 In uncertain situations, when the outcome of the transaction involving the rendering of services cannot be estimated reliably, the standard recommends a **no loss/no gain approach**. Revenue is recognised only to the extent of the expenses recognised that are recoverable.

5.38 This is particularly likely during the **early stages of a transaction**, but it is still probable that the enterprise will recover the costs incurred. So the revenue recognised in such a period will be equal to the expenses incurred, with no profit.

5.39 Obviously, if the costs are not likely to be reimbursed, then they must be recognised as an expense immediately. **When the uncertainties cease to exist**, revenue should be recognised as laid out in Paragraph 5.34 above.

Amendment to FRS 5: Revenue recognition

5.40 There is no specific UK standard which deals exclusively with revenue recognition, although it has featured in a number of standards including SSAP 9, the former SSAP 2, FRS 18 and UITF Abstract 26.

5.41 The IASB has a standard on Revenue (IAS 18), and is currently working on a project that will lead to a revision of both IAS 18 and the *Framework*. The intention is to publish an Exposure Draft in 2004. IASB is currently exploring an approach to revenue recognition which focuses on changes in assets and liabilities.

5.42 The ASB issued a Discussion Paper in July 2001, which is covered in Paragraphs 5.1-5.21. However, the ASB has no plans to produce an Exposure Draft or FRS on the subject because of its policy of only issuing full standards on topics of major concern that have been developed jointly with the IASB.

5.43 Nevertheless, the ASB has noted that **questions continue to arise** in relation to transactions affecting revenue recognition, and has therefore issued guidance on a number

of aspects of the topic. This guidance takes the form of an **Application Note to FRS** 5 *Reporting the substance of transactions*, which was published in November 2003.

5.44 The Application Note sets out a number of **basic principles**, which may be summarised as follows.

Exchange transaction

5.45 A seller enters into exchange transactions with its customers under **contractual arrangements** (formal or informal) under which it obtains the **right to be paid**.

5.46 Turnover is the revenue resulting from exchange transactions under which the seller transfers to customers the **goods or services that it is in business to provide.**

5.47 Payments derived from **other exchange transactions** (eg fixed asset sales) **do not normally give rise to turnover** as they do not fall within the class of transactions above (ie 'goods or services that it is in business to provide').

Reporting of revenue

5.48 At the point of performance of its contractual obligations, an entity will recognise either:

(a) An **increase in assets**, or

(b) A **decrease in liabilities** (eg where an entity previously received payment in advance of performance and is now released from the liability)

5.49 The asset increase or liability decrease is simultaneously reported as **revenue**.

Payment in advance of performance

5.50 When a seller receives payment from a customer in advance of performance, it recognises a **liability:**

(a) This liability equals the consideration received and represents the seller's contractual obligation to provide goods or services to that value.

(b) When performance takes place, the gross amount of the reduction in liability is simultaneously reported as revenue.

Measurement of revenue

5.50 Revenue (represented by the seller's new asset or by derecognition of a liability) should be measured at the **fair value of the consideration receivable.**

5.51 Fair value (FV) is defined as the amount at which goods or services could be exchanged in an arm's length transaction between informed and willing parties, other than in a forced or liquidation sale.

5.52 The FV of the consideration receivable will normally be the amount specified in the contractual arrangement as adjusted for:

- Discounts
- The time value of money and risk (where material)

The statement also gives **detailed guidance** on the following five areas.

(a) Long-term contractual performance
(b) Separation and linking of contractual arrangements
(c) Bill and hold arrangements
(d) Sales with rights of return
(e) Presentation of turnover as a principal or agent.

5.53 These are the main areas which have been subject to **differing interpretation** in practice. The intention is to ensure that entities report turnover in accordance with the **substance of their contractual arrangements** with customers, and **at the point at which their performance entitles them to recognise** either an **increase in assets** or a **decrease in liabilities**.

Long-term contractual performance

5.54 A contractual arrangement may require a seller to design, manufacture or construct a single substantial asset or provide a service for a customer which is significant to the business and which straddles the seller's year-end.

5.55 The Application note proposes the following approach to such transactions.

(a) Assess how changes in a seller's assets or liabilities, and related turnover, that arise from its performance under an incomplete long-term contract, should be recorded in the seller's financial statements.

(b) Amounts recognised should represent the **stage of completion of contractual obligations, derived from an assessment of the fair value of goods or services provided** to the reporting date as **proportion of the total fair value of the contract**. This is preferred to considering expenditure to date as a proportion of total expenditure.

(c) Fair values should represent those applicable on **inception of contract** (except where contractual terms specify that changes in prices will be passed on to the customer).

(d) **Payments in instalments** may be (but will not necessarily be) **indicative** of extent to which seller has performed its contractual obligations.

(e) Where payment is received in **arrears**, seller should take the following into account when valuing changes in assets or liabilities and related turnover:

(i) Risk
(ii) Time value of money

(f) Where contractual arrangements give the customer the **right to cancel** at an interim stage of contract completion, the seller should have regard to the effect of **additional risk** arising.

Separation and linking of contractual arrangements

5.56 A single contractual arrangement may require a seller to provide a number of different goods or services (or 'components') to its customers. Three possibilities arise.

(a) The components are unrelated and capable of being sold separately.

(b) Two or more components are so closely related that their individual sale is not commercially feasible from viewpoint of either party.

(c) A number of goods or services are provided in which the amount payable is set below the price at which the items would be sold individually.

The approach to be followed in the case of such arrangement is to **determine whether 'unbundling' or 'bundling' is appropriate.**

(a) **Unbundling.** This arises when the seller, as a result of performance, decides to recognise a change in its assets or liabilities, and turnover, in respect of its right to be paid for each component on an individual basis.

(b) **Bundling.** This is where a seller combines two or more components and recognises turnover on that basis.

In each case the commercial substance of the transaction needs to be considered.

Question: 'bundling' and 'unbundling'

State whether 'bundling' or 'unbundling' is appropriate in each of the following situations.

(a) Fiona buys an 'off the shelf' software package from Seager Software Ltd. Seager Software offers separately a support service that provides helpline assistance and advice about the package's operation.

(b) Total Software Solutions plc enters into a contractual arrangement for the supply of bespoke software, together with its maintenance and the customer's right to future upgrades for a period of three years.

Answer

(a) An analysis of the arrangement shows that Fiona has no commercial obligation or requirement to purchase the support service; it is not needed in order that the software package operates satisfactorily. Seager Software Ltd's performance is made up from two components and it should recognise turnover separately for each.

(b) An analysis of the arrangement shows that the maintenance and upgrades are required in order to ensure that the software continues to operate satisfactorily throughout the three year period and that these services are offered only by the supplier of the software, Total Software Solutions plc. The commercial substance of the arrangement is therefore that the customer is paying for a three year service agreement. The seller should treat all three components as linked, and recognise turnover on a long-term contractual basis.

Bill and hold arrangements

5.57 A seller may enter into a contractual arrangement with a customer for the supply of goods where there is **transfer of title but physical delivery is delayed to a later date.** These are commonly known as 'bill and hold' arrangements. It is necessary to determine whether, at any point, the seller has the right to recognise changes in its assets or liabilities, and turnover, in relation to the bill and hold arrangement.

5.58 In order to recognise these changes, the seller needs to have performed its contractual obligations by **transferring to the customer the principal benefits and risks of the goods**.

5.59 **Benefits** include:

(a) The right to obtain the goods as and when required

(b) The sole right to the goods for their sale to a third party, and the future cash flows from such a sale

(c) Insulation from changes in prices charged by the seller (for example, arising from revisions to the seller's standard price list)

5.60 **Risks** include:

(a) Slow movement (resulting in increased holding costs) and obsolescence

(b) Being compelled to take delivery of goods that have become obsolescent or not readily saleable

For changes in assets/liabilities and turnover to be recognised, the contractual arrangements between seller and customer should include *all* of the following characteristics.

(a) The bill and hold terms should **fulfil the commercial objectives of the customer**.

(b) Subject to any normal rights of return, the **seller should have the right to be paid regardless of whether the goods are shipped**, at the customer's request, to its delivery address.

(c) The **seller should not have retained any performance obligations** other than the safekeeping of the goods, and their shipment when the customer requests this.

(d) The **goods should be identified separately from the seller's other stock** and should not be capable of being used to fill other orders that are received between the date of the bill and hold sale and shipment of the goods to the customer.

(e) The goods should be **complete and ready for delivery**.

Sales with right of return

5.61 The terms of contractual arrangements may allow customers to return goods that they have purchased and either obtain a refund or be released from the obligation to pay. Rights of return may be included explicitly or implicitly within contractual arrangements, or arise through statutory requirements.

5.62 Including rights of return in a contractual arrangement **may affect either the quantification of the seller's right to be paid** (compared with a transaction which does not have these rights), **or the point at which the seller should recognise that right**. In some cases, 'right of return' could oblige the seller to defer recognition of the sales transaction so long as the seller retains substantially all of the risks associated with the related goods.

5.63 The seller's recognition of its right to be paid and contractual obligation to transfer economic benefits to its customer in respect of rights of return are linked transactions. In consequence, **changes in the seller's assets or liabilities should reflect the loss expected to arise from the rights of return. Turnover should exclude the sales value of estimated returns**.

5.64 The seller will generally be able reliably to estimate the sales value of returns, having regard to risk, which may be less than its maximum potential obligation. This may be derived from historic experience of comparable sales.

5.65 In extreme cases **where no reliable estimate can be made, substantially all of the risks of the related goods remain with the seller and turnover should not be recognised**. Any payments received should be included within creditors as **payments in advance**.

Presentation of turnover as principle or agent

5.66 A seller may act on its own account (as 'principal') when contracting with customers for the supply of goods or services. Alternatively a seller may act as an intermediary ('agent'),

earning a fee or commission in return for arranging the provision of goods or services on behalf of a principal.

5.67 It is necessary to determine whether a seller should be regarded as acting as principal or agent in relation to an exchange transaction with a customer. **For a seller to account for exchange transactions as a principal, the seller should normally have exposure to all significant benefits and risks** associated with at least one of the following.

(a) **Selling price**. The seller must be able to establish the selling price, directly or indirectly (for example through provision of additional goods or services).

(b) **Stock**. The seller must be exposed to risks of damage, slow movement and obsolescence and changes in suppliers' prices.

5.68 Other indications that the **seller acts as principal** include:

(a) Performance of part of the services, or modification to the goods supplied
(b) Assumption of credit risk
(c) Discretion in supplier selection
(d) No disclosure of agency relationship

Other indications that the **seller acts as agent** include the following.

(a) Once the customer's order has been confirmed with a third party, the seller has no further involvement in performance of ultimate supplier's contractual obligations.

(b) The amount the seller earns is predetermined (a fixed fee or percentage of amount billed to customer).

(c) The seller bears no stock or credit risk.

(d) The seller has disclosed the fact that it is acting as agent.

Question: principal or agent?

Consider whether the seller is acting as principal or agent in the following situations.

(a) Buildit Ltd acts as a building contractor for the construction of a new office block. An analysis of the arrangement shows that the terms of the Buildit's contract with its customer include a negotiated selling price, credit risk for amounts due from the customer, primary responsibility for the construction and quality of the new building and discretion as to whether it carries out the work itself or employs subcontractors.

(b) Kwikbreak.com acts as an online retailer from a website, where it advertises discounted holidays. An analysis of the arrangement shows that it acts as an intermediary between its customers and the ultimate sellers of the holidays and that it does not set the selling price. Its contractual terms of business include an exclusion of any liability to its customers once they have been put in touch with the ultimate sellers. Kwikbreak.com is paid a fee for each customer that purchases a holiday from an ultimate seller and has no involvement in the transaction after it has put the customer in touch with the ultimate seller.

Answer

(a) Buildit Ltd is acting as principal and should account for the gross amount of turnover, regardless of whether it carries out the work itself or employs subcontractors to carry out part or all of the construction activities.

(b) Kwikbreak.com is acting as agent and its turnover should include only the fees it receives from the ultimate seller.

Chapter roundup

- The subject of **off balance sheet finance** is a complex one which has plagued the accountancy profession. In practice, off balance sheet finance schemes are often very sophisticated and they are beyond the range of this syllabus. FRS 5 embodies the concept of **substance over form**.
- Make sure that you have memorised the definitions for **assets and liabilities** and the criteria for their **recognition and derecognition** given in FRS 5.
- **FRS 5** embodies the concept of **substance over form**.
- You also need to understand the methods of presentation described in FRS 5, particularly *offset* and **linked presentation**.
- The major types of off balance sheet finance are discussed in the **Application Notes** to FRS 5.
- **Revenue recognition** is an important problem, so the ASB has issued a Discussion Paper about it.
- The ASB has also issued an **Application Note on revenue recognition** in the form of an **Amendment to FRS 5**. This gives both general principles and specialist guidance.

Quick quiz

1 Off balance sheet transactions are always fraudulent.

True ☐

False ☐

2 Give three examples of ways in which the principle of substance over form is enforced.

3 When should an asset be recognised on the balance sheet?

4 Assets must be recognised or not appear at all.

True ☐

False ☐

5 What is 'linked presentation'?

6 FRS 5 allows offset of assets and liabilities only in very limited cases.

Fill in the blanks.

(a) The parties owe each other .... amounts.

(b) The reporting entity has the ability to insist on a ....

(c) The above is ....

7 Factotem Ltd brings in a debt factor. The terms of the agreement are that the factor pays Factotem 90% of the value of the outstanding debtors. Interest is charged on this amount. The factor then collects the debts and reduces this amount accordingly. Factotem is responsible for any uncollected debts. What is the substance of the transaction?

8 The ASB's Discussion Paper on revenue recognition deals with specific industries.

True ☐

False ☐

9 Why would a sale of fixed assets not give rise to revenue?

Answers to quick quiz

1 False. There may be genuine reasons for excluding items from the balance sheet.

2 (a) Leasing
(b) Quasi subsidiaries
(c) Joint arrangement which are not entities.

3 See para 3.7.

4 False. FRS 5 allows the in-between case of partial derecognition.

5 This requires non-recourse finance to be shown on the face of the balance sheet as a deduction from the asset to which it relates, rather than in the liabilities section.

6 (a) Determinable monetary amounts
(b) Net settlement
(c) Assured beyond doubt

7 The form is likely to be that Factotem has sold its debtors to the factor. The substance is that Factotem is still responsible for bad debts and the factor has provided a commercial loan with the debtors as security.

8 False. It is a discussion of the underlying principles.

9 Under the ASB's recent Application Note to FRS 5, such a transaction would not give rise to revenue because it does not fall within the category of goods or services that the entity is in business to provide.

Now try the question below from the Exam Question Bank

Number	Level	Marks	Time
Q27	Introductory	n/a	n/a

Chapter 20

LEASES

Topic list		Syllabus reference
1	Forms of lease	1(a) – (f), 4(e)
2	Lessee accounting	1(a) – (f), 4(e)
3	Lessor accounting	1(a) – (f), 4(e)
4	Criticism and new approach	1(a) – (f), 4(e)

Introduction

Leasing transactions are extremely common in business and you will often come across them in both your business and personal capacity. You should be familiar with the more straightforward aspects of this topic from your earlier studies. Leasing is strongly associated with **off balance sheet finance** and SSAP 21 interacts with FRS 5 in sale and leaseback transactions.

Study guide

Section 16 – Leases

- Discussion of problem areas in lease accounting including classification, termination, tax variation clauses
- Accounting for sale and leaseback transactions and recognition of income by lessors
- Discussion of and accounting for proposed changes in lease accounting and its impact on corporate financial statements

Exam guide

As you can see from the Study Guide, the emphasis is on current developments in leasing.

1 FORMS OF LEASE

1.1 You should know the distinction between finance leases and operating leases from your earlier studies. Look back to your study material if anything in this summary is unfamiliar.

Knowledge brought forward from earlier studies

Finance lease

- Transfers substantially all the risks and rewards of ownership of an asset to the lessee
- Presumed if at the inception of a lease the PV of the minimum lease payments ≥ 90% of the FV of leased asset
- *PV*: calculate using the interest rate implicit in the lease
- The minimum lease payments are the minimum payments over the remaining part of the lease term (except charges for services and taxes to be paid by the lessor) *and*
    - (Lessee) any residual amounts guaranteed by him, *or*
    - (Lessor) any residual amounts guaranteed by the lessee or by an independent third party
- *Lease term*: the period for which the lessee has contracted to lease the asset (primary *and* secondary periods)

Operating lease

A lease other than a finance lease.

2 LESSEE ACCOUNTING

Finance leases

2.1 From the lessee's point of view there are two main **accounting problems**.

- Should the assets be **capitalised** as if it had been purchased?
- How should the **lease charge** allocated between different accounting periods?

2.2 **SSAP 21 requirements**

(a) A finance lease should be recorded in the balance sheet of a lessee as an asset and as an obligation to pay future rentals. At the inception of the lease the sum to be recorded both as an asset and as a liability should be the **present value of the minimum lease payments**, derived by discounting them at the interest rate implicit in the lease.

(b) In practice in the case of a finance lease the **fair value** of the asset will often be a sufficiently close approximation to the present value of the minimum lease payments and may in these circumstances be substituted for it.

(c) The combined benefit to a lessor of regional development and other **grants** together with **capital allowances**, which reduce tax liabilities, may enable the minimum lease payments under a finance lease to be reduced to a total which is less than the fair value of the asset. In these circumstances, the amount to be capitalised and depreciated should be restricted to the **minimum lease payments**. A negative finance charge should not be shown.

(d) **Rentals payable** should be apportioned between the **finance charge** and a **reduction of the outstanding obligation for future amounts payable**. The total finance charge under a finance lease should be allocated to accounting periods during the lease term so as to produce a **constant periodic rate of charge** on the remaining balance of the obligation for each accounting period, or a reasonable approximation thereto.

(e) An asset leased under a finance lease should be **depreciated** over the shorter of the lease term or its useful life. However, in the case of a hire purchase contract which has the characteristics of a finance lease, the asset should be depreciated over its useful life.

2.3 In interpreting the above these definitions from SSAP 21 should be borne in mind. We have seen that **the main argument in favour of capitalisation is substance over form**.

KEY TERMS

- **Fair value** is the price at which an asset could be exchanged in an arm's length transaction less, where applicable, any grants receivable towards the purchase or use of the asset.
- **Finance charge** is the amount borne by the lessee over the lease terms, representing the difference between the total of the minimum lease payments (including any residual amounts guaranteed by him) and the amount at which he records the leased asset at the inception of the lease.
- The **interest rate implicit in a lease** is the discount rate which at the inception of the lease, when applied to the amounts which the lessor expects to receive and retain produces an amount (the present value) equal to the fair value of the leased asset. The amounts which the lessor expects to receive and retain comprise:

  (a) The minimum lease payments to the lessor (as defined below); *plus*
  (b) Any unguaranteed residual value; *less*
  (c) Any part of (a) and (b) for which the lessor will be accountable to the lessee

  If the interest rate implicit in the lease is not determinable, it should be estimated by reference to the rate which a lessee would be expected to pay on a similar lease.

2.4 **Main arguments against capitalisation**

(a) **Legal position.** The benefit of a lease to a lessee is an intangible asset, not the ownership of the equipment. It may be misleading to users of accounts to capitalise the equipment when a lease is legally quite different from a loan used to purchase the equipment. Capitalising leases also raises the question of whether other executory contracts should be treated similarly, for example contracts of employment.

(b) **Complexity**. Many small businesses will find that they do not have the expertise necessary for carrying out the calculations required for capitalisation.

(c) **Subjectivity**. To some extent, capitalisation is a somewhat arbitrary process and this may lead to a lack of consistency between companies.

(d) **Presentation**. The impact of leasing can be more usefully described in the notes to financial statements. These can be made readily comprehensible to users who may not understand the underlying calculations.

IMPORTANT!

These are outweighed by the main argument in favour: **Substance over form**.

2.5 There are two main ways of **allocating the finance charge** between accounting periods:

- The actuarial method (before tax)
- The sum of the digits method.

Each of these is illustrated in an example later in this chapter. The actuarial method is to be preferred as it most exactly reflects the way in which the finance charges are incurred. The sum of the digits method produces a reasonable approximation to the actuarial method.

Operating leases

2.6 SSAP 21 requires that the **rentals** under operating leases should be **written off as an expense** on a **straight line basis** over the lease term even if the payments are not made on such a basis, unless another systematic and rational basis is justified by the circumstances.

Hire purchase contracts

2.7 Assets acquired under hire purchase agreements should be **capitalised** in the same way as those under finance leases if the HP contracts are of a financing nature. Otherwise (eg, if the option to purchase is not to be taken up) they should be accounted for on a basis similar to that used for operating leases.

Disclosure requirements: lessees

2.8 SSAP 21 requires lessees to disclose the following information.

(a) The gross amounts of **assets held under finance leases**⋆ together with the related accumulated depreciation, analysed by class of asset must be shown. This information may be consolidated with the corresponding information for owned assets, and not shown separately. In that case, the net amount of assets held under finance leases⋆ included in the overall total should also be disclosed.

(b) The amounts of **obligations related to finance leases**⋆ (net of finance charges allocated to future periods) should be disclosed. These should be shown separately from other obligations and liabilities and should be analysed between amounts payable in the next year, amounts payable in the second to fifth years inclusive from the balance sheet date and the aggregate amounts payable thereafter.

(c) The **aggregate finance charges** allocated for the period in respect of finance leases must appear.

(d) Disclosure should be made of the amount of any **commitments** existing at the balance sheet date in respect of finance leases which have been entered into but whose inception occurs after the year end.

(e) The total of **operating lease rentals** charged as an expense in the profit and loss account should be disclosed, analysed between amounts payable in respect of hire of plant and machinery and in respect of other operating leases.

(f) In respect of **operating leases**, the lessee should disclose the payments which he is **committed** to make during the next year, analysed between those in which the commitment expires within that year, in the second to fifth years inclusive and over five years from the balance sheet date, showing separately the commitments in respect of leases of land and buildings and other operating leases.

⋆ Including the equivalent information in respect of **hire purchase contracts**.

Exam focus point

Rather than learn this list by heart, take a look at a set of company accounts and see how those disclosures work in practice.

2.9 EXAMPLE: ACTUARIAL AND SUM OF DIGITS METHODS

A lessee enters a leasing agreement on 31 December 20X3 for a piece of equipment costing £47,460. The lease requires the payment of an annual rental of £13,610 payable in advance. The primary period of the lease is for four years. After the end of the primary period, the lessee has the right to extend the lease indefinitely on payment of a nominal annual rental. The lessee believes that the equipment will last for four years and will have no scrap value at the end of that period. The lessee depreciates assets of this type using the straight line basis. Both the lessor and the lessee have accounting periods ending on 31 December.

2.10 SOLUTION: ACTUARIAL METHOD

Under the actuarial method, the first problem is to find the implied rate of interest in the lease. To do this the following steps should be followed.

Step 1. Establish the amount of money that has been advanced. This will be equal to the cost of the equipment less any deposit and/or rental payable at the start of the lease.

	£
Cost	47,460
Initial rental	13,610
Amount advanced	33,850

Step 2. Divide the amount advanced by the period rental to give the annuity (or cumulative discount) factor.

$$\text{Annuity factor} = \frac{33{,}850}{13{,}610} = 2.487$$

Step 3. Establish how many rentals are payable excluding, if appropriate, that payable at the start of the lease. Here it is 3 rentals.

Step 4. Inspect the annuity table for the number of periods equal to the number of rentals found in Step 3. The implied rate will have the same annuity factor as that found in Step 2.

From the table reproduced towards the end of this Study Text it can be seen that a rate of 10% has an annuity factor of 2.487.

In some cases it will be found that the annuity factor calculated in Step 2 does not equate exactly to one in the table. It will then be necessary to find the implied rate by interpolation.

Note. This calculation assumes that the secondary period rental is nominal and ignores the residual value of the equipment.

In the present case, the purchase cost is known to the lessee. The liability and the value of the machine will, therefore, be recorded at £47,460 at the start of the lease. The liability will of course be reduced immediately by the first rental. Since the lease started on the last day of the lessee's accounting period to 31 December 20X3, there will be no finance charge in respect of that year.

It is now possible to establish the amount of the finance charges in each period.

Period	Liability at start of period	Rental payment	Liability during period	Finance charge = 10% of liability during period	Liability at end of period
	£	£	£	£	£
1	47,460	13,610	33,850	3,385	37,235
2	37,235	13,610	23,625	2,362	25,987
3	25,987	13,610	12,377	1,233	13,610
4	13,610	13,610			

Notes

(a) The periods (1 - 4) are years under the lease rather than accounting periods (see below).

(b) The format of the table would obviously need to be adjusted if the rentals were payable in arrears.

(c) As suggested in the standard the allocation 'produces a constant periodic rate of return (10%) on the remaining balance of the liability'.

(d) Payment in arrears would be calculated differently.

Charges to the P&L account

Year ending 31 December	Finance charge	Depreciation	Total
	£	£	£
20X3	-	-	-
20X4	3,385	11,865	15,250
20X5	2,362	11,865	14,227
20X6	1,233	11,865	13,098
20X7	-	11,865	11,865
	6,980	47,460	54,440

Note that the total charge to the P&L account over the life of the machine is equal to the total rentals paid (£13,610 × 4 = £54,440).

Balance sheet presentation

	As at 31 December				
	20X3	20X4	20X5	20X6	20X7
	£	£	£	£	£
Assets					
Equipment acquired under finance leases	47,460	47,460	47,460	47,460	47,460
Less accumulated depreciation	-	11,865	23,730	35,595	47,460
	47,460	35,595	23,730	11,865	-
Liabilities					
Obligations under finance leases					
Within 2 - 5 years	23,625	12,377	-	-	-
Within 1 year	10,225	11,248	12,377	-	-
	33,850	23,625	12,377	-	-

Note that the obligations under the lease can be found from the main table constructed above. It is, of course, necessary to ensure that the finance charges are allocated to the correct accounting periods.

SSAP 21 also permits this alternative analysis.

Leasing commitments: finance leases

The future minimum lease payments under finance leases to which the company is committed as at 31 December 20X3 are as follows.

Year ending 31 December	£		
20X4	13,610		
20X5	13,610		
20X6	13,610		
20X7	-	)	This part of the table has been included
20X8	-	)	for illustrative purposes as the standard
20X9 and after	-	)	suggests that the figures for the next
	40,830		five years should be shown separately
Less finance charged allocated			and those thereafter in aggregate.
to future periods	6,980		
	33,850		This figure will be the same as that in the balance sheet

2.11 SOLUTION: SUM OF THE DIGITS METHOD

The sum of the digits (or rule of 78) method gives an acceptable approximation to the actuarial method and, because of its relative simplicity, has been more popular in practice. Although you should already be familiar with the technique, it is as well to revise the main steps.

Step 1. Calculate the total finance charges. This will be equal to the total rentals less the value of the equipment.

	£
Cost	54,440
Initial rental	47,460
Amount advanced	6,980

Step 2. Establish how many rentals are payable excluding if appropriate, that payable at the start of the lease (see note below). Here it is 3 rentals

Step 3. Calculate the sum of the digits. For large numbers it is best to use the formula below where n is the number found in Step 2.

$$\text{Sum of digits} = \frac{n(n+1)}{2}$$

$$1 + 2 + 3 = 6 \quad \frac{3(3+1)}{2} = 6$$

Step 4. Calculate the appropriate proportion of the finance charges starting with the number obtained in Step 2 for the first period of the lease.

Period	*Finance charges*
1	3/6 × £6,980 = £3,490
2	2/6 × £6,980 = £2,327
3	1/6 × £6,980 = £1,163

Note. In the present case, although the primary period of the lease is four years, the liability under the lease will be discharged after three years (and one day) as all four rentals will then have been paid. For this reason, the finance charges will be allocated to the accounting periods 20X4, 20X5 and 20X6 (as under the actuarial method) and no charge will arise in the final year of the primary period, 20X7. If the rentals had been payable in arrears, it would have been necessary to calculate a finance charge for each year of the primary period and the sum of the digits would be 10 (1 + 2 + 3 + 4).

Charges to the P&L account

Year ending 31 December	*Finance charge*	*Depreciation*	*Total*
	£	£	£
20X4	3,490	11,865	15,355
20X5	2,327	11,865	14,192
20X6	1,163	11,865	13,028
20X7	-	11,865	11,865
	6,980	47,460	54,440

The balance sheet presentation for the asset will be the same as under the actuarial method. The obligation under the lease could be arrived at by preparing a table similar to that used before. In this case, however, let us consider the entries in the liability account.

OBLIGATIONS UNDER FINANCE LEASE

Date		£	*Date*		£
31.12.X3	Cash	13,610	31.12.X3	Fixed assets	47,460
31.12.X3	Balance c/f	33,850			
		47,460			47,460
31.12.X4	Cash	13,610	1.1.X4	Balance b/f	33,850
31.12.X4	Balance c/f	23,730	31.12.X4	Finance charge: P&L	3,490
		37,340			37,340
31.12.X5	Cash	13,610	1.1.X5	Balance b/f	23,730
31.12.X5	Balance c/f	12,447	31.12.X5	Finance charge: P&L	2,327
		26,057			26,057
Date		£	*Date*		£
31.12.X6	Cash	13,610	1.1.X6	Balance b/f	12,447
			31.12.X6	Finance charge: P&L	1,163
		13,610			13,610

Summary

2.12 The two main methods of allocating the finance charges are summarised below.

	Actuarial	*Sum of the digits*
	£	£
20X4	3,385	3,490
20X5	2,362	2,327
20X6	1,233	1,163
	6,980	6,980

Question: finance lease

On 31 December 20X3 Cradlebrake Ltd entered into a leasing arrangement with Heathcliffe Finance for a large packaging machine. The terms of the lease require quarterly payments in arrears for four years of £1,107.24. Cradlebrake depreciates all plant and machinery on a straight line basis. The engineering manager estimates that the packaging machine will last 4 years and will have no scrap value. The rate of interest implicit in the lease is 5% per quarter. The company intends to capitalise the machine and show as a liability the outstanding rentals (excluding interest).

You are required to calculate the relevant P&L account and balance sheet figures for incorporation in the annual accounts for the accounting periods ending 30 September 20X4, 20X5, 20X6, 20X7 and 20X8.

Answer

	Balance sheet		P&L account	
	Leased assets	Leasing creditor	Depreciation charge	Interest
Year ending	£	£	£	£
30.9.X4	9,750	10,401	2,250	1,723
30.9.X5	6,750	7,870	3,000	1,898
30.9.X6	3,750	4,794	3,000	1,353
30.9.X7	750	1,055	3,000	690
30.9.X8	-	-	750	53

Working

Using the table towards the end of the Study Text, the present value of the payments under the lease is equal to £1,107.24 × 10.838 = £12,000 at the start of the lease.

Period	Liability at start of period	Finance charge	Rental payment	Liability at end of period
	£	£	£	£
1	12,000.00	600.00	(1,107.24)	11,492.76
2	11,492.76	574.64	(1,107.24)	10,960.16
3	10,960.16	548.01	(1,107.24)	10,400.93
4	10,400.93	520.05	(1,107.24)	9,813.74
5	9,813.74	490.69	(1,107.24)	9,197.19
6	9,197.19	459.86	(1,107.24)	8,549.81
7	8,549.81	427.49	(1,107.24)	7,870.06
8	7,870.06	393.50	(1,107.24)	7,156.32
9	7,156.32	357.82	(1,107.24)	6,406.90
10	6,406.90	320.34	(1,107.24)	5,620.00
11	5,620.00	281.00	(1,107.24)	4,793.76
12	4,793.76	239.69	(1,107.24)	3,926.21
13	3,926.21	196.31	(1,107.24)	3,015.28
14	3,015.28	150.76	(1,107.24)	2,058.80
15	2,058.80	102.94	(1,107.24)	1,054.50
16	1,054.50	52.74	(1,107.24)	Nil

The finance charges for each year can be found by adding together those for the appropriate quarters.

Where a large number of payments are involved, it is probably simpler to look at accounting periods rather than the periods within the lease. The liability at any point of the lease is equal to the present value of payments due thereafter. Thus the liability at 30.9.X4 when there are 13 instalments outstanding will be £1,107.24 × 9.394 (see cumulative discount table) = £10,401. The finance charge can then be found as follows.

	£
Rentals paid to 30.9.X4 (£1,107.24 × 3)	3,322
Capital repayment (reduction in liability)	
£12,000 – £10,401	1,599
Finance charge	1,723

The calculations for the remaining periods are shown below.

Year ending 30.9.X5

Liability at 30.9.X5 with 9 instalments to pay:

£1,107.24 × 7.108 = £7,870; £10,401 – £7,870 = £2,531;

Interest = (4 × £1,107.24) – £2,531 = £1,898

Year ending 30.9.X6

Liability at 30.9.X6 with 5 instalments to pay:

£1,107.24 × 4.329 = £4,794; £7,870 – £4,794 = £3,076

Interest = (4 × £1,107.24) – £3,076 = £1,353

Year ending 30.9.X7

Liability at 30.9.X7 with 1 instalment to pay:
£1,107.24 × 0.952 = £1,055; £4,794 – £1,055 = £3,739
Interest = (4 × £1,107.24) – £3,739 = £690

Year ending 30.9.X8

Interest = £1,107.24 – £1,055 = £52

3 LESSOR ACCOUNTING

3.1 The following SSAP 21 definitions are relevant to lessor accounting.

KEY TERMS

- **Initial direct costs** are those costs incurred by the lessor that are directly associated with negotiating and consummating leasing transactions, such as commissions, legal fees, costs of credit investigations and costs of preparing and processing documents for new leases acquired.
- **Gross earnings** comprise the lessor's gross finance income over the lease term, representing the difference between his gross investment in the lease and the cost of the leased asset less any grants receivable towards the purchase or use of the asset.
- The **gross investment** in a lease at a point in time is the total of the minimum lease payments and any unguaranteed residual value accruing to the lessor.
- The **net investment** in a lease at a point in time comprises:

  (a) The gross investment in a lease (as defined above)
  (b) Less gross earnings allocated to future periods.

- The **net cash investment** in a lease at a point in time is the amount of funds invested in a lease by a lessor, and comprises the cost of the asset plus or minus the following related payments or receipts:

  (a) Government/other grants receivable towards the purchase or use of the asset
  (b) Rentals received
  (c) Taxation payments and receipts, including the effect of capital allowances
  (d) Residual values, if any, at the end of the lease term
  (e) Interest payments (where applicable)
  (f) Interest received on cash surplus
  (g) Profit taken out of the lease *(SSAP 21)*

3.2 EXAMPLE: GROSS INVESTMENT

Willco Ltd has just purchased a lorry from Drogon Trucks Ltd for £50,000. The lorry has been leased to Newton Freight Ltd on a two year lease requiring annual payments in arrears of £13,500. Drogon Trucks have agreed to buy the truck back at open market value at the end of the lease. Newton Freight Ltd have guaranteed that the value of the lorry after two years will be not less than £30,000. A realistic estimate of its value at that time is £33,000, ie the unguaranteed residual value is £3,000.

What is the gross investment in the lease at the start of the lease?

3.3 SOLUTION

At the start of the lease the 'minimum lease payments' will be the rentals due of £27,000 plus the guaranteed residual of £30,000 giving £57,000. The gross investment in the lease will be the minimum lease payments of £57,000 plus the unguaranteed residual of £3,000 (£33,000 – £30,000) giving £60,000.

It will be apparent from the definition of net investment above that when any residual amount receivable by the lessor is insignificant (as is usually the case in normal full payout leases) the net investment in the lease will be equal to the cost of the equipment less any grant receivable.

Standard accounting practice for lessors

3.4 The requirements of SSAP 21 for accounting by lessors are as follows.

(a) The **amount due from the lessee** under a finance lease should be recorded in the balance sheet of a lessor as a *debtor* at the amount of the **net investment in the lease** after making provisions for items such as bad and doubtful rentals receivable.

(b) The **total gross earnings** under a finance lease should normally be allocated to accounting periods to give a **constant rate of return** on the lessor's net cash investment in the lease in each period. In the case of a hire purchase contract which has characteristics similar to a finance lease, allocation of gross earnings so as to give a constant periodic rate of return on the finance company's net investment will in most cases be a suitable approximation to allocation based on the net cash investment.

In arriving at the constant periodic rate of return, a reasonable approximation may be made.

(c) As an alternative to (b) above, an **allocation** may first be made out of gross earnings of an amount equal to the lessor's estimated cost of finance included in the net cash investment calculation, with the balance being recognised on a systematic basis.

(d) **Tax free grants** which are available to the lessor against the purchase price of assets acquired for leasing should be spread over the period of the lease and dealt with by treating the grant as non-taxable income (see below).

(e) An **asset** held for use in operating leases by a lessor should be recorded as a fixed asset and depreciated over its useful life.

(f) **Rental income from an operating lease**, excluding charges for services such as insurance and maintenance, should be recognised on **a straight-line basis** over the period of the lease, even if the payments are not made on such a basis, unless another systematic and rational basis is more representative of the time pattern in which the benefit from the leased asset is receivable.

(g) **Initial direct costs** incurred by a lessor in arranging a lease may be apportioned over the period of the lease on a systematic and rational basis.

Amendment to SSAP 21

3.5 Until recently, SSAP 21 allowed an alternative treatment for the **tax free grants** mentioned in Paragraph 3.4(d) above. Such tax free grants were still spread over the period of the lease, but could be dealt with by grossing up the grant and including the grossed-up amount in arriving at profit before tax. Where this treatment was adopted, the lessor had to disclose the amount by which the profit before tax and the tax charge had been increased as a result of grossing up the grant.

3.6 EXAMPLE: NET INVESTMENT

Consider again the example first given in Paragraph 2.9, this time from the point of view of the lessor.

3.7 SOLUTION

	Years ending 31 December				
	20X3	*20X4*	*20X5*	*20X6*	*Total*
	£	£	£	£	£
Rentals receivable	13,610	13,610	13,610	13,610	54,440
Capital repayment	13,610	10,225	11,248	12,377	47,460
Finance charge	-	3,385	2,362	1,233	6,980
Average sum outstanding during period		33,850	23,625	12,377	
Finance charge expressed as a % return on the average sum outstanding in the period		10%	10%	10%	

As suggested in the standard, this return is constant.

The lessor's balance sheet and notes will include the following amounts for each year.

	As at 31 December		
	20X3	*20X4*	*20X5*
	£	£	£
Debtors			
Net investment in finance lease	33,850	23,625	12,377
Of which the following is due in more than one year	23,625	12,377	-

3.8 Note that under the assumptions of this question the total net investments shown above are the same as the obligations shown in the lessee's balance sheet. This would not have been the case had the lessee based its disclosure on a present value found using its cost of borrowing rather than the implied rate in the lease.

3.9 The best methods of obtaining a **constant periodic rate of return** on the lessor's net *cash* investment are:

(a) The actuarial method *after* tax
(b) The investment period method (IPM)

3.10 The **main difference** between these two methods and the methods discussed above (actuarial method before tax and sum of the digits) is that the former methods take into account the impact of tax relief on the lessor's cash flow.

Disclosure requirements: lessors

3.11 The disclosure requirements of SSAP 21 are as follows.

(a) The **net investment** in (i) finance leases and (ii) hire purchase contracts at each balance sheet date should be disclosed.

(b) The **gross amounts of assets** held for use in operating leases*, and the related accumulated depreciation charges, should be disclosed.

(c) Disclosure should be made of:

(i) The **policy adopted** for accounting for operating leases* and finance leases* and, in detail, the policy for accounting for finance lease income*

(ii) The **aggregate rentals receivable** in respect of an accounting period in relation to (i) finance leases⋆ and (ii) operating leases⋆

(iii) The **cost of assets acquired**, whether by purchase or finance leases⋆, for the purpose of letting under finance leases⋆

⋆ Including the equivalent information in respect of **hire purchase contracts** which have characteristics similar to that type of lease.

Selling profit

3.12 A manufacturer or dealer lessor should not recognise a selling profit under an operating lease. The selling profit under a finance lease should be **restricted** to the excess of the fair value of the asset over the manufacturer's or dealer's cost less any grants receivable by the manufacturer or dealer towards the purchase, construction or use of the asset.

Sale and leaseback transactions

3.13 These should be dealt with as follows.

(a) **Accounting by the seller/lessee**

(i) In a sale and leaseback transaction which results in a **finance lease**, any apparent profit or loss (that is, the difference between the sale price and the previous carrying value) should be deferred and amortised in the financial statements of the seller/lessee over the shorter of the lease term or the useful life of the asset.

(ii) If the leaseback is an **operating lease**:

(1) Recognise any profit or loss recognised immediately, provided it is clear that the transaction is established at a **fair value**

(2) If the **sale price is below fair value**, any profit or loss should be recognised immediately except that if the apparent loss is compensated by future rentals at below market price it should to that extent be deferred and amortised over the remainder of the lease term (or, if shorter, the period during which the reduced rentals are chargeable)

(3) If the **sale price is above fair value**, the profit based on fair value may be recognised immediately. The balance of profit in excess of fair value should be deferred and amortised over the shorter of the remainder of the lease term and the period to the next rent review (if any). In some cases **where the sales price is significantly above fair value, the operating lease rentals are likely to have been adjusted for the excess price paid for the assets. According to FRS 5, the substance of the transaction is one of sale of an asset and a loan equalling the deferred income element**. The excess over fair value can be shown as a loan and part of the operating lease cost as a repayment of capital and interest on this amount.

(b) **Accounting by the buyer/lessor**

A buyer/lessor should account for a sale and leaseback in the same way as he accounts for other leases.

Exam focus point

A leasing question may be connected to off balance sheet finance in general. In particular, you may be asked to discuss the links between SSAP 21 and FRS 5.

UITF 28 *Operating lease incentives*

3.14 Abstract 28 deals with the way in which both lessors and lessees should account for incentives given by the lessor to the lessee. The Abstract is based on a draft that was published for comment in October 2000, the proposals of which were supported by most of those who responded.

3.15 The Abstract reflects the UITF's view that the rental, net of any incentive, should be recognised as rental expense or income over the period of the lease or, as appropriate, the period to the next rent review.

3.16 The Abstract replaces Abstract 12 *Lessee accounting for reverse premiums and similar incentives*, which, as its title implies, deals only with accounting by the lessee. No major changes are made to the requirements of Abstract 12, the main purpose of the new Abstract being to extend the requirements to lessors, who are also covered by the equivalent international requirements.

4 CRITICISM AND NEW APPROACH — PILOT PAPER

4.1 SSAP 21 has not been without its critics. Although it closed many loopholes in the treatment of leases, it is still open to abuse and manipulation. A great deal of this topic is tied up in the off balance sheet finance debate discussed in Chapter 19.

Unguaranteed residual value

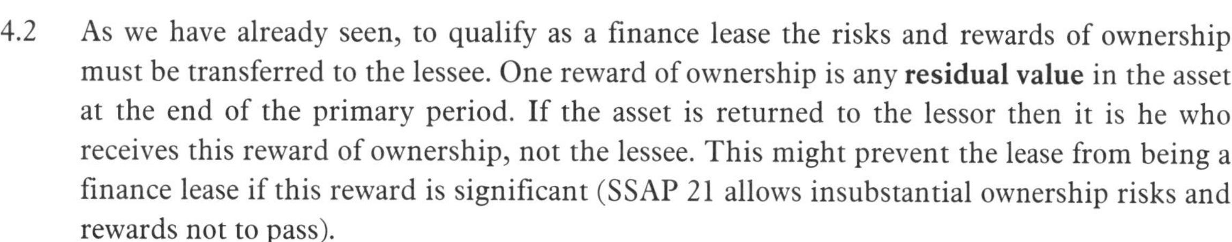

KEY TERM

Unguaranteed residual value is that portion of the residual value of the leased asset (estimated at the inception of the lease), the realisation of which by the lessor is not assured or is guaranteed solely by a party related to the lessor. *(SSAP 21)*

4.2 As we have already seen, to qualify as a finance lease the risks and rewards of ownership must be transferred to the lessee. One reward of ownership is any **residual value** in the asset at the end of the primary period. If the asset is returned to the lessor then it is he who receives this reward of ownership, not the lessee. This might prevent the lease from being a finance lease if this reward is significant (SSAP 21 allows insubstantial ownership risks and rewards not to pass).

4.3 SSAP 21 states that it should normally be presumed that a transfer of substantially all the risks and rewards of ownership occurs if, at the beginning of the lease, the present value of the minimum lease payments amounts to 90% or more of the fair value of the leased asset. This is an application of **discounting principles** to financial statements. The discounting equation is:

Present value of minimum lease payment	+	Present value of unguaranteed residual amount accruing to lessor	=	Fair value of leased asset

Note. Any **guaranteed residual amount** accruing to the lessor will be included in the minimum lease payments.

4.4 If there is an unguaranteed residual amount due to the lessor, it can be seen that its present value must be **less than 10% of the fair value** of the leased asset if the lease is to qualify as a finance lease, since only then will the present value of the minimum lease payments amount to 90% or more of that fair value under the 90% rule.

4.5 You should now be able to see the **scope for manipulation** involving lease classification.

(a) Whether or not a lease is classified as a finance lease can **hinge on the size of the unguaranteed residual amount** due to the lessor, and that figure will **only be an estimate**.

(b) A lessor might be persuaded to estimate a larger residual amount than he would otherwise have done and **cause the lease to fail the 90% test**, rather than lose the business.

(c) While the test is only intended to be presumptive and does not provide a precise mathematical definition of a finance lease, it would be a **brave auditor** who would contend that a lease which failed the test was still a finance lease.

4.6 EXAMPLE: UNGUARANTEED RESIDUAL VALUE

A company enters into two leasing agreements.

	Lease A	*Lease B*
	£'000	£'000
Fair value of asset	210	120
Estimated residual value (due to lessor)	21	30
Minimum lease payments	238	108

How should each lease be classified?

4.7 SOLUTION

You should note that it is unnecessary to perform any calculations for discounting in this example.

Lease A: it is obvious that the present value of the unguaranteed lease payments is less than £21,000, and therefore less than 10% of the fair value of the asset. This means that the present value of the minimum lease payments is over 90% of the fair value of the asset. Lease A is therefore a finance lease.

Lease B: the present value of the minimum lease payments is obviously less than £108,000 and therefore less than 90% of the fair value of the asset. Lease B is therefore an operating lease.

Implicit interest rate

4.8 It will often be the case that the lessee does not know the unguaranteed residual value placed on the asset by the lessor and he is therefore unaware of the interest rate implicit in the lease. In such a case, SSAP 21 allows the lessee to provide his **own estimate**, to calculate the implicit interest rate and perform the 90% test. It is obviously very easy to estimate a residual amount which fails the test. This situation would also lead to different results for the lessee and the lessor.

Omission of material assets and liabilities

4.9 The ASB and other standard setters regard existing leasing standards as deficient.

(a) They **omit material assets and liabilities** arising from operating lease contracts.

(b) The approach of SSAP 21 is '**all or nothing**', while modern transactions are more complex than this.

(c) Classification of leases has important implications, eg for gearing, interest cover and return on capital employed. **Investment analysts** and credit rating agencies often **re-work** financial statements by calculating the assets and liabilities implicit in off balance sheet operating leases.

Discussion paper: Leases: implementation of a new approach

4.10 For some time, users have called for finance leases and operating leases to be treated consistently.

4.11 The ASB published a Discussion Paper *Leases: implementation of a new approach* in December 1999. The Discussion Paper presents a Position Paper that has been developed by the G4+1.

4.12 The paper recommends that **all leases should be reflected in financial statements in a consistent manner** and it explores the principles that should determine the extent of the assets and liabilities that lessees and lessors would recognise under leases.

4.13 At the beginning of a lease the lessee would **recognise an asset and a liability equivalent to the fair value of the rights and obligations that are conveyed by the lease** (usually the present value of the minimum payments required by the lease). Then the accounting for the lease asset and liability would **follow the normal requirements for accounting for fixed assets and debt**. The lessor would report financial assets (representing amounts receivable from the lessee) and residual interests as separate assets.

4.14 Leases that are now treated as operating leases and therefore off balance sheet would give rise to assets and liabilities. However, the difference may not be significant. **Where a lease is for a small part of an asset's useful economic life, only that part would be reflected in the lessee's balance sheet.**

4.15 The Discussion paper also examines the principles for accounting for more complex features of lease contracts. These include renewal options, contingent rentals, residual value guarantees and sale and leaseback transactions.

Sale and leaseback transactions

4.16 SSAP 21 requires a different treatment for sale and leaseback transactions depending on whether the leaseback is a finance or an operating lease. To recap:

- **Operating lease**: treat the transaction as a **sale**
- **Finance lease:** continue to recognise the **asset in the balance sheet**; recognise a **liability for the lease payment**

4.17 The Discussion Paper considers two possible approaches to accounting for sale and leaseback transactions.

(a) **One transaction approach.** This views a sale and leaseback as **one transaction with a double purpose.**

(i) The raising of finance
(ii) The partial disposal of an interest in property

(b) **Two transactions approach.** A sale and leaseback is viewed as **two separate transactions.**

(i) A sale of property
(ii) A subsequent lease of different property rights

The two transactions would be accounted for separately.

4.18 EXAMPLE: SALE AND LEASEBACK TRANSACTION

Newlease Ltd sells a property for £240,000. The property has a carrying value of £200,000 and a fair value of £240,000.

Under the one transaction approach, the accounting entries are as follows.

DEBIT Cash	£240,000	
CREDIT Lease creditor		£240,000

The property remains in the balance sheet at its carrying value of £200,000. This is similar to the current treatment.

The two transactions approach splits the transaction into two components, as follows.

Sale

DEBIT Cash	£240,000	
CREDIT Asset		£200,000
CREDIT Profit on disposal		£40,000

Leaseback

DEBIT Asset	£240,000	
CREDIT Lease liability		£240,000

In effect, the asset has been revalued to its fair value of £240,000.

4.19 The Discussion Paper favours the **one transaction approach.** The main reason for this is that although there are technically two transactions, these are negotiated together.

4.20 A sale and leaseback is generally a **partial disposal**. At one extreme, the transaction may be a financing arrangement with only an immaterial part of the asset sold. At the other extreme, the transaction could be closer to a sale, with only an immaterial amount of finance raised. To deal with this situation, the Discussion Paper proposes the following accounting treatment.

Step 1. Recognise a liability for the lease payments.

Step 2. The excess of cash received over this liability is deemed to be consideration for the part of the asset that is sold.

Step 3. Apportion the carrying amount of the asset immediately before the transaction between the amount sold and the amount retained.

Step 4. The difference between the carrying amount apportioned as sold and the consideration calculated in Step 3 would be recognised as a gain or loss.

Step 5. The part of the asset that is retained, in other words the right to use the asset for the term of the lease would be carried as a proportion of the previous carrying amount, as calculated in Step 3.

4.21 EXAMPLE: SALE AND LEASEBACK WITH 'PARTIAL DISPOSAL'

Goodlease Ltd has a building with a carrying value of £200,000 and a fair value of £240,000. It sells the property to Greatlease Ltd for £240,000 and leases it back. The liability for lease payments is £140,000.

As this is a partial disposal, we need to apportion the carrying amount of the asset between the part sold and the part retained. As the liability for lease payments is £140,000 and the total proceeds are £240,000, £100,000 of the proceeds can be deemed to have been received for selling part of the asset.

The accounting entries would be as follows.

DEBIT Cash	£240,000	
CREDIT Liability for lease payments		£140,000
CREDIT Asset (200 × 100/240)		£83,333
CREDIT Profit on disposal		£16,667

Note that the profit that would arise if the whole asset had been sold would be £240,000 – £200,000, ie £40,000. This needs to be apportioned to the part of the asset that has been sold, ie 100/240 × £40,000 = £16,667.

The carrying value of the building is now £200,000 – £83,333 = £116,667.

Not the last word

4.22 The Discussion Paper has met with some criticism. It has been argued (by KPMG's technical accounting director Kevin Singleton in *Accountancy,* March 2000) that FRS 5, with its emphasis on substance over form, can adequately deal with leases, and that ways will be found to bend the rules. The proposals would be particularly contentious for land and buildings, which are normally held on long leases. Lessees would have to recognise significant additional assets and liabilities in their balance sheets.

Exam focus point

The Pilot paper contained a question asking you to consider the effect of the treatment under the Discussion Paper.

Chapter roundup

- SSAP 21's requirements are not as tricky as they seem at first reading. You should understand the distinction between:
  - **Finance leases**
  - **Operating leases**
- **Finance leases** are **capitalised** – an example of the application of substance over form.
- You should understand the reasons why an **Amendment to SSAP 21** was required.
- You must also have a sound grasp of the **disclosure requirements** of SSAP 21 for both lessors and lessees in respect of finance leases, operating leases and HP contracts.
- You must be able to discuss the **arguments for and against capitalisation** of finance leased assets.
- You should be able to understand the treatment of **sale and leaseback** transactions.
- You should be aware of the reasons why SSAP 21 has been **criticised**.

Quick quiz

1. Distinguish between a finance lease and an operating lease.
2. List the arguments against lessees capitalising leased assets?
3. List the disclosure requirements for lessees.
4. Alpha plc enters into a lease with Omega Ltd of an aircraft which had a fair value of £240,000 at the inception of the lease. The terms of the lease require Alpha to pay 10 annual rentals of £36,000 in arrears.

   Taking into account the residual value of the aircraft accruing to Omega Ltd at the end of 10 years, the interest rate implicit in the lease is approximately 10%.

   The present value of the ten annual rentals of £36,000, discounted at the interest rate implicit in the lease, is £220,000.

   Applying the provisions of SSAP 21 to this lease by how much will the assets of Alpha plc be increased?
5. SSAP 21 requires a lessee to capitalise a finance lease at the amount of the:

   A Arm's length price
   B Arm's length price less government grants
   C Minimum lease payments less residual value
   D Present value of the minimum lease payments
6. On 1 January 20X0 Melon plc entered into a finance lease in respect of a machine. The terms of the agreement were:

	£
Cash price	18,000
Deposit	(6,000)
	12,000
Interest (9% for two years)	2,160
Balance – payable in two annual instalments commencing 31 December 20X0	14,160

   The rate of interest implicit in the contract is approximately 12%. Applying the provisions of SSAP 21, *Accounting for leases and hire purchase contracts*, what is the finance charge in the profit and loss account for the year ended 31 December 20X0?
7. What is the main change proposed by the ASB's Discussion Paper?

Answers to quick quiz

1 See key term

2 (a) Legal position
(b) Complexity
(c) Subjectivity
(d) Presentation

3 See Para 2.8.

4 £220,000. Per SSAP 21 the value should be the present value of the minimum base payments.

5 D

6 The rate of interest used should be the rate implicit in the lease. This rate takes account of the reducing balance on the amount outstanding.

£12,000 × 12% = £1,440.

7 Leases that are now treated as operating leases and therefore off balance sheet would give rise to asset and liabilities.

Now try the questions below from the Exam Question Bank

Number	Level	Marks	Time
Q28	Introductory	n/a	n/a
Q29	Introductory	n/a	n/a

Chapter 21

RETIREMENT BENEFITS

Introduction

An increasing number of companies now provide a **pension** as part of their employees' remuneration package. In view of this trend, it was important to standardise best practice for the way in which pension costs are **recognised and disclosed** in the accounts of sponsoring companies, and the way in which pension schemes themselves draw up sets of accounts. SSAP 24 *Accounting for pension costs* was criticised for being too ambiguous, and FRS 17 *Retirement benefits* was published to address the criticisms. In this chapter SSAP 24 and FRS 17 are both covered, as you may, at this stage be asked to compare the two. Furthermore, FRS 17 has a three year implementation period.

Study guide

Section 18 – Accounting for retirement benefits

- Describing the nature of defined contribution, multi-employers and defined benefit schemes
- Explaining the recognition of defined benefit schemes under current proposals
- Discussion of the measurement of defined benefit schemes under current proposals
- Accounting for defined benefit schemes including the amounts shown in the balance sheet, statement of total recognised gains and losses, profit and loss account and notes to the accounts
- Discussion of perceived problems with current proposals on accounting for retirement benefits

1 BACKGROUND

1.1 Before we look at FRS 17, and to be absolutely clear as to how a pension scheme operates, let us examine a scheme in very simple terms.

KEY TERMS

Retirement benefits. All forms of consideration given by an employer in exchange for services rendered by employees that are payable after the completion of employment.

A **pension scheme** is an arrangement (other than accident insurance) to provide pension and/or other benefits for members on leaving service or retiring and, after a member's death, for his/her dependants. *(SSAP 24)*

1.2 The basic roles of the participants are as follows.

(a) The **trustees** administer the scheme and safeguard its assets.

(b) The **company** pays over both its own contributions and, in practice, those of its employees (if they are required to contribute), deducted from their salaries.

(c) The trustees invest the contributions with a **fund manager**, who in turn invests in the stock market or other assets for the scheme. The return is either reinvested or paid back to the scheme.

(d) The scheme pays out **pensions to employees** who have reached retirement age and also pays **transfer values** to other funds when employees leave.

(e) If allowed, the company contributions might be **refunded** to the company when the scheme is in surplus. Alternatively, the company's future contributions may be cut to use up a surplus.

(f) The role of the **actuary** is very important. He or she is responsible for determining the future contributions required from the company, based on the value of the fund, expected rate of growth, profile of employees and so on.

Consider the diagram below.

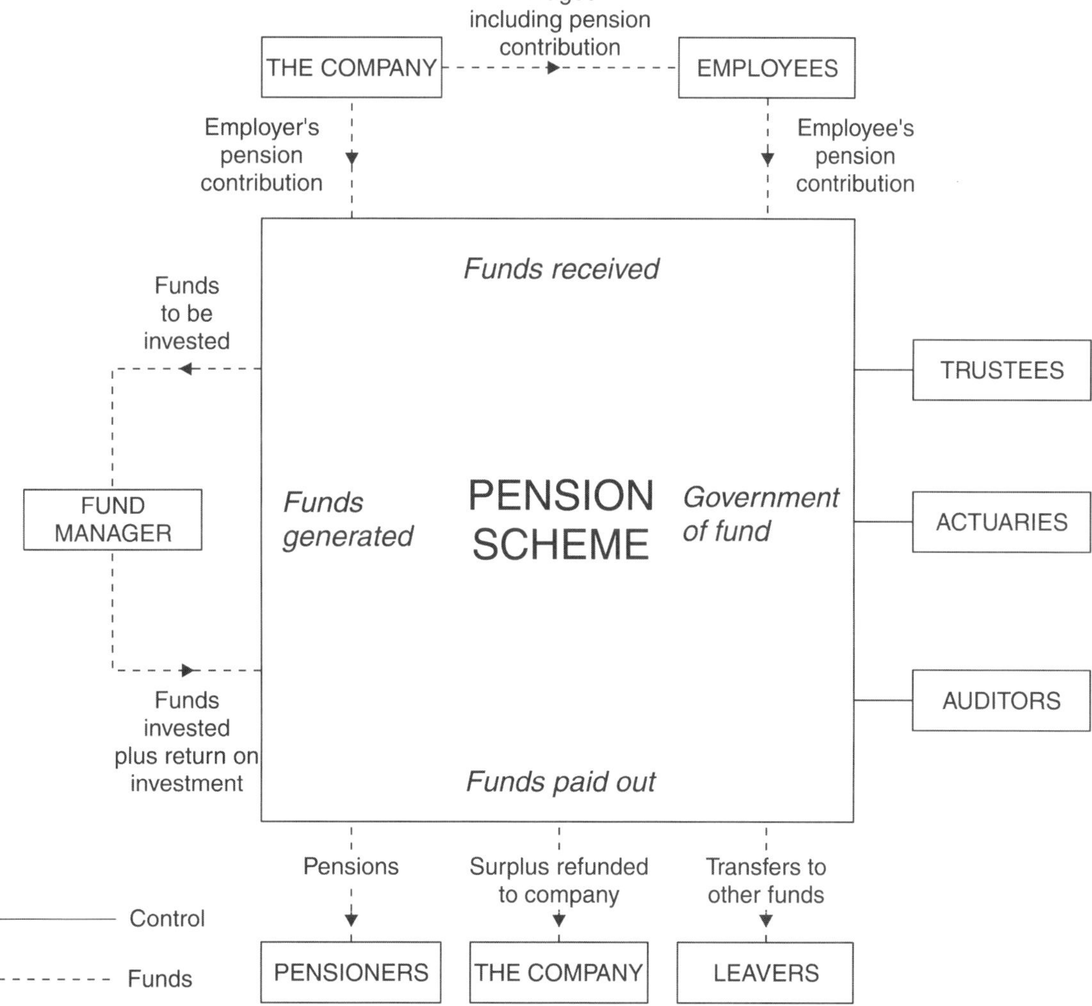

The conceptual nature of pension rights and costs

1.3 When a company employs a new worker and that worker is offered a chance to participate in the company's pension scheme, then the company is, in effect, saying that the

contributions given by the employee and employer will secure an income in the future for the employee in the form of a **pension**.

1.4 The **cost of the pension** to the employer can be viewed in various ways. It could be described as a deferred salary to the employee. Alternatively, it is a deduction from the employee's true gross salary, used as a tax-efficient means of saving. The tax efficiency arises because the employer's contributions are not taxed on the employee, but they are a deduction from taxable profits for the employer. The income and capital gains made by the fund are tax free as well. It is only when the pension is received by the retired employee that the funds become taxable.

Accounting for pension costs

1.5 Accounting for pension costs is difficult. This is because of the **large amounts** involved, as well as the **long time scale**, **complicated estimates** and **uncertainty** surrounding the many assumptions which must be made. **Before SSAP 24**, the forerunner of FRS 17, the usual accounting practice was to charge the employer company's P&L account on the basis of the actual payments made to the pension fund. The company's reported profit was therefore subject to fluctuations as the contribution payments varied. Other disclosed information was sparse: little was said about commitments to pay pensions or any assets held in the pension funds to meet such obligations.

Types of scheme

1.6 There are two types of pension schemes.

Defined contribution schemes

KEY TERM

Defined contribution scheme. A pension or other retirement benefit scheme into which an employer pays regular contributions fixed as an amount or as a percentage of pay and will have no legal or constructive obligation to pay further contributions if the scheme does not have sufficient assets to pay all employee benefits relating to employee service in the current and prior periods.

An individual member's benefits are determined by reference to contributions paid into the scheme in respect of that member, usually increased by an amount based on the investment return on those contributions.

Defined contribution schemes may also provide death-in-service benefits. For the purposes of this definition, death-in-service benefits are not deemed to relate to employee service in the current and prior periods.

1.7 These schemes **do not present a problem** for the reporting company, as they should simply **charge the contributions** payable in respect of the accounting period **within operating profit**. If the amount actually paid is more or less than the amount payable, a prepayment or accrual will appear in the balance sheet in accordance with normal accounting practice.

1.8 The FRS 17 treatment of these schemes is identical to that required by SSAP 24.

Defined benefit schemes

> **KEY TERM**
>
> **Defined benefit scheme.** A pension or other retirement benefit scheme other than a defined contribution scheme.
>
> Usually, the scheme rules define the benefits independently of the contributions payable, and the benefits are not directly related to the investments of the scheme. The scheme may be funded or unfunded.

Problems

1.9 This type of scheme presents problems in respect of:

(a) **Valuing** the scheme **assets**
(b) **Estimating** the scheme **liabilities**
(c) **Measuring** and recognising the **cost** to the employing company

The solutions to these problems in FRS 17 represent a substantial change from the previous treatment under SSAP 24.

Treatment required under SSAP 24

1.10 (a) The **assets and liabilities** of the pension fund would be **valued by an actuary** (on an actuarial basis, although no single method was specified).

(b) The **cost** would be made up of **two elements:**

(i) **Regular cost** - amount which the actuary would regard as a sufficient contribution to the scheme to provide the eventual pensions to be paid in respect of future service, provided present actuarial assumptions about the future were borne out in practice and there were no future changes to the terms of the scheme.

- usually expressed as a percentage of pensionable earning.

(ii) **Variations** - resulting from the unknowns affecting the pension liability and the pension fund assets. The most common were known as 'experience surpluses or deficits' which arose because actuarial assumptions were not borne out.

(c) **Accounting treatment**

(i) Regular costs - usually taken to the profit and loss account

(ii) Variations - *normally* spread over the remaining service lives

Effect of SSAP 24

1.11 SSAP 24 was orientated towards the **P&L account** rather than the balance sheet and sought to even out the impact of pension contributions on earnings. As such, the asset or liability recorded in the balance sheet was a balancing figure, the cumulative difference between the P&L charge and the amount paid. It could be either a prepayment or an accrual, depending on whether contributions are in advance or arrears of 'cost' in P&L terms.

1.12 EXAMPLE: SPREADING TREATMENT UNDER SSAP 24

The actuarial valuation at 31 December 20X0 of the pension scheme of A Ltd showed a surplus of £260m. The actuary recommended that A Ltd eliminate the surplus by taking a contribution holiday in 20X1 and 20X2 and then paying contributions of £30m pa for eight years. After that the standard contribution would be £50m pa. The average remaining service life of employees in the scheme at 31 December 20X0 was 10 years. B Ltd's year end is 31 December.

1.13 SOLUTION

Assuming no change in circumstances, the annual charge in the P&L account for the years 20X1 to 20Y0 will be:

$$\text{Regular cost} - \frac{\text{Surplus}}{\text{Average remaining service life}} = £50\text{m} - \frac{£260\text{m}}{10} = £24\text{m}$$

The funding in these periods will be:

20X1 to X2	Nil
20X3 to Y0	£30m pa

The difference between the amounts funded and the amounts charged in the P&L account will be recognised as a provision as follows.

Year	*Funded*	*Charged*	*(Provision)*
	£m	£m	£m
20X1	-	24	(24)
20X2	-	24	(48)
20X3	30	24	(42)
20X4	30	24	(36)
20X5	30	24	(30)
20X6	30	24	(24)
20X7	30	24	(18)
20X8	30	24	(12)
20X9	30	24	(6)
20Y0	30	24	-

UITF Abstract 13 *Accounting for ESOP Trusts*

1.14 **Employee share ownership plans** (ESOPs) are designed to facilitate employee shareholdings and are often used as vehicles for distributing shares to employees under remuneration schemes. In the light of FRS 5 *Reporting the substance of transactions* (see Chapter 19), questions arose regarding:

(a) The nature and extent of the sponsoring company's assets and liabilities
(b) The timing of expense recognition under such arrangements

1.15 In basic terms, the abstract requires that the assets and liabilities of the ESOP trust be brought **on to the balance sheet of the sponsoring company** where the company 'has *de facto* control of the shares held by the ESOP trust and bears their benefits or risks'.

1.16 The detailed structures of individual ESOPs are varied, as are the reasons for establishing them. However, the **main features** are normally as follows.

(a) The trust uses interest-free finance from the sponsoring company to purchase shares in that company which it 'warehouses' - holding them to sell or transfer to the employees of the company in future.

(b) The sponsoring company will guarantee any third party loans and pay interest, ie any shortfall in capital or revenue is made up by the company.

(c) Shares held by the ESOP trust are distributed to employees through an employee share scheme, by one of a variety of arrangements.

(d) Although the trustees of the ESOP trust must act in the interests of the beneficiaries, the schemes are generally designed to serve the interests of the sponsoring company. The sponsoring company therefore has *de facto* control.

1.17 The accounting requirements and disclosures required by the UITF consensus include the following.

(a) **Shares held by the ESOP trust** should be recognised as assets of the sponsoring company until the shares vest unconditionally in employees. The shares should be classified as 'own shares', either as fixed or current assets. They will generally be held for the continuing benefit of the sponsoring company's business and classified as **fixed assets.**

(b) Where the shares are classified as fixed assets, any **permanent diminution** in their value should be recognised immediately.

(c) Where the shares are **gifted conditionally** or are under option to employees at below the book value of the shares, 'the difference between book value and residual value should be charged as an operating cost over the period of service of the employees in respect of which the gifts or options are granted'.

(d) Any **borrowings** of the ESOP trust that are guaranteed (formally or informally) by the sponsoring company should be regarded as a liability of the company.

(e) **Dividend income** arising on the shares should be **excluded** in arriving at profit before tax and deducted from the aggregate of dividends paid and proposed. Until such time as the shares vest unconditionally in employees, the shares should also be excluded from earnings per share calculations as, under FRS 14 *Earnings per share*, they are treated as if they were cancelled.

1.18 Sufficient information should be **disclosed** as to enable readers of the sponsoring company's accounts to understand the significance of the ESOP trust in the context of the sponsoring company.

2 FRS 17 RETIREMENT BENEFITS 6/01, 6/04

2.1 Criticisms of SSAP 24

(a) There is too much scope for employers to adjust the pension cost in the short term.

(b) There are too many different valuation methods.

(c) The disclosure requirements do not necessarily lead to an adequate explanation of the pension costs and related balances.

(d) It is inconsistent with international standards.

Objective of FRS 17

2.2 The objective of the FRS is to ensure that:

(a) Financial statements reflect at fair value the assets and liabilities arising from an employer's retirement benefit obligations and any related funding

(b) The operating costs of providing retirement benefits to employees are recognised in the accounting period(s) in which the benefits are earned by the employees, and the related finance costs and any other changes in value of the assets and liabilities are recognised in the accounting periods in which they arise

(c) The financial statements contain adequate disclosure of the cost of providing retirement benefits and the related gains, losses, assets and liabilities

Scope

2.3 The FRS applies to **all financial statements that are intended to give a true and fair view** of a reporting employer's financial position and profit or loss (or income and expenditure) for a period.

2.4 The FRS covers **all retirement benefits** that an employer is committed to providing, whether the commitment is statutory, contractual or implicit in the employer's actions. It applies to retirement benefits arising overseas, as well as those arising in the UK and the Republic of Ireland. Retirement benefits include, for example, pensions and medical care during retirement.

2.5 The FRS covers **funded and unfunded retirement benefits**, including schemes that are operated on a pay-as-you-go basis, whereby benefits are paid by the employer in the period they fall due and no payments are made to fund benefits earned in the period.

2.6 The FRS requires a liability to be recognised as the benefits are earned, not when they are due to be paid. The fact that the employer is funded by central government (or any other body) is not a reason for the employer not to recognise its own liabilities arising under the FRS.

Multi-employer schemes

2.7 Multi-employer schemes are pension schemes are schemes which have been set up for a number of employers or for a whole industry. Such schemes **expose** participating employers to the actuarial **risks associated with other entities' employees**, both current and former.

2.8 Where more than one employer participates in a **defined contribution scheme**, the employer's cost is limited to the contributions payable, so **no special problems** arise.

2.9 Where more than one employer participates in a **defined benefit scheme**, the employer should **account for the scheme as a defined benefit** scheme except in limited circumstances.

(a) The employer's contributions are set in relation to the **current service period only**, and are therefore not affected by any surplus or deficit in the scheme relating to past service of its own employees or any other members of the scheme. In this case the employer should account for the contributions to the scheme as if it were a defined contribution scheme.

(b) The employer's contributions are affected by a surplus or deficit in the scheme but the employer is **unable to identify its share of the underlying assets and liabilities** in the scheme on a consistent and reasonable basis. If this is the case, the employer should account for the contributions to the scheme as if it were a defined contribution scheme but, in addition, disclose:

(i) The fact that the scheme is a defined benefit scheme but that the employer is unable to identify its share of the underlying assets and liabilities

(ii) Any available information about the existence of the surplus or deficit in the scheme and the implications of that surplus or deficit for the employer

Question: group schemes

Many group schemes are run on a basis that does not enable individual companies within the group to identify their share of the underlying assets and liabilities.

How should the individual companies within the group account for such schemes?

Answer

In these circumstances, the individual companies (including the parent company) within the group will account for the scheme as a defined contribution scheme and will give the additional disclosures required above. From the point of view of the group entity, a group defined benefit scheme is not a multi-employer scheme and is treated as any other defined benefit scheme.

Defined contribution schemes

2.10 You met the definition of a defined contribution scheme earlier.

KEY TERM

Defined contribution scheme. A pension or other retirement benefit scheme into which an employer pays regular contributions fixed as an amount or as a percentage of pay and will have no legal or constructive obligation to pay further contributions if the scheme does not have sufficient assets to pay all employee benefits relating to employee service in the current and prior periods. *(FRS 17)*

2.11 The **cost of a defined contribution** scheme is **equal to the contributions payable** to the scheme for the accounting period. FRS 17 requires that the cost should be recognised **within operating profit** in the profit and loss account.

Defined benefit schemes

2.12 You also met the definition of a defined benefit scheme earlier.

KEY TERM

Defined benefit scheme. A pension or other retirement benefit scheme other than a defined contribution scheme *(FRS 17)*

Scheme assets

2.13 **Assets** in a defined benefit scheme should be measured at their **fair value at the balance sheet date.** FRS 17 defines fair value for each type of asset.

(a) For **quoted securities**, the **mid-market value** is taken as the fair value. For **unquoted securities**, an **estimate of fair value** is used. The fair value of unitised securities is taken to be the average of the bid and offer prices.

(b) **Property** should be valued at **open market value** or on another appropriate basis of valuation determined in accordance with the Appraisal and Valuation Manual published by the Royal Institution of Chartered Surveyors.

(c) **Insurance policies** that exactly match the amount and timing of some or all of the benefits payable under the scheme should be measured **at the same amount as the related obligations**. For **other insurance policies** there are a number of possible valuation methods. A method should be chosen which gives the **best approximation** to fair value given the circumstances of the scheme.

2.14 Scheme assets include current assets as well as investments. Any liabilities such as accrued expenses should be deducted. Notional funding of a pension scheme does not give rise to assets in a scheme for the purposes of the FRS.

Scheme liabilities

2.15 Defined benefit scheme **liabilities** should be measured on an **actuarial basis using the projected unit method**. The scheme liabilities comprise:

(a) Any benefits promised under the formal terms of the scheme

(b) Any constructive obligations for further benefits where a public statement or past practice by the employer has created a valid expectation in the employees that such benefits will be granted

2.16 As there is no active market for defined benefit scheme liabilities, fair value must be estimated using actuarial techniques. FRS 17 has certain rules relating to the valuation.

(a) The benefits should be attributed to periods of service according to the scheme's benefit formula, except where the benefit formula attributes a disproportionate share of the total benefits to later years of service. In such cases, the benefit should be attributed on a straight-line basis over the period during which it is earned.

(b) The assumptions underlying the valuation should be mutually compatible and lead to the best estimate of the future cash flows that will arise under the scheme liabilities. The assumptions are ultimately the responsibility of the directors (or equivalent) but should be set upon advice given by an actuary. Any assumptions that are affected by economic conditions (financial assumptions) should reflect market expectations at the balance sheet date.

(c) The actuarial assumptions should reflect expected future events that will affect the cost of the benefits to which the employer is committed (either legally or through a constructive obligation) at the balance sheet date.

Question: scheme liabilities

Which of the following expected future events will affect the cost of the benefits to which the employer is committed?

A Expected cost of living increases provided for in the scheme rules
B In the case of final salary schemes, any expected increase in salary
C Expected future redundancies
D Expected early retirement where the employee has that right under the scheme rules

Answer

A, B and D. Expected future redundancies are not reflected in the actuarial assumptions because the employer is not committed (either legally or constructively) to making such redundancies in advance. When the employer does become committed to making the redundancies, any impact on the defined benefit scheme is treated as a settlement and/or curtailment (see later).

Discounting

2.17 Defined benefit scheme **liabilities should be discounted** at a rate that reflects the time value of money and the characteristics of the liability. The rate should be assumed to be the **current rate of return on a high quality corporate bond** of equivalent currency and term to the scheme liabilities.

2.18 The discounting requirement is in line with other recent FRSs such as FRS 19, and reflects the fact that the scheme's liabilities are long-term and should take into account the time value of money.

Actuarial valuations

2.19 At intervals **not exceeding three years, full actuarial valuations** by a professionally qualified actuary should be obtained for a defined benefit scheme. The actuary should review the most recent actuarial valuation at the balance sheet date and update it to reflect current conditions.

2.20 The actuarial valuations required for the FRS may use different assumptions and measurement methods from those used for a scheme's funding valuation.

2.21 Full actuarial valuations under the FRS are not needed at every balance sheet date. Some aspects of the valuation will need to be updated at each balance sheet date, for example the fair value of the assets and financial assumptions such as the discount rate. Other assumptions, such as the expected leaving rate and mortality rate, may not need to be updated annually.

Recognition of defined benefit schemes in the balance sheet

Assets

2.22 The employer should **recognise an asset** to the extent that it is able to **recover** a surplus through **reduced contributions** in the future or through **refunds** from the scheme.

KEY TERMS

A **surplus** in a defined benefit scheme is the excess of the value of the assets in the scheme over the present value of the scheme liabilities.

A **deficit** is the shortfall of the value of the assets below the present value of the scheme liabilities. *(FRS 17)*

2.23 A surplus in the scheme gives rise to an asset of the employer to the extent that:

(a) The employer controls its use, ie has the ability to use the surplus to generate future economic benefits for itself, either in the form of a reduction in future contributions or a refund from the scheme, and

(b) That control is a result of past events (contributions paid by the employer and investment growth in excess of rights earned by the employees)

2.24 The amount of the asset that can be recovered is the present value of the liability expected to arise from future service by current and future scheme members less the present value of future employee contributions. The amount to be recovered from refunds should reflect only refunds that have been agreed by the pension scheme trustees at the balance sheet date.

Liability

2.25 Conversely, the employer has a **liability** if it has **a legal or constructive obligation to make good a deficit** in the defined benefit scheme. In general, the employer will either have a legal obligation under the terms of the scheme trust deed or will have by its past actions and statements created a constructive obligation as defined in FRS 12 *Provisions, contingent liabilities and contingent assets.*

Presentation in the balance sheet

2.26 The presentation is illustrated in the disclosure example at the end of this section. Note that **the defined benefit asset or liability is presented separately on the face of the balance sheet**, after accruals and deferred income, but before capital and reserves.

2.27 Unpaid contributions are presented as a creditor due within one year. Deferred tax relating to the asset or liability is not included with other deferred tax, but is offset against the defined benefit asset or liability.

Recognition of defined benefit schemes in the performance statements

2.28 The pension **cost** is the change in the defined benefit asset or liability, other than through contributions paid to the scheme. It is analysed into **periodic costs and non-periodic costs.**

Periodic costs	Non-periodic costs
Current service cost	Past service costs
Interest cost	Gains and losses on settlements or curtailments
Expected return on assets	
Actuarial gains and losses	

2.29 Look carefully at the following definitions. Read them through several times to make sure you understand them so the treatment will make sense.

KEY TERMS

Current service cost. The increase in the present value of the scheme liabilities expected to arise from employee service in the current period.

Interest cost. The expected increase during the period in the present value of the scheme liabilities because the benefits are one period closer to settlement.

Expected return on assets. The average rate of return, including both income and changes in fair value but net of scheme expenses, expected over the remaining life of the related obligation on the actual assets held by the scheme.

Actuarial gains and losses. Changes in actuarial deficits or surpluses that arise because:

(a) Events have not coincided with the actuarial assumptions made for the last valuation (experience gains and losses), or

(b) The actuarial assumptions have changed

Past service costs. The increase in the present value of the scheme liabilities related to employee service in prior periods arising in the current period as a result of the introduction of, or improvement to, retirement benefits.

Settlement. An irrevocable action that relieves the employer (or the defined benefit scheme) of the primary responsibility for a pension obligation and eliminates significant risks relating to the obligation and the assets used to effect the settlement. Settlements include:

(a) A lump-sum cash payment to scheme members in exchange for their rights to receive specified pension benefits

(b) The purchase of an irrevocable annuity contract sufficient to cover vested benefits

(c) The transfer of scheme assets and liabilities relating to a group of employees leaving the scheme

Curtailment. An event that reduces the expected years of future service of present employees or reduces for a number of employees the accrual of defined benefits for some or all of their future service. Curtailments include:

(a) Termination of employees' services earlier than expected, for example as a result of closing a factory or discontinuing a segment of a business

(b) Termination of, or amendment to the terms of, a defined benefit scheme so that some or all future service by current employees will no longer qualify for benefits or will qualify only for reduced benefits

(FRS 17)

Question: past service cost

Can you think of an example of a past service cost?

Answer

Creation of a pension benefit for a spouse where benefit did not previously exist, or added on years of service on retirement.

Current service cost, interest cost and expected return on assets

2.30 These items should all be recognised in the profit and loss account.

(a) The **current service cost** should be based on the most recent actuarial valuation at the beginning of the period with the financial assumptions updated to reflect conditions at that date. **Include it within operating profit**. Any contributions from employees should be set off against it.

(b) The **interest cost** should be based on the discount rate and the present value of liabilities at the start of the period. It should also reflect changes in the scheme liabilities during the period. It should be shown **in the profit and loss account, adjacent to interest and netted off against the expected return on assets.**

(c) The **expected return on assets** should be shown in the **profit and loss account, netted off against the interest cost.** It should be based on long-term expectations at the start of the period, for example, for quoted government or corporate bonds, the redemption yield × market value at the start of the period. It should reflect changes in assets through contributions paid in and benefits paid out of the scheme.

Actuarial gains and losses

2.31 **Actuarial gains and losses** arising from any new valuation and from updating the latest actuarial valuation to reflect conditions at the balance sheet date should be recognised in the **statement of total recognised gains and losses**. They should **never be re-cycled to the profit and loss account** in future periods.

Non-periodic costs

2.32 **Past service costs** should be **recognised in the profit and loss account on a straight-line basis over the period in which the increases in benefit vest**. If benefits vest immediately, recognise immediately.

2.33 **Gains and losses on settlements and curtailments** should be recognised **in the profit and loss account in operating profit** except where they attach to an exceptional item shown after operating profit. This would be the case with closure of business. This only refers to settlements and curtailments **not covered by actuarial assumptions.**

Question: events affecting pension plan

Consider how the following events might affect a pension plan and how any gains or losses would be recognised. Fill in the table below.

Event	Effect and treatment
The law changes to recognise the rights of cohabitees to be treated as if they were a legally married couple.	
Unexpected falls in property values and global stock markets have adversely affected the value of the scheme assets.	
A company makes 40% of its workforce redundant.	

Answer

Event	Effect and treatment
The law changes to recognise the rights of cohabitees to be treated as if they were a legally married couple	This event has increased the pension liability, and to the extent that the additional benefits attach to past years' services, the past service cost should be recognised immediately.
Unexpected falls in property values and global stock markets have adversely affected the value of the scheme assets.	The difference between the estimated year-end value of the scheme net asset/liability based on expected return and the value from the year-end valuation will be recognised in the STRGL as an actuarial loss.
A company makes 40% of its workforce redundant.	This will reduce the scheme liabilities and a gain will result. This is a curtailment which would fall outside actuarial assumptions so it should be recognised in the profit and loss account. If the redundancies relate to the sale or termination of an operation or fundamental reorganisation or reconstruction, the gain would be included in the exceptional items. In other circumstances it should be included in operating expenses.

Disclosures

2.34 *Defined benefit contribution schemes*

(a) The nature of the scheme (ie defined contribution)
(b) The cost for the period
(c) Any outstanding or prepaid contributions at the balance sheet date

2.35 *Defined benefit schemes – a summary*

(a) The main assumptions underlying the scheme

(b) An analysis of the assets in the scheme into broad classes and the expected rate of return on each class

(c) An analysis of the amounts included:

(i) Within operating profit
(ii) Within other finance costs
(iii) Within the statement of total recognised gains and losses

(d) A five-year history of:

(i) The difference between the expected and actual return on assets
(ii) Experience gains and losses arising on the scheme liabilities
(iii) The total actuarial gain or loss

(e) An analysis of the movement in the surplus or deficit in the scheme over the period and a reconciliation of the surplus/deficit to the balance sheet asset/liability.

2.36 The disclosure requirements in full are very extensive, and are best learnt by reference to the example below, taken from FRS 17.

2.37 EXAMPLE: FRS 17 DISCLOSURES

Below is an example, taken from the FRS, of the disclosures required.

Balance sheet presentation

	20X2	*20X1*
	£m	£m
Net assets excluding pension asset	700	650
Pension asset	335	143
Net assets including pension asset	1,035	793

Reserves note

	20X2	*20X1*
	£m	£m
Profit and loss reserve excluding pension asset	400	350
Pension reserve	335	143
Profit and loss reserve	735	493

Pension cost note

Composition of the scheme

The group operates a defined benefit scheme in the UK. A full actuarial valuation was carried out at 31 December 20X1 and updated to 31 December 20X2 by a qualified independent actuary. The major assumptions used by the actuary were:

	At 31.12.X2	*At 31.12.X1*	*At 31.12.X0*
Rate of increase in salaries	4.0%	5.5%	6.5%
Rate of increase in pensions in payment	2.0%	3.0%	3.5%
Discount rate	4.5%	7.0%	8.5%
Inflation assumption	2.5%	4.0%	5.0%

The assets in the scheme and the expected rate of return were:

	Long-term rate of return expected at 31/12/X2	*Value at 31.12.X2*	*Long-term rate of return expected at 31.12.X1*	*Value at 31.12.X1*	*Long-term rate of return expected at 31.12.X0*	*Value at 31.12.X0*
		£m		£m		£m
Equities	7.3%	1,116	8.0%	721	9.3%	570
Bonds	5.5%	298	6.0%	192	8.0%	152
Property	6.0%	74	6.1%	49	7.9%	33
Total market value of assets		1,488		962		760
Present value of scheme liabilities		(1,009)		(758)		(608)
Surplus in the scheme		479		204		92
Related deferred tax liability		(144)		(61)		(28)
Net pension asset		335		143		64

Analysis of the amount charged to operating profit

	20X2	*20X1*
	£m	£m
Service cost	34	25
Past service cost	12	-
Total operating charge	46	25

Analysis of amount credited to other finance income

	20X2	*20X1*
	£m	£m
Expected return on pension scheme assets	73	68
Interest on pension liabilities	(53)	(57)
Net return	20	11

Analysis of amount recognised in statement of total recognised gains and losses (STRGL)

	20X2	*20X1*
	£m	£m
Actual return less expected return on pension scheme assets	480	138
Experience gains and losses arising on the present value of the scheme liabilities	(58)	(6)
Changes in financial assumptions underlying the present value of the scheme liabilities	(146)	(41)
Actuarial gain/(loss) recognised in STRGL	276	91

Movement in surplus during the year

	20X2	*20X1*
	£m	£m
Surplus in scheme at beginning of year	204	92
Movement in year:		
Current service cost	(34)	(25)
Contributions	25	35
Past service costs	(12)	-
Other finance income	20	11
Actuarial gain/(loss)	276	91
Surplus in scheme at end of the year	479	204

The full actuarial valuation at 31 December 20X1 showed an increase in the surplus from £92 million to £204 million. Improvements in benefits costing £12 million were made in 20X1 and contributions reduced to £25 million (8 per cent of pensionable pay). It has been agreed with the trustees that contributions for the next three years will remain at that level.

History of experience gains and losses

	20X2	*20X1*	*20X0*	*20W9*	*20W8*
Difference between the expected and actual return on scheme assets:					
amount (£m)	480	138	(6)	94	(73)
Percentage of scheme assets	32%	14%	(1%)	16%	(26%)
Experience gains and losses on scheme liabilities:					
amount (£m)	(58)	(6)	34	25	(23)
Percentage of scheme liabilities	(4%)	(1%)	5%	2%	(2%)
Total amount recognised in statement of total recognised gains and losses:					
amount (£m)	276	91	1	66	(158)
Percentage of scheme liabilities	27%	12%	0%	5%	(14%)

Question: FRS 17

The net pension liability of Sonya plc as at 1 January 20X3 comprised the following:

	£
Pension fund assets	10,000,000
Pension fund liabilities	(10,400,000)
	400,000

The following information relates to the year ended 31 December 20X3.

Current service cost	£800,000
Interest rate	5%
Expected return on assets	3%
Contributions paid	£1,020,000
Pensions paid	£560,000
Actual return on assets	£400,000
Actuarial valuation of liabilities at 31.12.X3	£11,000,000

Required

Show how the pension scheme assets, liabilities, gains and losses will be recognised in the financial statements for the year ended 31 December 20X3.

Answer

Balance sheet	£
Pension liability (W1)	(140,000)
Pension reserve	(140,000)

Profit and loss account	
Included in operating expenses	800,000
Other finance charges - 520,000 (journal (a)) – 300,000 (journal (c))	220,000

Statement of total recognised gains and losses	
Actual return less expected return on pension scheme (journal (f))	100,000
Experience gains and losses arising on the scheme liabilities (journal (g)	160,000

Working: Pension liability

	Journal	*Asset* £	*Liability* £
B/f		10,000,000	10,400,000
Current service cost	(a)		800,000
Interest	(b)		520,000
Expected return	(c)	300,000	
Contributions	(d)	1,020,000	
Pensions paid	(e)	(560,000)	(560,000)
		10,760,000	11,160,000
Actuarial gains	(f)/(g)	100,000	(160,000)
		10,860,000	11,000,000

Net deficit = £140,000

Journals		£	£
(a) DEBIT	P&L account operating profits	800,000	
CREDIT	Obligations		800,000
	Current service cost		
(b) DEBIT	P&L account interest charge	520,000	
CREDIT	Obligation		520,000
	Restatement of opening liability (10,400,000 × 5%)		
(c) DEBIT	Pension fund assets	300,000	
CREDIT	P&L account interest receivable		300,000
	Expected return (10,000,000 × 3%)		
(d) DEBIT	Pension fund assets	1,020,000	
CREDIT	Cash		1,020,000
	Contributions		
(e) DEBIT	Obligations	560,000	
CREDIT	Pension fund assets		560,000
	Pensions paid		
(f) DEBIT	Pension fund assets	100,000	
CREDIT	STRGL		100,000
	Re actual return (400,000 – 300,000)		
(g) DEBIT	Pension fund obligations	160,000	
CREDIT	STRGL		160,000
	Re actuarial gain obligations		

Date from which effective and transitional arrangements

2.38 The standard is complex and therefore has a three year implementation period.

Financial statements for periods ending on or after 22 June 2001

2.39 The following disclosures only are required, all relating only to the closing balance sheet.

(a) Nature of scheme, date of latest valuation, contributions paid, age profile
(b) Main financial assumptions
(c) Fair value and expected return on assets
(d) Reconciliation to balance sheet figure and analysis of movements in surplus or deficit

Financial statements for periods ending on or after 22 June 2002

2.40 (a) The disclosures in 2.37 plus corresponding details for the opening balance sheet

(b) The disclosures of the separate components of the cost which would be reflected in the performance statements (without comparatives)

(c) The disclosures of actuarial gains and losses as amounts and percentages for the current period only.

None of these need be recognised in the primary financial statements for these periods.

Financial statements for periods ending on or after 22 June 2003

2.41 (a) All the requirements of the FRS must be followed.

(b) Gains and losses arising on the initial recognition of items in the primary statements under the FRS should be dealt with as prior period adjustments in accordance with FRS 3. It is not required to create retrospectively the five year history of amounts recognised in the statement of total recognised gains and losses beyond those figures already disclosed in the financial statements of previous years.

Proposed extended transitional regime

2.42 The ASB has published an Exposure Draft proposing that the mandatory requirement for the adoption of FRS 17 be deferred. The ASB's proposal is a direct result of the IASB announcement last week that it had added to its agenda a project to reconsider the provisions of the corresponding international standard, IAS 19 *Employee benefits*. An equivalent deferral is proposed in respect of the FRSSE.

2.43 The ASB chairman, Mary Keegan, states that the purpose of this deferral is to **ease the transition to the adoption of IAS in 2005**; the ASB is not responding to public criticism of FRS 17 (see below).

2.44 **Benefits of FRS 17**

(a) FRS 17 has brought the UK into line with **international practice** on measurement of pension scheme assets and liabilities. The only major difference is in the recognition of actuarial gains and losses. The FRS requires these to be recognised immediately they occur in the STRGL. IAS 19 requires actuarial gains and losses to be recognised in the profit and loss account to the extent that they exceed 10% of the greater of the gross assets or gross liabilities in the scheme. Recognition of actuarial gains and losses exceeding the 10% corridor may be spread forward over the expected average remaining working lives of the employees participating in the scheme.

(b) **Market values for assets are easier to understand** than actuarial values.

(c) The ASB believes that it has found a better way of **recognising the volatility** and risk inherent in a defined benefit pension scheme, **while protecting the P & L from massive swings** that could swamp the results of the employer's operations.

(d) By recognising the actuarial gains and losses immediately, a clear picture emerges in the accounts of the scheme's potential **impact on cash flows.**

(e) The **profit and loss account** and EPS are protected from market changes affecting the pension scheme. However, the ongoing operating and financing costs associated with providing a pension are recorded.

2.45 **Potential problems with FRS 17**

(a) **Market values** may **not** bear much relation to the **economic reality** of a pension scheme, since most scheme assets are held for the long term. A similar criticism could be made of the proposal to fair value financial instruments. Actuarial valuations take into account long term assumptions.

(b) The pension scheme **asset** (surplus) is treated as an **asset of the employer**, while the **legal position** is that it belongs to the **scheme members.**

(c) Market values cause **volatility**. Although the profit and loss account is protected from such fluctuations, the balance sheet may fluctuate.

(d) **The STRGL is often overlooked** by many users of accounts. The treatment could be viewed as a fudge, presenting the predictable in the profit and loss account and hiding the unpredictable.

(e) The standard is, arguably, even more **complex** than SSAP 24

UITF 35 Death-in-service and incapacity benefits

2.46 Abstract 35 was issued in May 2002. It clarifies the accounting required by FRS 17 *Retirement benefits* for the cost of death-in-service and incapacity benefits, where such benefits are provided through a defined benefit pension scheme.

2.47 The Abstract requires that, where the benefits are not wholly insured, the uninsured scheme liability and the cost for the accounting period should be measured, in line with other retirement benefits, using the projected unit method.

2.48 The effect is that the valuation of uninsured benefits reflects the current period's portion of the full benefits ultimately payable in respect of current members of the scheme; the cost of insured benefits is determined by the relevant insurance premiums.

Exam focus point

Keep an eye on the financial press to see how FRS 17 is working in practice.

3 FUTURE REGULATIONS

3.1 The world of pension schemes was struck by a thunderbolt when it was discovered that the **Mirror Group Newspaper (MGN) Pension Funds** had lost between £300m and £400m as a result of the apparently fraudulent activities of at least one of those entrusted with fiduciary responsibility for them. This was in spite of the fact that the main provisions of the Social Security Act 1990, which sought to protect pensions, were already in force.

3.2 In the subsequent debate, several weaknesses in the regulation of pension schemes came to light. One of the most significant flaws is the problem of **trust law**. Trusts are only effective in separating the assets of the pension scheme from those of the employer company as long as trustees honour their trusts.

Problems with pension funds

3.3 The main areas of concern were as follows.

(a) The then current accounting (annual) and actuarial (triennial) reporting requirements were ineffective to prevent abuse, because the information contained in them was **out of date** at the time of publication.

(b) Requirements of **accountability** to scheme members were susceptible to manipulation.

(c) **Third parties** who handled pension fund assets did not have to be bonded (ie insured) and were generally entitled to retain the proceeds of fraud if they received them in good faith.

(d) There was no **fit and proper person test** for the trustees of occupational pension schemes.

(e) Confronted with **dishonest trustees**, even well informed scheme members were prevented from taking effective action by financial constraints and lack of adequate information.

(f) The investment and administration of pension funds was subject to the vagaries of the **law of trusts** and the expense of High Court proceedings. Conflicts of interest between employers and beneficiaries were built into the system.

(g) Pension fund members whose benefits could not be paid ranked as **unsecured creditors** in an insolvency and the receiver/liquidator who was appointed over the employer owed them no duty whatsoever. In addition, administrative receivers and liquidators who might have encountered some of the more obvious cases of abuse were under no clear statutory duty to report such abuse. It was not usually within their powers to pursue those responsible for committing the abuse if there was no hope of recovering assets for the creditors.

3.4 The area of **transfers between pension schemes**, particularly in a take-over situation, also gave cause for concern. There was no requirement for transfer values to be earmarked for the benefit of transferring employees, and so any surplus over the cash equivalents might be used by the buyer for a contribution holiday, a loan or a straightforward return of surplus. This was not actually illegal, although it might have been if deliberate misrepresentations were used.

3.5 In a **take-over situation**, the buyer and seller companies will include the pension scheme as part of the consideration. This undermines the independence of the trustees: the trust is supposed to separate the assets of the scheme from that of the company. Unfortunately, commercial reality dictates that corporate profitability and welfare takes precedence over the interests of pension scheme beneficiaries. The trustees should be more involved in sale negotiations, perhaps, to ensure that pensioners' rights are properly catered for.

3.6 The Government has now enacted those parts of the Social Security Act 1990 relating to the **limit of 5% on self-investment**.

Pensions Act 1995

3.7 The Pensions Act 1995 has now come into force. There are six components of this enormous piece of legislation.

(a) 'Post-Maxwell' security measures
(b) Sex discrimination in pensions
(c) Equalisation of retirement ages
(d) Terms governing contracting out from SERPs
(e) Treatment of pension rights and divorce
(f) Miscellaneous matters

Although all those parts of the Act are of general interest to us, from the accountant's or auditor's point of view the provisions relating to part (a) are of fundamental importance.

3.8 These provisions place trustee boards at the heart of good pension practice: note particularly points (d), (e), (f) and (h).

(a) The Act set up a new watchdog body called **the Occupational Pensions Regulatory Authority (OPRA)** with power to impose penalties on any person not complying with their duties under an occupational pension scheme.

(b) The **Pensions Ombudsman's duties** were extended so that he can investigate complaints against employers as well as against trustees and managers of the scheme, and complaints by trustees, managers and employers against other trustees and managers.

(c) A **Pensions Compensation Board** was set up to administer a compensation scheme in cases where the employer becomes insolvent and the scheme's assets have been reduced by certain acts or omissions (not yet defined). The amount of compensation is likely to be 90% of the assets lost (see Maxwell!).

(d) The Act introduced a **minimum solvency requirement** for final salary schemes. Trustees are required to agree a schedule of contribution payments which is certified by the actuary as adequate to maintain the minimum solvency level. If the employer fails to meet these payments when due, trustees must notify OPRA.

(e) The Act requires that arrangements for **member-nominated trustees** are set up. The arrangements must provide for at least one-third of the trustees to be member-nominated, subject to a minimum of two (or one for small schemes).

(f) The Act spells out **trustees' duties** regarding investments, and places a duty on the trustees to consult with the employer in determining investment policy. Trustees must keep a written statement of investment principles.

(g) The idea of **Limited Price Indexation** (introduced in SSA 1990) has come into force. All pensions in payment earned after 6 April 1997 must, when they come into payment, be increased in line with price inflation subject to a maximum of 5% pa.

(h) The Act restricts the ability to **make changes** to a scheme which would affect members' rights. The trustees must approve such changes and members must give their consent unless an actuary certifies that they will be no worse off.

(i) The Act specifies the **order of winding-up liabilities** in a final salary pension scheme and what is to be done in the case of a deficiency/surplus on winding up.

(j) A new procedure applies to the provision of **transfer value quotations** to members of salary-related schemes to avoid a situation where a member receives a transfer payment less than the amount quoted due to market fluctuations over time.

'Whistle-blowing' by auditors

3.9 The Act also introduced a 'whistle-blowing' obligation for scheme **auditors and actuaries** to report to OPRA if they believe legal duties concerned with the administration of the scheme are not being carried out. Other professionals and trustees are encouraged, but not obligated, to 'blow the whistle'. This is something of a double-edged sword for accountants: 'whistle-blowing' will lead to worse client relations, but auditors will benefit from the need for better systems and audited accounts in pension funds. It is highly likely that auditors may avoid conflict with clients by refusing to act as auditors to the pension fund.

Chapter roundup

- **Company pension schemes** have become more and more important as supplements to or replacements for the state pension, as a means of support after retirement. With an increasingly large pensioned population, the importance of this topic can only increase.
- **FRS 17** *Retirement benefits* has recently replaced SSAP 24, with a three year implementation period.
- **Scheme assets** are measured at **market value** (previously actuarial value).
- **Scheme liabilities** are discounted at a high-quality corporate bond rate.
- Actuarial gains and losses are **recognised immediately** in the STRGL, rather than spread forward in the P&L account.
- As a consequence, the **balance sheet reflects the surplus/deficit** in the scheme
- You should understand the **ASB's proposals on pension costs**, contained in **FRED 20** ***Retirement benefits***.
- The topic of pensions is still in the news, particularly as far as regulation is concerned. The **1995 Pensions Act** has tightened up the security surrounding pension funds in light of the Maxwell scandal. Auditors and accountants play a large part in providing this security.

Quick quiz

1 Assets of a pension scheme are valued at market value/actuarial value. (Delete as appropriate).

2 How is surplus defined?

3 Should the surplus be recognised as an asset?

4 Past service costs are not recognised because they are in the past.

True ☐

False ☐

5 How, under FRS 17, is the reserves note made up?

Answers to quick quiz

1. Market value
2. The excess of the value of the scheme assets over that of scheme liabilities.
3. Yes, to the extent that the employee is able to recover the surplus through reduced contributions or refunds from the scheme.
4. False. They relate to service in prior periods, but arise in current periods, for example as a result of improvements to benefits. They should be recognised in the P&L.
5.

	£m
Profit and loss reserve excluding pension assets	X
Pension reserve	X
Profit and loss reserve	X

Now try the question below from the Exam Question Bank

Number	Level	Marks	Time
Q30	Introductory	n/a	n/a

Chapter 22

TAXATION

Topic list		Syllabus reference
1	FRS 16 *Current tax*	1(a) – 1(f), 4(e)
2	FRS 19 *Deferred tax*	1(a) – 1(f), 4(e)

Introduction

FRS 16 *Current tax* is straightforward and should not cause too many problems. FRS 19 *Deferred tax* replaced SSAP 15 recently. It changes the method of providing for deferred tax from partial provision to full provision. This is a topical issue, so you should study this chapter carefully.

Study guide

Section 19 – Taxation

- Discussion of the different approaches to accounting for deferred taxation
- Discussion of the recognition of deferred taxation in the balance sheet and performance statements under current proposals including revaluations, unremitted earnings of group companies and deferred tax assets
- Explaining the nature of the measurement of deferred taxation under current proposals including tax rates and discounting
- Discussion of the differences between the recognition requirements of International Accounting Standards and proposed UK regulation, and related problem areas
- Calculating deferred tax amounts in financial statements under current proposals

Exam guide

As you can see from the Study Guide, you may be asked to compare different approaches to deferred tax. Accordingly this chapter shows the partial provision method as well as the full provision method.

1 FRS 16 CURRENT TAX

1.1 Companies pay corporation tax at 30%, usually nine months after the year end. **FRS 16 Current tax** specifies how current tax should be reflected in the financial statements. This should be done in a '**consistent and transparent manner**'.

1.2 Specifically, the FRS deals with **tax credits** and **withholding tax**. Consider these definitions.

KEY TERMS

- **Current tax**. The amount of tax estimated to be payable or recoverable in respect of the taxable profit or loss for a period, along with adjustments to estimates in respect of previous periods.
- **Withholding tax**. Tax on dividends or other income that is deducted by the payer of the income and paid to the tax authorities wholly on behalf of the recipient.
- **Tax credit**. The tax credit given under UK tax legislation to the recipient of a dividend from a UK company. The credit is given to acknowledge that the income out of which the dividend has been paid has already been charged to tax, rather than because any withholding tax has been deducted at source. The tax credit may discharge or reduce the recipient's liability to tax on the dividend. Non-taxpayers may or may not be able to recover the tax credit.

1.3 You can see from these definitions that a tax credit is different from a withholding tax.

- A tax credit **gives credit for** tax paid by a company
- A **withholding tax withholds** the taxable part of the income

Accordingly, the tax credit and the withholding tax are treated differently in the financial statements.

Treatment in financial statements

1.4 Learn this treatment.

Outgoing dividends paid and proposed, interest or other amounts payable

- Include withholding tax
- Exclude tax credit

Incoming dividends, intérest or other amounts payable

- Include withholding tax
- Exclude tax credit
- Include the effect of withholding tax suffered as part of the tax charge

1.5 EXAMPLE: CURRENT TAX

Taxus Ltd made a profit of £1,000,000. It received a dividend of £80,000 on which there was a tax credit of £20,000. From an overseas company it received a dividend of £3,000 on which 25% withholding tax had been deducted. The corporation tax charge was £300,000.

Required

Show how this information would be presented in the financial statements in accordance with FRS 16 *Current tax*.

1.6 SOLUTION

	£
Operating profit	1,000,000
Income from fixed asset investments	
UK (note 1)	80,000
Foreign (note 2)	4,000
Profit before tax	1,084,000
Taxation (note 3)	301,000
Profit after tax	783,000

Notes

1 Excludes tax credit.

2 Includes withholding tax: £3,000 + £1,000 = £4,000. Read the question carefully - 25% had been deducted already.

3 Add back withholding tax of £1,000.

Other requirements of FRS 16

1.7 Current tax should be recognised in the **profit and loss account**. But if it is attributable to a gain or loss that has been recognised in the statement of total recognised gains and losses, it should be recognised in that statement.

1.8 Current tax should be **measured** using tax rates and laws that have been enacted or **substantially enacted** by the balance sheet date.

1.9 Generally (apart from the treatment of withholding tax) income and expenses are **not adjusted** to reflect a **notional amount** of tax that would have been paid or received if the transaction had been taxable or allowable on a different basis. Income and expenses are included in pre-tax results on the basis of amounts **actually receivable or payable**.

Tax disclosure in the notes

1.10 This example, taken from the appendix to FRS 16, illustrates one method of showing by way of a note the tax items required to be disclosed under CA 1985 and the FRS.

	£'000	£'000
UK corporation tax		
Current tax on income for the period	X	
Adjustments in respect of prior periods	X	
	X	
Double taxation relief*	(X)	
		X
Foreign tax		
Current tax on income for the period	X	
Adjustments in respect of prior periods	X	
		X
Tax on profit on ordinary activities		X

*Don't worry about this - it's unlikely to come up in your exam.

SSAP 5 *Accounting for value added tax*

1.11 SSAP 5 *Accounting for value added tax* is one of the most straightforward of all the SSAPs. A summary of the provisions is given here, but you should make sure you understand how VAT operates.

> **Knowledge brought forward from earlier studies**
>
> ***SSAP 5 Accounting for VAT***
>
> - **Turnover** shown in the P&L account should exclude VAT on taxable outputs. If gross turnover must be shown, then the VAT included in that figure must also be shown as a deduction in arriving at the turnover exclusive of VAT.
> - **Irrecoverable VAT** allocated to fixed assets and other items separately disclosed should be included in their cost where material and practical.
> - The **net amount due to or from Customs & Excise** should be included in the total for creditors or debtors, and need not be separately disclosed.
> - **CA 1985** also requires disclosure of the cost of sales figure in the published accounts. This amount should exclude VAT on taxable inputs.

2 FRS 19 DEFERRED TAX 6/04

2.1 You may already be aware from your studies of taxation that accounting profits and taxable profits are not the same. There are several reasons for this but they may conveniently be considered under two headings.

(a) **Permanent differences** arise because certain expenditure, such as entertainment of UK customers, is not allowed as a deduction for tax purposes although it is quite properly deducted in arriving at accounting profit. Similarly, certain income (such as UK dividend income) is not subject to corporation tax, although it forms part of accounting profit.

(b) **Timing differences** arise because certain items are included in the accounts of a period which is different from that in which they are dealt with for taxation purposes.

Deferred taxation is the tax attributable to timing differences.

> **KEY TERM**
>
> **Deferred tax.** Estimated future tax consequences of transactions and events recognised in the financial statements of the current and previous periods.

2.2 Deferred taxation is therefore a means of ironing out the tax inequalities arising from timing differences.

(a) In years when **corporation tax is saved** by timing differences such as accelerated capital allowances, a charge for deferred taxation is made in the P&L account and a provision set up in the balance sheet.

(b) In years when **timing differences reverse**, because the depreciation charge exceeds the capital allowances available, a deferred tax credit is made in the P&L account and the balance sheet provision is reduced.

Deferred tax is the subject of a new standard, FRS 19 *Deferred tax*. Before we look at the detailed requirements of FRS 19, we will explore some of the issues surrounding deferred tax.

2.3 You should be clear in your mind that the tax actually payable to the Inland Revenue is the **corporation tax liability**. The credit balance on the deferred taxation account represents an estimate of tax saved because of timing differences but expected ultimately to become payable when those differences reverse.

2.4 FRS 19 identifies the main categories in which timing differences can occur.

(a) **Accelerated capital allowances.** Tax deductions for the cost of a fixed asset are accelerated or decelerated, ie received before or after the cost of the fixed asset is recognised in the profit and loss account.

(b) **Pension liabilities** are accrued in the financial statements but are allowed for tax purposes only when paid or contributed at a later date.

(c) **Interest charges or development costs** are capitalised on the balance sheet but are treated as revenue expenditure and allowed as incurred for tax purposes.

(d) **Intragroup profits in stock**, unrealised at group level, are reversed on consolidation.

(e) **Revaluations.** An asset is revalued in the financial statements but the revaluation gain becomes taxable only if and when the asset is sold.

(f) **Unrelieved tax losses.** A tax loss is not relieved against past or present taxable profits but can be carried forward to reduce future taxable profits.

(g) **Unremitted earnings of subsidiaries.** The unremitted earnings of subsidiary and associated undertakings and joint ventures are recognised in the group results but will be subject to further taxation only if and when remitted to the parent undertaking.

2.5 Deferred taxation is therefore an accounting convention which is introduced in order to apply the accruals concept to income reporting where timing differences occur. However, **deferred tax assets** are not included in accounts as a rule, because it would not be prudent, given that the recovery of the tax is uncertain.

Basis of provision

2.6 A comprehensive tax allocation system is one in which deferred taxation is computed for every instance of timing differences: **full provision**. The opposite extreme would be the **nil provision** approach ('**flow through** method'), where only the tax payable in the period would be charged to that period.

SSAP 15

2.7 SSAP 15, the forerunner of FRS 19, rejected both these approaches and prescribe a middle course, called **partial provision**.

> 'Tax deferred or accelerated by the effect of timing differences should be accounted for to the extent that it is probable that a liability or asset will crystallise. Tax deferred or accelerated by the effect of timing differences should not be accounted for to the extent that it is probable that a liability or asset will not crystallise.'

2.8 The **probability** that a liability or asset would crystallise was assessed by the directors on the basis of **reasonable assumptions**. They had to take into account all relevant information available up to the date on which they approved the financial statements, and also their intentions for the future. Ideally, financial projections of future plans had to be made for a number (undefined) of years ahead. The directors' judgement had to be exercised with prudence.

2.9 If a company predicted, for example, that capital expenditure would **continue at the same rate** for the foreseeable future, so that capital allowances and depreciation would remain at the same levels, then no originating or reversing differences of any significance to the continuing trend of the tax charge would arise and so no change to the provision for deferred tax needed to be made (unless there were other significant timing differences).

The three different methods compared

2.10 Under the **flow-through method**, the tax liability recognised is the expected legal tax liability for the period (ie no provision is made for deferred tax). The main **advantages** of the method are that it is straightforward to apply and the tax liability recognised is closer to many people's idea of a 'real' liability than that recognised under either full or partial provision.

2.11 The main **disadvantages** of flow-through are that it can lead to large fluctuations in the tax charge and that it does not allow tax relief for long-term liabilities to be recognised until those liabilities are settled. The method is not used internationally.

2.12 The **full provision method** has the **advantage** that it is consistent with general international practice. It also recognises that each timing difference at the balance sheet date has an effect on future tax payments. If a company claims an accelerated capital allowance on an item of plant, future tax assessments will be bigger than they would have been otherwise. Future transactions may well affect those assessments still further, but that is not relevant in assessing the position at the balance sheet date. The **disadvantage** of full provision is that, under certain types of tax system, it gives rise to large liabilities that may fall due only far in the future. The full provision method is the one prescribed by FRS 19.

2.13 The **partial provision method** addresses this disadvantage by providing for deferred tax only to the extent that it is expected to be paid in the foreseeable future. This has an obvious intuitive appeal, but its effect is that deferred tax recognised at the balance sheet date includes the tax effects of future transactions that have not been recognised in the financial statements, and which the reporting company has neither undertaken nor even committed to undertake at that date. It is difficult to reconcile this with the ASB's *Statement of Principles*, which defines assets and liabilities as arising from past events.

Exam focus point

Calculations under all three methods could be required in the exam. FRS 19 is relatively new, so you could be asked to compare different methods.

2.14 It is important that you understand the issues properly so consider the example below.

2.15 EXAMPLE: THE THREE METHODS COMPARED

Suppose that Girdo plc begins trading on 1 January 20X7. In its first year it makes profits of £5m, the depreciation charge is £1m and the capital allowances on those assets is £1.5m. The rate of corporation tax is 33%.

2.16 SOLUTION: FLOW THROUGH METHOD

The tax liability for the year is 33% £(5.0 + 1.0 – 1.5)m = £1.485m. The potential deferred tax liability of 33% × (£1.5m – £1m) is completely ignored and no judgement is required on the part of the preparer.

2.17 SOLUTION: FULL PROVISION

The tax liability is £1.485m again, but the debit in the P&L account is increased by the deferred tax liability of 33% × £0.5m = £165,000. The total charge to the P&L account is therefore £1,650,000 which is an effective tax rate of 33% on accounting profits (ie 33% × £5.0m). Again, no judgement is involved in using this method.

2.18 SOLUTION: PARTIAL PROVISION

Is a deferred tax provision necessary under partial provision? It is now necessary to look ahead at future capital expenditure plans. Will capital allowances exceed depreciation over the next few years? If *yes*, no provision for deferred tax is required. If *no*, then a reversal is expected, ie there is a year in which depreciation is greater than capital allowances. The deferred tax provision is made on the maximum reversal which will be created, and any not provided is disclosed by note.

If we assume that the review of expected future capital expenditure under the partial method required a deferred tax charge of £82,500 (33% × £250,000), we can then summarise the position.

Summary

2.19 The methods can be compared as follows.

Method	*Provision*	*Disclosure*
	£	£
Flow-through	-	-
Full provision	165,000	-
Partial provision	82,500	82,500

2.20 Now try the question below. This question is based on the tax system prior to the 1984 Finance Act. It illustrates the important effect of 100% FYAs.

Question: methods compared

Cuthbert Ltd buys a machine for £100,000 in 20X1. It is to be depreciated evenly over four years, has no scrap value, and will attract a 100% FYA. The company plans to buy a similar machine in 20X4 and its long term plans are for general expansion. Corporation tax is assumed to be 50% and pre-tax profit can be assumed to be £90,000 per annum before adjustments for tax in years 20X1-20X3. In 20X4 it will be £210,000. Calculate the figures for deferred tax for the years 20X1 to 20X4, using the nil, full and partial provision bases.

Answer

Nil provision would give rise to the following figures.

	20X1	*20X2*	*20X3*	*20X4*
	£'000	£'000	£'000	£'000
Pre-tax profit	90	90	90	210
Add depreciation	25	25	25	50
Less FYA	(100)	0	0	(100)
Taxable profit	15	115	115	160
Tax payable (50%)	7.5	57.5	57.5	80
Deferred tax charge	-	-	-	-
Tax charge in P & L a/c	7.5	57.5	57.5	80

Full provision of deferred tax requires that at each year end the deferred tax account in the balance sheet contains full provision for tax on all timing differences to date, which are equal to the excess of FYAs claimed over depreciation charged. The deferred tax calculations are as follows.

	20X1	*20X2*	*20X3*	*20X4*
	£'000	£'000	£'000	£'000
WDV of machines (tax)	-	-	-	-
NBV of machines (accounts)	75	50	25	75
Excess of NBV over WDV (= accelerated capital allowances)	75	50	25	75
Deferred tax provision (total) needed, at 50%	37.5	25	12.5	37.5
Deferred tax charge/(credit) for the year (= movement required on provision)	37.5	(12.5)	(12.5)	25
Tax payable (as above)	7.5	57.5	57.5	80
Deferred tax charge/(credit)	37.5	(12.5)	(12.5)	25
Tax charge in P & L a/c	45.0	45.0	45.0	105
Deferred tax provision in balance sheet	37.5	25.0	12.5	37.5

Note. The deferred tax figures could also be found as follows.

	FYA	*Depreciation*	*Difference*	*Deferred tax charge/(credit) (50% of difference)*
	£'000	£'000	£'000	£'000
20X1	100	25	75	37.5
20X2	-	25	(25)	(12.5)
20X3	-	25	(25)	(12.5)
20X4	100	50	50	25

Partial provision of deferred tax would involve making provision only for reversing differences foreseen. These must therefore be analysed. The deferred tax calculations are as follows.

	FYA	*Depreciation*	*Originating/ (reversing) difference*
	£'000	£'000	£'000
20X1	100	25	75
20X2	-	25	(25)
20X3	-	25	(25)
20X4	100	50	50

At the end of 20X1 reversing differences (excess of depreciation over FYAs) are foreseen for 20X2 and 20X3; therefore provision is made for them (50% × 50 = 25). This provision will reverse during 20X2 and 20X3. No provision is made in 20X4 as general expansion is foreseen.

	20X1	20X2	20X3	20X4
	£'000	£'000	£'000	£'000
Tax payable (as above)	7.5	57.5	57.5	80
Deferred tax charge/(credit)	25.0	(12.5)	(12.5)	-
Tax charge in P & L a/c	32.5	45.0	45.0	80
Deferred tax provision in balance sheet	25.0	12.5		

Problems with SSAP 15

2.21 SSAP 15 is **conceptually inconsistent** with other standards in that it requires deferred tax to be recognised only where it is not expected to remain a permanent feature of the balance sheet. Other standards do not have this rule. For example, a liability for unfunded pension costs is recognised, even if it is never expected to reduce (because new liabilities will arise as old ones are settled).

2.22 There are other disadvantages to SSAP 15, namely its inconsistency with **international practice** and the fact that it requires **estimation** of future transactions (which is against the *Statement of Principles*). These problems led to the development of FRS 19.

FRS 19 *Deferred tax*

2.23 In December 2000 the ASB published FRS 19. The FRS replaced SSAP 15 and comes into effect for accounting periods ending on or after 23 January 2002, although earlier adoption is encouraged. It requires entities to provide for tax timing differences on a **full, rather than partial provision basis.**

Objective

2.24 The objective of FRS 19 is to ensure that:

(a) Future tax consequences of past transactions and events are recognised as liabilities or assets in the financial statements

(b) The financial statements disclose any other special circumstances that may have an effect on future tax charges.

Scope

2.25 The FRS applies **to all financial statements that are intended to give a true and fair view** of a reporting entity's financial position and profit or loss (or income and expenditure) for a period.

2.26 The FRS applies to taxes calculated on the basis of taxable profits, including withholding taxes paid on behalf of the reporting entity.

Recognition of deferred tax assets and liabilities

REMEMBER!

Deferred tax should be recognised in respect of **all timing differences that have originated but not reversed by the balance sheet date.**

Deferred tax should not be recognised on permanent differences.

Question: timing differences

Can you remember some examples of timing differences?

Answer

- Accelerated capital allowances
- Pension liabilities accrued but taxed when paid
- Interest charges and development costs capitalised but allowed for tax purposes when incurred
- Unrealised intra-group stock profits reversed on consolidation
- Revaluation gains
- Tax losses
- Unremitted earnings of subsidiaries, associates and joint ventures recognised in group results.

KEY TERM

Permanent differences. Differences between an entity's taxable profits and its results as stated in the financial statements that arise because certain types of income and expenditure are non-taxable or disallowable, or because certain tax charges or allowances have no corresponding amount in the financial statements.

Allowances for fixed asset expenditure

2.27 Deferred tax **should be recognised** when the **allowances** for the cost of a fixed asset are **received before or after the cost of the fixed asset is recognised in the profit and loss account.** However, if and when **all conditions** for retaining the allowances have been met, the **deferred tax should be reversed.**

2.28 If an asset is not being depreciated (and has not otherwise been written down to a carrying value less than cost), the timing difference is the amount of capital allowances received.

2.29 Most capital allowances are received on a **conditional basis**, ie they are repayable (for example, via a balancing charge) if the assets to which they relate are sold for more than their tax written-down value. However, some, such as industrial buildings allowances, are repayable only if the assets to which they relate are sold within a specified period. Once that period has expired, all conditions for retaining the allowance have been met. At that point, deferred tax that has been recognised (ie on the excess of the allowance over any depreciation) is reversed.

Question: industrial buildings allowance

An industrial building qualifies for an IBA when purchased in 20X1. The building is still held by the company in 20Z6. What happens to the deferred tax?

Answer

All the conditions for retaining tax allowances have been met. This means that the timing differences have become permanent and the deferred tax recognised should be reversed. Before the 25 year period has passed, deferred tax should be provided on the difference between the amount of the industrial building allowance and any depreciation charged on the asset.

Marked to market non-monetary assets

2.30 **Deferred tax must be provided for** when the timing difference arises on assets that are marked to market, with gains and losses recorded in the profit and loss account.

2.31 This reflects the view that, when gains and losses are recognised in the profit and loss account, it is because they are for the most part readily realisable. To give a true and fair view of the entity's performance, the additional tax that would be payable on realising the gains should also be recognised.

Revaluations

2.32 **Deferred tax should not be recognised** on timing differences arising when other non-monetary assets are **revalued**, unless, by the balance sheet date, the reporting entity has:

(a) Entered into a **binding agreement to sell** the revalued assets
(b) **Recognised the gains and losses** expected to arise on sale

2.33 Deferred tax **should not be recognised** on timing differences arising when non-monetary assets (other than marked to market assets) are revalued or sold if, on the basis of all available evidence, it is more likely than not that the taxable gain will be **rolled over**, being charged to tax only if and when the assets into which the gain has been rolled over are sold.

REMEMBER!

Even if you have a binding agreement to sell and the gain/loss recognised is expected to arise on sale, those gains expected to be rolled over will not necessarily result in a future liability to tax and deferred tax should not be provided.

2.34 Gains subject to **holdover relief** do **not** receive the same exemption as those attributed to rollover relief.

2.35 The reason for this treatment is that, where rollover relief has been obtained, the entity retains the discretion to avoid paying tax on the chargeable gain. That tax will be paid only if and when the replacement assets are sold.

Unremitted earnings

2.36 Tax that could be payable (taking account of any double taxation relief) on any future remittance of the past earnings of a subsidiary, associate or joint venture **should be provided for only to the extent that**, at the balance sheet date:

(a) **Dividends** have been **accrued as receivable**

(b) **A binding agreement to distribute the past earnings in future** has been entered into by the subsidiary, associate or joint venture.

2.37 It is **considered unlikely** that there will be a binding agreement to distribute the past earnings of the subsidiary, associate or joint venture.

Deferred tax assets

2.38 Deferred tax assets should be recognised to the extent that they are considered **recoverable,** which will be the case if **it is more likely than not** that **suitable tax profits** will exist from which the reversal of the timing difference giving rise to the asset can be deducted.

2.39 The need for prudence would suggest that more evidence of the likelihood of future profits was needed for recognition of a deferred tax asset than for recognition of a deferred tax liability.

2.40 *Suitable taxable profits*

(a) The profits are generated by the same taxable entity and assessed by the same taxation authority.

(b) Set off is compliant with tax authority rules, for example carry back, carry forward relief.

(c) They arise from the future reversal of deferred tax liabilities recognised at the balance sheet date.

2.41 Account may be taken of tax planning opportunities, ie actions that the entity would take if necessary to create suitable taxable profits.

Recognition in the statements of performance

REMEMBER!

Recognise deferred tax in the performance statement where related timing differences have been recognised.

2.42 **Deferred tax** should be **recognised in the profit and loss account** for the period, **except** to the extent that it is **attributable to a gain or loss** that is or has been **recognised** directly **in the statement of total recognised gains and losses.**

2.43 Where a gain or loss is or has been recognised directly in the statement of total recognised gains and losses, deferred tax attributable to that gain or loss should also be recognised directly in that statement.

Measurement – tax rates

2.44 Deferred tax should be measured at **the average tax rates expected to apply when timing differences reverse**, based on tax rates and laws **substantially enacted** by the balance sheet date.

2.45 Average tax rates only need to be calculated if different rates of tax are expected to apply to different levels of taxable income.

2.46 Tax rates are substantially enacted:

(a) Once a Bill has passed through the House of Commons but not the Lords

(b) When a resolution having statutory effect is passed under the Provisional Collection of Taxes Act 1968

Measurement – discounting

2.47 Reporting entities are **permitted but not required** to discount deferred tax assets and liabilities to reflect the time value of money.

2.48 The ASB believes that, just as other long-term liabilities such as provisions and debt are discounted, so too in principle should long-term deferred tax balances. The FRS therefore permits discounting and provides guidance on how it should be done. However, the ASB stopped short of making discounting mandatory, acknowledging that there is as yet **no internationally accepted methodology** for discounting deferred tax, and that for some entities **the costs might outweigh the benefits.** Entities are encouraged to select the more appropriate policy, taking account of factors such as materiality and the policies of other entities in their sector.

Question: discounting

Can you think of a situation where it might be appropriate to discount deferred tax liabilities?

Answer

Where the reversal is fairly slow, for example with industrial buildings allowances.

2.49 Discounting should be **applied consistently** to all tax flows on timing differences where the effect is expected to be **material** and where the **tax flows have not already been discounted**. Certain timing differences such as those arising on provisions for pension costs or the lessor's investment in finance leases are measured by reference to cash flows that have already been discounted. The deferred tax provisions to which they give rise already incorporate discounting, so they are not eligible for further discounting.

2.50 **No account** should be taken of **future timing differences** including future tax losses.

2.51 The **scheduling of the reversals** should take account of the **remaining tax effect of transactions already reflected in the financial statements**, for example tax losses at the balance sheet date.

2.52 The **discount rate** should be the **post tax return** that could be obtained at the balance sheet date on **government bonds** with **similar maturity dates** and in **currencies similar to those of the deferred tax assets or liabilities.** It may be possible to use average rates without introducing material errors. The examples below are taken from the FRS.

2.53 EXAMPLE: SCHEDULING OF REVERSAL OF ACCELERATED CAPITAL ALLOWANCES ON A SINGLE ASSET

An entity purchases an asset for £100,000 at the start of 20X0. It is estimated that the asset will have a useful economic life of ten years and no residual value. Capital allowances can be claimed at a rate of 25 per cent of cost in each of the first four years.

At the end of 20X0, there is a timing difference of £15,000, which is the difference between the allowances of £25,000 received and the depreciation of £10,000. The timing difference is treated as reversing according to the following schedule (even if the entity expects to make losses at some point during the life of the asset):

Years from now:	1	2	3	4	5	6	7	8	9	Total
Depreciation (£'000)	10	10	10	10	10	10	10	10	10	90
Allowances (£'000)	25	25	25	-	-	-	-	-	-	75
(ACA)/ Reversal – leading to increase in PCTCT	(15)	(15)	(15)	10	10	10	10	10	10	15

Published information				**Post-tax return (bid yield less tax of 30%)**
Years to Maturity	Coupon rate %	Bid Price	Bid Yield %	
1	6	99.37	6.67	4.7
3	7	102.82	6.01	4.2
5	6.5	104.27	5.55	3.9
9	7.2	114.16	5.29	3.7
30	6	114.00	5.09	3.6

Years from now	Timing difference (increase)/reversal £000	Deferred tax (asset)/liability @ 30% £000	Discount rate %	Deferred tax (asset)/liability Discounted £000
1	(15)	(4.5)	4.7	(4.3)
2	(15)	(4.5)	4.4	(4.1)
3	(15)	(4.5)	4.2	(4)
4	10	3	4	2.6
5	10	3	3.9	2.5
6	10	3	3.8	2.4
7	10	3	3.8	2.3
8	10	3	3.2	2.2
9	10	3	3.2	2.2
Total	15	4.5		1.8

2.54 MORE COMPLICATED EXAMPLE: DISCOUNTING

This example is taken from an appendix to the FRS. It illustrates how deferred tax arising from accelerated capital allowances on a plant and machinery pool is discounted.

Assumptions

A company that operates solely in the UK depreciates its plant and machinery on a straight-line basis over 10 years. Residual value is estimated to be 1/11th of cost. The company receives capital allowances at a rate of 25 per cent per year on a reducing balance basis. It is taxed on its profits at 30 per cent.

The company has three groups of assets costing £1,100 each, purchased six years, three years and one year ago (in each case at the end of the financial year). The net book value of plant and machinery at the balance sheet date (year 0) is:

	£
Original cost	3,300
Cumulative depreciation	(1,000)
Net book value	2,300

The tax written-down values of the plant and machinery pool, and the consequential timing difference, at the balance sheet date are:

	£
Net book value	2,300
Tax written-down value	(1,114)
Timing difference at end of year 0	1,186

Scheduling the reversal of the deferred tax liability

The future reversals of the liability are scheduled in Table 1 below. The future depreciation of the existing pool of fixed assets (column b) is compared with the future writing-down allowances available on the pool (column c) to determine the years of reversal of the capital allowances (column d). When forecasting capital allowances for future periods, it is assumed that allowances will be claimed as early as possible and that the residual values of the assets will equal those forecast for depreciation purposes.

Table 1

Years from now	Depreciation	Capital allowances	Reversal of timing differences	Deferred tax liability (undiscounted)
	£	£	£	£
a	b	c	d = b – c	e = d × 30%
1	300	278	22	7
2	300	209	91	27
3	300	157	143	43
4	300	93	207	62
5	200	69	131	39
6	200	52	148	44
7	200	14	186	56
8	100	11	89	27
9	100	(17)	117	35
10	-	(52)	52	16
Total	2,000	814	1,186	356

Where do the capital allowances figures come from?

You will not need to calculate these figures in an exam, but it may help to know where they come from. Take the figure of £278 at the end of year 1.

At balance sheet date the three lots of assets will have had allowances for seven, four and two years respectively (as they were bought at the end of the financial years). So the tax written down values at the balance sheet dare are:

	£		£
Group 1	1,100	$\times 75\%^7$	147
Group 2	1,100	$\times 75\%^4$	348
Group 3	1,100	$\times 75\%^2$	619
Total			1,114

The capital allowances arising in the next year are therefore (£1,114 × 25%) = £278.5

Discount rates

The prices of and yields on UK Treasury gilts are published in the *Financial Times.* An appropriate post-tax rate is obtained by deducting the rate of tax that the entity pays on investment income (30 per cent) from these returns.

Table 2

Published information				Post-tax return (bid yield less tax of 30%)
Years to Maturity	Coupon rate %	Bid Price	Bid Yield %	
1	6	99.37	6.67	4.7
3	7	102.82	6.01	4.2
5	6.5	104.27	5.55	3.9
9	7.2	114.16	5.29	3.7
30	6	114.00	5.09	3.6

Appropriate rates of return for other maturity dates are estimated by interpolation. See column f of Table 3 below.

Discounting the liability

Table 3 below illustrates how the discounted liability of £290 is calculated. The guidance in the FRS notes that it may be possible to use simplifying assumptions without introducing material errors into the measurement of the discounted liability. In this example, all timing differences reversing in years 10 onwards are treated as reversing in year 10.

Table 3

Years from now	Deferred tax liability (undiscounted) £	Discount rate %		Deferred tax liability (discounted) £
a	e (from Table 1)	f (from Table 2)		$g = e/[(1+f)^a]$
1	7	4.7		7
2	27	4.4	i	25
3	43	4.2		38
4	62	4.0	i	53
5	39	3.9		33
6	44	3.8	i	35
7	56	3.8	i	43
8	27	3.7	i	20
9	35	3.7		25
10+	16	3.7	i	11
Total	356			290

i = estimate based on interpolation of rates known for years 1, 3, 5, 9 and 30*

The discount reduces the deferred tax liability at year 0 by £66, ie from £ 356 to £290.

Presentation

2.55 In the **balance sheet** classify:

- Net deferred tax liabilities as 'provisions for liabilities and charges'

- Net deferred tax assets as debtors, as a separate subhead if material where taxes are levied by the same tax authority or in a group where tax losses of one entity can reduce the taxable profits of another.

2.56 Balances are to be **disclosed separately** on the face of the balance sheet **if** so **material** as to distort the financial statements.

2.57 In the **profit and loss account** classify as part of **tax on profit or loss on ordinary activities.**

Disclosures

2.58 FRS 19 has detailed disclosures relating to deferred tax, which are best learnt by studying the illustrative example below, taken from the Appendix.

IMPORTANT!

Note in particular that the FRS requires information to be disclosed **about factors affecting current and future tax charges. A key element** of this is a requirement to disclose a **reconciliation of the current tax charge for the period to the charge that would arise if the profits reported in the financial statements were charged at a standard rate of tax.**

2.59 EXAMPLE: DISCLOSURES

The following illustrates how the disclosures required by the FRS could be presented in the notes to the accounts. The reconciliation of the tax charge, illustrated as a reconciliation of monetary amounts in note 1 (b) below, could alternatively be given as a reconciliation of the standard rate of tax to the effective rate.

1 TAX ON PROFIT ON ORDINARY ACCOUNTS

(a) *Analysis of charge in period*

	20X1		*20X0*	
	£m	£m	£m	£m
Current tax				
UK corporation tax on profits of the period	40		26	
Adjustments in respect of previous periods	4		(6)	
		44		20
Foreign tax		12		16
Total current tax (note 1(b))		56		36
Deferred tax				
Origination and reversal of timing differences	67		60	
Effect of increased tax rate on opening liability	12		-	
Increase in discount	(14)		(33)	
Total deferred tax (note 2)		65		27
Tax on profit on ordinary activities		121		63

(b) *Factors affecting the tax charge for period*

The tax assessed for the period is lower than the standard rate of corporation tax in the UK (31 per cent). The differences are explained below.

	20X1	20X0
	£m	£m
Profit on ordinary activities before tax	361	327
Profit on ordinary activities multiplied by standard rate of corporation tax in the UK of 31% (20X0: 30%)	112	98
Effects of		
Expenses not deductible for tax purposes (primarily goodwill amortisation)	22	10
Capital allowances for period in excess of depreciation	(58)	(54)
Utilisation of tax losses	(17)	(18)
Rollover relief on profit on disposal of property	(10)	-
Higher tax rates on overseas earnings	3	6
Adjustments to tax charge in respect of previous periods	4	(6)
Current tax charge for period (note 1 (a))	56	36

(c) *Factors that may affect future tax charges*

Based on current capital investment plans, the group expects to continue to be able to claim capital allowances in excess of depreciation in future years but at a slightly lower level than in the current year.

The group has now used all brought-forward tax losses, which have significantly reduced tax payments in recent years.

No provision has been made for deferred tax on gains recognised on revaluing property to its market value or on the sale of properties where potentially taxable gains have been rolled over into replacement assets. Such tax would become payable only if the property were sold without it being possible to claim rollover relief. The total amount unprovided for is £21 million. At present, it is not envisaged that any tax will become payable in the foreseeable future.

The group's overseas tax rates are higher than those in the UK primarily because the profits earned in country X are taxed at a rate of 45 per cent. The group expects a reduction in future tax rates following a recent announcement that the rate of tax in that country is to reduce to 40 per cent.

No deferred tax is recognised on the unremitted earnings of overseas subsidiaries, associates and joint ventures. As the earnings are continually reinvested by the group, no tax is expected to be payable on them in the foreseeable future.

2 PROVISION FOR DEFERRED TAX

	31.12.20X1	31.12.20X0
	£m	£m
Accelerated capital allowances	426	356
Tax losses carried forward	-	(9)
Undiscounted provision for deferred tax	426	347
Discount	(80)	(66)
Discounted provision for deferred tax	346	281
Provision at start of period	281	
Deferred tax charge in profit and loss account for period (note 1)	65	
Provision at end of period	346	

International comparisons

2.60 The move to full provision accounting reflects an acceptance of the need to harmonise with international practice in the area of deferred tax. However, there are **differences** between the requirements of the FRS and those of the equivalent international standard IAS 12 *Income taxes*.

2.61 The **ASB does not agree** with the rationale underlying the '**temporary difference**' **approach** adopted in the IAS.

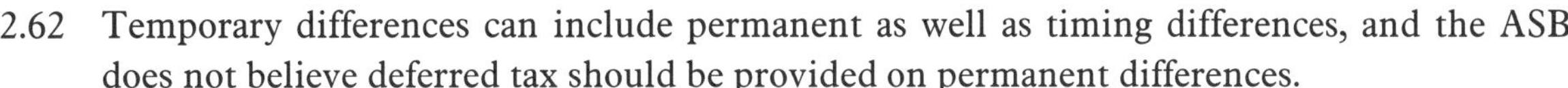

KEY TERM

Temporary difference. Any difference between the amount at which an asset or liability is recognised in financial statements and its tax base. The tax base is the amount that will be deductable or taxable in respect of the asset or liability in the future.

2.62 Temporary differences can include permanent as well as timing differences, and the ASB does not believe deferred tax should be provided on permanent differences.

2.63 In practical terms, the requirements of the FRS are similar to IAS 12's. Both standards require full provision on most timing differences, and both permit deferred tax assets to be recognised only if there is evidence that there will be taxable profits in the future against which the assets can be recovered.

2.64 *Areas of difference*

(a) The FRS does not require or permit deferred tax to be provided for when non-monetary assets are revalued.

(b) No deferred tax can be provided when a taxable gain is rolled over into replacement assets and will become taxable only if and when the assets are sold.

(c) No deferred tax is provided when group accounts incorporate retained earnings of associates and joint ventures, which would become subject to further taxation on remittance to the parent company.

2.65 In each of the above cases there is no obligation to pay more tax until the entity commits itself to selling the assets or remitting the earnings.

Problems

2.66 The FRS makes a significant change. It will have the effect of **increasing the liabilities** reported by entities that at present have **large amounts of unprovided deferred tax** arising from capital allowances in excess of depreciation.

2.67 Criticisms that may be made of the FRS 19 approach include the following.

(a) The provisions on **discounting** are somewhat **confusing**. The full reversal basis of discounting deferred tax liabilities may turn them into assets in the early years of an asset's life because capital allowances exceed depreciation before the timing differences reverse.

(b) The standard is **complicated,** and there is **scope for manipulation and inconsistency**, since discounting is optional.

(c) It is **open to question whether deferred tax is a liability** as defined in the *Statement of Principles*. It is not, strictly speaking, a present obligation arising as a result of a past event. However, it is being recognised as such under the FRS.

(d) Arguably the flow-through or **nil provision method is closer to the ASB definition**, but this method, although much simpler, has been rejected to bring the standard closer to the IAS.

(e) The standard may '**fall between two stools**', as it is different from IAS 12 and not really what the UK wants either.

2.68 **Section summary**

- Deferred tax is tax relating to timing differences.
- Full provision must be made for tax timing differences.
- Deferred tax must not be recognised on revaluation unless there is a commitment to sell, when a gain on sale is rolled over or on unremitted earnings of subsidiaries, associates or joint ventures.
- Discounting is allowed but not required.

Chapter roundup

- **FRS 16 *Current tax*** requires dividends, interest and other income or expenditure to be presented in the financial statements:
  - Excluding the tax credit
  - Including any withholding tax
  - Including the effect of withholding tax suffered as part of the tax charge
- **FRS 19** requires **full provision,** although assets/liabilities may be discounted. In particular you should know about deferred tax and:
  - Revalued assets
  - Overseas earnings not yet remitted to the UK
  - Discounting

Quick quiz

1 A company receives a dividend of £4,000 on which 20% withholding tax has been paid. At what amount should be dividend be shown in the financial statements?

2 What are the three bases under which deferred tax can be computed?

3 Which method does FRS 19 require to be used?

4 Temporary differences are the same as timing differences

True ☐

False ☐

5 Under FRS 19 deferred tax assets and liabilities may/must be discounted. (Delete as applicable.)

Answers to quick quiz

1 £5,000

2 The nil provision bases, the full provision basis and the partial provision basis

3 Full provision

4 False. Temporary differences include permanent differences.

5 May

Now try the question below from the Exam Question Bank

Number	Level	Marks	Time
Q31	Introductory	n/a	n/a

Chapter 23

REPORTING FINANCIAL PERFORMANCE 1

	Topic list	Syllabus reference
1	**FRS 3** ***Reporting financial performance***	**1(a), 4(e)**
2	**FRED 32** ***Disposal of non-current assets and presentation of discontinued operations***	**1(a), 4(e)**
3	**FRS 14** ***Earnings per share***	**1(a), 4(e)**
4	**FRED 26** ***Earnings per share***	**1(a), 4(e)**

Introduction

We have already discussed the problems perceived by companies when they report their results, and how they feel 'obliged' to **manipulate** those results to avoid adverse reaction in the market. **FRS 3** represents the ASB's attempt to prevent some of the worst abuses.

FRED 32 proposes, amongst other things, separate presentation of assets held for disposal. These proposals are topical.

Section 2 summarises the description of **EPS**, the mechanics of its calculation and the disclosure required by FRS 14. EPS is an important indicator of a company's performance. Because of the changes introduced by FRS 3, there has been a movement in the business community towards producing **another standard EPS figure**, which companies could disclose alongside the FRS 14 figure.

Study guide

Section 20 – Reporting financial performance and earnings per share

- Discussion of proposed changes to reporting financial performance
- Explaining the rationale behind the proposed changes in reporting financial performance
- Calculation of diluted earnings per share by reference to dilutive potential ordinary shares, loss per share and particular types of dilutive instruments including partly paid shares, employee incentive schemes and contingently issuable shares

1 FRS 3 REPORTING FINANCIAL PERFORMANCE 12/01, 12/02, 6/03

1.1 The P&L account is arguably the most significant single indicator of a company's success or failure. It is very important to ensure that it is not presented in such a way as to be misleading. This could happen either through an inadvertent lack of consistency within a company or between different companies; or it could arise as a result of deliberate manipulation of accounting figures by unscrupulous directors.

1.2 One particular area where this might happen is the practice known as **reserve accounting**. This involves deducting items of expenditure not from the profits for the current year, but

from the balance of accumulated profits brought forward. By eliminating such items from the **current** year's P&L account a more favourable presentation of the year's results may be achieved; only a close inspection of the previous year's balance sheet will disclose that the figure for reserves brought forward has been manipulated.

1.3 Possible **justifications** for excluding items in this way from the current year's P&L account include the following.

(a) The item might have **arisen in a previous year** without becoming apparent until the current year. It is really a charge against previous year's profits and would have appeared in an earlier year's P&L account if the directors had been aware of it.

(b) The item is **unique in nature** and unlikely to recur. It would be a misleading distortion of the trend of reported profits if such an item were charged against the current year's profits.

1.4 Each of these arguments may be valid in certain circumstances, but it is clear that scope is available for unscrupulous manipulation of the P&L account unless those circumstances are very clearly defined. The old SSAP 6 attempted to standardise the treatment of **prior year adjustments** and **extraordinary items**, which are respectively the two categories of items referred to in Paragraph 1.3 above.

1.5 You have covered FRS 3 in your earlier studies, but here is a reminder of its main reading.

Exceptional and extraordinary items

1.6 FRS 3 practically outlawed extraordinary items.

Knowledge brought forward from earlier studies

Exceptional and extraordinary items

Exceptional items

Exceptional items are **material items** which derive from events or transactions that fall **within the ordinary activities** of the reporting entity and which need to be disclosed by virtue of their **size or incidence** if the financial statements are to give a true and fair view. Show on the face of the P&L a./c:

- Profit *and* loss (no offset) on the **sale/termination of an operation**
- Costs of a **fundamental reorganisation** or restructuring that has a material effect on the nature and focus of the reporting entity's operations
- Profit *and* loss (no offset) on **disposal of fixed assets** (difference between sale proceeds and the **carrying value** of the investment)

Other exceptional items should be allocated to the appropriate **statutory format heading** and attributed to continuing or discontinued operations as appropriate. If sufficiently material disclose on the face of the P&L a/c.

Extraordinary items

Extraordinary items are material items possessing a **high degree of abnormality** which arise from events or transactions that fall **outside the ordinary activities** of the reporting entity and which are not expected to recur. Note that **ordinary activities** include infrequent and unusual events.

- Largely **redundant** as the ASB has stated that such items are not expected to appear in P&L accounts in future.
- Should be shown on the **face of the P&L account** before dividends and other minority interests; tax and MI in the extraordinary item shown separately; a description should be given in the notes.

The profit and loss account

1.7 The face of the P&L account was altered by FRS 3 to give further information.

Knowledge brought forward from earlier studies

The P & L account

Structure

- All statutory headings from turnover to operating profit are subdivided: **continuing vs discontinued operations.**
- Turnover and operating profit are fully analysed: **existing vs newly acquired operations.**
- Only figures for turnover and operating profit need to be shown on the **face of the P&L account**; others are by note.

Discontinued operations

A discontinued operation needs *all* these conditions

- Sale/termination must be **completed** before the earlier of 3 months after the y/e or the date the FS approved (terminations not completed by this date: disclose by note)
- Former activity must have **ceased permanently**
- Sales/termination has a **material effect** on the **nature and focus** of the entity's operations and represents a **material reduction** in its operating facilities resulting from either a:
    - Withdrawal from a market (business/geographical), or
    - Material reduction in turnover in its continuing markets
- Assets, liabilities, results of operations and activities are **clearly distinguishable**, physically, operationally and for financial reporting purposes

Accounting for the discontinuation involves the following.

- The **results** of the discontinued operation up to the date of sale/termination or the balance sheet date should be shown under each of the relevant P&L account headings.
- **Profit/loss on (or costs of) discontinuation**: disclose as exceptional item after operating profit, before interest
- Figures for the **previous year** must be adjusted for any activities which are now discontinued in the current year
- Once a business is committed to dispose of an operation (eg by signing a sale agreement) it should **provide for direct costs of sale or termination**; and any **operating losses** up to the date of sale/termination.
    - If the operation continues during the whole of the accounting period then the provision should be included under the continuing column
    - If the operation is discontinued in the next accounting period, the provision will be utilised and disclosed

Acquisitions

- Business combinations that are accounted for as **mergers** and/or as **acquisitions.**
- Associates that **become subsidiaries**, on further acquisition of shares.
- **Start-ups** and **acquisitions of associates** are *not* acquisitions.

Statement and notes

1.8 A new statement and various notes were introduced by FRS 3.

Knowledge brought forward from earlier studies

New statement and notes

Statement of total recognised gains and losses

Presented with the same prominence as the P&L account, balance sheet and cash flow statement, as a **primary statement**.

- **Contents**

Profit for the year (per P&L a/c)	X
Items taken directly to reserves (not goodwill written off to reserves)	X
Unrealised surplus on revaluation of fixed assets	X
Surplus/deficit on revaluation of investment properties	X
Currency translation differences on foreign currency net investments	X
Total recognised gains and losses for the year	X
Prior period adjustments (see later)	(X)
Total gains and losses recognised since last annual report	X

- Once an unrealised gain or loss is recognised in the statement, transfer for inclusion in the P&L when it **becomes realised** at a later date is *not* allowed.
- **Transactions with shareholders** are excluded (dividends paid and proposed, share issues, redemptions): these transactions do not represent gains/losses.
- Where the profit/loss for the year is the **only recognised gain/loss**, state this below the P&L account.
- In the consolidated statement of total recognised gains and losses, include the investor's share of the total recognised gains and losses of its associates, shown separately under each heading if the amounts are material, either in the statement or a note.

Reconciliation of movements in shareholders' funds

- In the notes to the accounts *or* a primary statement
- Pulls together **financial performance** as shown in the:
  - P&L account
  - Other movements in shareholders' funds as in STRGL
  - All other changes in shareholders' funds
- **Example**

Profit for the financial year	X
* Dividends	(X)
	X
Other recognised gains and losses (per STRGL)	X
* New share capital	X
Net addition to shareholders' funds	X
Opening shareholders' funds	X
Closing shareholders' funds	X

* Items not appearing in the primary statements

Note of historical cost profits and losses

Reported profit is not the same as HC profit where **alternative accounting rules** are used. If the difference is material, then include a **reconciliation** statement after the STRGL or the P&L account. Reconcile profit before tax; however, the retained profit for the year must also be restated.

Prior period adjustments

1.9 FRS 3 defines prior period adjustments and states when they should be used.

Knowledge brought forward from earlier studies

Prior period adjustments

- **Definition**: material adjustments applicable to prior periods arising from changes in accounting policies or from the correction of fundamental errors; it does *not* include normal recurring adjustments or corrections of account estimates made in prior periods.
- **Accounting treatment**
  - Restate prior year P&L account and balance sheet
  - Restate opening reserves balance
  - Include in the reconciliation of movements in shareholders' funds
  - Note at the foot of the STRGL of the current period
- **Fundamental error**: an error which is so significant that the truth and fairness of the financial statements is not achieved.
- **Change in accounting policy**: based on the fundamental accounting concept of **consistency**; reasons for a change in policy:
  - Gives fairer presentation of financial position/result
  - Introduction of, or change to a standard/legislation

1.10 The following exercises will be useful revision.

Question: discontinued operation

B&C plc's P&L account for the year ended 31 December 20X2, with comparatives, is as follows.

	20X2	*20X1*
	£'000	£'000
Turnover	200,000	180,000
Cost of sales	(60,000)	(80,000)
Gross profit	140,000	100,000
Distribution costs	(25,000)	(20,000)
Administration expenses	(50,000)	(45,000)
Operating profit	65,000	35,000

During the year the company sold a material business operation with all activities ceasing on 14 February 20X3. The loss on the sale of the operation amounted to £2.2m. The results of the operation for 20X1 and 20X2 were as follows.

	20X2	*20X1*
	£'000	£'000
Turnover	22,000	26,000
Operating loss	(7,000)	(6,000)

In addition, the company acquired a business which contributed £7m to turnover and an operating profit of £1.5m.

Required

Prepare the profit and loss account and related notes for the year ended 31 December 20X2 complying with the requirements of FRS 3 as far as possible.

Answer

B&C PROFIT AND LOSS ACCOUNT FOR THE YEAR ENDED 31 DECEMBER

	20X2		20X1	
	£'000	£'000	£'000	£'000
Turnover				
Continuing operations				
(200 – 22 – 7)/(180 – 26)		171.0		154
Acquisitions		7.0		-
		178.0		154
Discontinued		22.0		26
		200.0		180
Cost of sales		(60.0)		(80)
Gross profit		140.0		100
Distribution costs		(25.0)		(20)
Administration expenses (50 – 2.2)		(47.8)		(45)
Operating profit				
Continuing operations	72.7		41	
Acquisitions	1.5		-	
	74.2		41	
Discontinued	(7.0)		(6)	
		67.2		35
Loss on sale of operation		(2.2)		-
		65.0		35

Note to the P&L account

	20X2			20X1(as restated)		
	Continuing	*Discontinued*	*Total*	*Continuing*	*Discontinued*	*Total*
	£'000	£'000	£'000	£'000	£'000	£'000
Cost of sales	X	X	60.0	X	X	80
Net operating expenses						
Distribution costs	X	X	25.0	X	X	20
Admin expenses	X	X	47.8	X	X	45
	X	X	72.8	X	X	65

Question: STRGL and reconciliation

Extracts from Z Ltd's P&L account for the year ended 31 December 20X1 were as follows.

	£'000
Profit after tax	512
Dividend	(120)
Retained profit	392

During the year the following important events took place.

(a) Assets were revalued upward by £120,000.

(b) £300,000 share capital was issued during the year.

(c) Certain stock items were written down by £45,000.

(d) The company's investment properties previously revalued by £81,000 were written down by £110,000. This deficit is expected to be temporary.

(e) Opening shareholders' funds = £4m

Show how the events for the year would be shown in the statement of total recognised gains and losses and the reconciliation of movements in shareholders' funds.

Answer

	£'000
Profit after tax	512
Asset	120
Devaluation of investments properties *	(110)
	522

* An amendment to SSAP 19 allows a temporary debit balance on the investment revaluation reserve (IRR).

RECONCILIATION OF MOVEMENTS IN SHAREHOLDERS' FUNDS

	£'000
Profit after tax	512
Dividend	(120)
	392
Other recognised gains and losses (522 – 512)	10
New share capital	300
Net addition to shareholders' funds	702
Opening shareholders' funds	4,000
Closing shareholders' funds	4,702

Question: historical cost profit reconciliations

A Ltd reported a profit before tax of £162,000 for the year ended 31 December 20X1. During the year the following transactions in fixed assets took place.

(a) An asset with a book value of £40,000 was revalued to £75,000. The remaining useful life is estimated to be five years.

(b) An asset (with a five year useful life at the date of revaluation) had been revalued upwards by £20,000 (book value £30,000). It was sold during the current year (one year after revaluation) for £48,000.

Show the reconciliation of profit to historical cost profit for the year ended 31 Dec 20X1.

Answer

RECONCILIATION OF PROFIT TO HISTORICAL COST PROFIT
FOR THE YEAR ENDED 31 DECEMBER 20X1

	£'000
Reported profit on ordinary activities before taxation	162
Realisation of property revaluation gains	20
Difference between historical cost depreciation charge and the actual depreciation charge of the year calculated on the revalued amount (75,000 – 40,000)/5	7
	189

Question: change of accounting policy

Wick Ltd was established on 1 January 20X0. In the first three years' accounts deferred development expenditure was carried forward as an asset in the balance sheet. During 20X3 the directors decided that for the current and future years, all development expenditure should be written off as it is incurred. This decision has not resulted from any change in the expected outcome of development projects on hand, but rather from a desire to favour the prudence concept. The following information is available.

(a) Movements on the deferred development account:

Year	*Deferred development expenditure incurred during year*	*Transfer from deferred development expenditure account to P & L account*
	£'000	£'000
20X0	525	-
20X1	780	215
20X2	995	360

(b) The 20X2 accounts showed the following.

	£'000
Retained reserves b/f	2,955
Retained profit for the year	1,825
Retained profits carried forward	4,780

(c) The retained profit for 20X3 after charging the actual development expenditure for the year was £2,030,000.

Required

Show how the change in accounting policy should be reflected in the statement of reserves in the company's 20X3 accounts. Ignore taxation.

Answer

If the new accounting policy had been adopted since the company was incorporated, the additional profit and loss account charges for development expenditure would have been as follows.

	£'000
20X0	525
20X1 (780 – 215)	565
	1,090
20X2 (995 – 360)	635
	1,725

This means that the reserves brought forward at 1 January 20X3 would have been £1,725,000 less than the reported figure of £4,780,000; while the reserves brought forward at 1 January 20X2 would have been £1,090,000 less than the reported figure of £2,955,000. The statement of reserves in Wick Ltd's 20X3 accounts should, therefore, appear as follows.

STATEMENT OF RESERVES (EXTRACT)

	20X3	*20X2*	
	£'000	£'000	
Retained profits at the beginning of year			
Previously reported	4,780	2,955	
Prior year adjustment (note 1)	1,725	1,090	
Restated	3,055	1,865	
Retained profits for the year	2,030	1,190	(note 2)
Retained profits at the end of the year	5,085	3,055	

Notes

1 The accounts should include a note explaining the reasons for and consequences of the changes in accounting policy. (See above workings for 20X3 and 20X2.)

2 The retained profit shown for 20X2 is after charging the additional development expenditure of £635,000.

Effect of FRS 3

1.11 First of all, FRS 3 makes **extraordinary items virtually non-existent**. This means that some of the manipulation of results which went on under SSAP 6 will be avoided. All exceptional items, apart from a few important exceptions, will be included under the relevant P&L heading. Those exceptional items requiring disclosure on the face of the P&L account are indicators of important events during the accounting period and they would usually have been shown under extraordinary items under the old SSAP 6. FRS 3 introduced **new definitions** for most of the important terms.

1.12 The effect on **prior year adjustments** is negligible. The effect on **EPS** will be studied in Section 2.

1.13 A **new format** for the P&L account was introduced, splitting continuing and discontinued operations. The definitions of these terms will again prevent manipulation. **Disclosure** is much fuller than under SSAP 6, where only a one line extraordinary item was given.

1.14 A **statement of total recognised gains and losses** (STRGL) must be provided. The ASB's aim here has been to turn attention away from particular numbers or indicators and to encourage users to make their own judgements about a company's performance based on the set of information given. This statement cannot be lost in the notes as the reserve movement note was under SSAP 6, because it must be given equal prominence with the other primary statements. (Note that one of the main reasons why this statement came into existence was the collapse of Polly Peck. The size of the exchange movements going through reserves was considerable and, although they had been disclosed, they had not been highlighted.) The really important figure here is that of **total gains and losses** for the year. This will probably be of great importance to all users in the future, as much as the profit for the year.

1.15 Consideration was given to extending the statement of recognised gains and losses to provide a **reconciliation of movements in shareholders' funds** for the period. Instead, a separate reconciliation was suggested, which could be shown as either a note or a primary statement. This statement includes dividends and goodwill written off. Note that dividends are shown as a deduction from profit for the financial year rather than from total recognised gains and losses, because dividends cannot be paid out of unrealised profits.

1.16 The overall effect of FRS 3 can be seen as a great improvement on its predecessor (SSAP 6), particularly in the way it highlights reserve movements and restricts the use of extraordinary items. It has been **criticised**, however, and the following points show the major criticisms.

(a) Restricting extraordinary items and calculating EPS after extraordinary items will make earnings and EPS too **volatile** to obtain meaningful results over time. Analysts will probably exclude items they consider extraordinary for their purposes, thus undermining the impact of FRS 3.

(b) The old and new primary statements and the new notes are not necessarily easy to relate to each other. The formats could have been adjusted to allow the **relationships to be clearer**.

(c) FRS 3, by introducing new statements and notes, has made financial statements even **more confusing** for the lay user, particularly since the non-columnar layout is allowed.

(d) Allowing companies to prepare **alternative EPS figures** will lead to confusion as different methods will be used in each case. Analysts also believe that the market, by its very nature, will aim for one 'across the board' earnings figure (see Section 4).

1.17 You may be able to think of other problems associated with FRS 3 but remember that it has many advantages, not the least of which is the fact that it discloses *more* information. You will be able to see this if you obtain some recent sets of company accounts. It also reflects the ASB's aim to avoid the use of just one earnings measure, such as EPS.

Exam focus point

Although you may be faced with a question based specifically on FRS 3, you may also find that questions requiring a consolidated P&L account will involve FRS 3 disclosures.

2 FRED 32 DISPOSAL OF NON-CURRENT ASSETS AND PRESENTATION OF DISCONTINUED OPERATIONS 6/04

Background

2.1 FRED 32 *Disposal of non-current assets* and *presentation of discontinued* operations was published in July 2003. It was the result of a short-term convergence project with the US Financial Accounting Standards Board (FASB). In due course as part of its programme to converge UK standards with IFRSs, the ASB proposes to issue a UK standard based on this exposure draft, which would replace FRS 3 and introduce new requirements for non-current assets held for disposal.

2.2 FRED 32 requires assets and groups of assets that are 'held for sale' to be **presented separately** on the face of the balance sheet and the results of discontinued operations to be presented separately in the income statement. This is required so that users of financial statements will be better able to make **projections** about the financial position, profits and cash flows of the entity.

KEY TERM

- **Disposal group**: a group of assets to be disposed of, by sale or otherwise, together as a group in a single transaction, and liabilities directly associated with those assets that will be transferred in the transaction. (In practice a disposal group could be a subsidiary, a cash-generating unit or a single operation within an entity.) *(FRED 32)*

2.3 FRED 32 does not apply to certain assets covered by other accounting standards:

(a) Goodwill
(b) Deferred tax assets
(c) Financial assets
(d) Assets arising from employee benefits
(e) Financial assets arising under leases

Classification of assets held for sale

2.4 A non-current asset (or disposal group) should be classified as **held for sale** if its carrying amount will be recovered **principally through a sale transaction** rather than **through continuing use**. A number of detailed criteria must be met:

(a) The asset must be **available for immediate sale** in its present condition.
(b) Its sale must be **highly probable** (ie, significantly more likely than not).

2.5 For the sale to be highly probable, the following must apply.

(a) Management must be **committed** to a plan to sell the asset.

(b) The asset should be available for immediate sale in its present condition.

(c) There must be an active programme to **locate a buyer.**

(d) The asset must be marketed for sale at a **price that is reasonable** in relation to its current fair value.

(e) The sale should be highly probably and should be expected to take place **within one year** from the date of classification.

(f) It is unlikely that significant changes to the plan will be made or that the plan will be withdrawn.

2.6 An asset (or disposal group) can still be classified as held for sale, even if the sale has not actually taken place within one year. However, the delay must have been **caused by events or circumstances beyond the entity's control** and there must be sufficient evidence that the entity is still committed to sell the asset or disposal group. Otherwise the entity must cease to classify the asset as held for sale.

2.7 If an entity acquires a disposal group (eg, a subsidiary) exclusively with a view to its subsequent disposal it can classify the asset as held for sale only if the sale is expected to take place within one year and it is highly probable that all the other criteria will be met within a short time (normally three months).

2.8 An asset that is to be **abandoned** should not be classified as held for sale. This is because its carrying amount will be recovered principally through continuing use. However, a disposal group to be abandoned may meet the definition of a discontinued operation and therefore separate disclosure may be required (see below).

Question: held for sale?

On 1 December 20X3, a company became committed to a plan to sell a manufacturing facility and has already found a potential buyer. The company does not intend to discontinue the operations currently carried out in the facility. At 31 December 20X3 there is a backlog of uncompleted customer orders. The subsidiary will not be able to transfer the facility to the buyer until after it ceases to operate the facility and has eliminated the backlog of uncompleted customer orders. This is not expected to occur until spring 20X4.

Required

Can the manufacturing facility be classified as 'held for sale' at 31 December 20X3?

Answer

The facility will not be transferred until the backlog of orders is completed; this demonstrates that the facility is not available for immediate sale in its present condition. The facility cannot be classified as 'held for sale' at 31 December 20X3. It must be treated in the same way as other items of property, plant and equipment: it should continue to be depreciated and should not be separately disclosed.

Measurement of assets held for sale

KEY TERMS

- **Fair value:** the amount for which an asset could be exchanged, or a liability settled, between knowledgeable, willing parties in an arm's length transaction.
- **Costs to sell:** the incremental costs directly attributable to the disposal of an asset (or disposal group), excluding finance costs and income tax expense.
- **Recoverable amount:** the higher of an asset's fair value less costs to sell and its value in use.
- **Value in use:** the present value of estimated future cash flows expected to arise from the continuing use of an asset and from its disposal at the end of its useful life.

2.9 A non-current asset (or disposal group) that is held for sale should be measured at the **lower of** its **carrying amount** and **fair value less costs to sell**. Fair value less costs to sell is equivalent to net realisable value.

2.10 An impairment loss should be recognised where fair value less costs to sell is lower than carrying amount. Note that this is an exception to the normal rule. FRS 11 *Impairment of fixed assets and goodwill* requires an entity to recognise an impairment loss only where an asset's recoverable amount is lower than its carrying value. Recoverable amount is defined as the higher of net realisable value and value in use. FRS 11 does not apply to assets held for sale.

2.11 A gain must be recognised for any subsequent increase in fair value less costs to sell, but not in excess of the cumulative impairment loss that has been recognised under this FRS or FRS 11.

2.12 Non-current assets held for sale **should not be depreciated**, even if they are still being used by the entity.

2.13 A non-current asset (or disposal group) that is **no longer classified as held for sale** (for example, because the sale has not taken place within one year) is measured at the **lower of**:

(a) Its **carrying amount** before it was classified as held for sale, adjusted for any depreciation that would have been charged had the asset not been held for sale

(b) Its **recoverable amount** at the date of the decision not to sell

Presenting discontinued operations

KEY TERMS

- **Discontinued operation:** a component of an entity that has either been disposed of, or is classified as held for sale, and:
  (a) The operations and cash flows of that component have been (or will be) eliminated from the ongoing operations of the entity as a result of its disposal
  (b) The entity will have no significant continuing involvement in that component after its disposal
- **Component of an entity:** operations and cash flows that can be clearly distinguished, operationally and for financial reporting purposes, from the rest of the entity.

(FRED 32)

2.14 An entity should **present and disclose information** that enables users of the financial statements to evaluate the financial effects of **discontinued operations** and disposals of non-current assets or disposal groups.

2.15 An entity should also disclose for all periods presented:

(a) The revenue, expenses and pre-tax profit or loss of discontinued operations

(b) The related income tax expense

(c) The gain or loss recognised on the measurement to fair value less costs to sell or on the disposal of the assets or the discontinued operation

(d) The related income tax expense

This may be presented either on the face of the income statement or in the notes. If it is presented on the face of the income statement it should be presented in a section identified as relating to discontinued operations, ie separately from continuing operations. This analysis is not required where the discontinued operation is a newly acquired subsidiary that has been classified as held for sale.

2.16 An entity should disclose the **net cash flows** attributable to the operating, investing and financing activities of discontinued operations. These disclosures may be presented either on the face of the cash flow statement or in the notes.

2.17 Gains and losses on the remeasurement of a non-current asset or disposal group that is not a component of an entity should be included in profit or loss from continuing operations.

Illustration

2.18 The following illustration is taken from the implementation guidance to IFRS 5, the International Standard based on an equivalent exposure draft. Profit for the period from discontinued operations would be analysed in the notes.

XYZ GROUP
INCOME STATEMENT
FOR THE YEAR ENDED 31 DECEMBER 20X2

	20X2	*20X1*
Continuing operations	$'000	$'000
Revenue	X	X
Cost of sales	(X)	(X)
Gross profit	X	X
Other income	X	X
Distribution costs	(X)	(X)
Administrative expenses	(X)	(X)
Other expenses	(X)	(X)
Finance costs	(X)	(X)
Share of profit of associates	X	X
Profit before tax	X	X
Income tax expense	(X)	(X)
Profit for the period from continuing operations	X	X
Discontinued operations		
Profit for the period from discontinued operations	X	X
Profit for the period	X	X
Attributable to:		
Equity holders of the parent	X	X
Minority interest	X	X
	X	X

2.19 An alternative to this presentation would be to analyse the profit from discontinued operations in a separate column on the face of the income statement.

Question: closure

On 20 October 20X3 the directors of a parent company made a public announcement of plans to close a steel works. The closure means that the group will no longer carry out this type of operation, which until recently has represented about 10% of its total turnover. The works will be gradually shut down over a period of several months, with complete closure expected in July 20X4. At 31 December output

had been significantly reduced and some redundancies had already taken place. The cash flows, revenues and expenses relating to the steel works can be clearly distinguished from those of the subsidiary's other operations.

Required

How should the closure be treated in the financial statements for the year ended 31 December 20X3?

Answer

Because the steel works is being closed, rather than sold, it cannot be classified as 'held for sale'. In addition, the steel works is not a discontinued operation. Although at 31 December 20X3 the group was firmly committed to the closure, this has not yet taken place and therefore the steel works must be included in continuing operations. Information about the planned closure could be disclosed in the notes to the financial statements.

Presentation of a non-current asset or disposal group classified as held for sale

2.20 Non-current assets and disposal groups classified as held for sale should be **presented separately** from other assets in the balance sheet. The liabilities of a disposal group should be presented separately from other liabilities in the balance sheet.

(a) Assets and liabilities held for sale **should not be offset.**

(b) The **major classes** of assets and liabilities held for sale should be **separately disclosed** either on the face of the balance sheet or in the notes.

Additional disclosures

2.21 In the period in which a non-current asset (or disposal group) has been either classified as held for sale or sold the following should be disclosed.

(a) A description of the **facts and circumstances** of the disposal and the expected manner and timing of the disposal

(b) Any **gain or loss** recognised when the item was classified as held for sale

(c) If applicable, the **segment** in which the non-current asset (or disposal group) is presented in accordance with SSAP 25 *Segment reporting.*

2.22 Where an asset previously classified as held for sale is **no longer held for sale,** the entity should disclose a description of the facts and circumstances leading to the decision and its effect on results.

3 FRS 14 EARNINGS PER SHARE 12/01

3.1 Earnings per share (EPS) is widely used by investors as a **measure of a company's performance** and is of particular importance in:

(a) Comparing the results of a company over a period of time

(b) Comparing the performance of one company's equity shares against the performance of another company's equity, and also against the returns obtainable from loan stock and other forms of investment

The purpose of any earnings yardstick is to achieve as far as possible clarity of meaning, comparability between one company and another, one year and another, and attributablity

of profits to the equity shares. FRS 14 *Earnings per share* goes some way to ensuring that all these aims are achieved.

3.2 The standard applies to all companies who have publicly traded shares or who are in the process of issuing shares publicly. However, where companies present EPS on a voluntary basis, FRS 14 **must** be adopted.

3.3 The ASB stated that earnings per share (EPS) was not a priority, but the development of new **international standards** on the area led to efforts to adopt a similar approach.

3.4 The following key terms may be useful for the remainder of this section.

KEY TERMS

- **Equity instrument:** any contract that evidences a residual interest in the assets of an entity after deducting all of its liabilities.
- **Fair value:** the amount for which an asset could be exchanged, or a liability settled, between knowledgeable, willing parties in an arm's length transaction.
- **Financial instrument**: any contract that gives rise to both a financial asset of one entity and a financial liability or equity instrument of another entity.
- **Ordinary shares:** any equity instrument that is subordinate to all other classes of equity instruments.
- **Potential ordinary share:** a financial instrument or other contract that may entitle its holder to ordinary shares.
- **Warrants or options**: financial instruments that give the holder the right to purchase ordinary shares. *(FRS 14)*

Basic EPS

3.5 The standard has been developed with the user of the accounts in mind. EPS is a popular measure of profitability. The ASB have actively discouraged reliance on EPS, preferring a more rounded approach. The aim of the standard is to provide a consistent approach to EPS which will allow:

(a) Comparisons between entities' results
(b) Comparison of an entity's results over the years

KEY TERM

EPS is profit in pence attributable to each equity share.

The basic EPS calculation is:

$$\frac{\text{Earnings}}{\text{Issued ordinary shares}}$$

KEY TERMS

Earnings are the net profits after tax, interest, minority earnings and dividends on other classes of shares (also after extraordinary items, but in practice, these are rare).

Issued ordinary shares are all ordinary shares in circulation during the year. The weighted average approach is taken to calculate this amount.

Changes to ordinary share numbers

Share issues at market value

3.6 The following example will show how this issue is treated. Note that:

(a) The weighted average number for the period is used
(b) There is no retrospective effect

3.7 EXAMPLE: WEIGHTED AVERAGE NUMBER OF SHARES

Consider the following issues and buy-backs of shares. What is the weighted average number of shares?

	Issued shares	*Shares bought back*	*Balance*
1 January 20X9	10,000	-	10,000
31 March 20X9 Issue of new shares for cash	2,000	-	12,000
1 July 20X9 Purchase of shares for cash	-	4,000	8,000
31 December 20X9 Year end balance	12,000	4,000	8,000

3.8 SOLUTION

Weighted average

$(10{,}000 \times 3/12) + (12{,}000 \times 3/12) + (8{,}000 \times 6/12) = 9{,}500$

or

$10{,}000 + (2{,}000 \times 9/12) - (4{,}000 \times 6/12) = 9{,}500$

3.9 There are a number of events which will alter the number of ordinary shares issued by a company. These include:

- Bonus issues
- Bonus elements (ie rights issues)
- Share splits
- Share consolidation

3.10 These events must be reflected in the EPS calculations. The basic EPS should reflect issues of ordinary shares from the date consideration is receivable. An event should be included in the diluted EPS calculation even if it occurs after the balance sheet date. All events must be allowed for up to the date of approval of the accounts.

Bonus issues

3.11 A bonus issue involves an increase in the issued shares without a corresponding increase in capital. The adjustment for bonus issues should be made back to the earliest possible period. This means that

(a) The issue is included for the full year.
(b) The issue applies to the prior year.

3.12 The following example shows how a bonus issue should be treated.

3.13 EXAMPLE: BONUS ISSUE

	20X8	*20X9*
Net profit 31 December	£1,000	£1,500
Ordinary shares until 30 June 20X9	500	

Bonus issue 1 July 20X9: one share for every two ordinary shares held at 30 June 20X9

3.14 SOLUTION

Bonus issue $500 \times 1/2 = 250$

EPS for 20X9 $\frac{\text{£}1{,}500}{(500 + 250)} = 200\text{p}$

Adjusted EPS for 20X8 $\frac{\text{£}1{,}000}{(500 + 250)} = 133.3\text{p}$

Note that, as the bonus issue involved no consideration, it is treated as though it had occurred at the **earliest period reported**.

Rights issues

3.15 A rights issue usually involves shares issued for an exercise price, that is, less than the fair value of the currently issued shares. The current year's ordinary shares are multiplied by an adjustment factor:

$$\frac{\text{Fair value of current shares}}{\text{Theoretical ex-rights value per share}}$$

3.16 The following example shows how a rights issue should be calculated. Note that fair value is the average price of the ordinary shares during the period.

3.17 EXAMPLE: RIGHTS ISSUE

	20X7	*20X8*	*20X9*
	£	£	£
Net profit as at 31 December	6,000	7,600	9,000
Shares before the rights issue	100,000		

The rights issue is to be one share for every five currently held (giving 20,000 new shares). Exercise price £1.00. The last date to exercise rights is 1 April 20X8.

The fair value of an ordinary share before the issue is £2.20.

3.18 SOLUTION

Theoretical ex-rights value per share is

$$\frac{\text{Fair value of current shares} + \text{Amount received from exercise of rights}}{\text{Number of current shares} + \text{Number of shares issued}}$$

$$\frac{(£2.20 \times 100{,}000 \text{ shares}) + (£1.00 \times 20{,}000)}{100{,}000 \text{ shares} + 20{,}000 \text{ shares}}$$

Theoretical ex-rights value per share = £2

Adjustment factor

$$\frac{\text{Fair value of current shares}}{\text{Theoretical ex-rights value per share}} = \frac{£2.20}{£2.00} = 1.1$$

Earnings per share

	20X7	*20X8*	*20X9*
20X7 EPS as originally stated:			
£6,000/100,000 shares	6p		
20X7 EPS restated for rights issue:			
£6,000/(100,000 shares × 1.1)	5.5p		
20X8 EPS allowing for rights issue:			
$\frac{£7{,}600}{(100{,}000 \times 1.1 \times 3/12) + (120{,}000 \times 9/12)}$		6.5p	
20X9 EPS			
£9,000/120,000			7.5p

Note that the adjustment factor is used on the original number of shares. Once the rights issue has taken place, the new number of shares (in this case 120,000) is included. For 20X8 the weighted average principle is applied.

Contingently issuable shares

3.19 Contingently issuable shares are issued after certain conditions have been fulfilled. They are not included in the basic EPS calculation until all the criteria have been met fully.

Part paid shares

3.20 If shares are part paid, then only the element which has been paid up is included in the calculation.

Alternative EPS

3.21 It should be noted that the adjustments covered so far affect the number of shares in the EPS calculation. This figure is the **denominator.**

KEY TERM

The **denominator** is the number of shares which are deemed to be entitled to the earnings of the entity.

3.22 The standard's emphasis is strongly upon the weighted average number of ordinary shares as opposed to the earnings figure. Many companies provide alternative EPS figures. The standard is very clear on this.

(a) The basic EPS and the diluted EPS must have the same prominence as any other EPS figure disclosed.

(b) The weighted average ordinary shares may only be calculated on the basis prescribed by the standard.

(c) The reason for the alternative calculation should be disclosed.

(d) The alternative calculation must be calculated on a consistent basis, year on year.

3.23 Alternative EPS calculations will therefore only have an alternative earnings figure; the **numerator.**

KEY TERM

The **numerator** is the earnings figure used in the EPS calculation.

3.24 If this amount is different from the reported net profit of the entity then a reconciliation must be provided to show how the numerator has been derived.

3.25 The EPS calculation in simple terms is therefore:

$$\frac{\text{Numerator}}{\text{Denominator}}$$

3.26 A favoured alternative EPS is the **headline EPS.**

'Headline' EPS

3.27 The ASB effectively destroyed the analysts' favourite EPS figure with the publication of FRS 3 and the subsequent publication of FRS 14, making clear that it did not believe anyone should rely on a single earnings figure. FRS 3 did allow for an EPS, but the figure was calculated after every conceivable expense, including extraordinary items if companies are able to identify any in future. The publication of FRS 3 drew loud protests from some investment houses, which felt that the new EPS figure would prove **volatile and confusing** to users. This is the EPS taken up by FRS 14.

3.28 The Institute of Investment Management and Research (IIMR) set up a sub-committee to investigate whether a definition for some kind of maintainable earnings could be developed. The sub-committee concluded that a standard measure for maintainable earnings, which could be used as a basis for forecasts, was not feasible, as too much **conjecture and subjectivity** are involved. This view falls in line with the ASB's.

3.29 Instead, the IIMR defines a **'headline' figure for earnings** which, it acknowledges, 'is inferior to maintainable earnings as a basis for forecasts', but is nevertheless robust and factual. 'The number is justified by its practical usefulness, even if it cannot encapsulate the company's performance in itself.'

3.30 The headline earnings figure **includes** all the trading profits and losses for the year, including interest, and profits and losses arising from operations discontinued or acquired at any point during the year. **Excluded** from the figure are profits or losses from the sale or termination of a discontinued operation, from the sale of fixed assets or businesses or from any permanent diminution in their value or write-off (except for assets acquired for resale). Abnormal trading items (any defined by FRS 3 as extraordinary or exceptional), says the IIMR, should be included in the figure but prominently displayed in a note if they are significant.

3.31 When the IIMR's original ED was published, the *Financial Times* announced that it would use the method to calculate **price/earnings ratios**, and Extel also announced that it would

use the figure. The statement was specifically not directed at companies, but many are expected to take up the definition. A large number of listed companies already disclose an EPS figure in addition to the one required by FRS 3 (and 14).

3.32 As with all EPS figures which are offered as an alternative to the FRS 3 and 14 figure, a **reconciliation** of the two EPS figures must be shown. Also, the alternative method must be applied consistently from year to year. No companies are *required* to produce the IIMR figure.

Example of 'headline' EPS

3.33 An **example** of the reconciliation between EPS as calculated under FRS 3 and 14 and 'headline' EPS might be as follows.

	20X6	*20X5*
	pence	pence
EPS as required by FRS 14	63.9	58.6
Exceptional items		
Classification of restructuring costs	-	6.3
Sale of property adjustments	13.8	2.6
'Headline' EPS	77.7	67.5

Diluted EPS

Exam focus point

You should pay particular attention to this area as it may cause problems in the exam.

3.34 At the end of an accounting period a company may have securities which do not have a claim to equity earnings, but they may do **in the future**. These include:

(a) **Separate classes of equity share** not yet entitled to a share of equity earnings, but becoming so at a future date

(b) **Convertible loan stock** or **convertible preference shares** which enable their holders to exchange their securities at a later date for ordinary shares at a predetermined rate

(c) **Options** or **warrants**

3.35 These securities have the potential effect of increasing the number of equity shares ranking for dividend and so diluting or 'watering down' the EPS. These securities may be **dilutive potential ordinary shares.**

KEY TERM

A **dilutive** potential ordinary share is one which decreases the share of net profit, or increases the loss shared.

3.36 The diluted EPS gives users of the accounts a view on the potential ordinary shares of the entity. There is the potential to forecast the future EPS from the amounts given. Again, the ASB is careful to point out that a number of measures should be used in order to assess the returns from an entity, stating that no one measure is accurate enough to rely on.

Pro forma calculations

3.37 The following are the simple pro forma calculations for the three main sets of securities.

(a) **Shares not yet ranking for dividend**

(i) *Earnings*

	£
Earnings	X

(ii) *Number of shares*

	No
Basic weighted average	X
Add shares that will rank in future periods	X
Diluted number	X

(b) **Convertible loan stock or preference shares**

(i) *Earnings*

	£
Earnings	X
Add back loan stock interest net of CT (or preference dividends) 'saved'	X
	X

(ii) *Number of shares*

	No
Basic weighted average	X
Add additional shares on conversion (using terms giving maximum dilution available after the year end)	X
Diluted number	X

(c) **Options or warrants**

(i) *Earnings*

	£
Earnings	X

(ii) *Number of shares*

	No
Basic weighted average	X
Add additional shares issued at nil consideration	X
Diluted number	X

Share options

3.38 A share option allows the purchase of shares at a favourable amount which is less than the fair value of existing shares. The calculation of diluted EPS includes those shares deemed as issued for no consideration. For this purpose, the following calculation is used.

$$\frac{\text{Shares under option} \times \text{exercise price}}{\text{Fair value of ordinary shares}}$$

3.39 This gives the number of shares that are to be excluded from the EPS calculation. This will become more clear in the following example

3.40 EXAMPLE: EFFECTS OF SHARE OPTIONS ON DILUTED EARNINGS PER SHARE

Net profit for 20X9	£1,000,000
Weighted average number of ordinary shares for 20X9	10 million
Average fair value of one ordinary share	£2.50
Weighted average number of shares under option during 20X9	3 million
Exercise price for shares under option in 20X9	£2.00

3.41 SOLUTION

	Shares	*Net profit*	*EPS*
Net profit for 20X9		£1,000,000	
Weighted average shares for 20X9	10m		
Basic EPS			10p
Number of shares on option	3m		
Number of shares that would have been issued at fair value: (3m × £2)/£2.50	(2.4m)		
Diluted EPS	10.6m	£1,000,000	9.4p

Note that the net profit has not been increased. This is because the calculation only includes shares deemed to be issued for no consideration.

Employee share option schemes

3.42 Employee share option schemes are becoming increasingly popular as an incentive scheme in organisations. Many schemes relate to performance criteria which mean that they are contingent on certain conditions being met. The section on contingently issuable shares further on in this chapter explains how these schemes should be treated when calculating diluted EPS.

3.43 Certain schemes do not have performance measures. As with the share option approach, only those shares deemed as issued for no consideration are included. UITF 17 also affects the calculation as the cost of the scheme is written off to the profit and loss account over its life and these costs are effectively included in the option proceeds. The following example shows how these schemes should be treated.

3.44 EXAMPLE: SHARE OPTION SCHEME (NOT PERFORMANCE RELATED)

A company runs a share option scheme based on the employee's period of service with the company.

As at 31 December 20X7 the provisions of the scheme were:

Date of grant	1 January 20X7
Market price at grant date	£2.00
Exercise price of option	£1.25
Date of vesting	31 December 20X9
Number of shares under option	3 million

Under UITF 17, 25p per option (£2.00 – £1.25/3 years) is charged to the profit and loss in each of the three years 20X7-20X9.

Net profit for the year 20X7	£1,000,000
Weighted average number of ordinary shares	10 million

Average fair value of an ordinary share	£2.50
Assumed proceeds from each option	£1.75 (Exercise price of £1.25 plus the cost relating to future service not recognised of two years at 25p:50p). The following year would be £1.50 (ie £1.25 plus 25p).

3.45 SOLUTION

	Shares	*Net profit*	*EPS*
Net profit for 20X7		£1,000,000	
Weighted average shares for 20X7	10m		
Basic EPS			10p
Number of shares on option	3m		
Number of shares that would have been issued at fair value: (3m × £1.75)/£2.50	(2.1m)		
Diluted EPS	10.9m	£1,000,000	9.2p

Contingently issuable shares

3.46 These are shares issued after certain criteria have been met. For the purposes of the diluted EPS calculation these shares are included in full.

3.47 The following example gives two contingent events arising after the acquisition of a business. Most contingent events will be based on target sales or profit. The example includes the opening of new branches. This is also a measure of the entity's successful expansion. Note that many employee share option schemes operate in this manner.

3.48 EXAMPLE: CONTINGENTLY ISSUABLE SHARES

A company has 500,000 ordinary shares in issue at 1 January 20X7. A recent business acquisition has given rise to the following contingently issuable shares.

- 10,000 ordinary shares for every new branch opened in the three years 20X7-20X9
- 1,000 ordinary shares for every £2,000 of net profit in excess of £900,000 over the three years ended 31 December 20X9

(Shares will be issued on 1 January following the period in which a condition is met.)

A new branch was opened on 1 July 20X7, another on 31 March 20X8 and another on 1 October 20X9.

Reported net profits over the three years were £350,000, £400,000 and £600,000 respectively.

3.49 SOLUTION

Basic EPS

	20X7		*20X8*		*20X9*	
	£		£		£	
Numerator	350,000		400,000		600,000	
Denominator						
Ordinary shares	500,000		510,000		520,000	
Branch contingency	5,000	(i)	7,500	(i)	2,500	(i)
Earnings contingency	-	(ii)	-	(ii)	-	(ii)
Total shares	505,000		517,500		522,500	
Basic EPS	69.3p		77.3p		114.8p	

Diluted EPS

	20X7		20X8		20X9	
	£		£		£	
Numerator	350,000		400,000		600,000	
Denominator						
Ordinary shares in basic EPS	505,000		517,500		522,500	
Additional shares:						
Branch contingency	5,000	(iii)	2,500	(iii)	7,500	(iii)
Earnings contingency	-		-		225,000	(iv)
Total shares	510,000		520,000		755,000	
Diluted EPS	68.6p		76.9p		79.5p	

(i) This figure is simply the shares due for opening a branch pro-rated over the year.

(ii) It is not certain the net profit condition has been satisfied until after the three year period.

(iii) The contingently issuable shares are included from the start of the period they arise so these figures are increasing the denominator by the full 10,000 shares.

(iv) This is (£1,350,000 – £900,000)/£2,000 × 1,000. This figure will be included in the basic EPS figure in the following year 20X0. Note that the £900,000 criteria was not exceeded in the prior year.

3.50 The example highlights FRS 14's emphasis on the denominator as opposed to the numerator. All of the adjustments in this case were to the number of shares.

Convertible bonds

3.51 In cases where the issue of shares will affect earnings, the numerator should be adjusted accordingly. This occurs when bonds are converted. Interest is paid out on the bond. When conversion takes place this interest is no longer payable.

3.52 EXAMPLE: CONVERTIBLE BONDS

Net profit	£500
Ordinary shares in issue	1,000
Basic EPS	50p
Convertible 15% bonds	200

Each block of 5 bonds is convertible to 8 ordinary shares. The tax rate (including any deferred tax) is 40%.

3.53 SOLUTION

Interest expense relating to the bonds 200 @ 15% =	£30
Tax @ 40%	£12
Adjusted net profit £500 + £30 – £12 =	£518
Number of ordinary shares resulting from the bond conversion	320
Number of ordinary shares used for the diluted EPS calculation 1,000 + 320 =	1,320

Diluted EPS $\frac{£518}{1{,}320} = 39.2\text{p}$

3.54 Earnings should be adjusted for savings or expenses occurring as a result of conversion. Other examples of this are:

(a) Preference dividends saved when preference shares are converted

(b) Additional liability on a profit sharing scheme as a result of higher profits (ie if conversion of bonds increases profit, a higher amount will be payable to members of a profit related pay scheme)

Ranking dilutive securities

3.55 The approach prescribed by FRS 14 involves including only dilutive potential ordinary shares. Antidilutive shares are not to be included. This is a prudent approach which recognises potential reduction of earnings but not increases.

3.56 The following examples show how dilutive potential ordinary shares are identified and included in the calculation of EPS. The standard also states that the dilutive shares should be ranked and taken into account from the most dilutive down to the least dilutive. Potential ordinary shares likely to have a dilutive effect on EPS include options, convertible bonds and convertible preference shares.

3.57 EXAMPLE: RANKING DILUTIVE SECURITIES FOR THE CALCULATION OF WEIGHTED AVERAGE NUMBER OF SHARES

Net profit attributable to ordinary shareholders	£20 million
Net profit from discontinued activities	£5 million
Ordinary shares outstanding	50 million
Average fair value of one ordinary share	£5.00

Potential ordinary shares

Convertible preference shares	500,000 entitled to a cumulative dividend of £5. Each is convertible to 3 shares
3% convertible bond	Nominal amount £50 million. Each £1,000 bond is convertible to 50 shares. There is no amortisation of premium or discounting affecting the interest expense
Options	10 million with exercise price of £4
Tax rate	30%

3.58 SOLUTION

The effect on earnings on conversion of potential ordinary shares

	Increase in earnings £	*Increase in ordinary shares* Number	*Earnings per share* £
Convertible preference shares			
Increase in net profit (£5 × 500,000)	2,500,000 (i)		
Incremental shares (3 × 500,000)		1,500,000	1.67
3% convertible bonds			
Increase in net profit			
50,000,000 × 0.03 × (1 – 0.3) (ii)	1,050,000		
Incremental shares (50,000 × 50)		2,500,000	0.42
Options			
Increase in earnings:	Nil		
Incremental shares 10 million × (£5 – £4)/£5		2,000,000	Nil

Identifying the dilutive shares to include in the diluted EPS

	Net profit from continuing operations	*Ordinary shares*	*Per share*	
	£	Number	£	
Reported	15,000,000	50,000,000	0.30	
Options	-	2,000,000		
	15,000,000	52,000,000	0.29	Dilutive
3% convertible bonds	1,050,000	2,500,000		
	16,050,000	54,500,000	0.29	Antidilutive
Convertible preference shares	2,500,000	1,500,000		
	18,550,000	56,000,000	0.33	Antidilutive

Note that:

- The potential share issues are considered from the most dilutive to the least dilutive.
- The diluted EPS is increased by both the bonds and the preference shares. These are therefore ignored in the diluted EPS calculation.

Basic EPS

Net profit	£20 million
Weighted average number of shares	50 million
Basic EPS	40p

Diluted EPS

Net profit (remains at)	£20 million
Weighted average number of shares	52 million
	38.5p

(i) The cumulative dividend on the preference shares is not taken into consideration. Only the dividend for the year is included in the increase in earnings.

(ii) It is important to remember the tax element in the bond interest.

3.59 It should be noted that the **numerator,** for the purposes of ranking the dilutive shares, is net profit from continuing operations only. This is net profit after preference share dividends but excluding discontinued operations and extraordinary items. The EPS calculation includes the full amount of net profit attributable to ordinary shareholders.

3.60 The following question is based on the previous example but with dilutive convertible bonds

Question: diluted EPS

Details as above except that the convertible bonds are 1.5% bonds.

Answer

Effect on earnings on conversion of potential ordinary shares

	Increase in earnings	*Increase in ordinary shares*	*Earnings per share*
	£	Number	£
1.5% Convertible bonds			
Increase in net profit (50,000 × 0.015 × (1 – 0.3)	525,000		
Incremental shares (50,000 × 50)		2,500,000	0.21

Identifying the dilutive shares to include in the diluted EPS

	Net profit from continuing operations	*Ordinary shares*	*Per share*	
	£	Number	£	
Reported	15,000,000	50,000,000	0.30	
Options	-	2,000,000		
	15,000,000	52,000,000	0.29	Dilutive
1.5% convertible bonds	525,000	2,500,000		
	15,525,000	54,500,000	0.28	Dilutive

The convertible preference shares will remain antidilutive and basic EPS will remain at 40p.

Diluted EPS

Net profit (20,000,000 + 525,000 bond interest)	£20,525,000
Weighted average number of shares	54.5 million
Diluted EPS	37.7p

3.61 The example in the above question emphasises the adjustments made to earnings and the use of net profit from continuing operations as the numerator.

Disclosure

3.62 Note the following.

(a) FRS 14 requires that **basic EPS** and **diluted EPS** are disclosed on the face of the profit and loss account, even if the amounts are negative. Comparative figures are also required.

(b) A basic and diluted EPS figure is required for every set of ordinary shares with different rights.

(c) The standard requires inclusion of all potential ordinary shares which will have a dilutive effect on the diluted EPS, regardless of materiality.

(d) The nil basis EPS is no longer required as this information can be derived from other disclosures in the financial statements.

(e) EPS need only be presented in the consolidated results of a group where the parent's results are shown as well.

4 FRED 26 EARNINGS PER SHARE

4.1 As part of its programme of convergence (see Chapter 13) between FRS and IFRS, the ASB published FRED 26 *Earnings per share* in May 2002.

Main points

4.2 FRED 26 proposes a replacement for FRS 14, based on a revised IAS 33 *Earnings per share*. The **changes** proposed to FRS 14 by FRED 26 are **limited and largely restricted to disclosure.**

(a) **Basic and diluted earnings per share** (EPS) must be disclosed on the **face of the profit and loss account both for net profit or loss for the period and for profit or loss from continuing operations.**

(b) **Basic and diluted EPS for discontinued operations** (if reported) may be shown **either on the face of the statement or in a note.**

(c) **Additional per share amounts** can only be disclosed by way of note.

4.3 FRED 26 covers the same ground as the revised IAS 33. Additionally, however, there is a section dealing with shares held by an ESOP trust and reflected as assets in the balance sheet.

More detail

4.4 The **content and the text of FRED 26 is similar to FRS 14**. The main differences between the proposals in the exposure draft and the existing requirements of FRS 14 are set out below.

Presentation and disclosure of earnings per share

4.5 FRED 26 proposes that basic and diluted earnings per share should be disclosed **on the face of the profit and loss account both for net profit or loss for the period and also for profit or loss from continuing operations.**

4.6 Basic and diluted earnings per share for **discontinued operations** (if reported) should be reported **either on the face of the profit and loss account or in a note to the accounts.**

4.7 Entities will be permitted to present **additional per share amounts** but **only in the notes to the accounts,** not on the face of the profit and loss account.

4.8 This is a departure from FRS 14 which requires disclosure as follows.

(a) Basic and diluted earnings per share for net profit or loss are disclosed on the face of the profit and loss account.

(b) Companies are encouraged to provide additional per share amounts which they can disclose where they wish providing they are no more prominent than the per share amounts required by the standard.

4.9 EXAMPLE: DISCLOSURE OF EARNINGS PER SHARE

The following example, taken from FRED 26, illustrates how a company might present its earnings per share data on its income statement. Note that the amounts per share for the loss from discontinued operations is not required to be shown on the face of the income statement.

EARNINGS PER ORDINARY SHARE
FOR THE YEAR ENDED 31 DECEMBER 20X1

Profit from continuing operations	193p
Loss from discontinued operations	(33p)
Net profit	160p

DILUTED EARNINGS PER ORDINARY SHARE
FOR THE YEAR ENDED 31 DECEMBER 20X1

Profit from continuing operations	178p
Loss from discontinued operations	(30p)
Net profit	148p

4.10 Where **additional** earnings per share amounts are presented, **FRS 14 requires a reconciliation** to the amounts required by the standard, listing the items for which an adjustment is being made and their individual effect on the calculation. The **reason** for the additional per share amount must also be given. Under **FRED 26** there will be **less disclosure** where additional per share amounts are presented. If the component of the income statement used for the additional earnings per share amount is not reported as a line item in the income statement, a reconciliation should be provided between the component and a line item.

Basic earnings per share

4.11 FRED 26 contains **more detailed guidance** than FRS 14 on the adjustments that need to be made when calculating basic earnings per share. An example of this is the proposed requirements in respect of a **repurchase of preference shares.**

(a) Any **loss on settlement** is **deducted** in calculating **income** for the period **attributable to ordinary shareholders**.

(b) Sometimes preference shares may be **converted early** because of favourable changes in the conversion terms. In such cases, FRED 26 proposes that the **excess of fair value** of the ordinary shares issued over the fair value of the ordinary shares issuable under the original conversion terms should also be **deducted** in calculating **income** for the period **attributable to ordinary shareholders.**

4.12 FRS 14 deals with company **shares that are held by a group company** and are not cancelled, stating that these are to be **treated as if they were cancelled** and excluded from the calculation of earnings per share.

4.13 Similarly, shares that are held in an **Employee Share Option Plan ('ESOP') trust** and reflected as assets in the company's balance sheet are **treated as if they were cancelled** until they vest unconditionally in employees. Such arrangements are common in the UK.

4.14 Because the international exposure draft on EPS is not explicit on this point, the ASB proposes to include **additional text** requiring own shares acquired and shares that are held in ESOP trusts to be treated as if they were cancelled when calculating earnings per share.

Diluted earnings per share

4.15 When establishing whether potential ordinary shares are dilutive or anti-dilutive, both FRS 14 and FRED 26 use profit or loss from continuing operations as the control number. **FRS 14** gives **additional guidance** on how to **allocate interest and tax** in order to achieve a reasonable estimate of profit or loss from continuing operations. This is because FRS 3 requires an analysis of continuing operations, acquisitions and discontinued operations only to the level of profit before interest.

4.16 **FRED 26 does not provide any guidance** on how to estimate this number, which is also required for basic earnings per share disclosure purposes.

4.17 Another change from FRS 14 concerns the **number of potential ordinary shares** to be included and the **market price** to be applied in the calculation of diluted earnings per share. Under FRED 26, this should be an **average of those used in each interim period** rather than for the year to date period.

4.18 A further difference concerns contracts that may be settled in ordinary shares or cash.

4.19 Under **FRS 14** the treatment depends on the facts available each period. Unless past experience or a stated policy provide a basis for concluding how the contract will be satisfied, it is **presumed that the contract will be settled by the more dilutive method.**

4.20 FRED 26 distinguishes between those contracts where settlement is to be determined by the entity and those by the holder.

(a) For those contracts that may be **settled at the holder's option**, the **more dilutive** of cash or share settlement should be used.

(b) For those contracts that may be settled in cash or shares at the **entity's option,** it should be **presumed** for the purpose of calculating diluted earnings per share that the **contract will be settled in shares.** This will be the case unless past experience or a stated policy provides a reasonable basis for believing that the contract will be paid in cash.

4.21 FRED 26 contains specific guidance on **written put options**. These are contracts that require the entity to repurchase its own shares. They are **included in the calculation of diluted earnings per share if the effect is dilutive,** ie the contracts are 'in the money' during the period. FRS 14 is less specific on this point.

Disclosure

4.22 There are two further differences relating to disclosure.

(a) **FRS 14** includes additional guidance in respect of the presentation of **financial statistics in historical summaries.** There is no equivalent guidance in FRED 26.

(b) **FRED 26** requires **disclosure of securities** that could potentially dilute basic earnings per share in the future but which were **not included in the calculation because they were anti-dilutive** for the periods presented.

Chapter roundup

- It is important that you appreciate how great an impact **FRS 3** has on reporting financial performance. You may be called on to discuss the changes and comment on them.
- Try to remember the **important terms**.
  - Reserve accounting
  - All inclusive concept
  - Extraordinary items
  - Exceptional items
  - Prior year adjustments
  - Discontinued operations
  - Total recognised gains and losses
- Jot down the format for the **statement of total recognised gains and losses** and the **reconciliation of movements in shareholders' funds**. This will help you, but you need to understand their purpose and the implications of their contents.
- **FRED 32** requires assets **'held for sale'** to be **presented separately** on the face of the balance sheet.
- The results of **discontinued operations** should be **presented separately** in the income statement.
- FRS 14 has superseded SSAP 3. This has brought the UK's treatment of the EPS calculation in line with international standards.
- Disclosure of the basic EPS and diluted EPS on the face of the profit and loss is required, along with comparatives for both figures. This is the case even if the figures are negative.
- Other EPS figures can be disclosed in the accounts.
  - These must use the same basis for calculating the denominator.
  - The reason for the method used must be disclosed.
  - They must be consistent year on year.
  - The required EPS figures should have the same prominence within the accounts.
- The denominator is calculated by finding the weighted average number of ordinary shares in issue in the year.
- Any effect that conversion to ordinary shares has on the earnings figure must be reflected in the calculation of the diluted EPS.
- Only dilutive shares are included in the diluted EPS. Anti-dilutive shares are ignored.
- **FRED 26** proposes limited changes to FRS 14, mainly in the area of disclosures.

Quick quiz

1 Reserve Ltd profit and loss account for the year ended 31 December 20X9 was as follows.

	£'000
Turnover	420
Costs and expenses	(180)
Operating profit	240
Interest	(20)
Profit before tax	220
Taxation	(70)
Profit after tax	150
Dividends	(60)
Retained profit	90

What amount would be included in the statement of total recognised gains and losses for the year ended 31 December 20X9?

2 Which of the following items has no impact on the STRGL?

A Rights issue of ordinary shares
B Impairment in the value of a tangible fixed asset previously revalued
C Prior year adjustment
D Upward revaluation of a fixed asset investment

3 When can a non-current asset be classified as held for sale?

4 How should an asset held for sale be measured?

5 How does FRED 32 define a discontinued operation?

6 How is basic EPS calculated?

7 Give the formula for the 'bonus element' of a rights issue.

8 Define 'dilutive potential ordinary share'.

9 Which numerator is used to rank dilutive shares?

10 Why is the numerator adjusted for convertible bonds when calculating diluted EPS?

11 Under FRED 26, basic and diluted EPS for discontinued operations must be disclosed in the face of the profit and loss account. True of false?

Answers to quick quiz

1 £150,000. Ignore all transactions with shareholders, ie dividends.

2 A Statement of total recognised gains and losses (STRGL) does not include transactions with shareholders.

Part of the impairment in the value of a tangible fixed asset previously revalued will reduce the total recognised gains and losses. The amount of the impairment taken to the STRGL is the difference between the carrying value of the asset and the depreciated historic cost.

The other items will be stated as such on the STRGL.

3 See Paragraph 2.4

4 At the lower of its carrying amount and fair value less costs to sell

5 See Paragraph 2.13, key terms

6 See KBF box.

7 $\dfrac{\text{Actual cum-rights price}}{\text{Theoretical ex-rights price}}$

8 See Para 3.35

9 Net profit from continuing operations only.

10 Because the issue of shares will affect earnings.

11 False. It may be disclosed in a note.

Now try the question below from the Exam Question Bank

Number	Level	Marks	Time
Q32	Introductory	n/a	n/a

Chapter 24

REPORTING FINANCIAL PERFORMANCE 2

	Topic list	Syllabus reference
1	Segmental reporting	1(a), 4(e)
2	Related party disclosures	1(a), 4(e)
3	Share based payment	1(a), 4(e)
4	FRS 18 Accounting policies	4(b)

Introduction

Section 1 covers segmental reporting, which you have looked at in your earlier studies. The ASB has issued a **discussion paper on segmental reporting** in response to an IASB proposal. Section 2 deals with related party disclosures, and Section 3 deals with FRS 20, a new standard on share based payment, a controversial area.

Study guide

Section 17 – Segmental reporting

- Discussion of the problem areas in segmental reporting including definition of segments, common costs, inter-segment sales etc
- Discussion of the different approaches
- Discussion of the importance of segmental information to users of financial statements

Section 22 – Related parties and share based payment

- Discussion of the related party issue
- Identifying related parties (including deemed and presumed) and the disclosure of related party transactions
- Discussion of the effectiveness of current regulations on disclosure of related party transactions
- Describing the current proposals for the recognition and measurement of share based payment
- Showing the impact of the proposals on the performance statements of the entity

1 SEGMENTAL REPORTING

1.1 CA 1985 and the Stock Exchange both require the disclosure of segmental information. The **purpose** of SSAP 25 *Segmental reporting* is twofold.

(a) It provides guidance to all companies on how best to comply with **Companies Act requirements** on segmental information.

(b) It requires plcs and large private companies to disclose **more segmental information** than CA 1985 requires.

A summary is given below as you have studied SSAP 25 for Paper 10.

Reasons for segmental information

1.2 Segmental information is considered **useful** for the following reasons.

(a) Segmental information can **explain factors** which have contributed to company results.

(b) Users can compare the results of **different products** from year to year.

(c) Users can compare performance with companies **within the same market**.

(d) Users can assess the **future risks and rewards** associated with the business.

Arguments against reporting by segment

1.3 Those who argue against this form of disclosure generally emphasise the practical problems, which include:

(a) **identifying segments** for reporting purposes;

(b) **allocating common income and costs** among the different segments;

(c) reporting **inter-segment transactions**;

(d) providing information in such a way as to **eliminate misunderstanding** by investors;

(e) avoiding any **potential damage** that may be done to the reporting entity by disclosing information about individual segments.

Knowledge brought forward from earlier studies

SSAP 25 and CA 1985 on segmental reporting

Reportable segment: definition

- **SSAP 25**
  - A **class of business** is a distinguishable component of an enterprise that provides a separate product or a separate group of related products or services.
  - A **geographical segment** is an area comprising an individual country or group of countries in which a company operates or to which it supplies products or services.
- **CA 1985 (directors' opinion)**
  - A **class of business** is a component of an enterprise that differs substantially from other elements of the business.
  - A **geographical segment** is a market supplied by a business which differs substantially from other geographical markets supplied.
- ≥ 10% of third party turnover/net assets/profit should be used to **identify a segment**.

Scope

- SSAP 25 **applies only** to plcs, banks/insurance companies, and companies exceeding medium-sized company criteria × 10.
- Companies can dispense with the disclosure of segmental information if, in the opinion of the directors, it would be **seriously prejudicial** to the interests of the company: a statement to that effect is required.

Knowledge brought forward from earlier studies (cont.)

Disclosure

An example of disclosure is shown on the next two pages. Note the individual disclosures for the following.

- **Turnover**
  - Geographical
  - Class of business
- **Results for the year** (SSAP 25 only)
  - PBIT
  - Interest is stated separately
  - Common costs relate to more than one segment and should be apportioned or deducted from the total
- **Capital employed**
  - Treat interest-bearing assets/liabilities as interest was treated
  - Common assets/liabilities should be treated as common costs were treated
- **Associated companies** are shown separately with extra disclosure for associates' results where they are ≥ 20% of the entity's net assets/results.
- The **average number of employees** by category of employee should be disclosed (CA 1985).

CLASSES OF BUSINESS

	Industry A		Industry B		Other Industries		Group	
	20X2	20X1	20X2	20X1	20X2	20X1	20X2	20X1
	£'000	£'000	£'000	£'000	£'000	£'000	£'000	£'000
Turnover								
Total sales	33,000	30,000	42,000	38,000	26,000	23,000	101,000	91,000
Inter-segment sales	(4,000)	-	-	-	(12,000)	(14,000)	(16,000)	(14,000)
Sales to third parties	29,000	30,000	42,000	38,000	14,000	9,000	85,000	77,000
Profit before taxation								
Segment profit	3,000	2,500	4,500	4,000	1,800	1,500	9,300	8,000
Common costs							(300)	(300)
Operating profit							9,000	7,700
Net interest							(400)	(500)
							8,600	7,200
Group share of the profit before taxation of associated undertakings	1,000	1,000	1,400	1,200	-	-	2,400	2,200
Group profit before taxation							11,000	9,400
Net assets								
Segment net assets	17,600	15,000	24,000	25,000	19,400	19,000	61,000	59,000
Unallocated assets*							3,000	3,000
							64,000	62,000
Group share of the net assets of associated undertakings	10,200	8,000	8,800	9,000	-	-	19,000	17,000
Total net assets							83,000	79,000

* Unallocated assets consist of assets at the group's head office in London amounting to £2.4 million (19X1: £2.5 million) and at the group's regional office in Hong Kong amounting to £0.6 million (19X1: £0.5 million).

GEOGRAPHICAL SEGMENTS

	United Kingdom		North America		Far East		Other		Group	
	20X2	20X1	20X2	20X1	20X2	20X1	20X2	20X1	20X2	20X1
	£'000	£'000	£'000	£'000	£'000	£'000	£'000	£'000	£'000	£'000
Turnover										
Turnover by destination										
Sales to third parties	34,000	31,000	16,000	14,500	25,000	23,000	10,000	8,500	85,000	77,000
Turnover by origin										
Total sales	38,000	34,000	29,000	27,500	23,000	23,000	12,000	10,500	102,000	95,000
Inter-segment sales	-	-	(8,000)	(9,000)	(9,000)	(9,000)	-	-	(17,000)	(18,000)
Sales to third parties	38,000	34,000	21,000	18,500	14,000	14,000	12,000	10,500	85,000	77,000
Profit before taxation										
Segment profit	4,000	2,900	2,500	2,300	1,800	1,900	1,000	900	9,300	8,000
Common costs									(300)	(300)
Operating profit									9,000	7,700
Net interest									(400)	(500)
									8,600	7,200
Group share of the profit before taxation of associated undertakings	950	1,000	1,450	1,200	-	-	-	-	2,400	2,200
Group profit before taxation									11,000	9,400
Net assets										
Segment net assets	16,000	15,000	25,000	26,000	16,000	15,000	4,000	3,000	61,000	59,000
Unallocated assets*									3,000	3,000
									64,000	62,000
Group share of the net assets of associated undertakings	8,500	7,000	10,500	10,000	-	-	-	-	19,000	17,000
Total net assets									83,000	79,000

* Unallocated assets consist of assets at the group's head office in London amounting to £2.4 million (19X1: £2.5 million) and at the group's regional office in Hong Kong amounting to £0.6 million (19X1: £0.5 million).

ASB *Segmental reporting* (discussion paper)

1.4 In May 1996, the ASB issued a discussion paper on segmental reporting. The paper seeks comments on two **international proposals**:

(a) E 51 *Reporting financial information by segment* (IASC); and
(b) *Reporting disagregated information about a business* (US FASB).

1.5 The **key issues** in this area are:

(a) the division of operations into segments;
(b) the information to be given for each segment; and
(c) whether the information given is verifiable and easy to understand.

1.6 The **IASC proposals** develop the risks and returns approach used in the current UK SSAP 25. The IASC envisages that segments should be identified by the different **risks and returns** an entity faces, either through providing different products or services or through providing products or services in different geographical locations.

1.7 The IASC proposes that **more information** should be given for each primary segment (the dominant source of risk for the entity) than is currently required for a segment under SSAP 25. The information should be prepared on the same basis as that given in the external financial statements.

1.8 The **FASB proposals** reflect a **managerial approach** under which segments reflect the way management disaggregates the entity for making operating decisions. Amounts reported by segment would be based on the information used internally by the chief executive or equivalent management committee to manage the business.

1.9 Although the IASC and the FASB approaches differ, the effect in practice, at least in the identification of segments, may be similar in that the IASC notes that the **dominant source of risk** affects how most enterprises are organised and managed. An enterprise's organisational structure and its internal financial reporting system should thus normally be the basis for identifying its segments under the IASC proposals.

2 RELATED PARTY DISCLOSURES — Pilot paper

2.1 The basics of this should be familiar to you from your earlier studies.

Knowledge brought forward from earlier studies

FRS 8

FRS 8 covers related party disclosures.

Definition: related parties

Two or more parties are related parties when at any time during the financial period:

- One party has direct or indirect control of the other party, *or*
- The parties are subject to common control from the same source, *or*
- One party has influence over the financial and operating policies of the other party to an extent that the other party might be inhibited from pursuing at all times its own separate interests, *or*

Knowledge brought forward from earlier studies (cont.)

- The parties, in entering a transaction, are subject to influence from the same source to such an extent that one of the parties to the transaction has subordinated its own separate interests

The FRS states that the most important factor in deciding whether two parties are related is the *substance* of their relationship.

'Deemed' and 'presumed' related parties

Examples of related parties are divided into two categories (lists not exhaustive).

- Those where the nature of the relationship is *deemed* to result in the parties being related
  - Ultimate/intermediate parent(s), (fellow) subsidiaries
  - Associates, JVs of itself or any of above
  - Investor/venturer to entity's associate/JV
  - Directors of entity/parent(s), plus immediate family
  - Pension fund of entity or its related parties
- Those where the nature of the relationship is *presumed* to result in the parties being related unless there is evidence to the contrary
  - Key management of entity/parent plus their direct families
  - Owns/controls > 20% voting rights in entity (nominees, direct family, holdings etc)
  - Concert parties exercising control/influence
  - Entity managed by the reporting entity under a management contract
  - Partnerships, companies, trusts, other entities of which directors/people listed above have a controlling interest

Further definitions

- *Control*: the ability to direct the financial and operating policies of an entity with a view to gaining economic benefits from its activities
- *Related party transactions*: the transfer of assets or liabilities or the performance of services by, to or for a related party irrespective of whether a price is charged

Disclosure of transactions and balances

Financial statements should disclose material transactions undertaken with a related party by the entity, irrespective of whether a price is charged, as follows.

- Names of the related parties
- Description of the relationship between the parties
- Description of the transactions
- Amounts involved
- Any other explanations required
- Amounts due to/from related parties at the B/S date
- Amounts w/off related party debts

Disclosure can be on aggregate basis for similar transactions.

Disclosure of control

When the reporting entity is controlled by another party, there should be disclosure of the name of that party and, if different, that of the ultimate controlling party (if not known, that fact should be disclosed). Disclose irrespective of whether any transactions have taken place between the controlling parties and the reporting entity.

Exemptions from disclosure

FRS 8 does *not* require disclosure of the following.

- In consolidated financial statements, of any transactions or balances between group entities that have been eliminated on consolidation

Knowledge brought forward from earlier studies (cont.)

- In a parent's own financial statements when those statements are presented together with its consolidated financial statements
- In the financial statements of > 90% voting subsidiary undertakings, of transactions with entities that are part of the group or investees of the group qualifying as related parties, *if* consolidated a/cs are available (state exemption taken)
- Of pension contributions paid to a pension fund
- Of emoluments in respect of services as an employee of the reporting entity

CA 1985 and the SE require disclosures covering transactions with directors, substantial shareholders and associates.

Exam focus point

The Pilot Paper contained a question on related parties, which was fairly straightforward.

Question: FRS 8

Fancy Feet Ltd is a UK company which supplies handmade leather shoes to a chain of high street shoe shops. The company is also the sole importer of some famous high quality Greek stoneware which is supplied to an upmarket shop in London's West End.

Fancy Feet Ltd was set up 30 years ago by Georgios Kostades who left Greece when he fell out with the military government. The company is owned and run by Mr Kostades and his three children.

The shoes are purchased from a French company, the shares of which are owned by the Kostades Family Trust (Monaco).

Required

Identify the financial accounting issues arising out of the above scenario.

Answer

(a) The basis on which Fancy Feet trades with the Greek supplier and the French company owned by the Kostades family trust.

(b) Whether the overseas companies trade on commercial terms with the UK company or do the foreign enterprises control the UK company.

(c) Who owns the Greek company: is this a related party under the provisions of FRS 8?

(d) Should the nature of trade suggest a related party controls Fancy Feet Ltd? Detailed disclosures will be required in the accounts.

FRED 25 Related party disclosures

2.2 As part of the ASB's programme of convergence between FRS and IFRS (see Chapter 13), in May 2002, it published FRED 25 *Related party disclosures.*

2.3 IAS 24 *Related party disclosures* covers similar ground to FRS 8. This standard has now been revised, and FRED 25 essentially adopts the revised IAS. The main difference between FRED 25 and IAS 24 is that **FRED 25** retains the requirement that an **entity's controlling party should be named**, while IAS 24 does not.

Changes from current UK requirements

2.4 Implementation of FRED 25 would mean:

(a) Changes in the **definitions** of related parties

(b) Changes in the **detail of the disclosure requirements**. For example, the FRED does not propose that the names of the transacting related parties should be disclosed

(c) Changes in the **exemptions from disclosure**. For example, the proposed exemption for subsidiaries' disclosure extends only to wholly-owned subsidiaries, while FRS 8 exempts 90% subsidiaries. However, the proposed exemption will cover all related party transactions and balances

Exam focus point

The above summary is sufficient for December 2002 candidates.

More detail

2.5 However, much of FRED 25 is the same as FRS 8, differences being of terminology and wording. We will therefore focus on the **changes to existing UK requirements** which the proposals would introduce.

Exemptions from disclosure requirements

2.6 The table below compares the exemptions from disclosure requirements.

FRS 8	**FRED 25**
Consolidated financial statements: transactions or balances between group entities that have been eliminated on consolidation.	*Equivalent exemption* included.
Parent's own financial statements: where they are presented together with its consolidated financial statements.	*Equivalent exemption* included.
Subsidiary undertakings, 90% or more of whose voting rights are controlled within the group, are exempted from disclosing transactions with group entities or investees of the group qualifying as related parties, provided that the consolidated financial statements in which the subsidiary is included are publicly available.	Financial statements of *wholly owned subsidiaries* that are made available or published with consolidated financial statements for the group to which the subsidiary belongs are not required to disclose related party transactions and outstanding balances.
Pension contributions paid into a pension fund. (However, disclosure is required by FRS 17.)	*No equivalent exemption* is included.
Emoluments in respect of services as an *employee of the reporting entity.*	*Management compensation, expense allowances and similar items* paid in the ordinary course of an entity's operations.

FRS 8	FRED 25
Disclosures *do not override* an entity's *duties of confidentiality* arising by *operation of law* (for example, banker/client confidentiality).	*No equivalent exemption* is included. However the FRED does *not* require disclosure of the names of the transacting related parties.

Definition of related parties

2.7 When defining related parties, **FRS 8** identifies various parties that **are related parties** and other parties that **are presumed to be related parties**. In other words, the presumption may be rebutted. The parties identified in **FRED 25** are all considered related parties, and there is **no rebuttable presumption**.

2.8 The parties identified are broadly equivalent. However, FRED 25 makes no reference to shadow directors or to persons acting in concert to exercise control or influence.

2.9 As regards the concept of **influence** that triggers related party status, **FRED 25 is less comprehensive** than FRS 8. FRS 8 talks about the level of influence being such that the party influenced might be **inhibited** from pursuing at all times its **own separate interests**. FRS 8 also accords related party status to transacting parties that are subject to **common influence from the same source** to such an extent that one of the parties has **subordinated its own separate interests**. The FRED does not go into this kind of detail in its definitions, as you can see in the table below.

FRS 8	FRED 25
Relationships	*The relationships and the parties listed below are all related parties*
Parties are in a *direct or indirect control* relationship.	*Equivalent.*
One party has *influence* over the financial and operating policies of the other party to the extent that the other party might be *inhibited from pursuing at all times its own separate interests.*	A party has an interest that gives it *significant influence.*
Parties entering a transaction are subject to *influence from the same source* to such an extent that *one of the parties has subordinated its own separate interests.*	*Does not deal* with such circumstances
Parties that are deemed to be related parties	*Parties that are related parties*
Associates and *joint ventures*	*Equivalent.*
Investor or *venturer* in respect of which the *entity* is an *associate or a joint venture.*	*Equivalent.*
Directors (including shadow directors) of the entity and directors of its ultimate and intermediate parent undertakings.	*Key management personnel* of the entity or its parent including any director (executive or non-executive) or officer. (No mention of shadow directors.)
Pension funds for the benefit of the entity's employees or of any entity that is a related party of the entity.	*Equivalent.*

FRS 8	**FRED 25**
Parties that are presumed to be related parties (presumption may be rebutted)	*Parties that are related parties (no rebuttable presumption*
Key management of the entity and its parent undertakings.	*Key management personnel (as above).*
A person owning or able to exercise control over *20% or more of the entity's voting rights*, whether directly or through nominees.	*No specific equivalent.* However, *any party* that has an interest that gives it *significant influence* is considered to be a related party.
Persons *acting in concert* to exercise control or influence.	*No equivalent.*
An entity managing or managed by the entity under a *management contract.*	*No equivalent.*
Close members of the family of individuals that are referred to as related parties are *presumed* related parties.	*Close members of the family* of individuals that are referred to as related parties *are* related parties.
Partnerships, companies, trusts or other entities in which any individual (or close family member) referred to as related parties has a *controlling interest.*	An *entity* in which any individual referred to as a related party *owns a controlling or jointly controlling interest in, or significant influence over the voting power* is a related party.

Disclosure of control

2.10 Where an entity is under the control of another party, **FRS 8 requires more detailed disclosure** than the international exposure draft. In developing FRS 8, the ASB took the view that disclosure of the **identity, as well as the existence, of a controlling party is relevant information for users.** Accordingly, it required the following disclosures.

- The related party relationship
- The name of that party and, if different, that of the ultimate controlling party
- If the controlling party or ultimate controlling party is not known, disclosure of that fact

2.11 In contrast, the international exposure draft merely requires disclosure of the relationships between parents and subsidiaries; it does not require a controlling party to be named.

2.12 This is an area in which FRED 25 departs from the international equivalent. It proposes that the **revised UK standard should include the requirement to disclose the names of controlling parties.**

Disclosure of transactions

2.13 FRS 8 requires disclosures in respect of **material transactions** with related parties. Furthermore it gives **guidance** on materiality.

(a) Transactions are material when their disclosure might **reasonably be expected to influence decisions** made by the users of general purpose financial statements.

(b) FRS 8's guidance considers the situation when a **transaction has been undertaken** directly or indirectly **with an individual in a position to influence** an entity, for example a director or substantial shareholder.

2.14 FRED 25 **does not specifically address materiality** in the context of the disclosure requirements.

2.15 FRED 25 and FRS 8 have **broadly similar disclosure requirements.** The **main exceptions** is that **FRS 8** requires disclosure of the **names** of transacting related parties. FRED 25 **does not require names** to be disclosed, but it **does** require **disclosures with categories** of related parties.

FRS 8	**FRED 25**
Names of transacting related parties.	*Not required.*
Description of the *relationship.*	*Nature* of the relationship.
Description of the *transactions*	*Information* about the transactions.
Amounts	*Amounts*
Any other elements necessary for an understanding of the financial statements.	*Information about the transactions and outstanding balances* necessary for an understanding of the potential effect of the relationship on the financial statements.
Amounts due to or from related parties.	*Amounts due to or from* related parties. In addition, disclosure of the *terms and conditions, the nature of the consideration* and details of any *guarantees* given or received.
Provision for doubtful debts	*Provision for doubtful debts.*
Amounts written off in respect of debts due to or from related parties.	*Expense recognised* in respect of bad or doubtful debts due from related parties.
	The above *disclosures* should be *made separately* for each of the following *categories:* The parent, entities with joint control or significant influence over the entity, subsidiaries, associates, joint ventures in which the entity is a venturer, key management personnel of the entity or its parent and other related parties.

3 SHARE BASED PAYMENT

Background

3.1 Transactions whereby entities purchase goods or services from other parties, such as suppliers and employees, by **issuing shares or share options** to those other parties are **increasingly common.** Share schemes are a common feature of director and executive remuneration and in some countries the authorities may offer tax incentives to encourage more companies to offer shares to employees. Companies whose shares or share options are regarded as a valuable 'currency' commonly use share-based payment to obtain employee and professional services.

3.2 The increasing use of share-based payment has raised questions about the accounting treatment of such transactions in company financial statements.

3.3 Share options are often granted to employees at an exercise price that is equal to or higher than the market price of the shares at the date the option is granted. Consequently the options have no intrinsic value and so **no transaction is recorded in the financial statements**.

3.4 This leads to an **anomaly:** if a company pays its employees in cash, an expense is recognised in the income statement, but if the payment is in share options, no expense is recognised.

Arguments against recognition of share-based payment in the financial statements

3.5 There are a number of arguments against recognition. The ASB and the IASB has considered and rejected the arguments below.

(a) **No cost therefore no charge**

There is no cost to the entity because the granting of shares or options does not require the entity to sacrifice cash or other assets. Therefore a charge should not be recognised.

This argument is unsound because it ignores the fact that a transaction has occurred. The employees have provided valuable services to the entity in return for valuable shares or options.

(b) **Earnings per share is hit twice**

It is argued that the charge to the income statement for the employee services consumed reduces the entity's earnings, while at the same time there is an increase in the number of shares issued.

However, the dual impact on earnings per share simply reflects the two economic events that have occurred.

(i) The entity has issued shares or options, thus increasing the denominator of the earnings per share calculation.

(ii) It has also consumed the resources it received for those shares or options, thus reducing the numerator.

(c) **Adverse economic consequences**

It could be argued that entities might be discouraged from introducing or continuing employee share plans if they were required to recognise them on the financial statements. However, if this happened, it might be because the requirement for entities to account properly for employee share plans had revealed the economic consequences of such plans.

A situation where entities are able to obtain and consume resources by issuing valuable shares or options without having to account for such transactions could be perceived as a **distortion**.

FRS 20 *Share-based payment*

3.6 In April 2004, the ASB, issued FRS 20 *Share based payment*. This implements IFRS 2 of the same name.

Objective and scope

3.7 FRS 20 requires an entity to **reflect the effects of share-based payment transactions** in its profit or loss and financial position.

3.8 FRS 20 applies to all share-based payment transactions. There are three types.

(a) **Equity-settled share-based payment transactions**, in which the entity receives goods or services in exchange for equity instruments of the entity (including shares or share options)

(b) **Cash-settled share-based payment transactions**, in which the entity receives goods or services in exchange for amounts of cash that are based on the price (or value) of the entity's shares or other equity instruments of the entity

(c) Transactions in which the entity receives or acquires goods or services and either the entity or the supplier has a **choice** as to whether the entity settles the transaction in cash (or other assets) or by issuing equity instruments

3.9 Certain transactions are **outside the scope** of the FRS:

(a) Transactions with employees and others in their capacity as a holder of equity instruments of the entity (for example, where an employee receives additional shares in a rights issue to all shareholders)

(b) The issue of equity instruments in exchange for control of another entity in a business combination

KEY TERMS

Share-based payment transaction A transaction in which the entity receives goods or services as consideration for equity instruments of the entity (including shares or share options), or acquires goods or services by incurring liabilities to the supplier of those goods or services for amounts that are based on the price of the entity's shares or other equity instruments of the entity.

Share-based payment arrangement An agreement between the entity and another party (including an employee) to enter into a share-based payment transaction, which thereby entitles the other party to receive cash or other assets of the entity for amounts that are based on the price of the entity's shares or other equity instruments of the entity, or to receive equity instruments of the entity, provided the specified vesting conditions, if any, are met.

Equity instrument A contract that evidences a residual interest in the assets of an entity after deducting all of its liabilities.

Equity instrument granted The right (conditional or unconditional) to an equity instrument of the entity conferred by the entity on another party, under a share-based payment arrangement.

Share option A contract that gives the holder the right, but not the obligation, to subscribe to the entity's shares at a fixed or determinable price for a specified period of time.

Fair value The amount for which an asset could be exchanged, a liability settled, or an equity instrument granted could be exchanged, between knowledgeable, willing parties in an arm's length transaction.

Grant date The date at which the entity and another party (including an employee) agree to a share-based payment arrangement, being when the entity and the other party have a shared understanding of the terms and conditions of the arrangement. At grant date the entity confers on the other party (the counterparty) the right to cash, other assets, or equity instruments of the entity, provided the specified vesting conditions, if any, are met. If that agreement is subject to an approval process (for example, by shareholders), grant date is the date when that approval is obtained.

Intrinsic value The difference between the fair value of the shares to which the counterparty has the (conditional or unconditional) right to subscribe or which it has the right to receive, and the price (if any) the other party is (or will be) required to pay for those shares. For example, a share option with an exercise price of £15 on a share with a fair value of £20, has an intrinsic value of £5.

Measurement date The date at which the fair value of the equity instruments granted is measured. For transactions with employees and others providing similar services, the measurement date is grant date. For transactions with parties other than employees (and those providing similar services), the measurement date is the date the entity obtains the goods or the counterparty renders service.

Vest To become an entitlement. Under a share-based payment arrangement, a counterparty's right to receive cash, other assets, or equity instruments of the entity vests upon satisfaction of any specified vesting conditions.

Vesting conditions The conditions that must be satisfied for the counterparty to become entitled to receive cash, other assets or equity instruments of the entity, under a share-based payment arrangement. Vesting conditions include service conditions, which require the other party to complete a specified period of service, and performance conditions, which require specified performance targets to be met (such as a specified increase in the entity's profit over a specified period of time).

Vesting period The period during which all the specified vesting conditions of a share-based payment arrangement are to be satisfied.

(FRS 20)

Recognition: the basic principle

3.10 An entity should **recognise goods or services received or acquired in a share-based payment transaction when it obtains the goods or as the services are received.** Goods or services received or acquired in a share-based payment transaction **should be recognised as expenses unless they qualify for recognition as assets**. For example, services are normally recognised as expenses (because they are normally rendered immediately), while goods are recognised as assets.

3.11 If the goods or services were received or acquired in an **equity-settled** share-based payment transaction the entity should recognise **a corresponding increase in equity** (reserves). If the goods or services were received or acquired in a **cash-settled** share-based payment transaction the entity should recognise a **liability.**

Equity-settled share-based payment transactions

Measurement

3.12 The issue here is how to measure the 'cost' of the goods and services received and the equity instruments (eg, the share options) granted in return.

3.13 The general principle in FRS 20 is that when an entity recognises the goods or services received and the corresponding increase in equity, it should measure these at the **fair value of the goods or services received**. Where the transaction is with **parties other than**

employees, there is a rebuttable presumption that the fair value of the goods or services received can be estimated reliably.

3.14 If the fair value of the goods or services received cannot be measured reliably, the entity should measure their value by reference to the **fair value of the equity instruments granted.**

3.15 Where the transaction is with a party other than an employee fair value should be measured at the date the entity obtains the goods or the counterparty renders service.

3.16 Where shares, share options or other equity instruments are granted to **employees** as part of their remuneration package, it is not normally possible to measure directly the services received. For this reason, the entity should measure the fair value of the employee services received by reference to the **fair value of the equity instruments granted**. The fair value of those equity instruments should be measured at **grant date**.

Determining the fair value of equity instruments granted

3.17 Where a transaction is measured by reference to the fair value of the equity instruments granted, fair value is based on **market prices** if available, taking into account the terms and conditions upon which those equity instruments were granted.

3.18 If market prices are not available, the entity should estimate the fair value of the equity instruments granted using a **valuation technique**. (These are beyond the scope of this exam.)

Transactions in which services are received

3.19 The issue here is **when** to recognise the transaction. When equity instruments are granted they may vest immediately, but often the counterparty has to meet specified conditions first. For example, an employee may have to complete a specified period of service. This means that the effect of the transaction normally has to be allocated over more than one accounting period.

3.20 If the equity instruments granted **vest immediately**, (ie, the counterparty is not required to complete a specified period of service before becoming unconditionally entitled to the equity instruments) it is presumed that the services have already been received (in the absence of evidence to the contrary). The entity should **recognise the services received in full**, with a corresponding increase in equity, **on the grant date**.

3.21 If the equity instruments granted do not vest until the counterparty completes a specified period of service, the entity should account for those services **as they are rendered** by the counterparty during the vesting period. For example if an employee is granted share options on condition that he or she completes three years' service, then the services to be rendered by the employee as consideration for the share options will be received in the future, over that three-year vesting period.

3.22 The entity should recognise an amount for the goods or services received during the vesting period based on the **best available estimate** of the **number of equity instruments expected to vest**. It should **revise** that estimate if subsequent information indicates that the number of equity instruments expected to vest differs from previous estimates. On **vesting date**, the entity should revise the estimate to **equal the number of equity instruments that actually vest**.

3.23 Once the goods and services received and the corresponding increase in equity have been recognised, the entity should make no subsequent adjustment to total equity after vesting date.

3.24 EXAMPLE: EQUITY-SETTLED SHARE-BASED PAYMENT TRANSACTION

On 1 January 20X1 an entity grants 100 share options to each of its 400 employees. Each grant is conditional upon the employee working for the entity until 31 December 20X3. The fair value of each share option is £20.

During 20X1 20 employees leave and the entity estimates that 20% of the employees will leave during the three year period.

During 20X2 a further 25 employees leave and the entity now estimates that 25% of its employees will leave during the three year period.

During 20X3 a further 10 employees leave.

Required

Calculate the remuneration expense that will be recognised in respect of the share-based payment transaction for each of the three years ended 31 December 20X3.

3.25 SOLUTION

FRS 20 requires the entity to recognise the remuneration expense, based on the fair value of the share options granted, as the services are received during the three year vesting period.

In 20X1 and 20X2 the entity estimates the number of options expected to vest (by estimating the number of employees likely to leave) and bases the amount that it recognises for the year on this estimate.

In 20X3 it recognises an amount based on the number of options that actually vest. A total of 55 employees left during the three year period and therefore 34,500 options (400 – 55 × 100) vested.

The amount recognised as an expense for each of the three years is calculated as follows:

		Cumulative expense at year-end	*Expense for year*
		£	£
20X1	40,000 × 80% × 20 × 1/3	213,333	213,333
20X2	40,000 × 75% × 20 × 2/3	400,000	186,667
20X3	34,500 × 20	690,000	290,000

Question: equity settled share-based payment

On 1 January 20X3 an entity grants 250 share options to each of its 200 employees. The only condition attached to the grant is that the employees should continue to work for the entity until 31 December 20X6. Five employees leave during the year.

The market price of each option was £12 at 1 January 20X3 and £15 at 31 December 20X3.

Required

Show how this transaction will be reflected in the financial statements for the year ended 31 December 20X3.

Answer

The remuneration expense for the year is based on the fair value of the options granted at the grant date (1 January 20X3). As five of the 200 employees left during the year it is reasonable to assume that 20 employees will leave during the four year vesting period and that therefore 45,000 options (250 × 180) will actually vest.

Therefore the entity recognises a remuneration expense of £135,000 (45,000 × 12 × ¼) in the income statement and a corresponding increase in equity of the same amount.

Cash-settled share-based payment transactions

3.26 Examples of this type of transaction include:

(a) **Share appreciation rights** granted to employees: the employees become entitled to a future cash payment (rather than an equity instrument), based on the increase in the entity's share price from a specified level over a specified period of time or

(b) An entity might grant to its employees a right to receive a future cash payment by granting to them a **right to shares that are redeemable**

3.27 The basic principle is that the entity measures the goods or services acquired and the liability incurred at the **fair value of the liability**.

3.28 The entity should **remeasure** the fair value of the liability **at each reporting date** until the liability is settled **and at the date of settlement**. Any **changes** in fair value are recognised in **profit or loss** for the period.

3.29 The entity should recognise the services received, and a liability to pay for those services, **as the employees render service.** For example, if share appreciation rights do not vest until the employees have completed a specified period of service, the entity should recognise the services received and the related liability, over that period.

3.30 EXAMPLE: CASH-SETTLED SHARE-BASED PAYMENT TRANSACTION

On 1 January 20X1 an entity grants 100 cash share appreciation rights (SARS) to each of its 500 employees, on condition that the employees continue to work for the entity until 31 December 20X3.

During 20X1 35 employees leave. The entity estimates that a further 60 will leave during 20X2 and 20X3.

During 20X2 40 employees leave and the entity estimates that a further 25 will leave during 20X3.

During 20X3 22 employees leave.

At 31 December 20X3 150 employees exercise their SARs. Another 140 employees exercise their SARs at 31 December 20X4 and the remaining 113 employees exercise their SARs at the end of 20X5.

The fair values of the SARs for each year in which a liability exists are shown below, together with the intrinsic values at the dates of exercise.

	Fair value	*Intrinsic value*
	£	£
20X1	14.40	
20X2	15.50	
20X3	18.20	15.00
20X4	21.40	20.00
20X5		25.00

Required

Calculate the amount to be recognised in the income statement for each of the five years ended 31 December 20X5 and the liability to be recognised in the balance sheet at 31 December for each of the five years.

3.31 SOLUTION

For the three years to the vesting date of 31 December 20X3 the expense is based on the entity's estimate of the number of SARSs that will actually vest (as for an equity-settled transaction). However, the fair value of the liability is **re-measured** at each year-end.

The intrinsic value of the SARs at the date of exercise is the amount of cash actually paid.

	Liability at year-end		*Expense for year*
	£	£	£
20X1 Expected to vest (500 – 95):			
405 × 100 × 14.40 × 1/3	194,400		194,400
20X2 Expected to vest (500 – 100):			
400 × 100 × 15.50 × 2/3	413,333		218,933
20X3 Exercised:			
150 ×100 × 15.00		225,000	
Not yet exercised (500 – 97 – 150):			
253 × 100 × 18.20	460,460	47,127	
			272,127
20X4 Exercised:			
140 × 100 × 20.00		280,000	
Not yet exercised (253 – 140):			
113 × 100 × 21.40	241,820	(218,640)	
			61,360
20X5 Exercised:			
113 × 100 × 25.00		282,500	
	Nil	(241,820)	
			40,680
			787,500

Transactions which either the entity or the other party has a choice of settling in cash or by issuing equity instruments

3.32 If the entity has incurred a liability to settle in cash or other assets it should account for the transaction as a cash-settled share-based payment transaction

3.33 If no such liability has been incurred the entity should account for the transaction as an equity-settled share-based payment transaction.

Disclosures

3.34 FRS 20 requires entities to disclose information that enables users of the financial statements to understand the **nature and extent** of share-based payment **arrangements that existed during the period**

(a) A **description** of each type of share-based payment arrangement that existed at any time during the period, including the general terms and conditions of each arrangement;

(b) The **number and weighted average exercise prices** of share options for each of the following groups of options.

(i) Outstanding at the beginning of the period
(ii) Granted during the period
(iii) Forfeited during the period
(iv) Exercised during the period

 (v) Expired during the period
 (vi) Outstanding at the end of the period
 (vii) Exercisable at the end of the period

(c) For share options **exercised** during the period, the **weighted average share price** at the date of exercise

(d) For share options **outstanding** at the end of the period, the **range of exercise prices** and **weighted average remaining contractual life**

3.35 In addition, FRS 20 requires disclosure of information that enables users of the financial statements to **understand how the fair value** of the goods or services received, or the fair value of the equity instruments granted, during the period **was determined**.

3.36 Entities should also disclose information that enables users of the financial statements to understand the effect of share-based payment transactions on the entity's **profit or loss for the period** and on its **financial position**.

(a) the **total expense recognised for the period** arising from share-based payment transactions, including separate disclosure of that portion of the total expense that arises from transactions accounted for as equity-settled share-based payment transactions;

(b) For **liabilities** arising from share-based payment transactions:

 (i) The **total carrying amount** at the end of the period

 (ii) The **total intrinsic value** at the end of the period of liabilities for which the counterparty's right to cash or other assets had vested by the end of the period

3.37 Section summary

FRS 20 requires entities to **recognise** the goods or services received as a result of **share based payment transactions.**

- **Equity settled transactions**: DEBIT Asset/Expense, CREDIT **Equity**
- **Cash settled transactions**: DEBIT Asset/Expense, CREDIT **Liability**
- Transactions are **recognised when goods/services are obtained/received** (usually over the performance period)
- Transactions are **measured at fair value**

4 FRS 18 ACCOUNTING POLICIES 6/02, 6/03

Exam focus point

You may be required to discuss the differences between SSAP 2 and FRS 18 in the exam. The examiner could ask you to highlight and discuss the improvements that FRS 18 has made on the old SSAP, or relate FRS 18 to the accounting framework provided by the *Statement of Principles*.

4.1 FRS 18 *Accounting policies* replaced SSAP 2 *Disclosure of accounting policies*. SSAP 2 has been a **corner stone** of accounting for the last two decades and FRS 18 is an attempt to bring UK accounting into the new millennium. However, FRS 18 does **not** seem to be a great departure from SSAP 2 and very little ground seems to have been broken by it.

Bedrocks of accounting

4.2 The most obvious change is the relegation of two fundamental accounting concepts.

- Prudence
- Consistency

These concepts are now **desirable features** of financial statements.

4.3 The bedrocks of accounting are:

- **Accruals** (matching)
- **Going concern**

4.4 FRS 18 places great **importance** upon these concepts. There is no tangible increase in emphasis on accruals (except that it is a great deal more important than prudence and consistency). Going concern is a different matter.

4.5 Entities are required to **consider going concern** and disclose the following

(a) **Material uncertainties.** Conditions or events which present **significant doubts** about the entity's ability to continue as a going concern.

(b) **Foreseeable future.** Where the future has been restricted to **less than one year** from the approval of the financial statements.

(c) **Going concern.** Where the financial statements are **not prepared on a going concern basis**, the reason for this and the method under which they have been prepared.

Statement of Principles

4.6 FRS 18 is designed to sit alongside the *Statement of Principles* framework. This helps explain the downplaying of the previously important prudence and consistency concepts.

4.7 The preparers of financial statements must now consider

- Relevance
- Reliability
- Comparability
- Understandability

4.8 There is an assumption that, in considering these objectives, the concepts of **prudence and consistency will be followed** in the majority of cases anyway. The objectives will need to be weighed against each other and a course of action taken which **best fits all four.**

4.9 All four objectives overlap and none of them should be compromised by the accounting policies adopted by the entity. By fulfilling the reliability and comparability objectives an accounting policy is likely to fulfil the consistency concept. If a policy provides information which is relevant and reliable then it is likely that amounts are not overstated and so the prudence concept is indirectly adhered to.

Accounting policies

4.10 FRS 18 prescribes the **regular consideration of the entity's accounting policies**. The **best** accounting policy should be adopted at all times. This is the major reason for downplaying consistency (and to a lesser extent prudence). An entity **cannot retain** an accounting policy merely because it was used last year or because it gives a prudent view.

4.11 However, the entity should consider how a **change** in accounting policy may affect **comparability**. Essentially a **balance** must be struck between selecting the **most appropriate policies** and presenting **coherent and useful** financial statements. The overriding guidance is that the financial statements should give a **true and fair view** of the entity's business. Chopping and changing accounting policies year on year is likely to jeopardise the true and fair view but so too is retaining accounting policies which do not present the most useful information to the users of the accounts.

Disclosure

4.12 FRS 18 requires the disclosure of:

- A **description of each accounting policy** which is material to the entity's financial statements
- A description of any significant estimation technique
- **Changes** to accounting policies
- The effects of any material change to an estimation technique

Estimation techniques

4.13 An estimation technique is material **only where a large range** of monetary values may be arrived at. The entity should vary the assumptions it uses, to assess how sensitive monetary values are under that technique. In most cases the range of values will be relatively narrow. Consider the useful life of motor vehicles, for example.

Changes to accounting policies

4.14 The disclosure of new accounting policies also requires:

- An explanation of the **reason for change**
- The **effects of a prior period adjustment** on the previous years results (in accordance with FRS 3)
- The **effects of the change in policy** on the previous year's results

If it is **not possible** to disclose the last two points then the **reason** for this should be disclosed instead.

Exam focus point

You need to be confident about the application of FRS 18. Make sure that you can **identify** a change in accounting policy and the **reason** that it is a change in accounting policy as opposed to a change in estimation technique. You will have to **discuss** the decision you have reached **and justify** your conclusions.

4.15 The most complex aspect to FRS 18 is the **application of the terms and definitions** within the standard. SSAP 2 defined accounting policies and accounting bases. There was some confusion as to what an accounting base was. FRS 18 has dispensed with the term accounting base. However, the term which seems to replace it, **estimation technique**, may prove difficult to apply in practice.

4.16 It is essential that you **learn the following definitions**. However, once you have read them you should **apply them** to the questions later in this section to make sure that you understand them.

KEY TERM

Accounting policies. The principles, conventions, rules and practices applied by an entity that prescribe how transactions and other events are to be reflected in its financial statements.

4.17 Accounting policies are **not** estimation techniques.

4.18 An accounting policy includes the

- Recognition
- Presentation
- And measurement basis

Of assets, liabilities, gains, losses and changes to shareholders' funds.

KEY TERM

Estimation technique. The methods used by an entity to establish the estimated monetary amounts associated with the measurement bases selected for assets, liabilities, gains, losses and changes to shareholders' funds.

4.19 Estimation techniques are used to **implement the measurement basis** of an accounting policy. The accounting policy specifies the measurement basis and the estimation technique is used when there is an uncertainty over this amount.

4.20 The method of **depreciation is an estimation technique**. The accounting policy is to spread the cost of the asset over its useful economic life. Depreciation is the measurement basis. The estimation technique would be, say, straight line depreciation as opposed to reducing balance.

4.21 A change of estimation technique should **not** be accounted for as a prior period adjustment unless the following apply.

- It is the correction of a fundamental error
- The Companies Act, an accounting standard or a UITF Abstract **requires the change to be accounted** for as a prior period adjustment.

Application of FRS 18

4.22 FRS 18 gives a number of examples of its application in an appendix to the standard. When a change is required to an accounting policy then **three criteria** must be **considered** to ensure that the change is affecting the accounting policy and not an estimation technique.

Criterion 1. Recognition
Criterion 2. Presentation
Criterion 3. Measurement basis

4.23 If **any one of the criteria apply** then a change has been made to the accounting policy. If they do **not** apply then a change to an estimation technique has taken place.

4.24 You should note that where an **accounting standard gives a choice** of treatments (ie SSAP 9 states that stock can be recognised on a FIFO or weighted average cost basis) then adopting the alternative treatment is a **change of accounting policy.** Also note that FRS 15 states that a **change in depreciation method is not** a change in accounting policy.

Example		*Recognition*	*Change to Presentation*	*Measurement basis?*	*Change of Accounting Policy*
1	Changing from capitalisation of finance costs associated with the construction of fixed assets to charging them through the profit and loss	Yes	Yes	No	Yes
2	A reassessment of an entity's cost centres means that all three will have production overheads allocated to them instead of just two	No	No	No	No
3	Overheads are reclassified from distribution to cost of sales	No	Yes	No	Yes
4	Change from straight-line depreciation to machine hours	No	No	No	No
5	Reallocate depreciation from administration to cost of sales	No	Yes	No	Yes
6	A provision is revised upwards and the estimates of future cash flows are now discounted in accordance with FRS 12. They were not discounted previously as the amounts involved were not material	No	No	No	No
7	Deferred tax is now reported on a discounted basis. It was previously undiscounted	No	No	Yes	Yes
8	A foreign subsidiary's profit and loss account is now to be translated at the closing rate. It was previously translated at the average rate	No	No	Yes	Yes
9	Fungible stocks are to be measured on the weighted average cost basis instead of the previously used FIFO basis	No	No	Yes	Yes

Fungible assets

KEY TERM

Fungible assets are similar assets which are grouped together as there is no reason to view them separately in economic terms. Shares and items of stock are examples of fungible assets.

4.25 The last example (example 9) is based on a **change to fungible assets.** The standard states that when fungible assets are considered in **aggregate** a change from weighted average cost to FIFO (or vice versa), is a change to the **measurement base.** The standard also recommends that fungible assets should **always be considered in aggregate** in order to enhance **comparability** of financial statements.

Question: change of accounting policy (1)

The board of Beezlebub plc decide to change the depreciation method they use on their plant and machinery from 30% reducing balance to 20% straight line to better reflect the way the assets are used within the business. Is this a change of accounting policy ?

Answer

No. This is a change to the **estimation technique**. The same measurement basis is used. The historic cost is allocated over the asset's estimated useful life.

Question: change of accounting policy (2)

The board of Beezlebub plc also decide to change their stock valuation. They replace their FIFO valuation method for an AVCO method to better reflect the way that stock is used within the business. Is this a change in accounting policy?

Answer

Yes. This is a change to the **measurement basis**. The paragraphs on fungible assets discuss this further.

Question: change of accounting policy (3)

The board of Beezlebub plc decide in the following year that the development costs the business incurs should not be capitalised and presented on the balance sheet. Instead they agree that all development expenditure should be expended in the profit and loss account. Is this an accounting policy change?

Answer

Yes. The choice to capitalise or not is given in SSAP 13. The criteria affected by this decision are **recognition and presentation.**

Question: change of accounting policy (4)

Beezlebub plc's board are also considering reallocating the depreciation charges made on its large fleet of company cars to administration expenses, they were previously shown in cost of sales. Is this an accounting policy change?

Answer

Yes. Beezlebub would be changing the way they **presented** the depreciation figure.

SORPs

4.26 If an entity's financial statements **fall within the scope of a SORP** the entity should **identify** the SORP and state **whether** it has been **complied with.** Any departure from the SORP must be **disclosed together with the reason for the departure.** The effect of the departure does not need to be quantified unless quantification would provide a **true and fair view.**

4.27 An entity can **choose** to comply with a SORP even if its financial statements do not fall within its scope. Entities **should disclose this fact** in their financial statements.

4.28 Section summary

- FRS 18 requires an entity to conduct a review on an annual basis in order to ensure that it is using the most appropriate accounting policies. The three criteria:
  - Recognition
  - Presentation
  - Measurement basis
- Are considered in order to establish whether there has been a change of accounting policy or merely a change of estimation technique. The objectives of:
  - Reliability
  - Relevance
  - Comparability
  - Understandability
- Must be fulfilled by the accounting policies adopted. This requirement helps prevent entities from changing accounting policies too often.
- Prudence and consistency have a lesser role in the accounting policy framework but despite this, FRS 18 is not a major departure from SSAP 2.

Chapter roundup

- **SSAP 25 *Segmental Reporting*** requires listed companies to provide a breakdown of their operations in different geographical and business areas.
- The ASB has issued a **discussion draft** on segmental reporting as a response to international developments.
- **FRS 8** is primarily a disclosure standard. It is concerned to improve the quality of information provided by published accounts and also to strengthen their stewardship roles.
- **FRED 25** proposes limited changes to FRS 8.
- **Share-based payment** transactions should be recognised in the financial statements. You need to understand and be able to advise on:
  - Recognition
  - Measurement
  - Disclosure

  of both equity settled and cash settled transactions.
- **FRS 18** *Accounting policies* replaced SSAP 2.
- Prudence and consistency are now less important
- **Going concern and accruals** are the **bedrocks** of accounting.
- An important distinction is made between **accounting policies and estimation techniques**.
- FRS 18 was written in the light of the *Statement of Principles.*

Quick quiz

1 Why is segmental reporting considered useful?

2 What are the arguments against segmental reporting?

3 What are the key issues in segmental reporting identified by the ASB's discussion draft?

4 A managing director of a company is deemed a related party.

True ☐

False ☐

5 Under FRED 25, names of the transacting parties in a related party transaction need to be disclosed.

True ☐

False ☐

6 What is grant date?

7 If an entity has entered into an equity-settled share based payment transaction, what should it recognise in its financial statements?

8 Where an entity has granted share options to its employees in return for services, how is the transaction measured?

9 An employee is granted share options on condition that he completes five years' service. When should the transaction be recognised?

10 FRS 18 abolished the concept of prudence.

True ☐

False ☐

Answers to quick quiz

1 See Para 1.2

2 See Para 1.3

3 (a) Division of operations into segments
(b) The information to be given for each segment
(c) Whether the information is verifiable and easy to understand

4 False. He is presumed to be a related party unless there is evidence to the contrary.

5 False. They do not need to be disclosed under the FRED, although they do under FRS 8.

6 The date on which the entity and another party (including an employee) agree to a share-based payment agreement, being when the entity and the other party have a shared understanding of the terms and conditions of the agreement.

7 The goods or services received and a corresponding increase in equity.

8 By reference to the fair value of the equity instruments granted, measured at grant date.

9 The entity should account for the employee's services as they are rendered, over the five year vesting period.

10 False. Prudence has been relegated to the status of a desirable feature.

Now try the question below from the Exam Question Bank

Number	Level	Marks	Time
Q33	Exam	25	45 mins

Chapter 25

POST BALANCE SHEET EVENTS, PROVISIONS AND CONTINGENCIES

Topic list		Syllabus reference
1	FRS 21 *Events after the balance sheet date*	1(a), 4(e)
2	FRS 12 *Provisions, contingent liabilities and contingent assets*	1(a), 4(e)
3	Discounting	1(a), 4(e)

Introduction

FRS 21 is a new standard based on IAS 10 *Events after the balance sheet date.* The principles are the same as SSAP 17, with which you should be familiar. However, note the treatment of dividends. **Provisions** are a topical area in the light of FRS 12, a recent standard on the subject.

Discounting is of increasing importance in the light of FRS 17 and FRS 19.

Study guide

Section 21– Post balance sheet events, provisions and contingencies

- Discussion of the problems of accounting for post balance sheet events including reclassification, window dressing etc
- Discussion of the issues relating to recognition and measurement of provisions including 'best estimates', discounting, future events
- Explaining the use of restructuring provisions and other practical uses of provisioning
- Discussion of the problems with current standards on provisions and contingencies including definitional and discounting problems

1 FRS 21 EVENTS AFTER THE BALANCE SHEET DATE

1.1 The financial statements are significant indicators of a company's success or failure. It is important, therefore, that they include all the information necessary for an understanding of the company's position.

1.2 FRS 21 *Events after the balance sheet date* and FRS 12 *Provisions, contingent liabilities and contingent assets* both require the provision of additional information in order to facilitate such an understanding. FRS 21 deals with events *after* the balance sheet date which may affect the position at the balance sheet date. FRS 12 *Provisions, contingent liabilities and contingent assets* deals with matters which are **uncertain** at the balance sheet date.

1.3 The standard gives the following definition.

KEY TERMS

Events after the balance sheet date are those events, both favourable and unfavourable, that occur between the balance sheet date and the date on which the financial statements are authorised for issue. Two types of events can be identified.

- Those that provide further evidence of conditions that existed at the balance sheet date (adjusting events after the balance sheet date)
- Those that are indicative of conditions that arose after the balance sheet date (non-adjusting events after the balance sheet date) *(FRS 21)*

Events after the balance sheet date

1.4 Between the balance sheet date and the date the financial statements are authorised (ie for issue outside the organisation), events may occur which show that assets and liabilities at the balance sheet date should be adjusted, or that disclosure of such events should be given.

Events requiring adjustment

1.5 The standard requires entities to **adjust** the amounts recognised in its financial statements to reflect adjusting events after the balance sheet date.

1.6 An **example** of additional evidence which becomes available after the balance sheet date is where a **customer goes bankrupt, thus confirming that the trade account receivable balance at the year end is uncollectable.**

1.7 In relation to going concern, the standard states that, where operating results and the financial position have deteriorated after the balance sheet date, it may be necessary to reconsider whether the going concern assumption is appropriate in the preparation of the financial statements.

Examples of adjusting events

1.8 The following examples of adjusting events are given in FRS 21.

(a) The resolution after the balance sheet date of a court case giving rise to a liability

(b) Evidence of impairment of assets, such as news that a major customer is going into liquidation, or the sale of inventories (stocks) below cost

(c) Determination of the price of assets bought or sold before the balance sheet date

(d) Determination of employee bonuses or profit shares

(e) Discovery of fraud or errors showing that the financial statements were incorrect

Events not requiring adjustment

1.9 The standard then looks at events which do **not** require adjustment. Entities **must not adjust** the amounts recognised in their financial statements to reflect these non-adjusting events.

1.10 The **example** given by the standard of such an event is where the **value of an investment falls between the balance sheet date and the date the financial statements are authorised** for issue. The fall in value represents circumstances during the current period, not conditions existing at the previous balance sheet date, so it is not appropriate to adjust the value of the investment in the financial statements. Disclosure is an aid to users, however, indicating 'unusual changes' in the state of assets and liabilities after the balance sheet date.

1.11 The rule for **disclosure** of events occurring after the balance sheet date which relate to conditions that arose after that date, is that disclosure should be made if non-disclosure would hinder the user's ability to made **proper evaluations** and decision based on the financial statements. An example might be the acquisition of another business.

Examples of non-adjusting events

1.12 The following examples of non-adjusting events are given in FRS 21.

(a) Major business combination

(b) Announcement of a plan to discontinue an operation

(c) Major purchases and disposals of assets

(d) Destruction of a major production plant by a fire

(e) Announcement of or beginning of major restructuring

(f) Major share transactions

(g) Abnormally large changes in asset prices or foreign exchange rates

(h) Changes in tax rates having a significant effect on current and deferred tax assets and liabilities

(i) Entering into significant guarantees

(j) Commencing major litigation arising out of events after the balance sheet date

Dividends

1.13 **Equity dividends proposed or declared after the balance sheet date should not be recognised as a liability at the balance sheet date**. Such dividends are disclosed in the notes to the financial statements.

Disclosures

1.14 The following **disclosure requirements** are given **for events** which occur after the balance sheet date which do *not* require adjustment. If disclosure of events occurring after the balance sheet date is required, the following information should be provided.

(a) The nature of the event
(b) An estimate of the financial effect, or a statement that such an estimate cannot be made

Question: adjustment

State whether the following events occurring after the balance sheet date require an adjustment to the assets and liabilities of the financial statements.

(a) Purchase of an investment

(b) A change in the rate of corporate tax, applicable to the previous year

(c) An increase in pension benefits

(d) Losses due to fire

(e) A bad debt suddenly being paid

(f) The receipt of proceeds of sales or other evidence concerning the net realisable value of inventory

(g) A sudden decline in the value of property held as a long-term asset

Answer

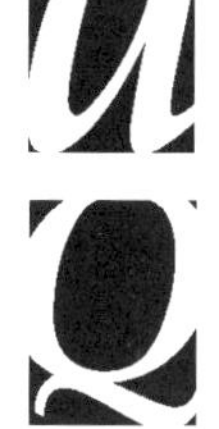

(b), (e) and (f) are adjusting; the others are non-adjusting.

Question: events

Fabricators Ltd, an engineering company, makes up its financial statements to 31 March in each year. The financial statements for the year ended 31 March 20X1 showed a turnover of £3m and trading profit of £400,000.

Before approval of the financial statements by the board of directors on 30 June 20X1 the following events took place.

(a) The financial statements of Patchup Ltd for the year ended 28 February 20X1 were received which indicated a permanent decline in that company's financial position. Fabricators Ltd had bought shares in Patchup Ltd some years ago and this purchase was included in unquoted investments at its cost of £100,000. The financial statements received indicated that this investment was now worth only £50,000.

(b) There was a fire at the company's warehouse on 30 April 20X1 when stock to the value of £500,000 was destroyed. It transpired that the stock in the warehouse was under-insured by some 50%.

(c) It was announced on 1 June 20X1 that the company's design for tank cleaning equipment had been approved by the major oil companies and this could result in an increase in the annual turnover of some £1m with a relative effect on profits.

Answer

The treatment of the events arising in the case of Fabricators Ltd would be as follows.

(a) The fall in value of the investment in Patchup Ltd has arisen over the previous year and that company's financial accounts for the year to 28 February 20X1 provide additional evidence of conditions that existed at the balance sheet date. The loss of £50,000 is material in terms of the trading profit figure and, as an adjusting event, should be reflected in the financial statements of Fabricators Ltd as an exceptional item in accordance with FRS 3.

(b) The destruction of stock by fire on 30 April (one month after the balance sheet date) must be considered to be a non-adjusting event (ie this is 'a new condition which did not exist at the balance sheet date'). Since the loss is material, being £250,000, it should be disclosed by way of a note to the accounts. The note should describe the nature of the event and an estimate of its financial effect. Non-reporting of this event would prevent users of the financial statements from reaching a proper understanding of the financial position.

(c) The approval on 1 June of the company's design for tank cleaning equipment creates a new condition which did not exist at the balance sheet date. This is, therefore, a non-adjusting event and if it is of such material significance that non-reporting would prevent a proper understanding of the financial position it should be disclosed by way of note. In this instance non-disclosure should not prevent a proper understanding of the financial position and disclosure by note may be unnecessary.

---

2 FRS 12 PROVISIONS, CONTINGENT LIABILITIES AND CONTINGENT ASSETS 12/01

2.1 As we have seen with regard to post balance sheet events, financial statements must include **all the information necessary for an understanding of the company's financial position**. Provisions, contingent liabilities and contingent assets are 'uncertainties' that must be accounted for consistently if are to achieve this understanding.

Objective

2.2 FRS 12 *Provisions, contingent liabilities and contingent assets* aims to ensure that appropriate **recognition criteria** and **measurement bases** are applied to provisions, contingent liabilities and contingent assets and that **sufficient information** is disclosed in the **notes** to the financial statements to enable users to understand their nature, timing and amount.

Provisions

2.3 You will be familiar with provisions for depreciation and doubtful debts from your earlier studies. The sorts of provisions addressed by FRS 12 are, however, rather different.

2.4 Before FRS 12, there was no accounting standard dealing with provisions. Companies wanting to show their results in the most favourable light used to make large '**one off' provisions** in years where a high level of underlying profits was generated. These provisions, often known as '**big bath**' provisions, were then available to shield expenditure in future years when perhaps the underlying profits were not as good.

2.5 In other words, **provisions were used for profit smoothing**. Profit smoothing is misleading.

Exam focus point

The key aim of FRS 12 is to ensure that provisions are made only where there are valid grounds for them.

2.6 FRS 12 views a provision as a **liability**.

KEY TERMS

A **provision** is a **liability** of uncertain timing or amount.

A **liability** is an obligation of an entity to transfer economic benefits as a result of past transactions or events. *(FRS 12)*

2.7 The FRS distinguishes provisions from other liabilities such as trade creditors and accruals. This is on the basis that for a provision there is **uncertainty** about the timing or amount of the future expenditure. Whilst uncertainty is clearly present in the case of certain accruals the uncertainty is generally much less than for provisions.

Recognition

2.8 FRS 12 states that a provision should be **recognised** as a liability in the financial statements when:

- An entity has a **present obligation** (legal or constructive) as a result of a past event
- It is probable that a **transfer of economic benefits** will be required to settle the obligation
- A **reliable estimate** can be made of the obligation

Meaning of obligation

2.9 It is fairly clear what a legal obligation is. However, you may not know what a **constructive obligation** is.

KEY TERM

FRS 12 defines a **constructive obligation** as

'An obligation that derives from an entity's actions where:

- by an established pattern of past practice, published policies or a sufficiently specific current statement the entity has indicated to other parties that it will accept certain responsibilities; and
- as a result, the entity has created a valid expectation on the part of those other parties that it will discharge those responsibilities.

Question: recognising a provision

In which of the following circumstances might a provision be recognised?

(a) On 13 December 20X9 the board of an entity decided to close down a division. The accounting date of the company is 31 December. Before 31 December 20X9 the decision was not communicated to any of those affected and no other steps were taken to implement the decision.

(b) The board agreed a detailed closure plan on 20 December 20X9 and details were given to customers and employees.

(c) A company is obliged to incur clean up costs for environmental damage (that has already been caused).

(d) A company intends to carry out future expenditure to operate in a particular way in the future.

Answer

(a) No provision would be recognised as the decision has not been communicated.

(b) A provision would be made in the 20X9 financial statements.

(c) A provision for such costs is appropriate.

(d) No present obligation exists and under FRS 12 no provision would be appropriate. This is because the entity could avoid the future expenditure by its future actions, maybe by changing its method of operation.

Probable transfer of economic benefits

2.10 For the purpose of the FRS, a transfer of economic benefits is regarded as '**probable**' if the event is **more likely than not** to occur. This appears to indicate a probability of more than 50%. However, the standard makes it clear that where there is a number of similar obligations the probability should be based on considering the population as a whole, rather than one single item.

2.11 EXAMPLE: TRANSFER OF ECONOMIC BENEFITS

If a company has entered into a warranty obligation then the probability of transfer of economic benefits may well be extremely small in respect of one specific item. However, when considering the population as a whole the probability of some transfer of economic benefits is quite likely to be much higher. If there is a **greater than 50% probability** of some transfer of economic benefits then a **provision** should be made for the **expected amount**.

Measurement of provisions

IMPORTANT

The amount recognised as a provision should be the best estimate of the expenditure required to settle the present obligation at the balance sheet date.

2.12 The estimates will be determined by the **judgement** of the entity's management supplemented by the experience of similar transactions.

2.13 Allowance is made for **uncertainty**. Where the provision being measured involves a large population of items, the obligation is estimated by weighting all possible outcomes by their discounted probabilities, ie **expected value**.

Question: warranty

Parker plc sells goods with a warranty under which customers are covered for the cost of repairs of any manufacturing defect that becomes apparent within the first six months of purchase. The company's past experience and future expectations indicate the following pattern of likely repairs.

% of goods sold	*Defects*	*Cost of repairs*
		£m
75	None	-
20	Minor	1.0
5	Major	4.0

What is the expected cost of repairs?

Answer

The cost is found using 'expected values' (75% × £nil) + (20% × £1.0m) + (5% × £4.0m) = £400,000.

2.14 Where the effect of the **time value of money** is material, the amount of a provision should be the **present value** of the expenditure required to settle the obligation. An appropriate **discount** rate should be used.

2.15 The discount rate should be a **pre-tax rate** that reflects current market assessments of the time value of money. **The discount rate(s) should not reflect risks for which future cash flow estimates have been adjusted.**

2.16 The **unwinding of the discount** should be included as a financial item adjacent to interest but it should be **shown separately** from other interest either on the face of the profit and loss account or in a note.

Future events

2.17 **Future events** which are reasonably expected to occur (eg new legislation, changes in technology) may affect the amount required to settle the entity's obligation and should be taken into account.

Expected disposal of assets

2.18 Gains from the expected disposal of assets should not be taken into account in measuring a provision.

Reimbursements

2.19 Some or all of the expenditure needed to settle a provision may be expected to be recovered form a third party. If so, the **reimbursement should be recognised only when it is virtually certain that reimbursement will be received if the entity settles the obligation**.

- The reimbursement should be treated as a separate asset, and the amount recognised should not be greater than the provision itself.
- The provision and the amount recognised for reimbursement may be netted off in the profit and loss account.

Changes in provisions

2.20 Provisions should be renewed at each balance sheet date and adjusted to reflect the current best estimate. If it is no longer probable that a transfer of economic benefits will be required to settle the obligation, the provision should be reversed.

Use of provisions

2.21 **A provision should be used only for expenditures for which the provision was originally recognised.** Setting expenditures against a provision that was originally recognised for another purpose would conceal the impact of two different events.

Recognising an asset when recognising a provision

2.22 Normally the setting up of a provision should be charged immediately to the profit and loss account. But **if the incurring of the present obligation recognised as a provision gives access to future economic benefits an asset should be recognised.**

2.23 EXAMPLE: RECOGNISING AN ASSET

An obligation for decommissioning costs is incurred by commissioning an oil rig. At the same time, the commissioning gives access to oil reserves over the years of the oil rig's operation. Therefore an asset representing future access to oil reserves is recognised at the same time as the provision for decommissioning costs.

Future operating losses

2.24 **Provisions should not be recognised for future operating losses.** They do not meet the definition of a liability and the general recognition criteria set out in the standard.

Onerous contracts

2.25 If an entity has a contract that is onerous, the present obligation under the contract **should be recognised and measured** as a provision. An example might be vacant leasehold property.

KEY TERM

An **onerous contract** is a contract entered into with another party under which the unavoidable costs of fulfilling the terms of the contract exceed any revenues expected to be received from the goods or services supplied or purchased directly or indirectly under the contract and where the entity would have to compensate the other party if it did not fulfil the terms of the contract.

2.26 EXAMPLES OF POSSIBLE PROVISIONS

It is easier to see what FRS 12 is driving at if you look at examples of those items which are possible provisions under this standard. Some of these we have already touched on.

(a) **Warranties**. These are argued to be genuine provisions as on past experience it is probable, ie more likely than not, that some claims will emerge. The provision must be estimated, however, on the basis of the class as a whole and not on individual claims. There is a clear legal obligation in this case.

(b) **Major repairs**. In the past it has been quite popular for companies to provide for expenditure on a major overhaul to be accrued gradually over the intervening years between overhauls. Under FRS 12 this will no longer be possible as FRS 12 would argue that this is a mere intention to carry out repairs, not an obligation. The entity can always sell the asset in the meantime. The only solution is to treat major assets such as aircraft, ships, furnaces etc as a series of smaller assets where each part is depreciated over shorter lives. Thus any major overhaul may be argued to be replacement and therefore capital rather than revenue expenditure.

(c) **Self insurance**. A number of companies have created a provision for self insurance based on the expected cost of making good fire damage etc instead of paying premiums to an insurance company. Under FRS 12 this provision would no longer be justifiable as the entity has no obligation until a fire or accident occurs. No obligation exists until that time.

(d) **Environmental contamination**. If the company has an environment policy such that other parties would expect the company to clean up any contamination or if the company has broken current environmental legislation then a provision for environmental damage must be made.

(e) **Decommissioning or abandonment costs**. When an oil company initially purchases an oilfield it is put under a legal obligation to decommission the site at the end of its life. Prior to FRS 12 most oil companies applied the SORP on *Accounting for abandonment costs* published by the Oil Industry Accounting Committee and they built up the provision gradually over the field so that no one year would be unduly burdened with the cost.

FRS 12, however, insists that a legal obligation exists on the initial expenditure on the field and therefore a liability exists immediately. This would appear to result in a large charge to profit and loss in the first year of operation of the field. However, the FRS takes the view that the cost of purchasing the field in the first place is not only the cost of the field itself but also the costs of putting it right again. Thus all the costs of abandonment may be capitalised.

(f) **Restructuring**. This is considered in detail below.

Provisions for restructuring

2.27 One of the main purposes of FRS 12 was to target abuses of provisions for restructuring. Accordingly, FRS 12 lays down **strict criteria** to determine when such a provision can be made.

KEY TERM

FRS 12 defines a **restructuring** as:

A programme that is planned and is controlled by management and materially changes either:

- The scope of a business undertaken by an entity, or
- The manner in which that business is conducted.

2.28 The FRS gives the following **examples** of events that may fall under the definition of restructuring.

- The **sale or termination** of a line of business
- The **closure of business locations** in a country or region or the **relocation** of business activities from one country region to another
- **Changes in management structure**, for example, the elimination of a layer of management
- **Fundamental reorganisations** that have a material effect on the **nature and focus** of the entity's operations

2.29 The question is whether or not an entity has an obligation - legal or constructive - at the balance sheet date.

- An entity must have a **detailed formal plan** for the restructuring.
- It must have **raised a valid expectation** in those affected that it will carry out the restructuring by starting to implement that plan or announcing its main features to those affected by it

IMPORTANT

A mere management decision is not normally sufficient. Management decisions may sometimes trigger off recognition, but only if earlier events such as negotiations with employee representatives and other interested parties have been concluded subject only to management approval.

2.30 Where the restructuring involves the **sale of an operation** then FRS 12 states that no obligation arises until the entity has entered into a **binding sale agreement**. This is because until this has occurred the entity will be able to change its mind and withdraw from the sale even if its intentions have been announced publicly.

Costs to be included within a restructuring provision

2.31 The FRS states that a restructuring provision should include only the **direct expenditures** arising from the restructuring, which are those that are both:

- **Necessarily entailed** by the restructuring; and
- Not associated with the **ongoing activities** of the entity.

2.32 The following costs should specifically **not** be included within a restructuring provision.

- **Retraining** or relocating continuing staff
- **Marketing**
- **Investment in new systems** and distribution networks

Disclosure

2.33 Disclosures for provisions fall into two parts.

- Disclosure of details of the **change in carrying value** of a provision from the beginning to the end of the year
- Disclosure of the **background** to the making of the provision and the uncertainties affecting its outcome

Contingent liabilities

2.34 Now you understand provisions it will be easier to understand contingent assets and liabilities.

KEY TERM

FRS 12 defines a **contingent liability** as:

- A possible obligation that arises from past events and whose existence will be confirmed only by the occurrence or non-occurrence of one or more uncertain future events not wholly within the entity's control; or
- A present obligation that arises from past events but is not recognised because:
    - It is not probable that a transfer of economic benefits will be required to settle the obligation; or
    - The amount of the obligation cannot be measured with sufficient reliability.

2.35 As a rule of thumb, probable means more than 50% likely. **If an obligation is probable, it is not a contingent liability** - instead, a **provision is needed**.

Treatment of contingent liabilities

2.36 Contingent liabilities **should not be recognised in financial statements** but they **should be disclosed**. The required disclosures are:

- A brief description of the nature of the contingent liability
- An estimate of its financial effect
- An indication of the uncertainties that exist
- The possibility of any reimbursement

Contingent assets

KEY TERM

FRS 12 defines a **contingent asset** as:

A possible asset that arises from past events and whose existence will be confirmed by the occurrence of one or more uncertain future events not wholly within the entity's control.

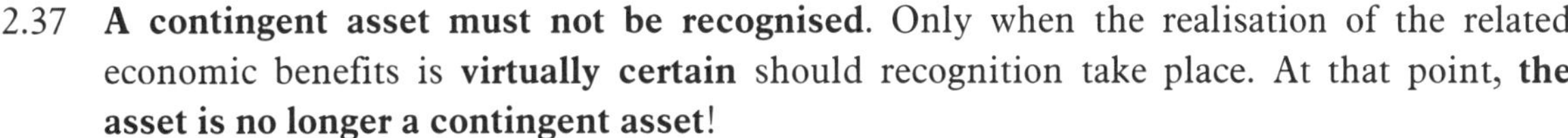

2.37 **A contingent asset must not be recognised**. Only when the realisation of the related economic benefits is **virtually certain** should recognition take place. At that point, **the asset is no longer a contingent asset**!

Disclosure: contingent liabilities

2.38 A **brief description** must be provided of all material contingent liabilities unless they are likely to be remote. In addition, provide

- An estimate of their **financial effect**
- Details of **any uncertainties**

2.39 *Disclosure: contingent assets*

Contingent assets must only be disclosed in the notes if they are **probable**. In that case a brief description of the contingent asset should be provided along with an estimate of its likely financial effect.

'Let out'

2.40 FRS 12 permits reporting entities to avoid disclosure requirements relating to provisions, contingent liabilities and contingent assets if they would be expected to **seriously prejudice** the position of the entity in dispute with other parties. However, this should only be employed in **extremely rare** cases. Details of the general nature of the provision/contingencies must still be provided, together with an explanation of why it has not been disclosed.

2.41 You must practise the questions below to get the hang of FRS 12. But first, study the flow chart, taken from FRS 12, which is a good summary of its requirements.

Exam focus point

If you learn this flow chart you should be able to deal with most of the questions you are likely to meet in the exam.

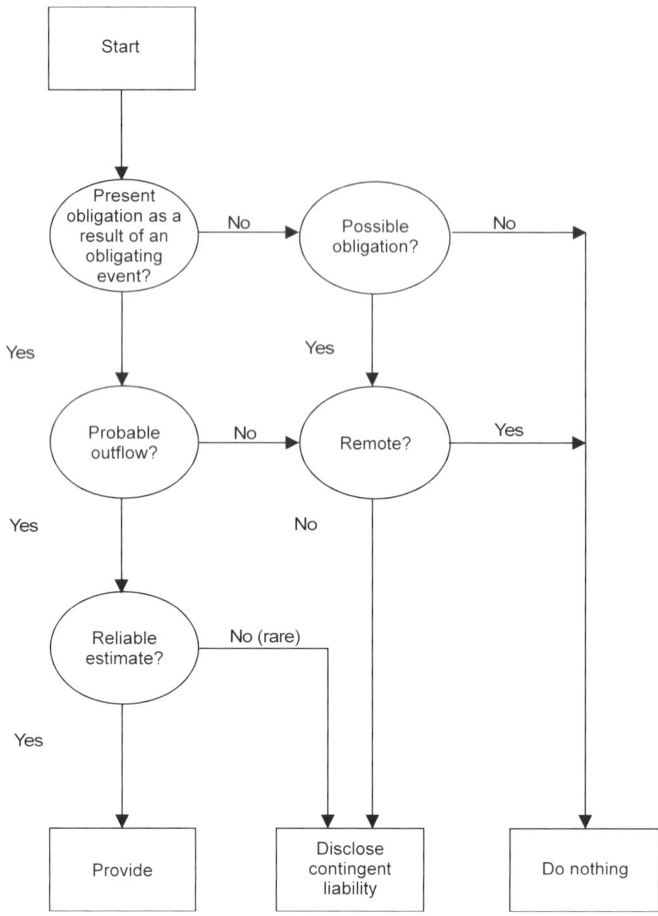

Question: provide or not? (1)

During 20X0 Smack Ltd gives a guarantee of certain borrowings of Pony Ltd, whose financial condition at that time is sound. During 20X1, the financial condition of Pony Ltd deteriorates and at 30 June 20x1 Pony Ltd files for protection from its creditors.

What accounting treatment is required:

(a) At 31 December 20X0?
(b) At 31 December 20x1?

Answer

(a) At 31 December 20X0

There is a present obligation as a result of a past obligating event. The obligating event is the giving of the guarantee, which gives rise to a legal obligation. However, at 31 December 20X0 no transfer of economic benefits is probable in settlement of the obligation.

No provision is recognised. The guarantee is disclosed as a contingent liability unless the probability of any transfer is regarded as remote.

(b) At 31 December 20X1

As above, there is a present obligation as a result of a past obligating event, namely the giving of the guarantee.

At 31 December 20X1 it is probable that a transfer of economic events will be required to settle the obligation. A provision is therefore recognised for the best estimate of the obligation.

Question: provide or not? (2)

Warren Ltd gives warranties at the time of sale to purchasers of its products. Under the terms of the warranty the manufacturer undertakes to make good, by repair or replacement, manufacturing defects that become apparent within a period of three years from the date of the sale. Should a provision be recognised?

Answer

Warren Ltd **cannot avoid** the cost of repairing or replacing all items of product that manifest manufacturing defects in respect of which warranties are given before the balance sheet date, and a provision for the cost of this should therefore be made.

Warren Ltd is obliged to repair or replace items that fail within the entire warranty period. Therefore, in respect of **this year's sales**, the obligation provided for at the balance sheet date should be the cost of making good items for which defects have been notified but not yet processed, **plus** an estimate of costs in respect of the other items sold for which there is sufficient evidence that manufacturing defects **will** manifest themselves during their remaining periods of warranty cover.

Question: provide or not? (3)

After a wedding in 20X0 ten people died, possibly as a result of food poisoning from products sold by Callow Ltd. Legal proceedings are started seeking damages from Callow but it disputes liability. Up to the date of approval of the financial statements for the year to 31 December 20X0, Callow's lawyers advise that it is probable that it will not be found liable. However, when Callow prepares the financial statements for the year to 31 December 20X1 its lawyers advise that, owing to developments in the case, it is probable that it will be found liable.

What is the required accounting treatment:

(a) At 31 December 20X0?
(b) At 31 December 20X1?

Answer

(a) *At 31 December 20X0*

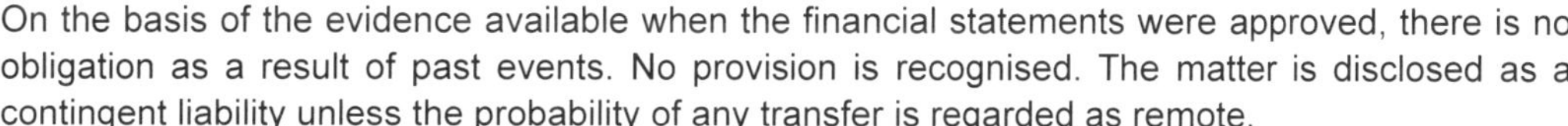

On the basis of the evidence available when the financial statements were approved, there is no obligation as a result of past events. No provision is recognised. The matter is disclosed as a contingent liability unless the probability of any transfer is regarded as remote.

(b) *At 31 December 20X1*

On the basis of the evidence available, there is a present obligation. A transfer of economic benefits in settlement is probable.

A provision is recognised for the best estimate of the amount needed to settle the present obligation.

2.42 Section summary

- The objective of FRS 12 is to ensure that **appropriate recognition criteria** and measurement bases are applied to **provisions and contingencies** and that **sufficient information** is disclosed.
- The FRS seeks to ensure that provisions are **only recognised** when a **measurable obligation** exists. It includes detailed rules that can be used to ascertain when an obligation exists and how to measure the obligation.
- The standard attempts to **eliminate** the '**profit smoothing**' which has gone on before it was issued.

3 DISCOUNTING

3.1 In April 1997 the ASB produced a **working paper** on *Discounting in financial reporting*, which is closely related to reporting the substance of transactions.

3.2 Discounting future cash flows is a technique for reflecting in the valuation of an asset or liability two factors that are taken into account in all rational economic decisions: the **time value of money** and the **risk** associated with the cash flows. Discounting is widely used in financial management and is part of most modern asset-pricing models and most option-pricing models.

3.3 In financial statements, discounting is used in the financial reporting of leases and pension costs. It has also been considered in a number of the ASB's projects, in particular goodwill, impairment of tangible fixed assets, provisions and deferred tax.

3.4 In these projects the ASB is concerned that, if items are recorded in financial statements at an amount based on undiscounted future cash flows, **unlike items will appear alike**. For example, a riskless cash inflow of £1 million due tomorrow, a riskless cash inflow of £1 million due in ten years and a risky cash inflow of £1 million due in ten years would all be recorded at £1 million. However, no entity would regard these assets as equal nor would they cost the same to acquire. In fact, £1 million is an economically meaningless value to attribute to the two assets that generate cash flows in ten years' time. If they are recorded at £1 million, relevant information is lost to the user of the financial statements and misleading information given instead.

3.5 Notwithstanding the fundamental economic truths that discounting can reflect, the ASB believes that it is not necessary or desirable to apply discounting to every item in the balance sheet that is measured by reference to future cash flows, as the period over which the cash flows arise is often **too short** for the effect to be material. In particular, the ASB does not envisage any need to apply discounting to the vast majority of current assets and current liabilities. However, in certain circumstances the effect of discounting on **long-term assets and liabilities** may be very significant and needs to be considered.

3.6 The working paper is not a prelude to a future FRS on this topic and the decision on whether discounting will be prescribed in any particular circumstance will form part of the development of the relevant standard. However, some respondents to Discussion Papers have asked for a **general approach to discounting** to be developed. The working paper is published in response to that request. It seeks to establish principles on how discounting should be applied so that any future FRSs involving discounting will be prepared on a consistent basis. It is a working paper for the ASB's own reference as the ASB considers discounting with various projects.

3.7 The working paper goes on to discuss the different **aspects** of discounting under the following headings.

- Time value of money
- Risk
- Measurement of assets
- Measurement of liabilities
- Inflation
- Tax
- Presentation in financial statements
- Change of rate

We will not go into any detail about these here, but you should be familiar with these issues or terms either within this text or in your management accounting studies.

Chapter roundup

- **FRS 21** defines ***events after the balance sheet date.***
- **Events** after the balance sheet date which provide **additional evidence** of conditions existing at the balance sheet date, will cause **adjustments** to be made to the assets and liabilities in the financial statements.
- **Events** which **do not affect the situation at the balance sheet date** should **not be adjusted for**, but should be **disclosed** in the financial statements.
- Where events indicate that the **going concern concept** is no longer appropriate then the **accounts may have to be restated** on a break-up basis.
- Under FRS 12, a **provision** should be recognised
  - When an entity has a **present obligation**, legal or constructive
  - It is probable that a **transfer of economic benefits** will be required to settle it
  - A **reliable estimate** can be made of its amount
- An entity **should not recognise a contingent asset or liability**, but they **should be disclosed.**
- The ASB has produced a **working paper** on *Discounting* which particularly applies to:
  - Impaired fixed assets (see Chapter 17)
  - Pensions (see Chapter 21)
  - Provisions for environmental liabilities (this chapter)

Quick quiz

1 Dividends declared after the balance sheet date are a liability under FRS 21.

True ☐

False ☐

2 FRS 12 *Provisions, contingent liabilities and contingent assets* requires that material contingent assets and liabilities, existing at the balance sheet date, should be treated as follows.

A Contingent assets and contingent liabilities must always be disclosed in the financial statements.

B Contingent assets must always be accrued and contingent liabilities must always be disclosed in the financial statements.

C Contingent liabilities must always be either accrued or disclosed and contingent assets must always be disclosed in the financial statements.

D Contingent liabilities must always be disclosed (unless remote) and contingent assets must sometimes be disclosed in the financial statements.

3 Castigliano plc has received a claim of £100,000 from one of its customers for defective yarn, which was sold in the year. The customer's claim is *bona fide* and Castigliano's solicitors have advised that it is probable that the claim will be successful.

Catigliano has insured itself against such a risk and the insurance company has agreed to reimburse Castigliano £80,000 of the cost. How should these transactions be represented in the balance sheet and profit and loss account?

Answers to quick quiz

1 False. Such dividends are disclosed in the notes.

2 D Contingent liabilities must be disclosed.

Contingent assets are only disclosed if they are probable, but not virtually certain.

3 FRS 12 requires the reimbursement to be shown as a separate asset in the balance sheet. In the profit and loss account the expense relating to the provision may be presented net of the amount recognised for a reimbursement.

Therefore the most appropriate treatment would be

Balance sheet	P&L
Asset of £80,000 Provision	Net expense of £20,000

Now try the question below from the Exam Question Bank

Number	Level	Marks	Time
Q34	Introductory	n/a	n/a

Mathematical tables

PRESENT VALUE TABLE

Present value of 1 = $(1+r)^{-n}$ where r = discount rate, n = number of periods until payment.

This table shows the present value of £1 per annum, receivable or payable at the end of *n* years.

Periods					Discount rates (r)					
(n)	**1%**	**2%**	**3%**	**4%**	**5%**	**6%**	**7%**	**8%**	**9%**	**10%**
1	0.990	0.980	0.971	0.962	0.952	0.943	0.935	0.926	0.917	0.909
2	0.980	0.961	0.943	0.925	0.907	0.890	0.873	0.857	0.842	0.826
3	0.971	0.942	0.915	0.889	0.864	0.840	0.816	0.794	0.772	0.751
4	0.961	0.924	0.888	0.855	0.823	0.792	0.763	0.735	0.708	0.683
5	0.951	0.906	0.863	0.822	0.784	0.747	0.713	0.681	0.650	0.621
6	0.942	0.888	0.837	0.790	0.746	0.705	0.666	0.630	0.596	0.564
7	0.933	0.871	0.813	0.760	0.711	0.665	0.623	0.583	0.547	0.513
8	0.923	0.853	0.789	0.731	0.677	0.627	0.582	0.540	0.502	0.467
9	0.914	0.837	0.766	0.703	0.645	0.592	0.544	0.500	0.460	0.424
10	0.905	0.820	0.744	0.676	0.614	0.558	0.508	0.463	0.422	0.386
11	0.896	0.804	0.722	0.650	0.585	0.527	0.475	0.429	0.388	0.350
12	0.887	0.788	0.701	0.625	0.557	0.497	0.444	0.397	0.356	0.319
13	0.879	0.773	0.681	0.601	0.530	0.469	0.415	0.368	0.326	0.290
14	0.870	0.758	0.661	0.577	0.505	0.442	0.388	0.340	0.299	0.263
15	0.861	0.743	0.642	0.555	0.481	0.417	0.362	0.315	0.275	0.239
16	0.853	0.728	0.623	0.534	0.458	0.394	0.339	0.292	0.252	0.218
17	0.844	0.714	0.605	0.513	0.436	0.371	0.317	0.270	0.231	0.198
18	0.836	0.700	0.587	0.494	0.416	0.350	0.296	0.250	0.212	0.180
19	0.828	0.686	0.570	0.475	0.396	0.331	0.277	0.232	0.194	0.164
20	0.820	0.673	0.554	0.456	0.377	0.312	0.258	0.215	0.178	0.149

Periods					Discount rates (r)					
(n)	**11%**	**12%**	**13%**	**14%**	**15%**	**16%**	**17%**	**18%**	**19%**	**20%**
1	0.901	0.893	0.885	0.877	0.870	0.862	0.855	0.847	0.840	0.833
2	0.812	0.797	0.783	0.769	0.756	0.743	0.731	0.718	0.706	0.694
3	0.731	0.712	0.693	0.675	0.658	0.641	0.624	0.609	0.593	0.579
4	0.659	0.636	0.613	0.592	0.572	0.552	0.534	0.516	0.499	0.482
5	0.593	0.567	0.543	0.519	0.497	0.476	0.456	0.437	0.419	0.402
6	0.535	0.507	0.480	0.456	0.432	0.410	0.390	0.370	0.352	0.335
7	0.482	0.452	0.425	0.400	0.376	0.354	0.333	0.314	0.296	0.279
8	0.434	0.404	0.376	0.351	0.327	0.305	0.285	0.266	0.249	0.233
9	0.391	0.361	0.333	0.308	0.284	0.263	0.243	0.225	0.209	0.194
10	0.352	0.322	0.295	0.270	0.247	0.227	0.208	0.191	0.176	0.162
11	0.317	0.287	0.261	0.237	0.215	0.195	0.178	0.162	0.148	0.135
12	0.286	0.257	0.231	0.208	0.187	0.168	0.152	0.137	0.124	0.112
13	0.258	0.229	0.204	0.182	0.163	0.145	0.130	0.116	0.104	0.093
14	0.232	0.205	0.181	0.160	0.141	0.125	0.111	0.099	0.088	0.078
15	0.209	0.183	0.160	0.140	0.123	0.108	0.095	0.084	0.074	0.065
16	0.188	0.163	0.141	0.123	0.107	0.093	0.081	0.071	0.062	0.054
17	0.170	0.146	0.125	0.108	0.093	0.080	0.069	0.060	0.052	0.045
18	0.153	0.130	0.111	0.095	0.081	0.069	0.059	0.051	0.044	0.038
19	0.138	0.116	0.098	0.083	0.070	0.060	0.051	0.043	0.037	0.031
20	0.124	0.104	0.087	0.073	0.061	0.051	0.043	0.037	0.031	0.026

CUMULATIVE PRESENT VALUE TABLE

This table shows the present value of £1 per annum, receivable or payable at the end of each year for *n* years.

Periods (n)	Discount rates (r) 1%	2%	3%	4%	5%	6%	7%	8%	9%	10%
1	0.990	0.980	0.971	0.962	0.952	0.943	0.935	0.926	0.917	0.909
2	1.970	1.942	1.913	1.886	1.859	1.833	1.808	1.783	1.759	1.736
3	2.941	2.884	2.829	2.775	2.723	2.673	2.624	2.577	2.531	2.487
4	3.902	3.808	3.717	3.630	3.546	3.465	3.387	3.312	3.240	3.170
5	4.853	4.713	4.580	4.452	4.329	4.212	4.100	3.993	3.890	3.791
6	5.795	5.601	5.417	5.242	5.076	4.917	4.767	4.623	4.486	4.355
7	6.728	6.472	6.230	6.002	5.786	5.582	5.389	5.206	5.033	4.868
8	7.652	7.325	7.020	6.733	6.463	6.210	5.971	5.747	5.535	5.335
9	8.566	8.162	7.786	7.435	7.108	6.802	6.515	6.247	5.995	5.759
10	9.471	8.983	8.530	8.111	7.722	7.360	7.024	6.710	6.418	6.145
11	10.37	9.787	9.253	8.760	8.306	7.887	7.499	7.139	6.805	6.495
12	11.26	10.58	9.954	9.385	8.863	8.384	7.943	7.536	7.161	6.814
13	12.13	11.35	10.63	9.986	9.394	8.853	8.358	7.904	7.487	7.103
14	13.00	12.11	11.30	10.56	9.899	9.295	8.745	8.244	7.786	7.367
15	13.87	12.85	11.94	11.12	10.38	9.712	9.108	8.559	8.061	7.606
16	14.718	13.578	12.561	11.652	10.838	10.106	9.447	8.851	8.313	7.824
17	15.562	14.292	13.166	12.166	11.274	10.477	9.763	9.122	8.544	8.022
18	16.398	14.992	13.754	12.659	11.690	10.828	10.059	9.372	8.756	8.201
19	17.226	15.678	14.324	13.134	12.085	11.158	10.336	9.604	8.950	8.365
20	18.046	16.351	14.877	13.590	12.462	11.470	10.594	9.818	9.129	8.514

Periods (n)	Discount rates (r) 11%	12%	13%	14%	15%	16%	17%	18%	19%	20%
1	0.901	0.893	0.885	0.877	0.870	0.862	0.855	0.847	0.840	0.833
2	1.713	1.690	1.668	1.647	1.626	1.605	1.585	1.566	1.547	1.528
3	2.444	2.402	2.361	2.322	2.283	2.246	2.210	2.174	2.140	2.106
4	3.102	3.037	2.974	2.914	2.855	2.798	2.743	2.690	2.639	2.589
5	3.696	3.605	3.517	3.433	3.352	3.274	3.199	3.127	3.058	2.991
6	4.231	4.111	3.998	3.889	3.784	3.685	3.589	3.498	3.410	3.326
7	4.712	4.564	4.423	4.288	4.160	4.039	3.922	3.812	3.706	3.605
8	5.146	4.968	4.799	4.639	4.487	4.344	4.207	4.078	3.954	3.837
9	5.537	5.328	5.132	4.946	4.772	4.607	4.451	4.303	4.163	4.031
10	5.889	5.650	5.426	5.216	5.019	4.833	4.659	4.494	4.339	4.192
11	6.207	5.938	5.687	5.453	5.234	5.029	4.836	4.656	4.486	4.327
12	6.492	6.194	5.918	5.660	5.421	5.197	4.988	4.793	4.611	4.439
13	6.750	6.424	6.122	5.842	5.583	5.342	5.118	4.910	4.715	4.533
14	6.982	6.628	6.302	6.002	5.724	5.468	5.229	5.008	4.802	4.611
15	7.191	6.811	6.462	6.142	5.847	5.575	5.324	5.092	4.876	4.675
16	7.379	6.974	6.604	6.265	5.954	5.668	5.405	5.162	4.938	4.730
17	7.549	7.120	6.729	6.373	6.047	5.749	5.475	5.222	4.990	4.775
18	7.702	7.250	6.840	6.467	6.128	5.818	5.534	5.273	5.033	4.812
19	7.839	7.366	6.938	6.550	6.198	5.877	5.584	5.316	5.070	4.843
20	7.963	7.469	7.025	6.623	6.259	5.929	5.628	5.353	5.101	4.870

Exam question and answer bank

1 CHARACTERISTICS

The following characteristics have been suggested as being essential in the preparation of financial accounting reports

(a) Understandable
(b) Objective
(c) Comparable
(d) Realistic (ie complete in form and substance)
(e) Relevant
(f) Reliable
(g) Consistent
(h) Timely
(i) Prudent
(j) Economy of presentation

Required

Comment on the suggested characteristics saying whether in your view year end accounts and statements prepared in accordance with normally accepted accounting rules and practices meet these criteria and whether the needs of the various users groups are being met. Give your reasons and if necessary suggest other criteria that you may consider important.

2 STATEMENT OF PRINCIPLES

'A major achievement of the ASB was the development of its *Statement of Principles*. However, it is too theoretical to be applied to accounting standards.'

What are the merits of the *Statement of Principles* and do you agree with the criticism that it is too theoretical.

3 EXCLUSION OF SUBSIDIARIES

In large and complex groups of companies, there are often difficulties in deciding how to treat certain companies when preparing the consolidated financial statements for the year.

Required

(a) State the treatments, required by legislation and by UK accounting standards, of subsidiaries which are unsuitable for inclusion in the consolidated accounts.

(b) Comment on the validity of each of the treatments so required.

4 JASMIN (25 marks)

45 mins

Relevant balance sheets as at 31 March 20X4 are set out below.

	Jasmin (Holdings) plc	*Kasbah plc*	*Fortran plc*
	£'000	£'000	£'000
Tangible fixed assets	289,400	91,800	7,600
Investments			
Shares in Kasbah (at cost)	97,600		
Shares in Fortran (at cost)	8,000		
	395,000		
Current assets			
Stock	285,600	151,400	2,600
Cash	319,000	500	6,800
	604,600	151,900	9,400
Creditors: amounts falling due within one year	289,600	238,500	2,200
Net current assets	315,000	(86,600)	7,200
Total assets less current liabilities	710,000	5,200	14,800

	£'000	£'000	£'000
Capital and reserves			
Called up share capital			
Ordinary £1 shares	60,000	20,000	10,000
10% £1 preference shares		4,000	
Revaluation reserve	40,000		1,200
Profit and loss reserve	610,000	(18,800)	3,600
	710,000	5,200	14,800

You have recently been appointed chief accountant of Jasmin (Holdings) plc and are about to prepare the group balance sheet at 31 March 20X4.

The following points are relevant to the preparation of those accounts.

(a) Jasmin (Holdings) plc owns 90% of the ordinary £1 shares and 20% of the 10% £1 preference shares of Kasbah plc. On 1 April 20X3 Jasmin (Holdings) plc paid £96 million for the ordinary £1 shares and £1.6 million for the 10% £1 preference shares when Kasbah's reserves were a credit balance of £45 million.

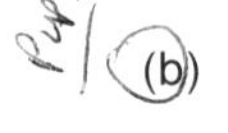

(b) Jasmin (Holdings) plc sells part of its output to Kasbah plc. The stock of Kasbah plc on 31 March 20X4 includes £1.2 million of stock purchased from Jasmin (Holdings) plc at cost plus one third.

(c) The policy of the group is to revalue its tangible fixed assets on a yearly basis. However, the directors of Kasbah plc have always resisted this policy preferring to show tangible fixed assets at historical cost. The market value of the tangible fixed assets of Kasbah plc at 31 March 20X4 is £90 million. The directors of Jasmin (Holdings) plc wish you to follow the requirements of FRS 2 *Accounting for subsidiary undertakings* in respect of the value of tangible fixed assets to be included in the group accounts.

(d) The ordinary £1 shares of Fortran plc are split into 6 million 'A' ordinary £1 shares and 4 million 'B' ordinary £1 shares. Holders of 'A' shares are assigned 1 vote and holders of 'B' ordinary shares are assigned 2 votes per share. On 1 April 20X3 Jasmin (Holdings) plc acquired 80% of the 'A' ordinary shares and 10% of the 'B' ordinary shares when the profit and loss reserve of Fortran plc was £1.6 million and the revaluation reserve was £2 million. The 'A' ordinary shares and 'B' ordinary shares carry equal rights to share in the company's profit and losses.

(e) The fair values of Kasbah plc and Fortran plc were not materially different from their book values at the time of acquisition of their shares by Jasmin (Holdings) plc.

(f) Goodwill arising on acquisition is amortised over five years.

(g) Kasbah plc has paid its preference dividend for the current year but no other dividends are proposed by the group companies. The preference dividend was paid shortly after the interim results of Kasbah plc were announced and was deemed to be a legal dividend by the auditors.

(h) Because of its substantial losses during the period, the directors of Jasmin (Holdings) plc wish to exclude the financial statements of Kasbah plc from the group accounts on the grounds that Kasbah plc's output is not similar to that of Jasmin (Holdings) plc and that the resultant accounts therefore would be misleading. Jasmin (Holdings) plc produces synthetic yarn and Kasbah plc produces garments.

Required

(a) List the conditions for exclusion of subsidiaries from consolidation for the directors of Jasmin (Holdings) plc and state whether Kasbah plc may be excluded on these grounds. (4 marks)

(b) Prepare a consolidated balance sheet for Jasmin (Holdings) Group plc for the year ending 31 March 20X4. (All calculations should be made to the nearest thousand pounds.) (18 marks)

(c) Comment briefly on the possible implications of the size of Kasbah plc's losses for the year for the group accounts and the individual accounts of Jasmin (Holdings) plc. (3 marks)

5 WATER (25 marks) *45 mins*

Fire Ltd, Brimstone Ltd and Water Ltd are three companies which work in association within the music industry. So close is their association that they operate a current account system for transactions between themselves, and have adopted 31 December as their accounting date.

On 1 January 20X0 Fire Ltd purchased 80,000 ordinary shares of 50p each in Brimstone Ltd for £55,000. On 31 December 20X0 Water Ltd purchased 60,000 ordinary shares of 50p each in Brimstone Ltd for £48,000 and the entire share capital of Fire Ltd for £280,000.

Draft accounts in respect of the year ended 31 December 20X0 reveal balance sheets for the three companies as follows.

	Water Ltd	Fire Ltd	Brimstone Ltd
	£	£	£
Credits			
Called up share capital			
Ordinary shares of £1 each	500,000	200,000	-
Ordinary shares of 50p each	-	-	100,000
Capital reserves 1 January 20X0	80,000	35,000	24,000
Profit and loss account as at 1 January 20X0	18,000	4,900	6,000
Profit for the year ended 31 December 20X0	77,219	31,200	12,000
Provision for depreciation of plant	60,406	45,215	14,623
Overdraft	-	1,613	-
Trade creditors	42,068	37,917	32,989
Current accounts	8,300	-	-
	785,993	355,845	189,612
Debits			
Freehold land and buildings	200,000	150,000	102,000
Plant and machinery	122,415	80,690	25,081
Investments at cost			
Shares in Fire Ltd	280,000	-	-
Shares in Brimstone Ltd	48,000	55,000	-
Stocks	65,820	37,820	34,215
Debtors	58,931	31,615	18,097
Current accounts	-	720	7,800
Cash	10,827	-	2,419
	785,993	355,845	189,612

The following additional information is available.

(a) The current account balances are made up as follows.

Water Ltd	Fire Ltd - £820 Cr, and Brimstone Ltd - £7,480 Cr.
Fire Ltd	Water Ltd - £820 Dr, and Brimstone Ltd £100 Cr.
Brimstone Ltd	Water Ltd - £7,700 Dr, and Fire Ltd - £100 Dr.

(b) A cheque for £220, drawn by Water Ltd in favour of Brimstone Ltd, is in transit at 31 December 20X0.

(c) 20% of the closing stock of Fire Ltd has been sold to that company by Water Ltd at a mark-up of $33\frac{1}{3}$ % on cost.

(d) Water Ltd proposed to pay a dividend of 2%. The dividend was declared before the year end.

(e) The estimated liability of the three companies for corporation tax for the year to 31 December 20X0 is as follows: Water Ltd - £24,300; Fire Ltd - £9,600; Brimstone Ltd - £4,800. Tax has not yet been provided for in the accounts.

(f) Any goodwill is to be capitalised as an asset in the balance sheet, subject to an annual impairment review.

You are required to prepare the consolidated balance sheet of Water Ltd and its subsidiary companies as at 31 December 20X0.

6 PHILLIPS, BYLETT AND MAGGS (25 marks) *45 mins*

Phillips Ltd has two subsidiaries, Bylett Ltd and Maggs Ltd. The draft accounts of the three companies are as follows.

PROFIT AND LOSS ACCOUNTS
FOR THE YEAR ENDED 31 DECEMBER 20X7

	Phillips Ltd	*Bylett Ltd*	*Maggs Ltd*
	£'000	£'000	£'000
Turnover	800	640	310
Operating costs	660	540	390
Profit before tax	140	100	(80)
Dividends received	19		
	159		
Taxation	69	40	-
	90	60	(80)
Dividends	40	30	-
Retained for the year	50	30	(80)

BALANCE SHEETS AS AT 31 DECEMBER 20X7

	Phillips Ltd	*Bylett Ltd*	*Maggs Ltd*
	£'000	£'000	£'000
Tangible assets (NBV)	2,195	1,789	761
Investment in Bylett Ltd (950,000 £1 shares at cost)	1,250	-	-
Investment in Maggs Ltd (800,000 £1 shares at cost)	(50)	-	-
Current assets			
Stock	1,120	1,362	949
Debtors	2,950	894	1,320
Cash	250	78	-
Liabilities			
Creditors	(1,895)	(967)	(1,234)
Proposed dividends	(40)	(10)	-
Bank overdraft	-	-	(642)
13% Loan stock	(1,200)	-	-
10% Debentures	-	(500)	-
Deferred tax	(980)	(746)	(129)
	3,600	1,900	1,025

	Phillips Ltd	*Bylett Ltd*	*Maggs Ltd*
	£'000	£'000	£'000
Share capital and reserves			
£1 ordinary shares	2,000	1,000	1,000
Profit and loss	1,600	900	25
Shareholders' funds	3,600	1,900	1,025

Notes

(a) Phillips acquired its holdings in Bylett Ltd and Maggs Ltd on 1 January 20X4 when the reserves of those companies were £400,000 and £100,000 respectively. Goodwill is capitalised as an intangible asset in the balance sheet and amortised over a useful economic life of five years.

(b) During the year Phillips Ltd made the following disposals.

On 30 September 200,000 shares in Bylett Ltd for £650,000.
On 30 December its entire holding in Maggs Ltd for £1,050,000.

In each case the proceeds were credited against the appropriate 'investment in subsidiary' account leaving the balances shown above.

(c) It is thought that tax payable in connection with the sale of shares in Bylett Ltd and Maggs Ltd will be £75,000 and £15,000 respectively.

(d) Bylett Ltd paid a dividend of £20,000 on 30 June 20X7. All proposed dividends were proposed before the year end.

Required

(a) Prepare the draft summarised consolidated profit and loss account of Phillips Ltd for the year to 31 December 20X7. (10 marks)

(b) Prepare the draft summarised consolidated balance sheet as on that date. (10 marks)

(c) Analyse the movement on consolidated reserves for the year. (5 marks)

7 TWO GROUPS (25 marks) *45 mins*

Greene plc, Ross plc, Benton Ltd and Carter Ltd produced the following draft financial statements as at 31 December 20X7.

BALANCE SHEETS AT 31 DECEMBER 20X7

	Green plc	*Ross plc*	*Benton Ltd*	*Carter Ltd*
	£'000	£'000	£'000	£'000
Fixed assets				
Tangible assets	87,500	13,750	1,500	2,250
Investment in Ross plc	22,500			
Investment in Benton Ltd		2,250		
Investment in Carter Ltd	1,250			
	111,250	16,000		
Net current assets	45,750	10,000	1,750	1,500
Creditors falling due after 1 year	3,250	750	250	125
	153,750	25,250	3,000	3,625
Capital and reserves				
Called up share capital of £1	33,750	2,500	750	500
Share premium account	38,750	2,500	250	500
Profit and loss account	81,250	20,250	2,000	2,625
	153,750	25,250	3,000	3,625

PROFIT AND LOSS ACCOUNTS FOR THE YEAR ENDED 31 DECEMBER 20X7

	Green plc	*Ross plc*	*Benton Ltd*	*Carter Ltd*
	£'000	£'000	£'000	£'000
Turnover	200,000	75,000	8,125	13,250
Cost of sales	125,000	50,000	4,875	8,000
Gross profit	75,000	25,000	3,250	5,250
Administrative and distribution costs	50,000	10,000	875	3,125
Income from group companies	325	100	-	-
Operating profit before taxation	25,325	15,100	2,375	2,125
Taxation	7,500	5,000	1,000	625
Profit on ordinary activities after tax	17,825	10,100	1,375	1,500
Dividends paid	750	250	125	125
Retained profit for year	17,075	9,850	1,250	1,375

(a) The following demerger was carried out on 31 December 20X7, to split the group into two separate groups.

(i) Greene plc disposed of its holding in Ross plc to a new company RE plc, in return for which 7.5m ordinary shares in RE plc were issued and given to the shareholders of Greene plc. There was no profit or loss on disposal because the demerger only involved a distribution to the shareholders of Greene plc of the shares in RE plc.

(ii) As result of the demerger two new and distinct groups were created. Greene plc controlled one group consisting of Greene plc and Carter Ltd. RE plc controlled a group consisting of RE plc and the Ross plc group.

(iii) The transaction qualifies as a merger and the group wishes to take advantage of the provisions of CA 1985 regarding group reconstruction relief.

(b) The dates of acquisitions, holdings and other relevant information on the group companies is as follows.

Holding company	Company acquired	% holding acquired	Dates	Share premium a/c	P&L account
				£'000	£'000
Greene plc	Ross plc	100	1.8 X4	2,500	6,250
Green plc	Carter Ltd	60	1.12 X5	500	750
Ross plc	Benton Ltd	80	1.1 X6	250	1,500

(c) The recipient companies have accounted for dividends received from group companies. The demerger of the Ross plc group and the distribution to RE plc will be shown in the Greene plc P&L account rather than as a movement on reserves.

(d) No fair value adjustments are required. The group policy is to capitalise goodwill as an asset in the balance sheet. To date no write down for impairment has been considered necessary.

Required

(a) Prepare the consolidated balance sheet of the Ross group plc for the year ended 31 December 20X7. (7 marks)

(b) For the Greene group plc, prepare the consolidated P&L account and balance sheet, after the demerger, as at 31 December 20X7. The provisions of FRS 3 should be followed. (16 marks)

(c) Calculate the share capital and reserves of the RE Group plc as at 31 December 20X7. (2 marks)

8 PLANS (Pilot paper - 25 marks) *45 mins*

X, a public limited company, owns 100 per cent of companies Y and Z which are both limited companies. The X group operates in the telecommunication industry and the directors are considering three different plans to restructure the group. The directors feel that the current group structure is not serving the best interests of the shareholders and wish to explore possible alternative group structures.

The balance sheets of X and its subsidiaries Y and Z at 31 May 20Y1 are as follows:

	X plc	*Y plc*	*Z plc*
	£m	£m	£m
Tangible fixed assets	600	200	45
Cost of investment in Y	60		
Cost of investment in Z	70		
Net current assets	160	100	20
	890	300	65
Share capital - ordinary shares of £1	120	60	40
Profit and loss account	770	240	25
	890	300	65

X acquired the investment in Z on 1 June 20X5 when the profit and loss account balance was £20 million. The fair value of the net assets of Z on 1 June 20X5 was £60 million. Company Y was incorporated by X and has always been a 100 per cent owned subsidiary. Goodwill is written off over four years. The fair value of the assets of Y at 31 May 20Y1 is £310 million and of Z is £80 million.

The directors are unsure as to the impact or implications that the following plans are likely to have on the individual accounts of the companies and the group accounts.

The three different plans to restructure the group are as follows.

Plan 1

Y is to purchase the whole of X's investment in Z. The directors are undecided as to whether the purchase consideration should be 50 million £1 ordinary shares of Y or a cash amount of £75 million. (10 marks)

Plan 2

A new company, W, is to be formed which will issue shares to the shareholders of X in exchange for X's investment in Y and Z. W is to issue 130 million ordinary shares of £1 to the shareholders of X in exchange for their shares held in Y and Z. The group is being split into two separate companies W and X which will be quoted on the Stock Exchange.

(8 marks)

Plan 3

The assets and trade of Z are to be transferred to Y. Company Z would initially become a non-trading company. The assets and trade are to be transferred at their book value. The consideration for the transfer will be £60 million which will be left outstanding on the inter company account between Y and Z. (7 marks)

Required

Discuss the key considerations and the accounting implications of the above plans for the X group. Your answer should show the potential impact on the individual accounts of X, Y and Z and the group accounts after each plan has been implemented.

(The mark allocation is shown in brackets next to each 'plan'.)

9 ELIZABETH

The summarised balance sheets of four companies as at 30 November 20X2 were as follows.

	Elizabeth Ltd	*Jane Ltd*	*Kitty Ltd*	*Lydia Ltd*
	£'000	£'000	£'000	£'000
Fixed assets (NBV)	300	250	190	220
Current assets	261	139	142	201
Creditors: amounts falling due within one year	(168)	(141)	(92)	(174)
Creditors: amounts falling due after more than one year	(62)	(72)	(54)	(62)
Provisions for liabilities and charges	(8)	-	-	(14)
	323	176	186	171
Called up share capital	200	100	100	100
Share premium account	50	-	20	15
Revaluation reserve	-	-	13	19
Other reserves	12	-	3	-
Profit and loss account	61	76	50	37
	323	176	186	171
Fixed assets at fair value (£'000)	400	300	250	270
Market value of ordinary shares	£2.50	£2.00	£1.30	£1.90

Additional information

(a) The share capital of Elizabeth Ltd, Jane Ltd and Kitty Ltd consists entirely of fully paid up £1 ordinary shares. Each share carries one vote. Lydia Ltd has two classes of equity share capital as follows.

50,000 fully paid up £1 ordinary shares (voting);
50,000 fully paid up £1 ordinary 'A' shares (non-voting).

(b) On 1 December 20X2 Elizabeth acquired the following investments.

(i) 90,000 shares in Jane Ltd as the result of an offer to all the shareholders in that company. The concession was 10 shares in Elizabeth Ltd for every 9 acquired in Jane Ltd.

(ii) 83,000 shares in Kitty Ltd in a share for share exchange. Elizabeth Ltd had previously acquired 12,000 shares in Kitty Ltd for £2.50 cash each.

(iii) 50,000 ordinary voting shares of Lydia Ltd in a share for share exchange.

(c) Apart from the 12,000 shares in Kitty Ltd which are included in the figure for fixed assets, Elizabeth Ltd had no previous investments.

Required

(a) Define 'equity share capital'.

(b) Prepare:

(i) The balance sheet of Elizabeth Ltd
(ii) The consolidated balance sheet of Elizabeth Ltd

as at 1 December 20X2 in accordance with FRS 6 and the Companies Act 1985 as amended by the Companies Act 1989.

Note. For the purposes of this question, assume that all the FRS 6 requirements for merger accounting have been met, where the CA 1985 criteria have not been breached.

10 BARRY

Barry plc has owned 18,000 shares in Coupar Ltd for many years and on 30 September 20X4 increased its shareholding in Coupar Ltd by purchasing 120,000 shares. The consideration comprised:

50,000	ordinary shares of £1 in Barry plc
£20,000	unsecured loan stock issued by Barry plc
£10,000	cash to be paid on 30 September 20X5
20,000	ordinary shares of £1 in Barry plc, dependent on profits of Coupar Ltd increasing by 10% for each of the two years to 30 September 20X6.

The summarised balance sheets of the companies as on 30 September 20X4 show:

	Barry plc	*Coupar Ltd*
Fixed assets	£	£
Freehold property	1,400,000	100,000
Plant and machinery	300,000	50,000
Motor vehicles	100,000	20,000
Investment in Coupar Ltd	50,000	-
	1,850,000	170,000
Current assets		
Stock	180,000	40,000
Debtors	190,000	30,000
Prepayments	30,000	10,000
Cash and bank	80,000	5,000
	480,000	85,000
Current liabilities	(210,000)	(65,000)
Net current liabilities	270,000	20,000
Long term liabilities		
Unsecured loan stock	(200,000)	-
	1,920,000	190,000
Share capital - ordinary shares of £1 each	1,300,000	150,000
Reserves	620,000	40,000
	1,920,000	190,000

Other information

(a) The recent purchase of 120,000 shares has not yet been reflected in Barry plc's balance sheet as on 30 September 20X4.

(b) The recent spread of market prices of Barry plc's securities have been:

Ordinary shares of £1 each	120 - 130p
Unsecured loan stock	55 - 65p

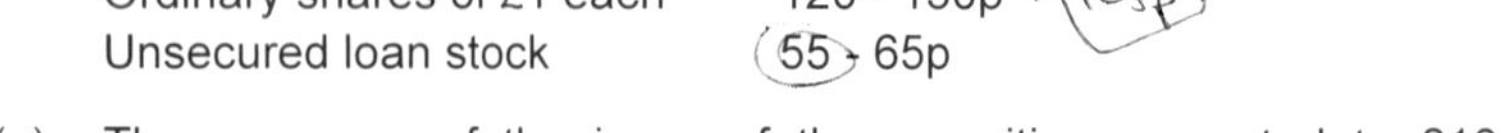

(c) The expenses of the issue of the securities amounted to £10,000 and have not yet been accounted for.

(d) Barry plc's bankers have recently made loans to the company at 10% pa rate of interest.

(e) The history of Coupar Ltd's profitability has shown that profits have risen evenly by 15% pa over the last three years.

(f) The fair values of the assets of Coupar Ltd as on 30 September 20X4 are the same as book values, except for the valuation of:

	£
Freehold property	170,000
Plant and machinery	40,000
Motor vehicles	10,000
Stock	30,000
Prepayments	Nil

(g) Barry plc's investigations into Coupar Ltd have revealed an outstanding claim from a customer against the company for £50,000. Legal advice has been sought and it is probable that this amount will be paid.

Required

Prepare the consolidated balance sheet of Barry plc as on 30 September 20X4 using the Companies Acts merger relief provisions. Goodwill is to be capitalised as an asset in the consolidated balance sheet.

11 TILES (25 marks) *45 mins*

On 30 September 20X1 Tiles plc acquired 90% of the issued ordinary capital of Ceramic Inc which trades in Pinto where the currency is Pin.

The following are balance sheets as at 31 December 20X1.

	Tiles plc	*Ceramic Inc*
	£'000	Pin ('000)
Tangible fixed assets	35,640	47,376
Investment in subsidiary	37,200	
Current assets less current liabilities	51,072	34,920
Long term loans	(22,320)	(14,400)
	101,592	67,896
Ordinary share capital £1/1 Pin	50,000	36,000
Retained reserves		
As at 31 December 20X0	30,064	25,920
Year to 31 December 20X1	21,528	5,976
	101,592	67,896

You are provided with the following information.

(a) The holding company's long term loans include the following.

(i) A loan from the Bank of Pinto, repayable in 20Y9, used to finance the purchase of the shares. £15.84m was received at the rate of 5.4 Pins = £1.

(ii) £5,760,000 borrowed from an Australian bank (to build a new factory) on 1 April 20X0 at 2.1 A$ -= £1. The rate at 31 December 20X1 was 2.3.

The loans are included in the balance sheet at the amount originally received.

(b) The fair value of Ceramic's fixed assets was considered to be 108 million Pins on 30 September 20X1. No adjustments have been made in the subsidiary's books and the depreciation charge for the year is 10,944,000 Pins. Based on the revalued amount, the depreciation for the post acquisition period would be 3,600,000 Pins. The fixed assets were acquired two years ago when the rate was 6 Pins = £1.

(c) It is the company's policy to capitalise goodwill as an asset and carry out annual impairment reviews. No impairment is considered to have taken place since acquisition.

(d) The company's policy is to translate the profit and loss account at the average rate and the directors wish to take advantage of the hedging provisions.

(e) Rates of exchange have been as follows:

	Pins = £1
31 September 20X1	5.4
Average for the three months to 31 December 20X1	4.8
31 December 20X1	4.2

Required

(a) Discuss the reasons for having two methods of translating foreign currency, the closing rate method and the temporal method. Is the decision of which to use not objective enough? Is it important? (8 marks)

(b) Prepare the consolidated balance sheet and a statement of consolidated reserves of Tiles plc and subsidiary at 31 December 20X1 under the closing rate method. (17 marks)

Work to the nearest £'000.

12 HASELEY (25 marks) *45 mins*

You are the group financial controller of Haseley Services Ltd and are currently drafting the group accounts for the year ended 30 June 20X7. You asked your assistant to prepare the consolidated cash flow statement and he has prepared the workings set out below. He has now asked for your assistance in completing the statement.

		Consolidated balance sheet at 30 June		*Movement*
		20X7	*20X6*	*in year*
	Note	£'000	£'000	£'000
Tangible fixed assets	1	3,345	2,103	1,242
Goodwill	2	12,322	1,300	11,022
Stock		2,365	1,803	562
Debtors		4,587	3,024	1,563
Short term deposits	3	564	1,532	(968)
Cash		322	2,505	(2,183)
Trade creditors		(3,578)	(2,035)	(1,543)
Accruals		(3,019)	(1,270)	(1,749)
Lease creditors	4	(989)	(545)	(444)
Corporation tax		(393)	(450)	57
Interest payable		(24)	0	(24)
Bank overdraft		(279)	0	(279)
Bank loans	5	(6,000)	0	(6,000)
Proposed dividend		(840)	(720)	(120)
Deferred taxation		(526)	(425)	(101)
		7,857	6,822	1,035
Share capital		(3,200)	(3,200)	0
Share premium account		(2,400)	(2,400)	0
Revaluation reserve		(1,240)	(560)	(680)
Profit and loss account	6	(1,017)	(662)	(355)
		(7,857)	(6,822)	(1,035)

Notes to cash flow workings

1 *Tangible fixed assets*

The movement in the year was as follows.

	£'000
Brought forward	2,103
Additions - leased	345
- other	456
Disposals at net book value	(425)
Revaluation	1,000
Acquisition of subsidiary	679
Disposal of subsidiary	(240)
Depreciation	(573)
Carried forward	3,345

Disposals comprise:

- Equipment with a net book value of £25,000 which gave rise to a loss on disposal of £5,000

- Freehold property with a net book value of £400,000 which was sold for £1 million. It had previously been revalued and the relevant balance of £320,000 on the revaluation reserve was transferred to the profit and loss account reserve

2 *Acquisition and disposal of subsidiaries*

Disposal of Wheatley Ltd

	£'000
Fixed assets	240
Stock	491
Trade debtors	553
Cash	103
Trade creditors	(672)
Accruals	(304)
Net assets	411

At the date of disposal, goodwill of £1.2 million relating to the original acquisition of Wheatley Ltd was included in the group balance sheet.

Cash consideration of £2.5 million was received during February 20X7.

Acquisition of Cuxham Ltd

Cuxham Ltd was acquired for total consideration of £14 million, of which £12 million was paid in cash on 30 June 20X7. The remaining £2 million is to be paid on 30 June 20X8.

Cuxham Ltd's net assets at the date of acquisition were as follows.

	£'000
Fixed assets	679
Stock	1,235
Trade debtors	2,364
Cash	335
Trade creditors	(1,979)
Accruals	(504)
Lease creditors	(331)
Deferred taxation	(121)
	1,678

Goodwill of £12,322,000 has been capitalised and will be written off over 20 years.

3 *Short-term deposits*

Short-term deposits can be analysed as follows.

	20X7	*20X6*
	£'000	£'000
Bank deposits available on demand	164	132
3 month deposits	400	1,400
	564	1,532

4 *Lease creditors*

The movement in the year can be summarised as follows.

	£'000
Brought forward	(545)
Additions	(345)
Capital payments	232
Acquisition of subsidiary	(331)
	(989)

5 *Bank loans*

The bank loan was taken out on 25 June 20X7 to fund the acquisition of Cuxham Ltd. It is repayable in annual instalments over five years.

6 *Profit and loss account*

The movement in the year can be summarised as follows.

	£'000
Brought forward	662
Profit for year	
Operating profit	1,300
Gain on disposal of fixed assets	595
Gain on disposal of subsidiary	889
Interest received	200
Interest paid on finance leases	(39)
Other interest paid	(30)
Taxation	(680)
Dividends	(2,200)
	35
Transfer from reserves	320
Carried forward	1,017

Required

(a) Using the workings prepared by your assistant, draft the consolidated cash flow statement for Haseley Services Ltd for the year ended 30 June 20X7. The cash flow statement should be in a format suitable for inclusion in the group accounts but the associated notes are not required. All workings should be shown. (19 marks)

(b) Prepare brief notes for a discussion with Mr Littlemore, the new owner/manager of Haseley Services Ltd. Mr Littlemore, who has no accounting experience, has asked you to explain to him what the cash flow statement for Haseley Services Ltd shows and, in particular, what information it gives him about the group's future ability to generate cash. (6 marks)

13 WIMBORNE

Wimborne plc is the holding company of an international trading group. The draft profit and loss account and balance sheet of the Wimborne group are as follows.

CONSOLIDATED PROFIT AND LOSS ACCOUNT

		Year ended 30 September 20X7
	Note	£'000
Turnover		112,430
Cost of sales		(58,583)
Gross profit		53,847
Distribution costs and administrative expenses		(31,456)
Operating profit		22,391
Interest payable		(1,350)
Income from fixed asset investments		175
Exceptional item	1	(2,500)
Profit before tax		18,716
Tax	2	(6,750)
Profit after tax		11,966
Minority interests		(1,545)
Dividends		(1,800)
Retained profit for the year	3	8,621

CONSOLIDATED BALANCE SHEET

	Note	30 Sept 20X7 £'000	30 Sept 20X6 £'000
Fixed assets			
Tangible	4	25,700	22,430
Investments		3,400	6,900
Current assets			
Stocks		19,773	17,702
Debtors		12,470	12,358
Cash at bank and in hand	5	10,125	5,100
Creditors due within one year			
Trade creditors		(23,365)	(25,592)
Dividend payable to shareholders		(1,200)	(1,100)
Dividends payable to minorities		(350)	(325)
Corporation tax		(6,370)	(4,829)
Creditors due after more than one year			
Loan from banks		(7,500)	(11,850)
Deferred taxation		(4,300)	(3,094)
		28,383	17,700
Capital and reserves			
Share capital		3,000	3,000
Reserves	3	20,283	11,300
Minority interests		5,100	3,400
		28,383	17,700

Notes

1 *Exceptional item*

This arose on the disposal of the group's 15% interest in Ringwood Ltd. Ringwood Ltd had cost £4.5m in 19W6 and was disposed of in the year to 30 September 20X7 for £2m.

2 *Tax*

The tax charge is made up as follows.

	£'000
Corporation tax	5,544
Deferred tax	1,206
	6,750

3 *Reserves*

Movements on reserves in the year ended 30 September 20X7 were as follows.

	£'000
Reserves at 1 October 20X6	11,300
Retained profit for the year	8,621
Exchange gain on translation	1,762
Revaluation of property	(1,400)
Reserves at 30 September 20X7	20,283

The exchange gain is made up as follows.

	£'000
Fixed assets	2,117
Stocks	205
Debtors	158
Cash	140
Loans	(476)
Other creditors	(124)
Minority interests	(258)
	1,762

4 *Fixed assets*

The depreciation charge for the year ended 30 September 20X7 was £3,197,000. Fixed asset additions were £5,750,000.

5 *Cash at bank and in hand*

This comprises:

	20X7	*20X6*
	£'000	£'000
Six months term deposits	7,500	5,000
30-day money market deposit	2,000	-
Current balances	625	100
	10,125	5,100

Required

Prepare the consolidated cash flow statement for the Wimborne plc group for the year ended 30 September 20X7 in accordance with FRS 1. State clearly any assumptions you make and list any further information which would be helpful.

You are *not* required to produce the reconciliation of movement in cash to movement in net debt or the notes to the cash flow statement other than reconciliation of operating profit to net cash flow from operating activities.

14 PORTAL (Pilot paper - 25 marks) *45 mins*

Portal Group, a public limited company, has prepared the following group cash flow statement for the year ended 31 December 20X0.

PORTAL GROUP PLC
GROUP STATEMENT OF CASH FLOWS
FOR THE YEAR ENDED 31 DECEMBER 20X0 (DRAFT)

	£m	£m
Net cash inflow from operating activities		875
Returns on investments and servicing of finance		
Interest received	26	
Interest paid	(9)	
Minority interest	(40)	
		(23)
Taxation		31
Capital expenditure		
Purchase of tangible fixed assets	(380)	
Disposals and transfers of fixed assets at carrying value	1,585	
		1,205
Acquisitions and disposals		
Disposal of subsidiary	(25)	
Purchase of interest in joint venture	(225)	
		(250)
Net cash inflow before management of liquid resources and financing		1,838
Management of liquid resources		
Decrease in short term deposits		(143)
Increase in cash in the period		1,695

The accountant has asked your advice on certain technical matters relating to the preparation of the group cash flow statement. Additionally the accountant has asked you to prepare a presentation for the directors on the usefulness and meaning of cash flow statements generally and specifically on the group cash flow statement of Portal.

The accountant has informed you that the actual change in the cash balance for the period is £165 million, which does not reconcile with the figures in the draft group cash flow statement above of £1,695 million.

The accountant feels that the reason for the difference lies in the incorrect treatment of several elements of the cash flow statement of which he had little technical knowledge. The following information relates to these elements.

(a) Portal has disposed of a subsidiary company, Web plc, during the year. At the date of disposal (1 June 20X0) the following balance sheet was prepared for Web plc.

		£m	£m
Tangible fixed assets:	valuation		340
	depreciation		(30)
			310
Stocks		60	
Debtors		50	
Cash at bank and in hand		130	
		240	
Creditors: amounts falling due within one year (including taxation £25 million)		(130)	
			110
			420
Called up share capital			100
Profit and loss account			320
			420

The loss on the sale of the subsidiary in the group accounts comprised:

		£m
Sales proceeds:	ordinary shares	300
	cash	75
		375
Net assets sold (80% of 420)		(336)
Goodwill		(64)
Loss on sale		(25)

The accountant was unsure as to how to deal with the above disposal and has simply included the above loss in the cash flow statement without further adjustments.

(b) During the year, Portal has transferred several of its tangible assets to a newly created company, Site plc, which is owned jointly with another company.

The following information relates to the accounting for the investment in Site plc.

		£m
Purchase cost:	fixed assets transferred	200
	cash	25
		225
Dividend received		(10)
Profit for year on joint venture after tax		55
Revaluation of fixed assets		30
Closing balance per balance sheet - Site plc		300

The cash flow statement showed the cost of purchasing a stake in Site plc of £225 million.

(c) The taxation amount in the cash flow statement is the difference between the opening and closing balances on the taxation account. The charge for taxation in the profit and loss account is £191 million of which £20 million related to the taxation on the joint venture.

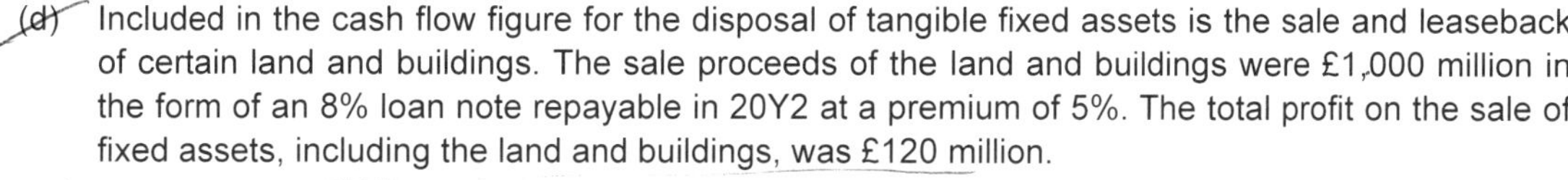

(d) Included in the cash flow figure for the disposal of tangible fixed assets is the sale and leaseback of certain land and buildings. The sale proceeds of the land and buildings were £1,000 million in the form of an 8% loan note repayable in 20Y2 at a premium of 5%. The total profit on the sale of fixed assets, including the land and buildings, was £120 million.

(e) The minority interest figure in the statement comprised the difference between the opening and closing balance sheet totals. The profit attributable to the minority interest for the year was £75 million.

(f) The net cash inflow from operating activities is the profit on ordinary activities before taxation adjusted for the balance sheet movement in stocks, debtors and creditors and the depreciation charge for the year. The interest receivable credited to the profit and loss account was £27 million and the interest payable was £19 million.

Required

(a) Prepare a revised group cash flow statement for Portal plc, taking into account notes (a) to (f) above. (18 marks)

(b) Prepare a brief presentation on the usefulness and information content of group cash flow statements generally and specifically on the group cash flow statement of Portal plc. (7 marks)

15 UPERAND (25 marks) *45 mins*

Uperand plc is a family controlled company that has grown in 10 years from having 10 employees to 350 employees. The company is now considering a listing on the AIM (Alternative Investment Market) through an offer for sale.

Uperand's managing director believes that, as the company has assets with a book vale of £22 million and reserves of more than £10 million, the company's value when listed should be at least £32 million. He proposes that 400,000 new shares should be issued to the public to raise approximately £2.5 million for future expansion.

The company's financial performance for the last three years is summarised below.

PROFIT AND LOSS ACCOUNTS FOR THE YEARS ENDED 31 MARCH

	20X6	*20X7*	*20X8*
	£'000	£'000	£'000
Sales	13,300	16,200	19,000
Cost of goods sold	9,000	11,500	14,400
Gross profit	4,300	4,700	4,600
Administrative expenses	800	900	950
Selling, distribution and other expenses	600	700	750
Interest payable	500	700	800
Taxable profit	2,400	2,400	2,100
Taxation	840	840	735
Retained profit	1,560	1,560	1,365

BALANCE SHEETS AS AT 31 MARCH

	20X6	*20X7*	*20X8*
	£'000	£'000	£'000
Fixed assets (net)	8,500	10,000	12,000
Current assets			
Stock	3,600	4,500	5,400
Debtors	2,800	3,500	4,500
Cash	100	100	100
Total assets	15,000	18,100	22,000
Represented by			
Ordinary shares (10p par value)	500	500	500
Reserves	7,800	9,360	10,750
Shareholders' funds	8,300	9,860	11,225
Long-term funds	2,000	3,500	5,000
Current liabilities			
Bank loans	1,400	500	587
Trade creditors	2,500	3,400	4,400
Taxation	800	840	788
	15,000	18,100	22,000

Additional notes relating to the 20X8 accounts are as follows.

(a) Sales are expected to grow by approximately 20% per year.

(b) The company owns a patent which could be sold for £1m more than its book value.

(c) Two per cent of debtors are expected to default.

(d) Ten per cent of stock (by value) is considered to be obsolete.

(e) Machinery has an estimated realisable value £500,000 less than its book value, and buildings £1.5 million more that their written-down value.

(f) Land has never been revalued. Land costing £50,000 was purchased 10 years ago and a further plot at a cost of £300,000 six years ago. The value of industrial land has increased by an average of 15% during the last 10 years.

Uperand's management has obtained some financial information on the AIM listed companies in the same industry, which have the same number of listed ordinary shares as Uperand.

	Stiver plc	*Gogetor plc*
Market capitalisation	35 million	£4.2 million
Earnings per share	46 pence	5.5 pence
Beta coefficient	1.4	1.35

Acting as an external consultant to Uperand prepare a report for the board of directors of Uperand which discusses:

(a) The accuracy of the managing director's assessment of the company's value
(b) The number of shares that should be issued

If you do not agree with the managing director you are required:

(a) To produce a revised estimate (or estimates) of the value of Uperand for purposes of an AIM listing

(b) To estimate the number of shares which should be issued

16 ANDREWS (25 marks) *45 mins*

Andrews Ltd, a manufacturer and retailer of golf clubs, disposed of its retail outlets in January 20X5. Extracts from the company's draft financial statements show:

PROFIT AND LOSS ACCOUNT
FOR THE YEAR ENDED 31 OCTOBER 20X5

	20X5	*20X4*
	£'000	£'000
Turnover	3,900	4,300
Cost of sales	(2,652)	(2,795)
Gross profit	1,248	1,505
Distribution costs	(302)	(430)
Administrative costs	(107)	(210)
Operating profit	839	865
Exceptional item - sale of retail outlets	16	-
	855	865
Interest payable	(4)	(15)
	851	850
Taxation	(290)	(285)
	561	565
Dividends	(96)	(105)
	465	460

BALANCE SHEET AS AT 31 OCTOBER 20X5

	20X5		*20X4*	
	£'000	£'000	£'000	£'000
Fixed assets		970		810
Current assets				
Stocks	470		340	
Debtors	420		360	
Investments	50		-	
Cash at bank and in hand	20		40	
	960		740	
Current liabilities	(590)		(725)	
Net current assets		370		15
Long term liabilities		-		(150)
		1,340		675

	£'000	£'000	£'000	£'000
Capital and reserves				
Share capital		350		350
Revaluation reserve		200		-
Profit and loss account		790		325
		1,340		675

Average ratios for the appropriate industrial sector for 20X5 and for Andrews Ltd are as follows.

	Industrial sector	*Andrews Ltd*	
	20X5	*20X5*	*20X4*
Gross margin	33%	32%	35%
Net margin (before taxation)	22%	21.5%	20.1%
Fixed asset turnover	4.5 times	4.0 times	5.3 times
Current ratio	1.5:1	1.63:1	1.02:1
Quick ratio	1.0:1	0.83:1	0.55:1
Return on shareholders' funds	48%	42.2%	85.9%

Required

Comment on the 20X5 profitability and liquidity of Andrews Ltd in the light of the available information.

17 PETER HOLDINGS

Peter Holdings plc is a large investment conglomerate.

Required

Explain how divisional performance should be measured in the interest of the group's shareholders.

18 ALTMAN FORMULA (25 marks) *45 mins*

The Altman formula for prediction of bankruptcy is as follows.

1.2(A) + 1.4(B) + 3.3(C) + 1(D) + 0.6(E)

where A = working capital/assets
B = retained earnings/assets
C = pre-tax earnings/assets
D = sales/assets
E = market value of equity/liabilities

A company which has a Z-score of less than 1.81 is regarded as being at risk.

You are given the following information in respect of four listed companies.

	Working capital	*Retained earnings*	*Pre-tax earnings*	*MV of equity*	*Assets*	*Liabilities*	*Sales*
Andrea plc	4,000	60,000	10,000	20,000	200,000	120,000	200,000
Chenier plc	2,000	20,000	0	5,000	100,000	80,000	120,000
Maddalena plc	6,000	20,000	(30,000)	48,000	800,000	740,000	900,000
Roucher plc	40,000	200,000	30,000	100,000	1,800,000	1,000,000	2,000,000

All figures are in £'000

Required

(a) Calculate the Z score for each of the companies and comment on your results. (11 marks)

(b) Describe the way in which the Altman formula was produced. (7 marks)

(c) Discuss the argument that other ratios ought to be regarded as better predictors of bankruptcy. (7 marks)

19 GO-GO

The following is an extract from *Accountancy* magazine.

'Take profit before tax divided by current liabilities; current assets as a proportion of total liabilities; current liabilities as a proportion of total tangible assets; take into account the no-credit interval; mix them in the right proportions and you can tell whether a company will go bust.'

The no-credit interval is defined as (current assets - current liabilities) ÷ (operating costs excluding depreciation).

The following are the summarised accounts of Go-Go Products Ltd and Numerous Inventions Ltd for the year ended 30 September 20X1 and 20X0.

	Go-Go Products		*Numerous Inventions*	
	20X1	*20X0*	*20X1*	*20X0*
Turnover	30,067	25,417	9,734	8,044
Costs				
Depreciation	311	284	331	195
Other	28,356	24,198	8,313	6,571
Profit before tax	1,400	935	1,090	1,278
	30,067	25,417	9,734	8,044
Intangible fixed assets	918	937	-	-
Tangible fixed assets	4,644	5,228	1,950	1,530
Stock	6,243	6,773	986	1,257
Debtors	4,042	4,680	3,234	2,236
Bank	516	184	2,578	1,366
	16,363	17,702	8,748	6,389
Creditors	5,261	5,144	1,297	972
Current taxation	312	379	483	321
Short term borrowing	2,357	4,447	2,577	1,174
Long term loans	1,409	1,168	55	38
Capital and reserves	7,024	6,564	4,336	3,884
	16,363	17,702	8,748	6,389

Required

(a) Calculate three of the stated factors for the two companies and two others you consider relevant to the going concern status.

(b) Compare the two companies stating clearly which of your calculated ratios have moved in an unfavourable direction.

(c) Describe and discuss the limitations of ratio analysis as a predictor of failure.

20 GERMAN COMPETITOR (25 marks) *45 mins*

You are the chief accountant of Tone plc. The managing director has provided you with the financial statements of Tone plc's main competitor, Hilde GmbH, a German company. He finds difficulty in reviewing these statements in their non-UK format, presented below.

HILDE GmbH
BALANCE SHEET AS AT 31 MARCH 20X5 (in DM million)

	31.3.X5	*31.3.X4*		*31.3.X5*	*31.3.X4*
ASSETS			CAPITAL AND LIABILITIES		
Tangible fixed assets			Capital and reserves		
Land	1,000	750	Share capital	850	750
Buildings	750	500	Share premium	100	-
Plant	200	150	Legal reserve	200	200
	1,950	1,400	Profit & loss b/fwd	590	300
			Profit & loss for year	185	290
Current assets			NET WORTH	1,925	1,540
Stock	150	120			
Trade debtors	180	100	Creditors		
Cash	20	200	Trade creditors	170	150
	350	420	Taxation	180	150
			Other creditors	75	50
Prepayments and accrued income				425	350
Prepayments	50	70			
	2,350	1,890		2,350	1,890

HILDE GmbH
INCOME STATEMENT FOR THE YEAR ENDED 31 MARCH 20X5 (in DM million)

	20X5	20X4		20X5	20X4
EXPENSES			INCOME		
Operating expenses:			Operating income:		
Purchase of raw materials	740	400	Sale of goods produced	1,890	1,270
Variation in stocks thereof	90	40	Variation in stock of finished goods and WIP	120	80
Taxation	190	125	Other operating income	75	50
Wages	500	285	Total operating income	2,085	1,400
Valuation adjustment on fixed assets: depreciation	200	150			
Valuation adjustment on current assets: amounts written off	30	20			
Other operating expenses	50	40			
Total operating expenses	1,800	1,060			
Financial expenses					
Interest	100	50			
Total financial expenses	100	50			
TOTAL EXPENSES	1,900	1,110	TOTAL INCOME	2,085	1,400
Balance: PROFIT	185	290			
SUM TOTAL	2,085	1,400		2,085	1,400

Required

Prepare a report for the managing director:

(a) Analysing the performance of Hilde GmbH using the financial statements provided (18 marks)

(b) Explaining why a direct comparison of the results of Tone plc and Hilde GmbH may be misleading (7 marks)

21 GLOWBALL (Pilot paper - 25 marks) *45 mins*

The directors of Glowball, a public limited company, had discussed the study by the Institute of Environmental Management which indicated that over 35% of the world's 250 largest corporations are voluntarily releasing green reports to the public to promote corporate environmental performance and to attract customers and investors. They have heard that the main competitors are applying the *Global Reporting Initiative* (GRI) in an effort to develop worldwide format for corporate environmental reporting. However, the directors are unsure as to what this initiative actually means. Additionally they require advice as to the nature of any legislation or standards relating to environmental reporting as they are worried that any environmental report produced by the company may not be of sufficient quality and may detract from and not enhance their image if the report does not comply with recognised standards. Glowball has a reputation for ensuring the preservation of the environment in its business activities.

Further the directors have collected information in respect of a series of events which they consider to be important and worthy of note in the environmental report but are not sure as to how they would be incorporated in the environmental report or whether they should be included in the financial statements.

The events are as follows.

(a) Glowball is a company that pipes gas from offshore gas installations to major consumers. The company purchased its main competitor during the year and found that there were environmental liabilities arising out of the restoration of many miles of farmland that had been affected by the

laying of a pipeline. There was no legal obligation to carry out the work, but the company felt that there would be a cost of around £150 million if the farmland was to be restored.

(b) Most of the offshore gas installations are governed by operating licences which specify limits to the substances which can be discharged to the air and water. These limits vary according to local legislation and tests are carried out by the regulatory authorities. During the year the company was prosecuted for infringements of an environmental law in the USA when toxic gas escaped into the atmosphere. In 20X9 the company was prosecuted five times and in 20X8 eleven times for infringement of the law. The final amount of the fine/costs to be imposed by the courts has not been determined but is expected to be around £5 million. The escape occurred over the sea and it was considered that there was little threat to human life.

(c) The company produced statistics which measure their improvement in the handling of emissions of gases which may have an impact on the environment. The statistics deal with:

 (i) Measurement of the release of gases with the potential to form acid rain. The emissions have been reduced by 84% over five years due to the closure of old plants.

 (ii) Measurement of emissions of substances potentially hazardous to human health. The emissions are down by 51% on 20X5 levels.

 (iii) Measurement of emissions to water which removes dissolved oxygen and substances that may have an adverse effect on aquatic life. Accurate measurement of these emissions is not possible but the company is planning to spend £70 million on research in this area.

(d) The company tries to reduce the environmental impacts associated with the siting and construction of its gas installations. This is done in a way that minimises the impact on wildlife and human beings. Additionally when the installations are at the end of their life, they are dismantled and are not sunk into the sea. The current provision for the decommissioning of these installations is £215 million and there are still decommissioning costs of £407 million to be provided as the company's policy is to build up the required provision over the life of the installation.

Required

Prepare a report suitable for presentation to the directors of Glowball in which you discuss the following elements.

(a) Current reporting requirements and guidelines relating to environmental reporting (10 marks)

(b) The nature of any disclosure which would be required in an environmental report and/or the financial statements for the evens (a) – (d) above (15 marks)

22 RECENT DEVELOPMENTS

List the current Exposure Drafts and Discussion/Consultation Papers.

23 LARGE COMPANY

C & R plc is a large company which operates a number of retail stores throughout the United Kingdom. The company makes up financial statements to 30 September each year.

On 1 October 20X6 the company purchased two plots of land at two different locations, and commenced the construction of two retail stores. The construction was completed on 1 October 20X7.

Details of the costs incurred to construct the stores are as follows.

	Location A	*Location B*
	£'000	£'000
Cost of land	500	700
Cost of building materials	500	550
Direct labour	100	150
Site overheads	100	100
Fixture and fittings	200	200

The construction of the stores was financed out of the proceeds of issue of a £10 million zero coupon bond on 1 October 20X6. The bond is redeemable at a price of £25,937,000 on 30 September 20Y6. This represents the one and only payment to the holders of the bond.

Both stores were brought into use on 1 October 20X7. The store at Location A was used by C & R plc but, due to a change of plan, the store at Location B was let to another retailer at a commercial rent.

It is the policy of C & R plc to depreciate freehold properties over their anticipated useful life of 50 years, and to depreciate fixtures and fittings over 10 years. The cost of such properties (including fixtures and fittings) should include finance costs, where this is permitted by the regulatory framework in the United Kingdom.

Required

(a) Compute the amounts which will be included in fixed assets in respect of the stores at Locations A and B on 30 September 20X7.

Give full explanations for the amounts you have included.

(b) Compute the change to the profit and loss account for depreciation on the fixed assets at the two locations for the year to 30 September 20X8, stating clearly the reasons for your answers.

24 FRS 11

A new FRS has been produced, FRS 11 *Impairment of fixed assets and goodwill*, under which it may be necessary to calculate an asset's value in use to compare with its carrying value. Where the income stream of an asset cannot be identified separately, it can be grouped with other assets in an 'income-generating unit'. In relation to the allocation of assets to such units, consider the following two scenarios, and answer the related questions.

(a) Suppose an entity has three independent streams, A, B and C, with net asset directly involved in the income streams with carrying amounts of £100m, £150m and £200m respectively. In addition there are head office net assets with a carrying amount totalling £150m. The relative amounts of the net assets are a reasonable indication of the proportion of head office resources devoted to each income stream. The income-generating units are defined as follows.

Income-generating unit	*A*	*B*	*C*	*Total*
	£m	£m	£m	£m
Net assets directly involved in				
income-generating unit	100	150	200	450
Head office net assets	33	50	67	150
Total	133	200	267	600

Required

Suppose that there is an indication that a fixed asset in Unit B is impaired and a value in use calculation was done. To which figure would the recoverable amount be compared?

(b) Suppose an entity acquires a business comprising three income-generating units, X, Y and Z. After five years, the carrying amount of the net assets in the income-generating units and the purchased goodwill compares with the value in use as follows.

Income-generating unit	*X*	*Y*	*Z*	*Goodwill*	*Total*
	£m	£m	£m	£m	£m
Carrying amount	80	120	140	50	390
Value in use	100	140	120		360

Required

What should be recognised by way of an impairment loss?

25 INVEST

(a) Invest plc has a number of subsidiaries. The accounting date of Invest plc and all its subsidiaries is 30 April. On 1 May 20X8, Invest plc purchased 80% of the issued equity shares of Target Ltd. This purchase made Target Ltd a subsidiary of Invest plc from 1 May 20X8. Invest plc made a cash payment of £31 million for the shares in Target Ltd. On 1 May 20X8, the net assets which were included in the balance sheet of Target Ltd had a fair value to Invest plc of £30 million. Target Ltd sells a well-known branded product and has taken some steps to protect itself legally against unauthorised use of a brand name. A reliable estimate of the value of this brand to the Invest group is £3 million. It is further considered that the value of this brand can be maintained or even increased for the foreseeable future. The value of the brand is *not* included in the balance sheet of Target Ltd.

For the purposes of preparing the consolidated financial statements, the directors of Invest plc wish to ensure that the charge to the profit and loss account for the amortisation of intangible fixed assets is kept to a minimum. They estimate that the useful economic life of the purchased goodwill (or premium on acquisition) of Target Ltd is 40 years.

Required

(i) Compute the charge to the consolidated profit and loss account in respect of the goodwill on acquisition of Target Ltd for its year ended 30 April 20X9, in accordance with FRS 10 *Goodwill and intangible assets.*

(ii) Explain the action which Invest plc must take in 20X8/X9 and in future years arising from the chosen accounting treatment of the goodwill on acquisition of Target Ltd.

(b) You are the management accountant of Investor plc, a listed company with a number of subsidiaries located throughout the United Kingdom. Investor plc currently appraises investment opportunities using a cost of capital of 10 per cent. Goodwill on consolidation is normally written off on a *pro rata* basis over twenty years.

On 1 April 20X9 Investor plc purchased 80 per cent of the equity share capital of Cornwall Ltd for a total cash price of £60m. Half the price was payable on 1 April 20X9; the balance was payable on 1 April 20Y1. The net identifiable assets that were actually included in the balance sheet of Cornwall Ltd had a carrying value totalling £55m at 1 April 20X9. With the exception of the pension provision (see below), you discover that the fair values of the net identifiable assets of Cornwall Ltd at 1 April 20X9 are the same as their carrying values. When performing the fair-value exercise at 1 April 20X9 you discover that Cornwall Ltd has a defined-benefit pension scheme that was actuarially valued three years ago and found to be in deficit. As a result of that valuation, a provision of £6m has been built up in the balance sheet. The fair-value exercise indicates that on 1 April 20X9, the pension scheme was in deficit by £11m. This information became available on 31 July 20X9.

Assume that today's date is 31 October 20X9. You are in the process of preparing the consolidated financial statements of the group for the year ended 30 September 20X9. Your financial director is concerned that profits for the year will be lower than originally anticipated. She is therefore wondering about extending to 40 years the period of the write-off of goodwill on acquisition of Cornwall Ltd.

Required

Calculate the write-off of goodwill on acquisition of Cornwall Ltd in the consolidated accounts of Investor plc for the year ended 30 September 20X9. You should fully explain and justify all parts of the calculation. Assume that the twenty year write-off policy is followed.

26 TALL (25 marks) *45 mins*

You are the management accountant of Tall plc. The company is planning a number of acquisitions in 20Y0 and so you are aware that additional funding will be needed. Today's date is 30 November 20X9. The balance sheet of the company at 30 September 20X9 (the financial year-end of Tall plc) showed the following balances.

	£m
Equity share capital	100.0
Share premium account	35.8
Profit and loss account	89.7
	225.5
Net assets	225.5

On 1 October 20X9 Tall plc raised additional funding as follows.

(a) Tall plc issued 15 million £1 bonds at par. The bonds pay no interest but are redeemable on 1 October 20Y4 at £1.61 – the total payable on redemption being £24.15m. As an alternative to redemption, bondholders can elect to convert their holdings into £1 equity shares on the basis of one equity share for every bond held. The current price of a £1 share is £1.40 and it is reckoned that this will grow by at least 5 per cent per annum for the next five years.

(b) Tall plc issued 10 million £1 preference shares at £1.20 per share, incurring issue costs of £100,000. The preference shares carry no dividend and are redeemable on 1 October 20Y5 at £2.35 per share – the total payable on redemption being £23.5m.

Your assistant is unsure how to reflect the additional funding in the financial statements of Tall plc. He expresses the opinion that both of the new capital instruments should logically be reflected in the shareholders' funds section of the balance sheet. He justifies this as follows.

(a) The preference shares are legally shares and so shareholders' funds is the appropriate place to present them.

(b) The bonds and the preference shares seem to have very similar terms of issue and it is quite likely that the bonds will *become* shares in five years' time, given the projected growth in the equity share price.

He has no idea how to show the finance costs of the capital instruments in the profit and loss account. This is because he has never before encountered a capital instrument where no payments will be made to the holders of the instrument until the date of redemption.

Required

(a) Write a memorandum to your assistant which evaluates the comments he has made and explains the correct treatment where necessary. Your memorandum should refer to the provisions of relevant accounting standards. (10 marks)

(b) Prepare the relevant balances in the balance sheet of Tall plc immediately after the issue of the bonds and the preference shares. (5 marks)

(c) Calculate the finance cost that will be required to be shown in the profit and loss account of Tall plc for the year ended 30 September 20Y0 for the bonds and the preference shares. You should state where in the profit and loss account the costs should be shown. (10 marks)

27 FRS 5 SCENARIOS

Scenario I

Shakey plc enters into an agreement with Farout Factors plc with the following principal terms.

(a) Shakey plc will transfer (by assignment) to Farout Factors plc such trade debts as Shakey plc shall determine, subject only to credit approval by Farout Factors plc and a limit placed on the proportion of the total that may be due from any one debtor. Farout Factors plc levies a charge of 0.15% of turnover, payable monthly, for this facility.

(b) Shakey plc continues to administer the sales ledger and handle all aspects of collection of the debts.

(c) Shakey plc may draw up to 80% of the gross amount of debts assigned at any time, such drawings being debited in the books of Farout Factors plc to a factoring account operated by Farout Factors plc for Shakey plc.

(d) Weekly, Shakey plc assigns and sends copy invoices to Farout Factors plc as they are raised.

(e) Shakey plc is required to bank the gross amounts of all payments received from debts assigned to Farout Factors plc direct into an account in the name of Farout Factors plc. Credit transfers made by debtors direct into Shakey's own bank account must immediately be paid to Farout Factors plc.

(f) Farout Factors plc credits such collections from debtors to the factoring account, and debit the account monthly with interest calculated on the basis of the daily balances on the account using a rate of base rate plus 2.5%. Thus this interest charge varies with the amount of finance drawn by Shakey plc under the finance facility from Farout Factors plc, the speed of payment of the debtors and base rate.

(g) Farout Factors provides protection from bad debts. Any debts not recovered after 90 days are credited to the factoring account, and responsibility for their collection is passed to Farout Factors plc. A charge of 1% of the gross value of all debts factored is levied by Farout Factors plc for this service and debited to the factoring account.

(h) Farout Factors plc pays for the debts, less any advances, interest charges and credit protection charges, 90 days after the date of purchase, and debits the payment to the factoring account.

(i) On either party giving 90 days' notice to the other, the arrangement will be terminated. In such and event, Shakey plc will transfer no further debts to Farout Factors plc, and the balance remaining on the factoring account at the end of the notice period will be settled in cash in the normal way.

Required

Consider the nature of the above agreement and resulting transactions and state how these should be reflected in the accounts of Shakey plc.

Scenario II

You are the management accountant of D Ltd which has three principal activities. These are the sale of motor vehicles (both new and second-hand), the provision of spare parts for motor vehicles, and the servicing of motor vehicles.

During the financial year ended 31 August 20X6, the company has entered into a type of business transaction not previously undertaken. With effect from 1 January 20X6, D Ltd entered into an agreement whereby it received motor vehicles on a consignment basis from E plc, a large manufacturer. The terms of the arrangement were as follows.

(a) On delivery, the stock of vehicles remains the legal property of E plc.

(b) Legal title to a vehicle passes to D Ltd either when D Ltd enters into a binding arrangement to sell the vehicle to a third party or six months after the date of delivery by E plc to D Ltd.

(c) At the date legal title passes, E plc invoices D Ltd for the sale of the vehicles. The price payable by D Ltd is the normal selling price of E plc *at the date of delivery*, increased by 1% for every complete month the vehicles are held on consignment by D Ltd. Any change in E plc's normal selling price between the date of delivery and the date legal title to the goods passes to D Ltd does not change the amount payable by D Ltd to E plc.

(d) At any time between the date of delivery and the date legal title passes to D Ltd, the company (D Ltd) has the right to return the vehicles to E plc *provided they are not damaged or obsolete*. D Ltd does not have the right to return damaged or obsolete vehicles. If D Ltd exercises this right of return then a return penalty is payable by D Ltd as follows.

Time since date of delivery	*Penalty as a percentage of invoiced price **
Three months or less	50%
Three to four months	75%
More than four months	100%

* ie, the price that would otherwise be payable by D Ltd if legal title to the vehicles had passed at the date of return.

(e) E plc has *no right to demand* return of vehicles on consignment to D Ltd unless D Ltd becomes insolvent.

The managing director suggests that the vehicles should be shown as an asset of D Ltd only when title passes, and the purchase price becomes legally payable.

Required

Using the details of the agreement between D Ltd and E plc outline with reasons the appropriate accounting treatment in D Ltd's book.

28 AXE

The financial director of Axe, a public limited company, has heard of the recent discussions over accounting for leases but us unsure as to the current position. Additionally the company has undergone certain transactions in the year and the director requires assistance as to how these transactions should be dealt with in the financial statements. The financial year end of the company is 31 December 20X0.

On 1 January 20X0, Axe sold its computer software and hardware to Lake, a public limited company, for £310 million. The assets were leased back for four years under an operating lease whereby Lake agreed to maintain and upgrade the computer facilities. The fair value of the assets sold was £190 million and the carrying value based on depreciated historic cost was £90 million. The lease rental payments were £45 million per annum, payable on 1 January in advance, which represented a premium of fifty per cent of the normal cost of such a lease.

Additionally, on 1 January 20X0 Axe sold plant with a carrying value of £200 million. The fair value and selling price of the plant was £330 million. The plant was immediately leased back over four years which is the remaining useful life of the asset. Axe has guaranteed a residual value of £30 million and the plant is to be sold for scrap at the end of the lease. Axe will be liable for any shortfall in the residual value. The lease cannot be cancelled and requires equal rental payments of £87 million at the commencement of each financial year. The 'normal' cost of such a lease without the residual value guarantee would have been £95 million per annum. Axe pays the costs of all maintenance and insurance of the plant.

The company has also leased motor vehicles on 1 January 20X0 for the first time. Fifty vehicles were leased at an annual rental of £5,000 each, payable on 1 January in advance. In addition an extra 20p per mile is payable if the mileage exceeds 60,000 miles over the three year rental period. The excess mileage charge reflects fair compensation for the additional wear and tear of the vehicle. Axe returns the vehicle to the lessor at the end of the lease. The lessee maintains and insures the vehicles. (A discount rate of 10% should be used in all calculations. The present value of an ordinary annuity of £1 per period for three years at 10% is £2.49.)

Required

(a) Discuss the new approach to accounting for leases which is being developed by the Accounting Standards Board in its Discussion Paper *Leases: implementation of a new approach.*

(b) Advise the financial director on the way in which the above transactions would be dealt with under SSAP 21.

29 ELLIOT

The accountant of Elliot Ltd, a book wholesaler, decided that the time had come to computerise the company's accounting records. The difficulty was that, at that moment, Elliot did not have sufficient funds to meet the capital cost of the hardware. Instead, the company approached Better Leasing plc to finance the purchase through a lease. The agreed terms of the lease were as follows.

Start date:	1 July 20X2
Monthly payments:	£1,989.00
Number of payments:	20

The computer cost £30,600. Better Leasing plc pays tax at 35% and obtains capital allowances of 25% on a reducing balance basis on the cost of the computer.

The cash flow statement for the computer lease from the point of view of Better Leasing (actuarial methods after tax) for the year to 30 June 20X3 was as follows.

Quarter to	*Net cash investment at beginning of period*	*Cash outflow*	*Cash inflow*	*Average net cash investment*	*Interest paid*	*Profit after tax taken out of lease*	*Net cash investment at end*
	£	£	£	£	£	£	£
30.9.X2	-	(30,600)	1,989	(28,611)	(715)	(115)	(29,441)
31.12.X2	(29,441)	-	1,989	(27,452)	(686)	(110)	(28,248)
31.3.X3	(28,248)	-	1,989	(26,259)	(657)	(104)	(27,020)
30.6.X3	(27,020)	-	1,989	(25,031)	(626)	(99)	(25,756)

Required

(a) Demonstrate how the lease would be shown in the balance sheet of Better Leasing at 30 June 20X3, and in the profit and loss account for the year. Produce a note on accounting policy for leases.

(b) State the main assumptions underlying the net cash investment calculation.

(c) State how the profit is produced which is taken out of the lease. On what basis is this profit allocated to accounting periods?

(d) Assuming Better Leasing used the investment period method rather than the actuarial method after tax, state how the gross earnings should be allocated.

30 **FRS 17**

In November 2000, the ASB issued FRS 17 *Retirement benefits.* This covers the treatment of pensions and other retirement benefits in the employer's accounts, and replaces SSAP 24 *Accounting for pension costs.* The main changes are to defined benefit schemes.

(a) What are the main criticisms of SSAP 24 which gave rise to the need for change?
(b) What are the main provisions of FRS 17?
(c) What drawbacks can you foresee to the new approach?

31 **HARMONISE**

Harmonise plc is a plastic toy manufacturer. its toy sales have been adversely affected by imports and it has been changing towards the supply of plastic office equipment. Profits are expected to continue to fall for the next four years when they are expected to stabilise at the 20X9 level. There will be a regular programme of plant renewal.

The following information is available.

Year ended 30 April	*Profit before depreciation and tax*	*Capital allowances*	*Depreciation*
	£	£	£
20X6	1,250,000	400,000	80,000
20X7	1,200,000	80,000	160,000
20X8	1,100,000	80,000	240,000
20X9	1,000,000	560,000	160,000

Assume a corporation tax rate of 33%. On 1 March 20X5 there was a nil balance on the deferred tax account.

Required

Prepare the profit and loss and balance sheet extracts for corporation tax and deferred taxation for the four years 20X6/20X9 using the following methods.

(a) Flow-through
(b) Full provision
(c) Partial provision

Notes to the profit and loss account and balance sheet are *not* required.

32 **ANGUS**

During the completion of the financial statements of Angus plc for the year ended 28 February 20X7, the following matters have been brought to your attention.

(a) On 1 March 20X6, the company revalued its freehold land and buildings (for the first time) to £20 million (land element £4 million) and the accounting records were adjusted to this value. The property originally cost £16 million on which annual depreciation of £280,000 had been charged. Accumulated depreciation to 29 February 20X6 was £2.8 million. Depreciation of £400,000 has been charged to the profit and loss account for the year ended 28 February 20X7.

(b) The company's accounting policy for research and development has been to capitalise the cost and amortise this over 10 years. On 1 March 20X6, when deferred development expenditure of £1.5 million was held as an intangible fixed asset, this policy was changed to immediate write off of development expenditure.

(c) The company announced the intended closure of its European operations on 31 January 20X7 when a formal closure plan was approved and adopted. On 10 March 20X7, the company contracted to terminate various operating leases and sell other fixed assets. The fixed assets had a net book value of £10.5 million and an agreed sale value of £9 million. The lessors of the assets held under operating leases agreed to terminate the contracts for a payment of £350,000. The European operations contributed 10% of turnover and profit.

(d) As a result of the closure in (c) above, the company will need to carry out a fundamental reorganisation of its other activities at a cost of £1.25 million.

(e) After accounting for the above items, the company's draft financial statements show turnover of £200 million, profit before taxation of £18 million and a tax charge of £6 million. The company has proposed a dividend of £2 million. Shareholders' funds at 1 March 20X6 were £500 million.

Required

(a) Prepare the following statements, suitable for publication, for Angus plc for the year ended 28 February 20X7:

- (i) Profit and loss account
- (ii) Statement of total recognised gains and loses
- (iii) Reconciliation of movements in shareholders' funds
- (iv) Note of historical cost profits and losses

(b) Explain briefly:

- (i) The purpose of the statement of total recognised gains and losses
- (ii) The extent to which a user of the accounts will be better able to make decisions by referring to a statement of total recognised gains and losses rather than the statement of movements on reserves that is produced to comply with the Companies Act 1985

33 ENGINA (Pilot paper - 25 marks) *45 mins*

Engina, a foreign company, has approached a partner in your firm to assist in obtaining a Stock Exchange listing for the company. Engina is registered in a country where transactions between related parties are considered to be normal but where such transactions are not disclosed. The directors of Engina are reluctant to disclose the nature of their related party transactions as they feel that although they are a normal feature of business in their part of the world, it could cause significant problems politically and culturally to disclose such transactions.

The partner in your firm has requested a list of all transactions with parties connected with the company and the directors of Engina have produced the following summary.

(a) Every month, Engina sells £50,000 of goods per month to Mr Satay, the financial director. The financial director has set up a small retailing business for his son and the goods are purchased at cost price for him. The annual turnover of Engina is £300 million. Additionally Mr Satay has purchased his company car from the company for £45,000 (market value £80,000). The director, Mr Satay, owns directly 10% of the shares in the company and earns a salary of £500,000 a year, and has a personal fortune of many millions of pounds.

(b) A hotel property had been sold to a brother of Mr Soy, the Managing Director of Engina, for £4 million (net of selling cost of £0.2 million). The market value of the property was £4.3 million but in the overseas country, property prices were falling rapidly. The carrying value of the hotel was £5 million and its value in use was £3.6 million. There was an over supply of hotel accommodation due to government subsidies in an attempt to encourage hotel development and the tourist industry.

(c) Mr Satay owns several companies and the structure of the group is as follows.

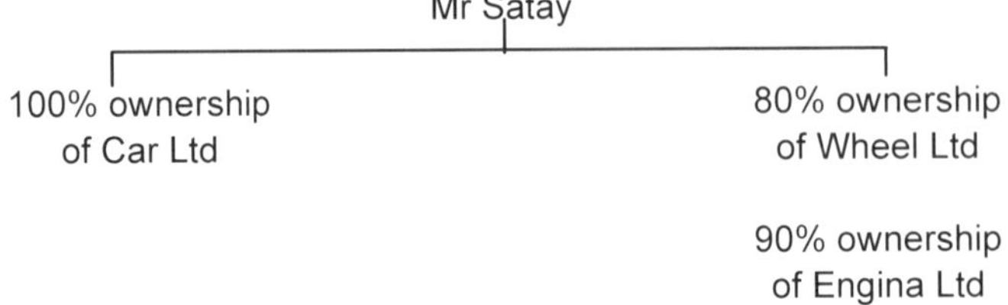

Engina earns 60% of its profit from transactions with Car and 40% of its profit from transactions with Wheel.

Required

Write a report to the directors of Engina setting out the reasons why it is important to disclose related party transactions and the nature of any disclosure required for the above transactions under the UK regulatory system before a Stock Exchange quotation can be obtained.

The mark allocation will be as follows:

		Marks
Style/layout of report		4
Reasons		8
Transaction	(a)	4
	(b)	5
	(c)	4
		25

34 LEASED WAREHOUSE

A leased warehouse has been modified to include offices, mezzanines, etc and under the terms of the lease the company, when it moves out, is obliged to return the building to its original state. If the business continues to expand, the directors believe they will have to move out in the next two to three years. The lease does not expire until 2010. The company received a quote for the reinstatement costs of £200,000 and have started to build this up last year at £50,000 a year.

How does FRS 12 *Provisions, contingent liabilities and contingent assets* affect the accounting treatment the company adopts?

35 BIG, SMALL AND TINY (25 marks) *45 mins*

The balance sheets of Big plc, Small Ltd and Tiny Ltd at 30 September 20X9 (the accounting date for all three companies) are given below.

	Big plc		*Small Ltd*		*Tiny Ltd*	
	£'000	£'000	£'000	£'000	£'000	£'000
Fixed assets						
Tangible assets	56,000		66,000		56,000	
Investments (Notes 1-3)	104,000		29,000		-	
		160,000		95,000		56,000
Current assets						
Stocks (Note 5)	45,000		44,000		25,000	
Debtors (Note 6)	40,000		30,000		16,000	
Cash in hand	8,000		6,000		3,000	
	93,000		80,000		44,000	
Creditors falling due within one year						
Trade creditors (Note 6)	16,000		12,000		8,000	
Taxation	7,000		6,000		4,000	
Proposed dividend	9,000		8,000		3,000	
Bank overdraft	12,000		10,000		9,000	
	44,000		36,000		24,000	
Net current assets		49,000		44,000		20,000
Long-term loans		(50,000)		-		(25,000)
		159,000		139,000		51,000
Capital and reserves						
Share capital (Notes 2 and 3)		90,000		80,000		32,000
Profit and loss account		69,000		59,000		19,000
		159,000		139,000		51,000

Notes to the financial statements

1 On 1 October 20X3, when the reserves of Small Ltd showed a balance of £22 million, Big plc purchased 64 million of Small Ltd's £1 equity shares for a consideration of £91.5 million, payable in cash. On 1 October 20X3, a large property owned by Small Ltd had a balance sheet value of £7 million and a fair value to Big plc of £11 million. With the exception of this property, the fair values of all the identifiable net assets of Small Ltd were the same as their carrying values in the balance sheet of Small Ltd. The property that had a fair value of £11 million on 1 October 20X3 was sold by Small Ltd on 30 June 20X7.

2 On 1 April 20X5, when the reserves of Tiny Ltd stood at £10m, Big plc purchased 8 million of Tiny Ltd's £1 equity shares for a cash consideration of £12.5 million. A fair-value exercise was carried out but all of the net identifiable assets of Tiny Ltd at 1 April 20X5 had a fair value that was the same as their carrying values in the balance sheet of Tiny Ltd.

3 On 1 April 20X9, Small Ltd purchased 16 million of Tiny Ltd's £1 equity shares for a cash consideration of £29 million. A fair-value exercise was carried out but all of the net identifiable assets of Tiny Ltd at 1 April 20X9 had a fair value that was the same as their carrying values in the balance sheet of Tiny Ltd. During the year ended 30 September 20X9, Tiny Ltd made a profit after taxation of £8 million and paid no interim dividends. This profit accrued evenly over the year.

4 The policy of Big plc is to write off goodwill on consolidation over a twenty-year period, with a full year's write off in the year of acquisition.

5 A key reason behind the purchases of shares in Tiny Ltd by Big plc and Small Ltd was that Tiny Ltd supplied a component that was used by both companies. Until 1 April 20X9, the component was supplied by Tiny Ltd at cost plus a mark-up of 30 per cent. From 1 April 20X9, the mark-up changed to 20 per cent. On 30 September 20X9, the stocks of components purchased from Tiny Ltd (all purchases since 1 April 20X9) were as follows.

- In Big plc's books, £9 million
- In Small Ltd's books, £7.8 million

6 The debtors of Big plc and Small Ltd include the correct dividends receivable from Small Ltd and Tiny Ltd. The creditors of Big plc and Small Ltd shows amounts of £6 million and £5 million respectively as being payable to Tiny Ltd, and these balances have been agreed. There was no other inter-group trading.

You are the management accountant responsible for the consolidation of the Big plc group. Your assistant is aware of the basic principles and procedures to be followed in preparing consolidated financial statements. She is clear on what is required to consolidate Small Ltd but is much less sure of what to do with Tiny Ltd. She is particularly puzzled by the fact that both Big plc and Small Ltd have made investments in Tiny Ltd and that one of these investments took place in the current financial year.

Required

(a) Write a memorandum to your assistant that explains how the investment in Tiny Ltd should be dealt with in the consolidated financial statements of the Big plc group for the year ended 30 September 20X9. Your memorandum should refer to relevant accounting standards and specifically address the particular concerns your assistant has expressed. (7 marks)

(b) Prepare the consolidated balance sheet of the Big plc group at 30 September 20X9. (18 marks)

Approaching the answer

The balance sheets of Big plc, Small Ltd and Tiny Ltd at 30 September 20X9 (the accounting date for all three companies) are given below.

	Big plc		*Small Ltd*		*Tiny Ltd*	
	£'000	£'000	£'000	£'000	£'000	£'000
Fixed assets						
Tangible assets	56,000		66,000		56,000	
Investments (Notes 1-3)	104,000		29,000		-	
		160,000		95,000		56,000
Current assets						
Stocks (Note 5)	45,000		44,000		25,000	
Debtors (Note 6)	40,000		30,000		16,000	
Cash in hand	8,000		6,000		3,000	
	93,000		80,000		44,000	
Creditors falling due within one year						
Trade creditors (Note 6)	16,000		12,000		8,000	
Taxation	7,000		6,000		4,000	
Proposed dividend	9,000		8,000		3,000	
Bank overdraft	12,000		10,000		9,000	
	44,000		36,000		24,000	
Net current assets		49,000		44,000		20,000
Long-term loans		(50,000)		-		(25,000)
		159,000		139,000		51,000
Capital and reserves						
Share capital (Notes 2 and 3)		90,000		80,000		32,000
Profit and loss account		69,000		59,000		19,000
		159,000		139,000		51,000

Notes to the financial statements

Small is therefore a subsidiary of Big

1 On 1 October 20X3, when the reserves of Small Ltd showed a balance of £22 million, Big plc purchased 64 million of Small Ltd's £1 equity shares for a consideration of £91.5 million, payable in cash. On 1 October 20X3, a large property owned by Small Ltd had a balance sheet value of £7 million and a fair value to Big plc of £11 million. With the exception of this property, the fair values

of all the identifiable net assets of Small Ltd were the same as their carrying values in the balance sheet of Small Ltd. The property that had a fair value of £11 million on 1 October 20X3 was sold by Small Ltd on 30 June 20X7.

> Therefore deduct the fair value adjustment from reserves

2 On 1 April 20X5, when the reserves of Tiny Ltd stood at £10m, Big plc purchased 8 million of Tiny Ltd's £1 equity shares for a cash consideration of £12.5 million. A fair-value exercise was carried out but all of the net identifiable assets of Tiny Ltd at 1 April 20X5 had a fair value that was the same as their carrying values in the balance sheet of Tiny Ltd.

> 25% stak gives significar influence

3 On 1 April 20X9, Small Ltd purchased 16 million of Tiny Ltd's £1 equity shares for a cash consideration of £29 million. A fair-value exercise was carried out but all of the net identifiable assets of Tiny Ltd at 1 April 20X9 had a fair value that was the same as their carrying values in the balance sheet of Tiny Ltd. During the year ended 30 September 20X9, Tiny Ltd made a profit after taxation of £8 million and paid no interim dividends. This profit accrued evenly over the year.

> What are the implications for Big's investment in Tiny?

4 The policy of Big plc is to write off goodwill on consolidation over a twenty-year period, with a full year's write off in the year of acquisition.

5 A key reason behind the purchases of shares in Tiny Ltd by Big plc and Small Ltd was that Tiny Ltd supplied a component that was used by both companies. Until 1 April 20X9, the component was supplied by Tiny Ltd at cost plus a mark-up of 30 per cent. From 1 April 20X9, the mark-up changed to 20 per cent. On 30 September 20X9, the stocks of components purchased from Tiny Ltd (all purchases since 1 April 20X9) were as follows.

- In Big plc's books, £9 million
- In Small Ltd's books, £7.8 million

> Straight-forward unrealised profit adjustment

6 The debtors of Big plc and Small Ltd include the correct dividends receivable from Small Ltd and Tiny Ltd. The creditors of Big plc and Small Ltd shows amounts of £6 million and £5 million respectively as being payable to Tiny Ltd, and these balances have been agreed. There was no other inter-group trading.

> Straight-forward inter company adjustme

You are the management accountant responsible for the consolidation of the Big plc group. Your assistant is aware of the basic principles and procedures to be followed in preparing consolidated financial statements. She is clear on what is required to consolidate Small Ltd but is much less sure of what to do with Tiny Ltd. She is particularly puzzled by the fact that both Big plc and Small Ltd have made investments in Tiny Ltd and that one of these investments took place in the current financial year.

Required

(a) Write a memorandum to your assistant that explains how the investment in Tiny Ltd should be dealt with in the consolidated financial statements of the Big plc group for the year ended 30 September 20X9. Your memorandum should refer to relevant accounting standards and specifically address the particular concerns your assistant has expressed. (7 marks)

> Must be in clear English – the assistant knows less than you

(b) Prepare the consolidated balance sheet of the Big plc group at 30 September 20X9.

(18 marks)

1 CHARACTERISTICS

> **Tutorial note.** This is revision from your earlier studies and a test of your ability to structure your answer.

Characteristics of financial reports

The suggested characteristics are, in general, present in company accounts prepared in accordance with normally accepted accounting rules and practices. SSAP 2 *Disclosure of accounting policies*, identifies **consistency** and **prudence** as two of the four fundamental accounting concepts. We could therefore assume that these characteristics are always present in audited company accounts. FRS 18, which replaced SSAP 2, put more emphasis on **reliability** and less on prudence. Moreover, one purpose of the entire series of SSAPs and FRSs is to improve **comparability** between companies by narrowing the range of valuation and reporting procedures available to them. However, in many areas alternative procedures remain permissible and a great deal of variety persists.

The use of historical cost as the basis for preparing financial reports is justified on the ground that it makes these statements more **objective**. On the other hand, use of historical cost conflicts, to some extent, with the need to provide *relevant* data; for many business decisions current values are more relevant than historical cost.

The need for company accounts to be **realistic** (complete in form and substance) to some extent conflicts with the desire for **economy of presentation** and the need for the data to be **understandable** to user groups. The accounts contain a comprehensive range of financial data within the constraints imposed by the money measurement concept, which requires transactions to be accurately expressed in financial terms before they are reported. For this reason resources such as human assets and created goodwill are excluded from the accounts. The preparation of final accounts inevitably involves a great deal of summarisation; it is impossible to report everything as an excessive amount of detail makes it difficult to identify the more important developments.

It is the job of the auditors to check that the information published is **reliable** and fairly reflects progress during the year. The preparation of the final accounts is a relatively slow process. Often the accounts are not made available to the shareholders until three or four months after the year end and, except for quoted companies which must publish interim results, no further information is received for another year.

Uses of accounting information

The users of accounting information are **many and varied**. They include the following.

(a) The equity investor group which includes existing and potential shareholders.

(b) The loan creditor group, including existing and potential holders of debentures and loan stock, and providers of short-term secured and unsecured loans and finance.

(c) The employee group, including existing, potential and past employees.

(d) The analyst/advisor group including financial analysts and journalists, economists, statisticians, stockbrokers and other providers of advisory services.

(e) The business contact group, ranging from customers, trade creditors and suppliers to business rivals.

(f) The government including tax authorities, departments and agencies concerned with the supervision of commerce and industry, and local authorities.

(g) The public including tax payers, rate payers, consumers and other community and special interest groups such as political parties, consumer and environmental protection societies.

Satisfying user needs

Obviously, a set of published accounts **cannot satisfy all the needs** of this diverse range of user groups. The accounts are principally designed for the shareholders and one must assume that their requirements are met more effectively than those of any other group. A number of the groups can of course insist on the supply of extra data. For example, a bank manager may insist on the preparation of detailed management accounts and forecasts as a pre-condition for granting a loan. Similarly, the government can oblige companies to fill in substantial forms for a variety of purposes.

Specialist accounts

Some companies prepare specialist accounts, which often make use of pictorial presentations in the form of graphs and bar charts, for employees. Probably the main weaknesses of final accounts are that they contain out of date historical costs rather than up to date values, and that they omit valuable assets that cannot be expressed accurately in financial terms. They are also the victim of 'window dressing' in order to conceal the full extent of a company's liabilities.

2 STATEMENT OF PRINCIPLES

> **Tutorial note.** As the UK goes over to IFRS the IASB's *Framework* will play an important role.

The merits of the ASB's *Statement of Principles* should, ideally, be summarised in its objective, which is given in the *Foreword to Accounting Standards*:

> 'to provide a framework for the consistent and logical formulation of individual accounting standards (and to provide) a basis on which others can exercise judgement in resolving accounting issues.'

The following points may be made in favour of the *Statement of Principles.*

(a) The principles have in fact been used in the formulation of standards, for example its definitions of assets and liabilities have been used in FRS 5 *Reporting the substance of transactions*.

(b) The *Statement* helps reduce scope for individual judgement and the potential subjectivity that this implies.

(c) Financial statements should be more comparable because, although alternative treatments will still be available, there will be a consistent and coherent framework on which to base one's choice of a particular alternative.

(d) The *Statement* puts forward a consistent terminology and consistent objectives, for example in the definitions and the qualitative characteristics.

It could be argued that the *Statement of Principles* is too theoretical. It is certainly general rather than particular. However, as has been seen with FRS 5 and FRS 15, the general principles can be applied to very specific issues in accounting standards. Moreover, in areas not at present covered by accounting standards, the statement can give general guidance. Nevertheless, in the short term, the principles in the *Statement* may conflict with some accounting standards which had already been issued before it was written.

3 EXCLUSION OF SUBSIDIARIES

> **Tutorial note.** The option of excluding subsidiaries had, in the past, led to off balance sheet finance transactions by companies. CA 1989 and FRS 2 tightened up the rules on exclusion.

(a) In certain circumstances and under certain conditions, UK accounting standards and UK company law allows subsidiaries to be accounted for other than by consolidation in group accounts. The relevant accounting standard is FRS 2 *Accounting for subsidiary undertakings* and s 229 of the Companies Act 1985 (as amended by CA 1989) contains the statutory rules.

S 229 CA 1985 (as amended by the CA 1989) provides that a subsidiary may be omitted from the consolidated accounts of a group in one of the following cases.

(i) In the opinion of the directors, its inclusion 'is not material for the purpose of giving a true and fair view; but two or more undertakings may be excluded only if they are not material taken together'

(ii) In the opinion of the directors, its inclusion is undesirable because the business of the holding company and subsidiary are so different that they cannot reasonably be treated as a single undertaking. 'This .... does not apply merely because some of the undertakings are industrial, some commercial and some provide services, or because they carry on industrial or commercial activities involving different products or provide different services'

(iii) There are severe long-term restrictions in exercising the parent company's rights

(iv) The holding is exclusively for resale

(v) The information cannot be obtained 'without disproportionate expense or undue delay'

(b) *Dissimilar activities*

The validity of excluding a subsidiary on the grounds of the dissimilarity of business activities is questionable. The proponents of this treatment argue that the combination of the financial statements of very different businesses produces consolidated accounts of limited meaning. They claim, for example, that the balance sheet ratios and profitability indicators produced by such accounts would be misleading.

This shortcoming is, moreover, largely overcome by appropriate segmental analysis which is a requirement of company law and of SSAP 25. The exclusion of subsidiaries from consolidated accounts has undoubtedly permitted considerable abuses in the area of 'off balance sheet finance' and the additional detail and disclosure that would follow from a requirement to consolidate such subsidiaries is warranted by the need to curb such practices. FRS 2 requires the subsidiary's accounts to be presented separately in the group accounts and the group holding to be accounted for on an equity basis.

Severe long term restrictions

Where control is impaired the use of 'frozen' equity accounting is probably preferable to reverting to a cost and dividend basis particularly where the activities of the subsidiary are material to the results or financial position of the group. The treatment is, however, potentially confusing where the holding company has investments in other associated companies and clear disclosure is required. Where this treatment is used there is a clear implication that it is expected that the impairment of control will be temporary and this assumption has to be reviewed periodically. On balance it is considered that this treatment is preferred to the cost and dividend basis so long as impairment of control does not become permanent.

Temporary control

Where control is temporary, it is appropriate that the investment should be treated as a current asset, since the intention that the investment is to be liquidated in the near future should be reflected in the accounts. The proviso is that the investment has never been consolidated as there was *always* an intention to sell.

Disproportionate expense/undue display

This argument is rejected entirely by FRS 2.

4 JASMIN

> **Tutorial note.** There is a catch in part (b) which you will work out if you begin by looking at the group structure, shares held *and* voting power.

(a) FRS 2 *Accounting for subsidiary undertakings* states that a subsidiary must be excluded from consolidation in the following circumstances.

(i) Severe long-term restrictions are substantially hindering the exercise of the parent's rights over the subsidiary's assets or management.

(ii) The group's interest in the subsidiary's undertaking is held exclusively with a view to subsequent resale *and* the subsidiary has not been consolidated previously.

(iii) The subsidiary undertaking's activities are so different from those of other undertakings to be included in the consolidation that its inclusion would be incompatible with the obligation to give a true and fair view.

The FRS requires the circumstances in which subsidiary understandings are to be excluded from consolidation to be interpreted strictly.

The Companies Act 1985 allows an additional ground for exclusion, namely that the information cannot be obtained 'without disproportionate expense or undue delay', but this is not allowed by FRS 2.

The directors of Jasmin (Holdings) plc have no grounds under FRS 2 for excluding Kasbah plc from consolidation. The activities of Kasbah plc are not materially different from those of Jasmin (Holdings) plc, in fact they are quite similar. It is apparent that the real reason the directors of

Jasmin (Holdings) plc wish to exclude this subsidiary is because it is making losses: this is not sufficient reason under FRS 2.

(b) JASMIN (HOLDINGS) GROUP PLC
CONSOLIDATED BALANCE SHEET AS AT 31 MARCH 20X4

	£'000	£'000
Fixed assets		
Intangible fixed assets (W3)		30,640
Tangible fixed assets (W2)		379,400
Investment in associate (W4)		8,438
		418,478
Current assets		
Stocks (285,600 + 151,400 – 300 (W5))	436,700	
Cash (319,000 + 500)	319,500	
	756,200	
Creditors due in under one year		
(289,600 + 238,500)	528,100	
Net current assets		228,100
Total assets less current liabilities		646,578
Capital and reserves		
Share capital: £1 ordinary shares		60,000
Revaluation reserve (W7)		37,964
Profit and loss account (W8)		545,474
		643,438
Minority interests (W6)		3,140
		646,578

Workings

1 *Group structure*

(a) *Kasbah plc*

Jasmin (Holdings) plc owns 90% of the ordinary shares of Kasbah plc, so Kasbah is a subsidiary of Jasmin. Jasmin also owns 10% of the preference shares of Kasbah.

(b) *Fortran plc*

	Jasmin	*Others*	*Total*
Shares			
'A' shares	80%	20%	100%
	4,800,000	1,200,000	6,000,000
'B' shares	10%	90%	100%
	400,000	3,600,000	4,000,000
Overall	52%	48%	100%
	5,200,000	4,800,000	10,000,000
Votes			
'A' shares	4,800,000	1,200,000	6,000,000
'B' shares	800,000	7,200,000	8,000,000
Overall	5,600,000	8,400,000	14,000,000
%	40%	60%	100%

Fortran plc should be classified as an associate because Jasmin (Holdings) plc does not control over 50% of the voting power in the company. However, Jasmin (Holdings) plc is entitled to 52% of the profits of Fortran plc, so the calculation of profits and losses attributable to the shares is based on this amount.

2 *Tangible fixed assets*

	£'000
Jasmin	289,400
Kasbah	91,800
Fair value loss	(1,800)
	379,400

3 *Goodwill*

	£'000	£'000
Cost of investment in Kasbah plc		97,600
Net assets acquired		
Ordinary shares	20,000	
Profit and loss account	45,000	
	65,000	
Group share: 90%		58,500
10% preference shares		800
Goodwill		38,300
Less amortisation $^1/_5$		7,660
		30,640

4 *Investment in associate*

	£'000	£'000
Cost of investment		8,000
Net assets acquired		
Share capital	10,000	
Profit and loss a/c	1,600	
Revaluation reserve	2,000	
	13,600	
Group share (52%)		7,072
Goodwill		928
Amortisation $^1/_5$		186
		742
Share of net assets as at 31 March 20X4		
14,800 × 52%		7,696
		8,438

5 *Unrealised profit on stock*

	£'000
Cost to Jasmin	9,000
Cost to Kasbah	1,200
Profit 25%	300

6 *Minority interests*

	£'000
Ordinary shares: 10% × 20,000	2,000
Preference shares: 80% × 4,000	3,200
Profit and loss a/c (debit) × 10%	(1,880)
Loss on revaluation: 10% × 1,800	(180)
	3,140

7 *Revaluation reserve*

	£'000
Jasmin	40,000
Kasbah (loss): 90% × 1,800	(1,620)
Fortran 52% × (1,200 – 2,000)	(416)
	37,964

8 *Profit and loss account*

	Jasmin	*Kasbah*	*Fortran*
	£'000	£'000	£'000
Per question	610,000	(18,800)	3,600
Pre-acquisition		(45,000)	(1,600)
		(63,800	2,000
Unrealised profit on stock	(300)		
Share of Kasbah 90% × (63,800)	(57,420)		
Share of Fortran 52% × 2,000	1,040		
Goodwill amortised (7,660 + 180)	(7,846)		
	545,474		

(c) The impact of the substantial losses at Kasbah plc may require the value of Jasmin's holding in Kasbah to be written down. This would reflect any impairment in its value. This would also apply to the goodwill figure in the group accounts. The question may also arise as to whether Kasbah plc is still a going concern, and consequently on what basis the company's accounts should be prepared and whether group support of the company may be necessary.

5 WATER

> **Tutorial note.** It is often useful, as a first looking, to lay out the group structure. You should then use it to check that you have the correct shareholding %. Look out for shares < £1 nominal value etc.

Workings

1 *Group structure*

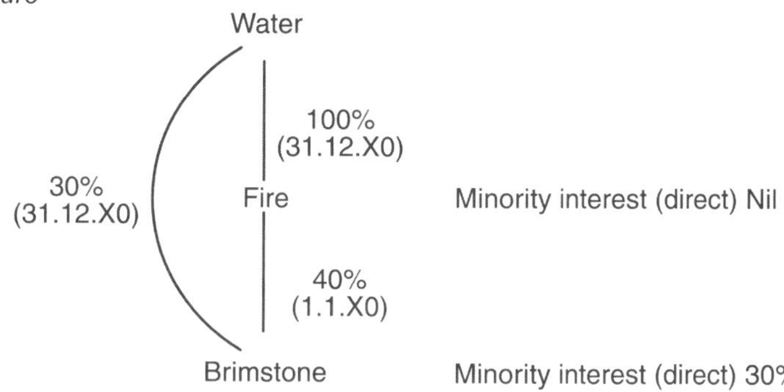

2 *Minority interests*

		£
Brimstone		
Share capital		100,000
Capital reserve		24,000
P&L account reserve		6,000
Profit for the year (12,000 – 4,800)		7,200
		137,200
	× 30%	41,160

3 *Goodwill*

	£	£
Fire Ltd		
Cost of investment		280,000
Share of consolidated net assets acquired as represented by:		
Share capital	200,000	
Capital reserve	35,000	
Consolidated reserves (see below)	26,380	
		261,380
		18,620

Consolidated reserves of Fire Ltd as at 31.12.X0

		£	£
Fire (4,900 + 31,200 – 9,600)			26,500
Brimstone (12,000 – 4,800) × 40%			2,880
Goodwill on Brimstone			
Cost of investment		55,000	
Net assets acquired			
Share capital	100,000		
Capital reserve	24,000		
P&L account reserve	6,000		
	130,000		
× 40%		52,000	
			(3,000)
			26,380

Brimstone	£	£
Cost of investment		48,000
Share of net assets acquired		
Share capital	100,000	
Capital reserve	24,000	
P&L account (6,000 + 12,000 – 4,800)	13,200	
	137,200	
	× 30%	41,160
		6,840

Total goodwill	£
Fire	18,620
Brimstone	6,840
	25,460

4 *Capital reserve*

Water Ltd	£80,000

5 *Profit and loss account*

	£
Water £(18,000 + 77,219 – 24,300)	70,919
Stocks: unrealised profit 20% (£37,820 × 25%)	(1,891)
Dividend	(10,000)
	59,028

WATER LIMITED
CONSOLIDATED BALANCE SHEET A AT 31 DECEMBER 20X0

	£	£
Fixed assets		
Intangible assets - goodwill (W3)		25,460
Tangible assets		
Freehold land and buildings		452,000
Plant and machinery at cost	228,186	
Less depreciation	(120,244)	
		107,942
		585,402
Current assets		
Stocks £(137,855 – 1,891)	135,964	
Debtors	108,643	
Cash and cash in transit £(10,827 + 2,419 + 220)	13,466	
	258,073	
Creditors: amounts falling due within one year		
Bank overdraft	1,613	
Creditors	112,974	
Current taxation	38,700	
Proposed dividend	10,000	
	163,287	
		94,786
		680,188
Capital and reserves		
Ordinary shares of £1 each, fully paid		500,000
Capital reserves		80,000
Profit and loss account		59,028
Shareholders' funds		639,028
Minority interest		41,160
		680,188

6 PHILLIPS, BYLETT AND MAGGS

> **Tutorial note.** This is a comprehensive question, including the movement on reserves, so you should be able to see the total effect of disposals on the consolidated accounts.

(a) PHILLIPS LIMITED
CONSOLIDATED PROFIT AND LOSS ACCOUNT
FOR THE YEAR ENDED 31 DECEMBER 20X7

	£'000	£'000
Turnover		
Continuing activity (800 + 640)	1,440	
Discontinued activity	310	
		1,750
Operating costs (660 + 540 + 390 + 132 (W1))		(1,722)
Operating profit		
Continuing activity (140 + 100 – 108)	132	
Discontinued activity (80 + 24)	(104)	
Operating profit/(loss)		28
Continuing operations		
Sale of business (W2)	241	
Discontinued operations		
Sale of business (W2)	206	
		447
Profit before tax		475
Taxation (69 + 40 + 75 + 15)		199
Profit after tax		276
Minority interest (W3)		10
Profit after minority interest		286
Dividends		40
Retained for year		246

Workings

1 *Goodwill*

Bylett Ltd

	£'000	£'000
Cost		1,900
Net assets acquired		
Share capital	1,000	
Profit and loss	400	
	1,400	
	× 95%	
		1,330
		570

	On shares disposed of (200/950) £'000	£'000	*On shares retained (750/950)* £'000	£'000
Total goodwill		120		450
Amortisation				
b/f (× 3/5)	72		270	
to 30.9/31.12	18		90	
		90		360
		30		90

Maggs Ltd

	£'000	£'000
Cost		1,000
Net assets acquired		
Share capital	1,000	
Profit and loss	100	
	1,100	
	× 80%	
		880
		120
Amortisation		
B/f (3/5)	72	
to 31.12	24	
		96
		24

	£'000
Total charge to P&L account	
Bylett (18 + 90)	108
Maggs	24
	132
Goodwill amortised b/f	
Bylett (72 + 270)	342
Maggs	72
	414

2 *Exceptional item*

	Bylett		*Maggs*	
	£'000	£'000	£'000	£'000
Holding company gain				
Sale proceeds		650		1,050
Less cost of shares				
(200/950 × 1,900)		400		1,000
		250		50
Tax		75		15
		175		35
Group gain				
Sale proceeds		650		1,050
Net assets at disposal				
Bylett:				
Share capital	1,000			
P&L account b/f				
(900 – 30)	870			
to 30.9 (60 × 9/12)	45			
dividend	(20)			
	1,895			
	× 20%	379		
		271		
Maggs:				
Share capital			1,000	
P&L account			25	
			1,025	
			× 80%	820
				230
Unamortised goodwill				
(W1)		(30)		(24)
		241		206

or

Alternative calculation

	£'000	£'000	£'000	£'000
Holding company gain		250		50
Less post acquisition profits				
Bylett				
P&L account b/f				
(900 – 30 – 400)	470			
to 30.9 (60 × 9/12)	45			
Dividend	(20)			
	495			
× 20%		(99)		
Maggs (25 – 100) × 80%				60
Goodwill amortised to date (W1)		90		96
		241		206

3 *Minority interest (P&L A/C)*

	£'000
5% × 60 × 9/12	2.25
25% × 60 × 3/12	3.75
20% × (80)	(16.00)
	(10.00)

(b) PHILLIPS LIMITED
CONSOLIDATED BALANCE SHEET AS AT 31 DECEMBER 20X7

	£'000	£'000
Fixed assets		
Intangible asset: goodwill (W1)		90.0
Tangible		3,984.0
		4,074.0
Current assets		
Stock	2,482.0	
Debtors	3,844.0	
Cash	328.0	
	6,654.0	
Current liabilities		
Creditors (W4)	2,954.5	
Proposed dividend	40.0	
	2,994.5	
Net current assets		3,659.5
13% loan stock		1,200.0
10% debentures		500.0
Deferred tax		1,726.0
		4,307.5
Capital and reserves		
Share capital		
£1 ordinary shares		2,000.0
Group reserves		1,832.5
Shareholders' funds		3,832.5
Minority interest (W5)		475.0
		4,307.5

Workings

4 *Creditors*

	£'000
Phillips	1,895.0
Bylett	967.0
Minority interest in dividend (25% × 10)	2.5
Tax (75 + 15)	90.0
	2,954.5

5 *Minority interest in Bylett Ltd*

	£'000
Share capital	1,000
Reserves	900
	1,900
25% thereof	475

6 *Reserves b/f*

	Phillips	*Bylett*	*Maggs*
	£'000	£'000	£'000
As at 31.12.X7	1,600	900	25
Less retained for year	(50)	(30)	(-80)
As at 1.1.X7	1,550	870	105
Pre-acquisition		(400)	(100)
		470	5
Share of Bylett : 95% × 470	446.5		
Share of Maggs : 80% × (15)	4.0		
Goodwill (W1)	(414.0)		
	1,586.0		

7 *Retained profit of Phillips Ltd*

	£'000
Profit	140.0
Divs received	19.0
Divs receivable (75% × 10)	7.5
	166.5
Tax	69.0
	97.5
Profit on disposals (175 + 35)	210.0
	307.5
Dividend	40.0
Retained	267.5

8 *Reserves c/f*

	Phillips	*Bylett*
	£'000	£'000
As at 1.1.X7	1,550.0	
Retained profit for year (W7)	267.5	
Per question		900
Pre-acquisition		(400)
		500
Share of Bylett : 75% × 500	375.0	
Goodwill (W1)	(360.0)	
	1,832.5	

(c) MOVEMENT ON CONSOLIDATED RESERVES

	£'000
Reserves at 1.1.X7 (W6)	1,586.5
Profit for the year	246.0
Reserves at 31.12.X7 (W8)	1,832.5

7 TWO GROUPS

> **Tutorial note**. The term 'demerger' here is a red herring. If you know how to deal with a disposal and follow the instructions in the question, then this is a very straightforward transaction to deal with.

The first thing to do in a question of this sort is to sort out the group structure pre- and post-demerger. This makes everything a lot clearer.

Pre-demerger

Post-demerger

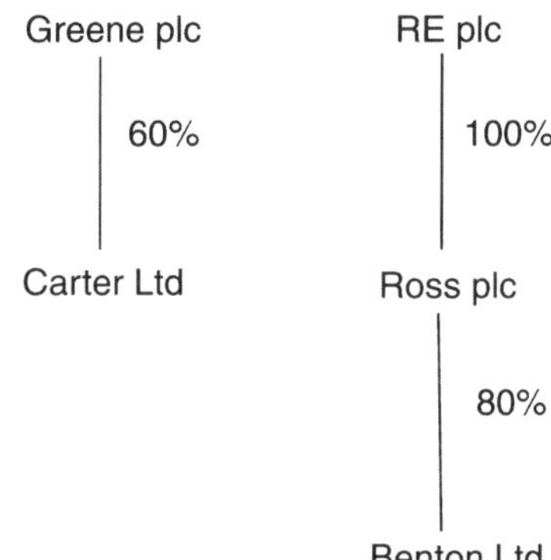

(a) ROSS GROUP PLC
BALANCE SHEET AS AT 31 DECEMBER 20X7

	£'000
Intangible asset - goodwill (W1)	250
Tangible assets (13,750 + 1,500)	15,250
Net current assets (10,000 + 1,750)	11,750
Creditors due after 1 year (750 + 250)	(1,000)
	26,250
Share capital	2,500
Share premium	2,500
Profit and loss account (W2)	20,650
Shareholders' funds	25,650
Minority interest (W3)	600
	26,250

Workings

1 *Goodwill*

	£'000	£'000
Cost of investment		2,250
Share of net assets acquired		
Share capital	750	
Share premium	250	
P&L account	1,500	
	2,500	
Group share (80%)		2,000
Goodwill		250

2 *Profit and loss account*

	£'000
Ross plc	20,250
Benton plc: group share of post-acquisition reserves (2,000 – 1,500) × 80%	400
	20,650

3 *Minority interest*

	£'000
Share capital: 750 × 20%	150
Share premium: 250 × 20%	50
P&L account: 2,000 × 20%	400
	600

(b) GREEN GROUP PLC
CONSOLIDATED PROFIT AND LOSS ACCOUNT
FOR THE YEAR ENDED 31 DECEMBER 20X7

	£'000	£'000
Turnover		
Continuing (200,000 + 13,250)	213,250	
Discontinued (75,000 + 8,125)	83,125	
		296,375
Cost of sales		
Continuing (12,5000 + 8,000)	133,000	
Discontinued (50,000 + 4,875)	54,875	
		187,875
Gross profit		
Continuing	80,250	
Discontinued	28,250	
		108,500
Net operating expenses		
Continuing (50,000 + 3,125)	53,125	
Discontinued (10,000 + 875)	10,875	
		64,000
Operating profit		
Continuing	27,125	
Discontinued	17,375	
		44,500
Goodwill on discontinued operations (W1)		(11,500)
Profit before tax		33,000
Taxation (7,500 + 5,000 + 1,000 + 625)		14,125
Profit after tax		18,875
Minority interests (W2)		875
Profit for year		18,000
Dividends (W3)		26,150
Retained loss for year		(8,150)

Workings

1 *Goodwill on discontinued operations*

	£'000	£'000
Cost of investment		22,500
Share of net assets acquired		
Share capital	2,500	
Share premium	2,500	
Reserves	6,250	
	11,250	
Group share (100%)		11,250
Goodwill		11,250
Goodwill on acquisition of Benton Ltd (see part (a))		250
Goodwill on discontinued operations		11,500

2 *Minority interest*

	£'000
Carter Ltd: 40% × 1,500	600
Benton Ltd: 20% × 1,375	275
	875

3 *Dividends*

	£'000
Greene plc	750
Dividend *in specie*: net assets of Ross Group plc (part (a)) (26,000 – 600)	25,400
	26,150

GREEN GROUP PLC
CONSOLIDATED BALANCE SHEET AS AT 31 DECEMBER 20X7

	£'000
Intangible asset - goodwill (W1)	200
Tangible assets (87,500 + 2,250)	89,750
Current assets (45,750 + 1,500)	47,250
Creditors due after 1 year (3,250 + 125)	(3,375)
	133,825
Share capital	33,750
Share premium	38,750
Reserves (W2)	59,875
Shareholders' funds	132,375
Minority interest (W3)	1,450
	133,825

Workings

1 *Goodwill: Carter Ltd*

	£'000	£'000
Cost of investment		1,250
Share of net assets acquired		
Share capital	500	
Share premium	500	
Reserves	750	
	1,750	
Group share (60%)		1,050
Goodwill		200

2 *Reserves*

	Green	*Carter*
	£	£
Per question	81,250	2,625
Pre acquisition		(750)
		1,875
Demerger: cost of investment in Rose Group	(22,500)	
Share of Carter 60% × 1,875	1,125	
	59,875	

3 *Minority interest*

	£'000
Share capital: 500 × 40%	200
Share premium: 500 × 40%	200
P&L account: 2,625 × 40%	1,050
	1,450

(c) RE GROUP PLC

	£'000
Share capital	7,500
Reserves (W)	17,900
	25,400

Working: reserves

	£'000	£'000
Ross plc (part (a)		20,400
Less difference on consolidation		
Re plc share capital	7,500	
Less Ross plc's share capital	(2,500)	
Less Ross plc's share premium	(2,500)	
		(2,500)
		17,900

8 PLANS

> **Tutorial note.** This is not a particularly difficult question, but it is time consuming and involves a lot of number crunching.

There are a number of reasons why a group may re-organise.

- To reduce gearing by floating a business
- Companies may be transferred to another business during a divisionalisation process
- To create efficiencies of group structure for tax purposes

The impact of each of the proposed structures is discussed below.

Plan 1

The implications of this plan will be different, depending on the choice of purchase consideration.

Share for share exchange

If the purchase consideration is in the form of shares, then a share premium account will need to be set up in the books of Y. This share premium account must comprise the minimum premium value, which is the excess of the book value of the investment over the nominal value of the shares issued: £70m – £50m = £20m.

The impact on the individual company accounts and on the group accounts is as follows.

X GROUP
PLAN 1: SHARE FOR SHARE EXCHANGE

	Note	*X*	*Y*	*Z*	*Group*
		£m	£m	£m	£m
Tangible fixed assets		600	200	45	845
Cost of investment in Y	1	130			
Cost of investment in Z	2		70		
Net current assets		160	100	20	280
		890	370	65	1,125
Share capital	3	120	110	40	120
Share premium	4		20		
Profit and loss account	5	770	240	25	1,005
		890	370	65	1,125

Notes

1 *Cost of investment in Y*

This is increased by the total value of the shares issued: £50m + £20m = £70m.

2 *Cost of investment in Z*

Transferred to Y. The book value of the investment is preserved.

3 *Share capital*

Y's share capital is increased by the nominal value of the shares issued, £50m.

4 *Share premium*

This is as discussed above.

5 *Profit and loss account*

Goodwill arising on the purchase of Z is £10m (£70m – (£40m + £20m)). This will have been written off to reserves. The group profit and loss account is calculated as follows.

	£m
X	770
Y	240
Z's PARR (25 – 20)	5
Goodwill	(10)
	1,005

Cash purchase

If the purchase consideration is in the form of cash, a gain or loss on the sale of Z will arise in the books of X. This does not count as a distribution as the cash price of £75m is not in excess of the fair value of the net assets of Z, £80m. The effect on the accounts would be as follows.

	Note	*X*	*Y*	*Z*	*Group*
		£m	£m	£m	£m
Tangible fixed assets		600	200	45	845
Cost of investment in Y		60			
Cost of investment in Z	1		75		
Net current assets	2	235	25	20	280
		895	300	65	1,125
Share capital		120	60	40	120
Profit and loss account	3	775	240	25	1,005
		895	300	65	1,125

Notes

1 *Cost of investment in Z*

This is the cash consideration of £75m.

2 *Net current assets*

X's cash increases by £75m and Y's cash decreases by £75m.

3 *Profit and loss account*

X's profit and loss account has been increased by £5m, being the profit on the sale of the investment in Z. This is eliminated on consolidation as it is an intra-group transaction. The consolidated profit and loss account is calculated in exactly the same way as in the share for share exchange.

Plan 2

This restructuring plan involves a demerger of Y and Z from the X group and the formation of a separate W group. The transaction may be viewed as a distribution by X to its shareholders in the form of shares in W.

It is likely that this group reconstruction will qualify as a merger under FRS 6 *Acquisitions and mergers.* This will get round the necessity of creating a share premium account. Assuming that the FRS 6 criteria are met, and that no other inter-company transactions involving transfers of shares and cash had taken place, the effect on the accounts will be as follows.

	Note	*X*	*W Group*
		£m	£m
Tangible fixed assets		600	245
Net current assets		160	120
		760	365
Share capital	1	120	130
Profit and loss account	2	640	235
		760	365

Notes

1 *Share capital*

W issued 130m £1 shares.

2 *Profit and loss account*

		£m
X		
Per question		770
Less distribution		(130)
		640

	£m	£m
W		
Y's profit and loss		240
Z's profit and loss		25
		265
Share capital balance on merger account		
W shares issued	130	
Y share capital	(60)	
Z share capital	(40)	
		(30)
		235

Plan 3

This restructuring plan is a rationalisation, aimed at simplifying the group structure. An important point to take into account is that the investment in Z in the books of X may be impaired. Z was originally purchased for £70m, with goodwill of £10m arising, but the assets have been transferred to Y at book value of £60m. Z will be a shell company with a net asset value of £60m and this will be shown as an intercompany account with Y. The cost of X's investment in Z should be reduced to £60m, with a corresponding charge to the profit and loss account. The accounts would appear as follows.

	Note	X	Y	Z	Group
		£m	£m	£m	£m
Tangible fixed assets		600	245		845
Cost of investment in Y		60			
Cost of investment in Z	1	60			
Net current assets	2	160	60	60	280
		880	305	60	1,125
Share capital		120	60	40	120
Revaluation reserve	3		5		
Profit and loss account	4	760	240	20	1,005
		880	305	60	1,125

Notes

1 *Cost of investment in Z*

	£m
Per question	70
Less impairment	(10)
	60

2 *Net current assets*

Y's net current assets are £100m + £20m less intercompany creditor £60m.

Note that this calculation is based on the assumption that the £10m loss in X's books, the revaluation gain in Y's books and the loss on the transfer of assets to Y in Z's books are intercompany items and can be ignored. The calculation of group profit and loss account is then the same as for Plan 1.

3 *Revaluation reserve*

This is the gain on the purchase of the assets from Z: £65m – £60m.

4 *Profit and loss account*

X's individual profit and loss account is £770m less the impairment of £10m, which gives £760m.

The group profit and loss account is calculated as follows.

	£m
X	770
Y	240
Z (post-acquisition)	5
	1,015
Less goodwill	(10)
	1,005

Z's profit and loss account is £20m, ie £25m less £5m loss on transfer of assets.

Summary and conclusion

There are advantages and disadvantages to each of the three plans. Before we could make a recommendation we would need more information about why the group wishes to restructure.

Plan 1 does not change the group financial statements. From an internal point of view it results in a **closer relationship** between Y and Z. This may be advantageous if Y and Z are close geographically or in terms of similarity of business activities. Alternatively, it might be advantageous for tax reasons.

Plan 2 does have a **dramatic effect on the group financial statements**. Total **distributable profits fall** from £1,005 to £875m (X £640m, W group £235m). However, the W group may benefit from being more closely knit, and this may enhance overall growth.

Plan 3 is an example of **divisionalisation**: the assets and trade of Z are transferred to Y and Z becomes a shell company. This could result in cost savings overall. Furthermore, Z becomes a non-trading company and this could be used for some other purpose. It should be noted that, with Plan 3, there is no effect on the group financial statements.

9 ELIZABETH

> **Tutorial note.** You must ensure that the CA 1985 requirements on merger accounting have not been breached. Questions on merger accounting in the exam should not be more difficult than this.

(a) 'Equity share capital' means, in relation to a company, its issued share capital excluding any part of that capital which, neither as respects dividends nor as respects capital, carries any right to participate beyond a specified amount in a distribution (s 744 Companies Act 1985). Alternatively, see FRS 4 definition in this Study Text.

(b) (i) ELIZABETH LIMITED
BALANCE SHEET AS AT 1 DECEMBER 20X2 (W1)

	£'000	£'000
Fixed assets (NBV)		732.5
Current assets	261	
Creditors: amounts falling due within one year	168	
Net current assets		93.0
Total assets less current liabilities		825.5
Creditors: amounts falling due after more than one year		62.0
Provisions for liabilities and charges		8.0
		755.5
Capital and reserves		
Called up share capital		433.0
Share premium account (W1)		125.0
Other reserves		136.5
Profit and loss account		61.0
		755.5

(ii) ELIZABETH LIMITED
CONSOLIDATED BALANCE SHEET AS AT 1 DECEMBER 20X2

	£'000	£'000
Intangible fixed asset: goodwill (W2)		18.3
Tangible fixed assets (W3)		1,040.0
Current assets	743.0	
Creditors: amounts falling due within one year	575.0	
Net current assets		168.0
Total assets less current liabilities		1,226.3
Creditors: amounts falling due after more than one year		250.0
Provisions for liabilities and charges		22.0
Minority interest (W4)		140.0
		814.3
Capital and reserves		
Called up share capital		433.0
Share premium account		125.0
Other reserves		137.0
Profit and loss account		119.3
		814.3

Workings

1 *Entries in Elizabeth's books on 1 December 20X2*

		£'000	£'000
DEBIT	Investment in Jane Ltd	100.0	
CREDIT	Ordinary share capital		100.0
DEBIT	Investment in Kitty Ltd	207.5	
CREDIT	Ordinary share capital		83.0
	Reserve (unrealised)		124.5

		£'000	£'000
DEBIT	Investment in Lydia Ltd	125.0	
CREDIT	Ordinary share capital		50.0
	Share premium		75.0

(*Note*. The investment in Kitty cannot be treated as a merger because the cash paid exceeds 10% of the nominal value of the shares issued (CA 1985). The investment in Lydia cannot be treated as a merger because Elizabeth does not hold 90% of the 'relevant' shares (Sch 4A (10) CA 1985: shares holding an unrestricted rights to participate in distributions and liquidation surpluses.)

Lydia is a subsidiary of Elizabeth because Elizabeth controls all Lydia's voting shares.

The investments are shown as fixed assets in Elizabeth's balance sheet. The £30,000 existing investment in Kitty is already included in Elizabeth's fixed assets.

2 *Goodwill*

	Kitty	*Lydia*
	£'000	£'000
Market value of shares issued	207.5	125.0
Cash paid for 12,000 shares	30.0	
Less share of net assets acquired		
95% × (186 + 60)	(233.7)	
50% × (171 + 50)		(110.5)
	3.8	14.5

3 *Fixed assets*

	£'000
Elizabeth (NBV 300, less investment 30)	270
Jane (NBV)	250
Kitty (fair value)	250
Lydia (fair value)	270
	1,040

4 *Minority interest*

	£'000
Jane 10% × 176	17.6
Kitty 5% × (186 + 60)	12.3
Lydia 50% × (171 + 50)	110.5
	140.4

5 *Profit and loss account*

	£'000
Elizabeth	61.0
Jane (90% × 76) – 10	58.4*
Kitty	-
Lydia	-
	119.4

*__Tutorial note.__ The deduction of £10,000 represents the difference between the nominal value of the shares issued in Elizabeth(£100,000) and the nominal value of the shares acquired in Jane (£90,000). It has to be deducted from the P&L account because Jane has no unrealised reserves.

10 BARRY

Tutorial note. The merger reserve (W6) is calculated in the same way as a share premium, using the mid-market price of 125p : (50,000 × £1.25) – (50,000 × £1) = £12,500.

BARRY PLC
CONSOLIDATED BALANCE SHEET AS AT 30 SEPTEMBER 20X4

	£'000	£'000
Intangible fixed asset - goodwill (W3)		2.1
Tangible fixed assets		
Freehold property (1,400 + 100 + 70)		1,570.0
Plant and machinery (300 + 50 – 10)		340.0
Motor vehicles (100 + 20 – 10)		110.0
		2,022.1
Current assets		
Stock (180 + 40 – 10)	210	
Debtors (190 + 30)	220	
Prepayments (30 + 10 – 10)	30	
Cash (80 + 5)	85	
	545	
Current liabilities (W5)	(294)	
Net current assets		251.0
		2,273.1
Long term liabilities (200 + 12)		(212.0)
Provision		(50.0)
		2,011.1
Capital and reserves		
Ordinary share capital (1,300 + 50)		1,350.0
Contingent shares (W2)		25.0
Reserves (W6)		622.5
		1,997.5
Minority interest (W4)		13.6
		2,011.1

Workings

1 *Group structure*

$$\frac{18+120}{150} = 92\%$$

$\therefore$ MI = 8%

(Previously only 12% holding)

2 *Cost of investment*

	£	£
On original investment		50,000
On new acquisition		
Share capital (50,000 × 1.25)	62,500	
Loan stock (20,000 × 60p)	12,000	
Cash to be paid (10,000 × 1/1.1)	9,000	
Contingent consideration (20,000 × 1.25)	25,000	
		108,500
		158,500

3 *Goodwill*

	£'000	£'000
Cost of investment		158.50
Share of net assets - per question	190	
Fair value of adjustments		
Freehold	70	
Plant and machinery	(10)	
Motor vehicles	(10)	
Stock	(10)	
Prepayment	(10)	
Provision for claim from customer	(50)	
	170	
	× 92%	156.40
Goodwill		2.10

4 *Minority interest*

		£
	8% × 170,000	13,600

5 *Current liabilities*

	£'000
Barry + Coupar per question	275
Deferred cash consideration	9
Accrued issue expenses for loan stock	10
	294

6 *Reserves*

	£
Per question	620.0
Merger reserve	12.5
Expenses on issue	(10.0)
	622.5

11 TILES

Tutorial note. This question may seem daunting, but it is *comprehensive*, so you should work through it very carefully and make sure you understand all the calculations.

(a) SSAP 20 requires that the method to be used for translating the financial statements of a foreign enterprise should reflect the financial and other operational relationship which exists between the holding company and its foreign enterprise. It recognises that in most cases this means that the consolidated accounts will be prepared using the closing rate/net investment method. However, in certain circumstances the standard requires the temporal method to be used.

The method used for translating the financial statements of a foreign enterprise should only be changed when the financial and other operational relationship changes and renders the method used inappropriate.

Closing rate/net investment method

For most investing companies in the UK where foreign operations are carried out by foreign enterprises it is normally the case that the foreign enterprises operate as separate or quasi-independent entities. The day to day operations of the foreign enterprise will be based in its local currency, are likely to be financed wholly or partly in its own currency, and will not be dependent on the reporting currency of the holding company. The foreign enterprise will be managed so as to maximise the local currency profits attributable to the holding company. Consequently the financial statements of the foreign enterprise expressed in its local currency will be the best available indicator of its performance and value to the group. In order to preserve the inherent relationships included in these local currency financial statements it is therefore necessary to use a single rate of exchange when translating the financial statements when preparing the consolidated financial statements.

Temporal method

In circumstances where it would be inappropriate to use the closing rate/net investment method for translating the financial statements of a foreign enterprise, the temporal method should be used.

Such a method is to be used where the trade of the foreign enterprise is more dependent on the economic environment of the investing company's currency than that of its own reporting currency. By using the temporal method the consolidated accounts reflect the transactions of the foreign enterprise as if they had been carried out by the investing company itself.

It is impossible to specify any one factor which would indicate when the temporal method should be used. The standard indicates that the following factors should be taken into account.

(i) The extent to which the cash flows of the enterprise have a direct impact upon those of the investing company. For example, whether there is a regular and frequent movement of cash between the holding company and the foreign enterprise or whether there are only occasional remittances of, for example, dividends.

(ii) The extent to which the functioning of the enterprise is dependent directly upon the investing company. For example, whether management is based locally or at head office

and whether pricing decisions are based on local competition and costs or are part of a worldwide decision process.

(iii) The currency in which the majority of the trading transactions are denominated, for example, whether the foreign currency is used for both invoicing goods and paying expenses, or whether the majority of such items are denominated in the currency of the investing company.

(iv) The major currency to which the operation is exposed in its financing structure.

For example whether the company is dependent on local financing or whether the majority of the financing is in the currency of the investing company and possibly obtained through, or guaranteed by, that company.

The choice of method is also important because of the direct impact on the consolidated results. Both profit before tax and capital employed will be different under each method because of the different rates used to translate P&L items and assets and liabilities. The choice of method may be abused to manipulate results.

(b) TILES PLC
CONSOLIDATED BALANCE SHEET AS AT 31 DECEMBER 20X2

	£'000
Intangible fixed asset: goodwill (W2)	16,485
Tangible fixed assets (35,640 + 24,857)	60,497
Current assets less current liabilities (51,072 + 8,314)	59,386
Long term loans (W4) (26,345 + 3,428)	(29,773)
	106,595
Share capital	50,000
Retained reserves	53,621
	103,621
Minority interest (W5)	2,974
	106,595

STATEMENT OF CONSOLIDATED RESERVES	£'000
Reserves brought forward	30,064
Retained profit for the year	22,147
Exchange differences	1,410
	53,621

Workings

1 *Translate balance sheet of Ceramic Inc*

CERAMIC INC
BALANCE SHEET AS AT 31 DECEMBER 20X1

	£'000
Fixed assets (108,000,000 – 3,600,000) @ 4.2	24,857
Net current asset (34,920 @ 4.2)	8,314
Long term loans (14,400 @ 4.2)	(3,428)
	29,743
Net assets at acquisition	23,017
Post acquisition reserves	6,726
	29,743

2 *Goodwill*

		£'000
Cost of investment		37,200
	Pins ('000)	
Fair value of net assets acquired		
Share capital	36,000	
Reserves b/f	25,920	
To 30.9.X1	4,482	
Revaluation	57,888	
	124,290	
@ 5.4	23,017	
× 90%		20,715
		16,485

3 *Fair value of fixed assets*

	£'000
NBV at end of year	47,376
Add back 10,944 × 3/12	2,736
	50,112
Fair value	108,000
Surplus	57,888

4 *Long-term loans*

		£'000
(i)	85,536,000 @ 4.2	20,366
(i)	12,096,000 @ 2.3	5,259
		25,625
Other		720
		26,345

On loan (i) therefore a loss of (20,366 – 15,840) £4,526 arises which is hedged in reserves in W7.

On loan (ii) therefore a gain of (5,760 – 5,259) £501 arises which is added to Tiles' profit for the year in W6.

5 *Minority interest*

29,743 (W1) × 10% = 2,974

6 *Retained profit for the year*

	£
Tiles	21,528
Add gain on A$ loan (5,259 (W4) – 5,760)	501
	22,029
Ceramic 90% × 131 (W7))	118
	22,147

7 *Exchange differences*

	£'000	£'000
Closing net assets at the closing rate (W1)	29,743	
Opening net assets at the opening rate (W2)	(23,017)	
Retained profit for the period		
(5,976 × 3/12) – (3,600 – 2,736) @ 4.8	(131)	
Exchange gain on investment	6,595	
Group share (90%)		5,936
Hedged against loss on loan (W4)		(4,526)
Net movement on reserves		1,410

8 *Proof of reserves*

	£'000
Tiles plc (51,592 – 4,526 (W7) +501 (W6))	47,567
Ceramic (6,726 (W1) × 90%)	6,054
	53,621

12 HASELEY

> **Tutorial note.** Don't rush Part (b) – this examiner puts a lot of emphasis on interpretation.

(a) HASELEY SERVICES LIMITED
GROUP CASH FLOW STATEMENT FOR THE YEAR ENDED 30 JUNE 20X7

	£'000	£'000
Cash flow from operating activities		2,188
Returns on investments and servicing of finance		
Interest received	200	
Interest paid (30 – 24)	(6)	
Finance charge on finance leases	(39)	
		155
Taxation		
Corporation tax paid		(757)
Capital expenditure and financial investment		
Purchase of tangible fixed assets	(456)	
Disposal of tangible fixed assets	1,020	
		564
Acquisitions and disposals		
Disposal of subsidiary	2,500	
Less cash sold	(103)	
	2,397	
Acquisition of subsidiary	(12,000)	
Less cash acquired	335	
	(11,665)	
		(9,268)
Equity dividends paid		(2,080)
Management of liquid resources		
Cash released from 3 months deposit		1,000
Financing		
Capital paid on finance leases	(232)	
New loan received	6,000	
		5,768
Decrease in cash		(2,430)

Workings

1 *Cash flow from operating activities*

	£'000
Operating profit	1,300
Depreciation	573
Decrease in debtors (1,563 – 2,364 + 553)	248
Increase in trade creditors (1,543 – 1,979 + 672)	236
Increase in accruals (1,749 – 504 + 304 – 2,000)	(451)
Decrease in stock (562 – 1,235 + 491)	182
Amortisation of goodwill (1,300 – 1,200)	100
	2,188

2 *Equity dividends paid*

DIVIDENDS PROPOSED

	£'000		£'000
∴ Cash	2,080	b/f	720
c/d	840	P&L	2,200
	2,940		2,920

3 *Taxation*

TAXATION

	£'000		£'000
∴ Cash	757	b/f Corporation tax	450
c/d Corporation tax	393	Deferred tax	425
Deferred tax	526	Acquisition	121
		P&L	680
	1,676		1,676

(b) (i) We can see the net movement in the company's cash position over the year for 20X7 Haseley Services had a net flow of £2,430,000.

(ii) Then using the standard headings within the cash flow proforma we can see where cash has been generated and what it has been spent on.

(iii) In terms of using it to get an indication of the businesses future cash generating ability, what I would look at is how sustainable the cash generation is and the ongoing nature of the expenditure.

(iv) The business generated £2,188,000 from its operating activities and £6,000,000 from debt. The most significant outflows were in connection with the acquisition of the subsidiary and in the payment of equity dividends.

(v) There has been a major inflow of cash from a one off source, raising of debt, however this has in the main been used to acquire a potentially cash generating business.

(vi) The cash flow statement alone cannot give complete information about future cash generation. The balance sheet is necessary to add meaning to the individual flows this year. For instance, interest received in 20X7 was £200,000. This is unlikely to be repeated as we can see from the balance sheet that 3 month deposits have significantly reduced.

(vii) Interest and loan repayments are likely to rise in future due to the loan being raised in the period.

13 WIMBORNE

> **Tutorial note.** You need to make a number of assumptions to do this question. These should be clearly stated.

WIMBORNE GROUP
CONSOLIDATED CASH FLOW STATEMENT
FOR THE YEAR ENDED 30 SEPTEMBER 20X7

	£'000	£'000
Operating activities (note 1)		21,417
Returns on investments and servicing of finance		
Dividends received (175 – 44)	175	
Dividends paid to minority interests (W1)	(78)	
Interest paid	(1,350)	
		(1,253)
Taxation		
Corporation tax paid (W3)		(4,003)
Capital expenditure and financial investment		
Sales of investments (2,000 + 5,000)	7,000	
Purchase of investments (W4) + 7,500	(8,500)	
Payments to acquire tangible assets	(5,750)	
		(7,250)
Equity dividends paid (W2)		(1,700)
Financing		
Loans repaid		(4,826)
Increase in cash		2,385

Note

1 *Operating activities*

	£'000
Operating activities	22,391
Depreciation	3,197
Decrease in debtors (12,470 – 12,358 – 158)	46
Increase in stock (19,773 – 17,702 – 205)	(1,866)
Decrease in creditors (23,365 – 25,592 – 124)	(2,351)
Operating cash flow	21,417

Assumptions

(a) Operating activities disclosed on a net basis.

(b) No interest accruals included within creditors.

(c) Ringwood Ltd was not an associate hence loss on disposal was calculated by reference to cost.

(d) All additions to tangible fixed assets were paid for in cash during the year.

(e) No new loans were taken out during the year.

(f) Six months term deposits of £5 million were cashed and a further £7.5 million was invested - there were no other movements.

(g) There were no disposals of tangible fixed assets.

(h) No interest was capitalised during the year.

(i) VAT has been ignored.

Further information

(a) Why was only £78,000 paid to minority shareholders during the year when there was a creditor for £323,000 at the end of the previous year?

(b) In view of (i) above, is it appropriate to include £350,000 dividend creditor with respect to the minority as an obligation falling due within one year?

Workings

1 MINORITY INTEREST

	£'000		£'000
Cash paid (balance)	78	B/f	3,400
		B/f	325
		P&L	1,545
C/f	5,100	Exchange gain	258
C/f	350		
	5,528		5,528

2 DIVIDENDS

	£'000		£'000
Cash paid (balance)	1,700	B/f	1,100
		P&L	1,800
C/f	1,200		
	2,900		2,900

3 TAXATION

	£'000		£'000
Cash paid (balance)	4,003	B/f	4,829
		B/f	3,094
		P&L	5,544
C/f	6,370	P&L	1,206
C/f	4,300		
	14,673		14,673

4 INVESTMENTS

	£'000		£'000
B/f	6,900	Disposal	4,500
Cash paid (balance)	1,000	C/f	3,400
	7,900		7,900

5 FIXED ASSETS

	£'000		£'000
B/f	22,430	P&L	3,197
Additions	5,750	Revaluation	1,400
X gain	2,117	C/f	25,700
	30,297		30,297

6 LOANS

	£'000		£'000
Cash paid (balance)	4,826	B/f	11,850
C/f	7,500	Exchange loss	476
	12,326		12,326

14 PORTAL

> **Tutorial note.** The examiner for the new syllabus paper has stated that the emphasis is on advising management and on realistic scenario's. part (b) could come under the heading of advice and Part (a), which involves using your knowledge to correct the accountant's work, could come under both headings

(a) PORTAL GROUP
CASH FLOW STATEMENT FOR THE YEAR ENDED 31 DECEMBER 20X0

	Working	£m	£m
Net cash inflow from operating activities			692
Returns on investments and servicing of finance			
Interest received		26	
Interest paid		(9)	
Dividend paid to minority interest	2	(31)	
Dividend received from joint venture		10	
			(4)
Taxation	3		(115)
Capital expenditure			
Purchase of tangible fixed assets		(380)	
Sale of tangible fixed assets	4	195	
			(185)
Acquisitions and disposals			
Disposal of subsidiary		75	
Cash of subsidiary disposed of		(130)	
Purchase of interest in joint venture		(25)	
			(80)
Net cash inflow before use of liquid resources and financing			308
Decrease in short term deposits			(143)
Net cash inflow			165

Workings

1 *Net cash inflow from operating activities*

	£m
Per question	875
Add back loss on disposal	25
Adjustments for current assets/liabilities of subsidiary*	
Stock	(60)
Debtors	(50)
Creditors (130 – 25)	105
Deduct pre-tax profit on joint venture (55 + 20)	(75)
Interest receivable	(27)
Interest payable	19
Deduct profit on sale of fixed assets	(120)
	692

**Note.* The movements in current assets used by the accountant to calculate net cash inflow from operating activities incorrectly include amounts relating to the subsidiary disposed of.

2 *Dividend paid to minority interest*

	£m
Difference per question (balance sheet movement)	40
Profit for year	75
Sale of subsidiary (20% × 420)	(84)
	31

3 *Taxation*

	£m
Per question (balance sheet movement)	31
Tax on joint venture	20
Tax on subsidiary disposed of	25
Tax on profit	(191)
Cash outflow	(115)

4 *Sale of tangible fixed assets*

	£m
Per question (carrying value)	1,585
Transferred to joint venture	(200)
Subsidiary disposed of	(310)
Sale and leaseback	(1,000)
Profit on sale	120
Cash inflow	195

(b) *Cash flow statements: presentation to directors of Portal plc*

General purpose

The purpose of cash flow statements is to **provide information which is not shown in the other financial statements**. This information is important because the success and survival of every reporting entity depends on its ability to generate or obtain cash. For example, the tax authorities require an **actual cash payment**, which will differ for a number of reasons from the tax charge shown in the profit and loss account. Some of the information, such as the purchase or sale of tangible fixed assets, is apparent or can easily be computed from the balance sheet or profit and loss account, but the **complexity** of the financial statements may make this hard to see in respect of some items.

Group cash flow statements

Consolidated profit and loss accounts and balance sheets can hide the amount of cash actually paid to acquire a subsidiary, or received on disposal, in situations where part of the consideration is in the form of shares. FRS 1 requires **cash flows relating to the consideration** to be reported under acquisitions and disposals in the consolidated cash flow statement. Similarly, the dividend paid to minority interest is shown, as is the dividend received from associates or joint ventures.

However, a possible limitation of consolidated cash flow statements is that they can **obscure the cash profile of companies within the group**. For example, if there were two subsidiaries, one with a high cash flow from operations and one with high returns on investments, consolidation would obscure this. This is a limitation of consolidated accounts generally.

Accounting ratios

Useful information derived from the cash flow statement can be used in **accounting ratios** for analysis purposes. In the case of Portal plc, it might be useful to show proportion of net cash inflow from operating activities which has been spent on purchasing fixed assets:

$$\frac{\text{Purchase of tangible fixed assets}}{\text{Net cash inflow from operating activities}} = \frac{380}{692} = 54.9\%$$

It would be useful to know how much of this relates to maintenance of existing operating capacity and how much relates to increasing capacity with a view to enhancing future earnings. However, this information cannot be derived from the cash flow statement.

It would also be useful to know **how the cash flow after investment has been utilised.** This can be done by comparing the net cash inflow before use of liquid resources and financing with the net cash increase in the period. In the case of Portal this works out as (308 – 165)/308 = 46.4%. In other words 46.4% of this net cash inflow has been used to pay off short term deposits.

Another useful ratio is **interest cover**, based not on profit before interest and tax as in conventional ratio analysis, but on operating cash flow:

$$\frac{\text{Net cash flow from operating activities}}{\text{Interest paid}} = \frac{692}{9} = 76.8 \text{ times}$$

Further limitations

- The cash flow statement does not provide information about future cash flows.
- The reconciliation can be misinterpreted. Naïve investors may perceive the adding back of depreciation/amortisation as sources of funds.
- Some regard the cash flow statement as derivative.

15 UPERAND

Tutorial note. You must use your common sense in questions of this nature: don't make any silly suggestions.

To: Board of directors of Uperand
From: External consultant Date: 10 December 20X9

VALUATION OF UPERAND FOR AIM LISTING

Introduction

This report proposes two potential methods of valuation with regard to obtaining a AIM listing. Unfortunately it will not be possible to use the figures suggested by the Managing Director for a number of reasons.

(a) The figures are based on book values. It is more appropriate to use market values in arriving at a valuation for listing purposes.

(b) The addition of total assets and reserves is to double count since the reserves represent one of the sources of finance used to acquire the existing assets.

(c) The liabilities should have been deducted from the total assets figure in order to arrive at the net asset position of the company.

(d) The issue of 400,000 new shares would bring the total number of shares in the company to 5.4m. If only the new shares are offered on the AIM this represents 7.4% of the total number of shares. The minimum percentage that can be offered on the market is 10%.

(e) In view of the problems with the net assets valuation, and taking into account the valuation estimates given below, Uperand is unlikely to achieve the price of 625 pence per share which would be necessary to raise £2.5m from 400,000 shares.

The valuation of shares in unquoted companies always presents problems, and a number of approaches are available. On the basis of the information given, two alternative approaches will be considered below, namely the net assets basis and the earnings method. There is insufficient information available to use the CAPM in this case, and since the company has not paid a dividend in the last three years, the dividend valuation method cannot be applied.

Net assets basis valuation

A valuation based on net asset value can be found by adjusting the book values of the assets to reflect the market situation, as follows.

		£'000	£'000
Fixed assets			12,000
Add:	Additional value of patent	1,000	
	Additional value of buildings	1,500	
	Additional value of land	152	
	Additional value of land	394	
Less:	Loss on machinery	(500)	
			2,456
			14,546
Current assets			10,000
Less:	Obsolete stock	(540)	
	Risky debts	(90)	
			(630)
			23,916
Total assets			(10,775)
Less total liabilities			13,141

Tutorial notes

1 Obsolete stock is assumed to have no scrap value.
2 Total liabilities includes long-term loans, bank loans, trade creditors and taxation.

Uperand has 5m ordinary shares in issue. The theoretical share price based on asset values is therefore 263 pence (£13.141/5m).

Earnings based valuation

An estimate of the market value of Uperand may be obtained by applying a P/E ratio similar to that in other companies in the sector to the current earnings. It is assumed that the relative growth rates, financial structures and risk profiles of Striver plc and Gogetor plc are similar to those of Uperand.

The first step is to calculate the P/E ratios of Striver and Gogetor.

	Striver	*Gogetor*
No of shares	5m	5m
EPS	46p	5.5p
Total earnings	£2.3m	£0.275m
Market capitalisation	£35m	£4.3m
P/E ratio	15.2	15.6

It would therefore appear reasonable to assume a P/E ratio of 15 for Uperand. This gives a market capitalisation of £20.475 based on the 20X8 earnings figure (£1.365m). The theoretical share price is therefore 409.5 pence (£20.475m/5m).

In practice, it is unlikely that Uperand could achieve this share price since earnings are falling and there is no record of dividend payments to attract investors. It is assumed that Striver and Gogetor have stable or growing earnings and are paying a dividend.

Conclusions

The valuations calculated above suggest that the shares could be issued at between 263 pence and 409 pence per share. In practice, it will be necessary to issue the shares at a discount to the theoretical share price in order to make them attractive to investors. Thus a price towards the lower end of the range of perhaps 300 pence per share might be appropriate. This would mean that Uperand will need to issue at least 833,333 shares in order to raise £2.5m. In fact a larger number of share are likely to be necessary in order to cover issue costs.

Other factors that should be considered include the effect of such an issue on the structure of ownership and control: this could cause a weakening in the family's control of the company. The

directors should also consider the need to pay a dividend, and it might be wise to make a statement to this effect, outlining the proposed dividend policy at the time of offer.

It would be helpful for the company to direct some attention to its working capital situation. This has grown from £1.8m in 20X6 to £4.225m in 20X8, mainly due to the increase in stock and debtors. At the same time turnover has increased by 42.8%, but gross margins have fallen from 32.3% to 24.2%. If the levels of stock and debtors could be reduced to the same percentage of sales as in 20X9, this would release £757,000. If gross margins could also be restored, this would further reduce the need for additional external financing.

16 ANDREWS

The financial statements provided for Andrews Ltd in 20X4 and 20X5 represent two very different sectors. The 20X4 statements include retailing as well as manufacturing, whereas 20X5 statements represent manufacturing alone. We are not provided with a breakdown of how much turnover and profits or losses are associated with the discontinuation of the retail sector. Applying FRS 3 to the profit and loss account would therefore have given us more useful information to work from.

It must also be taken into consideration that the industrial sector ratios are more likely to be relevant to the 20X5 financial statements than to the 20X4 statements. Bearing these differences and incomplete information in mind it is not possible to comment fully on the 20X5 profitability and liquidity of Andrews Ltd, but using available information the following can be said.

Profitability

The gross margin fell 3% from 20X4 to 20X5 indicating that there was probably a higher gross return on retail sales than from manufacturing goods. The 32% achieved in 20X5 is very close to the industry average and hence acceptable. Net profit margin (excluding exceptional gain on sale of retail outlets) has risen to approach the industry norm following the sell-off of retail outlets. This would indicate that the shops were expensive to run which is probably one reason why they were sold.

Despite selling off all the retail outlets the fixed asset turnover appears to have fallen and is disappointingly below the industry average. However this is principally due to the effect of a revaluation in the year. If this revaluation was stripped out the fixed asset turnover in 20X5 would increase to 5.1 times which is much in line with the previous year and healthily above the average for the industry. The return on shareholders' funds appears to have halved from 20X4 to 20X5. This ratio, however, does not take into account the influencing factors, ie the revaluation in 20X5 and the long term liability in 20X4. However even if alternative ratios were used taking these factors into consideration it still appears that ordinary shareholders will be less happy in the short term with their investment.

Inc conclusion, as like is not being compared with like it is very difficult to make accurate comparisons. The sell-off of retail outlets appears to have depressed profitability and efficiency but it may be that the figures given in the financial statements are misleading.

Liquidity

In 20X4 Andrews Ltd appears to have a severe liquidity problem. Both its current and quick ratios were below the industry average. However the sale of its retail outlets appears to have boosted the cash flow to the company. As well as paying off its long term loan both the current and quick ratios have improved markedly. The current ratio is above the industry average whilst the quick ratio is close to it albeit slightly below average.

There is a worrying trend, however, in that stock has increased by more than a third in 20X5 compared to 20X4. As there are no further retail outlets this is clearly all stock from manufactured goods. It indicates that the company is having difficulty finding alternative outlets for its stock.

Another worrying indicator is that debtor collection period has increased from 31 days to 40 days. However, it is possible that this increase is entirely due to the fact that the retail outlets operated on a cash sales basis and now goods are being sold to other retailers all sales are credit sales.

Summary

From the limited information available it would appear that Andrews Ltd has improved its liquidity position due to selling off its retail outlets. Time will show whether or not this relief is temporary or longer term.

In the short term at least profitability is not so good, but once again the figures given are distorted due to year on year differences.

17 PETER HOLDINGS

> **Tutorial note.** It is not yet clear how the examiner will test this area.

Divisional performance should be measured, in the interests of the group's shareholders, in such a way as to indicate what sort of return each subsidiary is making on the **shareholder's investment**. Shareholders themselves are likely to be interested in the performance of the group as a whole, measured in terms of return on shareholders' capital, earnings per share, dividend yield, and growth in earnings and dividends. These performance ratios cannot be used for subsidiaries in the group, and so an alternative measure has to be selected, which compares the return from the subsidiary with the value of the investment in the subsidiary.

Two performance measures could be used. Both would provide a suitable indication of performance from the point of view of the group's shareholders.

(a) Return on capital employed, which from the shareholders' point of view would be:

$$\frac{\text{Profit after interest}}{\text{Net assets at current valuation minus long - term liabilities (eg long - term borrowings)}}$$

(b) Alternatively, residual income could be used. This might be:

	Profit after debt interest
Minus	A notional interest charge on the value of assets financed by shareholders' capital
Equals	Residual income.

Residual income might be measured instead as:

	Profit before interest (controllable by the subsidiary's management)
Minus	A notional interest charge on the controllable investments of the subsidiary
Equals	Residual income.

Each subsidiary would be able to increase its residual income if it earned an incremental profit in excess of the notional interest charges on its incremental investments – ie in effect, if it added to the value of the group's equity.

18 ALTMAN FORMULA

> **Tutorial note**. It is unlikely that you would get a full calculation on Z-scores in the exam, but here is a comprehensive question just in case.

(a)

	Working capital	*Retained earnings*	*Pre-tax earnings*	*MV of equity*	*Assets*	*Liabilities*	*Sales*
	£'000	£'000	£'000	£'000	£'000	£'000	£'000
Andrea	4,000	60,000	10,000	20,000	200,000	120,000	200,000
Chenier	2,000	20,000	0	5,000	100,000	80,000	120,000
Maddalena	6,000	20,000	(30,000)	48,000	800,000	740,000	900,000
Roucher	40,000	200,000	30,000	100,000	1,800,000	1,000,000	2,000,000

Calculate the factors in the formula for each company.

	A	*B*	*C*	*D*	*E*
Andrea	0.020	0.300	0.050	1.000	0.167
Chenier	0.020	0.200	0.000	1.200	0.063
Maddalena	0.008	0.025	-0.038	1.125	0.065
Roucher	0.022	0.111	0.017	1.111	0.100

Calculate the Z-score for each company.

	1.2(A)	1.4(B)	3.3(C)	1(D)	0.6(E)	Z-score
Andrea	0.024	0.420	0.165	1.000	0.100	1.709
Chenier	0.024	0.280	0.000	1.200	0.038	1.541
Maddalena	0.009	0.035	-0.124	1.125	0.039	1.084
Roucher	0.027	0.156	0.055	1.111	0.060	1.408

In each case, the Z-score is less than the critical level of 1.8, and therefore all the companies appear to be at risk from bankruptcy. Maddalena plc would appear to be the firm most at risk, since it has the lowest Z-score. It is followed in order of vulnerability by Roucher plc, Chenier plc and Andrea plc.

(b) Altman worked in the US using a relatively small sample of failed companies and going concerns. He undertook the simultaneous analysis of more than 20 variables, both accounting and non-accounting. From this, five variables emerged as being key factors in determining the financial soundness of a company. These factors could be weighted, as in the expression applied above, and combined to produce a single Z-score. In addition to contending that there is a threshold Z-score which a company needs to exceed for financial safety, he identified a 'grey area' or range of Z-scores for which the eventual survival or demise of the company is uncertain. This middle range was represented by Z-scores in the band 1.81 to 2.99.

(c) As explained above, Altman's work dealt only with a small sample of US firms, and was wholly empirical in nature. It is therefore unreasonable to expect the same formula to have equal validity in different countries, economic sectors, and stages in the economic cycle. In recognition of this, Altman's approach has been applied by a number of subsequent researchers seeking to find key predictors in other situations. They have come up with expressions using both different weightings and different key ratios to predict financial failure in other environments.

Another widely used approach in failure prediction is the analysis of liquidity ratios. The two most important of these are the current ratio and the quick ratio.

(i) *Current ratio.* This is the ratio of current assets to current liabilities. The current ratio is based on the premise that a company should have enough current assets to suggest that it will be able to meet its future commitments to pay off its current liabilities. A ratio in excess of 2.0 is needed for safety, although this will obviously depend on the nature of the industry - the relationship between credit periods allowed and taken - and the level of stockholdings.

(ii) *Quick ratio.* This is the ratio of current assets excluding stock to current liabilities. Stock is excluded because, particularly in the case of manufacturing companies, it is not always possible to convert stock to cash quickly. The current ratio (including stock) can therefore give a misleading picture of a firm's actual ability to meet commitments to its creditors. A ratio in excess of 1.0 is a general indicator of financial safety, but in firms where stock turnover is fast, a ratio of less than 1.0 does not necessarily indicate a liquidity problem.

Research indicates however that, contrary to expectations, the level of these ratios and trends over time for a single company do not provide a reliable means of predicting business failure.

Debt ratios can also be used to provide a measure of financial security. These include the following.

(i) *Total debts: total assets.* This ratio shows the extent to which assets are financed by borrowings. A maximum level of 50% is considered appropriate for safety.

(ii) *Interest cover (profit before interest and tax: interest).* This indicates the ability of the company to pay the interest charge out of earnings, and it can also be used to give a measure of sensitivity to interest rate fluctuations. A ratio greater than 2.0 or ideally 3.0 is considered to be necessary for safety.

To conclude, the empirical evidence suggests that some form of simultaneous ratio analysis of the kind undertaken by Altman is the most useful quantitative method available for predicting business failure. However the exact nature and relative combination of ratios will depend on the economic and geographic sector being studied. No single ratio in isolation can be used as a reliable failure predictor. In addition to ratio analysis, other more general indicators can be used to form a view of the financial stability of the firm. These include changes in the company's operating environment, such as new legislation or technological developments, which might jeopardise the success of existing operations. Other figures within the accounts, when considered together, might also indicate potential instability. Examples of this are very large provisions, increases in intangible fixed assets, and significant post balance sheet events. Thus ratios are useful in failure prediction, but cannot be used on their own to forecast the future of a company with any degree of certainty.

19 GO-GO

> **Tutorial note.** This question looks back to the chapter on corporate failure as well as considering the limitations of ratio analysis.

(a)

	Go-Go Products		Numerous Inventions	
	20X1	20X0	20X1	20X0
Profit before tax / Current liabilities	1,400 / 7,930	935 / 9,970	1,090 / 4,357	1,278 / 2,467
	0.18	0.094	0.25	0.52
Current assets / Total liabilities	10,801 / 9,339	11,537 / 11,138	6,798 / 4,412	4,859 / 2,505
	1.16	1.03	1.54	1.94
Current liabilities / Total tangible assets	7,930 / 15,445	9,970 / 16,765	4,357 / 8,745	2,467 / 6,389
	0.51	0.59	0.50	0.39
Working capital / Operating costs exc depn	2,871 / 28,356	1,567 / 24,198	2,441 / 8,313	2,392 / 6,571
	0.10	0.06	0.29	0.36

Aspects of performance which are of great relevance to the going concern status are as follows.

(i) *Liquidity:* although aspects of liquidity are revealed in the ratios already calculated, the current ratio and/or 'quick' ratio could usefully be added.

(ii) *Profitability:* although concerned with a different problem from the previous ratios, it is important to earn a sufficient profit for shareholders, and a ROCE could be calculated.

	Go-Go Products		Numerous Inventions	
	20X1	20X0	20X1	20X0
Current assets / Current liabilities	10,801 / 7,930	11,537 / 9,970	6,798 / 4,357	4,859 / 2,467
	1.36	1.16	1.56	1.97
Quick assets / Current liabilities	4,558 / 7,930	4,764 / 9,970	5,812 / 4,357	3,602 / 2,467
	0.57	0.48	1.33	1.46
ROCE: Profit before tax / Capital & reserves	1,400 / 7,024	935 / 6,564	1,090 / 4,336	1,287 / 3,884
	19.9%	14.2%	25.1%	33.1%

(b) Go-Go Ltd has improved its performance over the past year, and this is reflected in improved ratios. (*Note.* The 'no credit interval' indicates the amount of working capital employed to sustain operations.) Provided that the amount of working capital is not excessive (which is unlikely), Go-Go Ltd is moving away from a position of under capitalisation.

The ratios of Numerous Inventions Ltd have, in contrast, worsened. The fall in profits/current liabilities by over one half threatens a situation where the company might be hard pressed to generate sufficient funds from operations to sustain the current level of activity; and it is noticeable that stock levels have fallen sharply. It has been suggested that this ratio more than any other is a guide to possible company insolvency.

It is also noticeable that the proportion of current liabilities to total tangible assets has risen considerably. (*Note.* The overall debt: total tangible assets ratio has similarly declined to:

$$\frac{4,412}{8,748} = 0.50 \text{ in 20X1 from} \qquad \frac{2,505}{6,389} = 0.39 \text{ in 20X0.)}$$

Although the ratios of Go-Go are improving and those of Numerous Inventions declining, it is important to remember that Numerous Inventions Ltd still compares favourably with Go-Go Ltd. For example, the quick ratio of Numerous Inventions seems very sound, whereas the quick ratio of Go-Go is well below the 'ideal' ratio. Go-Go Ltd must therefore still be vulnerable to any unfavourable movements in its liquidity position in the future, and the management of both companies have considerable cause for concern.

(c) Various ratios have been used fairly widely in the United States to provide predictions of failure (by constructing 'Z'-scores for companies from a weighted average calculation based on the selected ratios). Management should perhaps concern itself more with ratio analysis of this sort as a means of identifying problems before they become critical. 'Failure analysis' does have limitations.

(i) *Subjectivity*: the weighting applied to various ratios is a subjective decision by the analyst. A formula that may provide accurate predictions for one company may be totally inadequate for another;

(ii) *Timing*: ratios may turn bad only very late in the day, when it is too late to prevent the company's failure. This is especially true of liquidity ratios;

(iii) *Ratio analysis* ignores factors having some influence in the future, for example government policy (loans and other forms of aid), take-over bids, and so on.

(iv) Analysis of accounts prepared by the historical cost convention may give a totally misleading impression (for example of profit and fixed asset values).

20 GERMAN COMPETITOR

> **Tutorial note**. You do not need to know about German accounting practice to answer this question, just a basic knowledge of the differences between the European and UK models and your common sense! Think of this as an interpretation of accounts questions.

To: Managing Director
From: An Accountant
Date: xx.xx.xx
Re: *Hilde GmbH*

(a) *Analysis of performance plus commentary (DM million)*

Profit and loss a/c	*20X4*	*20X5*	*% Increase (decrease)*
Sales	1,270	1,890	49
Cost of sales			
Material purchased	400	740	
De-stocking of materials	40	90	
Material cost	440	830	89
Labour cost	285	500	75
Depreciation	150	200	33
Current assets written off	20	30	50
Other operating expenses	40	50	25
Finished goods stock increase	(80)	(120)	50
	855	1,490	
Operating profit before other income	415	400	(4)

Profit and loss a/c	*20X4*	*20X5*	*% Increase (decrease)*
Profit rate on turnover	32%	21%	
Other operating income	50	75	50

Cash flows

	DM million
Share capital issued	200
Increased creditors	75
Increased accruals	20
Profit ploughed back (185 + 200)	385
	680

These flows were used to finance:

Purchases of plant (550 + 200)	750
Net stocks	30
More credit to customers	80
	860
Difference: reduction in cash reserves	180

Other relevant performance measures

	20X4	*20X5*
Debtors' turnover		
$= \dfrac{\text{Trade debtors}}{\text{Sales}} \times 365$	$\dfrac{100}{1{,}270} \times 365$ = 29 days	$\dfrac{180}{1{,}890} \times 365$ = 35 days
Current ratio		
$= \dfrac{\text{Current assets}}{\text{Current liabilities}}$	$\dfrac{420 + 70}{350}$ = 1.4	$\dfrac{350 + 50}{425}$ = 0.94
Quick ratio		
$= \dfrac{\text{Current assets} - \text{Stock}}{\text{Current liabilities}}$	$\dfrac{100 + 200 + 70}{350}$ = 1.06	$\dfrac{180 + 20 + 50}{425}$ = 0.59

Commentary

(i) Material costs and labour costs have risen at an alarming rate in 20X5 and to a certain extent other costs have also increased substantially. These increases are far greater than the increase in turnover. A lack of co-ordination of production to sales has created a substantial build up of finished goods in stock.

(ii) Interest costs and other operating income have both increased substantially, but because debt and investments (respectively) are not shown on the balance sheet it is not possible to judge why these rises have taken place. One possibility is that the increases in the value of land and buildings represent additions which are being rented out.

(iii) Creditors have increased only slightly considering the increases in stock purchases during the year. This may indicate that the company's trade creditors are taking a very firm line with the company and thus the trade creditors balance is being held firm.

(iv) Although shares were issued during the year, at a premium of 100%, the fact that appropriations are not disclosed in the P&L account makes it very difficult to determine what type of dividend policy the company is following, and hence what kind of return shareholders have received over the two years.

(v) The length of credit period given to debtors has increased (if all sales are on credit). While trading conditions may make this slip in credit control a necessity, it is regrettable that the company cannot obtain the same more relaxed terms from its creditors; this would balance out working capital requirements, at least to some extent.

(vi) The stock situation is what has changed most dramatically between 20X4 and 20X5. The rise in balance sheet stocks of DM 30m may appear moderate, but it represents a rise of DM 120m in finished goods and a fall of DM 90 m in raw materials. It may be the case that the company is manufacturing less and buying in more finished goods, but the increase in labour costs would tend to negate this. It seems more likely that the company has greatly over-estimated the level of sales for 20X5, and has therefore ended 20X5 with an anomalous stock position.

(vii) The cash levels held by the business, while perhaps on the high side at the beginning of the year, now appear far too low. The company is verging on an overdraft situation, in spite of receiving cash from a share issue during the year. The working capital situation, and in particular the stock levels, must be resolved in order to recover the liquidity position of the business. If not, then there will be some difficulty in paying creditors and taxes in the near future.

(b) A direct comparison of the results of Tone plc and Hilde GmbH may be misleading for the following reasons.

(i) It is unlikely that the two companies follow the same, or even similar, accounting policies, for example on stock valuation, depreciation, valuation of land and buildings etc. Also, the general approach to debtor recoverability may be more or less prudent in the UK than under Tone's approach. These policies would have to be investigated to discover whether comparison is really feasible.

(ii) Hilde GmbH's creditors are not split between short and long term, ie those due within one year and in more than one year (if any). Gearing ratios cannot be calculated, and the current and quick ratios calculated in (a) are of limited value.

(iii) There may be local or country-specific types of relationships between debtors and creditors which are different from the UK methods of doing business.

(iv) There is an interest charge shown in the P&L account but the balance sheet shows no separate disclosure of loans. The explanation may be that an interest charge is payable on the share capital in place of dividends.

(v) A legal reserve is shown. There is no indication of what type of reserve this may be comparable with (if any) in UK financial statements.

(vi) The P&L account does not show a figure of gross profit making it difficult to compare margins.

(vii) The expenses include valuation adjustments for fixed asset depreciation and current assets. It is not clear how these arise. They may simply comprise the normal depreciation charge and, say, a provision against doubtful debts and obsolete stock. It is true of many of the P&L account figures, that a lack of knowledge about how, say, 'cost of sales' is computed, prevents comparison with UK accounts.

21 GLOWBALL

Tutorial note. A good test of report writing skills. To produce a good answer here you need to be able to explain the main issues in environmental reporting and to identify these in a scenario. Don't forget to think about FRSs, especially FRS 12 when reading the scenario. Your answer should read well as a report to the directors, as well as addressing all the technical issues.

REPORT

To: The Directors
Glowball plc

From: A N Accountant
Date: 12 May 20X1

Environmental Reporting

Introduction

The purpose of this report is to provide information about current reporting requirements and guidelines on the subject of environmental reporting, and to give an indication of the required disclosure in relation to the specific events which you have brought to my attention. We hope that it will assist you in preparing your environmental report.

Current reporting requirements and guidelines

Most business, certainly those in the UK, have generally ignored environmental issues in the past. However, the use and misuse of natural resources all lead to environmental costs generated by business, both large and small.

There are very few rules, legal or otherwise, to ensure that companies disclose and report environmental matters. Any **disclosures tend to be voluntary**, unless environmental matters happen to fall under standard accounting principles. Environmental matters may be reported in the accounts of companies in the following areas.

- Contingent liabilities
- Exceptional charges
- Profit and capital expenditure focus
- Operating and financial review comments
- Profit and capital expenditure focus

The voluntary approach contrasts with the position in the United States, where the SEC/FASB accounting standards are obligatory.

While nothing is compulsory, there are a number of **published guidelines** and **codes of practice**, including:

- The *Valdez Principles*
- The Confederation of British Industry's guideline *Introducing Environmental Reporting*
- The ACCA's *Guide to Environment and Energy Reporting*
- The Coalition of Environmentally Responsible Economies (CERES) formats for environmental reports
- The Friends of the Earth *Environmental Charter for Local Government*
- The Eco Management and Audit Scheme Code of Practice

The question arises as to verification of the environmental information presented. Companies who adopt the Eco Management and Audit Scheme must have the report validated by an external verifier. In June 1999, BP Amoco commissioned KPMG to conduct an independent audit of its greenhouse gas emissions in the first ever **environmental audit**.

Comments on 'environmental events'

(a) Of relevance to the farmland restoration is FRS 12 *Provisions, contingent liabilities and contingent assets*. Provisions for environmental liabilities should be recognised where there is a **legal or constructive obligation** to rectify environmental damage or perform restorative work. The mere existence of the restorative work does not give rise to an obligation and there is no legal obligation. However, it could be argued that there is a constructive obligation arising from the company's approach in previous years, which may have given rise to an **expectation** that the work would be carried out. If this is the case, a provision of £150m would be required in the financial statements. In addition, this provision and specific examples of restoration of land could be included in the environmental report.

(b) The treatment of the **fine** is straightforward: it is an obligation to transfer economic benefits. An estimate of the fine should be made and a **provision** set up in the financial statements for £5m. This should be mentioned in the environmental report. The report might also **put the fines in context** by stating how many tests have been carried out and how many times the company has passed the tests. The directors may feel that it would do the company's reputation no harm to point out the fact that the number of prosecutions has been falling from year to year.

(c) These statistics are good news and need to be covered in the environmental report. However, the emphasis should be on **accurate factual reporting** rather than boasting. It might be useful to provide target levels for comparison, or an industry average if available. The emissions statistics should be split into three categories:

- Acidity to air and water
- Hazardous substances
- Harmful emissions to water

As regards the aquatic emissions, the £70m planned expenditure on **research** should **be mentioned in the environmental report**. It shows a commitment to benefiting the environment. However, **FRS 12 would not permit a provision** to be made for this amount, since an obligation does not exist and the **expenditure is avoidable**. Nor does it qualify as development expenditure under SSAP 13.

(d) The environmental report should mention the steps the company is taking to minimise the harmful impact on the environment in the way it sites and constructs its gas installations. The report should also explain the policy of dismantling the installations rather than sinking them at the end of their useful life.

Currently the company builds up a provision for decommissioning costs over the life of the installation. However, FRS 12 does not allow this. Instead, the **full amount must be provided** as soon as the obligation to transfer economic benefits exists. The obligation exists right at the beginning of the installation's life, and so the full £407m must be provided for. A corresponding asset is created.

22 RECENT DEVELOPMENTS

> **Tutorial note.** This may have changed by the time you take your exam.

(a) Financial instruments (Consultation Paper)

(b) Revision of certain IAS (Consultation Paper)

(c) The Convergence Handbook

(d) Converge Strategy (Discussion Paper)

(e) 'One-stop shop' FRSSE (Discussion Paper)

(f) FREDs 23-29, bringing in IAS requirements

(g) FRED 30 Financial instruments

(h) FRED 32 Discontinued operations

23 LARGE COMPANY

> **Tutorial note**. This question required candidates to compute the amounts which should be capitalised in respect of two retail stores' developments and also the subsequent depreciation.
>
> In part (a) notice that the requirement asked for 'full explanations' as well as the numbers. Make sure you do both. The calculation of the interest charge on the bond was potentially tricky. You could have worked it out from first principles, or used tables. Even if you couldn't work it out, you could guess (always guess 10% - you'll actually be right in a huge number of questions) or at least explain the treatment – no one detail will carry many marks. In part (b) again the key to a good pass mark here is to give sufficient effort to the 'reasons', not just the calculations.

(a) This is a zero coupon bond and FRS 4 requires the premium on redemption to be treated as an **interest cost**.

The effective rate is 0.38555 $\left(\frac{10{,}000{,}000}{25{,}937{,}000}\right)$ which from tables gives an interest rate of 10% pa over ten years.

Interest incurred whilst the assets are under construction can be capitalised, hence each building can include an interest cost of 10%.

Amounts to be included in fixed assets are as follows.

	A	*B*
	£'000	£'000
Land	500	700
Building materials	500	550
Labour	100	150
Overheads	100	100
Fixtures and fittings	200	200
	1,400	1,700
10% interest	140	170
Capitalise	1,540	1,870

(b) *Location A*

The store is retained for the **company's own use**. It should therefore be **depreciated** under the principles of FRS 15.

Depreciation to be charged (£'000s).

Land: nil
Buildings: (500 + 100 + 100+ 70)/50 = 15.4
Fixtures and fittings: (200 + 20)/10 = 22

Location B

This store meets the criteria of SSAP 19 *Accounting for investment properties* to be treated as an **investment property**. Hence only the fixtures and fittings will be depreciated with a charge of £22,000. The land and buildings will be **carried in the balance sheet at open market value.**

If this exceeds the cost of £1,700,000 (700 + 550 + 150 + 100 + 200) then any surplus will be credited to a revaluation reserve. If there is a deficit it will need to be charged to the profit and loss account. This is because there is no balance on the revaluation for reserve against which it can be charged.

24 FRS 11

Tutorial note. A quick introductory question. More detailed questions are found in the Kit.

(a) If there were an indication that a fixed asset in income-generating unit B was impaired, the value in use of B would be compared with £200m, not £150m.

(b) An impairment loss of £20m is recognised in respect of income-generating unit Z, reducing its carrying amount to £120m and the total carrying amount to £370m. A further impairment loss of £10m is then recognised in respect of the goodwill.

25 INVEST

Tutorial note. Review your answer carefully, as every paper this examiner writes tends to include goodwill in the main consolidation question and/or a stand-alone question like this.

(a) (i) The net assets of Target included in the calculation of goodwill have a fair value of £30m which excludes a brand valued at £3m.

The brand should only be included as an intangible asset if its value can be reliably measured on initial recognition, the question states the value is 'reliable'.

However, the ASB took the view under FRS 10 that internally developed intangible assets such as brands are very difficult to value and the recognition of internally generated brands is effectively prohibited.

Therefore it is assumed that **although the value of the brand can be reliably measured** by an estimate and that the value will increase or be maintained, the value of the brand is **subsumed within the valuation of goodwill.** Goodwill is thus calculated as follows.

	£m
Fair value of purchase price	31
Fair value of net assets acquired (30 × 80%)	(24)
Fair value of brand (3 × 80%)	(2.4)
Positive purchased goodwill	4.6

Amortisation of goodwill

1 May 20X8 to 30 April 20X9 = £4.6m/40 = £115,000

Note. there is no amortisation of the brand, as it is considered to have an indefinite useful life. However, there will need to be an annual impairment review of the brand.

(ii) Under FRS 10, where goodwill and intangible assets have limited useful lives, they should be amortised to the profit and loss account over those lives. Normally the **rebuttable presumption** under FRS 10 is that the life is considered to be 20 years or less.

The useful economic life of goodwill may exceed 20 years provided that:

(1) The asset justifies using a longer write off period (ie the goodwill is considered sufficiently durable)

(2) The goodwill is capable of continued measurement

However, the directors of the Invest Group must subject the carrying value of goodwill to an **annual impairment review** at the end of each reporting period (beginning 31 March 20X9) and the carrying value revised if the value is impaired. The revised carrying value will then be written off over the remaining life (or the shorter life) and the resulting impairment loss charged to the P&L account. Impairment means that the carrying value of the goodwill is compared o the recoverable amount of the goodwill (the greater of net realisable value and economic value). FRS 11 deals with impairment reviews.

(b) *Fair value of consideration*

	£'000
Fair value of consideration payable now	30,000
Fair value of consideration deferred £30m/1.10^2	24,793
	54,793

Note. Per FRS 7 *Fair values in acquisition accounting* deferred consideration should be valued at its present value. The consideration is payable in two years' time and is discounted accordingly.

Fair value of net assets

	£'000
Per balance sheet	55,000
Add back: provision	6,000
Deduct: deficit	(11,000)
	50,000

Note. FRS 7 requires that defined benefit pension schemes should be shown at their fair value. As the pension scheme was in deficit by £11m at the date of acquisition, this must be deducted in arriving at the net assets figure. The provision of £6m already in the balance sheet is no longer needed and must be added back.

Calculation of goodwill

	£'000
Cost of investment	54,793
Share of net assets acquired	
80% × 50m	40,000
Goodwill	14,793

Write off in the year to 30 September 20X9:

14,793/20 × 6/12 = £369,825

26 TALL

Tutorial note. Part (a) has the examiner's favourite 'memorandum' requirement. Presentation is important and will carry marks, as is your ability to set out sufficient distinct and relevant points.

The calculations in (b) and (c) are similar to examples which have appeared many times in the past so it's worth taking time reviewing your answer carefully to make sure you can get them right.

(a) MEMORANDUM

To: Assistant Accountant
From: Management Accountant
Date: 10 October 20X9

Treatment of Capital Instruments

Although there may be some similarities between the bonds and the preference shares, they should not be treated in the same way. The accounting standard governing their treatment is FRS 4 *Capital instruments.*

The **bonds** are not legally shares and they carry an **obligation to transfer economic events** on redemption. Under FRS 4 they would therefore be regarded as **debt instruments** and shown as **a long-term liability** in the creditors section of the balance sheet. The **finance cost** should be allocated to individual accounting periods so that a **uniform percentage** of the amount outstanding is charged in the period. This is unaffected by the fact that no payments are made until redemption.

The **preference shares**, by contrast, would be shown in as part of **shareholders' funds** in the balance sheet under FRS 4. They are **non-equity** shares – although legally shares they are redeemable at a fixed future date and are therefore less 'permanent' than equity shares. FRS 4 requires that they be **disclosed separately from equity shares**, but the disclosure can be given in a note to the financial statements.

The **finance cost** should be **allocated uniformly** to individual accounting periods, despite the fact that no payments are to be made until redemption.

(b)

	£'000
Equity shares capital	100,000
Non equity share capital	
Preference shares	10,000
Share premium account (W1)	37,700
Profit and loss account	89,700
	237,400
Net assets (W2)	237,400

Workings

1 *Share premium account*

	£'000	£'000
Existing balance		35,800
Premium on issue of preference shares	2,000	
Less issues costs	100	
		1,900
New balance		37,700

2 *Net assets*

	£'000
Existing balance	225,500
Net proceeds of preference	
Share issue (10,000 + 1,900)	11,900
Net proceeds from issue of bonds	15,000
Creditor for bonds	(15,000)
New balance	237,400

(c) Fixed cost of bonds

$$\frac{\text{Carrying value}}{\text{Value on redemption}} = \frac{15}{24.15} = 0.621$$

From present value tables, implicit intercept rate (5 years) is 10%.

∴Interest for the year is 10% × £15m = £1.5m. this should be shown under 'interest payable and similar charges'.

Finance cost of preference shares

$$\frac{\text{Carrying value}}{\text{Value on redemption}} = \frac{11.9}{23.5} = 0.506$$

From present value tables, implicit interest rate (6 years) is 12%.

∴Interest for the year is £11.9m × 12% = £1,428,000. This should be shown as an appropriation of profit.

27 FRS 5 SCENARIOS

Scenario I

> **Tutorial note**. This scenario is based on an illustration in FRS 5 and it demonstrates the thought processes required to determine how an item should be treated.

The commercial effect of this arrangement is that, although the debts have been legally transferred to Farant Factors plc, Shaky plc continues to bear significant benefits and risks relating to them. Shaky plc continues to bear slow payment risk as the interest charged by Farant Factors plc varies with the speed of collections of the debts. Hence, the gross amount of the debts should continue to be shown on its balance sheet until the earlier of collection and transfer of all risks to Farant Factors plc (ie 90 days.).

However, Shaky plc's maximum downside loss is limited since any debts not recovered after 90 days are in effect paid for by Farant Factors plc, which then assumes all slow payment and credit risk beyond this time. Thus, even for debts that prove to be bad, Shaky plc receives some proceeds. (For a debt of £100 that subsequently proves to be bad, the proceeds received would be £100, less the credit protection fee of £1, less an interest charge calculated for 90 days at base rate plus 2.5%.)

Hence, assuming the conditions given in FRS 5 for linked presentation for certain non-recourse finance arrangements are met, a linked presentation should be adopted. The amount deducted on the face of the balance sheet should be the lower of the proceeds received and the gross amount of the debts less all charges to the factor in respect of them. In the above example, for a debt of £100 this latter amount would be calculated at £100 less the credit protection fee of £1 and the maximum finance charge (calculated for 90 days at base rate plus 2.5%). Assuming the proceeds received of £80 are lower than this, and accrued interest charges at the year end are £2, the arrangement would be shown as follows.

	£	£
Current assets		
Stock		X
Debts factored without recourse		
Gross debts (after providing for credit protection fee and accrued interest	97	
Less non-returnable proceeds	(80)	
		17
Other debtors		X

In addition, the non-returnable proceeds of £80 would be included within cash and the P&L account would include both the credit protection expense of £1 and the accrued interest charges of £2.

Scenario II

REPORT

To: Managing Director
From: An Accountant
Date: 30 September 20X6
Re: *Reporting the substance of transactions*

D Ltd's transactions with E plc

The nature of these transactions can be assessed by looking at each aspect (a) to (e) in turn.

(a) *Legal title on delivery*

The legal title is irrelevant under FRS 5 as it is the substance of the transaction which is important, not its legal form.

(b) *Legal title when sold/after 6 months*

At either of these dates the entire risks and benefits associated with the cars have definitely transferred to D Ltd and they are therefore assets of the company. The question remains: how to account for the cars before this date.

(c) *Price payable*

The date at which D Ltd is invoiced for the cars is also irrelevant. The monetary cost of the asset is known and this cannot be changed because of increases in the normal selling price (ie D Ltd is insulated from the risk of price rises - a benefit). If the cars are recognised as an asset, the corresponding liability owed to E plc can be recorded. The liability will then be increased by 1% per month. The 1% per month charge can also be included in the asset cost as a capitalised finance charge. The pricing situation indicates that the cars are an asset of D Ltd as the company bears the slow-movement risk.

(d) *Obsolescence etc*

D Ltd bears the entire risk of obsolescence and damage to the cars, ie there is no right to return obsolete or damaged vehicles. D Ltd has the right to return vehicles but is prevented from doing so because of the harshness of the penalty payments. These points would imply that the vehicles are assets of D Ltd from delivery.

(e) *Return to manufacturer*

E plc has no right to demand return of the stock and again this indicates that the cars are an asset of D Ltd. The right to claim the cars back if D Ltd becomes insolvent is merely a Romalpa-type clause which is fairly standard when any type of stock is sold on credit.

Summary and accounting treatment

In summary, the cars should be treated as assets from the date of delivery. The asset should be recognised *and* the corresponding liability to E plc, from the date of delivery.

28 AXE

> **Tutorial note.** When you review your answer, consider whether you addressed the requirements properly.
>
> In (a), the 'discussion' should look at the reasons for the new proposals, not just list out rules.
>
> In (b), the requirement gives a good indication as to where to find marks. Three are three lease transactions to consider under two sets of rules. As long as you can find at least one point to make on each of these six 'sub-requirements' and two on a few of them, the 50% needed to pass should be straightforward, even if some of the more complicated calculations went wrong.

(a) The current treatment of leases under SSAP 21 is open to criticism.

(i) The distinction between treatment as a finance lease or operating lease is based on **quantitative rather than qualitative cri**teria.

(ii) Many operating lease transactions have been **designed to fit** the quantitative criteria when in substance they are finance leases.

(iii) The 90% present value criterion may be satisfied by using a **contingent rental clause**. Contingent rentals would not come into the calculation.

(iv) The interest rate implicit in the lease may not be available, in which case an alternative estimated rate can be used. This can lead to the **present value criterion being circumvented.**

(v) **Material assets and liabilities** arising from operating lease contracts are **omitted**.

(vi) The approach of SSAP 21 is 'all or nothing', while modern transactions are more complicated than this.

For some time, users have called for **finance leases and operating leases to be treated consistently.**

The ASB published a Discussion Paper *Leases: implementation of a new approach* in December 1999. The Discussion Paper presents a Position Paper that has been developed by the G4+1.

The paper recommends that **all leases should be reflected in financial statements in a consistent manner** and it explores the principles that should determine the extent of the assets and liabilities that lessees and lessors would recognise under leases.

At the beginning of a lease the lessee would **recognise an asset and a liability equivalent to the fair value of the rights and obligations that are conveyed by the lease** (usually the present value of the minimum payments required by the lease). Then the accounting for the lease asset and liability would **follow the normal requirements for accounting for fixed assets and debt**. The lessor would report financial assets (representing amounts receivable from the lessee) and residual interests as separate assets.

Leases that are now treated as operating leases and therefore off balance sheet would give rise to assets and liabilities. However, the difference may not be significant. **Where a lease is for a small part of an asset's useful economic life, only that part would be reflected in the lessee's balance sheet.**

The Discussion paper also examines the principles for accounting for more complex features of lease contracts. These include renewal options, contingent rentals, residual value guarantees and sale and leaseback transactions.

(b) **Computer software and hardware**

Under SSAP 21 *Accounting for leases and hire purchase contracts* the computer software and hardware **sold and leased back** should be treated as **a sale** and the operating lease rentals charged against profit. The lease is not shown on the balance sheet. If the transaction is at **fair value**, the profit or loss on the sale should be **recognised immediately**. If the transaction is **above fair value**, the **profit based on fair value** (£190m – £90m, ie £100m) may be **recognised immediately**. The balance of profit in **excess of fair va**lue (£310 – £190m, ie £120m) should be

deferred and amortised over the shorter of the lease term and the period to the next lease rental review. In this case this would be amortised over four years, ie £30m per annum.

However, as the sales value is not the fair value, the operating lease rentals (£45m) are likely to have been adjusted for the excess price paid for the assets. For Axe plc, the sale value is considerably more than the fair value, and according to FRS 5 *Reporting the substance of transactions*, **the substance** of the transaction is one of **sale of asset and a loan** equalling the deferred income element. The premium of £15m would be viewed as a financing cost, with the excess over the fair value of £120m being shown as a loan, with part of the costs of the operating lease being treated as repayment of the loan plus interest.

Plant

The sale and leaseback appears to create a **finance lease** as the present value of the minimum lease payments is greater than 90% of the fair value of the plant. The lease runs for the useful life of the plant and Axe has a guaranteed residual amount of £30m. Therefore the minimum lease payments are:

	£m
£87m + (£87m × 2.49)	303.6
£30m residual value discounted at 10%	20.5
	324.1

Under FRS 5 the asset should **remain in the lessee's balance sheet at carrying value** and the sale proceeds (£330m) are shown as a creditor representing the finance lease liability. As payments are made they are treated partly as a repayment of the creditor and partly as a finance charge against income. The rental payments have been reduced because Axe has guaranteed a residual value of £30m, which is probably more than its scrap value, which is likely to be low.

Motor vehicles

SSAP 21 would treat the lease of the motor vehicles as an **operating lease**. The rentals would be charged to the profit and loss account on a straight line basis over the term of the lease, regardless of the due dates for payment.

29 ELLIOT

> **Tutorial note.** This question looks at the methods of lessor accounting. The numbers are quite straightforward.

(a) PROFIT AND LOSS ACCOUNT
FOR THE YEAR ENDED 30 JUNE 20X3
(EXTRACT)

	£
Rental (£1,989 × 4)	7,956
Less capital repayment (balance)	4,614
	3,342
Less interest (£715 + £686 + £657 + £626)	2,684
Profit before tax (£428 × $^{100}/_{65}$)	658
Taxation (W)	832
	1,490
Deferred tax (balance)	1,062
Net profit (£115 + £110 + £104 + £99)	428

Working

	£
Rental	7,956
WDA (25% × £30,600)	(7,650)
	306
Interest payable	(2,684)
	(2,378)
Taxation @ 35%	832

BALANCE SHEET
AS AT 30 JUNE 20X3 (EXTRACT)

	£
Debtors	
Investment in finance leases (£30,600 – £4,614)	25,986

The balances relating to taxation and deferred tax will be included in the balance sheet.

The notes to the accounts will also disclose the rentals receivable under finance leases of £7,956 and the £30,600 cost of assets acquired to let under finance leases.

Accounting policy note

Income from finance leases is credited to the P&L account to give a constant periodic rate of return on the net cash investment. Assets under finance leases are stated in the balance sheet as debtors at the total value of rental receivable less finance charges relating to future periods.

(b) The major assumptions used in the calculation of net cash investment relate to the variables involved as follows.

(i) Interest rates and taxation charges will occur as predicted in the future.

(ii) The company will generate sufficient taxable profits to absorb the tax deductible expenses and capital allowances which have been predicted.

(iii) Other costs, such as administrative costs, will be immaterial.

(iv) The lease continues for its full term.

Any change in the above assumptions will require a new calculation as at the date when the change occurred.

(c) The profit on the lease arises because there is a difference between:

(i) The rental payments made

(ii) The sum of the interest suffered on the average net cash investment (calculated at the cost of funds to the lessor) and taxation

The profit is allocated to individual accounting periods based on the proportion of the average net cash investment during the period to the total average net cash investment.

(d) As opposed to the actuarial method after tax, the investment period method allocates gross earnings over that part of the lease in which the lessor has a net cash investment, in proportion to the net cash investment at each interval.

30 FRS 17

> **Tutorial note.** In an exam you should expect a numerical element as well as a discussion. Study the example in the chapter on retirement benefits carefully.

(a) Under **SSAP 24** the assets and liabilities in a defined benefit pension scheme were valued on an **actuarial basis**. The objective was to arrive at a regular pension cost each year that was a substantially level percentage of the pensionable payroll. Any **variations from regular** cost were spread forward and **recognised** gradually **over the average remaining service lives** of the employees. SSAP 24 was criticised for several reasons.

(i) There were **too many options** available to the preparers of accounts, leading to inconsistency in accounting practice and allowing a great deal of flexibility to adjust results on a short-term basis.

(ii) The **disclosure requirements** did **not** necessarily ensure that the pension cost and related amounts in the balance sheet were **adequately explained**.

(iii) It is **inconsistent** with **international accounting standards**.

(b) **FRS 17** abandons the use of actuarial values for assets in a pension scheme in favour of a **market value approach**. They are to be measured at **fair value**. Likewise, pension **liabilities** must be measured on a **market basis**, using the **projected unit basis**. Liabilities will be discounted at the current rate of return on a high quality corporate bond of equivalent term and currency to the liability.

An asset will be recognised to the extent that an employer can recover a surplus through reduced contributions and refunds. A liability will be recognised to the extent that the deficit reflects the employer's legal or constructive obligation. The resulting asset or liability is presented separately on the face of the balance sheet after other net assets.

The use of market values at the balance sheet date introduces **volatility** into the measurement of the surplus or deficit in the pension scheme. Such volatility was largely absent from the actuarial values used under SSAP 24. Internationally the volatility stemming from market values is dealt with by averaging the market values over a number of years and/or spreading the gains and losses forward in the accounts over the service lives of the employees. There are problems with this approach.

(i) It gives rise to figures in the balance sheet that do not represent the current surplus or deficit in the scheme.

(ii) It creates charges in the profit and loss account that are contaminated by gains and losses that occurred up to fifteen years previously.

The ASB has developed an alternative approach to cope with the volatility. The **profit and loss account** shows the relatively stable ongoing **service cost, interest cost** and **expected return** on assets measured on a basis consistent with international standards. The effects of the **fluctuations in market values**, on the other hand, are not part of the operating results of the business and are treated in the same way as revaluations of fixed assets, ie are recognised immediately in the second performance statement, the **statement of total recognised gains and losses**. This has two advantages over the international approach.

(i) The balance sheet shows the deficit or recoverable surplus in the scheme.

(ii) The total profit and loss charge is more stable than it would be if the market value fluctuations were spread forward.

(c) There are possible disadvantages to the new approach.

(i) The new standard is very **complicated**.

(ii) It could be argued that the disclosure requirements are so extensive that preparers and users of accounts will get **lost in the detail**.

(iii) Concerns about the new accounting standard may cause more **employers to move to defined contribution schemes**, thereby putting the risk on the employee.

(iv) The standard aims to aid consistency by the use of market values. However, much depends on the 'expected return on assets' which the actuary will be free to choose. Using a high expected return will increase profits, but since variations in future years go through the STRGL and not the profit and loss account, profits will not suffer in future years if the expected return is not realised. In other words **there will still be room for manoeuvre**.

31 HARMONISE

Tutorial note. As FRS 19 is relatively recent, you may still be asked to compare full and partial provision.

(a) *Flow-through method*

	20X6	*20X7*	*20X8*	*20X9*
	£'000	£'000	£'000	£'000
Profit and loss				
Taxable profit (W1)	850	1,120	1,020	440
Taxation @ 33%	280.5	369.6	336.6	145.2

Balance sheet. No provision required for flow though method.

(b) *Full provision*

	20X6	*20X7*	*20X8*	*20X9*
	£'000	£'000	£'000	£'000
Profit and loss				
Taxable profit (from (a))	850	1,120	1,020	440
Taxation @ 33%	280.5	369.6	336.6	145.2
Deferred tax (W2)	105.6	(26.4)	52.8)	132.0

	20X6	20X7	20X8	20X9
	£'000	£'000	£'000	£'000
Balance sheet				
Provision for liabilities and charges	105.6	79.2	26.4	158.4

(c) *Partial provision*

£79,200 of timing difference will reverse in 20X7 and 20X8.

	20X6	20X7	20X8	20X9
	£'000	£'000	£'000	£'000
Profit and loss				
Taxable profit	850	1,120	1,020	440
Taxation @ 33% (from (a))	280.5	369.6	336.6	145.2
Deferred tax (W2)	79.2	(26.4)	(52.8)	-
Balance sheet				
Provision for liabilities and charges	79.2	52.8	Nil	Nil

Workings

1 *Taxable profit*

20X6: 1,250 – 400 = 850
20X7: 1,200 – 80 = 1,120
20X8: 1,100 – 80 = 1,020
20X9: 1,000 – 560 = 440

2 *Deferred tax* (full provision)

	CA	Depreciation	Cum difference	@ 33%	Movement
20X6	400	80	320	105.6	105.6
20X7	80	160	240	79.2	(26.4)
20X8	80	240	80	26.4	(52.8)
20X9	560	160	480	158.4	132.0

32 ANGUS

> **Tutorial note**. Aspects of FRS 3 could come up in all types of question - make sure you are familiar with all its statements and notes.

(a) (i) ANGUS PLC
PROFIT AND LOSS ACCOUNT FOR THE YEAR ENDED 28 FEBRUARY 20X7

	Continuing	Discontinued	Total
	£'m	£'m	£'m
Turnover	180.00	20.00	200.00
Operating profit (W1)	18.99	2.11	21.10
Loss on disposal of fixed asset (W2)	-	(1.50)	(1.50
Loss on disposal of discontinued operations		(0.35)	(0.35)
Cost of fundamental reorganisation	(1.25)	(0.35)	(1.25)
Profit on ordinary activities before taxation	17.74	0.26	18.00
Tax on profit on ordinary activities			(6.00)
Profit on ordinary activities after taxation			12.00
Dividends			(2.00)
Retained profits for the financial year			10.00

(ii) STATEMENT OF TOTAL RECOGNISED GAINS AND LOSSES

	£m
Profit for the year	12.0
Surplus on revaluation of fixed assets (W3)	6.8
Total recognised gains and losses	18.8
Prior year adjustment	(1.5)
Total gains and losses recognised since last annual report	17.3

(iii) RECONCILIATION OF MOVEMENTS IN SHAREHOLDERS' FUNDS

	£m
Profit for the financial year	12.0
Dividends	(2.0)
	10.0
Other recognised gains and losses	6.8
Net addition to shareholders funds	16.8
Opening shareholders' funds (originally £500m before deducting prior year adjustment of £1.5m)	498.5
Closing shareholders' funds	515.3

(iv) NOTE OF HISTORICAL COST PROFITS AND LOSSES

	£m
Reported profit on ordinary activities before taxation	18.00
Difference between a historical cost depreciation charge and the actual depreciation charge for the year calculated on the revalued amount (400k – 280k)	0.12
Historical cost profit on ordinary activities before taxation	18.12

	£m
Historical cost profit for the year retained after taxation, minority interests, extraordinary items and dividends (18.12 – 6 – 2)	10.12

Workings

1 *Operating profit*

	£'m
Profit before tax	18.00
Add back losses	
Fixed assets	1.50
Termination	0.35
Reorganisation	1.25
	21.10

2 *Loss on sale of fixed assets*

	£'m
NBV	10.5
Proceeds	(9.0)
	(1.5)

3 *Surplus on revaluation*

	£'m
Revalued amounts	20
NBV at 28.2.X6 (16m – 2.8m)	(13.2)
Surplus	6.8

(b) (i) The purpose of the STRGL is to be an 'all inclusive' statement of gains and losses occurring in an enterprise during a period.

The P&L account excludes items deemed to be unrealised such as revaluations/forex differences that go directly to the reserves. These can, however, represent very material amounts. FRS 3 therefore requires companies to provide this extra statement to give increased prominence to these items.

(ii) As illustrated in parts (a) and (b) the two statements differ as dividends are not shown in the gains and losses statements as it represents a distribution of gains made not a loss.

By only including true gains and losses, not anything which changes net assets, the statement has a clearer purpose than the reserve statement.

Reserve notes are usually included at the end of the financial statements. The STRGL is a primary statement and must therefore be given due prominence within the financial statements.

One explanation might be that the statement of movement on reserves has not a regulatory or mandatory format so that it is clear that the movements contained in the statement are not presented in a uniform format and are not well understood by the user.

The efforts to improve the presentation of information in the accounts is designed to produce decision useful information. By advocating additional primary statements the ASB might be setting the scene for further primary statements that could be used to accommodate future developments, eg value statements with a reconciliation to the historical cost profit.

33 ENGINA

> **Tutorial note.** A good test of your ability to apply FRS 8 to a practical scenario.
>
> Notice the mark allocation before starting to produce your answer. Take time to think about the presentation and structure of the report and ensure you allocate your rime appropriately over the headings and keep sentences and paragraphs short to make your answer easy to mark.
>
> When you review your answer think abut whether it is written in a good professional style as well as checking the technical details.

REPORT

To: The Directors
Engina Co
Zenda
Ruritania

From: A N Accountant

Date: 12 May 20X1

Related Party Transactions

The purpose of this report is to explain why it is necessary to disclose related party transactions. We appreciate that you may regard such disclosure as politically and culturally sensitive. However, there are **sound reasons for the required disclosures**. It should be emphasised that related party transactions are a normal part of business life, and the disclosures are required to give a fuller picture to the users of accounts, rather than because they are problematic.

Prior to the issue of FRS 8, disclosures in respect of related parties were concerned with directors and their relationship with the group. The ASB extended this definition and also the required disclosures. This reflects the objective of the ASB to provide useful data for investors not merely for companies to report on stewardship activities.

Unless investors know that transactions with related parties have not been carried out at '**arm's length**' between independent parties, they may fail to ascertain the true financial position.

Related party transactions typically take place on **terms which are significantly different** from those undertaken on normal commercial terms.

FRS 8 brings the UK more into line with **international practice** and requires all material related party transactions to be disclosed.

It should be noted that related party transactions are not necessarily fraudulent or intended to deceive. Without proper disclosures, investors may be disadvantaged – FRS 8 seeks to remedy this.

Sale of goods to the directors

Disclosure of related party transactions is only necessary when the transactions are **material.** FRS 8 applies only to material related party transactions. For the purposes of FRS 8, however, transactions are material when their disclosure might be expected to influence decisions made by users of the financial statements, irrespective of their amount. Moreover, the materiality of a related party transaction with an individual, for example a director, must be judged by reference to that individual and not just the company. In addition, disclosure of contracts of significance with directors is required by the Stock Exchange.

Mr Satay has purchased £600,000 (12 × £50,000) worth of goods from the company and a car for £45,000, which is just over half its market value. The transactions are not material to the company, and because Mr Satay has considerable personal wealth, they are not material to him either. However, **while not material**, any transactions with directors could be viewed as **sensitive**, and therefore ought to be disclosed in accordance with **best practice and good corporate governance.**

Hotel property

The hotel property sold to the Managing Director's brother is a **related party transaction**, and it appears to have been undertaken at **below market price**. FRS 8 requires disclosure of 'any other elements of the transactions necessary for an understanding of the financial statements'.

However, not only must the transaction be disclosed, but the question of **impairment** needs to be considered. The value of the hotel has become impaired due to the fall in property prices, so the carrying value needs to be adjusted in accordance with FRS 11 *Impairment of fixed assets and goodwill.* The hotel should be shown at the lower of carrying value (£5m) and the recoverable amount. The recoverable amount is the higher of net realisable value (£4.3m – £0.2m = £4.1m) and value in use (£3.6m). Therefore the hotel should be shown at £4.1m.

The sale of the property was for £100,000 below this impaired value, and it is this amount which needs to be disclosed.

Group structure

Companies legislation and the Stock Exchange require **disclosure of director's interests** in a company's share capital. Thus Mr Satay would need to disclose his ownership of the share capital of Engina, being 10% direct and 90% through his ownership of Wheel.

The rules in FRS 8 are not consistent with this. The FRS **exempts from the disclosure** requirements group companies where the parent company owns **90% or more** of the subsidiary's share capital. Engina does not therefore need to disclose transactions with Wheel Ltd, provided that Wheel Ltd prepares consolidated accounts.

However, Engina's transactions with Car Ltd will need to be disclosed. FRS 8 states that companies under **common control** are related parties, and the two companies are under the common control of Mr Satay. Car is not part of the Wheel group and so will not be entitled to exemption on that basis.

34 LEASED WAREHOUSE

> **Tutorial note.** FRS 12 has generally come up as part of a multi-standard questions, a question type increasingly popular with this examiner. You may also get FRS 12 in the context of an environmental question.

In this situation, an obligation to restore the building to its original state arises at the time the alterations were made. If there is nothing the company can do to avoid the obligation, then full provision for the estimated reinstatement costs of £200,000 should be made by means of a prior year adjustment, assuming that discounting the provision is unlikely to have any material effect.

The company should also set up a corresponding asset in accordance with para 66 of FRS 12. This is because an obligation to return the property to its original state is incurred as a result of constructing the offices, which represent access to future economic benefits that are to be enjoyed over more than one period. Therefore, an asset is recognised at the same time as the provision. In practice, this would be added to the cost of the offices etc and depreciated over the shorter of the lease term and their useful life.

The prior year adjustment made should take account of the effect of any backlog depreciation. Care should also be taken to ensure that capitalising the provision does not result in stating the asset at above its recoverable amount. Therefore, it may be necessary to test the asset for impairment under FRS 11 *Impairment of fixed assets and goodwill.*

35 BIG, SMALL AND TINY

> **Tutorial note**. Think carefully about the group structure (Part (a)) before you more on to the calculations in Part (b).

(a) MEMORANDUM

To: Assistant Accountant
From: Management Accountant
Date: 10 October 20X9

Treatment of Investment in Tiny Ltd

The investment in Tiny Ltd is more complicated than the sort of investments you have come across before in your consolidations. The main point to note is that **the group's interest in the company changed during the year**.

For the six months to 31 March 20X9 Big plc owned a 25% stake in Tiny Ltd, that is 8 million equity shares out of 32 million. Assuming that no other shareholder has a major stake in Tiny, this gives us **significant influence** over the company, which is not the same as a controlling interest. Tiny Ltd is therefore an **associate** of Big plc. Following FRS 9 *Associates and joint ventures* Tiny Ltd will be **equity accounted** for the first six months of the year.

The position changed on 1 April 20X9, following the acquisition by Small Ltd of a 50% equity stake in Tiny Ltd (16 million shares out of 32 million). Small Ltd is a subsidiary of Big plc so Big plc **controls** what Small Ltd controls, that is 50%, which, when added to its original holding of 25%, gives 75% (25% direct and 50% indirect). This makes Tiny Ltd a **subsidiary** of Big plc, and the correct treatment according to FRS 2 *Accounting for subsidiary undertakings* is **line by line consolidation**.

You should not confuse **control**, for the purpose of determining the status of the investment, with **effective interest.** Big plc's effective interest in Tiny Ltd is 25% + **80%** × **50%** = 65%. But when it comes to deciding on the status of the investment, the figure of 75% is used because Big plc controls **all** of Small Ltd, its subsidiary.

(b) BIG GROUP PLC
CONSOLIDATED BALANCE SHEET
AS AT 30 SEPTEMBER 20X9

	£'000	£'000
Fixed assets		
Intangible goodwill (W1)		9,990
Tangible (W3)		178,000
		187,990
Current assets		
Stocks (W4)	111,200	
Debtors (W5)	66,350	
Cash in hand	17,000	
	194,550	
Current liabilities		
Trade creditors (W6)	25,000	
Other creditors (W7)	50,350	
Proposed dividend	9,000	
	84,350	
Net current assets		110,200
Total assets less current liabilities		298,190
Long-term loans		75,000
		223,190
Share capital and reserves		
Share capital		90,000
Profit and loss account		93,560
		183,560
Minority interest		39,630
		223,190

Workings

1 *Goodwill*

Investment in Small Ltd:

	£'000	£'000
Cost of investment		91,500
Share of net assets acquired		
Share capital	80,000	
Reserves	22,000	
Revaluation (11 – 7)	4,000	
	106,000	
Group share: 80%		84,800
Goodwill		6,700

Big's investment in Tiny:

	£'000	£'000
Cost of investment		12,500
Share of net assets acquired		
Share capital	32,000	
Reserves	10,000	
	42,000	
Group share: 25%		10,500
Goodwill		2,000

Small's investment in Tiny:

	£'000	£'000
Cost of investment		29,000
Share of net assets acquired		
Share capital	32,000	
Reserves 19 – (8 – 3) + (6/12 × 8)	18,000	
	50,000	
Small's share: 50%		25,000
Goodwill		4,000

> **Tutorial note.** The goodwill arising on the subsidiary's acquisition of the sub-subsidiary is consolidated gross, like any other asset owned by the subsidiary. This is consistent with FRS 10.

Amortisation of goodwill:

	Goodwill £'000	*Amortisation* £'000	*To CBS* £'000
Big in Small	6,700		
6/20		2,010	4,690
Big in Tiny	2,000		
5/20		500	1,500
Small in Tiny	4,000		
1/20		200	3,800
Total amortisation/goodwill	12,700	2,710	9,990

2 *Minority interests*

	£'000	£'000
Tiny Ltd: 35% × (51 – 2.8 (wk) £8		16,870
Small Ltd		
Share capital	80,000	
Profit and loss	59,000	
Goodwill on acquisition of Tiny	3,800	
	142,800	
Less cost of acquisition of Tiny	(29,000)	
	138,000	
20% interest		22,760
		39,630

3 *Tangible fixed assets*

	£m
Big	56
Small	66
Tiny	56
	178

4 *Stocks*

	£'000	£'000
Sum of balance sheets (45 + 44 + 25)		114,000
Provision for unrealised profit		
Big: 20/120 × 9	1,500	
Small: 12/120 × 7.8	1,300	
		2,800
		111,200

5 *Debtors*

	£'000	£'000
Sum of balance sheets		86,000
Dividends receivable		
Big from Small (8,000 × 80%)	6,400	
Big from Tiny (3,000 × 25%)	750	
Small from Tiny (3,000 × 50%)	1,500	
		8,650
		77,350
Intercompany (6 + 5)		11,000
		66,350

6 *Trade creditors*

	£'000
Sum of balance sheets (16 + 12 + 8)	36,000
Intercompany (W5)	11,000
	25,000

7 *Other creditors*

	£'000
Dividends payable to minority	
Small (8,000 × 20%)	1,600
Tiny 25% × 3,000	750
	2,350
Bank overdraft (12 + 10 + 9)	31,000
Taxation (7 + 6 + 4)	17,000
	50,350

8 *Profit and loss account*

	Big	*Small*	*Tiny*
	£'000	£'000	£'000
Reserves per question	69,000	59,000	19,000
Less unrealised profit (W6)			(2,800)
Fair value adjustment		(4,000)	
	69,000	55,000	16,200
Less pre-acquisition reserves of Small		(22,000)	
		33,000	
Small: 80% × 33,000	26,400		
Tiny: 25% (16.2 – 10)	1,550		
40% (16.2 – 18)	(720)		
Amortisation of goodwill			
Big in Small (W2)	(2,010)		
Big in Tiny (W2)	(500)		
Small in Tiny (80% × 200 (W2))	(160)		
	93,560		

Note. Tiny is piecemeal acquisition: two different acquisition dates.

9 *Fair value adjustments (in Small)*

	At acquisition	*Now*
	£'000	£'000
Property	4,000	-*
	4,000	-

* sold

Index

Note: Key Terms and their references are given in **bold**

REVIEW FORM & FREE PRIZE DRAW

All original review forms from the entire BPP range, completed with genuine comments, will be entered into a draw on 31 January 2005 and 31 July 2005. The names on the first four forms picked out will be sent a cheque for £50.

Name: ______________________________ **Address**: ______________________________

____

How have you used this Text?
(Tick one box only)

- ☐ Home study (book only)
- ☐ On a course: college ____________
- ☐ With 'correspondence' package
- ☐ Other ____________

Why did you decide to purchase this Text?
(Tick one box only)

- ☐ Have used complementary Kit
- ☐ Have used BPP Texts in the past
- ☐ Recommendation by friend/colleague
- ☐ Recommendation by a lecturer at college
- ☐ Saw advertising
- ☐ Other ____________

During the past six months do you recall seeing/receiving any of the following?
(Tick as many boxes as are relevant)

- ☐ Our advertisement in *ACCA Student Accountant*
- ☐ Our advertisement in *Pass*
- ☐ Our advertisement in *PQ*
- ☐ Our brochure with a letter through the post

Which (if any) aspects of our advertising do you find useful?
(Tick as many boxes as are relevant)

- ☐ Prices and publication dates of new editions
- ☐ Information on Text content
- ☐ Facility to order books off-the-page
- ☐ None of the above

Which BPP products have you used?

Text	☑	**Success CD**	☐	**i-Learn**	☐
Kit	☐	**Success Tape**	☐	**i-Pass**	☐
Passcard	☐	**Big Picture Poster**	☐	**Virtual Campus**	☐

Your ratings, comments and suggestions would be appreciated on the following areas of this Text.

	Very useful	*Useful*	*Not useful*
Introductory section (Key study steps, personal study)	☐	☐	☐
Chapter introductions	☐	☐	☐
Key terms	☐	☐	☐
Quality of explanations	☐	☐	☐
Case examples and other examples	☐	☐	☐
Questions and answers in each chapter	☐	☐	☐
Chapter roundups	☐	☐	☐
Quick quizzes	☐	☐	☐
Exam focus points	☐	☐	☐
Question bank	☐	☐	☐
Answer bank	☐	☐	☐
List of key terms and index	☐	☐	☐
Icons	☐	☐	☐

	Excellent	*Good*	*Adequate*	*Poor*
Overall opinion of this Text	☐	☐	☐	☐

Do you intend to continue using BPP Products? ☐ Yes ☐ No

Please note any further comments and suggestions/errors on the reverse of this page. The BPP author of this edition can be e-mailed at: katyhibbert@bpp.com

Please return to: Catherine Watton, ACCA Range Manager, BPP Professional Education, FREEPOST, London, W12 8BR

REVIEW FORM & FREE PRIZE DRAW (continued)

TELL US WHAT YOU THINK

Please note any comments and suggestions/errors below.

FREE PRIZE DRAW RULES

1 Closing date for 31 January 2005 draw is 31 December 2004. Closing date for 31 July 2005 draw is 30 June 2005.

2 No purchase necessary. Entry forms are available upon request from BPP Professional Education. No more than one entry per title, per person. Draw restricted to persons aged 16 and over.

3 Winners will be notified by post and receive their cheques not later than 6 weeks after the draw date.

4 The decision of the promoter in all matters is final and binding. No correspondence will be entered into.

See overleaf for information on other
BPP products and how to order

Mr/Mrs/Ms (Full name)

Daytime delivery address

Postcode

Daytime Tel | Date of exam (month/year) | Scots law variant Y / N

	6/04 Texts	1/04 Kits	1/04 Passcards	***Success CDs	Big Picture Posters	8/04 i-Learn	8/04 i-Pass	Virtual Campus
PART 1								
1.1 Preparing Financial Statements	£24.95 ☐	£10.95 ☐	£6.95 ☐	£14.95 ☐	£6.95 ☐	£34.95 ☐	£24.95 ☐	£90 ☐
1.2 Financial Information for Management	£24.95 ☐	£10.95 ☐	£6.95 ☐	£14.95 ☐	£6.95 ☐	£34.95 ☐	£24.95 ☐	£90 ☐
1.3 Managing People	£24.95 ☐	£10.95 ☐	£6.95 ☐	£14.95 ☐	£6.95 ☐	£34.95 ☐	£24.95 ☐	£90 ☐
PART 2								
2.1 Information Systems	£24.95 ☐	£10.95 ☐	£6.95 ☐	£14.95 ☐	£6.95 ☐	£34.95 ☐	£24.95 ☐	£90 ☐
2.2 Corporate and Business Law **	£24.95 ☐	£10.95 ☐	£6.95 ☐	£14.95 ☐	£6.95 ☐	£34.95 ☐	£24.95 ☐	£90 ☐
2.3 Business Taxation FA2003 (12/04 exams)	£20.95 ☐	£10.95 ☐	£6.95 ☐	£14.95 ☐	£6.95 ☐	£34.95 ☐	£24.95 ☐	£90 ☐
2.3 Business Taxation FA2004 (**8/04** for 6/05 exams)†	£24.95 ☐			£14.95 ☐	£6.95 ☐			£90 ☐
2.4 Financial Management and Control	£24.95 ☐	£10.95 ☐	£6.95 ☐	£14.95 ☐	£6.95 ☐	£34.95 ☐	£24.95 ☐	£90 ☐
2.5 Financial Reporting (7/04)	£24.95 ☐	£10.95 ☐	£6.95 ☐	£14.95 ☐	£6.95 ☐	£34.95 ☐	£24.95 ☐	£90 ☐
2.6 Audit and Internal Review (12/04 exams)	£24.95 ☐	£10.95 ☐	£6.95 ☐	£14.95 ☐	£6.95 ☐	£34.95 ☐	£24.95 ☐	£90 ☐
2.6 Audit and Internal Review (**9/04** for 6/05 exams)†	£24.95 ☐			£14.95 ☐	£6.95 ☐			£90 ☐
PART 3								
3.1 Audit and Assurance Services	£24.95 ☐	£10.95 ☐	£6.95 ☐	£14.95 ☐	£6.95 ☐		£24.95 ☐	
3.2 Advanced Taxation FA2003 (12/04 exams)	£20.95 ☐	£10.95 ☐	£6.95 ☐	£14.95 ☐	£6.95 ☐		£24.95 ☐	
3.2 Advanced Taxation FA2004 (**9/04** for 6/05 exams)†	£24.95 ☐			£14.95 ☐	£6.95 ☐			
3.3 Performance Management	£24.95 ☐	£10.95 ☐	£6.95 ☐	£14.95 ☐	£6.95 ☐		£24.95 ☐	
3.4 Business Information Management	£24.95 ☐	£10.95 ☐	£6.95 ☐	£14.95 ☐	£6.95 ☐		£24.95 ☐	
3.5 Strategic Business Planning and Development	£24.95 ☐	£10.95 ☐	£6.95 ☐	£14.95 ☐	£6.95 ☐		£24.95 ☐	
3.6 Advanced Corporate Reporting (7/04)	£24.95 ☐	£10.95 ☐	£6.95 ☐	£14.95 ☐	£6.95 ☐		£24.95 ☐	
3.7 Strategic Financial Management	£24.95 ☐	£10.95 ☐	£6.95 ☐	£14.95 ☐	£6.95 ☐		£24.95 ☐	
INTERNATIONAL STREAM								
1.1 Preparing Financial Statements	£24.95 ☐	£10.95 ☐	£6.95 ☐			£34.95 ☐	£24.95 ☐	
2.2 Corporate and Business Law	£24.95 ☐	£10.95 ☐	£6.95 ☐					
2.5 Financial Reporting	£24.95 ☐	£10.95 ☐	£6.95 ☐			£34.95 ☐	£24.95 ☐	
2.6 Audit and Internal Review	£24.95 ☐	£10.95 ☐	£6.95 ☐			£34.95 ☐	£24.95 ☐	
3.1 Audit and Assurance Services	£24.95 ☐	£10.95 ☐	£6.95 ☐					
3.6 Advanced Corporate Reporting	£24.95 ☐	£10.95 ☐	£6.95 ☐					
Success in Your Research and Analysis								
Project - Tutorial Text (10/04)	£24.95 ☐							
Learning to Learn (7/02)	£9.95 ☐							

SUBTOTAL £

ACCA Order

To BPP Professional Education, Aldine Place, London W12 8AW

Tel: 020 8740 2211 Fax: 020 8740 1184

email: publishing@bpp.com website: www.bpp.com

Order online www.bpp.com

Occasionally we may wish to email you relevant offers and information about courses and products.
Please tick to opt into this service. ☐

POSTAGE & PACKING

Study Texts

	First	Each extra	Online	
UK	£5.00	£2.00	£2.00	£
Europe*	£6.00	£4.00	£4.00	£
Rest of world	£20.00	£10.00	£10.00	£

Kits

	First	Each extra	Online	
UK	£5.00	£2.00	£2.00	£
Europe*	£6.00	£4.00	£4.00	£
Rest of world	£20.00	£10.00	£10.00	£

Passcards/Success Tapes/CDs

	First	Each extra	Online	
UK	£2.00	£1.00	£1.00	£
Europe*	£3.00	£2.00	£2.00	£
Rest of world	£8.00	£8.00	£8.00	£

Grand Total (incl. Postage)

I enclose a cheque for £
(Cheques to *BPP Professional Education*)

Or charge to Visa/Mastercard/Switch

Card Number

Expiry date Start Date

Issue Number (Switch Only)

Signature

We aim to deliver to all UK addresses inside 5 working days; a signature will be required. Orders to all EU addresses should be delivered within 6 working days. All other orders to overseas addresses should be delivered within 8 working days. * Europe includes the Republic of Ireland and the Channel Islands.† **For 6/05 exam, New edition Kit, Passcard, i-Learn and i-Pass available 2005 .** ** For Scots law variant students, a free **Scots Law Supplement** is available with the 2.2 Text. Please indicate in the name and address section if this applies to you. ***Alternatively, Success Tapes are available for the same papers, all £12.95.